CONGRESS'S CONSTITUTION

JOSH CHAFETZ

Congress's Constitution

LEGISLATIVE AUTHORITY AND
THE SEPARATION OF POWERS

Yale

UNIVERSITY PRESS

NEW HAVEN AND LONDON

Published with assistance from the Mary Cady Tew Memorial Fund.

Yale University Press books may be purchased in quantity for educational, business, or promotional use. For information, please e-mail sales.press@yale.edu (U.S. office) or sales@yaleup.co.uk (U.K. office).

Set in Times Roman and Scala Sans type by IDS Infotech, Ltd.
Printed in the United States of America.

Library of Congress Control Number: 2016957903
ISBN 978-0-300-19710-5 (hardcover : alk. paper)

A catalogue record for this book is available from the British Library.

This paper meets the requirements of ANSI/NISO Z39.48-1992
(Permanence of Paper).

10 9 8 7 6 5 4 3 2 1

To Kate,
who vetoed a more extravagant dedication:
I love you.

CONTENTS

ACKNOWLEDGMENTS

I HAVE BEEN WORKING ON THIS PROJECT for quite some time. Indeed, as is perhaps typical, I was working on this project for some time before I was aware that I was working on this project. In any such lengthy endeavor, one accumulates innumerable debts, and I have been especially fortunate in having so many friends and colleagues who have contributed to the work's progress and the author's well-being. This note merely acknowledges those debts; I am under no delusion that it even begins to repay them.

I presented portions of this project at the American Constitution Society Constitutional Law "Schmooze," the Boston University Legal History Workshop, the Cornell Law and Libations Reading Group, the Cornell Law School Summer Workshop Series, the European Consortium for Political Research Standing Group on Regulatory Governance biennial conference, the London School of Economics Legal and Political Theory Forum, the Notre Dame London Law Centre, the University of Oxford Rothermere American Institute Research Seminar on Constitutional Thought and History, the University of Chicago Constitutional Law Workshop, the University of Houston Law Center Faculty Colloquium, the University of North Carolina School of Law Faculty Workshop, the University of Pennsylvania Law School Constitutional Law Speaker Series, the University of Richmond School of Law Faculty Colloquium, the William & Mary Law School Faculty Workshop, and the Yale-Duke Foreign Relations Law Roundtable. I am deeply grateful for the questions and comments I received at each of those events.

I am also immensely grateful for conversations with and feedback on various parts of the book from Akhil Amar, Shyam Balganesh, Joseph Blocher, Aaron Bruhl, Jessica Bulman-Pozen, Neal Devins, Mike Dorf, David Fontana, Aziz Huq, Mary Katzenstein, Randy Kozel, Corinna Lain, Marin Levy, Paul MacMahon, Gerard Magliocca, Bill Marshall, Aziz Rana, Richard Re, Pat Sandman, Rogers Smith, David Strauss, Sid Tarrow, Kevin Walsh, Justin Zaremby, and Mariah Zeisberg. David Pozen went far above and beyond the calls of duty and friendship by reading the entire manuscript and giving detailed and immensely helpful comments. Also tremendously helpful were the comments from anonymous reviewers for Yale University Press. Bill Frucht, Karen Olson, and Mary Pasti at the Press have been helpful and supportive at every step, as has Otto Bohlmann.

I am deeply grateful to the librarians at Cornell Law School, who have diligently tracked down every source I could possibly need for this project. Thanks also to Jessica Barragan, Arthur Kutoroff, Phuc Le, Adam McCall, Samantha Ostrom, and Gerry Scott, who provided first-rate research assistance.

This book is, in some loose sense, an expansion of my article *Congress's Constitution*, 160 U. Pa. L. Rev. 715 (2012), and paragraphs here and there from that article have survived into the finished manuscript. Chapter 5 is a revised version of *Executive Branch Contempt of Congress*, 76 U. Chi. L. Rev. 1083 (2009), and a few paragraphs of *Whose Secrets?*, 127 Harv. L. Rev. F. 86 (2013), appear in chapter 6. Please consider my acknowledgments in those articles incorporated by reference here.

The further I progress into my career as a scholar, the more I realize how incredibly fortunate I have been in my mentors. Three, especially, have made indelible marks on my life and work. In the order in which they came into my life, they are Rogers Smith, Akhil Amar, and Guido Calabresi. Their influences are all over this work—probably in many places that I don't even realize—and I am deeply and ever increasingly grateful for their wisdom, their support, their guidance, and their friendship.

Finally, I am profoundly grateful to my father, Henry Chafetz, and to my parents-in-law, Janice Carlisle and Joseph Roach, all of whom have been wonderfully supportive and loving, as well as exemplars of scholarly achievement. Most importantly, I am grateful to my first reader, my partner in all things, and the love of my life, Catherine Roach. This book is for her.

Introduction

WHAT GOOD IS CONGRESS? This is not a new question: less than three months into the First Congress in 1789, Fisher Ames, a representative from Massachusetts, wrote to a friend that he "felt chagrined at the yawning listlessness" of his colleagues.[1] Five years later, John Adams would mark the rise of the Jeffersonian faction in the House of Representatives by writing to Abigail Adams that "[t]he Business of Congress this session is Dulness Flatness and Insipidity itself."[2] And as Ames (who was, like Adams, a Federalist) was preparing to retire from the House in 1796, he wrote to another friend, "Do not ask what good we do: that is not a fair question, in these days of faction."[3]

But even if questioning the value of Congress is as old as the Republic, it has taken on new life in recent years, as talk of gridlock and dysfunction have come to dominate much of the public discourse around our national legislature.[4] Observers call Congress "the broken branch" and lament that, "[g]ripped by stalemate, America's chief lawmaking body can barely muster the ability to make law."[5] Into the breach have stepped an increasingly imperial executive and an increasingly activist judiciary.[6] Complaints that the other branches have arrogated too much power to themselves abound, but almost no one looks to Congress for a solution. And so the question presents itself with renewed urgency: What good is Congress?

This book begins to answer that question by offering a new framework for thinking about congressional power in the American constitutional system. In particular, the book is interested in the ways that Congress and its constituent parts—individual houses and even individual members—can and do make use of constitutional powers *other than the power to pass laws*. Broadening the scope beyond legislation is essential if one truly hopes to understand Congress's ability to have an impact on our national political life.[7] After all, legislation must meet Article I, section 7's bicameralism and presentment requirements. If a president has enough allies in one house of Congress, then bills she opposes are unlikely to reach her desk; even if Congress can send such a bill to her desk, she can veto it, and vetoes are very seldom overridden. Moreover, legislation is subject to judicial interpretation and judicial review. If a court, especially the Supreme Court, disapproves of a statute, it can strike it down or interpret it into near oblivion. For anyone concerned about the power of the other branches or about Congress's ability to press its own position as against theirs, then, legislation is a singularly unpromising route. The close identification of Congress with legislation, combined with the recognition of the limitations of legislation, is likely responsible in large part for complaints of congressional fecklessness.

As the following chapters demonstrate, however, the exclusively legislation-focused view of Congress is far too narrow. Congress has numerous powers other than the power to pass bills into law, powers that tend to receive scant treatment even in isolation; they are almost never grouped together and conceptualized as a coherent set of legislative tools. And yet these tools together are potent, giving Congress the ability to assert itself vigorously against the other branches.

In Richard Neustadt's memorable phrase, the Constitution creates "a government of separated institutions *sharing* powers."[8] No account of such a system could focus on one institution to the exclusion of the others: to talk about any one of them is, to some extent, to talk about them all. Or, put differently, a book about congressional power is necessarily a book about the separation of powers. Part I of this book, comprising the first two chapters, lays the theoretical groundwork by offering a new account of the American constitutional separation of powers. I refer to this account as *multiplicity based*, because it highlights the ways in which claims of authority multiply and overlap in a nonhierarchical constitutional order. Chapter 1 offers an interpretive account of this system, with a special emphasis on the ways in which institutionally sited actors construct their own constitutional power through their engagements with the broader public. Nothing in the first chapter is specific to Congress: the chapter is meant to provide an account of the American separation-of-powers system as a whole. Chapter 2 then begins the turn to Congress in particular, arguing that the legislature has both the motivation and the capacity to assert itself in the constitutional system as I have described it.

Building on the separation-of-powers theory laid out in part I, parts II and III of the book turn to thick accounts of specific constitutional tools that Congress has at its disposal in its interactions with the other branches. For ease of presentation, these tools are divided into two categories, borrowed from the international relations literature: "hard powers" and "soft powers." Hard power is, quite simply, "the ability to coerce."[9] In the international arena, a nation's hard power is "usually associated with tangible resources like military and economic strength."[10] Soft power, by contrast, is "the ability to get what you want through attraction rather than coercion or payments."[11] In foreign affairs, it "arises from the attractiveness of a country's culture, political ideals, and policies. When our policies are seen as legitimate in the eyes of others, our soft power is enhanced."[12] A nation neglects its soft-power resources at its own peril in the international sphere[13]—and, as we shall see, an institution neglects its soft-power resources in the domestic sphere at its own peril as well. The three hard powers discussed in part II are the power of the purse, the personnel power, and the contempt power. Part III considers the "softer" powers associated with the freedom of speech or debate, the disciplinary power over members, and the cameral rule-making power. The reader is advised, however, not to mistake the book's organizational schema for a strong analytic claim about the distinctness of hard and soft powers: they exist on a continuum. Indeed, it is one of the central contentions of this book that these powers are best understood as parts of a suite: it makes little sense to think of them in hermetically sealed categories. The division into "hard" and "soft" is primarily useful, I think, because it emphasizes an often-overlooked feature of congressional procedure: the powers falling along the softer end of the spectrum are frequently regarded (to the extent that they are thought of at all) as mere housekeeping measures. Describing them as soft powers helps to emphasize the generally neglected fact that they are significant sources of legislative power vis-à-vis the other branches.

Within each of the six chapters discussing a specific congressional hard or soft power, the analysis is largely historical. This methodological approach follows from the theoretical account laid out in part I: if constitutional power is largely constructed within the practice of politics, then one cannot hope to understand a constitutional power without situating its exercise within a certain political context. And if one hopes to understand the political context in which a power is exercised in the present, then one must think about how the current web of institutional actions and interactions at any given time has come to be. As Karen Orren and Steve Skowronek have put it, "[B]ecause a polity in all its different parts is constructed historically, over time, the nature and prospects of any single part will be best understood within the long course of political forma-tion."[14] The historical construction of politics means that, "[a]t any given moment, the different rules, arrangements, and timetables put in place by changes negotiated at various points in the past will be found to impose them-selves on the actors of the present and to affect their efforts to negotiate changes of their own."[15] It is important to emphasize that this is not a deterministic account of politics—far from it. There is significant room for the play of contin-gency and agency, and these will be central factors in the historical accounts tracing the development of congressional powers. But that agency and contin-gency are always already sited within a politics that is up and running. In Mark Graber and Howard Gillman's words, "History creates some constitutional options while foreclosing others"[16]—at least for the time being. And, of course, actions in the present shape the landscape for the future, meaning that feedback, indeterminacy, and endogeneity are central to my accounts of the development of various congressional powers.[17]

Of course, the story must begin *somewhere*, and the stories traced in parts II and III all begin in earnest in England around the turn of the seventeenth century. This may at first glance seem a bit early, but there are some important parallels between seventeenth-century English constitutionalism and subsequent American constitutionalism that make it an apt starting point. Perhaps most centrally, conflicts between Parliament and the Stuart Crown involved contending claims by institutional actors with independent sources of constitu-tional authority. These conflicts occurred before the rise and solidification of parliamentary sovereignty and ministerial responsibility to Parliament in the early eighteenth century (a process that is traced in chapter 4). As a result, seventeenth-century conflicts between Parliament and the Crown looked quite familiar to eighteenth-century American colonists, who elected their own assem-blies only to see them engage in running conflicts with governors and other offi-cials appointed by the Crown. Small wonder, then, that numerous historians of colonial America have argued (in Jack Greene's words) that the behavior of the colonial assemblies was "deeply rooted" in parliamentary opposition to the

Stuart Crown.[18] Indeed, so pervasive was the specter of Stuart tyranny that "colonial legislators had a strong predisposition to look at each governor as a potential Charles I or James II, to assume a hostile posture toward the executive, and to define with the broadest possible latitude the role of the lower house as 'the main barrier of all those rights and privileges which British subjects enjoy.' "[19] Or, in Jack Rakove's formulation, "It is evident . . . that the vocabulary of American constitutional thinking was profoundly shaped by the great disputes between the Stuart monarchs and their opponents (in Parliament and out). . . . These positions remained vital . . . because the structure of colonial politics gave seventeenth-century arguments a continuing vitality in eighteenth-century America."[20] This constitutional vocabulary cashed out prominently in legislative procedure: the colonial assemblies looked closely to Parliament, especially to seventeenth-century Parliaments, for their understandings of their own privileges and procedures.[21]

The late eighteenth-century moment at which the American Constitution was first drafted, then, can be seen as something of a midpoint of the developmental stories that this book tells. Tracing the growth of legislative powers, procedures, and strategies from their English parliamentary context, into the New World in the colonial assemblies, and then across the Revolution into the early republican state constitutions and the Articles of Confederation helps to explain the form and texture they took in the written American Constitution. But the written document is only one part of American constitutional practice. As chapter 1 argues, the written Constitution constrains—it is certainly an important part of the historical construction of later politics—but that constraint still leaves a great deal of room for the operation of constitutional politics in shaping the institutional arrangements of those later politics. An attempt to understand the role of Congress in the American constitutional order that ended its developmental story in the late-eighteenth century would be radically incomplete. The chapters in parts II and III therefore trace the development of congressional powers under the American constitutional regime, not just the development leading up to it.

After tracing the development of a specific congressional power from the beginning of the seventeenth century through the end of the long nineteenth century (that is, up to roughly the outbreak of World War I), each chapter in parts II and III then turns to a thematic discussion of that power, considering important issues and controversies surrounding it in the twentieth and twenty-first centuries, as illuminated by the preceding history. In this way, for each of the congressional powers discussed, the reader should end the chapter with a sense of how it has developed over time, why it developed as it has, what live issues there are in the present, and how that developmental history bears on those live issues. One particular virtue of this approach is that, by illuminating both the fact of change across time and the agency and contingency that have factored into that change, it is a useful corrective to accounts of politics that treat extant institutional arrangements as inevitable. Contingency creates room for effective critique; put differently, the accounts offered here suggest that, to the extent that we do not like the institutional arrangements we have, there may be some room to alter them.

And I should be clear: some of our current institutional arrangements hardly strike me as likable. This book should certainly not be read to express deep satisfaction with our constitutional status quo, nor should it be read to suggest that Congress is in the habit of exercising its powers judiciously or thought-fully. The book foregrounds underappreciated congressional powers and high-lights the ways that they work in tandem to create a potent toolbox for Congress. But like all tools, they can be used poorly, and a pattern of injudicious uses of power can lead the public to shift its trust to other institutions, enhancing their governing authority at the expense of Congress's. Indeed, in tracing the devel-opment of each specific congressional power, we shall see numerous examples of both judicious and injudicious uses (and non-uses) of the power. It is a contention of this book that Congress has the capacity to behave so as to foster public trust and thereby enhance its own power; it is likewise a contention of this book that Congress has only sometimes taken advantage of that capacity.

We need, then, to modify the question with which this Introduction opened. The question is not: What good is Congress? Rather, the questions are what good it *can be*, what tools it can use in the process, how it can use those tools effectively, and how such a Congress fits into a larger constitutional framework. It is the project of this book to shed light on those questions.

PART ONE

SEPARATION-OF-POWERS MULTIPLICITY

Prelude

IN THE 2010 CASE *CITIZENS UNITED V. FEC*, the United States Supreme Court held unconstitutional a major provision of the Bipartisan Campaign Reform Act of 2002.[1] Specifically, the Court (by a five-to-four majority) held that "the Government may not suppress political speech on the basis of the speaker's corporate identity,"[2] and therefore that the act's provision barring independent corporate expenditures for electioneering communications violated the First Amendment.

Less than a week after the decision was handed down, President Barack Obama was discharging his constitutional duty to "from time to time give to the Congress Information of the State of the Union."[3] Obama and his aides were outraged by the decision, which they reportedly viewed as the work of "another group of Republicans, deserving no greater deference than GOP senators or congressmen."[4] About two-thirds of the way through his speech, the president remarked: "With all due deference to separation of powers, last week the Supreme Court reversed a century of law that I believe will open the floodgates for special interests—including foreign corporations—to spend without limit in our elections. I don't think American elections should be bankrolled by America's most powerful interests, or worse, by foreign entities. They should be decided by the American people. And I'd urge Democrats and Republicans to pass a bill that helps to correct some of these problems."[5] As Obama delivered those lines, cameras captured Justice Samuel Alito, who was seated in the second row of the House chamber, mouthing the words, "Not true."[6] Widely noted and discussed in the press,[7] Obama's criticism of the Court and Alito's reaction helped to crystallize the public perception that "the Obama White House and the Roberts Supreme Court were at odds."[8]

This conflict resurfaced a little more than two years later, when the tenor of oral arguments on the constitutionality of the 2010 Affordable Care Act suggested that the Court might strike down at least a significant portion of it. Obama went after the Court again, this time in a press conference:

> I just remind conservative commentators that for years we have heard the biggest problem on the bench was judicial activism or a lack of judicial restraint. That an unelected group of people would somehow overturn a duly constituted and passed law. Well, this is a good example and I am pretty confident that this Court will recognize that and not take that step. . . .
>
> As I said, we are confident this will be over—this will be upheld. I am confident this will be upheld because it should be upheld. And again, that is not just my opinion. That is the opinion of a whole lot of constitutional law professors and academics and judges and lawyers who have examined this law, even if they're not particularly sympathetic to this piece of legislation or my presidency.[9]

Once again, the press took intense notice,[10] with the *Wall Street Journal* editorializing that, "[a]s he runs for re-election, Mr. Obama's inner community organizer seems to be winning out over the law professor."[11] The implication— an odd one for an editorial page that often has quite a bit to say about Supreme Court cases—seems to have been that public mobilization and public discourse must be hermetically sealed off from discussions of the distribution of constitutional authority.

Nor were political pundits the only ones taken aback by Obama's assertiveness. Shortly after Obama made his comments, a conservative panel of the Fifth Circuit Court of Appeals, which was hearing a separate challenge to the healthcare law, ordered the government to file a letter "stating specifically and in detail in reference to [Obama's] statements what the authority is of the federal courts in this regard in terms of judicial review. That letter needs to be at least three pages single spaced, no less, and it needs to be specific. It needs to make specific reference to the president's statements and again to the position of the attorney general and the Department of Justice."[12] In response, the attorney general filed a letter—roughly two and a half pages long—agreeing that "[t]he power of the courts to review the constitutionality of legislation is beyond dispute,"[13] but also insisting that the courts are to approach legislation with a presumption of constitutionality and with respect for the constitutional and policy judgments of the elected branches.[14] Once again, the dustup received significant media attention.[15]

The public may well have taken note. In between oral arguments in the healthcare case and the Supreme Court's ruling in late June 2012, opinion polling gave "a fresh indication that the court's standing with the public has slipped significantly in the past quarter-century," with only 44 percent of respondents approving of the Supreme Court's performance, down more than twenty percentage points since the late 1980s.[16] In addition, more than three-quarters of respondents replied that the justices sometimes let their personal or political views influence their decisions.[17] As Lee Epstein noted, this and other recent polls undermined the conventional wisdom that the Supreme Court's approval rating will inevitably be higher than that of the other branches of the federal government.[18] Indeed, these numbers gave ammunition to those who argued that, should the Court strike down the healthcare law, the president and congressional Democrats should "come out swinging" against the Court.[19] As one observer noted, "A complete nullification of the health care law on the eve of a presidential election would put the Court at the center of the campaign, especially if the majority in the case consisted only of the five Republican appointees. Democrats, and perhaps Obama himself, would crusade against the Court, eroding its moral if not its legal authority."[20]

One can imagine that these poll results and political exhortations were met with significant consternation by Chief Justice John Roberts, who has repeatedly described his focus on maintaining the Court's "credibility and legitimacy as an institution."[21] For Roberts, stewardship of the Court's legitimacy involves making it clear that "[w]e're not politicians; we're judges, we're a court, and we're going to work real hard to be a court—partly because we don't like people thinking we're not."[22] Or, put differently, protecting the Court's institutional prestige might sometimes require putting a justice's own jurisprudential or political views on the back burner so as to avoid giving the appearance that judges are merely political partisans in robes.[23]

When the Supreme Court did finally rule on the healthcare law in *NFIB v. Sebelius*, it upheld the statute almost in its entirety.[24] The lineup was unexpected—on the most controversial issues, the vote was five to four, with Chief Justice Roberts voting to uphold the law and writing for the Court. Shortly after the opinions were released, it was reported that Roberts was originally the fifth vote to strike down the law and then subsequently changed his vote.[25] Even without definite knowledge of the Court's internal deliberative process, other observers speculated about the "political" motives behind Roberts's vote, suggesting that he put the institutional prestige of the Court above his own preferred outcome.[26] He was "almost certainly aware" of a great deal of "external pressure," including statements by political actors (like President Obama) and by media outlets "warning of damage to the court—and to Roberts' reputation—if the court were to strike down" the law.[27] By contrast, Roberts's act of "statesmanship"[28] in upholding the law was widely praised in the press, with observers suggesting that it "saved the Supreme Court from the stench of extreme partisanship,"[29] and that it brought "the Court back from the partisan abyss" by placing "the bipartisan legitimacy of the Court above [Roberts's] own ideological agenda."[30] *New York Times* columnist Thomas Friedman—the voice of elite centrism, if anyone is—praised Roberts's act of "simple noble leadership" aimed at "preserv[ing] the legitimacy and integrity of the Supreme Court as being above politics."[31] As another observer put it, Roberts acted to "save the court," because "[a] 5–4 decision to strike down [the healthcare law] along party lines, whatever its reasoning, would have been received by the general public as yet more proof that the court is merely an extension of the nation's polarized politics. Add the fact that the legal challenges . . . were at best novel and at worst frivolous, and suddenly a one-vote takedown of the [law] looks like it might undermine the court's very legitimacy."[32] Although it will be years, if ever, before we get a definitive version of the Court's decision-making process in the healthcare case, it certainly seems plausible—indeed, likely—that concerns about public reaction, concerns that were stoked and fed by public rhetoric by the president and others, played a role in shaping the outcome of this case.

But, of course, the battle over the Affordable Care Act was not over. Republican presidential candidate Mitt Romney was critical both of the law itself and of the Supreme Court's opinion.[33] Indeed, he promised that, if elected, he would sign a bill repealing the act "on my first day."[34] Repealing the Affordable Care Act was a plank in the 2012 Republican Party platform,[35] and it was a major theme for many Republican candidates on the campaign trail. Obama won reelection handily, and Democrats increased their margin in the Senate (despite having to defend more seats than the Republicans did) and narrowed the Republican margin in the House. Two days after the election,

Republican House Speaker John Boehner told a television interviewer that the quest to repeal the law was over: "I think the election changes that, it's pretty clear that the President was re-elected, Obamacare is the law of the land,"[36] a point subsequently echoed by Senator John McCain,[37] the Republican whose loss in the 2008 presidential election was a necessary precondition for the passage of the act in the first place. A poll taken in the aftermath of the election also showed support for repealing the law dropping to its lowest level since the bill was passed.[38] Subsequent efforts by Republicans to leverage their power of the purse to secure changes in the law (a topic discussed in detail in chapter 3) proved politically damaging to Republicans, and even the disastrous initial rollout of the act's online healthcare exchanges did not ultimately sink the act.[39] Indeed, by the 2014 midterm elections, commentators widely noted that Republicans had moved on to other campaign issues.[40]

When another challenge to the act (based on a statutory interpretation claim that, if successful, would have prohibited the payment of subsidies to low-income individuals in a number of states) was pending before the Supreme Court in 2015, Obama once again pursued an aggressive public strategy. "This should be an easy case. . . . Frankly, it probably shouldn't even have been taken up," he said at a press conference.[41] If one viewed the case as being about detailed questions of statutory interpretation, then perhaps the president was overstating his point. But if, instead, one viewed the case as being about whether the Supreme Court, having narrowly refused to destroy the act in 2012, would attempt to seriously undermine it in 2015, then Obama was on the mark. This was all the more true because, by 2015, people were already receiving the healthcare subsidies: a ruling against the administration this time would have meant taking away benefits that were already being enjoyed. The justices showed even less appetite for this: in *King v. Burwell*, they turned back the challenge by a six-to-three vote, with Justice Kennedy joining the five justices in the majority in *NFIB* (and with Chief Justice Roberts again writing for the Court).[42]

As a formal matter, the Affordable Care Act was no more entrenched after this sequence of events than it was the day after it was passed—it could still be repealed by a new statute, and the Court still had mechanisms (including overruling its own precedents) by which it could try to undermine or destroy the law. But as a political matter, the events traced above made those possibilities far more difficult. As this book goes to press, Donald Trump has won an upset victory in the 2016 presidential election, and Republicans have also retained control of both houses of Congress. It remains to be seen whether their election victories provide sufficient political impetus for Republicans to unwind the act, or whether they instead tinker around the edges (and perhaps rename it), while leaving many of its central features in place. Political events can entrench policies, but entrenchment is never absolute or final.

* * *

What is noteworthy about the multi-year back-and-forth between President Obama and the judiciary over campaign finance and healthcare is the sharp relief into which it throws the dynamics of the separation of powers. It demonstrates that, at its heart, the American constitutional separation of powers focuses on the creation of (or the attempt to create) space for conflict between branches of government without an overarching adjudicator to resolve the conflict in a principled, binding, and lasting way. These conflicts play out in public, and the branch that most successfully engages the public will accrete power over time. Part I of this book is devoted to fleshing out this conception of the separation of powers and demonstrating how it works in our constitutional structure.

1

Political Institutions in the Public Sphere

WHEN QUESTIONS OF INSTITUTIONAL POWER BECOME SALIENT, they generally do so in the context of some specific substantive controversy. When the conservative panel of the Fifth Circuit Court of Appeals snarkily demanded to know whether the Obama administration and the Department of Justice believed in the power of judicial review, it completely missed the point of Obama's comments (and it managed to do so in a politically tone-deaf way that further undermined the idea of a nonpartisan judiciary). Obama's comments were not about judicial review in the abstract, nor was he seeking a wholesale reevaluation of the legacy of *Marbury v. Madison*. He was, instead, making a highly contextualized argument about what the courts should do *about the healthcare law* in particular. He was, as the contemporary commentators noted, making it clear that, if the Court struck down the largest piece of social welfare legislation in decades, a legislative accomplishment that was, itself, decades in the making, and one that formed a cornerstone of his own successful presidential campaign, then he would do his best to ensure that there was hell to pay for the courts.

Constitutional text provides limited guidance as to questions of authority as they normally arise—that is, in the context of a particular political dispute within a particular political milieu. Using the standard toolbox of constitutional interpretation, the text can tell us what the scope of the federal judicial power is,[1] or what sort of authorization is necessary before the Treasury can disburse money.[2] But questions like "Can the courts review federal legislation for constitutionality?" and "How is the federal budget passed?" are classroom questions. "How deferential should the courts be toward the political branches' determination that the healthcare law is constitutional?" and "Who will decide the government's spending priorities for next year?" are political questions. These political questions *are* questions about the distribution of political authority among the branches, but they are *not* answerable by reference to the normal tools of constitutional interpretation. Text, history, structure, and precedent will not get us all the way to an answer here, because political context will necessarily play a sizable role. To put it more formally, the written Constitution (even as interpreted in light of the conventional modalities)[3] is substantially underdeterminate with respect to the separation of powers.[4] Our questions about judicial deference in the healthcare case or the allocation of budgetary authority in a particular context, then, like many of the most important separation-of-powers questions, ultimately are and must be answered through the process of *constitutional politics*.

The concept of constitutional politics will play a significant role throughout this book, and so it will be helpful to begin with a definition—with the understanding, of course, that this definition will be skeletal at first, with flesh to be added in the coming chapters. By *politics*, I mean to refer broadly to the processes and institutions of collective self-government.[5] This is, of course, a capacious definition; it covers, for example, the behavior of courts, especially when they issue wide-ranging opinions that have implications far beyond the parties before them. Any decision in the healthcare case, on this conception of politics, was necessarily political. Those observers who praised Roberts for transcending politics were, obviously, working with a much narrower conception of politics;[6] the most that can be said on my view is that he transcended partisanship.[7] By *constitutional*, I mean that which has to do with the distribution of governmental authority within a political community. Constituting, distributing, and restraining political power is the very heart of what constitutions do.[8] Putting them together, then, constitutional politics is the processes and structures of collective decision making about the distribution of authority to decide questions of collective self-government. Or, put differently, constitutional politics is meta-politics: if the question "How should we collectively regulate and pay for the provision of healthcare?" is a question of ordinary politics, then the question "Who should decide, and how should they decide, how we collectively regulate and pay for the provision of healthcare?" is a question of constitutional politics.[9] As this makes clear, in practice there almost never arise questions of *pure* constitutional politics. Rather, questions about the distribution of authority generally arise in the context of some dispute in the domain of normal politics. Understanding the dynamics of these separation-of-powers controversies in constitutional politics requires attentiveness to the concomitant questions of normal politics.

This chapter traces the ways in which constitutional politics shapes institutional power. In particular, the chapter is devoted to explicating the following claim: *Political power is largely endogenous to politics.* In other words, the authority possessed by political actors is neither static nor determined by something outside the process of politics. Rather, political power is, to a large extent, a *consequence* of political behaviors and interactions.

This claim may at first seem radical. After all, as noted above, if constitutions do anything, they constitute and distribute power among governmental institutions. One of the functions of a written constitution, then, would seem to be to make the distribution of political power immune to politics—to raise it to a higher plane.[10] It is this static conception of the separation of powers that seems to be behind the Fifth Circuit panel's reaction to President Obama's remarks. After all, surely it is a bit late in the day to be questioning whether federal courts can declare federal statutes unconstitutional. And there can be no doubt that there are a number of such relatively static separation-of-powers provisions in the Constitution. It is, for instance, clear that only the House can impeach and only the Senate can try impeachments.[11] Likewise, only the president may formally nominate Supreme Court justices and principal executive-branch officers, subject to confirmation that only the Senate can provide.[12] In addition to these clearly demarcated powers, each branch also has certain clearly defined protections against the other branches.[13] Members of Congress are privileged against civil arrest[14] and against being "questioned in any other Place" for "any Speech or Debate in either House."[15] Both the president and federal judges have protection against salary diminution.[16] And there are others; this list is not meant to be exhaustive. There is widespread consensus, cutting across nearly all ideological and interpretive divides, on the existence and location (if not the precise contours or normative desirability) of these powers and limitations, a consensus that is largely enabled by the precision and rule-like nature of the relevant portions of constitutional text. To put it succinctly, at least for the foreseeable future these provisions are most assuredly not subject to the play of politics.[17] In these particulars, the written Constitution can be said to be determinate—not everything is up for grabs, at least not all at once.[18]

But a lot more is up for grabs than we commonly realize. Questions like "Who should decide how we collectively regulate and pay for healthcare?"—and like

"Who has the authority to take us to war?," "Who has the authority to regulate greenhouse gases?," and "Who has the authority to determine the government's spending priorities?"—cannot be answered by reference to interpretation of the written constitutional text. Rather, constitutional interpretation allows us to understand the tools that different actors can use in the process of political contestation for this decision-making authority. In other words, written constitutional tools define the parameters of the field upon which the branches can fight with one another for the powers that they really care about. Political institutions are involved in constant contestation, not simply for the substantive outcomes they desire, but also for the authority to determine those outcomes. I refer to this understanding of the separation of powers as *multiplicity based* because it aims to highlight the ways in which claims of authority multiply and overlap in a nonhierarchical constitutional order.[19]

This claim that the distribution of political authority is largely generated through politics and is therefore not knowable in advance of politics is quite different from how we normally talk about the separation of powers. Indeed, one point of commonality between theories that fall under the "formalist" label and those that fall under the "functionalist" label[20] is that they all treat institutional power as a matter of institutional design, knowable in advance. For formalists, the allocation of governing authority is generally derivable from constitutional text, history, and structure.[21] For functionalists, it is generally a matter of associating certain design features with certain comparative competencies and allocating a power to the branch most competent to wield it.[22] For both, then, one does not need to know anything about the political circumstances in which authority will be exercised in order to state confidently to whom that authority belongs. By contrast, the multiplicity-based understanding focuses on the branches' contestation with one another for governing authority in specific political circumstances, with each making use of those relatively determinate constitutional tools that it possesses. On this understanding, one simply cannot describe the distribution of authority in advance of politics.

The rest of this chapter is devoted to describing more fully the dynamics of this conception of the separation of powers.

Consider again President Obama's public confrontations with the courts. This conflict has four defining features: (1) it involved nonhierarchical interbranch contestation; (2) it had no logical stopping point; (3) it took place in the public sphere and was essentially public focused; and (4) it privileged judicious, rather than maximal, combativeness. I shall elaborate each of these in turn.

First, the conflict between Obama and the courts involved interbranch contestation over the location of political authority where the Constitution itself provided no one with an unambiguous last word. What would have happened if Obama had defied a court ruling—say, by agreeing with the Federal Election Commission to enforce those provisions of campaign finance law that were struck down in *Citizens United* against parties other than Citizens United, thereby forcing the courts to rule against the government in every single instance? In doing so, he could have claimed the mantle of Abraham Lincoln, who insisted that, although he was bound by the *Dred Scott* decision with respect to the individual named Dred Scott, he would "refus[e] to obey it as a political rule"[23] because "the Supreme Court had no right to lay down a rule to govern a co-ordinate branch of the government, the members of which had sworn to support the Constitution."[24] Or, in a somewhat less strident vein, suppose that Obama had announced that a commitment to overturning *Citizens United* would be his litmus test for all future Supreme Court nominations (and perhaps even that he would seek to appoint lower-court nominees who would limit or stymie the principles announced in *Citizens United* to the greatest extent possible).[25] Or suppose he had simply announced that he would veto any appropriations bill that authorized any spending on the judiciary (except for judicial salaries, which are explicitly protected by determinate constitutional text)[26] until such time as *Citizens United* was overruled. What would have happened next? The Constitution's text provides no answer, and Obama could plausibly have claimed that none of these actions violated any determinate constitutional stricture. The simple point here is that there is no separation-of-powers equivalent of the Supremacy Clause;[27] rather, each branch has numerous powers that it can use against the others in a massively iterated—indeed, endless—separation-of-powers game. Parts II and III of this book are devoted to tracing a number of such powers possessed by the legislature and examining how those powers allow it to compete vigorously in that game.

This brings us to the second key feature of this confrontation: it highlights that interactions among the branches inevitably involve the possibility of conflict and that this conflict has no *logical* stopping point. The success or failure of Obama's attacks on *Citizens United* or his preemptive strike against an overturning of the healthcare law could not be determined by simply knowing the rules of the game. Those rules allow the branches to engage in continual contestation without any one of them having a decisive, final constitutional trump card. This does not mean, however, that any particular interbranch conflict is perpetual. The fact that there is no logical stopping point does not mean that there are no stopping points. Consider 2012 as a stopping point in the conflict over the authority to regulate healthcare. Roberts's decision, combined with the election results, had the effect of settling the issue temporarily. The House's renewed attacks on the law in 2013, however, suggested that the settlement remained open for renegotiation, under the right political circumstances. As the law further entrenched itself, those political circumstances became harder to conjure, and the surrounding politics adapted. But just because the new equilibrium is *harder* to disrupt does not make it *impossible* to disrupt; these settlements are never truly final, and Republican control of the House, Senate, and presidency as a result of the 2016 election will test how firmly entrenched the law's provisions really are. Such issues of interbranch power allocation are settled locally and contingently as they arise, often via compromise or negotiation, and without binding implications for the future—although, of course, each local institutional settlement alters (sometimes subtly, sometimes not) the playing field for future conflicts.[28]

But to say that such issues are always locally and provisionally settled is not really to say *how* they are settled. If constitutional text and structure simply define the parameters of the interbranch fight, then who picks the winner? Answering this question requires looking outside the institutions of government and focusing on the larger political community in which those institutions are embedded. The third key feature of these sorts of conflicts is that they are essentially *public focused.* This fact is often overlooked, as attention naturally gravitates toward the institutional actors actually engaged in the conflict. No one goes to a sporting event to watch the referee or to gawk at the trophy.[29] But an exclusive focus on the governmental actors obscures the nature of what they are fighting over. In brief, when struggling with one another for constitutional authority, the branches are engaged in what David Mayhew has described as the "public sphere."[30] As Mayhew has emphasized, "[P]olitical activity takes place before the eyes of an appraising public—not in a Washington, D.C., realm that can be theoretically or empirically isolated."[31] Actions in the public sphere can take a wide array of forms, from taking a stand on an issue to running for a different office to leading an impeachment drive to resigning from office.[32] The crucial thing about all of these actions is that they are public and, as such, both affect and are affected by public political discourse. It is generally through such active engagements with the people in the public sphere that the branches seek to expand their power vis-à-vis one another.

The process of engagement in the public sphere is murky[33]—indeed, I have deliberately used the somewhat wordy locution "engagement in the public sphere" to emphasize this murkiness. "Public opinion," with its association with snapshot polling and the attendant pretension to precision, fails to capture the dialogic and highly mediated complexity of public political interaction.[34] "Engagement," on the other hand, seems to point us in the direction of a more complicated and opaque process.[35] But despite this structural opacity, modern political science allows us to say at least a few things about political engagement in the public sphere. For one thing, public engagement affects the relative power of the branches. For instance, a president who enjoys high levels of public support will find it much easier to get his way with Congress in a wide variety of contexts than a president who does not.[36] This should not surprise us: as a review essay summarizes the literature, "[P]ublic opinion influences policy most of the time, often strongly."[37] But, of course, most members of the public do not have well-formed views on most specific issues. Rather, trust in specific decision makers stands in a dialectical relationship with views on particular issues: people will come to trust certain decision makers because those decision makers share their views on some issues (among other reasons), and people will come to take a position on certain issues because decision makers they trust take those views. Diffuse trust in and support for political actors thus plays an important role in the distribution of decision-making authority. In the context of the federal government as a whole, Marc Hetherington has concluded that "[o]nce government has earned the trust of its citizens, it follows that it will receive more leeway to pursue policy goals."[38] And at the level of individual members of Congress, Richard Fenno has noted that constituent trust can prevent them from being punished for the occasional vote with which their constituents disagree.[39] Indeed, Fenno quotes a member saying of his constituents, "If they trust you, you can vote the way you want, and it won't hurt."[40] What is true at both the macro and micro levels is also true in between: people can develop trust in institutions, and that trust can give the institution more power.[41] Philip Pettit has perceptively analyzed the link between trust and power: "Not only can the mechanisms of loyalty, virtue, and prudence make it sensible for me to believe in the motivating efficacy of manifesting reliance, and make it sensible for me to trust the person in question in a relevant domain.

The mechanisms can also explain why trust builds on trust: why trust tends to grow with use, not diminish. For it should be clear that as I test and prove someone suitably loyal, suitably virtuous, or suitably prudent, I have reason to be reinforced in my disposition to put those mechanisms to the test in future acts of trust."[42] Or, to use Hetherington's more vivid imagery, "If you come home and all is well, then your trust in the babysitter may increase. However, if you come home and your child is awake three hours after bedtime because his arm is hanging loosely from his shoulder socket, then you update your trust of the sitter downward dramatically."[43] As a result of this decrease in trust, you are, of course, much less likely to again place the babysitter in a position of power over your child. To combine these strands, then, the more trust the public has in an institution, the more leeway the public will give that institution in making future decisions—which is to say, the more power that institution has.

But how is that trust gained? Here, the story becomes somewhat more complicated, as there are at least two dialectical relationships at play: that between the general and the specific, and that between the political institution and the public. Trust is not given in the abstract—indeed, as both Pettit and Hetherington make clear, trust is earned by performing trustworthy actions, including by carrying through on one's promises.[44] An institution that is able to demonstrate trustworthiness to the public by performing well will find itself with a larger reservoir of trust—and, therefore, of power—from which to draw in the future. Moreover, demonstrating trustworthiness to the public is not simply a matter of pandering to public sentiment. Rather, as Mayhew has noted, political actors engage in both "opinion *expression*" and "opinion *formation*."[45] That is to say, not only do they often seek to speak and behave as their constituents want them to; sometimes, they "really do try to change the content of public opinion."[46] The result is a dialectical process "in which both elite actors and voters revise, to some degree, their policy preferences as they go along."[47] Or, more poetically, "[p]olicymaking is, among other things, a process of personal and national discovery."[48]

Consider, for example, the conversation that took place around President Reagan's nomination of Robert Bork to the Supreme Court in 1987. The Democrat-controlled Senate Judiciary Committee, by ensuring that "extended hearings would take place" gave "ample opportunity for Bork's opponents to elaborate the reasons for their position."[49] The result was "a national seminar on constitutional law" played out on live television,[50] one remarkable for the "heights [of public debate] that it repeatedly reached" and for the extent to which it "captivated and involved [the] citizenry."[51] It was out of these hearings, and the surrounding public debate on the airwaves, on op-ed pages, and around office water coolers, that "widespread popular opposition" to Bork arose.[52] Consider a sequence of three *Washington Post*–ABC News polls. The first, taken in early August 1987, roughly a month after Reagan had nominated Bork, found that only about 45 percent of respondents had heard or read about the Bork nomination; of those who were aware of it, 45 percent supported the nomination and 40 percent opposed it.[53] The second, taken during and after Bork's testimony before the Senate Judiciary Committee, found that 70 percent of respondents were aware of the nomination; of those who were aware, 44 percent supported Bork and 48 percent opposed him.[54] The third poll, taken about ten days before the Senate rejected his nomination, found that 78 percent of respondents were aware of the nomination, and of them, only 38 percent supported Bork, while 52 percent opposed him.[55] Clearly, the hearings and the attendant media attention not only significantly increased public awareness of the nomination; they also significantly increased opposition to it, and it was this opposition that sank Bork. Note the complicated and subtle back-and-forth here: Senate Democrats and their allies first had to accurately ascertain that there was a public willingness to endure a protracted fight over Bork's nomination. In this, they were undoubtedly bolstered by the fact that Reagan's popularity was sagging, due in large part to the Iran-Contra scandal.[56] Indeed, Democrats were only running the Bork hearings because they had made a net gain of eight Senate seats in the 1986 elections and taken control of the Senate for the first time during the Reagan presidency. Having ascertained that the public would at least be receptive to a substantial pushback against Bork, Senate Democrats then had to construct the hearings so as to convince the receptive public of Bork's unfitness. Meanwhile, the administration and its allies were engaged in attempting to construct a counternarrative. The vigor with which the supporters and opponents of the nomination engaged one another signaled to the public that this was a high-stakes fight, one to which it should pay attention. And, over the course of several months, Bork's opponents were more successful in convincing a significant segment of the population that it should oppose the nomination. As a result, the more centrist Anthony Kennedy wound up on the Supreme Court (but only after another Reagan nominee, Douglas Ginsburg, was forced to withdraw when allegations of marijuana use became public).

Political trust—and with it, political power—arises out of such conversations between political elites and the public. Constitutional text does not tell us whether the Senate will vigorously challenge a nomination, as it did with Bork, or deferentially support it, as it had done with Reagan's nomination of Antonin Scalia a year earlier. Constitutional text does, however, set the stage upon which such decisions play out—after all, if the Constitution gave the Senate no role in selecting judges, then there would have been no institutional actor capable of opposing Bork. But within the confines laid out by the text, it is political engagement in the public sphere that determines where, for any given nomination (or other decision), the power to decide really lies. The political actors who are the best public conversationalists, and who are seen to back up their talk with consistent actions, win power in the long run. Those who attempt to govern without paying attention to this public dynamic, or who engage inartfully in the public sphere, tend to lose. There should be nothing surprising about this; we are well used to seeing public officials, even those who will not face the voters for quite some time (indeed, even those who will never face the voters again) campaigning for public trust and support.[57]

The fourth and final essential aspect of these separation-of-powers conflicts emerges from the first three, and it goes to the question of the local and provisional settlements that arise out of specific interbranch confrontations. If the contestation is, at its heart, about winning over the public, then what is privileged is not maximal combativeness but rather *judicious* combativeness. Just as lawyers in an adversarial system are advised not to object too frequently, lest they lose the confidence or patience of the judge, so too institutional actors must not pick too many fights, lest they alienate the public and thereby cost themselves trust and power. Moreover, the issue is not simply one of how many fights to pick but also one of which fights to pick—sometimes one loses a fight simply by starting it.[58] It appears, for example, that House Republicans' decision to shut down the federal government in late 2013 as part of their attempt to defund the Affordable Care Act was a miscalculation that cost them significant public support, at least in the short run.[59] Importantly, however, the judiciousness of any particular confrontation cannot be established *a priori*. Rather, it is a function of the constitutional politics of the day. Or, put differently, the judiciousness of a branch's action arises out of and depends upon the success of its discursive engagement with the citizenry.

To whatever extent formalization is helpful, we might think of the preceding in broadly Bayesian terms.[60] Each branch has a wide variety of possible moves at any given moment, and it has limited information about both the state of the world and the strategies of the other branches. Formally, each decision node on the game tree faced by an actor presents that actor with a large number of branching choices. Moreover, the actor is never certain precisely which decision node it faces; rather, it constantly faces a massive information set of potential nodes.[61] It uses what information it does have to form beliefs—that is, conditional probabilities that it is at a particular node in the information set.[62] Those beliefs are always necessarily contingent; new information can (and, if the actors are behaving rationally, should) always cause them to be updated, with the consequence that the optimal strategy for the actor is in constant flux as new information comes in. The tools of interbranch contestation compose the choices available to the political actor at each node of the game. The invocation of one or more of those tools moves the actor to a different node, sends signals to the other actors, and—by engaging dialogically with the public—potentially alters the payoffs available to different actors at different points in the game. The local, one-off settlements reached in particular interbranch conflicts are unstable equilibria,[63] easily disturbed by changes in conditions. And the judiciousness of an actor's engagement in the public sphere is a function of the accuracy of its beliefs, as well as its skillfulness in choosing and implementing a strategy.

This, then, is how we might characterize Chief Justice Roberts's "statesmanship" in the first healthcare case: in this extremely high-profile case, faced with a president who had signaled his willingness to fight and with slipping public support for the Court as an institution, Roberts concluded that it would be injudicious for five Republican-appointed justices to strike down the signature accomplishment of a Democratic president and Congress. Or, to put it differently, he seems to have made the judgment that, if the law were struck down along partisan lines, the institution of which he views himself as the steward would emerge weakened from the resulting public fight.[64] Faced with the same political backdrop, President Obama seems to have come to the same conclusion—that is, he, too, seems to have calculated that, were the Supreme Court to strike down the healthcare law along partisan lines, he could win the ensuing public debate. He thus signaled to the Court that he was prepared to have that fight. The result was a local equilibrium outcome upholding the law. When the additional information generated by the 2012 elections was added to the mix, the equilibrium became more stable, and the Republican politicians who attempted in late 2013 to disturb that equilibrium both failed to do so and hurt their public standing in the process.

It is crucial to understand the role that political power, constituted and constrained by constitutional institutions, plays in these interactions in the public sphere. Stable, textual constitutional constraints may, as I have been arguing, be significantly underdeterminate of the separation of powers, but they are no less crucial for that. Effective engagement in the public sphere often requires political power, and the written Constitution provides the key framework.[65] Consider again the Bork nomination. I have argued above that it was the public's turn against Bork that sank his nomination; crucial to that turn were the Senate hearings, which happened because the Constitution requires Senate consent to Supreme Court appointments. It was, moreover, the constitutional structuring of Senate elections—the requirement that a third of the chamber be up for election every two years, for instance—that put control of the Senate into Democratic hands in 1987. The interaction of these hard-wired constitutional requirements with the political conditions of the day created the playing field upon which the Judiciary Committee was able to fight for and win public support.

In other words, the multiplicity-based understanding of the separation of powers does not posit a free-form free-for-all. Rather, it posits a dynamic, inter-institutional competition for public support, played out on a field that is given form and structure by the written Constitution. While some of these constitutional provisions, like the regular election of senators and the requirement of Senate consent for judicial nominees, are quite familiar, it is the task of parts II and III of this book to highlight others, ones that empower Congress in particular. Those chapters both describe these constitutional constraints and demonstrate the ways in which they create the conditions for public interbranch contestation.

But before getting to those chapters, there is still more work to be done in laying out the multiplicity-based view of the separation of powers. This chapter has offered an interpretive-descriptive account of the multiplicity-based view. The next chapter considers the political economy of this account—and, specifically, considers whether, and under what conditions, it is plausible that Congress will seek to make use of the tools at its disposal.

2

The Role of Congress

IT WILL NOT HAVE ESCAPED NOTICE THAT IN THIS, a book about congressional power, the two recent paradigm cases that I chose to illustrate separation-of-powers multiplicity involved clashes between the *other* two branches—between President Obama and the courts over campaign finance reform and healthcare legislation. This was a conscious choice, designed to illustrate the multiplicity-based understanding of the separation of powers without stealing the thunder of later chapters. But it also highlights a serious concern. Both the McCain-Feingold campaign finance reform law partially struck down in *Citizens United* and the Affordable Care Act largely upheld in the healthcare cases were, after all, congressionally passed statutes. Indeed, President Obama had taken a good deal of criticism in 2009 for leaving the drafting of the health-care law almost entirely to Congress.[1] But by 2012, the law had become widely known as "Obamacare," and Congress was largely absent from the public back-and-forth over its constitutionality. All of which raises the following questions: If the separation-of-powers game is as I have described it in the previous chapter, and if the constitutional tools available to Congress include those that I describe in the next six chapters, is it plausible to think that Congress will use those tools to engage in that game? And if it does engage, can it be effective? This chapter addresses those questions in turn. First, it addresses the question of whether Congress has the motivation to assert itself against the other branches. And second, it addresses the question of whether Congress is neces-sarily at a disadvantage when it competes against the other branches in the public sphere.

Congressional Motivation

The principal argument for the claim that Congress will inevitably lack the motivation to assert itself against the other branches sounds in partisanship. In particular, as Daryl Levinson and Rick Pildes have influentially written, the development of political parties "overwhelmed the Madisonian conception of separation of powers almost from the outset, preempting the political dynamics that were supposed to provide each branch with a 'will of its own' that would propel departmental '[a]mbition . . . to counteract ambition.'"[2] The reason, according to Levinson and Pildes, is that the separation-of-powers system "would seem to require government officials who care more about the intrinsic interests of their departments than their personal interests or the interests of the citizens they represent. Democratic politics is unlikely to generate such officials."[3] Instead, our political system channels "relatively stable lines of policy and ideological disagreement" through relatively stable political parties.[4] Accordingly, government officials develop primary loyalty to their parties—which both help them advance their personal goals and reflect the political and ideological issues salient to the voters—rather than to their branches. As a result, Levinson and Pildes assert, we will see vigorous interbranch contestation only under conditions of divided government—and even then, the interbranch contestation will really just be an epiphenomenal manifestation of the real, underlying conflict between the parties. Under unified government, we will see no such contestation. Indeed, "the structural position of the minority party under unified American government is more closely analogous to that of minority parties shut out of parliamentary governments than observers have recognized."[5] In neither case is the constitutional separation of powers doing much important work.

But Levinson and Pildes's account has a few problems of its own. First, it is important to note that the actual unity of unified government is very much a matter of degree. Levinson and Pildes understand unified government to involve control by a single party of the House, Senate, and presidency.[6] But given the prevalence of the filibuster[7] (about which, more in chapter 8), true control of the Senate could be said to require at least sixty votes, not fifty. What's more, truly unified government should be understood to involve the courts as well as Congress and the presidency. Because judges have good-behavior tenure, the partisan and ideological composition of the judiciary may be sharply different from that of the elected branches, and the courts, like the other branches, have tools that allow them to behave confrontationally. Franklin Roosevelt spent much of his first term "look[ing] on with increasing frustration as the [Supreme] Court invalidated one after another of the central elements of his New Deal,"[8] statutes that were passed through a Congress in which Democrats had dominant majorities in both chambers. In more recent years, as we saw in the prelude to this part, conservative judges on the Fifth Circuit and the Supreme Court attacked the Affordable Care Act—ultimately unsuccessfully—and their colleagues on the D.C. Circuit went after implementation of financial regulations,[9] environmental regulations,[10] labor regulations,[11] and agency appointments,[12] before the arrival of new personnel gave that court a more liberal tilt in late 2013. Examples could, of course, be multiplied; the key point is simply that a highly unified government would also involve control of the judiciary. Moreover, a highly unified government would look to the states as well as the federal government. As Jessica Bulman-Pozen has noted, given the large number of federal laws that depend on state cooperation in implementation (what are often called "cooperative federalism" statutes), a state government controlled by one party can often form an effective check to a unified federal government in the hands of the other party.[13] As all of this should make clear, however common unified government in the sense in which Levinson and Pildes use the term may be, a government in which one party truly has a strong grip on all of the important levers of power is far, far rarer.

And even as to institutions that are firmly controlled by a single party, as Levinson and Pildes note in passing, party discipline is by no means absolute in the American system.[14] Perhaps more importantly, the willingness of members of Congress to accede to the wishes of a same-party president is at least partly a function of that president's standing in the public sphere.[15] Consider several high-profile examples in recent years. At the beginning of his second term, President George W. Bush made a major push to partially privatize Social Security. In fact, more than a fifth of the 2005 State of the Union Address was dedicated to the subject of Social Security reform,[16] and the president followed that speech with a lengthy national tour of "well rehearsed" presentations meant to build support for his reform proposals.[17] Finally, in a nationally televised prime-time news conference in late April 2005, Bush laid out the specifics of his plan.[18] From a purely partisan perspective, things should have looked good for the plan: the Republicans had healthy majorities in both houses of Congress, although not a filibuster-proof supermajority in the Senate. But the broader political conditions were highly unfavorable—by the time of his late April press conference, Bush's poll ratings "equal[ed] the worst of his 51 months in office,"[19] and they were to continue heading south in the months ahead. Moreover, his stewardship of Social Security in particular had never been well regarded,[20] and, in the immediate aftermath of his press conference, a poll showed 38 percent support for his proposal, as against 54 percent opposition to it.[21] In this political climate, there was no need for a filibuster—the House simply declined to take up the proposals,[22] and the proposed reforms died. As Bush's popularity continued to slide throughout 2005, opposition by Senate Republicans was also responsible for sinking the nomination of Harriet Miers to the Supreme Court.[23]

President Obama, too, faced intraparty opposition from Congress. Consider, for example, his first-term nominations of Dawn Johnsen to head the Office of Legal Counsel in the Department of Justice and of Goodwin Liu to be a judge on the Ninth Circuit Court of Appeals. Despite the fact that Democrats had a filibuster-proof Senate supermajority for much of the time during which these nominations were pending, Johnsen and Liu—like Miers—were ultimately not confirmed.[24] Likewise, a revolt by Democrats was responsible for the decision by Lawrence Summers, reported to be Obama's top pick to chair the Board of Governors of the Federal Reserve System, to withdraw his name from consideration in 2013.[25] Consider also that certain Senate Democrats—most notably Senators Ron Wyden and Mark Udall—publicly pressured the Obama administration to be significantly less secretive about national security matters.[26] And, of course, such public examples of intraparty conflict may significantly understate the actual impact of members' willingness to stand up to same-party presidents: presidents who know, or have reason to believe, that they will face significant challenges from within their own ranks may choose instead to modify their positions preemptively. The point here is certainly not that party loyalty is not important—clearly, it is. But neither is intraparty deference automatic, which means that, even in times of unified government, Congress and its members can and sometimes do play a checking role. And, importantly, their willingness to play that role depends, in part, on the success of the various actors' discursive engagements in the public sphere.

A third factor that complicates Levinson and Pildes's claims about congressional behavior is that members of Congress do, on some occasions, care about their chamber's power, per se.[27] Consider the Senate's role in making treaties. Under the Treaty Clause, the president needs to secure the "Consent" of "two thirds of the Senators present" in order to ratify a treaty.[28] But, from the earliest days of the Republic, there has been a parallel means of making international agreements: the "congressional-executive agreement," passed under the usual Article I, section 7, lawmaking procedures.[29] Beginning in the 1940s, the use of congressional-executive agreements increased substantially,[30] such that "today they constitute the vast majority of international agreements entered into by the United States."[31] But there remain certain substantive areas—most notably, arms control agreements, military alliances, and human rights agreements— which continue to progress via the Article II Treaty Clause mechanism.[32] And the reason for this, as Curt Bradley and Trevor Morrison have noted, is that the Senate itself has insisted that it be so.[33] In particular, in ratifying arms control treaties on a number of occasions, the Senate has included a declaration insisting that such agreements must be ratified via the treaty power.[34] And they have insisted on this even against same-party presidents. So, for example, President Carter reportedly wanted to submit the SALT II treaty as a congressional-executive agreement.[35] This made some degree of sense—the Democrats had large majorities in both houses of the Ninety-fifth and Ninety-sixth Congresses, but they did not have a two-thirds supermajority in the Senate in either Congress. But when news that Carter was thinking of submitting SALT II as a congressional-executive agreement became public, a number of Democratic senators joined Republican colleagues in insisting that it be submitted as a treaty.[36] Indeed, Democratic Senate majority leader Robert Byrd all but taunted the Carter administration, telling the *Washington Post*: "If they don't feel they can get two-thirds [support in the Senate], then they must not feel they have a good case."[37] Carter retreated and submitted SALT II as an Article II treaty.[38] More recent presidents have faced similar pressures from the Senate. President Bill Clinton, who had originally sought to submit an update to the Treaty on Armed Conventional Forces in Europe as a congressional-executive agreement, bowed to pressure from the (Republican-controlled) Senate and submitted it as an Article II treaty instead.[39] Likewise, although Clinton failed to gain ratification for the Comprehensive Nuclear Test Ban Treaty, "his administration never publicly proposed—nor, so far as we know, even privately contemplated— concluding the treaty as a congressional-executive agreement."[40] In 2001, when President George W. Bush and Secretary of State Colin Powell indicated that the administration was considering negotiating a nuclear-arms-reduction treaty with Russia, the Democratic chairman of the Senate Foreign Relations Committee (Joe Biden) and the Republican ranking member (Jesse Helms) cosigned a letter insisting that any such treaty go through the Article II process.[41] The administration complied, and the treaty was ratified in 2003.[42] And in May 2010 President Obama sent the New START nuclear-arms-reduction treaty to the Senate via the Article II process,[43] despite the fact that the 111th Congress had large Democratic margins in both houses of Congress—but, again, not a two-thirds supermajority in the Senate. Harold Koh, who served as the State Department's top lawyer during the New START ratification process, described the ratification as "hard-won"[44] but explained that the congressional-executive agreement route was not politically available because "Congress has its own strong views on how certain types of agreements should be entered into and will fight for those outcomes as a matter of institutional and political preroga-tive."[45] As Bradley and Morrison summarize, it "seems highly unlikely" that the United States would enter into certain types of international agreements, such as joining the International Criminal Court treaty or the Law of the Sea Convention, through anything other than the Article II Treaty Clause process.[46] And senators—even senators of the president's party who support the treaty at issue—seem to be willing at least sometimes to put this institutional preroga-tive ahead of either partisan loyalty or substantive preferences.

Nor is the Senate treaty power the only area in which we see members acting in the interests of their houses, as such. On the House side, consider the Origination Clause, which provides that "[a]ll Bills for raising Revenue shall originate in the House of Representatives; but the Senate may propose or concur with Amendments as on other Bills."[47] The House protects this prerogative through "blue slips," resolutions of the House (usually printed on blue paper) that assert that a bill that has originated in the Senate, "in the opinion of this House, contravenes the first clause of the seventh section of the first article of the Constitution of the United States and is an infringement of the privileges of this House; and . . . shall be respectfully returned to the Senate with a message communicating this resolution."[48] If members of Congress cared only about party, then we might expect to see blue slips used merely strategically—in other words, we would expect them to be used when different parties controlled the House and the Senate. In fact, however, this is not what we see at all: the over-whelming majority of blue slips are sent to a Senate controlled by the *same* party that controls the House. According to a tally kept by the House Ways and Means Committee,[49] there were thirty-one blue slips, sending back thirty-six measures,[50] between the 98th Congress (1983–1985) and the 113th Congress (2013–2015), inclusive. Of those, a Democratic House sent eighteen blue slips, returning twenty-three measures, to a Democratic Senate. A Republican House sent eight blue slips, returning eight measures, to a Republican Senate. A Democratic House sent three blue slips, returning three measures, to a Republican Senate; and a Republican House sent two blue slips, returning two measures, to a Democratic Senate.[51] To pull out a few specific examples, in the 100th Congress (1987–1989), the Democratic House sent seven blue slips to the Democratic Senate; in the 104th Congress (1995–1997), the Republican House sent four blue slips to the Republican Senate; and in the 111th Congress (2009–2011), the Democratic House used one blue slip to send six measures back to the Democratic Senate.[52] This is not consistent with the hypothesis that blue slips are used as one more tool in partisan battle; it is, however, consistent with the hypothesis that they are, in fact, used by the House to protect its cameral prerogatives.

So far, I have offered three caveats to Levinson and Pildes's thesis: I have argued that the unity of unified government is a matter of degree and that *highly* unified government (that is, a situation in which a single party controls all of the significant levers of power) is vanishingly rare; I have argued that members of Congress do, on some occasions, defy presidents of their own party on policy grounds (especially when those presidents have lost significant public support); and I have argued that members have sometimes been known to put their cameral interests ahead of their partisan ones. But this is still not a full answer to Levinson and Pildes. After all, one would have to be willfully blind to the realities of government to claim that Congress checks the president as vigorously when the chambers are controlled by the president's party as it does when they are controlled by the other party.

But what Levinson and Pildes fundamentally miss is that this is a feature of the American governing system, not a bug. As the previous chapter emphasized, a branch's successful engagement in the public sphere requires judicious, not maximal, combativeness, with judiciousness understood as a function of the political circumstances of the day. The branches should not always have the same posture toward one another. And, crucially, the fact of unified or divided government goes a good way toward indicating what posture the branches should take. Levinson and Pildes treat the issue of unified versus divided government as an independent variable and then look to see what each possible value of this variable implies for constraints on the executive. But unified versus divided government is more properly understood as a dependent variable—dependent, that is, on the will of the people, as expressed through electoral mechanisms.

The different (but cross-cutting) constituencies and staggered electoral time-tables of the component parts of the federal government make it very difficult for a party to achieve (and even harder to sustain) unified government. Our representatives serve two-year terms; our presidents serve four-year terms with a two-term limit; and our senators serve six-year terms, with a third of the seats up for election every two years. Because of this staggered electoral cycle, a single election—even a single "transformative" election—is unlikely to result in unified government. The 1994 "Republican Revolution" swung both houses of Congress, but not the presidency, because 1994 was not a presidential election year. Only if the Republicans had been able to continue making a successful public case through the 1996 elections would they have been able to achieve unified government. Unified government under President George W. Bush did not arise ex nihilo—Republicans had held both houses of Congress (more or less) since 1995.[53] Likewise, the 2008 elections resulted in unified government, but that was a consequence of the 2006 Democratic takeover of both houses of Congress, and it lasted only until the Republicans retook the House in the 2010 elections. At Westminster, achieving unified government requires convincing a plurality of voters in a majority of constituencies to cast a single vote for your party's parliamentary candidates. In Washington, that will get you a House majority, but nothing more. You also need the voters to cast a second ballot for a senator of that party—and (barring a vacancy-necessitated special election) they will have the opportunity to vote for, at most, one of their senators in any given election cycle. And you need their vote in the presidential election, assuming it is a presidential election year, which it will not be in half of all House election years.[54] A lot can interfere with this: voters may split their tickets; they may change their preferences between election cycles; and the cross-cutting nature of the constituencies may result in different outcomes (for example, a state with a majority of Democrats—which therefore sends Democrats to the Senate and the Electoral College—may be districted in such a way as to send more Republicans than Democrats to the House). To put it succinctly, unified government in America requires a relatively broad, deep, and durable commitment by the electorate to the agenda of one of the parties. Because the parties have strong incentives to compete for the center, unified government will be the exception.[55] And under divided government, power is shared among actors with a strong interest in checking one another. As Levinson and Pildes acknowledge, interbranch checks can operate effectively under divided government.

What they overlook, however, is that unified government tells us something important. It tells us that, across these multiple election cycles and cross-cutting constituencies, one party has consistently outperformed the other. It tells us, in short, that one party is having significantly more success engaging in the public sphere than the other. Of course, this does not mean that there will be no disagreements within that party—as noted above, party discipline in America is far from absolute—but it does indicate a general, sustained preference for one party's governing agenda over the other's. And, in that context, it makes good democratic sense for there to be fewer checks on the implementation of that party's agenda. Divided government, by contrast, indicates that the American people have not seen fit to entrust the entirety of governmental operations to a single party. The multiplicity-based separation-of-powers framework provides institutional homes for both parties under such circumstances, and the Constitution provides them with ample powers to use from these institutional bases[56]—as parts II and III of this book demonstrate in the case of Congress. The motivating power of partisanship, then, does not suggest the inevitability of congressional passivity; rather, it is one factor that goes to the *judiciousness* of the exercise of congressional power.

Congressional Capacity

Of course, even if Congress, under the right conditions, has the motivation to assert itself against the other branches, we still have to ask whether it has the capacity to do so. While parts II and III of the book address specific capacities that individual members and houses of Congress possess in interbranch conflicts, here I want to address the broader question of whether Congress is inevitably at a disadvantage in such confrontations. The literature suggests two broad reasons Congress might be at such a disadvantage: first, the president may, in many situations, possess a power of unilateral action that forestalls effective congressional response; and second, the presidency, due to its unified nature, may have a definite advantage in communicating with the public. This section considers these two arguments in turn.

The first argument for inevitable executive predominance asserts that the president, in many situations, has the ability to act unilaterally, and that her doing so limits the options available to Congress (and the courts). As Terry Moe and William Howell put it, presidents often have a "formal capacity for taking unilateral action"—that is, they "can and do make new law—and thus shift the existing status quo—without the explicit consent of Congress."[57] To take the most common example, it is often said that when the president deploys troops overseas, it will not be politically feasible for Congress to cut off their funding or otherwise force them to be brought home (although, as the next chapter discusses, there are a number of examples of such action by Congress, including the Cooper-Church and Case-Church Amendments during the Vietnam War).[58] By contrast, Congress is "burdened by collective action problems and heavy transaction costs,"[59] thus making congressional action significantly more cumbersome. Congress, as Eric Posner and Adrian Vermeule put it, is destined to be "continually behind the pace of events in the administrative state" and therefore to "play an essentially reactive and marginal role."[60] Of course, there are limits to this argument; as Moe and Howell suggest, presidents have to "pick their spots," lest they "go too far or too fast, or move into the wrong areas at the wrong time," in which case they might "find that there are heavy political costs to be paid—perhaps in being reversed on the specific issue by Congress or the courts, but more generally by creating opposition that could threaten other aspects of the presidential policy agenda or even its broader success."[61] Posner and Vermeule likewise note that "politics and public opinion at least block the most lurid forms of executive abuse."[62] Still, as the grudging nature of those acknowledgments indicates, the central message remains clear: in contrast to the executive, which can act unilaterally and with resolve, the legislature is bound to remain slow, reactive, and distinctly secondary in importance. Given all that, how can it possibly play the separation-of-powers game effectively?

Clearly, there is a measure of truth in this argument. Especially in certain policy areas, the executive can and frequently does act unilaterally in ways that constrain the universe of feasible responses by other branches. This is a significant source of executive power. But, again, it is important not to put the point too strongly. David Mayhew, surveying every president from Franklin Roosevelt to Obama, points out that they all (with the possible exception of Lyndon Johnson) "have seen some of their major policy initiatives sink on Capitol Hill. That is the norm."[63] Even in moments of crisis, moments at which decisive action appears to be called for, scholars like Moe, Howell, Posner, and Vermeule may well overestimate the ability of executive actors to move unilaterally. As Aziz Huq has noted, in September 2008, at the height of the meltdown of the financial industry, (Republican) Treasury Secretary Henry Paulson literally got down on his knees and begged (Democratic) Speaker Nancy Pelosi to enact new statutory authority for the Treasury to act.[64] In the national security context, congressional opposition prevented Obama from closing the prison at Guantanamo Bay[65] and perhaps from intervening in the Syrian civil war.[66] Indeed, at least one study suggests that Congress acts as a significant constraint on presidents' ability to initiate major uses of military force.[67] As Huq concludes from these and other examples, "It is generally the case that even in the heart of crisis, and even on matters where executive competence is supposedly at an acme, legislators employ formal institutional powers not only to delay executive initiatives but also affirmatively to end presidential policies."[68] In other words, it turns out that the president's power to alter the status quo unilaterally is often robustly constrained by Congress.

Posner and Vermeule, especially, devote a great deal of energy to insisting that such constraints are a function of "politics," rather than "law" or the "separation-of-powers framework."[69] But this sharp distinction between politics and the "separation-of-powers framework" is an artifact of Posner and Vermeule's own creation. As chapter 1 argued, the separation-of-powers framework is best understood as the enabler and shaper of politics. The constitutional separation of powers constitutes our politics; it only muddies the waters to attempt to divorce the two and then argue about which actually constrains the president. In the end, what matters is that the executive is significantly constrained and that this constraint, far from being external to our constitutional design, is in fact the proper functioning of that design. For certain types of decisions and under certain circumstances, presidents will be able to act unilaterally in ways that effectively constrain the actions of the other branches. But this is certainly not true for all types of decisions or under all circumstances. And, as Huq points out, even in those situations in which it seems most plausible to imagine a wide scope for unilateral executive action, we do not always see it.

Moreover, the president is not the only actor capable of sometimes acting unilaterally and thereby forcing the other branches to respond on its terms. Court decisions often prod other actors, whether because they have brought an issue to the fore that those actors would have preferred not to address or because the other actors dislike the substantive outcome the court has reached and therefore react against it. Likewise, congressional committees can drive the national agenda by holding hearings that draw attention to certain issues, and "entrepreneurial" individual members of Congress, using the platform afforded by their offices (and, if necessary, the protection afforded by the Speech or Debate Clause, discussed in chapter 6), can play key roles in shaping the national discussion.[70] The feasibility and success of these actions—like those of unilateral actions by the president—will depend on how successful they are at engaging in the public sphere.

This brings us to the second argument for inevitable executive predominance: that presidents will always enjoy an advantage in engagements in the public sphere because of their ability to speak with a unified voice. On this view, presidents are inevitably better at communicating their position because they speak for the only branch that can be said to have a single will. Congressional communication, in contrast, is inevitably muddled by the cacophony of congressional views, interests, and speakers. Indeed, John Hibbing and Elizabeth Theiss-Morse, in a book tellingly titled *Congress as Public Enemy*, provocatively argued that, although Americans claim that they value robust debate and compromise, they in fact recoil from Congress precisely because it is the institution that most visibly instantiates those qualities.[71] In their pithy phrase, Americans want "stealth democracy"—that is, they "want democratic procedures, but they do not want to see them in action."[72] Congress's diversity and openness, on this view, are precisely what put it at a disadvantage vis-à-vis the other branches when doing battle in the public sphere.

While Hibbing and Theiss-Morse are not without their critics,[73] it would be petulant to deny that there is some truth here. On some issues, and in some circumstances, the president is better able to speak with a unified voice, which proves an advantage in the public sphere; likewise, Congress is frequently hampered by its internal divisions. But, once again, several factors complicate the simple story. For one thing, executive communication is not so unitary as many commentators make it out to be, because the executive faces a straightforward principal-agent problem. The federal bureaucracy is vast—for 2014, it was estimated that there were nearly 2.1 million civilian employees of the federal government, excluding postal service employees.[74] There were an additional 1.35 million active-duty members of the military.[75] In one sense, of course, these numbers demonstrate the executive branch's advantage—it may well have the personnel to overwhelm Congress. But they also make clear the impossibility of keeping close tabs on all of those agents to ensure that they are carrying out the president's priorities. It is simply impossible to monitor that many people at a high enough level of detail, and the predictable result is to decrease the unified nature of executive action.[76] Indeed, as David Pozen has documented, executive-branch leaks of secret information are a startlingly frequent phenomenon, and, while some leaks are intended to advance the president's agenda, others are intended to thwart or influence that agenda.[77] In recent years, for example, Army Private Chelsea Manning leaked a huge cache of secret documents, including a large number of State Department cables, to WikiLeaks,[78] and Edward Snowden, who had worked for the Central Intelligence Agency and the National Security Agency before taking a job with a consulting firm hired by the National Security Agency, leaked the details of a number of government surveillance programs.[79] That these leaks both came from within the supposedly unified executive branch makes it clear that, in practice, the executive, too, is beset by collective action problems and by cross-cutting agendas. Indeed, a number of influential Washington journalists (perhaps most famously Bob Woodward) serve as well-known conduits for internal executive-branch position taking and score settling.[80] Moreover, certain features of institutional structure may create a miniature version of the separation of powers *within* bureaucratic agencies, thereby frustrating attempts at top-down control.[81] These structural features may be reinforced by institutional customs that actively undermine the very idea of a unitary executive: as Adrian Vermeule has pointed out, the autonomy of various executive-branch agencies is protected by conventions of independence,[82] and this autonomy makes it possible for them to pursue policies that complicate the president's agenda.

And if the executive isn't quite so unified as some theorists seem to assume, neither are the houses of Congress always quite so divided. Specifically, party discipline—especially in the House of Representatives—can help overcome certain types of collective action problems typically associated with Congress. In moments of high-stakes interbranch conflict, legislative leaders, including especially the Speaker of the House, may be able to muster the same degree of political attention and support that the president does. As Matthew Green notes, Speakers "go public" for numerous reasons, but they are most often motivated by "a desire to contest the policies of the opposite party and advocate the House majority party's agenda."[83] Consider, for example, some of the recent budget showdowns (discussed in more detail in chapter 3) pitting Newt Gingrich against Bill Clinton and John Boehner against Barack Obama. In those cases, the news media generally treated the Speaker and the president as coequal spokesmen for their respective positions, allowing them to press their cases in the public sphere with equal vigor. And, with each side able effectively to press its point in the public sphere, members of the public are likely to throw their support behind the political actor who best makes his case.

The important point here is that, as noted in chapter 1, public support for a particular institution at a particular moment arises out of a complex calculus of diffuse support for the institution itself and specific support for the position that the institution is taking on particular substantive issues. Asking people whether they like Congress may prime them to think in terms of the messiness and divisiveness that Hibbing and Theiss-Morse identify; in contrast, asking them whether they support the budget proposals of the House of Representatives or those of the president may prime them to think in more partisan, ideological, or policy-oriented terms. Again, the two are deeply intertwined—people who do not have sophisticated views on the details of the competing budget proposals may use a number of heuristics, including general trust in the decision-making institution, to help them decide where to throw their support. Nevertheless, we need to keep in mind both general, diffuse, long-term support for an institution and specific, immediate support for a policy when thinking about the likelihood of successful congressional engagement in the public sphere. And when we think in those terms, we see that there is plenty of room for Congress successfully to compete with the president—prominent examples include the Bork nomination, discussed in the previous chapter, and some of the budget battles discussed in the next chapter.

Moreover, even in the realm of diffuse, general support, it is important to emphasize that there is nothing necessary or inevitable about popular disapproval of the legislature. Obviously, the fact that relative public approval of different institutions increases and decreases over time[84] indicates that their behavior can affect the public's perception of them. Indeed, Hibbing and Theiss-Morse emphasize this with their prescriptive conclusion: civic education.

"[W]e must attempt to communicate to as many people as possible that democratic processes are not naturally endearing," and that they should nevertheless appreciate them.[85] Hibbing and Theiss-Morse emphasize (rightly, in my view) that this is the duty both of legislators themselves and of educators at all levels. Indeed, the frequently remarked-upon fact that people approve of their member of Congress at much higher levels than they approve of the membership of Congress overall[86] opens up an important possibility here: it suggests that members, were they to commit to the educative role, could speak plausibly and persuasively to their constituents. This is a long game, to be sure, but no one ever suggested that institutional power could turn on a dime. As Justin Crowe has emphasized in his recent book on the accretion of institutional power by the federal judiciary, playing the long game can yield significant benefits: "Judicial institution building was not the result of fate or destiny but the architectonic work of influential political actors seeking to advance their own objectives. Indeed, the building of the American judiciary was not at all historically inevitable, but, instead, a contingent and continuous political process."[87] There is no reason that Congress is incapable of a similar trajectory.

Indeed, bringing the judiciary into the analysis should suffice to indicate the incompleteness of the arguments that a unified voice and the capacity for unilateral, agenda-setting action are the primary drivers of institutional power. After all, courts have to wait for cases to be brought to them, and one thing the public surely knows about high-profile court cases is that they often come with a dissent. And yet the American judiciary is undeniably powerful.[88]

None of this is meant to deny that the abilities to speak in a unified voice and to engage in unilateral, status-quo-altering action are important sources of power. Clearly, they are, insofar as they allow an actor to engage in effective ways in the public sphere. But the preceding discussion should make three things clear. First, the extent to which the executive in fact has these traits in operation is often overstated. Second, the extent to which Congress in fact has these traits in operation is often understated. And third, while these are sources of power, there are other ways that actors can engage in the public sphere— which is to say, there are other sources of institutional power.

The different branches have different ways of interacting in the public sphere, and this means that, under different political circumstances, they are likely to have different levels of power. The key contention of this chapter has been that there is nothing inherent in Congress's constitutional place that dooms it to play second (or third) fiddle. Partisanship works in conjunction with, not in contradistinction to, the separation of powers—partisanship can, in many circumstances, provide the motivation for conflict, with the separation of powers providing the institutional homes and tools for the contending parties. Where we see truly unified government and therefore a less confrontational posture among the branches, this is evidence not of the failure or breakdown of the separation-of-powers system but rather of its calibration to the interests of the voting public. And while different situations will lend advantages to different branches, Congress is certainly not at a necessary disadvantage across the board as against the other branches. It has tools at its disposal, as do they, and, as chapter 1 emphasized, actors that use those tools in the service of successful engagement in the public sphere will find themselves with growing power over time. To the extent that Congress has engaged inartfully in the public sphere and thereby lost power, that is a contingent fact, and one that can be reversed.

The two remaining parts of this book are devoted to specific tools available to individual houses and members of Congress. They examine these tools' origins, histories, contemporary uses, and potential for future uses. It is my hope that the reader will be surprised, both by the efficacy with which some of the tools have been (and are being) used, and also by their potential for use in future interbranch conflicts.

PART TWO

CONGRESSIONAL HARD POWERS

3

The Power of the Purse

IT MAY APPEAR ODD TO BEGIN THE DISCUSSION of specific congressional powers with the power of the purse, given that this book focuses on mechanisms that are available to individual houses or members of Congress. After all, the power of the purse is exercised via legislation,[1] which requires both bicameralism and presentment.[2] These are among the more specific and determinate of constitutional provisions. But notice the converse of this fact: if directing money to be spent requires the concurrence of the House, the Senate, and the president (or sufficiently large House and Senate supermajorities),[3] then either the House or the Senate, acting alone, can withhold money. Of course, this is true of any bill—the House and Senate are each absolute vetogates to the passage of legislation.[4] But appropriations laws are different in that their passage is necessary to the continued functioning of the entire government. An annual budget process guarantees that, every year, each house of Congress has the opportunity to give meaningful voice to its priorities and its discontentments. As we shall see in this chapter, this tool has been underappreciated and, perhaps, underutilized.

Historical Development

Annual legislative appropriations have their roots in English parliamentary practice and became entrenched in the aftermath of the 1688–1689 Glorious Revolution. Before that, parliamentary control over appropriations had been sporadic, at best. As Maitland put it, "[T]hroughout the Middle Ages the king's revenue had been in a very true sense the king's revenue, and parliament had but seldom attempted to give him orders as to what he should do with it."[5] This was in large part because most of the Crown's revenue at that point came from what Blackstone termed "ordinary" sources—that is, either those sources of revenue that have "subsisted time out of mind in the crown; or else [have] been granted by parliament, by way of purchase or exchange for such of the king's inherent hereditary rights."[6] Blackstone identified eighteen revenue sources that had traditionally been the Crown's, including everything from ecclesiastical revenues to rents on the king's demesne lands to feudal dues to custody of the persons and lands of idiots and lunatics.[7] Extraordinary revenue, by contrast, consisted of various forms of taxation.[8] The principle of parliamentary consent to taxation harkens back at least to Magna Carta's requirement that any general aid be levied only by common counsel,[9] and the requirement of consent by the Commons in particular dates back at least to the mid-fifteenth century.[10] But the need for extraordinary revenue for a long time arose only in extraordinary circumstances—most commonly in wartime.

So long as Crown revenues came primarily from money due the king in his own person—that is, from ordinary sources—Parliament had little claim to dictate how it was to be spent. But as early as the thirteenth century, the nascent parliamentary body[11] asserted the right to appropriate extraordinary revenue;[12] in other words, if they were going to have to pay taxes, the magnates were going to have some say as to how those taxes would be spent.[13] As Simon Payling has noted, it would be a mistake to view these medieval appropriations as evincing a right "of free refusal. For just as the representative nature of the Commons gave it this right of assent, the Crown had the right to demand a share of its subjects' goods in times of common necessity."[14] It is, nevertheless, telling that, when asked to hand over money to the Crown, Parliament in the later Middle Ages not infrequently specified how that money was to be spent.[15] To take just one example, in 1425 Parliament granted Henry VI certain extraordinary revenues "for the defense of the said Roialme of England"; in case that wasn't clear enough, after specifying the revenues granted, the law repeats the stipulation: "The whiche grauntes of subsidies be made by the seid Commens, on the conditions that folwith. That is to sey, that it ne no part therof be beset ne dispendid to no othir use, but oonly in and for the defense of the seid Roialme."[16]

Under the Tudors, Parliament was far more deferential to royal authority over expenditures—in Maitland's words, it "hardly dared to meddle with such matters."[17] But, as with so many other constitutional principles, conflict returned with the ascent of the Stuarts.[18] This was in no small part due to what Conrad Russell—speaking literally—called "the poverty of the Crown."[19] As Russell noted, the financial system facing Charles I on the eve of the Civil War "was, in essentials, that of the fourteenth century."[20] But, by the seventeenth century, the king's ordinary revenues were no longer even remotely sufficient to cover the normal costs of royal governance.[21] And the policies of the first two Stuart kings did not help: James I's "inability to manage money was notorious both in Scotland and in England,"[22] and Charles I began his reign with a series of expensive and unnecessary foreign policy adventures, each of which ended poorly.[23] This put Charles, especially, at the mercy of Parliament for the granting of extraordinary revenues; the combination of newfound parliamentary assert-iveness[24] and Charles's intransigence and remarkable "ability to rub people up the wrong way"[25] made it that much harder for him to get what he wanted out of Parliament. When Parliament refused to grant him supply or demanded too many concessions for doing so, he resorted to prerogative taxation—that is, essentially, collecting extraordinary revenues *without* parliamentary authoriza-tion. This, of course, further enraged an already alienated Parliament, rein-forcing a vicious cycle that led to the Civil War and, ultimately, to Charles's beheading.[26]

The Commonwealth accustomed people to the idea of "national finances managed by a parliamentary committee,"[27] and so it is not entirely surprising to see the practice of specific appropriations attached to large grants of supply pick up steam after the Restoration. Although, as Maitland notes, the practice was not invariably followed under Charles II,[28] the extent to which it was followed was remarkable. Several of the monarchy's "ordinary" sources of revenue (in the Blackstonian sense of the word) were abolished at the Restoration;[29] they were replaced with certain grants made to Charles II for life and others made to him and his heirs in perpetuity.[30] These grants, as was only natural, came with no strings attached; they were, after all, simply making up for lost sources of unencumbered revenue. But these grants were also indicative of the prevailing trust between the restored monarch and his Parliament[31]—with the exception of three grants of supply in 1660 that were intended to pay and decommission the bulk of the Republican army and navy,[32] no grant of extraordinary supply between 1660 and 1665 came with any sort of appropriation.[33]

As was so often the case with the Stuarts, it was the debts created by foreign entanglements that began to cause friction with Parliament. The outbreak of the

Second Anglo-Dutch War in 1665 "squandered" the "initial goodwill on the parts of both king and parliament,"[34] and this mistrust is apparent in the sudden profusion of specific appropriations provisions in revenue bills. Charles II first came to Parliament in late 1664 seeking the princely sum of £2.5 million to fight the war over two and a half years.[35] In the course of requesting the aid, he felt compelled to dismiss the "vile Jealousy, which some ill Men scatter abroad ... that, when you have given Me a noble and proportionable Supply for the Support of a War, I may be induced by some evil Counsellors ... to make a sudden Peace, and get all that Money for My own private Occasions."[36] This time, a majority of the House of Commons believed him—he was narrowly voted the funds he sought, without any specific appropriations attached.[37] But it seems the suspicion did not fully disappear; when in 1665 he sought and received an additional £1.25 million for the war, a clause was inserted in the revenue-raising legislation providing that "noe moneyes levyable by this Act be issued out of the Exchequer dureing this Warr but by such Order or Warrant mentioning that the moneyes payable by such Order or Warrant are for the service of Your Majestie in the said Warr respectively."[38] Indeed, to make sure that the appropriation was adhered to, the act also required specific and meticulous recordkeeping[39] and insisted that the records be open for public inspection.[40] The next year, when it was clear that yet more money was needed for the war, Parliament passed a poll tax containing not only a specific appropriation of the funds for the war,[41] and a right of anyone considering lending money to the Crown to inspect the books,[42] but also a specific limitation: "[T]hirty thousand pounds and noe more of the money to be raised by this Act may be applyed for the payment of His Majesties Guards."[43] This limitation was important— Charles's personal guard was the first royal standing army in England,[44] and it was created not by statute but by royal prerogative (the first standing army in England was, of course, Cromwell's New Model Army, parts of which were reformed into Charles's guard).[45] Once Charles's initial honeymoon period wore off, the maintenance of this force became a significant source of friction between the king and his people.[46] Indeed, the fear of a standing army under royal command was so pervasive that Charles soon felt the need to address it head-on: in a speech proroguing Parliament in July 1667, "His Majesty further said, He wondered what One Thing He had done since His coming into *England*, to persuade any sober Person that He did intend to govern by a Standing Army; He said He was more an *Englishman* than so."[47]

Perhaps because of this widespread suspicion of Charles's motives, the only other two revenue bills passed during the war contained appropriations provisions as well.[48] In one of those acts, Parliament directed that a sizable chunk of the revenue raised be used to pay seamen's wages, and it threatened the treasurer of the navy with treble damages if he diverted any of that money to any other purpose.[49] And to make sure that the funds were being used as directed, Parliament passed a law creating what we might anachronistically call an independent auditing board, charged with looking over the books of all of the officials who had received funds earmarked for the war and ensuring that the money was spent properly.[50]

Consistent with Patterson's observation that trust between king and Parliament was briefly "rebuilt" after the end of the Second Anglo-Dutch War,[51] grants of supply in the early 1670s did not generally come with appropriations provisions.[52] But the goodwill quickly dissipated, as a result of the Third Anglo-Dutch War and the fear that Charles was too friendly toward the French. Beginning again in 1677, nearly every grant of extraordinary revenue for the remainder of Charles II's reign came with an appropriating clause, an auditing provision to ensure that the appropriation was followed, and stiff penalties for any Crown official caught putting the money to any unsanctioned use.[53] Nor were these idle threats: in 1678, the House of Commons impeached the Earl of Danby, one of Charles's highest officials. There were six articles of impeachment, the second of which charged Danby as follows:

> [H]e did design the Raising of an Army, upon Pretence of a War against the *French* King; and then to continue the same as a Standing Army within this Kingdom: And an Army being so raised, and no War ensuing, an Act of Parliament having passed to pay off and disband the same, and a great Sum of Money being granted for that End, he did continue this Army contrary to the said Act, and misemployed the said Money, given for disbanding, to the Continuance thereof; and issued out of his Majesty's Revenue divers great Sums of Money for the said Purpose; and wilfully neglected to take Security from the Paymaster of the Army, as the said Act required; whereby the said Law is eluded, and the Army is yet continued, to the great Danger and unnecessary Charge of his Majesty and the whole Kingdom.[54]

In other words, Danby was charged with violating a specific appropriations provision, and with doing so in order to maintain a standing army on English soil. Before the Lords could vote on Danby's impeachment, Charles pardoned him, which led to a debate in Parliament as to whether a royal pardon was effective against impeachments. While that debate was still ongoing, both houses passed a bill of attainder against Danby, upon which he was arrested; he spent the next five years in the Tower of London.[55] While he was there, another royal official, Sir Edward Seymour, was impeached. The first article charged him with violating a specific appropriation that certain money was to be used only to build and outfit naval vessels; Seymour instead, as treasurer of the navy, lent some of that money for the purpose of maintaining the standing army past the date at which Parliament had ordered it disbanded, "whereby the said Two several Acts were eluded."[56] The second article against Seymour likewise charged him with violating a specific appropriation.[57] A snap dissolution of Parliament in January 1681 ended the proceedings against Seymour before the Lords could vote.[58]

After this dissolution, Charles, fed up with parliamentary interference, ruled without Parliament, and therefore without any parliamentary taxation, for the rest of his reign.[59] The overall trend in Charles's reign is clear: once the initial honeymoon period wore off around 1665, Parliament was largely unwilling to grant him additional money without specifying in some measure how it was to be used. In addition, Parliament got into the habit of providing monitoring mechanisms and penalties for disobedient royal officials.

When Charles's brother James came to the throne in 1685, the "Loyal Parliament"—so called because it was dominated by those loyal to the new, Catholic monarch—quickly confirmed all of the same life grants (that is, the substitutes for old sources of ordinary revenue) that had been made to his brother.[60] Shortly thereafter, it also granted him temporary customs duties on wine and vinegar,[61] tobacco and sugar,[62] and various cloths and liquors.[63] Although the last of these grants was meant to aid James in suppressing the Monmouth Rebellion,[64] none of them contained an appropriations provision. After the rebellion was suppressed, James, having been made financially comfortable by Parliament,[65] indicated that he had no intention of disbanding the standing army under his control.[66] This, combined with his determination to dispense with the Test Act (which prevented Catholics from holding public office),[67] turned even many of the Tories in Parliament against him,[68] and in November 1685, the House of Commons voted not to take up the matter of supply for the Crown.[69] A week later, James prorogued Parliament;[70] although it technically remained in existence until July 1687, it never sat again. There were to be no more parliaments in James II's brief reign.

And then, of course, came the second deposition of a Stuart monarch in as many generations. Afterward, a large part of Parliament's goal in stitching together the Revolution Settlement was to ensure that monarchs would no longer feel free to rule without Parliament. To this end, Parliament attacked, among other things, what were seen as two mutually reinforcing pillars of monarchical authority in Restoration England: royal revenues and royal control over a standing army. The Bill of Rights specifically criticized James II both for "Levying Money for and to the Use of the Crowne, by pretence of Prerogative for other time and in other manner then the same was granted by Parlyament" and for "raising and keeping a Standing Army within this Kingdome in time of Peace without Consent of Parlyament."[71] The Bill of Rights went on to prohibit both of these things, as well as to require the calling of frequent parliaments.[72]

But even before the passage of the Bill of Rights, Parliament had begun to take more concrete steps to put these principles into action. First, it took away almost all of the remnants of the Crown's ordinary revenue. It began by repealing the hearth tax, which had been perpetual, and replacing it with an annually granted land tax.[73] Grants of tonnage and poundage and duties on woolen cloth, which had been granted for life, were now granted for only four years.[74] Only a relatively small amount of revenue was granted William and Mary for life or longer.[75] The importance of this move to annual appropriations cannot be overstated. Blackstone described the loss of the Crown's ordinary revenue as "fortunate[] for the liberty of the subject,"[76] and Trevelyan explains why: "[T]he Commons took good care that after the Revolution the Crown should be altogether unable to pay its way without an annual meeting of Parliament. William had no large grant made him for life. Every year he and his Ministers had to come, cap in hand, to the House of Commons, and more often than not the Commons drove a bargain and exacted a quid pro quo in return for supply."[77] That is to say, the granting of revenue only for a short duration not only forced the regular calling of parliaments—something all four of the Stuart monarchs had tried, at one time or another, to do without—but also forced regular negotiation with Parliament, and those negotiations often led to concessions.

Moreover, after the Revolution, it became common practice (as it had been during much of Charles II's reign) for Parliament to specifically appropriate the funds that it raised for the Crown, and to threaten severe punishments upon any royal official using the funds for any other purpose.[78] Indeed, as Gill has noted, it was shortly after the Revolution that a proto-annual budget made its first appearance, a natural outgrowth of the new royal need for annual parliamentary grants.[79] And this proto-budget as passed by Parliament was not always identical to the budget the Crown requested.[80] Moreover, throughout the reigns of William and Mary and of Anne, Parliament regularly created Commissions of Public Accounts, staffed by members of Parliament, to look into how the Crown was spending appropriated funds.[81]

The second, and related, key element of the Revolution Settlement for our purposes was parliamentary control over the military. As we have already seen, there was deep suspicion of standing armies on English soil, and many of the Restoration fights over finance were intimately bound up with fights over a standing army. Thus, in the Mutiny Act, which created a criminal offense of mutiny against the army, Parliament provided that the penalties would sunset within a year.[82] Subsequent Mutiny Acts followed suit every year for nearly two centuries.[83] Each year, the monarchs were thus faced with a tripartite choice: they could disband the standing army; they could call a Parliament that year; or, if they did neither of those, they would run the risk of soldiers deserting without fear of consequence. If they chose either to disband the army or to call a Parliament, then they would be adequately constrained in their exercise of power.

What both of these elements of the Revolution Settlement have in common is their creation of an annual baseline. They did not require the monarch to call annual Parliaments, but they did make it very difficult for the monarch to exercise power without the aid of Parliament. The Revolutionary doctrine of parliamentary supremacy and the accompanying eighteenth-century rise of cabinet government and ministerial responsibility to Parliament[84] were the consolidation of these gains, and they inaugurated the modern British political system. But even after the advent and consolidation of parliamentary supremacy, Parliament continued to appropriate funds "with great minuteness,"[85] and violations of those appropriations are criminally punishable.[86] As Maitland put it, drawing together once again the two threads we have been discussing, "[E]ven at a pinch money appropriated to the navy cannot be applied to the army."[87] While monarchs would continue to—and indeed still today continue to—have certain sums appropriated to their personal and household use (long called the "civil list," and recently renamed the "Sovereign Grant"), these sums are granted by Parliament and are distinct from, and cannot be supplemented by, other taxpayer revenue.[88] The Revolution Settlement made clear that just as

Parliament must consent to the raising of funds so too it must consent to how, specifically, they are to be spent.

As we saw in the Introduction, seventeenth-century relations between Crown and Parliament made a big impression on the American colonists. It is, then, unsurprising that, in conjunction with the taxation power,[89] the colonial assemblies asserted a robust power of appropriation over all of the tax revenue they raised.[90] Indeed, despite the "extensive precautions" that officials in London took "to prevent that power from falling into the hands of the lower houses,"[91] Jack Greene found that, by the middle of the eighteenth century, the appropriations power wielded by the lower houses of colonial assemblies was "greater even than that of the British House of Commons."[92] This was because the colonial assemblies, in addition to strictly appropriating funds, maintained a substantial auditing power.[93]

Indeed, some colonial assemblies even successfully asserted the right to appropriate money without the approval of the royal governor or his council.[94] Consider the "Wilkes Fund Controversy" in South Carolina. In 1769, that colony's House of Commons voted a £1,500 grant to the Society of the Gentlemen Supporters of the Bill of Rights in London.[95] The society was what we would today call a legal defense fund for John Wilkes,[96] who was a major thorn in the side of the London government and a cause célèbre among English radicals and American colonists alike (and who is discussed in greater detail in chapter 7).[97] When imperial authorities got word of the grant, they immediately instructed the royal governor in South Carolina to withhold royal assent from any revenue bill that did not specifically appropriate the money that it raised to *local* matters (that is, not funding enemies of the ministry in London); they also instructed that all revenue bills were to contain a provision levying significant penalties upon the treasurer if he disbursed any further money on the authority of the lower house alone.[98] The South Carolinians were outraged and responded with both a formal protest from the Commons and an increase in pro-Wilkes editorials and demonstrations.[99] The Commons also issued a report rejecting the instruction that money could be appropriated only to local purposes.[100] The resulting impasse between the assembly and royal officials consumed South Carolina politics until the breakout of the Revolution mooted the point.[101] Indeed, so all-consuming was the controversy that "[n]o annual tax bill was passed in South Carolina after 1769 and no legislation at all after February 1771. For all practical purposes royal government in South Carolina broke down four years earlier than it did in any of the other colonies."[102] It is important to note the radicalism of the colonists' claim here: the Crown had not claimed any right to appropriate money on its own, nor had it denied that the assembly could attach detailed appropriations provisions to its revenue bills. The principle of legislative appropriation was sufficiently firmly established by this point that no one dared to deny it. All the Crown had insisted was that the consent of the governor and the council was *also* necessary in order to appropriate money. It was the lower house's resistance to *sharing* its appropriating power that brought the functions of the South Carolina colonial government to a halt and caused an early end to royal authority in the colony.

Moreover, it was not simply in the granting of appropriations that colonial assemblies clashed with royal officials. The assemblies were also prepared to withhold funds when they did not like the direction of royal government. As early as the late 1670s, "foot-dragging on appropriations and other bills became a favored tactic in the burgesses' struggles" with royal governors in Virginia.[103] In 1685, in the midst of a conflict with royal governor Baron Howard of Effingham over the details of an urban development bill, the House of Burgesses refused to pass an appropriations bill in an attempt to force Effingham's hand. The governor responded by proroguing the assembly.[104] Similarly, in 1720 the Massachusetts assembly, in the course of a fight with Crown officials in the colony, refused appropriations for the customary celebrations of the king's birthday, accession, and coronation. Perhaps more cruelly, in Herbert Osgood's telling, "[t]he semi-annual appropriation of the governor's salary was postponed until the close of the session and then it was reduced by one hundred pounds, though the depreciation of the currency in which it was paid was already great and was steadily increasing. The small grant to the lieutenant governor was also cut down to such an insignificant sum that he returned it in disgust."[105] Two years later, when the commanding officer of the royal army in the colony did not follow the Massachusetts assembly's orders, it refused to vote him any pay and thereby "compelled his discharge."[106] In 1734, the South Carolina House of Commons, angry that the royally appointed chief justice had sided with the royally appointed governor in a dispute with the legislature, provided no salary at all for the chief justice.[107] The only response available to the Crown in such circumstances was to find another way to pay its officers—in 1735, the Crown began paying the chief justice's salary out of its own funds.[108] Indeed, in order to avoid assembly domination of Crown officials, the Crown used imperial revenues to pay its officers in a number of colonies,[109] leading to the Declaration of Independence's complaint that the king "has made Judges dependent on his Will alone, for the Tenure of their Offices, and the Amount and Payment of their Salaries."[110] Even so, the colonial assemblies pulled what purse strings they did have: in 1751, the South Carolina House of Commons refused to pay the rent on the governor's house "because he had vetoed several of its favorite bills."[111] This use of the appropriations power to withhold the salaries or perks of royal officials was a strategy employed by assemblies across a number of colonies throughout the colonial period.[112] The power of colonial assemblies to appropriate—including their power to *refuse* to appropriate—thus provided significant leverage in policy disputes.

The Continental Congress under the Articles of Confederation had neither an executive to speak of (the "president" being nothing more than the presiding officer of the Congress)[113] nor much by way of revenue (it could only requisition money from the states, not levy taxes itself, and the states proved stingy).[114] Nevertheless, the Articles specifically allocated to Congress the power to appropriate money "for defraying the public expenses," so long as the delegations from at least nine states approved the appropriation.[115] And, indeed, we see the Congress appropriating specific sums for everything from buying "good musquets"[116] to reimbursing for troops' clothing that was "taken by the enemy"[117] to building "a fœderal town."[118]

At the time the American Constitution was drafted, seven state constitutions contained explicit provisions requiring appropriations by the legislature,[119] and nine states (including four that did not explicitly require legislative appropriations) provided that the state treasurer would be appointed by the legislature.[120] Given that the governments of Connecticut and Rhode Island were still operating under their seventeenth-century royal charters, this means that only one state that drafted a constitution between independence and the drafting of the federal Constitution, Georgia, did not include some explicit mechanism of legislative control over appropriations. The Georgia Constitution did, however, provide that "[e]very officer of the State shall be liable to be called to account by the house of assembly."[121] And when constitutional revisions in the late 1790s made the office of the Georgia governor more powerful, an explicit appropriations provision was added to the 1798 state constitution.[122] Gerhard Casper, summarizing the early republican state constitutions as a whole, concluded that they "confirm our understanding that during the founding period money matters were primarily thought of as a legislative prerogative."[123] On the specific issue of appropriating the salaries of state officers, the states were split: some, like Massachusetts and South Carolina, required fixed salaries for both the governor and judges;[124] other states had no such provision. New Hampshire, in adjacent provisions, drew a clear distinction between the two types of office: "Permanent and honorable salaries shall be established by law for the justices of the superior court,"[125] but "[t]he president and council shall be compensated for their services from time to time by such grants as the general court shall think reasonable."[126]

As we have seen, it was a favorite practice of the Stuart monarchs to rule without Parliament whenever they came to find parliamentary interference with their plans tiresome. In addition to the English Bill of Rights' requirement of frequent parliaments, the post-Revolutionary Parliament also kept the Crown dependent by moving much more heavily toward annually granted and specifically appropriated supply. The U.S. Constitution adopts a similar set of strategies. In place of the English Bill of Rights' admonition that "parliaments ought to be held frequently,"[127] the American Constitution substitutes the more specific requirement that Congress assemble at least once per year.[128] The desire to control how money is spent, which we saw growing during the late Stuart period, coming to maturity in the eighteenth century, and asserted emphatically in colonial and early republican America, found its expression in the requirement—wholly uncontroversial at the Constitutional Convention[129]— that "[n]o Money shall be drawn from the Treasury, but in Consequence of Appropriations made by Law; and a regular Statement and Account of the Receipts and Expenditures of all public Money shall be published from time to time."[130] The concern with auditing the books is familiar, too; it had been clear for centuries that appropriations were ineffectual without some means of ensuring that the money was actually spent for the purposes for which it was appropriated. The Constitution also speaks to the issue of governmental officials' salaries: it prohibits presidential salaries from being altered during a presidential term, judicial salaries from being diminished, and (in an amendment proposed in 1789 but not ratified until 1992) congressional salaries from "varying" until after the next election,[131] but it does not otherwise prevent officers' salaries from being reduced.

The Constitution moreover evinces discomfort with standing armies, a discomfort which we saw as early as the reign of Charles II and which appears in the Declaration of Independence and in the republican constitutions of both Maryland and Virginia.[132] Although the duration of most appropriations is not limited, the Constitution does specify that "no Appropriation of Money" for the purpose of "rais[ing] and support[ing] Armies . . . shall be for a longer Term than two Years."[133] This is, in some sense, a parallel to what the English Parliament accomplished with the Mutiny Act: if the king or the president wants to keep a standing army in the field, he will have to negotiate with Parliament or Congress about it on a regular basis.[134] And, like the Mutiny Act, the American Constitution is concerned specifically with *armies*, not navies. Hence, the neighboring clause, which allows Congress to "provide and maintain a Navy," places no time limit on naval appropriations.[135] The Third Amendment, which forbids the nonconsensual peacetime quartering of "Soldier[s]," not sailors, evinces a similar concern.[136] The reason sounds in domestic liberties: standing armies could be used to oppress the people and rule with an iron fist. In contrast, the navy was traditionally understood to face outward, serving to defend the political community from external threats and, less exaltedly, to engage in imperial expansion. In Blackstone's words, the navy serves as "the floating bulwark of the island . . . from which, however strong and powerful, no danger can ever be apprehended to liberty."[137] Madison, writing as Publius, echoed the sentiment, insisting that "our situation bears [a] likeness to the insular advantage of Great Britain. The batteries most capable of repelling foreign enterprises on our safety are happily such as can never be turned by a perfidious government against our liberties."[138]

Indeed, the separation of purse and sword was the Federalists' strongest rejoinder to Anti-Federalist fears of a tyrannical president. When Patrick Henry worried that "Your President may easily become king. . . . The army is in his hands, and . . . . the President, in the field, at the head of his army, can prescribe the terms on which he shall reign master,"[139] Madison answered by pointing to the fact that "[t]he purse is in the hands of the representatives of the people. They have the appropriation of all moneys."[140] Hamilton likewise told the New York ratifying convention that "where the purse is lodged in one branch, and the sword in another, there can be no danger."[141] Indeed, throughout the ratification debates, we see the Federalists' using congressional control over appropriations as a rejoinder to fears about presidential military might.[142]

Once the Constitution was ratified, one of the first tasks of the new Congress was setting up the three major departments of government—those of foreign affairs, war, and the treasury. As Casper has noted, the Treasury was singled out for special treatment.[143] The organic statutes for both the Foreign Affairs Department and the War Department explicitly termed them "Executive department[s]," provided that the secretary was to carry out "such duties as shall from time to time be enjoined on, or entrusted to him by the President of the United States," and created only a skeletal organization, consisting of a secretary and a chief clerk.[144] The organic statute for the Treasury Department, by contrast, did not refer to it as an "executive" department and specifically provided for the appointment of a comptroller, an auditor, a treasurer, a registrar, and an assistant to the secretary, in addition to the secretary himself.[145] Most strikingly, the duties of these various officers mention nothing about taking direction from the president; however, the duties of both the secretary and the treasurer specifically require them to report to the houses of Congress.[146] The First Congress, in Casper's words, seems to have viewed the secretary of the treasury as "an indispensable, direct arm of the House in regard to its responsibilities for revenues and appropriations."[147]

Notwithstanding the fact that the text of the Constitution allows for indefinite appropriations in all contexts other than the army, the practice from the beginning of the Republic has largely been one of annual appropriations. The nation's very first appropriations bill authorized the expenditure of sums not exceeding $639,000 "for the service of the present year."[148] Subsequent early appropriations bills followed suit.[149] These earliest appropriations laws, which essentially tracked estimates submitted to Congress by Treasury Secretary Alexander Hamilton,[150] were very brief and not very specific. Indeed, the first one divided that $639,000 into only four categories: the civil list (not more than $216,000), the War Department (not more than $137,000), the discharging of "warrants issued by the late board of treasury" (not more than $190,000), and pensions to invalids (not more than $96,000).[151] The second annual appropriations act, for 1790, introduced several innovations. Although it once again divided the total (just over $394,000) into broad categories (this time, only three: the civil list, the War Department, and invalid pensions), it incorporated by reference Hamilton's estimates, so that, for example, the civil list appropriation reads: "A sum not exceeding one hundred and forty-one thousand, four hundred and ninety-two dollars, and seventy-three cents, for defraying the expenses of the civil list, as estimated by the Secretary of the Treasury, in the statement annexed to his report made to the House of Representatives on the ninth day of January last. . . ."[152] The law also provided President Washington with a slush fund—up to $10,000 "for the purpose of defraying the contingent charges of government"—but required that he report how he spent that money to Congress at the end of the year.[153]

By the time we get to the mid-1790s, increasing tensions between the nascent Federalist and Jeffersonian factions led to an increase in the specificity of appropriations legislation.[154] In 1793, Representative William Branch Giles of Virginia introduced a series of resolutions censuring Hamilton for alleged violations of specific appropriations provisions.[155] The resolutions were handily defeated; it was not clear that Hamilton actually had violated the terms of the appropriations, and even if he had, the offense was minor—even Albert Gallatin, the staunch Republican financial expert, later wrote that Hamilton's transgression had been "rather a want of form than a substantial violation of the appropriation law."[156] Gallatin, however, remained a strong champion of legislative control over appropriations. As a freshman representative in 1795, he successfully pressed the House to lessen its reliance on the secretary of the treasury by establishing a Committee on Ways and Means that could develop its own expertise over matters of taxing and spending.[157] He also fought, with some success, for more specific and restrictive language in appropriations laws.[158] Gallatin would go on to be the United States' longest-serving secretary of the treasury, holding the post for the entire Jefferson administration and most of the Madison administration. In 1809, Gallatin helped shepherd through Congress a law specifying that all warrants drawn upon the Treasury "shall specify the particular appropriation or appropriations to which the same shall be charged" and that "the sums appropriated by law for each branch of expenditure in the several departments shall be solely applied to the objects for which they are respectively appropriated, and to no other." The sole exception was a provision allowing the president, during a congressional recess and only upon the application of a department head, to move money appropriated for one purpose to another purpose within the same department.[159]

It is true that some presidents, starting with George Washington in his response to the Whiskey Rebellion in 1794, have spent money without congressional appropriations in response to emergencies. But, as Richard Rosen has noted, the presidents who have done so have not claimed to be acting legally. Rather, they acknowledged their actions to be ultra vires, justified only by necessity, and they sought post hoc congressional authorization. Moreover, they have faced serious congressional scrutiny and criticism when they have done so.[160]

The nineteenth century would see two significant framework statutes meant to consolidate congressional control over appropriations.[161] The 1849 Miscellaneous Receipts Statute requires, with some exceptions, that all money coming into the federal government be paid into the Treasury,[162] so that departments could not place incoming funds into special accounts beyond congressional control. In 1870, in response to an increase in "coercive deficiencies"—situations in which an executive department created obligations in excess of appropriations, thus putting substantial moral pressure on Congress to make good on the departments' promises[163]—Congress passed the Anti-Deficiency Act, which made it illegal for "any department of the government to expend in any one fiscal year any sum in excess of appropriations made by Congress for that fiscal year, or to involve the government in any contract for the future payment of money in excess of such appropriations."[164] In response to continuing evasions, the 1905 Anti-Deficiency Act expanded the prohibition to "any contract *or obligation* for the future payment of money in excess of . . . appropriations." It prohibited any governmental department from accepting any voluntary service not authorized by law, except "in cases of sudden emergency involving the loss of human life or the destruction of property." It also required agencies to apportion their appropriations over the course of the year so as to prevent them from spending all of their money at the beginning of the year and then coming to Congress for more. Finally, it provided that any officer violating the act's terms would be summarily removed from office and could face fines or imprisonment.[165]

From this historical sketch up to the beginning of the twentieth century, we can trace a few enduring themes in the battle for appropriations power. First, and most basically, is the question of *who* has the power to determine how public moneys will be spent. The Revolution Settlement cemented the transfer of that power from the Crown to Parliament in the mother country; appropriations control became a bone of contention between the Crown and the restive North American colonies in the eighteenth century; and the Constitution, in no uncertain terms, requires that appropriations be made by law. Even so, we have seen political contention over how specific those appropriations should be. And this leads us to the second theme: *What* exactly is contained in the appropriations power? Should appropriations statutes simply provide broad outlines and sum totals, or should they involve minute details? Should military expenditures

be treated differently from other types? And how intermingled should appropriations decisions be with substantive policy decisions? In particular, we have
seen a variety of different approaches to the question of the extent to which it is
permissible to reduce or zero-out an official's salary. Finally, there is the question of *when* appropriations happen. As we have seen, when the Crown's "ordinary" sources of revenue covered the vast majority of its expenses, appropriations
were infrequent. Hereditary sources of revenue provided no opportunity for
parliamentary involvement, and life grants did not provide much more. The
shift to regular appropriations—beginning in earnest during the Restoration,
accelerating dramatically after the Glorious Revolution, and always the case in
the United States—was a significant one, but (with the exception of spending
on the army) the U.S. Constitution is silent on the duration of appropriations.

Each of these issues has been the subject of significant constitutional contention because, as we shall see in the remainder of this chapter, each has wide-
ranging constitutional implications.

The Structural Significance of Annual Appropriations

Consider first the timing of appropriations. Specific annual appropriations
serve much the same function as sunset provisions in substantive legislation:
both reset the legislative baseline.[166] Consider the following simple example: At
time t_1, Congress passes a law delegating a certain amount of power to an
executive-branch agency. If that law has no sunset provision, then, in order to
take that power back at time t_2, Congress would need to pass a second law—
which, of course, would require either presidential concurrence or two-thirds
supermajorities in both chambers.[167] But the t_1 law empowers executive-branch
actors (that is, the administrative agency) and thereby empowers the president,
so it is unlikely that the president would consent to giving that power back.
Under this scenario, Congress is likely stuck with the t_1 law. But now imagine
that Congress had included a sunset provision, so that at t_2, the delegation ceases
to have any legal force. Inaction now favors congressional power; only if the
House, Senate, and president once again agree to delegate the power will the
executive be able to exercise it at t_2. This, of course, is precisely why Parliament
in 1689 included a sunset clause in the Mutiny Act, and it is why Congress in
2001 included a sunset provision in the PATRIOT Act.[168] (It also explains why the
Bush administration opposed the PATRIOT Act's sunset provision.)[169]

An appropriations provision can be understood simply as a specific delegation of spending authority. A long-term or indefinite appropriation significantly
increases executive power. So long as the president is happy with the appropriation, she need only veto any attempt to change it. An annual appropriation,
however, resets to zero in the absence of congressional action and thereby
forces the president to negotiate with Congress each year, just as post–Glorious
Revolution monarchs were forced to negotiate annually with Parliament. Thus,
the larger the percentage of the budget that is subject to annual appropriations,
the more bargaining chips Congress has at its disposal.

It is, then, interesting to note that the percentage of the federal budget subject
to annual appropriations has been steadily declining for some time. The federal
budget now consists of two essential components: mandatory spending and
discretionary spending. Mandatory spending (also called "direct spending")
"involves a binding legal obligation by the Federal Government to provide
funding for an individual, program, or activity."[170] Once mandatory spending
has been authorized, "eligible recipients have legal recourse to compel payment
from the government if the obligation is not fulfilled."[171] Mandatory spending
is precisely that spending that does not require annual appropriations. It is
authorized in perpetuity, unless a new law is passed revoking it. The major
elements of mandatory spending are entitlements and interest payments on
debt.[172] All other spending—including the funding for all federal agencies—is
discretionary[173] and requires annual appropriations. For the 2016 fiscal year,
69 percent of the federal budget consisted of mandatory spending,[174] reflecting
a long-running trend of growth in the percentage of the federal budget devoted
to mandatory spending.[175] In other words, for 69 percent of the federal budget,
Congress has ceded the institutional advantage of annual appropriations[176] and
surrendered the institutional gains of 1689.

Moreover, even in the realm of discretionary spending, Congress has ceded
the first-mover advantage to the president. As we have seen, in the earliest years
of the Republic, Congress heavily deferred to Hamilton's spending priorities
and estimates. But with the rise of partisan competition, the House began to
take a more active, specific role, including the 1809, 1849, and 1870 statutes
discussed above. Indeed, when President Taft in 1912 submitted a proposed
budget to Congress, Congress simply ignored it and went about preparing its
own budget.[177] But the growth of the regulatory state put pressure on the frag-
mented manner in which Congress went about budgeting,[178] and the era of

"legislative dominance" of the budget process[179] came to an end shortly after World War I. Under the 1921 Budget and Accounting Act,[180] the president kicks off the annual appropriations process by submitting a budget proposal to Congress.[181] Of course, Congress could always depart from the president's proposal, but it is nevertheless the president's proposal that serves as the starting point for negotiation and therefore exerts a disproportionate impact on the subsequent process.[182] Furthermore, the 1921 act created the Budget Bureau in an effort to foster administrative coordination and centralization in budgetary matters. Although the Budget Bureau was initially located in the Treasury Department, its leadership from the beginning reported directly to the president.[183] When the Executive Office of the President was created in 1939, the bureau was moved into it,[184] and in 1970, it was renamed the Office of Management and Budget (OMB).[185] Throughout its history, the bureau/OMB has proven remarkably effective in centralizing and consolidating presidential control over the various component parts of the administrative state.[186] Congress was not wholly inattentive to the ways in which the 1921 act empowered the president: the act also created the General Accounting Office (GAO) as an independent agency headed by the comptroller general with the authority to investigate the receipt and spending of federal funds and report to both the president and Congress.[187] Moreover, at almost exactly the same time, both houses gave exclusive jurisdiction over appropriations legislation to their Appropriations Committees, thus creating a single power base in each chamber with appropriations expertise that might push back against the White House.[188] Still, the overall effect of these measures was clearly to inaugurate an era of "presidential dominance" of the budget process.[189]

In the mid-1970s, in the context of the Watergate scandal and the deepening distrust of the presidency it engendered, Congress began to push back against this executive budgetary dominance. A series of minor challenges—including exempting certain agencies from OMB review and instead having them send their budget requests directly to Congress, successfully pressuring the White House to turn over raw estimates in addition to a completed budget proposal, and requiring Senate confirmation of OMB leadership[190]—were prelude to the more sweeping changes in the Budget Act of 1974, signed into law less than a month before Nixon's resignation.[191] This act created the Budget Committees in both houses of Congress, as well as the Congressional Budget Office, in an attempt to provide counterweights to budget expertise at OMB. It also created the process by which the two houses pass a Budget Resolution to guide the appropriations process—a counterweight to the budget proposal submitted by the president.[192] Several subsequent statutes have created procedural mechanisms designed to limit budget deficits, but the essential structure of the budget process remains that of the combined 1921 and 1974 acts.[193]

The other big budgetary fight leading up to the 1974 act was over "impoundment," the refusal by the president to spend appropriated funds. Of course, Congress has the ability to authorize the expenditure of "up to" a certain amount, and, as we have seen, the nation's earliest appropriations bills authorized the expenditures of "sum[s] not exceeding" certain amounts for certain purposes. (Indeed, the example that is sometimes cited as the first instance of impoundment—President Jefferson's 1803 announcement to Congress that he would not spend an appropriated $50,000 for gunboats on the Mississippi because the recent "favorable and peaceful turn of affairs" rendered them unnecessary[194]—was in fact an instance of presidential adherence to an appropriation authorizing the expenditure of "a sum not exceeding fifty thousand dollars" for the purchase of "a number not exceeding fifteen gun boats.")[195] But what about when the statute does not include such permissive language? Presidents had long taken the position that, in the words of Judson Harmon, attorney general to Grover Cleveland, appropriations are "not mandatory to the extent that you are bound to expend the full amount if the work can be done for less."[196] Such "routine impoundments" have generally been uncontroversial.[197]

More controversial have been "policy impoundments"—refusals to spend appropriated funds because the president disagrees with the policies to be pursued by such expenditures. Policy impoundments did not begin in any significant degree until World War II; Presidents Franklin Roosevelt, Truman, Eisenhower, Kennedy, and Lyndon Johnson all made use of them to a limited extent.[198] But there is consensus among observers that the Nixon administration engaged in the practice on such an expanded scale as to constitute a difference in kind, not simply in degree.[199] Allen Schick estimates that Nixon impounded approximately $18 billion,[200] and he was frequently unable to convince Congress to come to an agreement to cancel the appropriations.[201] Several would-be recipients of impounded funds filed lawsuits, and in 1975 the Supreme Court, in *Train v. City of New York*, unanimously held that the Environmental Protection Agency was required to disburse the full amount authorized under the Federal Water Pollution Control Act Amendments of 1972, notwithstanding the president's order to the agency's administrator to disburse less money.[202] A series of lower-court decisions, dealing with impoundment of other funds, likewise found the impoundments impermissible.[203]

Congress also reacted swiftly. Title X of the 1974 Budget Act, commonly known as the Impoundment Control Act,[204] created two tightly controlled kinds of impoundment authority: rescission, which meant that the president did not wish to spend the funds at all, and deferral, which meant that he wanted to delay spending them. In both cases, the president was required to send a message to Congress laying out his reasons and supporting evidence. For rescissions, the funds could then be withheld for forty-five days; if at the end of that period both houses had not passed a "rescission bill"—that is, a joint resolution rescinding the spending in accordance with the president's wishes—then the president was obligated to spend the funds.[205] Deferrals were automatically effective, but the funds had to be released if either house adopted a resolution of disapproval.[206] In the aftermath of the Supreme Court's decision in *INS v. Chadha*,[207] invalidating legislative vetoes (about which, more in a few pages), a court held that the entire section of the act dealing with deferrals was invalid.[208] Congress soon amended the statute to allow for deferrals without the possibility of congressional override, but only in three tightly constrained situations: "to provide for contingencies"; "to achieve savings made possible by or through changes in requirements or greater efficiency of operations"; or "as specifically provided by law."[209] When its procedural ability to check deferrals was removed, Congress therefore responded by creating tighter substantive constraints on the deferral mechanism.

The Impoundment Control Act's checks have generally been effective, with studies finding that presidents have largely adhered to the act's requirement to report impoundments and that presidents have released funds when required to.[210] Moreover, presidential rescission proposals have been routinely rebuffed—between January 1983 and January 1989, Congress rejected 76 percent of Reagan's rescission requests, accounting for 98 percent of the funds that Reagan sought to impound.[211] Even under unified government, rescission bills were no guarantee—Congress refused to pass them 29 percent of the time during the Carter administration (accounting for 31 percent of the funds that Carter sought to impound), despite Democratic control of both houses.[212] A detailed study of rescission requests during the first year and a quarter of the act's existence—which was also the first year and a quarter of the Ford administration, with both houses of Congress under Democratic control—found that Congress generally approved "routine rescissions involving no change in government policy," while generally rejecting those that sought to accomplish some other policy objective.[213] Thus, the impoundment control provisions of the 1974 act, like its provisions structuring the congressional budget process, have been at least somewhat successful in their aim to counterbalance and constrain executive budgetary authority, as it had been growing since the 1921 act. (Whether they are successful in controlling deficits is another matter. In an attempt to reduce the deficit in the mid-1990s, the Republican-controlled Congress passed, and President Clinton signed into law, an enhanced presidential rescission power, the line-item veto.[214] Two years later, the Supreme Court struck it down.)[215] As several commentators have noted, the creation of these counter-weights has "institutionalized and expanded budgetary conflict."[216] And this increased budgetary capacity gives Congress more power to affect non-fiscal policy.

Spending Authority as Substantive Authority

Indeed, it is a mistake to think about the congressional power of the purse solely in terms of Congress's power to determine spending levels. Control over spending also provides Congress with significant leverage to use in negotiations over other policies, leverage that we have already seen Parliament and colonial assemblies put to good use. Madison, writing as Publius, had such leverage in mind when he wrote that the "power over the purse may, in fact, be regarded as the most complete and effectual weapon with which any constitution can arm the immediate representatives of the people, for obtaining a redress of every grievance, and for carrying into effect every just and salutary measure."[217] As Charles Black colorfully put it, "[B]y simple majorities, Congress could . . . reduce the president's staff to one secretary for answering social correspondence, and . . ., by two-thirds majorities, Congress could put the White House up at auction."[218] Along the same lines, Congress could presumably eliminate the salaries of judicial clerks and secretaries or even (most cruelly of all) cut the Supreme Court's air conditioning budget.[219] Indeed, as we have seen, refusing to pay the salaries of Crown officers and judges was a venerable tradition in the American colonies. The president himself,[220] like federal judges,[221] is protected against salary diminution, but the Constitution provides no other government official such protection, nor does it explicitly protect any other form of spending.

It is certainly not unknown for Congress to attach specific riders to appropriations measures forbidding the use of funds for specific purposes. As one observer complained at the end of the Reagan administration, "Congress discovered that it could intimidate the executive branch by uttering again and again the same seven words, 'Provided, that no funds shall be spent. . . .' "[222] Of course, this "discovery" was hardly new to the 1980s—Congress had been prohibiting the use of funds for specific purposes (including for specific salaries) since the early days of the Republic. For example, an 1810 law, signed by President Madison, provided that certain diplomatic officials, in order to be entitled to their salary, had to have been confirmed by the Senate, even though no substantive legislation actually *required* that these officials be confirmed by the Senate.[223] Such provisos, whether dealing with salaries or other forms of spending, became increasingly popular as the bureaucracy grew.[224] Indeed, this power has on occasion been used to zero-out the salaries of specific officials or categories of officials.[225] To take just one small example, an 1869 law provides that "no salary shall hereafter be allowed the marshal at" the Bangkok consulate.[226] Critics of the practice charge that it violates separation-of-powers principles by allowing Congress to interfere in the internal functioning of the executive or judicial branches,[227] but these criticisms presuppose that the allocation of power to each branch is static and predetermined. Understanding the interbranch allocation of powers as something that is continually being worked out through constitutional politics, by contrast, brings us to a very different view of Congress's authority to zero-out specific programs or officials' salaries: it is simply another one of the tools by which Congress can press for decision-making authority in substantive areas. (The Supreme Court weighed in on this topic in the 1946 case of *United States v. Lovett*,[228] striking down a provision forbidding the use of any government funds to pay the salaries of three named individuals who some members of Congress believed were Communist "subversives." Emphasizing that this was no "mere appropriation measure" and that the plaintiffs had been singled out "because of what Congress thought to be their political beliefs,"[229] the Court held the provision to be an unconstitutional bill of attainder. Given the traditional scope of the congressional power of the purse, *Lovett* is most sensibly read as a narrow decision pushing back against the McCarthyite punishment of individuals for political beliefs unrelated to the scope of their government duties, not as a broader limitation on Congress's power to attach defunding riders to appropriations bills.)[230]

Of course, perhaps Charles Black was wrong—perhaps simple majorities could not reduce the president's staff to a single social secretary because the president would veto any such appropriations bills. There would be an element of perversity in that: by doing so, the president would shut down (at least part of) the government, thereby reducing his staff to zero (or, more precisely, to only those personnel deemed "essential" and thus allowed to donate their time under the Anti-Deficiency Act).[231] But he would be banking on winning the ensuing public relations struggle, thereby forcing Congress (eventually) to back down and restore his full staff. Perhaps a president would even be willing to veto an appropriations bill simply because it zeroed-out the salary of one of his favored subordinates. After all, government shutdowns and near shutdowns are not entirely unknown in our system of government, with various policy disagreements motivating budgetary standoffs. For instance, after the 1878 elections gave Democrats control over both houses of Congress for the first time since the Civil War, they insisted on appropriations riders repealing Reconstruction-era laws protecting the exercise of the franchise and therefore the political power of the freedmen (and hence the Republicans) in the South.[232] President Hayes vetoed four separate appropriations bills in his insistence not to accept the riders.[233] The Democrats had miscalculated, however, and Hayes's public standing grew with each veto.[234] Eventually, the Democrats gave in and passed appropriations bills without the offending riders, with only days to spare before a shutdown. (Indeed, one part of the government did shut down— Hayes's final veto in the conflict was of a rider-laden appropriations bill for federal marshals, and Congress adjourned without passing a clean one.)[235] Although Hayes kept his promise to serve only one term, the conflict worked to the Republicans' advantage, with Garfield winning the presidency in 1880 and Republicans retaking control of both houses.

More recently, the federal government has shut down eighteen times since 1976, with some shutdowns as brief as a day and one as lengthy as three weeks.[236] In 1995 and 1996, the federal government shut down twice—once for less than a week and then again for three weeks—when President Clinton and the Republican-controlled Congress (led by Speaker Newt Gingrich) were unable to agree on a budget.[237] While Congress was the clear institutional loser in the 1995–1996 government shutdowns,[238] it would be a mistake (albeit a common mistake)[239] to infer from this example that Congress inevitably loses out in government shutdowns. The lesson of 1995–1996 was, rather, that a government shutdown throws interbranch conflict into sharp relief, increasing the public salience—and therefore the political stakes—of the fight. This dynamic presents both opportunities and pitfalls for Congress and the president alike. As Leon Panetta, the White House chief of staff during the 1995–1996 shutdowns, put it, "[I]t was a day-to-day crisis, and you never quite knew what the hell was going to happen."[240] A historian of the period concurs: "It was a high-risk gamble for both sides. No one really knew how the public would react."[241] Indeed, news accounts during the shutdowns made it clear that the president was at risk both of losing in the public arena and of losing enough Democratic votes in Congress that his veto could no longer be sustained.[242] But, as several commentators have noted, Gingrich made both tactical mistakes, such as personalizing the fight and thereby appearing petty,[243] and strategic ones, such as overreading his mandate to press for conservative fiscal policy.[244] Had he been more skilled, or had Clinton been less so, we might well remember the 1995–1996 budget showdown as a win for Congress. But to the extent that Congress internalizes the narrative that it is bound to lose any budget show-down with the White House, it correspondingly lessens its bargaining power.

Indeed, the contrast between two recent budget showdowns pitting the Obama administration and the Democratic-controlled Senate against the Republican-controlled House of Representatives is illuminating. The 2010 midterm election was a good one for the Republican Party, giving it control of the House by a comfortable margin and significantly narrowing the margin in the Senate; President Obama referred to it as a "shellacking" for Democrats.[245] House Republicans, led by Speaker John Boehner, claimed a mandate for a decidedly more conservative agenda than had predominated over the previous two years.[246] Because no budget for fiscal year 2011 had ever been completed, the government was being funded by a series of short-term continuing resolutions.[247] This meant that the new Republican House majority had an early crack at the budget.

By credibly threatening to allow the government to shut down, the House Republican leadership was able to bargain for a great deal of what it wanted.[248] Not only did House Republicans successfully negotiate for more than $38 billion in spending cuts that were opposed by the White House, they also used their budget power as leverage to achieve changes they sought in areas as diverse as environmental law, education policy, and abortion access.[249] They even took the opportunity to intervene in a separation-of-powers controversy, prohibiting the expenditure of funds for certain White House "czars."[250] Clearly, the House in this instance was able to use its power of the purse as a potent weapon in interbranch struggle.

By contrast, the 2012 election was a good one for the Democrats. Obama was handily reelected, and, despite having to defend more seats than the Republicans, the Democrats increased their margin in the Senate. Although they did not retake the House, they narrowed the Republicans' margin of control.[251] Because of the centrality of fiscal issues in the campaign, Democrats could plausibly claim a mandate for their positions on taxing and spending.[252] Indeed, in the immediate aftermath of the election, the lame-duck Congress passed a fiscal compromise that was largely favorable to Democratic priorities.[253] But as the next Congress progressed, Republicans became emboldened and sought to use the threat of a government shutdown as leverage in an attempt to secure significant changes in, if not outright repeal of, the Affordable Care Act. This time, Obama and Senate Democrats refused to compromise, and the government shut down on October 1, 2013. The Affordable Care Act was indeed unpopular, but even before the shutdown began, polls showed Americans overwhelmingly opposed shutting down the government in an attempt to secure changes to the law.[254] The shutdown hurt the approval ratings of everyone involved, but congressional Republicans bore the brunt of it, with their poll numbers continuing to slide throughout the sixteen-day shutdown.[255] With the stock market taking a hit[256] and key conservative interest groups and opinion leaders abandoning the Republican position,[257] House Republicans backed down and reopened the government almost entirely on Democrats' terms.[258] Presumably eager to avoid making the same tactical mistake again—and eager to focus on issues more advantageous to them, especially the glitch-laden launch of the Affordable Care Act's website—Republicans agreed in December 2013 to a two-year budget resolution with spending levels above the previous baseline, precisely the sort of deal that they had previously resisted.[259] In late 2015, with Republicans in control of both houses of Congress, they again agreed to a two-year budget resolution with higher spending levels.[260]

So, what was the difference between 2011, when Republicans used their control of the House to win both their preferred spending levels and significant changes in a variety of substantive policy fields, and 2013, when their effort to use budgetary power to secure changes in the healthcare law backfired, forcing them to back off their healthcare demands *and* agree to higher levels of spending? In both cases, the Republicans controlled only the House, with the Senate and the presidency in Democratic hands. But, of course, the political contexts were quite different. The 2010 election was, in large part, a repudiation of the previous two years of unified Democratic government. Had the Republicans successfully used the two intervening years to build trust with the voters, they might have captured unified government themselves in 2012. But they did not; instead, the pendulum swung back toward the Democrats. Little wonder, then, that Republicans were able to get a better deal in the politically friendly climate of 2011 than in the politically hostile one of 2013. And by injudiciously picking a budgetary fight over the Affordable Care Act in 2013, the House not only harmed its ability to get what it wanted in the present, it also created a political dynamic in which its best move was to agree to a series of *two-year* budget resolutions, thereby surrendering some of the power that comes with the annual budget process in even-numbered years (although, of course, the crafting of the individual appropriations bills remained an annual affair).

The crucial lesson of these budget fights is not that the president always wins; as 2011 showed, he does not. The lesson is that who wins—which is to say, who has more say in determining the government's spending levels and priorities, and who is able to leverage that budgetary power to gain power over other policy areas—is significantly affected by the artfulness with which the various actors engage in the public sphere. And the artfulness with which political actors exercise the power that they do have, in turn, significantly affects their future public-sphere engagements.

Of course, none of this is limited to the power to *shut down* the government—that is simply the limiting case. The power of the purse is continually exercised in small-bore ways as well, and there, too, the purse strings come with significant substantive power. Although modern appropriations bills usually allocate lump sums to various agencies and departments, those appropriations bills are generally "accompanied by detailed committee reports giving the specific amounts the department or agency should spend on each program within the budget account."[261] Given that the appropriations committees retain the power to specify detailed spending levels in the statutory language itself— and given that they retain the power to drastically cut those spending levels in future years or to attach unpleasant riders—the departments and agencies "treat those committee reports as the equivalent of legislation."[262] As Democratic representative (and chairman of the House Appropriations Committee) David Obey put it in 2009, "For any administration to say, Well, we will accept the money, but ignore the limitations is to greatly increase the likelihood that they will not get the money."[263] (This was especially noteworthy because the administration that Obey and a number of Democratic colleagues were implicitly threatening was that of a fellow Democrat, Barack Obama.)[264] When agencies do wish to "reprogram" funds (in other words, spend funds in ways that are consistent with the legislation but inconsistent with the committee report), they generally report to the relevant appropriations subcommittee and receive permission to do so.[265] Moreover, when Congress wishes to express its displeasure about an agency's performance, a not-so-gentle tug on the purse strings can be quite effective—in fiscal years 2014 and 2015, the budget of the Internal Revenue Service was slashed, which was clearly meant to convey congressional (and especially House Republican) displeasure at the agency's enhanced scrutiny of the tax-exempt status of certain political groups.[266]

Such pressures seem generally effective: there is a growing body of evidence suggesting that the federal bureaucracy is broadly responsive to congressional preferences.[267] As Morris Fiorina provocatively put it, "Congress controls the bureaucracy, and Congress gives us the kind of bureaucracy it wants."[268] And budgets are one (although, as later chapters indicate, certainly not the only one) of the primary mechanisms by which Congress both directly controls and, perhaps more importantly, signals its priorities to bureaucratic agencies.[269] Indeed, the desire to signal to an agency that congressional appropriators intend to keep a close eye on some particular policy area is likely responsible for the continuing popularity of "legislative vetoes," provisions in delegating legislation that authorize one house of Congress (or sometimes both houses acting jointly, but without presentment to the president) to override some type of agency action. The Supreme Court held legislative vetoes unenforceable in the 1983 case *INS v. Chadha*.[270] Nevertheless, between 1983 and 1999, Congress passed more than four hundred laws containing provisions authorizing legislative vetoes.[271] As Lou Fisher noted in the classic study of this phenomenon, although presidents routinely denigrate legislative-veto provisions in signing statements, "agencies have a different attitude. They have to live with their review committees, year after year, and have a much greater incentive to make accommodations and stick by them. ... Agencies cannot risk ... collisions with the committees that authorize their programs and provide funds."[272] Indeed, as Jessica Korn has noted, when Reagan administration officials initially took *Chadha* as an indication that they could ignore appropriations directives contained in committee reports (but not statutory language), threats from Congress to tie the administration's hands more explicitly forced them to beat a hasty retreat.[273] Nor is this budgetary pressure limited to the executive branch: Eugenia Toma's research suggests both that Congress uses the Supreme Court's budget to signal approval or disapproval of the general thrust of the Court's rulings and that the Court responds to these signals by bringing its decisions more in line with Congress's wishes.[274]

Furthermore, it is not simply the fact or the level of funding that is important; the form that funding takes also has important substantive implications. As Nick Parrillo has meticulously demonstrated, the long nineteenth century saw a large-scale transformation in official compensation, from a fee- and bounty-driven model to a salary model.[275] Broadly speaking, this development has two important implications for congressional power. First, the shift from fees paid by the recipients of government services to salaries meant a greater level of congressional control over government officials. After all, pulling the purse strings is only effective to the extent that the officials in question are paid out of the relevant purse; to the extent that they were paid by the recipients of their services, they naturally tended to take a customer-service attitude rather than an attitude governed by congressional priorities—and this was even more so when fees were not only paid by the recipients of government services but actually *negotiated* between the recipient and the provider.[276] Salarization allowed Congress, using precisely the types of mechanisms discussed in this chapter, to exert greater control. Second, and relatedly, the transition from fees and bounties to salaries had the effect of shifting officials' priorities, even when the fees and bounties had been paid by Congress all along. Thus, as Parrillo notes, the late nineteenth-century transition of federal prosecutors from a system of fees for trial (with a bonus for convictions) to a salary incentivized prosecutors to exercise more discretion, allowing some petty illegalities to go unpunished.[277] Even holding amounts constant, the form of payment was intentionally used as a tool to influence how prosecutors went about their duties.

Funding, and Defunding, the Military

Finally, let us return briefly to a theme that has run throughout this chapter: the connection between the power of the purse and one of the most potent substantive powers, that of the sword. We have seen the two bound tightly together in the constitutional imagination from the Restoration through the Revolution Settlement, into the New World, and in the constitutional ratification debates. It is worth contemplating briefly the ways in which they interact today.

In 2004, Secretary of Defense Donald Rumsfeld remarked, "You go to war with the Army you have, not [necessarily] the Army you might want or wish to have at a later time."[278] What Rumsfeld might have added is that, in many circumstances, the president's decision whether or not to go to war in the first place as well as her decision about what sort of war to prosecute are made in light of the military she has. And, of course, what kind of military she has is a function of the sort of military that Congress chooses to fund. For instance, a Congress that wants to curtail the military's nuclear capacities can refuse to fund them, as Congress did in 2004 when it eliminated funding for a nuclear bunker-busting bomb, known as the Robust Nuclear Earth Penetrator.[279] Likewise, a Congress that wanted to limit presidents' ability to project American power overseas could choose to reduce or eliminate funding for things like aircraft carriers and long-range bombers.[280] Future presidents' decisions about whether or not to initiate a conflict, and how to do so, would be made in the shadow of those past appropriations decisions.

Once a conflict has been initiated, we frequently hear claims that the presidential decision to send troops into the field essentially forces Congress to fund the operation. But despite this conventional wisdom, Congress has, in fact, repeatedly used its power of the purse to end, limit, or forestall military action. As public opinion began to turn against the Vietnam War, Congress enacted two such restrictions. First, the 1971 Cooper-Church Amendment provided that no funds could be used "to finance the introduction of United States ground combat troops into Cambodia, or to provide United States advisers to or for Cambodian military forces in Cambodia."[281] And the 1973 Case-Church Amendment— which passed with veto-proof, bipartisan majorities in both houses—effectively cut off all funding for the war: "Notwithstanding any other provision of law, on or after August 15, 1973, no funds herein or heretofore appropriated may be obligated or expended to finance directly or indirectly combat activities by

United States military forces in or over or from off the shores of North Vietnam, South Vietnam, Laos or Cambodia."[282] Nixon, despite resisting the amendments, complied with them.[283] Likewise, the Byrd Amendment in 1993 forbade the use of any funds for security operations in Somalia after March 31, 1994, and required that the troops currently engaged there be under the command of American officers.[284] President Clinton complied with the requirement, withdrawing U.S. troops in early March 1994. In the Obama administration, Congress repeatedly frustrated the president's goal of closing the detention camp at Guantanamo Bay Naval Base by forbidding the expenditure of any funds to transfer or release into the United States any prisoner held at the camp who is not a U.S. citizen.[285] Similarly, Congress has since 1986 routinely included an appropriations rider forbidding the payment of direct assistance to any foreign government whose elected head of state has been deposed in a military coup.[286] A recent study suggests that post–Cold War administrations have generally, albeit imperfectly and grudgingly, complied with this restriction.[287] And the existence of the restriction has posed problems when administrations do not want to comply: after the Egyptian coup in 2013, the Obama administration attempted to avoid the restriction by not making any formal declaration that a coup had occurred. The result was "extensive, and critical, media coverage," which eventually pressured the administration into partial, but meaningful, compliance.[288]

Of course, sometimes such funding restrictions are outright ignored. Despite the sweeping language of the Boland Amendments prohibiting the use of funds to support the Nicaraguan Contras,[289] the Reagan administration did indeed arrange to provide funds to the Contras. But the political fallout was severe, with the Iran-Contra scandal dominating the last two years of the Reagan administration in ways that had collateral consequences for other aspects of Reagan's agenda, such as the Bork nomination, discussed in chapter 1. Indeed, as Mariah Zeisberg has persuasively argued, a more deft handling of the scandal and resulting hearings by congressional Democrats might well have resulted in impeachment proceedings.[290] The Boland Amendments' specific prohibition on funding the Contras raised the political stakes, and the Reagan administration's flouting of that prohibition forced it to pay a significant price.

In other respects, however, Congress has used its power of the purse in ways that foster the expansion of executive military power. As Fisher has demonstrated, secret funding for the intelligence community has grown explosively since World War II, in some tension with the Constitution's requirement that a

"Statement and Account of the Receipts and Expenditures of all public Money shall be published from time to time."[291] Under the Central Intelligence Act, the CIA, with the approval of OMB, is authorized to take money from other government agencies for its own purposes.[292] The result is doubly misleading: Congress (and the public) can only guess at the scope of the intelligence budget, and the budgets of other agencies appear inflated because some of the money appropriated to them is subsequently funneled to the intelligence agencies.[293] In the aftermath of revelations that U.S. intelligence agencies have been carrying out a massive domestic surveillance program,[294] Congress may wish to reconsider the budgetary latitude that those agencies have been given. As we have seen, pulling the purse strings tighter has been an effective means of reining in executive power throughout Anglo-American constitutional history.

The aim of this chapter has been to survey the extent of the authority available to Congress under the rubric of "the power of the purse." By tracing the historical development of this power, we've been able to see the ideas and goals that have motivated it and to get a sense of what makes its use in a given context efficacious or inefficacious. Some developments—like the increasing percentage of the budget devoted to mandatory spending, certain ill-conceived budgetary showdowns, and the growth of the secret intelligence budget—have diminished congressional power. Others—like more opportunely timed budgetary showdowns, the development of budgetary expertise and institutions in Congress, and the pushback against impoundment—have increased congressional power. Crucially, as stressed in part I of this book, sensitivity to political context, to how certain actions will play out in the public sphere, is crucial to understanding and anticipating the effects of any given exercise of the power of the purse. The growth of mandatory spending may curtail congressional power, but that certainly does not mean that an indiscriminate slashing of entitlements will redound to Congress's benefit. Budget brinksmanship by House Republicans was so successful in 2011 that it won them a wide range of changes in substantive law, but similar brinksmanship in 2013 was such a failure that their best move was to agree to a two-year budget resolution, thus preemptively giving up that source of leverage the following year. And the success (from Congress's point of view) of the Cooper-Church, Case-Church, and Byrd amendments does not mean that Congress will inevitably come out smelling like roses when it cuts off funds for military conflicts. The relevant factor in all of these cases is the politics of the day, and how well the houses and members of Congress are able to use these tools to engage in the public sphere. Like all potent tools, the power of the purse can be used well or poorly.

Moreover, the highly potent versions of these powers, although attention grabbing, are the limiting cases. But while government shutdowns, or even the zeroing-out of some particular program or salary, may be rare, the existence of those extremes—and the ability of Congress plausibly to threaten to go to those extremes—means that all other interbranch bargaining takes place in their shadow. The power of the purse, we have seen, can cast a very long shadow.

4

The Personnel Power

WE MAY ASPIRE, IN THE WORDS John Adams drafted for the 1780 Massachusetts Constitution, to live under "a government of laws and not of men,"[1] but it would take an act of willful blindness to deny that the content of the substantive rules that govern our behavior depends significantly on the men and women who promulgate, adjudicate, and enforce them. It matters greatly who controls the levers of power—this is why we care so much about elections to Congress and the presidency. And it also explains why congressional power over who staffs executive agencies, independent agencies, and the federal judiciary matters so greatly. Personnel and policy are not the same thing, but having a say in personnel choices is certainly one of the ways in which Congress gets a say in policy matters. This chapter therefore considers Congress's role in appointing, removing, and impeaching officials in the other branches.

Historical Development

The development of legislative control over the personnel of the state is tied to the struggle for responsible government in Britain. As the leading historical treatment has defined it, responsible government is "those laws, customs, conventions, and practices that serve to make ministers of the King rather than the King himself responsible for the acts of the government, and that serve to make those ministers accountable to Parliament rather than to the King."[2] Vernon Bogdanor has described responsible government as "the most important of the [constitutional] conventions to develop in the eighteenth century,"[3] but understanding this development requires some attention to the preceding century.

To be sure, there were moments even earlier than the seventeenth century at which Parliament forced monarchs to dismiss odious servants. In particular, the procedure later known as impeachment arose out of the Plantagenet tumult of the fourteenth and fifteenth centuries,[4] and it was used against various ministers of Edward III, Richard II, and Henry VI, with eighteen royal officers and judges being impeached and convicted between 1376 and 1397 alone.[5] For example, in 1386 Parliament asked Richard II to remove the Earl of Suffolk from the chancellorship, accusing him of mismanagement of Crown finances, among other sins. Richard supposedly replied that he would not "remove the meanest scullion from his kitchen" upon parliamentary request, but Parliament's refusal to move on to any other business, combined with a (not terribly subtle) reference to the 1327 deposition of Edward II, convinced him to reverse course. The king removed Suffolk from office; once it was clear that the king would no longer protect him, Parliament impeached, convicted, and briefly imprisoned the earl.[6] Henry IV, who deposed Richard in 1399, was apparently more eager to remain in Parliament's good graces; in 1404, he removed from his service several officials and his confessor upon Parliament's request.[7]

But these medieval precedents were isolated instances in the midst of tumultuous reigns. There was certainly no entrenched general principle of responsibility to Parliament, and the use of impeachment as a mechanism of removal required Parliament to make a plausible argument that the odious official was guilty, not simply of misgovernment, but of treason,[8] which made impeachment "a poor instrument for controlling the King's policies."[9] Impeachment fell entirely into disuse under the Tudors, supplanted by bills of attainder. The explanation for this shift, as James Fitzjames Stephen noted, sounds in royal power: an impeachment, which required a trial but not royal assent, was useful for punishing those whom the monarch wanted to protect, but "[i]f the King himself wished to punish a minister a bill of attainder was more convenient than an impeachment because it superseded the necessity for a trial."[10] The complete replacement of impeachment by attainder during the Tudor dynasty is evidence that only officials who had made themselves obnoxious *to the king or queen* were punished; in no sense were the ministers responsible to Parliament.

Parliament was not, however, entirely subservient to the Tudor monarchs, and I have elsewhere traced the developments in late-Tudor parliamentary procedure that enabled the House of Commons vigorously to push back against the Stuart Crown.[11] In doing so, Stuart Parliaments made creative use of constitutional principles that had been developing for centuries. The first of these principles was that the king always acted through servants—that is, royal commands, to be effectual, had to bear the Great Seal, the Privy Seal, and/or the Signet, which could only be applied by officials in the Chancery, the Exchequer, or the Secretary's office, respectively.[12] And second was the principle that the king himself could do no wrong.[13] This second principle, as Blackstone would later explain it, entailed that "whatever may be amiss in the conduct of public affairs is not chargeable personally on the king; nor is he, but his ministers, accountable for it to the people."[14] The first principle entailed that there was always *some* minister—discoverable at least in theory if not always in fact—to hold accountable, since the king could do nothing without the assistance of some servant. Combined, these principles would come to mean that there was always a servant of the Crown, subject to parliamentary jurisdiction, who could be held responsible for any wrong done in the king's name. Over time, royal servants who knew they would be held *responsible* by Parliament for the policies of the Crown insisted on the power to *determine* those policies, resigning from royal service if their advice was not taken. Over the course of the seventeenth and eighteenth centuries, these practices solidified into the conventions of responsible government.

Shortly after ascending to the English throne, James I faced parliamentary demands for a greater say in the composition of his government. James insisted that he would allow no such thing, and, in large part due to his weariness with parliamentary meddling in issues of royal prerogative, no Parliament met between 1614 and 1621.[15] When financial necessity compelled him to call a new Parliament in 1621, the House of Commons assembled in a combative mood.[16] The House in 1621 arrested seven Crown servants and expelled three from sitting in the House; it also revived the power of impeachment, sending Sir Francis Michell and Sir Giles Mompesson (both commissioners charged with enforcing royal patents), as well as Sir Francis Bacon, the Lord Chancellor, to the House of Lords to be tried. The Lords pronounced sentences upon all three of them (Mompesson in absentia, as he had fled to France).[17] When it appeared that the Commons might impeach Henry Montagu, the Lord Treasurer, James insisted that impeachment should be reserved for corruption, not for mere error. The House, cognizant that the king could dissolve Parliament at will, refrained from going after Montagu.[18]

Here we can see the link between impeachment and the topic of the previous chapter, the power of the purse. The monarch could forestall impeachment by dissolving Parliament, but doing so meant abandoning any hope of receiving supply from Parliament. Thus, the king's ability to protect his servants was directly proportional to his financial independence, a fact of which both the Crown and Parliament were increasingly acutely aware. Thus, the remainder of those punished by the 1621 Parliament were "extortionists and receivers of bribes"[19]—not men whom the king was eager to protect—and that Parliament was dissolved in 1622. But when the expenses of foreign adventuring forced James to call another Parliament in 1624,[20] the houses resumed their attacks on royal officials, including the new Lord Treasurer, the Earl of Middlesex.[21] Middlesex was sentenced by the Lords before the new supply bill was passed; as soon as it was, James prorogued Parliament.[22]

James's reign also saw the opening salvos in another sort of dispute over personnel—that over judges. Although a well-defined judicial role began developing in England as early as the thirteenth century,[23] judges remained in many ways royal servants like any other.[24] It was this long-standing role to which James appealed when, in 1607, he summoned the common-law judges to berate them for deciding that they had jurisdiction to determine the jurisdiction of the ecclesiastical courts.[25] James insisted that, as "the Judges are but the delegates of the King," the king could take upon himself the determination of legal cases.[26] Edward Coke (at least in his own famous, but likely overstated, telling)[27] stood up to his sovereign, asserting that judgments at law could only be issued by the courts of law, and by judges learned in the "artificial reason and judgment of law, . . . which requires long study and experience, before that a man can attain to the cognizance of it."[28] Regardless of what actually passed between the king and his chief justice in 1607, James always had the upper hand. In 1616, he removed Coke from office, at least partly out of frustration at Coke's elevation of the common law, and therefore of the law courts, at the expense of royal prerogative.[29] Indeed, James and his son both frequently removed judges of the common-law courts for decisions they disliked.[30]

Nevertheless, in Coke's pushback against James, we can see nascent ideas about judicial independence from the Crown. More importantly, in Parliament's revival of impeachment and use of it to attack ministers of the Crown, at least one of whom must be responsible for any abuse, since the king himself must be blameless, we can see significant steps toward ministerial responsibility to Parliament.

This practice only picked up steam under Charles I, who saw two successive favorites impeached by the House of Commons. The Duke of Buckingham, who had been James's favorite at the end of his life, managed to strengthen his position even more in the court of James's son.[31] Buckingham was therefore the natural—and largely justifiable—target for parliamentary ire at Charles's expensive policies and highhanded tactics.[32] And one of the principal complaints directed at Buckingham was the extravagant number of important (and lucrative) offices of state with which Charles entrusted him. Complaints against Buckingham began in the first Parliament of Charles's reign in 1625, and Hume speculated that "spleen and ill-will" aimed at the duke were responsible for that Parliament's failure to grant Charles the funds he sought from it.[33] Because he was still in dire need of funds, Charles called another Parliament the following year; instead of being more generous than its predecessor, this House of Commons, in the words of a contemporary observer, "fell upon the Duke, as the chief cause of all publick Miscarriages."[34] Charles angrily insisted: "I must let you know, that I will not allow any of my servants to be questioned amongst you, much less such as are of eminent place, and near unto me. . . . I see you specially aim at the duke of Buckingham. . . . [I] can assure you, he hath not meddled, or done any thing concerning the public or common wealth, but by special directions and appointment, and as my servant."[35] The king, that is, sought to undermine the theoretical foundations of the nascent principle of ministerial responsibility by insisting that he himself—he who could do no wrong—was responsible for the policies of which the House disapproved. Charles ordered the Commons to "cease this unparliamentary inquisition" and get on with the business of granting him supply.[36] Instead, the Commons sent thirteen articles of impeachment against Buckingham to the House of Lords.[37] Rather than allow his favorite to face a trial, and without having received the money he sought, Charles dissolved his second Parliament a month later.[38]

Without Parliament, Charles was increasingly forced to resort to prerogative taxation (that is, taxes levied without parliamentary consent), which was widely decried as unconstitutional. He also chose 1627 to begin a war with France, likely on Buckingham's advice. Indeed, Buckingham led the expedition himself and lost two-thirds of his forces in a rout on the Île de Ré. The resultant expenses left Charles with no choice but to call a new Parliament in 1628,[39] a Parliament that assembled "with the conscious and deliberate aim of vindicating English liberties."[40] In the midst of a controversy over the king's response to the Petition of Right,[41] Coke—who had reentered Parliament after James dismissed him from the bench—took to the floor of the House of Commons to say, "I think the Duke of *Buckingham* is the cause of all our miseries; . . . that man is the Grievance of Grievances: let us set down the causes of all our disasters, and all will reflect upon him."[42] Upon giving satisfactory assent to the Petition, Charles expected that he would then be granted supply, but the House was more inclined to take Coke's advice. It quickly passed a resolution declaring that "the excessive Power of the Duke of *Buckingham*, is the cause of the Evils and Dangers to the King and Kingdom,"[43] and it went to work preparing a lengthy and detailed remonstrance laying out Buckingham's sins—real and imagined—in great detail.[44] This (and a simultaneous remonstrance on the topic of illegal taxation) was the final straw: Charles prorogued Parliament, without having received most of the funds he sought.[45]

During the prorogation, Buckingham was assassinated by a disgruntled army veteran named John Felton.[46] Felton made it clear that he was spurred on by the parliamentary charges against the duke: he admitted that reading the parliamentary remonstrance put the idea into his head, and he had even sewn several lines from the remonstrance into his hat to serve as explanation and justification in the event he was killed in the attack.[47] But while Parliament was able to provide the charges against Buckingham, it was unable to carry out the sentence without royal cooperation, as Charles's dissolution and prorogation had made clear. Indeed, William Fleetwood, a fellow disgruntled veteran who had become an opposition pamphleteer, had written in his account of the Île de Ré that he and several comrades had decided to assassinate Buckingham but then decided that it was better to let Parliament condemn him to death.[48] What Fleetwood missed but Felton saw was that, as of the 1620s, a determined monarch could frustrate parliamentary justice.

Indeed, so determined was Charles that, after dissolving Parliament in 1629, he ruled without it for more than a decade.[49] Although no courtier was able fully to replicate Buckingham's monopoly of offices or primacy in Charles's government, Thomas Wentworth (soon to be created Earl of Strafford), who had previously opposed Buckingham and therefore the Crown, entered Charles's service and quickly rose in prominence, becoming the king's chief councillor by the middle of 1639.[50] The rising tide of discontent that led Charles to dissolve Parliament in 1629, as well as the new grievances accumulated in the intervening decade,[51] meant that, when the financial burdens of the Bishops' Wars in

Scotland required the calling of Parliament in 1640, the members assembled in a combative mood. Charles dissolved the "Short Parliament" after a mere three weeks, when it became clear that it would demand redress of grievances before even considering granting supply.[52] But before the year was up, financial necessity compelled him to call a new Parliament and to keep it in existence, even as it grew increasingly confrontational.

Indeed, one of the first actions of the House of Commons in the Long Parliament was to vote impeachments against Strafford and other royal officials.[53] The articles of impeachment began by accusing Strafford of "traitorously endeavour[ing] to subvert the Fundamental Laws and Government of the Realms of *England* and *Ireland*, and instead thereof, to introduce an arbitrary and tyrannical Government, against Law,"[54] and went on to accuse him of, inter alia, enriching himself at public expense, encouraging Roman Catholics, fomenting hostility between England and Scotland, and violating parliamentary privilege. As Roberts has noted, Strafford's impeachment was not "the work of a faction, a party, or a handful of plotters"; rather, support for it (mirroring opposition to Crown policies) was widespread.[55] What was most distasteful to the political nation was not the means but the ends: it was the exercise of strong unilateral Crown power *in the service of* policies that were high church, conciliatory toward Catholics, and pro-monopoly in economic matters that created the zeal for impeachment.[56]

But this also pointed to the problematic nature of impeachment as a mechanism for controlling royal policy. Strafford compellingly argued before the upper house that he had not, in fact, treasonously attempted to undermine the English constitution, as many of the actions he advised and undertook had clear precedents stretching back to the Middle Ages. Within the juridical procedures of an impeachment trial, many of the Lords were uncomfortable condemning Strafford, even as they were opposed to royal policy.[57] With the impeachment proceedings collapsing, the House of Commons changed course and passed a bill of attainder against Strafford.[58] The Lords, believing Strafford to be a "danger to the realm" even if he was not guilty of treason, followed suit.[59] Charles threatened to withhold royal assent, and indeed promised Strafford that he would do so,[60] but that promise proved hollow. In the face of public baying for Strafford's head and the refusal of the Commons to grant supply until Charles assented to the attainder, he gave in.[61] Hume reported that, upon learning the news, Strafford quoted Psalms: "Put not your trust in princes, nor in the sons of men: For in them there is no salvation."[62] He was beheaded in May 1641.

The Strafford attainder shows Parliament groping its way toward a principle of ministerial responsibility, not simply for illegal conduct, but for distasteful policy. But Parliament's options remained limited: impeachment required a trial, and the Lords were deeply reluctant to convict a minister for treason over policy disagreements. What's more, the king could short-circuit an impeachment trial by proroguing or dissolving Parliament, as Charles did to save Buckingham. Attainder, meanwhile, required royal assent, which was only likely to be forthcoming when (as was the case with Strafford) Parliament had an unusual degree of leverage over the king. As the confrontations between Charles and Parliament intensified in the months after Strafford's death, the House of Commons began to look for other ways to ensure a voice in the composition of the ministry.

The year 1641 saw two important efforts by Parliament to gain a measure of control—or, at least, to limit Charles's control—over the personnel of the state. First, in January the Lords petitioned that Charles begin commissioning royal judges during good behavior, rather than at the pleasure of the Crown.[63] In other words, they wanted him to commit to removing judges only for misconduct, rather than being able to remove them for any reason (or none at all). Four days later, Charles announced to the Lords that he was "Graciously pleased to condescend" to their request,[64] a promise that he in fact kept for the brief remainder of his reign.[65] In addition, in the summer of that year a number of the leading members of the House of Commons pressed for a parliamentary voice in naming Crown servants.[66] Although the Lords were unwilling to assent to so radical a proposal, the Commons did in December 1641 include in the Grand Remonstrance a somewhat scaled-down demand that Charles "vouchsafe to imploy such persons in your great and publick Affairs, and to take such to be near you in Places of Trust, as your Parliament may have cause to confide in."[67] As we shall see in more detail in the next chapter, Charles responded to the Grand Remonstrance by attempting to arrest the parliamentary ringleaders; the resulting public backlash drove him from London.[68] The emboldened House of Commons, led by John Pym, now demanded that Charles employ only such ministers "as shall be recommended to Your Majesty, by Advice of both Houses of Parliament."[69] Pym and his colleagues mobilized public pressure to bring the Lords on board; in April 1642, they succeeded, and the Lords added their assent to the demand to nominate the king's ministers.[70] Edward Hyde penned a response for Charles, arguing that impeachment was the only legitimate means of parliamentary interference in the composition of the ministry.[71] Charles simultaneously insisted that it was his prerogative to take advice in secret, thus frustrating any parliamentary inquiry into which royal servant to hold responsible in any given instance.[72] The Civil War was certainly not fought solely, or even primarily, over the authority to name officers of state, but Charles's insistence upon maintaining that prerogative in its strictest form both enraged parliamentarians and ensured that no one in Charles's inner circle was likely to advise conciliation until it was too late.

Of course, the House of Commons' waging war against and ultimately executing Charles I was a vigorous denial of the proposition that the king can do no wrong. The parliamentarians' best attempts to surround it with the trappings of legality notwithstanding, the act can only be understood as revolutionary.[73] Partially because he refused to allow Parliament a greater say in the selection of his ministry, Charles lost the entire government, and, indeed, his life.

The great irony of the Commonwealth was that Parliament under Charles had never sought to exercise executive powers itself; it simply wanted those powers to be exercised by royal officials who were acceptable and responsive to it. But the outcome of the Civil War was, in fact, government by parliamentary committee.[74] Importantly, as Roberts has suggested, the Commonwealth inculcated in parliamentarians certain "habits" of control over the state, habits that would survive the Restoration.[75] While the experience of the Commonwealth would make parliamentarians wary of government by parliamentary committee, or even of demanding a role in naming the king's servants, it would also accustom them to demanding some measure of oversight over those whom the king chose as his servants. After the Commonwealth, "Englishmen never again placed the executive power immediately in Parliament. Yet they never ceased criticizing in Parliament those to whom the King entrusted it."[76]

The potency of such criticism was demonstrated early in the reign of Charles II. Edward Hyde, Charles I's servant and pamphleteer, had served Charles II in exile and returned with him in May 1660 as his Lord Chancellor. The following year, Charles created Hyde Earl of Clarendon.[77] But, as noted in the previous chapter, the Second Anglo-Dutch War soon undermined both public and parliamentary goodwill toward the restored monarch, and Clarendon took the brunt of the blame. By the summer of 1667, it became clear that "parliament would be impossible to manage unless [Clarendon] had gone" from office.[78] Charles ordered him to surrender the chancellor's seals.[79] More pointedly, in exchange for grants of supply and support for his policies, Charles agreed to support the impeachment of Clarendon.[80] In November of that year, Clarendon fled into exile in France.[81] Although many of Clarendon's opponents were opportunists, seeking to gain office when he fell, the impeachment nevertheless had a republican educative function, showing members of Parliament how legislative inquiry could be used to supervise the government.[82]

One of those who profited from Clarendon's fall was the second Duke of Buckingham, the louche son of Charles I's assassinated favorite. But as fates and alliances churned, he, too, soon found himself on the outs with Parliament. The proceedings against the second Buckingham mark an important turn in parliamentary practice, even if it was not fully perceived at the time. In January 1674, the House of Commons petitioned Charles "to remove the Duke of *Buckingham* from all his Employments that are held during his Majesty's Pleasure, and from his Presence and Councils for ever."[83] The move echoed the language used by the House to petition the Crown for redress of grievances, rather than the language used in impeachment. This was highlighted several weeks later, when the Commons narrowly voted *not* to request the concurrence of the Lords in the matter but rather to address it to the Crown directly.[84] By petitioning the Crown directly, the Commons dispensed with the need for a trial, along with the need for juridical forms and standards attendant upon impeachment. Relatedly, they dispensed with the idea that Buckingham should be deprived of anything more than the offices he held at the pleasure of the king—here was a theory that a politically accountable legislative body could hold a political officer responsible for poor policy, without purporting to judge him guilty of treason or deprive him of his life, liberty, or property. Moreover, the Lords were cut out entirely; on the view expressed by the Commons in 1674, ministers of the Crown should be responsible to their house alone. As with attainder, however, it suffered from the defect that the king could ignore it—so long as he did not need money. Mere days after the Commons sent their petition against Buckingham to the king, Charles announced the conclusion of a treaty ending the Third Anglo-Dutch War. No longer in need of funds, he prorogued Parliament immediately.[85]

The wheel of patronage continued to turn, and Buckingham was soon replaced in Charles's confidence by the Earl of Danby. As noted in the previous chapter, Danby himself was impeached by the House of Commons in 1678 for, among other things, violating specific appropriations provisions. Soon thereafter, Charles dissolved Parliament and called a new election. As Roberts notes, "The election of February 1679 has the distinction of being the first in English history in which the character, conduct, and future of the King's first minister played an important role."[86] It did not go well for Danby. When the newly returned Parliament sought to revive the impeachment against Danby, Charles set off a constitutional firestorm by claiming to have pardoned him. Forced to retreat, Charles allowed his former first minister to spend the next five years in the Tower of London.[87]

Importantly, Danby became a cautionary tale for other royal servants, some of whom began refusing to carry out direct commands of the king, for fear of parliamentary reaction. "No longer could the King exact obedience from his servants in doubtful matters, for neither his commands nor his pardons offered them protection; neither could he act himself, for 'the King can do no ministerial act.' "[88] The consequence, by the end of the reign of Charles II, was a Whig constitutional theory that made the king's ministers responsible to Parliament, not simply for the legality, but also for the wisdom of all actions taken by the Crown. On this theory, ministers had a duty to resign from Crown service before carrying out actions odious to the people as represented in Parliament, and the king had a duty to dismiss ministers who had lost the confidence of Parliament.[89]

It is also worth noting the tight grip that Charles II maintained on the judiciary for most of his reign. For the first few years after the Restoration, Charles continued his father's practice of appointing judges during good behavior.[90] But by 1668, he had "quietly reverted to the practice of appointing judges during pleasure."[91] And beginning in the mid-1670s, he began summarily replacing judges with those who "would doubtless support the king in [the] future against Parliament,"[92] a trend that continued through the remainder of his reign and into his brother's brief tenure. A sequence of events bridging the two reigns serves to make this plain. In 1682, Charles initiated quo warranto proceedings to strip the City of London of its charter. This was a bold attempt by the monarch to assert royal control over the city and to eliminate its long-standing rights and privileges.[93] In order to ensure success, during the pendency of the case Charles removed Justice William Dolben and Lord Chief Justice Francis Pemberton from the King's Bench. Dolben was replaced by Francis Wythens and Pemberton by Edmund Saunders, both of whom were deeply loyal to the Crown. Indeed, Saunders had drawn up the pleadings for the Crown in the quo warranto action before he was placed on the bench to decide that very case.[94] The king won unanimously.[95] Saunders, who had been too ill to attend when the judgment was rendered—but whose agreement was noted by his colleagues—died a week later.[96] Charles replaced him with the equally loyal George Jeffreys. Two years later, after James II had assumed the throne, Lord Chief Justice Jeffreys (joined by Wythens, among others) would go on to preside over the trials arising out of the Monmouth Rebellion in 1685. Owing to their haste and procedural irregularities, and to the severity of the sentences, these trials are known to history as the "Bloody Assizes."[97]

As noted in the previous chapter, Parliament met only very briefly at the beginning of the reign of James II. Indeed, had he allowed Parliament to meet, it might have been satisfied with impeaching some of his servants, rather than deposing him.[98] But he did not, and once again several aspects of the post-1688 Revolution Settlement are worth emphasizing. First, following a report by a special committee of the House of Commons finding that the judgment against the City of London in the quo warranto proceeding was "illegal, and a Grievance,"[99] William and Mary assented to a statute voiding the judgment and restoring the city's traditional rights and privileges.[100] Second, the new monarchs began voluntarily appointing judges during good behavior, rather than at the pleasure of the Crown.[101] This arrangement was formalized in 1701 by the Act of Settlement, which provided that, beginning with the Hanoverian succession, "Judges Commissions [shall] be made Quam diu se bene Gesserint [during good behavior] and their Salaries ascertained and established but upon the Address of both Houses of Parliament it may be lawfull to remove them."[102] And finally, the move toward ministerial responsibility to Parliament continued apace.

This last development was aided in no small part by those aspects of the Revolution Settlement, discussed in the previous chapter, that made the Crown increasingly dependent on Parliament for annual grants of supply. Partisan rancor ran high in the post-Revolution Parliaments, with each party seeking, not a proportional share, but rather a monopoly of offices.[103] This was buttressed by the gradual growth of two norms: first, the House of Commons' addresses against royal servants were increasingly meant for public consumption, not simply for the king's eyes.[104] And second, ministers whose advice was not followed were increasingly willing to resign from royal service rather than publicly defend policies of which they disapproved.[105] Combined, these changes were decisive for the development of responsible government. The Crown needed money, and only Parliament could grant it. Parliament was unwilling to grant supply to a Crown whose servants it distrusted. And political leaders were unwilling to serve a Crown that did not follow their advice, preferring instead to resign and take their case to the people. The result was dramatic: by 1697, the Whigs, who controlled Parliament, had a monopoly on high offices of state. William would have preferred a mixed ministry, but that option was no longer available: "[Whigs] alone could successfully manage his business in Parliament, could win him votes of supply, could secure him loans in the City. Only slowly, reluctantly, and painfully did he come to see that the logic of parliamentary supremacy required him to employ ministers in whom Parliament could confide. It was also his unhappiness to discover that Parliament would not confide in a ministry of men drawn from all parties. . . . He therefore had to choose his ministers from the dominant party in Parliament."[106] This constitutional theory, which was Whiggish in its origins, soon came to dominate Tory thinking as well. The 1698 elections returned a House of Commons that, if not dominated by the Tories, was at least hostile to the Whig ministry. Charles Montagu, the Whig chancellor of the exchequer and first commissioner of the treasury, resigned both posts in 1699, and the remainder of the Whig leaders followed suit.[107] By the middle of 1700, William—after his attempts to create a mixed ministry were thwarted by the unwillingness of Whigs to work with Tories, and vice versa—recognized the need to create a Tory ministry.[108] Both parties were now firmly committed to responsible government rather than Crown prerogative, and the king's ability to choose his own servants was largely at an end.[109]

Further buttressing parliamentary power was an effort to limit "placemen," members of Parliament who also held offices of trust or profit under the Crown. The concern was that the promise of royal patronage would induce members to support the Crown, thus allowing the monarch to get his way through parliamentary undertaking. Although there had been place bills—attempts to prevent the introduction of placemen by making parliamentary membership incompatible with royal service, sometimes also known as self-denying bills—introduced on a semiregular basis since 1641,[110] they had either failed in Parliament, been denied royal assent, or been hastily abandoned. The Revolution Settlement changed this: the Act of Settlement contained a sweeping prohibition on any "Person who has an Office or Place of Profit under the King or receives a Pention from the Crown" from sitting in the House of Commons.[111] Indeed, this provision was a little *too* sweeping: it prevented royal interference in Parliament at the expense of parliamentary leaders' ability to assume positions of power under the Crown. Before that provision could come into effect, it was repealed by the 1705 Regency Act. In its place, the act created a more nuanced scheme: no one could sit in the House of Commons while simultaneously holding certain enumerated Crown offices, a pension at the pleasure of the Crown, or any Crown office created after 1705. Moreover, any member of the House who accepted any "Office of Profit from the Crown" voided his election; however, so long as the office was not one of those enumerated incompatible offices, he could stand for reelection and, if reelected, hold both positions.[112] This struck a better balance for Parliament: it could prevent royal co-optation of its members while still preserving their ability to hold high offices of state.[113]

In addition to assenting to the Regency Act, Queen Anne made clear that she had thoroughly assimilated to the House of Commons' greatly increased control over the composition of the ministry when, in 1710, she decided that she could no longer live with the extant Whig government: she replaced the Whigs with Tories and then immediately dissolved Parliament. The 1710 general election would decide who governed Britain.[114] Anne had the political nation with her—the Tories routed the Whigs and remained in power.[115] But it was clear that the combination of the power of the purse and partisan alliances had won out over royal prerogative: the monarch would henceforth find it necessary to staff her government with the leaders of the party that controlled the House of Commons. Increasingly, this group of royal servants would be referred to as the Cabinet Council and would assume collective political responsibility for the actions of the Crown.[116] By 1717, George I stopped attending meetings of his cabinet on the grounds that he had no real voice in making the decisions of his government.[117]

It may not have escaped attention that this chapter has yet to use the title "prime minister," which today is most closely associated with Crown government. The title of prime minister was, in fact, unknown to the law until the twentieth century; the first legislation mentioning the title was the 1917 Chequers Estate Act, which designated Chequers as the official country residence of the prime minister of the day.[118] Although there is a case to be made for using the term as early as Clarendon under Charles II, Robert Walpole is generally regarded as the first prime minister, serving under George I and George II from 1721 to 1742.[119] The constitutional history of the eighteenth century consists largely in working out the details. But the general outlines were clear: Crown authority was exercised by the cabinet, presided over by an increasingly powerful prime minister; the cabinet was collectively responsible to Parliament; cabinet members would be drawn from the leaders of the party that had a majority in the House of Commons; and the monarch's personal discretion over both personnel and policy would be gradually but inexorably constricted.

The English colonies across the Atlantic were keen observers of the politics of the mother country, and eighteenth-century colonial legislatures, in particular, were eager to press for some of the same gains that the metropolitan Parliament had made in the previous century. Two American colonies were significant outliers when it came to personnel: by the terms of their royal charters (both issued by Charles II), Connecticut and Rhode Island both had elected governors and judges, in addition to the elected assemblies that were present in all of the colonies.[120] In the other colonies, the governors tended to be vice-regal, in both their formal powers and their outlooks.[121] In theory, this meant that the governors had broad authority over the appointment and removal of colonial officials.[122] But in practice this power came under pressure from two different directions. On one side, imperial authorities in London limited governors' discretion, both by requiring that certain appointments be made only with the advice and consent of the colony's council[123] and by reserving for themselves the right to make certain appointments, including the chief justiceship.[124] By the early 1750s, most of the significant colonial patronage was concentrated in the hands not of the governors but of the Earl of Halifax, the powerful president of the Board of Trade.[125] From the other direction, colonial assemblies were asserting increasing authority over appointments to colonial offices. Unsurprisingly, perhaps, this began with an assertion of control over those officials responsible for colonial finances. In nearly all of the colonies, the assemblies asserted the power to fill the post of treasurer, and in several colonies, they successfully pressed for the right to fill other revenue posts as well.[126] In South Carolina—the colony that gave us the Wilkes Fund Controversy, discussed in the previous chapter—the colonial House of Commons "succeeded in obtaining virtually complete control over all officers concerned in handling revenues arising from South Carolina laws."[127] The Georgia House of Commons, following South Carolina's lead, began in the mid-1760s to create new customs offices and to fill them with its own appointees.[128] Several colonies had a regular practice of making the Speaker of the lower house of the assembly the treasurer for the colony as well.[129] And assembly control over the appointment of these officers could have significant implications: in North Carolina in the early 1770s, the two state treasurers ignored the order of the governor to collect a certain tax, instead obeying the assembly's order to suspend collection of that tax.[130] In addition, several colonial assemblies passed laws establishing qualifications for, and limiting the tenure of, civil and even military offices.[131] Thus, although there were significant variations among colonies,[132] it is clear that by the time of the Revolution many of the assemblies were asserting substantial and meaningful control over who held colonial office.

It was widely accepted that colonial governors had the right to appoint those judges who were not appointed by imperial authorities in London, but, for much of the eighteenth century, there was "no uniform practice" as to the tenure of judicial offices.[133] Despite instructions from the Crown that judges should be appointed at pleasure, a number of governors appointed judges during good behavior. Moreover, in the late 1750s and early 1760s, several colonial assemblies passed statutes prescribing good-behavior tenure for judges. Imperial authorities were not pleased, and they both disallowed those statutes and threatened removal of any governors who issued good-behavior commissions to judges.[134] In New York and New Jersey, the assemblies threatened to withhold the salaries of any judges commissioned at the pleasure of the Crown; when Governor Josiah Hardy of New Jersey gave in and issued good-behavior commissions, he was removed from his post in 1762, and Attorney General Charles Yorke declared the judges' commissions void.[135] The Crown position on judicial tenure was a "lingering grievance" in a number of the colonies in the 1760s and 1770s.[136]

As we saw in the previous chapter, this grievance found airing in the Declaration of Independence's complaint that George III "made Judges dependent on his Will alone, for the Tenure of their Offices, and the Amount and Payment of their Salaries."[137] The Declaration also evinced a more general antipathy toward royally appointed officers in the colonies, using language tinged with Old Testament resonance: "He has erected a Multitude of new Offices, and sent hither Swarms of Officers to harass our People, and eat out their Substance."[138] Note that the concern is not simply about the number of colonial officers but about the fact that they were "sent hither"—that they were externally imposed. If the Revolutionary rallying cry of "No taxation without representation!" sounds in the conditions of *legislative* legitimacy, then this anti-swarming language, at least in part, makes a similar point about the conditions of *executive and judicial* legitimacy.

The national government under the Continental Congress did not have much of an executive, of course, but a few developments are worth noting. In 1775 and 1776, the Congress established a number of committees to transact the basic business of the confederation;[139] as the war dragged on, it became clear that some separate institution tasked with administrative work would be useful. In the late-1770s, Congress experimented with Boards of War, Treasury, and Admiralty, whose memberships were a mixture of members of Congress and commissioners appointed by Congress; these boards also hired their own staff members.[140] Finally, in 1780 Congress empowered a committee "to report a plan for the revision and new arrangement of the civil executive departments of the United States under Congress."[141] Upon its recommendation, Congress created four executive departments (Foreign Affairs, Finance, War, and Marine)[142] and appointed their heads.[143] Robert Morris, the superintendent of finance, was given the power to hire and dismiss his own subordinates only because he insisted upon it as a condition of accepting the office.[144] The Articles of Confederation, which came into effect in 1781, also had a few relevant provisions. First, they provided Congress with the authority to "appoint such . . . civil officers as may be necessary for managing the general affairs of the United States under [Congress's] direction."[145] Second, the Congress was to appoint all naval officers and all high-ranking army officers, with the lower-ranking army officers to be appointed by the legislature of the state that raised the regiment.[146] And third, there was an incompatibility provision: no member of the Continental Congress could simultaneously hold "any office under the United States, for which he, or another for his benefit, receives any salary, fees or emolument of any kind."[147] It was widely understood that judicial business under the Articles would be handled by state courts—the Articles allowed Congress to set up admiralty courts and, through a complicated process, to form a court out of its own body to resolve cases between two or more states.[148] Neither of these provisions played a significant role in the government of the confederation.

Early republican state constitutions took a variety of approaches to personnel, but the legislature had a strong role across the board. This should not be surprising, as early republican governors were notoriously weak—in Gordon Wood's words, "Americans' emasculation of their governors lay at the heart of their constitutional reforms of 1776."[149] In most of the states, the governors (called "presidents" in some)[150] were appointed by the legislature. The 1777 New York and 1780 Massachusetts Constitutions were the first to provide for popular election of the governor; New Hampshire and Vermont followed suit with their 1784 and 1786 revised constitutions.[151] Moreover, in most states the governors had little or no role in the lawmaking process: only in South Carolina between 1776 and 1778 did the executive have an absolute veto, mirroring that which the Crown had possessed.[152]

Although there was substantial variance across states, legislatures took a significant role in appointment matters as well. In no state did the governor or president exercise the appointment power alone.[153] At one end of the spectrum were North Carolina and New Jersey, whose constitutions "wrest[ed] every bit of control over appointments away from the governors" and gave it to the legislatures.[154] In some sense, Maryland and Pennsylvania were at the opposite extreme: with the exception of legislatively appointed treasurers (as noted in the previous chapter, nine states had legislatively appointed treasurers), the executive was empowered to fill all of the major civil and military offices.[155] But in neither case did the executive act unilaterally: in Maryland, appointments required the advice and consent of the five-member executive council (whose members were appointed by the assembly),[156] and in more democratic Pennsylvania, the appointing power resided in the president and the twelve-member, directly elected council, acting jointly.[157] In other states, the legislature appointed some officers, while the governor (generally with the advice and consent of the council) appointed others.[158] New York made use of an unusual "council of appointment," consisting of four members of the upper legislative house and presided over by the governor, who could only cast a vote if the four members were evenly divided.[159] The differences between the states are less significant than the states' key similarity: in every state, some legislative voice—and, in most states, a major legislative voice—was seen as crucial in appointments. The states also evinced their fear of the corrupting possibility of placemen: nearly every state prohibited members of the legislature from serving in executive positions.[160] (The 1780 Massachusetts Constitution, perhaps wisely, included Harvard professors on the list of those offices incompatible with legislative service; this disability was not removed until 1877.)[161]

Executive authority was also largely removed from judicial tenure. Most republican state constitutions specified that judges were to serve during good behavior, although Pennsylvania and New Jersey established fixed tenures (with the possibility of reappointment), and New York had a mandatory retirement age of sixty.[162] And even for nonjudicial officials, executive control over removal was limited. Some states, like Maryland, gave good-behavior tenure to officials other than judges;[163] Pennsylvania even specified that some officials (registers of wills and recorders of deeds) served "at the[] pleasure" of the legislature.[164] New York specified that military officers were appointed during pleasure, with the implication that the relevant pleasure was that of the governor,[165] and South Carolina did the same for justices of the peace.[166] In addition to these tenure provisions, many of the state constitutions provided specific removal mechanisms, including, but not limited to, impeachment.

The growth of other mechanisms of ministerial responsibility to Parliament had led to impeachment's largely going out of style in London in the early years of the eighteenth century; as a result, the American states had no widely understood model to follow, which may explain why they adopted a number of different approaches to the practice.[167] But crucially, nearly every state explicitly provided for some impeachment mechanism. New York, for example, allowed the lower legislative house, by a two-thirds vote, to impeach "all officers of the State, for mal and corrupt conduct in their respective offices." Impeachments were to be tried before a special court consisting of the senators, the chancellor, and the judges of the supreme court, which also needed a two-thirds vote to convict, and punishment could extend no further than removal from office and disqualification from future officeholding.[168] In Massachusetts, the lower legislative house impeached before the upper house for similarly described offenses, and the available punishments were similarly limited, but there were no supermajority requirements.[169] In unicameral Pennsylvania and Vermont, the assembly impeached before the governor and council; moreover, both specified that officers could be impeached either during their time in office or after their resignation or removal for maladministration.[170] Virginia and Delaware added the twist that the chief executive of the state could only be impeached after he had left office, although "others, offending against the State, either by mal-administration, corruption, or other means, by which the safety of the State may be endangered" could be impeached while in office.[171] Finally, a number of states provided legislative removal mechanisms other than impeachment. Delaware provided that "all officers shall be removed on conviction of misbehavior at common law, or on impeachment, or upon the address of the general assembly."[172] Maryland provided that state judges and the chancellor "shall be removed for misbehaviour, on conviction in a court of law, and may be removed by the Governor, upon the address" of two-thirds of each house of the assembly.[173] Pennsylvania and Vermont provided for legislative removal of judges without impeachment for "misbehaviour" and "mal-administration," respectively.[174] In Massachusetts and New Hampshire, the chief executive, with the consent of the council, could remove judges "upon the address of both houses of the legislature."[175] South Carolina removed the element of executive discretion, providing in its 1776 constitution that judges and various executive officers "shall be removed" upon the address of both legislative houses.[176] When it revised the constitution in 1778, the state kept the provision for judges but eliminated it for the executive officers, opting instead to reduce their tenure from good behavior to a fixed, two-year term.[177]

The delegates gathered in Philadelphia in 1787, then, had a number of models of the personnel power from which to work. The decision to create a chief executive who did not owe his appointment to support in Congress necessitated a different distribution of the power from that existing in Britain or in most of the states, and indeed most of the delegates at Philadelphia seemed convinced that the president should have a greater role in appointments than the chief executive in most of the states had.[178] As we have seen, however, the lessons of the Stuarts loomed large in the new Republic, and fear of an overweening executive balanced fear of an impotent one. In particular, the authors of the new constitutional order sought to ensure that gains in responsibility were not sacrificed on the altar of presidential power. The solution they settled upon was a division of responsibility, with some mechanisms to ensure officers' accountability to the president, some to ensure their responsibility to Congress, and some to be worked out in the politics of the moment.

The Constitution provides that

[The president] shall nominate, and by and with the Advice and Consent of the Senate, shall appoint Ambassadors, other public Ministers and Consuls, Judges of the supreme Court, and all other Officers of the United States, whose Appointments are not herein otherwise provided for, and which shall be established by Law: but the Congress may by Law vest the Appointment of such inferior Officers, as they think proper, in the President alone, in the Courts of Law, or in the Heads of Departments.

The President shall have Power to fill up all Vacancies that may happen during the Recess of the Senate, by granting Commissions which shall expire at the End of their next Session.[179]

Note that there are, in fact, three different appointment mechanisms here: the appointment of principal officers by the president, with the advice and consent of the Senate; the appointment of inferior officers, which Congress may vest in the president, the courts, or the heads of departments; and recess appointments, which the president can make unilaterally but which come with an expiration date. Note also that while the president may generally be the constitutional first mover in appointments, it was Congress that created and structured most of those offices in the first place. Thus, while the Constitution's text clearly contemplates the existence of ambassadors, judges, heads of departments, and so on, it leaves to Congress the details of what departments to create and how to structure them. Famously, it also leaves the structure of the federal judiciary up to Congress: other than a supreme court (of unspecified size), the Constitution simply gives Congress the power "to constitute Tribunals inferior to the supreme Court" and provides that the federal judiciary shall be composed of the Supreme Court and "such inferior Courts as the Congress may from time to time ordain and establish."[180] This was a consequence of deep disagreement at the Constitutional Convention over whether lower federal courts should exist at all, or whether most litigation should progress through the state courts, with the federal Supreme Court there to ensure that, in matters of federal law, the states' centrifugal tendencies did not get out of control.[181] In addition, the Constitution reflects the concerns about placemen that we saw gaining traction with the Revolution Settlement and reflected in the Declaration of Independence, the Articles of Confederation, and the states' republican constitutions: "[N]o Person holding any Office under the United States, shall be a Member of either House during his Continuance in Office."[182]

As far as removals from office go, the Constitution provides an impeachment mechanism: "The President, Vice President and all civil Officers of the United States" may be impeached for "Treason, Bribery, or other high Crimes and Misdemeanors."[183] The House of Representatives has the sole power of impeachment, and all impeachments are tried before the Senate, which requires a two-thirds vote to convict. Upon conviction, impeached officers are removed from office; they may also be disqualified from holding future office, but the penalties can extend no further (although they are still subject to criminal pros-ecution and/or civil liability arising out of the same conduct). The president's pardon power does not extend to impeachments, and when the president himself is impeached, the chief justice presides over the Senate trial.[184] Aside from the impeachment provisions, the Constitution says nothing about the removal of officers; it does, however, provide that federal judges are to have good-behavior tenure.[185]

Reflecting some measure of discontentment with the state constitutions' vesting the appointment power largely in the legislatures, Hamilton, writing as Publius, asserted that "one man of discernment is better fitted to analyze and estimate the peculiar qualities adapted to particular offices than a body of men of equal or perhaps even of superior discernment."[186] The reason, Hamilton thought, was that a single person would feel a stronger duty to invest resources in investigating an appointment for which he alone was responsible; moreover, a single person would have "*fewer* personal attachments to gratify."[187] To critics like Luther Martin, this singularity of responsibility was precisely the problem: "[T]his was giving the President a power and influence, which together with the other powers, bestowed upon him, would place him above all restraint or controul. In fine, it was urged, that the President as here constituted, was a KING, in every thing but the name."[188] But, retorted Hamilton, all of the benefits of a singular appointer "derived from the power of *nomination*" alone.[189] The Senate's check would have the effect of disciplining any latent monarchical tendencies. Indeed, Hamilton anticipated that the Senate's check would do most of its work below the surface, by preventing the president from even nominating unfit men for office.[190]

One other claim of Hamilton's is worth noting, for the light that it sheds on offices in the early Republic. In explaining the role of the Senate in appoint-ments, Hamilton wrote: "The consent of that body would be necessary to displace as well as to appoint. A change of the Chief Magistrate, therefore, would not occasion so violent or so general a revolution in the officers of the government as might be expected if he were the sole disposer of offices. Where a man in any station had given satisfactory evidence of his fitness for it, a new President would be restrained from attempting a change in favor of a person more agreeable to him by the apprehension that a discountenance of the Senate might frustrate the attempt, and bring some degree of discredit upon himself."[191] At first blush, this claim seems odd coming from the man usually regarded as the high apostle of executive power: was Hamilton in fact asserting that the consent of the Senate was necessary for the *removal* of executive officers? Seth Barrett Tillman has suggested that the answer is no; in context, he argues, "to displace" meant to remove *and appoint a replacement*, for which the consent of the Senate was undeniably necessary.[192] In that case, why would Hamilton find it necessary to make this point? The answer is that, given the structure of the early national administration, there were very few circumstances in which a chief executive would be comfortable *removing* an officer when he was not sure he could *displace* him (in Tillman's understanding of the word). Put simply, there were precious few federal officers. As noted in the previous chapter, the 1789 organic statutes for the Foreign Affairs and War Departments provided simply for a secretary and a chief clerk; the Treasury Department received the comparatively opulent staff of six, including the secretary.[193] Away from the capital, federal officials were even thinner on the ground: aside from a tax collector, a federal marshal, and a U.S. attorney, there might be no federal executive officers in an entire state.[194] Under those circumstances, removal without a replacement in hand might well have left no one to execute federal laws or promulgate federal policies in certain areas.[195]

This is important background against which to read the much-discussed "Decision of 1789," the name given to the debate in the First Congress over whether the president possessed unilateral constitutional authority to remove executive officers. As Madison originally drafted the three organic statutes, they specified that the secretaries were removable by the president alone; this provision was dropped, but attempts to insert a provision specifying that removals required the advice and consent of the Senate were defeated.[196] In the end, none of the three statutes contained an explicit removal provision; instead, each provided in nearly identical language that a specified underling (the chief clerk for Foreign Affairs and War; the assistant to the secretary for Treasury) would have custody of the department's records "whenever the Secretary shall be removed from office by the President of the United States, or in any other case of vacancy in the office of Secretary."[197] The debate was extensive, largely focusing on the constitutional question of removal authority, and the series of votes was complex.[198] Opinion is divided as to whether the final outcome indicates a majority in favor of a constitutional removal authority in the president or whether there was no majority for any particular constitutional position.[199] Another wrinkle was added by the subsequent debate over whether Congress might be able to limit the president's removal authority over certain "nonexecutive" officials. In debating the organic statute for the Treasury, Madison suggested that the comptroller was neither "executive or judicial" but rather "distinct from both, tho' it partakes of each." This observation by Madison was of a piece with the fact, noted in the previous chapter, that the Treasury Department, unlike the Foreign Affairs and War Departments, was not statutorily designated as "executive" in character. Madison argued that the hybrid nature of the office of comptroller necessitated "some modification accommodated to those circumstances . . . I would therefore make the officer responsible to every part of government" by establishing a limited term of office.[200] Although Madison eventually withdrew his proposal for term limits, the debates surrounding it suggest that many members understood there to be certain offices that were not purely legislative, executive, or judicial, and that not everyone who thought that the president had exclusive, inherent constitutional authority to remove purely executive officers also thought that he had similar authority to remove such hybrid officers. The debate was simply inconclusive on that point.[201] What's more, the debate implicitly raised the questions of what made an office "executive" and who got to decide that question. As we have seen in this chapter and the previous one, Anglo-American legislatures from the time of Charles II on had a tendency to regard the Treasury as more closely tied to the legislature than other offices were—or than executives perceived the Treasury to be. This view of the Treasury is implicit in the organic statute's refusal to label the Treasury as "executive" as well as in the requirement that several Treasury officials report to Congress, but it also came up in the Senate debates over the removability issue. The Senate sought to eliminate the removal text quoted above from the Treasury statute but not from the other two organic statutes. The House refused to go along, and the impasse only lifted when Vice President John Adams cast a tie-breaking vote in the Senate to approve the House bill, containing the same removal language as the organic statutes for the Foreign Affairs and War Departments.[202]

The next Congress turned its attention to the problem of filling temporary vacancies—both those that arose from illness or absence and those that arose when death or resignation vacated an office that had to be filled while the president and Senate contemplated a permanent replacement. A 1792 statute provided that if a cabinet officer or other executive official whose appointment was not vested in the head of his department (that is, who could not be immediately replaced by his superior) died, became ill, or was absent, then "it shall be lawful for the President of the United States, in case he shall think it necessary, to authorize any person or persons at his discretion to perform the duties of the said respective offices until a successor can be appointed, or until such absence or inability by sickness shall cease."[203] This provision appears to have been wholly uncontroversial at the time, but, as partisan competition picked up, the statute was amended in 1795 to forbid such acting appointments from lasting for more than six months.[204]

The transition from Washington to Adams gives us some sense of how different the context of appointments and removals was in the early Republic from what it is today. Upon assuming office, Adams retained Washington's cabinet in its entirety—he was, as one leading historical treatment puts it, "not inclined to go to the trouble of replacing them."[205] Indeed, the first removal of cabinet officers did not come until Adams fired Secretary of State Timothy Pickering and demanded the resignation of Secretary of War James McHenry in May 1800.[206]

Unsurprisingly, the new nation's first cross-partisan handover of power was accompanied by a flurry of activity relating to appointments and removals. Famously, after the election of 1800 returned a Republican president (Jefferson) and Republican majorities in both houses of Congress, the Federalist lame ducks passed the Judiciary Act of 1801. The act both increased the number of district and circuit courts and also, crucially, changed how the circuit courts were staffed—whereas those courts had previously been staffed by a combination of district judges and Supreme Court justices riding circuit, they would now be staffed by a new group of designated circuit judges.[207] As Alison LaCroix has demonstrated, the act was, at least in part, an attempt by the Federalists to respond to long-standing complaints about the judicial structure created by the 1789 Judiciary Act and to put into action their own theory of federal jurisdiction.[208] But the 1801 act also provided the opportunity for Adams to nominate, and for the Federalist-dominated Senate to confirm, a number of new federal judges with good-behavior tenure before the Republicans were inaugurated in March of that year. Adams took the opportunity, successfully appointing thirteen new circuit judges, who, because of the last-minute nature of their appointment, came almost immediately to be known as the "midnight judges."[209]

A few days after passing the Judiciary Act, Congress also passed the Organic Act for the District of Columbia, which, among other things, provided for the president to appoint a number of justices of the peace with five-year terms— conveniently structured to outlast Jefferson's first (and, the Federalists hoped, only) term as president.[210] As Michael McConnell has noted, these positions were important: they were the principal law-enforcement officers for the new national capital.[211] The Federalists had only to look across the Atlantic to France, where the streets of Paris had recently run red with blood, where Napoleon had only just seized power, and where he would soon be crowned emperor, to have reason to be concerned about who kept order in the capital city. It was not lost on the Federalists that the president-elect had been serving as the U.S. minister to France when the Bastille was stormed and had been broadly sympathetic to the aims of the French Revolution. On March 2, 1801— two days before his term ended—President Adams nominated twenty-three men to serve as justices of the peace for Washington, many of whom were staunch Federalists.[212] The next day, the Senate confirmed them all.[213] Adams spent the evening signing the commissions and then sent them to John Marshall (who was serving simultaneously as chief justice of the United States and acting secretary of state), who affixed the Great Seal of the United States. A few were delivered to their recipients, but many were still in the State Department offices when Jefferson took office the next day. He ordered his acting secretary of state, Levi Lincoln, not to deliver them. One of the undelivered commissions was for stalwart Federalist William Marbury.[214]

A year later, Congress repealed the Judiciary Act of 1801,[215] thus eliminating all of the new judgeships that had been created by that act and filled by President Adams. The subsequent 1802 Judiciary Act increased the number of circuits (as the 1801 act had) but did not create any circuit judges, so the circuit courts would once again be staffed by a combination of district judges and Supreme Court justices riding circuit.[216] The Federalists protested furiously that judges, once appointed, had good-behavior tenure and could not be summarily removed in this manner, but the Republicans argued that abolishing a judgeship (as opposed to removing a judge) was simply an exercise of Congress's power to shape the federal judiciary.[217] The Republicans, who had just received a decisive electoral mandate,[218] were in no mood to listen to what they perceived as hypo- critically principled arguments attempting to entrench a blatant power grab by the outgoing Federalists. In an effort to make sure that their own actions stuck,

Republicans deviously rearranged the judicial calendar. The 1802 Judiciary Act, which was passed at the end of April, canceled the Supreme Court term that was to have begun in August, instead directing that Supreme Court terms were to begin in February; it also required each of the circuit courts to meet in the fall.[219] This put Federalist justices in a bind: before they could meet as a court to discuss, and perhaps decide upon, the constitutionality of the Repeal Act or the 1802 Judiciary Act, they would have to decide individually whether to obey those acts by riding circuit. If they rode circuit and heard cases, they would appear to be acquiescing in the constitutionality of the acts; if they refused to ride circuit, they would risk impeachment, and they would have to do it without face-to-face consultation. After an exchange of letters, the justices all rode circuit,[220] thus "effectively ousting the midnight judges."[221] Republicans also made substantial gains in both houses in the 1802 midterm elections, making it even clearer to Federalists that the political winds were not at their backs.

While riding circuit, Chief Justice Marshall heard arguments in *Stuart v. Laird*, one of a number of suits brought by Federalist attorneys challenging the constitutionality of the Repeal Act. These challenges were brought in the context of cases that were already pending when the Repeal Act was passed, and they asserted that the act, by unconstitutionally divesting the circuit judges of their offices, effected an illegal transfer of their cases from the Adams-era circuit courts (that is, those constituted by judges appointed under the 1801 Act) to the Jefferson-era ones (that is, those constituted by district judges and circuit-riding justices, under the Repeal Act and the 1802 Judiciary Act). Marshall rejected this argument as circuit justice and then recused himself when the case was argued before the Supreme Court in 1803.[222] Justice Paterson, who wrote the Supreme Court's terse, four-paragraph opinion, said nothing about the removal of the circuit judges from office; instead, he affirmed Marshall's circuit-court ruling on the grounds that Congress had the authority to transfer cases from one court to another, and that was all that had been done here.[223] The justices' effective abandonment of their Federalist colleagues, combined with the midnight judges' own reading of the prevailing political winds, convinced the Federalists that the cause was lost. The judges petitioned Congress in 1802–1803 for their salaries, lost, and let the matter lie.[224]

A few days before the Court ruled in *Stuart*, it also disposed of William Marbury's case. Marbury had filed suit directly in the Supreme Court, seeking a writ of mandamus—an order from the Court to Secretary of State James

Madison ordering him to hand over Marbury's commission. Madison, making plain the administration's view that the Court had no authority to order him to hand anything over, did not show up and did not send counsel to the proceedings.[225] Despite the fact that John Marshall had been the one who sealed but failed to deliver the commission in the first place, he wrote the opinion for the Court. After insisting that the office had vested once the commission was signed and sealed, and therefore that Marbury had a legal right to it that the Jefferson administration had violated,[226] Marshall pivoted to make a highly strained argument that the Court lacked jurisdiction to afford Marbury any remedy for this violation of his rights.[227] It was in the course of this argument that Marshall famously defended the authority of federal courts to disregard unconstitutional acts of Congress, striking down a provision of the 1789 Judiciary Act that, in Marshall's reading (although probably not in actuality), purported to confer jurisdiction upon the Court to issue the remedy Marbury sought.[228] The opinion in *Marbury v. Madison* thus allowed Marshall to do three things: (1) emphatically assert that federal courts possessed a power of judicial review over acts of Congress; (2) strenuously chastise Madison (and, by implication, Jefferson) for violating the vested legal rights of poor William Marbury; and (3) meekly do both of the preceding while giving Jefferson the "win," thus making it impossible for the administration to defy the Court. Had the Court ruled in Marbury's favor, it seems almost certain that Jefferson would have refused to produce the commission, thus demonstrating the impotence of the Court at an early moment in its history.[229] Marshall, a brilliant political tactician, got as much as he dared, but there should be no doubt who won this conflict. The midnight judges vanished from the scene—and the fact that we still refer to them as "midnight judges" today suggests that history attaches more opprobrium to Adams and the Federalists for the appointments than to Jefferson and the Republicans for the removals. Marbury and the other appointees who had not received their commissions were denied their offices. The best Marshall could boast was, in Michael McConnell's apt phrasing, the "effective avoidance of judicial humiliation."[230] The Republican revolution of 1800 and its further entrenchment in 1802 effectively (if only temporarily) settled these questions over personnel: the midnight judges could be deprived of their offices, and appointees who had not yet received their commissions could be told that they were out of luck.

There is also one curious omission from the *Marbury* saga: no one seems to have suggested that Jefferson had the constitutional authority to *remove* William

Marbury from office, if indeed Marbury had been properly appointed to that office in the first place. After all, if Jefferson had such a power, then whether the office had vested or not hardly mattered—Jefferson could have handed over the commission in one instant and taken it away in the next. But no one at the time seems to have asserted this point; indeed, Marshall repeatedly made claims at odds with it, noting that, once a justice of the peace was properly appointed under the act, "the law continues him in office for five years, and he is entitled to the possession of those evidences of office, which, being completed, became his property."[231] And, speaking precisely to the removal question:

> Where an officer is removable at the will of the executive, the circumstance which completes his appointment is of no concern; because the act is at any time revocable; and the commission may be arrested, if still in the office. But when the officer is not removable at the will of the executive, the appointment is not revocable, and cannot be annulled. It has conferred legal rights which cannot be resumed.
>
> The discretion of the executive is to be exercised until the appointment has been made. But having once made the appointment, his power over the office is terminated in all cases, where, by law, the officer is not removable by him. The right to the office is then in the person appointed, and he has the absolute, unconditional, power of accepting or rejecting it.[232]

In Marshall's view, then—uncontested in these proceedings—there were at least some officers of the United States, appointed by the president with the advice and consent of the Senate, who were not Article III judges but who were not necessarily removable at the pleasure of the president. Congress could surely have made justices of the peace removable at will, but it also, on this view, could give them set terms of office.

Indeed, Jefferson himself appears to have acquiesced in this view. It has long been known that Jefferson decided to reduce the number of Washington justices of the peace from twenty-three to fifteen (the Organic Act had left the number to be appointed to the president's discretion), which allowed him to appear above the partisan fray by renominating most of the men Adams had nominated, while omitting the staunchest Federalists (like Marbury).[233] Of the fifteen men to whom Jefferson gave recess appointments for the position, thirteen had been on Adams's list.[234] Jefferson originally nominated all fifteen recess appointees for full terms, but three withdrew, and he named three others in their stead.[235] Although Jefferson renominated some relatively "apolitical" Federalists, David Forte has suggested that "he cut every one of the Adams' partisans but two."[236] One of the two partisans Forte identifies, Benjamin Stoddert, had been Adams's secretary of the navy and was still in office while Jefferson searched for a successor. Under those circumstances, refusing to nominate him might have caused too much tension in Jefferson's cabinet. Stoddert, however, had the good grace to refuse the appointment.[237] Forte's other staunch Federalist was William Hammond Dorsey, whose inclusion he describes as a "curious case,"[238] and who also declined the appointment. But Forte missed one of Jefferson's retentions: Thomas Peter, a stalwart Federalist who was, in fact, married to George Washington's step-granddaughter.[239] What did Peter and Dorsey have in common? *They both had taken physical custody of their commissions on the night they were signed.* Upon taking office, Jefferson compiled a list of Adams's nominees, divided into the columns "Justices' Commissions given out" and "Commissions not given."[240] For the Washington positions, there were three that had been delivered: William Thornton (a Republican), Dorsey, and Peter.[241] It is hard to imagine why Jefferson would have nominated Dorsey and Peter other than the fact that they had already received their commissions. In other words, Jefferson does not seem to have thought that they, having been appointed, were removable at his pleasure.

Of course, the fact that he did *re*nominate them, rather than simply treating them as appointed, may suggest that he did not believe that their commissions from Adams were valid.[242] Alternatively, much as Marshall would the next year make the best of a losing hand in *Marbury*, Jefferson may simply have been making the best of a losing hand with respect to the already-delivered commissions. He could put his name to the commissions, thereby making a statement about who the boss really was, but the Federalists could not complain about it, because they were, after all, getting to serve as justices of the peace. In other words, Jefferson may have realized that Dorsey and Peter—unlike other staunch Federalists whose commissions had not been delivered—had a strong case for having a vested right to their office, an office that was not held at his pleasure. Recommissioning them may simply have been the most assertive statement he thought he could make. Indeed, Jefferson's treatment of Dorsey and Peter stands in stark contrast to offices that were undoubtedly held at the pleasure of the president: there, Jefferson was highly active in forcing out Federalist holdovers.[243]

The Jeffersonians were, in fact, hoping to spend their first years in power making over all three branches: as noted above, they increased their control of Congress in 1802; Jefferson was steadily stocking the bureaucracy with Republicans wherever he could; and, in addition to the removal of the midnight judges and the restructuring of the circuit courts, there was a brief attempt to remake the judiciary through impeachment. The Jeffersonians began with John Pickering, a federal district judge in New Hampshire and a loyal Federalist. Although his service as chief justice of the state supreme court had been marred by charges that he was mentally unbalanced, George Washington appointed him to the federal bench in 1795. He continued to behave erratically in his new job, and by 1803 Jefferson suggested to the House that it might inquire into his conduct.[244] In March 1803, the House voted to impeach Pickering, with forty-five votes in the affirmative and eight (all of them Federalists) in the negative.[245] Three of the four articles of impeachment dealt with misconduct in a specific case; the fourth accused him of "being a man of loose morals and intemperate habits" and of blaspheming from the bench while drunk.[246] Pickering did himself no favors, refusing to attend his Senate trial and challenging Jefferson to a duel.[247] Several Federalists in the Senate, realizing that if Pickering were removed other Federalist judges would soon face impeachment proceedings, sought to slow or halt the trial; arguing that impeachment was a criminal proceeding, they claimed that his very mental incapacity should *preclude* his trial.[248] The Federalists lost: Pickering was convicted on all four articles of impeachment by a vote of nineteen to seven; he was then declared removed from office by a separate vote of twenty to seven, the first federal official of any sort removed by impeachment. All of the votes in the affirmative were by Republicans, and all of the votes in the negative were by Federalists.[249]

With that success in hand, the Republicans turned their sights on Samuel Chase, the arch-Federalist, ill-tempered justice who had issued a number of controversial decisions while riding circuit.[250] Especially vexing to Republicans had been his zealous jury charges in Sedition Act prosecutions.[251] Moreover, unlike Marshall and his more savvy Federalist colleagues, Chase "did not trim his sails after the Republican victories of 1800 and 1802."[252] The House voted to impeach Chase on March 12, 1804—the same day that the Senate convicted Pickering—and drew up articles of impeachment later that month.[253] The House adjourned without voting on the articles, and in the interim Jefferson was reelected and Republicans gained additional seats in both chambers. The

Federalists' hopes that the electorate would return them to power were dashed, and the Republicans were emboldened. The articles were reworked and expanded over the break, and the House passed them in December.[254] They accused Chase of misconduct while presiding over the treason trial of John Fries and the seditious libel trial of James Callender, haranguing a Delaware grand jury to issue a presentment against "a most seditious printer," and giving a Federalist political speech in the guise of a grand jury charge in Baltimore.[255] Many Federalists, including perhaps Marshall himself, feared that Marshall would be next if Chase were convicted.[256] But that fear did not come to pass: by skillfully conceding errors in judgment while denying that they rose to the level of impeachable misconduct, Chase picked off just enough Republican votes.[257] All Federalists voted to acquit, and a "handful of Republicans deserted their party on every one of the articles."[258] In fact, a bare majority voted to convict on only three of the eight articles (two dealing with the Callender trial and one dealing with Chase's partisan speech to the Baltimore grand jury), and none came close to the requisite two-thirds margin for conviction.[259] This ended the Republicans' impeachment drive against Federalists in the federal judiciary, but it would be a grave mistake to think that the Federalists "won." Chase himself came away humbled, "lack[ing] fire and determination" when he returned to the bench.[260] The circuit judges had lost their seats. Most of the staunch Federalists appointed (but with undelivered commissions) never served as justices of the peace. Jefferson and his Republican successors continued remaking the federal bureaucracy in their own image. The Marshall Court quietly made its peace with Republican politics.[261] And the Federalist Party would never again hold the presidency or control either chamber of Congress.

The near-total victory of Jefferson and the Republicans over the Federalists involved Congress and the president working together on personnel matters.[262] But this should certainly not be confused for congressional abdication in the personnel field. Indeed, the 1820 Tenure of Office Act, passed by a Republican-dominated Congress and signed by a Republican president, James Monroe, suggests that Congress maintained a vital power over appointments and removals. The act provided that a large number of officers were to be "appointed for the term of four years, but shall be removable from office at pleasure."[263] This, of course, meant that the Senate would have a say in who filled those offices at least every four years. Equally importantly, the act provided expiration dates for the commissions of *currently serving* officers,[264] thus suggesting that Congress could, by statute, remove at least certain executive-branch officers.[265] Congress thus indicated its continuing interest in having a significant say over executive-branch personnel policy.

The partisan spirit in appointments, begun by Adams and increasingly utilized by Jefferson, found its apotheosis in Andrew Jackson, who very explicitly ran on a platform of rewarding his supporters with appointments.[266] Consider the following anecdote as evidence of both the relative importance of offices and the importance that Jackson attached to patronage appointments: the post office was the largest potential source of patronage jobs in the federal government, making the postmaster general an important figure. John McLean, who had been postmaster general under James Monroe and John Quincy Adams but supported Jackson's 1828 presidential bid, was committed to meritocracy and opposed to the partisan replacement of his staff. Not wanting to anger other allies by getting rid of one of his supporters entirely, Jackson appointed McLean to the Supreme Court *in order to appoint someone more accommodating as postmaster general.*[267] The new postmaster general, William Barry, immediately went on a partisan replacement spree,[268] and the Jacksonians began developing an ideological defense of "rotation in office."[269] The "spoils system," as it came to be known, would remain a key feature of the American political landscape until postbellum civil service reforms.

But even Jackson at times had significant trouble with high-level appointments. Despite being controlled by Jacksonian Democrats, the Senate rejected ten of his nominations in his first year in office.[270] The 1832 election delivered a decidedly mixed message: Jackson ran partly against Senate obstruction of his nominees and was handily reelected; at the same time, his party lost control of the Senate itself.[271] The new Twenty-third Congress (1833–1835) twice rejected Roger Brooke Taney—first as secretary of the treasury, and then as a Supreme Court justice, reflecting significant displeasure with his role (while serving as treasury secretary under a recess appointment) in carrying out Jackson's program of removing deposits from the Bank of the United States.[272] Jackson's partisans picked up Senate seats in the midterm elections, and when John Marshall died in 1835, Taney was confirmed as his replacement.[273]

By 1834, Jackson's opponents had adopted the name "Whig" as a nod to traditional critics of overbearing executive power.[274] Central to the Whig constitutional vision was strong congressional control over the administration, including personnel matters.[275] Mike Gerhardt has provocatively suggested that the true significance of the first Whig president, William Henry Harrison, who served for only thirty-one days before he died, lies precisely in his confrontations with Henry Clay, the Whig leader in the Senate, and therefore in Harrison's abandonment of Whig principles upon election to the presidency.[276] Of course, such a brief presidency makes it difficult to draw any firm conclusions, and, on the available evidence, one might conclude that Harrison's deference to Daniel Webster made him not so much anti-Senate as anti-Clay. But it is clear that Harrison's vice president and successor, John Tyler, ran into a Whig-dominated Senate that had no interest in deferring to his nominees. Tyler, who became a Whig more out of frustration with Jackson than because he subscribed to the party's principles, immediately set about alienating his party by vetoing significant portions of its legislative platform.[277] Derided as "His Accidency" for the manner in which he assumed the office, Tyler soon found himself a president without a party or constituency—the Whigs expelled him from the party in September 1841, a mere five months after he became president. Tyler's political isolation was reflected in the fate of his nominations. As Gerhardt summarizes: "The Senate rejected seven of his twenty cabinet nominations—the largest number of cabinet nominations ever made by a single president to be rejected by the Senate. In Tyler's last two years in office, the Senate blocked a majority of his nominations (including four cabinet and two minister nominations), and the Senate rejected eight of his nine Supreme Court nominations—the largest number of unsuccessful Supreme Court nominations ever made by a single president."[278] The Whig constitutional vision was not dead; it was simply dependent on the political climate. A weak president, like Tyler, found himself unable to get the personnel he wanted.

The remainder of the antebellum period saw "[a]n enormous turnover in personnel . . . every four years . . . because control of the presidency changed parties in every election but one in that period."[279] The largest turnover in personnel came as Lincoln removed nearly everyone that he was entitled to remove who had served under Buchanan.[280] But while Lincoln may have used patronage to reward Republican supporters with most offices, it was his choice of a War Democrat, Andrew Johnson, as his second-term running mate that was to prove most consequential.[281] After Lincoln's assassination, Johnson, like Tyler before him, found himself a president without a mandate, and like Tyler, he quickly alienated congressional majorities.[282] Congress responded with legislation meant to constrain Johnson in various ways, especially in terms of the personnel around him. After having expanded the size of the Supreme Court to ten justices in 1863 in order to give Lincoln an extra appointment, it reduced the number of justices to seven in 1866 (with all existing justices keeping their seats) in order to prevent Johnson from making any appointments.[283] The 1867 Tenure of Office Act, which was passed over Johnson's veto, provided that most Senate-confirmed officers were entitled to remain in office until a replacement was confirmed by the Senate. Certain important officers, however—including the secretaries of state, treasury, and war—were entitled to remain in office "during the term of the President by whom they may have been appointed and for one month thereafter, subject to removal by and with the advice and consent of the Senate." The president could suspend such officers during a Senate recess, but if the Senate did not ratify the suspension and appoint a replacement when it reconvened, then the suspended officer would be immediately reinstated. Violations of the act were made a criminal offense.[284] The Army Appropriations Act, passed by Congress a few weeks later, required that all military orders from the president be issued via the General of the Army (Republican Ulysses S. Grant), who could not be dismissed without the consent of the Senate.[285] Because vetoing this bill would have meant defunding the army, Johnson signed it under protest.[286]

As his conflicts with congressional Republicans, and especially the radical wing of the Republican Party, continued, Johnson decided to up the ante by firing Secretary of War Edwin Stanton, whom he had inherited from Lincoln. When the Senate refused to concur, Johnson insisted that Stanton was removed from office anyway, on the grounds that the Tenure of Office Act was unconstitutional.[287] Three days later, the House impeached Johnson by a vote of 126 to 47, with nine of the eleven articles of impeachment charging him with attempting to circumvent congressionally imposed limits on his authority over personnel.[288] After a trial lasting several months, Johnson escaped conviction by a single vote: the final tally was thirty-five guilty votes to nineteen not-guilty votes.[289] Although Johnson was not removed from office, he served out the remainder of his term as a severely weakened president, constrained by promises that he had made to secure moderate Republican votes for acquittal. And a number of his nominations ran into trouble during the remainder of his term.[290] Indeed, the Senate had gone out of its way to make scrutiny of Johnson's nominees more likely—a mere five days before opening arguments in his impeachment trial began, the Senate adopted (for only the fourth time since 1789) a major overhaul of its rules.[291] As part of that overhaul, for the first time it became the default practice to refer nominations to committees,[292] thus ensuring greater opportunity for scrutiny. Moreover, a few months after his narrow acquittal, Johnson signed the Vacancies Act of 1868. The provision for filling temporary vacancies, established in the 1792 and 1795 statutes, had been tweaked slightly under Lincoln. An 1863 revision had retained the six-month limit and added a requirement that the acting appointee be either "the head of any other Executive Department, or other officer in either of said Departments, whose appointment is vested in the President, at his discretion."[293] In other words, the acting appointee had to be either Senate confirmed or an inferior officer appointed by the president. But the 1868 provision was much more restrictive: an acting head of a department or bureau had to be either the second-in-command at that department or bureau or some other Senate-confirmed presidential appointee. In addition, the acting head could serve for only ten days (in the case of the incumbent's death or resignation) or until the incumbent recovered from his illness or returned from his absence.[294] (In 1891, the ten-day period was extended to thirty days.)[295] As Jerry Mashaw has noted, Johnson's presidency had a lasting impact on appointments, with an "ascendant" Congress exercising greater control over appointments throughout the Gilded Age.[296]

Johnson failed to secure the Democratic nomination for the 1868 election, and the eventual Democratic nominee, Horatio Seymour, lost badly to Ulysses S. Grant. One of the first laws of the Grant presidency restored the Supreme Court to nine justices, giving Grant an early appointment.[297] Grant had campaigned on a platform of civil service reform, and a rider to an 1871 appropriations bill gave him the authority to "prescribe such rules and regulations for the admission of persons into the civil service of the United States as will best promote the efficiency thereof, and ascertain the fitness of each candidate" and authorized him to appoint officers to advise him in doing so.[298] Grant appointed several such officers, who collectively began to be called the Civil Service Commission, and he implemented the rules they recommended, including the administering of a competitive exam for applicants for certain positions. But congressional ascendance over patronage appointments in this period translated into congressional antipathy toward civil service reform, and political support dried up in Grant's second term. The commission was defunded in 1874, and shortly thereafter Grant disbanded the examination boards, putting an end to the first experiment in reform.[299]

Grant's successor, fellow Republican Rutherford B. Hayes, was strongly committed to civil service reform and attempted to do what he could by executive order, insisting that federal employees not "take part in the management of political organizations, caucuses, conventions, or election campaigns."[300] This meant taking on the New York political machine of Senator Roscoe Conkling, the leader of the "Stalwart" wing of the Republican Party, which was opposed to civil service reform. When Hayes asked for the resignation of a number of federal officials in New York, they refused. He nominated others in their places, but this meant winning over the Senate, and Conkling did everything possible to defeat the confirmation of their replacements. Although Hayes won their confirmation in the end, he was considerably weakened in the process, and no further movement on civil service reform happened during his presidency.[301]

Hayes kept his promise to retire after a single term, and the 1880 Republican Party convention was highly contentious, pitting the "Half-Breeds," the branch of the party that supported civil service reform, against the "Stalwarts," who opposed it. In the end, the party nominated Half-Breed James Garfield as its presidential candidate and, in the interests of preserving party unity, Stalwart Chester Arthur as the vice presidential candidate. Arthur, not coincidentally, had been the Collector of the New York Custom House whom Hayes had replaced as part of his fight with Conkling.[302] Four months after taking office, Garfield was shot by Charles Guiteau, a madman who thought himself entitled to appointment to high office. Before shooting Garfield, he wrote a justificatory statement, including the lines: "[Garfield]'s death was a political necessity. . . . I am a stalwart of the stalwarts." When apprehended, he repeated to the arresting officer, "I am a stalwart. . . . Arthur is now President of the United States."[303] This was not quite true—it took eighty days and medical care of questionable competence for Garfield to die[304]—but Arthur did indeed become president in September 1881. But the manner in which Arthur came to office made it impossible for him to resist civil service reform, as accounts of the assassination emphasized Guiteau's desire for office and downplayed his derangement. The day after Garfield was shot, the *New York Times*, then a Republican newspaper, wrote: "[I]t is impossible to ignore the causes which led immediately to this act. . . . [Guiteau] was a disappointed office-seeker, and he linked the bitterness of his personal disappointment with the passionate animosity of faction. . . . [T]he act was an exaggerated expression of a sentiment of narrow and bitter hatred which has been only too freely indulged. It is not too much to say, in the first place, that if

Mr. GARFIELD had not been the chief of a service in which offices are held out as prizes to men of much the same merit and much the same career as this murderer he would not have been exposed to this attack."[305] The following day, in an editorial titled "A Lesson," the same paper wrote: "If our civil and diplomatic service were properly organized, no President would ever incur the personal hostility of a disappointed hunter after Consulships."[306] With that narrative taking hold so quickly, the prospects of civil service reform had never looked so good.

And, indeed, Arthur signed the Pendleton Act into law in January 1883. The act created a permanent Civil Service Commission, which was required to have a bipartisan composition, and tasked it with establishing competitive, merit-based civil service exams. All "classified" federal government positions were required to be filled according to the results of those exams.[307] The act classified certain sets of customs and postal employees and Washington-based departmental clerks, and it allowed the president to direct heads of all the executive departments to create or modify classifications.[308] It also contained sundry provisions meant to prevent federal employees from either exercising or being subject to personal or partisan pressures.[309] In the immediate aftermath of the act's passage, only about 11 percent of the executive workforce was under the merit examination system, but the number expanded rapidly. By 1900, about 46 percent was subject to examination.[310] The reason for the rapid expansion appears to have been partisan: between 1881 and 1901, partisan control of the White House flipped every four years. During this time, lame-duck presidents would clean house in nonclassified positions, appoint their own partisans to fill those offices, and then classify the positions on their way out the door, so as to deny such opportunities for patronage appointments to their successors.[311] As Steve Skowronek has cautioned, we should be careful not to overstate the change: because of the significant growth of the postbellum administrative state, the number of *nonclassified* (that is, patronage) positions remained roughly the same over this time.[312] The Pendleton Act did, however, create a certain momentum—only one president, William McKinley, ever reversed a civil service classification,[313] and by the end of the 1920s, about 80 percent of federal positions were classified.[314] Moreover, classification mattered: in the first sixteen months after Democrat Grover Cleveland succeeded Chester Arthur, "there was a 90 percent turnover in presidential officers, a 68 percent turnover in unclassified executive officers, and a 6.5 percent turnover in classified executive officers."[315] And a dedication to civil service reform could be a career maker: Theodore Roosevelt began to make his national reputation as a hard-charging civil service commissioner under Presidents Benjamin Harrison and Grover Cleveland.[316] Room for patronage positions of course remained throughout the Gilded Age and beyond, but the large and growing federal bureaucracy as a whole would henceforth be generally subject to an examination-based appointments process.

The growth of the federal bureaucracy was also key to understanding the renewed fight in the 1920s and 1930s over the removability of executive officers. The Pendleton Act had classified certain postal clerks, but it had left unclassified the vast number of postmasters all over the country. As a result, the postal service remained "the great conspicuous example of the spoils system" in the Gilded Age.[317] Between 1908 and 1912, the huge number of fourth-class postmasters (which were largely part-time, rural posts that did not require Senate confirmation) were classified and brought into the competitive examination system.[318] But this did not affect more senior positions: upon his inauguration in 1913, Woodrow Wilson kicked Republicans out of all the first-, second-, and third-class postmasterships and replaced them with Democrats.[319] Wilson then followed the example of his nineteenth-century predecessors by classifying the positions in March 1917, so that his successors could not take advantage of the same patronage opportunities that he just had.[320]

One of the first-class postmasters Wilson installed in 1913 (with Senate confirmation) was Frank Myers. Under an 1876 statute, first-, second-, and third-class postmasters had four-year terms, although they could be removed midterm "by the President by and with the advice and consent of the Senate."[321] In 1917, Myers was renominated and reconfirmed (the classification ordered by Wilson did not apply to the reappointment of incumbents). During his second term, he managed to alienate both his political superiors and his post office underlings, and the postmaster general informed him in 1920 that he was removed from office.[322] Myers (and, after he passed away, his widow) sued for back pay for the remainder of his four-year term, arguing that, per the 1876 statute, he could only be removed with the consent of the Senate. The case ended up in the Supreme Court, where Chief Justice Taft—the only justice also to have served as president—wrote the opinion of the Court, holding that Myers was not owed back pay. Despite the fact that, as president, Taft had sought the consent of the Senate when he removed postmasters,[323] his opinion for the six-justice majority argued that the Article II Vesting Clause ("The executive Power

shall be vested in a President of the United States of America") gave the president inherent constitutional authority to remove Senate-confirmed executive
officials.[324] Taft's rather formalistic opinion drew heavily on historical analysis,
including a reading of the Decision of 1789, which he declared left "not the
slightest doubt" that the First Congress had read the Constitution as giving the
president a unilateral removal power.[325] He insisted that the Constitution kept
the branches hermetically sealed except where it explicitly provided for them to
check one another,[326] and he argued that this scheme served to promote accountability by allowing the people easily to determine who was responsible for
well- or poorly executed government policy.[327] Although the Johnson-era
Tenure of Office Act was not at issue in the case (and, indeed, had been repealed
in 1887),[328] Taft made explicit his conclusion that the act had been unconstitutional.[329] Justice Holmes wrote the pithiest of the three dissents, noting simply
that the office at issue "owes its existence to Congress," that Congress "may
abolish [it] tomorrow," and that, therefore, Congress ought to have the lesser
power of prescribing the terms on which officers could be removed from it.[330]
Justices McReynolds and Brandeis were more expansive, but to the same effect:
the Constitution provided no inherent executive power to remove, at least not
when a statute provided otherwise.[331]

Indeed, the Court took a very different tack a mere nine years later, in a case
called *Humphrey's Executor v. United States*. That case, also an action for back
pay, arose when President Franklin Roosevelt tried to remove a federal trade
commissioner over policy disagreements. The relevant statute provided for a
seven-year term but allowed the president to remove a commissioner for "inefficiency, neglect of duty, or malfeasance in office."[332] As a matter of statutory
interpretation, the Court held that inefficiency, neglect of duty, and malfeasance
were exclusive—that is, that the statute purported to limit the president to
removing commissioners for those reasons *only*.[333] And as a constitutional
matter, the Court held that this was permissible. In a passage that is almost a
parody of the judicial practice of "distinguishing away" inconvenient precedents, the Court described *Myers* as deciding "only that the President had power
to remove a postmaster of the first class, without the advice and consent of the
Senate as required by act of Congress."[334] Federal trade commissioners, of
course, were not postmasters of the first class—indeed, they were not really
executive officials at all but rather (in language echoing Madison's description
of the comptroller of the treasury almost 150 years earlier) "quasi-judicial and

quasi-legislative" officers.[335] The Court elaborated that the FTC "is an administrative body created by Congress to carry into effect legislative policies embodied in the statute in accordance with the legislative standard therein prescribed, and to perform other specified duties as a legislative or as a judicial aid. Such a body cannot in any proper sense be characterized as an arm or an eye of the executive."[336] This was odd, to say the least—after all, one might think that a less loquacious synonym for "carry into effect legislative policies embodied in the statute" would be "execute the law." Nevertheless, having characterized the FTC as nonexecutive, and therefore as distinguishable from the office at issue in *Myers*, the Court then held that independence in such agencies is important, and therefore that the president possesses no inherent constitutional power to remove such officers.[337] Noting that the two decisions combined created a "field of doubt" as to which offices were purely executive (and therefore governed by *Myers*) and which were quasi-legislative and quasi-judicial (and therefore governed by *Humphrey's Executor*), the Court punted, leaving such determinations "for future consideration and determination as they may arise."[338] It was not at all clear how such determinations were to be made—as Sai Prakash has noted, the claim that the FTC was not executive "was met with astonishment, even by those who favored [the] judgment."[339] Indeed, an observer steeped in the formalism of the *Myers* Court might well ask what in the Constitution authorizes the creation of federal offices that are not housed in either the legislative, executive, or judicial departments but rather partake of all three. By resolutely avoiding that question, the more functionalist *Humphrey's Executor* Court indicated that it had made its peace with one key pillar of the administrative state: independent agencies.

From this historical sketch emerge four central themes with regard to the personnel power. First, there is Congress's role in appointments. We have seen substantial development across time in how the apparatus of the state is structured. Which offices should be subject to Senate confirmation, and which should be filled without that body's advice and consent? For those offices that do require Senate confirmation, what factors is it appropriate for senators to take into account when deciding whether or not to consent? We have seen policy disagreements or even partisan rancor justify voting down nominees in some eras; in others, we have seen wide deference to the president's choice. For non-Senate-confirmed appointments, how may Congress structure the appointments process? Civil service reform has, as we have seen, led to large numbers of government employees over whose appointment the president has little or no say. Second, there are questions surrounding acting and recess appointments: When can the president make them, and what options does Congress have if it seeks to forestall them? Third, there is the question of removals—indeed, the power to remove officers of state was the central battleground in the development of responsible government in England. May Congress itself fire government personnel? And when and how may it limit the president's ability to do so? What is the line between *Myers* and *Humphrey's Executor*? Finally, there is the question of impeachment and the role it plays in ensuring responsible government today. The remainder of this chapter takes up these four central themes in turn.

Appointments

The first question to be asked about the congressional role in appointments deals with the *scope* of the Senate's advice-and-consent power. As we have seen, the Constitution distinguishes between principal officers, who must be appointed with Senate consent, and inferior officers, whose appointments Congress may vest "in the President alone, in the Courts of Law, or in the Heads of Departments."[340] And although the Constitution says nothing about them, it has long been accepted that there can be government personnel who are not "officers" in either sense but are rather employees of the government.[341] Indeed, the fifth law passed by the First Congress authorized various port officials (none of whom was the head of a department) to hire employees.[342] But how are we to know what falls into each of these categories? Are there certain officers who *must* be appointed with Senate consent? Are there certain officers for whom Congress *cannot* require Senate consent? Can Congress put other requirements or procedures in place for certain officers or employees?

Clearly, the Constitution requires Senate consent for certain officers— ambassadors and other consular officials and Supreme Court justices are listed as principal officers in Article II. But things become trickier when we consider the provision addressing "all other Officers of the United States": which of them should be confirmed by the Senate, and which of them might be left to appointment by the president alone, the courts, or the heads of departments? And how do we know if someone is an officer at all, rather than an employee?

In the 1988 case *Morrison v. Olson*, the Supreme Court upheld the scheme for appointing independent counsels created by the 1978 Ethics in Government Act. Under the act, the attorney general could ask a three-judge special court to appoint an independent counsel to investigate and prosecute potentially illegal activities by certain high-ranking government officials. Over a spirited dissent by Justice Scalia, the Court held that the independent counsel was an inferior officer because she was subject to removal by a superior officer; she had prescribed, limited duties; she had limited jurisdiction; and her tenure was limited to the single task for which she was appointed.[343] Scalia retorted that the independent counsel was structured so as to answer to no one, and that she could not be "an inferior officer because she is not *subordinate* to any officer in the Executive Branch (indeed, not even to the President)."[344] In the light of what was widely perceived as overreaching by independent counsel Kenneth Starr in his investigation into President Clinton, Scalia's dissent came to be looked upon more favorably across the political spectrum, including by Clinton's attorney general, Janet Reno, when she testified before a Senate committee in opposition to renewing the independent counsel statute (which contained a sunset provision).[345] In a subsequent case (not dealing with independent counsels), Scalia wrote for the Court, holding that "the term 'inferior officer' connotes a relationship with some higher ranking officer or officers below the President: whether one is an 'inferior' officer depends on whether he has a superior."[346]

On Scalia's view, the heads of departments and, presumably, of independent agencies must be principal officers, but this does not get us very far, as the Constitution says nothing about which departments should exist and how they should be structured. As we have seen, the First Congress created only three executive departments; today, there are fifteen cabinet-level departments. Nor is there any constitutional criterion for what sorts of duties are sufficiently important to make one a principal officer. Surely, the Department of Veterans Affairs could be located within the Department of Defense, with its head appointed by the secretary of defense or the president, rather than being a free-standing department with a Senate-confirmed head. But if that is so, then could not every department be made a subunit of, say, the State Department? Moreover, on Scalia's view, some White House positions that have never been thought to require Senate confirmation indeed would require it. The White House chief of staff, for instance, answers to no one but the president (that is, has no superior officer below the president) and yet has always been appointed by the president unilaterally.

Rather than attempting to determine what constitutes an inherently principal or inferior office, it makes more sense to say that this determination is part and parcel of Congress's ability to structure the bureaucracy (and, for that matter, the judiciary: note that nothing in the constitutional text prohibits Congress from vesting the appointment of lower-court judges in the Supreme Court). Indeed, this is the principal way in which the *House* gets a say over personnel matters, and we have seen the houses of Congress using the requirement of Senate confirmation as a cudgel in interbranch fights. Recall from the previous chapter that, during its fiscal fights with the Nixon administration, Congress began requiring Senate confirmation of the director of the Office of Management and Budget (OMB), a powerful office within the White House. Indeed, the Nixon administration saw Congress move to make a number of appointed positions Senate confirmed.[347] In 1980, Congress created the Office of Information and Regulatory Affairs (OIRA) within OMB. Originally, the OIRA administrator was appointed by the head of OMB.[348] In 1986, the statutory scheme was changed (via a rider to an appropriations bill) to require Senate confirmation, although, perhaps in deference to Reagan's then high approval ratings (the law was passed mere weeks before Iran-Contra hit the news), the incumbent OIRA head was allowed to continue in office without Senate confirmation.[349] (Similarly, when, toward the end of J. Edgar Hoover's long career, Congress moved to subject the position of FBI director to Senate confirmation, the requirement took effect with Hoover's successor.)[350] As Mike Gerhardt has noted, the growth in the administrative state has necessitated a corresponding growth in the number of officers, a trend that naturally empowers the president. Congress has pressed back by "assiduously preserv[ing]" the Senate's role in confirming those nominees it considers most important and by adding to that list when it considers more oversight warranted.[351] Relatedly, it appears that Congress (including the House) uses its power of *creating* offices to be held by Senate-confirmed appointees as a means of exercising power—in this vein, consider the expansion, shrinking, and reexpansion of the Supreme Court to give appointments to Lincoln and Grant but not Johnson.[352]

The fact that Congress's role in structuring the federal bureaucracy allows it to determine (for the most part) which offices should require Senate confirmation also means that Gerhardt is mistaken when he insists that there is "no doubt that a congressionally mandated requirement that certain high-level White House staff, such as the White House Counsel, should be subject to Senate confirmation is unconstitutional."[353] His choice of examples is especially ironic because, as Jed Shugerman has noted, the attorney general functioned "like a part-time White House Counsel" during the entire antebellum period.[354] Moreover, it is hard to see why the White House Counsel is somehow less appropriate for Senate control than, say, the OMB director or OIRA administrator, both of whom are likewise within the Executive Office of the President. A better understanding is that put forth by Bruce Ackerman, who argues that Congress both can and should require Senate confirmation for all significant White House staffers, as a means of reining in executive unilateralism.[355] This is all the more true when we remember that the origins of the legislative personnel power lie in the development of responsible government. Congress is well within its rights to seek responsibility and responsiveness from even, and perhaps especially, the president's closest advisers—his privy council, if you will.

Finally, in Congress's view, it may be more important *that* many positions are filled than *by whom* they are filled. One solution, of course, is to vest the appointment of these offices in the president, the heads of departments, or the courts, but for many of these positions, there may be two factors cutting against this. First, the position may not be sufficiently important to warrant this: does every low-level agency staffer really need a presidential or cabinet-level appointment? Second, the nineteenth-century spoils system provides a cautionary tale about letting political elites hand out well-paying government positions for purely partisan reasons. The solution has been to treat those positions as employees and, since the passage of the Pendleton Act, employees largely hired on the basis of performance on competitive exams.[356] As we've seen, the creation and expansion of civil service protections was itself an example of responsiveness to the politics of the day. And subsequent politics have continued to expand those protections. In the aftermath of Watergate, the Civil Service Reform Act of 1978 established a swath of new protections intended to enhance "merit-based" personnel practices for most employees and eliminate consideration of any factor not directly related to the government job at issue, including prohibiting "personnel action" taken on the basis of factors like race, sex, religion, political affiliation, and nepotism.[357]

Having considered congressional control over *who* should (and who must) receive Senate confirmation, the next question is how deferential the

Senate should be to the president's nominations, and what constitutes appropriate grounds for refusing to confirm them. It should, first, be recalled that the Constitution has some—but not much—to say about eligibility for offices. Specifically, reflecting long-standing concerns with placemen, the Incompatibility Clause forbids sitting members of Congress from also holding "any Office under the United States," and the neighboring Emoluments Clause, in a blow against self-dealing, forbids any member of Congress "during the Time for which he was elected" from taking any "civil Office under the Authority of the United States, which shall have been created, or the Emoluments whereof shall have been encreased during such time."[358] When presidents have wanted to nominate members to such positions, they have generally asked Congress to employ the so-called Saxbe fix (named for Senator, and subsequently Attorney General, William Saxbe), whereby the salary is statutorily reduced to its previous level before the nominee is confirmed.[359] In addition to the constitutional qualifications, Congress has created statutory qualifications for office from the beginning: the 1789 Judiciary Act required that the attorney general be "learned in the law,"[360] and beginning in the 1880s Congress required that certain boards have a bipartisan composition, a practice that increased substantially in the twentieth century.[361] Indeed, one of the earliest such requirements is found in the Pendleton Act, which specified that on the three-person Civil Service Commission "not more than two" of the commissioners could be "adherents of the same party."[362] Other legislatively imposed qualifications for office include everything from residency requirements to conflict-of-interest prohibitions.[363] Likewise, consider that, in the aftermath of what was widely regarded as an incompetent response by the Federal Emergency Management Agency to Hurricane Katrina, an appropriations rider in 2006 required the FEMA administrator to have experience in both management and disaster response. President Bush, in his signing statement for the bill, objected to those requirements, stating that they excluded "a large portion of those persons best qualified by experience and knowledge to fill the office."[364] This, of course, was a fight over who would exercise how much of the personnel power, but it played out in the neutral-sounding language of "qualifications." As Lou Fisher has noted, these provisions are enforced by the Senate; they are effective, not because a court will throw an unqualified appointee out of office, but rather because the Senate is likely to refuse to confirm such a nominee in the first place.[365] For non-Senate-confirmed positions, a president who disregards statutory requirements is likely to find himself opposed in other ways—perhaps involving the power of the purse, failure to confirm other nominees, or something else from the congressional toolbox. Of course, the extent to which Congress seeks to make use of that toolbox depends on the wider politics of the moment: a president who is doing well in the public sphere overall will generally have more leeway, and Congress will go along or implement Saxbe-fix-like solutions; a president doing worse—and perhaps especially a president perceived as appointing unqualified cronies to important positions—will face more serious pushback.

Assuming that a nominee requiring Senate confirmation does not contravene constitutional or statutory qualifications, how should the Senate evaluate him? Gerhardt has suggested that constitutional structure establishes a "presumption of confirmation,"[366] but if this is true, it is only in a very specific sense. After all, the Constitution says nothing about what qualifications or credentials are *sufficient* to hold appointed office, nor does it suggest that only certain sorts of reasons suffice for a senator to deny consent to a nomination. As a predictive matter, one might expect most nominees to be confirmed, if for no other reason than that presidents will generally seek to nominate people likely to be confirmed. But this tells us nothing about how individual senators will or should think about any particular nomination.

As a preliminary matter, it should be noted that nothing in the Constitution requires that the Senate consider a nominee at all. When Justice Scalia unexpectedly passed away in early 2016, the Republican leadership of the Senate wasted no time in announcing that it would refuse to consider any nominee put forward by President Obama.[367] Republicans framed their stance as letting "the American people" decide, via the mechanism of the 2016 elections. Democrats, predictably, were outraged, with many insisting that the Senate had a constitutional duty to at least consider any nominee.[368] Obama nominated Merrick Garland, a longtime D.C. Circuit judge who was widely regarded as a centrist and well-respected by Republicans and Democrats alike (and who was, at the age of sixty-three, the oldest of the plausible nominees).[369] The choice of Garland put pressure on Republicans, many of whom had to explain why they would refuse to hold hearings on a nominee many of them had publicly praised in the past. This pressure was most acutely felt by a number of incumbent Republican senators up for reelection in 2016 in swing or Democratic-leaning states (including Illinois, Wisconsin, Pennsylvania, New Hampshire, and Ohio).

Indeed, of the Senate elections expected to be competitive in 2016, the vast majority—more than enough to return control of the chamber to the Democrats—were for seats then held by Republicans. Moreover, as these Senate campaigns heated up in the spring and summer of 2016, it became increasingly clear that the Republicans would choose a generally unpopular candidate (either Ted Cruz or, as it turned out, Donald Trump) as their presidential nominee.[370] In this political climate, vulnerable Republicans eager to prove their moderation began breaking with their leadership, first agreeing to hold meetings with Garland and then calling for the Judiciary Committee to hold hearings.[371] Republican leadership ultimately declined to hold hearings on Garland, a decision presumably based on its judgment that continued intransigence would not be particularly harmful to the party in the public sphere.[372] This tactical decision was ultimately vindicated, as Trump pulled off a surprise win and Republicans retained control of the Senate.

Once the Senate has decided to consider a nominee, how should it do so? It is frequently suggested that the Senate is and ought to be more deferential to certain *types* of nominees—that, for instance, executive-branch nominees should nearly always be confirmed, on the grounds that the president has a right to have "his team" in place, while perhaps nominees to the judiciary and to independent agencies should face greater scrutiny.[373] As a description of confirmation rates for various positions, this may well be correct—although, as we have seen, senators have historically proven quite willing to vote down executive-branch nominations when they perceive that the politics favor them. And politically weaker presidents, knowing this, will likely choose to nominate someone broadly palatable—someone on the "elder statesman" model. Consider, in this regard, President Bush's nomination of Michael Mukasey as attorney general in 2007. Bush was near the nadir of his popularity, and Democrats had taken control of the Senate in the 2006 elections. Moreover, the Justice Department itself had been "buffeted by Congressional inquiries into the firing of federal prosecutors and the resignation of the previous attorney general, Alberto R. Gonzales."[374] In the days leading up to the nomination, Senate Democrats had vocally insisted that they would oppose various candidates whose names had been floated.[375] In that political context, Bush nominated Mukasey, a former federal judge who was not known as a political partisan and who, indeed, was criticized by a number of Republicans as "too close to Democrats."[376] Even so, Mukasey was confirmed by a narrow margin of fifty-three to forty.[377] Levels of deference may be sensitive to the office at issue, but they are at least as sensitive to the surrounding politics.

Nominations, and the deference they receive, are also shaped by one other key factor: senatorial courtesy. Senatorial courtesy is the practice, arising in the early Republic, of presidents "defer[ring] to Senators' judgments about the merits of appointees from their own states."[378] It is often justified in terms of the "advice" prong of "advice and consent."[379] We have already seen how congressional influence over appointments stymied civil service reform under Grant and how New York senator Roscoe Conkling used, and fought to retain, his own patronage powers over appointments to federal office in New York when President Hayes sought to initiate civil service reform. The eventual triumph of reform meant that there were fewer opportunities to build up that sort of patronage network, but senatorial courtesy has persisted, and to some extent ossified, as a means of ensuring some amount of control by senators over the federal officials in their state. Consider the Senate's "blue slip" process (not to be confused with the House procedure of the same name for dealing with Origination Clause violations, discussed in chapter 2): for a judicial nominee to move forward, both of that nominee's home-state senators must return a blue slip indicating their approval. By tradition, if either senator does not return the slip, the chairman of the Judiciary Committee usually will not schedule a hearing (although the degree of deference to home-state senators does vary somewhat across Judiciary Committee chairmen). Knowing the potency of a blue slip, presidents have generally waited for senators to recommend judicial appointments before nominating anyone, thus giving up even the first-mover advantage to the senators.[380] Consider that Texas, which had two Republican senators, had ten vacant federal judgeships in 2014 because the senators simply did not suggest nominees.[381] When the Obama administration went public in an attempt to shame the Texas senators, the logjam was at least partly broken, with the president nominating and the Senate confirming several people who had been recommended by the senators.[382]

Once a nomination (especially a judicial nomination) has been made, one sometimes hears the claim that senators should consider only "qualifications," not "ideology."[383] But it should be clear that there is no such thing as a qualification divorced from ideological concerns; moreover, even if there were, we would not actually want senators to blind themselves to ideology. First, consider some of the criteria usually put forward as "neutral" qualifications: good educational pedigree, a history of employment in a relevant field, integrity, and (specifically for judicial office) writing skill and a judicial temperament. Even if the ideological valences of these criteria do not line up along traditional partisan divides, that does not make them any less ideological. Concern for the educational pedigree of a nominee suggests that socialization in elite environments and inculcation in certain patterns and processes of thought are important.[384] Adrian Vermeule has suggested that there should be Supreme Court justices who lack legal training entirely, in favor of training in other fields;[385] obviously, this relies on a conception of educational pedigree and its value that is very different from the currently dominant position. Likewise, the types of employment history that count in this analysis are ideologically bounded. In recent years, for Supreme Court nominees this has tended to mean service on a federal appellate court—and, in many cases, service in the executive branch. When President Obama nominated Elena Kagan to the Court, for instance, opponents attacked her as unqualified because she had no judicial experience.[386] And yet this conception of "relevant experience" may have significant ideological consequences: people with long judicial careers and no experience in elected office, for example, may tend to see electoral politics as a degraded form of decision making, in contrast to the perceived purity of judging.[387] Judges with executive-branch experience but not legislative experience may have more expansive conceptions of the proper scope of executive power.[388] Whatever else they are, these qualifications are not neutral. And the same goes for issues of "good writing" and "temperament," where it may well be impossible fully to separate the views being expressed from the rhetorical skill or temperament of the person expressing them. Consider a 1990 study that used newspaper editorials (from a mixture of liberal and conservative papers) to measure the perceived qualifications of Supreme Court nominees. William Rehnquist was considered more than twice as qualified in 1971, when he was nominated as an associate justice, than he was in 1986, when he was nominated as chief justice.[389] His educational background was obviously the same, and his relevant work experience had only increased. Most plausibly, liberal editorialists the second time around were reacting to what his service as an associate justice revealed about his ideology, but they did so in the neutral-sounding language of "qualifications."

As another window onto the ideological valence of qualifications, consider whether it is possible to display a good judicial temperament while expressing views that are blatantly racist or sexist. If it is not possible, then temperament necessarily has an ideological component. And if it is possible, then we would certainly want to add an ideological qualification on top of the temperament-based one: a theory that would require a senator to vote to confirm a well-educated, calm-demeanored racist cannot be a good one. Indeed, even staunch defenders of the "qualifications only" approach to confirmations generally sneak ideology back in with a caveat that the nominee's views must be "main-stream."[390] The question, then, is not whether ideology should come into the confirmation process but rather how it manifests itself and, perhaps more importantly, *whose* ideological positions carry how much weight. To the extent that we continue to see the appointments process as tied to understandings of responsible government, to whom are appointees meant to be responsible, and to what degree?

Arguments that only "qualifications" should matter to senators often take as their implicit premise a belief that, just beyond the historical horizon, there was a golden age in which ideology was irrelevant. The first section of this chapter should suffice to put the lie to that notion. Indeed, as William III was made to realize, the concept of responsible government *required* him to take partisan-ship into account when selecting his ministers, and American presidents from the beginning have used partisan litmus tests. In 1795, George Washington wrote to Timothy Pickering, his secretary of war: "I shall not, whilst I have the honor to administer the government, bring a man into any office of consequence knowingly, whose political tenets are adverse to the measures, which the general government are pursuing; for this, in my opinion, would be a sort of political suicide."[391] And it was certainly not a coincidence that Adams chose his staunchly Federalist secretary of state, John Marshall, as chief justice, nor was the partisan composition of the midnight judges or the Washington justices of the peace coincidental. Likewise, Jefferson's elimination of the midnight judgeships and his choice of which justices of the peace to recommission bore clear partisan and ideological imprints, as did the turnover in cabinet officers upon his inauguration. With the rise of the spoils system, these influences made themselves felt at every level of the federal government. A recent study of all antebellum judicial nominations found that "every antebellum President took political considerations into account in making nominations."[392] Given this tendency in the executive, any argument that the Senate should ignore such considerations is not an argument for taking partisanship or ideology out of appointments; rather, it is an argument that only presidents should consider such factors in making nominations. And to the extent that such arguments tend to reinforce the idea that there is a neutral, nonideological craft of judging, they may also enhance judicial power—all at Congress's expense.

As the history traced above suggests, the amount of deference that the Senate gives to presidential nominations will and should depend on the politics of the day. As one study of Supreme Court confirmations put it, "Confirmation politics . . . differs from normal politics in significant ways, but it is still politics."[393] As such, the level of deference that senators show to presidential nominees will largely be shaped by the same factors that determine how supportive they will be of that president's desired legislative program or other initiatives. We therefore should not be surprised that higher presidential approval levels tend to translate into easier confirmation for a president's nominees—indeed, Epstein and Segal found that "[a]ll in all, an out-of-favor president can cost his nominee nearly 20 votes" in the Senate.[394] We can see this dynamic at play, for instance, in the extreme difficulty that John Tyler had in getting his nominees confirmed as well as the heightened scrutiny that Andrew Johnson's nominees faced, and we can see it much more recently in the George W. Bush administration. Despite the fact that Republicans controlled the Senate by a comfortable margin, Bush's 2005 nomination of Harriet Miers to the Supreme Court went disastrously, with bipartisan opposition forcing Miers to withdraw from consideration within a month of her nomination.[395] Bush was wildly unpopular at the time—the Democrats would recapture both houses of Congress in the 2006 elections[396]— and this freed members of his own party to push for a nominee more to their taste, while freeing Democrats to oppose Miers as a way of further damaging a weak Republican president. It does not seem much of a stretch to speculate that, had Bush been at the height of his popularity, Miers would have been confirmed.

And this is as it should be. As we have repeatedly seen, legislators care so much about appointees because appointees matter for policy. A politically strong president—which is to say, a president who enjoys both a Senate majority (reflecting both geographically and, given the staggered timetable of Senate elections, temporally diverse support) and strong, immediate public support— has a stronger democratic claim to be able to put into place his own personnel, and therefore his own policies. What's more, this is not simply a matter of diffuse support for or against a president: personnel politics plays out in the public sphere, where it both affects and is affected by the public standing of the president and the Senate. The Federalists unsuccessfully attempted to make

the Repeal Act an issue in the 1802 elections;[397] Andrew Jackson more successfully made an issue of Senate obstructionism in 1832 and 1834; the public reaction to the Garfield assassination meant that even the Stalwart Chester Arthur
had to support civil service reform in the early 1880s; and Theodore Roosevelt
began to build his reputation as a crusader for civil service reform. Indeed,
strategies of "going public" in an attempt to either support or derail a nominee
are a routine feature of our political landscape.[398] We have already seen, in
chapter 1, the complicated public strategies on both sides that ultimately
resulted in the defeat of the Bork nomination. Likewise, in the Obama administration, a carefully calibrated public campaign from the president's left forced
him to nominate Janet Yellen rather than Lawrence Summers as chair of the
Board of Governors of the Federal Reserve, undoubtedly one of the most
important appointed positions in American government (and, because the Fed
is a *Humphrey's Executor*–like independent agency, the chair, once appointed,
can only be removed for cause).[399] As the *New York Times* put it, "The ascendant
power of [Senator Elizabeth] Warren and her fellow populists is best captured
by their torpedoing this month of Lawrence H. Summers, . . . who was blocked
before President Obama could even nominate him to lead the Federal
Reserve."[400] Opponents of Summers were able both to tap into and to create
support for their position by their interactions in the public sphere. Likewise, as
noted above, both Democrats and Republicans used public-facing strategies in
the battle over replacing Justice Scalia. In such contests, it is ultimately political actors' success at engaging in the public sphere, not abstract attempts to
specify a presumption of confirmation, that determines the deference that will
be shown to nominees. And because presidents know this, it impacts their
choice of whom to nominate in the first place—after all, Summers was never
even nominated for the Fed job.[401]

   Moreover, the reminder that confirmation politics is "still politics" should
remind us that it neither can nor should be sealed off from the rest of politics.
One sometimes hears claims that, in the words of then Senate majority leader
Harry Reid, it is inappropriate for senators to vote "to block executive branch
nominees [when] they have no objection about the qualification of the
nominee."[402] But to do this—to talk not only as if there are neutral qualifications
for evaluating nominees but also as if nothing else should be allowed to influence a senator's confirmation vote—is to insist that appointments be severed
from the rest of politics. And to do that is to remove one of Congress's more

potent weapons in interbranch conflict. Opposition or the threat of opposition to a nominee is one way that senators can exert significant influence on underlying policy. Political science research confirms that the appointments power, in the right political context, can indeed be a potent source of legislative power.[403]

We might think of senatorial opposition to a nominee as lying along a continuum of motives, with opposition based on purely personal factors about the nominee (this could be anything from concerns about her performance in a past position to ethical concerns to ideological disagreement) on one end, to concerns about policies with which that nominee is specifically connected in the middle, to concerns about policies largely unconnected to the particular nominee at the far end. Senators' ability to maintain opposition to a nominee will depend, not only on the political circumstances surrounding the nomination, but also on where their opposition falls on this spectrum—in general, it may be easier to justify opposing a nominee on grounds specific to that nominee than to justify opposing her for other reasons. It should also be noted that not all opposition has as its end goal the defeat of the nominee: as one moves away from factors specific to the nominee, the purpose of the opposition may increasingly sound in factors *collateral* to the nomination itself—the desire to change (or at least call attention to) matters of underlying policy, for example. The wider political context, the nature of the nominee, and the reasons for opposing him will all affect one another.

Opposition based on a nominee himself is, in some sense, the simplest case. It was opposition to specific royal favorites like Buckingham and Strafford, after all, that began to give rise to principles of responsible government in England; in more recent times, ideological opposition sank Robert Bork's nomination to the Supreme Court (as we saw in chapter 1) and concerns about integrity sank Abe Fortas's nomination as chief justice in 1968. In this vein, consider the fate of Admiral Lewis Strauss. In hearings before the congressional Joint Committee on Atomic Energy in 1954, Strauss faced hostile questions—from both Republicans like Representative W. Sterling Cole and Democrats like Representative Chet Holifield—about the way in which he ran the Atomic Energy Commission and about his failure to turn over information to the Joint Committee in a timely manner. He also refused to answer questions about advice he had given President Eisenhower in his prior role as special adviser to the president on atomic energy.[404] When Democrats retook both houses in the 1954 elections, Senator Clinton Anderson became the chairman, and he and Strauss came to hate one another.[405] The Democrats won the 1958 congressional elections in a landslide, and they began to look hopefully toward the 1960 presidential election. It was into this political climate that Eisenhower nominated Strauss to be secretary of commerce (and gave him a recess appointment in that position while the nomination was pending).[406] Anderson and others assailed Strauss for his history of keeping information from congressional committees and (what they portrayed as) his difficulty with the truth when he did testify.[407] Strauss managed to alienate more members by his demeanor at his hearings, and by the time the nomination came to a floor vote there was a "growing sense that no Democratic senator who supported Strauss would have a chance at the party's presidential nomination."[408] In retrospect, it began to be clear that the recess appointment was a costly mistake, "insensitive to those latent animosities" surrounding the nominee and feeding their progression from latent to active.[409] Strauss's nomination was defeated by a vote of forty-nine against to forty-six in favor—only the eighth cabinet nominee ever to be voted down on the Senate floor. A furious Eisenhower called it "the second most shameful day in Senate history," after only the Andrew Johnson impeachment trial.[410] The *Washington Post* had a different take, editorializing that Strauss "too frequently exhibited a disregard of the right of Congress to know about the transactions of the executive departments. And he came before the Senate at a time when many Senators were feeling irritation at the exhibition of this same sort of executive arrogance by other officials."[411] The editorial went on to connect the appointments power to congressional power more broadly: "The Congress does not always have the power to compel members of the executive departments to be communicative about the operations of government for which it shares responsibility. However, to use an old truism of politics: although it cannot make them talk it can make them wish they had."[412] It is important to note that the opposition was rooted in reasons specific to the nominee, but its success depended very much on the wider political circumstances—specifically, the Democrats' landslide in 1958 and the pursuit of the 1960 presidential nomination by a number of Senate Democrats. And, of course, this sort of opposition is not always reducible to pure partisanship; in the Obama presidency, even Democratic control of the Senate did not secure the confirmation of nominees like Dawn Johnsen as head of the Office of Legal Counsel (OLC), Goodwin Liu as a Ninth Circuit judge, and Debo Adegbile as head of the Civil Rights Division of the Justice Department.

A bit further along the spectrum, consider opposition to nominees arising from "opposition to policies with which these individuals had been associated."[413] We saw this, for example, in congressional opposition to Jackson's withdrawal of funds from the Bank of the United States playing out in a refusal to confirm Taney, who had been instrumental in the withdrawals, as secretary of the treasury. This sort of opposition sometimes does not even take the form of a vote against confirmation; it may simply be a strategy for "exact[ing] pledges from the nominee before moving to confirm,"[414] or drawing attention to or securing compromises from the administration on issues related to the nominee. For instance, when Richard Holbrooke's nomination to be ambassador to the United Nations was pending in 1999, Senate Foreign Relations Committee chairman Jesse Helms secured from Holbrooke a promise to work to implement reforms at the United Nations that the committee had suggested.[415] More recently, Senator Rand Paul has used opposition to confirmations as a way to highlight what he views as presidential overreach in combatting terrorism. In March 2013, he made national headlines when he staged a rare, twelve-hour "talking filibuster" of the nomination of John Brennan to be director of the CIA. Paul's primary objection was to the administration's policy of using drone strikes to kill suspected terrorists, which Brennan had been instrumental in devising.[416] Although Brennan was easily confirmed at the end of the filibuster, Paul's theatrics—and the bipartisan statements of support that accompanied them— "generated extraordinary scrutiny of the Obama administration's drone-strike program and revealed some surprising divisions and alliances on Capitol Hill."[417] The filibuster also led Attorney General Eric Holder to send Paul a letter committing the administration to the position that it did not have the authority to use drones to kill Americans on American soil if they were not engaged in combat, a question that Paul had previously been pressing the administration to answer, without success.[418] The event helped catapult the issue of drone strikes to the top of the news and served notice to the administration that it was vulnerable on this issue. Paul continued his crusade the following year, both suing the administration over its surveillance of domestic phone calls[419] and opposing the nomination of David Barron to be a judge on the First Circuit Court of Appeals. Barron, while serving in OLC, had written the administration's legal memos justifying the use of drone strikes to kill an American citizen abroad, and Paul announced his intention to fight the Barron nomination until those memos were made public.[420] (The previous month, a federal court had ordered the memos released;[421]

the administration had not yet done so while it contemplated asking for rehearing en banc or for Supreme Court review.) Once again, Paul had bipartisan support,[422] and the administration caved, opting to forgo appeals and release a (redacted) version of the memo in order to garner the necessary votes for Barron's confirmation.[423] The release once again sparked serious public debate and criticism.[424]

Moving further along the spectrum, the appointments power is also available for even more capacious collateral uses. As Walter Oleszek has noted, "Senators regularly place holds on diplomatic and other nominations to extract concessions from the State Department and other federal agencies. Hostage holds . . . enable senators to gain leverage to achieve other objectives."[425] Consider again Senator Helms, who, by mid-1999, had used his position as chairman of the Foreign Relations Committee to "bottle[] up 493 of President Clinton's ambassadorial and other foreign relations nominations," in order to express his displeasure with the general thrust of the administration's foreign policy and to press for reorganization of the foreign policy agencies.[426] More recently, Senate Republicans between 2011 and 2013 filibustered Richard Cordray, President Obama's nominee to head the newly created Consumer Financial Protection Bureau, announcing that they would filibuster *any* nominee to lead the bureau until certain changes were made to the law establishing it.[427] Cordray was eventually confirmed in a deal that (temporarily) averted filibuster reform[428] (discussed in more detail in chapter 8), but the lengthy delay had the effect both of slowing down the bureau's work and of drawing public attention to Republican claims that the underlying law was in need of reform. The politics were not entirely with them—the Republicans were in the minority, after all, and fearful of rules reform that would cost them the filibuster altogether—but one can certainly imagine a Senate majority successfully refusing to confirm as a way of winning substantive concessions.

Acting and Recess Appointments

Of course, many of the processes described above are, and are intended to be, cumbersome, and this may well create lags between one officer's departure and her replacement's arrival. This gives rise to two temporary mechanisms: acting appointments and recess appointments.

We have seen the use of acting appointments from the earliest days of the Republic. Indeed, the 1801 transition saw Acting Secretary of State (and confirmed Chief Justice) John Marshall replaced by Acting Secretary of State (and confirmed Attorney General) Levi Lincoln. It would be a few months before James Madison would take up the State Department post.[429] Nevertheless, several scholars have recently suggested that the various acting appointments statutes are unconstitutional insofar as they allow the president to appoint a non-Senate-confirmed individual to hold an office requiring Senate confirmation.[430] This was most clearly the case in the 1790s provisions, which put no limitation on whom the president could appoint in an acting capacity, but it remains the case even after the 1860s provisions, which allowed for, variously, the first assistant, deputy, or chief clerk of an officer to replace that officer in an acting capacity,[431] an arrangement continued by the current statutory scheme.[432] In many cases, the first assistant of a Senate-confirmed officer will herself be Senate-confirmed, but in many other cases, she will not; moreover, the current statutory scheme explicitly allows the president to appoint certain civil service employees in an acting capacity in positions that are normally Senate confirmed.[433] In fact, it has never been the case that only Senate-confirmed officers are statutorily eligible to serve in acting positions when the permanent position requires Senate confirmation.[434] (And, indeed, there was no indication that anyone in the Second Congress, which passed the 1792 law, thought that only Senate-confirmed officers could serve as acting officers.)[435]

The argument that one must be Senate confirmed (in some position) in order to serve in an acting capacity for a Senate-confirmable position relies on the premise that acting appointments "are not really appointments at all." On this view, they are simply temporary reassignments of the duties of one office to another officer. Since those duties (by hypothesis) are the duties of a principal officer and can therefore be exercised only by someone who has been confirmed by the Senate, the person to whom they are temporarily reassigned must, likewise, have been confirmed by the Senate. But so long as that is the case, no new appointment has been made.[436]

That argument assumes that, whatever officer exercises them, certain duties are inherently principal-officer duties and therefore can be exercised only by a principal officer. Even though senators may not have thought about the fitness of, say, the deputy secretary of labor to serve as the administrator of the EPA, they would at least have had a chance to consider his fitness for government service generally when they confirmed him to the Labor post. Congress can, on this view, delegate the authority to the president to radically change the duties

of any Senate-confirmed officer, but it cannot delegate the authority to temporarily make a principal office into an inferior one. But this seems odd. If, as I
have argued above, we understand principal offices to be (for the most part)
whatever Congress chooses to designate as principal offices, then the allowance
for non-Senate-confirmed individuals to serve in an acting capacity in (otherwise) Senate-confirmable positions could be read as a temporary reclassifica-
tion of the office just as easily as it could be read as a temporary reassignment
of duties. At the end of the day, it is simply hard to understand what is gained
by the formalistic assertion that only Senate-confirmed officers can serve in an
acting capacity for otherwise Senate-confirmable offices.

Indeed, this is all the more so because Congress has shown itself willing and
able to adjust the terms on which individuals can serve in an acting capacity in
order to preserve its role. As we have seen, the earliest statute, in 1792, did not
limit acting appointments at all. In 1795, a six-month time limit was added. In
1863, the time limit was retained and limits on who could serve in an acting
capacity were added. In 1868, both the limits on who could serve and the limits
on how long were tightened—the latter to a mere ten days, subsequently
extended to thirty days once the specter of Andrew Johnson had passed. In
1988, the time limit was extended to 120 days; moreover, if confirmation of a
nominee was pending before the Senate (provided she was either the first or the
second nominee for this opening), then the time limit was suspended until she
was confirmed, rejected, or withdrawn. The language of the provision was also
tweaked to make it clear that this was the exclusive means of filling any vacancies in any executive agency—some agencies had apparently taken the position
that certain positions were not covered by the Vacancies Act and therefore that
acting appointments to those positions did not have to abide by the act's time
limitations. The 1988 amendments were meant to make clear to those agencies
the error of their ways.[437] Nevertheless, several controversies over acting
appointments during the Bill Clinton administration appeared, at best, to stretch
the Vacancies Act scheme.[438] In 1998, as part of an omnibus appropriations
statute (and therefore politically difficult for President Clinton to veto), Congress
passed the Federal Vacancies Reform Act.[439] The act extended the time limitation for an acting appointment to 210 days,[440] but it also contained a new section,
subtly titled "Exclusivity," intended to make it pellucidly clear that any acting
appointments would have to comply with the provisions of the act.[441] The act
also contained provisions requiring that vacancies and acting appointments be

reported to Congress.[442] Although the act did extend the time that a person could serve in an acting position, the price for that benefit to the president was the clearly expressed intention of the statute to cover nearly all offices and to do so exclusively, as well as the provision for enhanced monitoring mechanisms.[443] Clearly, when Congress has been concerned about presidential overreliance on acting officers, it has been willing and able to clamp down on it. Of course, it is more likely to do so when the party controlling Congress is not the party in the White House—but that is also when the president is most likely to rely on acting appointments to circumvent the Senate in the first place.

In addition to the statutory mechanism of the acting appointment, there is the constitutional mechanism of the recess appointment, which remains important for two main reasons: first, the Vacancies Act does not permit acting appointments to federal courts or *Humphrey's Executor*–like independent agencies;[444] and second, the Vacancies Act, as noted, substantially limits *who* can be appointed in an acting capacity—in particular, the Vacancies Act does not permit the acting appointment of someone from outside the executive branch.[445] A president who wanted to bring in, say, a governor or an academic would be barred by the Vacancies Act scheme. In either of those (relatively frequent) contexts, the president would have to rely on a recess appointment if he wanted to install someone in the position temporarily and without Senate confirmation.

Like acting appointments, recess appointments have a long pedigree in American constitutional practice—just to take a few examples, Jefferson recess appointed the Washington justices of the peace while awaiting their Senate confirmation; Jackson recess appointed Roger Brooke Taney as secretary of the treasury; and Eisenhower recess appointed Lewis Strauss as secretary of commerce. Importantly, recess appointments to Article III courts have also been prominent since early on: "The first five Presidents together made thirty-one such appointments, including five to the Supreme Court."[446] Indeed, George Washington recess appointed John Rutledge to the Supreme Court in 1795; Rutledge's nomination for a permanent seat was subsequently rejected by the Senate.[447] In the twentieth century, Eisenhower used recess appointments to place three justices—Earl Warren, William Brennan, and Potter Stewart—on the Supreme Court; all three were subsequently confirmed.[448] After the Stewart recess appointment, the Senate adopted a sense-of-the-Senate resolution insisting that recess appointments to the Supreme Court "should not be made except under unusual circumstances and for the purpose of preventing or ending a demonstrable breakdown in the administration of the Court's business,"[449] and no president since Eisenhower has made a recess appointment to the highest court.[450] Recess appointments to lower courts, however, have continued to the present day: President Bill Clinton recess appointed Roger Gregory to the Fourth Circuit, and President George W. Bush recess appointed Charles Pickering and William Pryor to federal appeals courts. Gregory and Pryor were subsequently confirmed by the Senate (Gregory after being renominated by President Bush); Pickering withdrew and retired when it became clear that he would not be confirmed.[451] In total, there have been more than three hundred recess appointments to Article III courts in the nation's history.[452]

It seems clear that, although they may recently have declined in popularity, recess appointments to the courts are permissible. Not only would any argument that they are not be incompatible with practice from the earliest years,[453] it would also have to contend with the fact that there is no judicial exception to the Recess Appointments Clause. It is true that Article III provides for good-behavior tenure for federal judges, but it should be remembered that good-behavior tenure was established as the antithesis of tenure at the pleasure of the Crown. A recess-appointed judge does not serve at the pleasure of the president; she serves until the end of the next congressional session. Of course, a recess-appointed judge may want to receive a permanent appointment and may therefore feel some pressure to adjudicate in conformity with her perceptions of the wishes of the president or the Senate. But this is no different from the assumption that many lower-court judges want promotion to higher courts or to executive-branch positions. Only by treating the good-behavior tenure and salary-protection provisions as synecdoche for a grand, and overriding, principle of judicial independence from the other branches can we create a carve-out for judges from the recess appointments power. But the Constitution creates certain sorts of judicial independence and certain sorts of judicial dependence; there is simply no reason to treat one as overridingly significant.

There remain two other questions about the recess appointment power. First, does the phrase "Vacancies that may happen during the Recess of the Senate" mean only vacancies that *arise* during a recess or does it encompass all vacancies that *exist* during a recess? And second, what counts as a recess: only intersession recesses (that is, recesses resulting from an adjournment *sine die*) or at least certain intrasession recesses (that is, recesses resulting from an adjournment to a day certain) as well?

Attorney General William Wirt considered the first of these questions in an 1823 opinion. Wirt noted that either interpretation was plausible, although he conceded that the *arise* interpretation was perhaps more so linguistically. Nevertheless, allowing for appointments to fill any vacancy that happens to exist during a Senate recess is more "compatible with [the clause's] spirit, reason, and purpose; while, at the same time, it offers no violence to its language."[454] He noted that the Senate might be forced to adjourn suddenly for all sorts of reasons, and it would be, in his view, foolish to require that any vacancies that existed when it did so had to remain unfilled until it reconvened.[455] But an 1863 report from the Senate Judiciary Committee strongly disagreed—it referred to Wirt's interpretation as "forced and unnatural," and suggested that it could "quickly open the way to a practical deprivation of all power of the Senate over executive appointments. For if the President may in the recess appoint to and fill an office which during a session of the Senate was vacant, he may omit to make any nomination at a subsequent session, and at the close of it again appoint him under the idea of filling a vacancy, and so on from session to session."[456] The Senate's response to this specter was to use the power of the purse. As a rider to that year's Army Appropriations Act, Congress passed the Pay Act, which provided that "no money shall . . . be paid out of the Treasury, as salary, to any person appointed during the recess of the Senate, to fill a vacancy in any existing office, which vacancy existed while the Senate was in session and is by law required to be filled by and with the advice and consent of the Senate, until such appointee shall have been confirmed by the Senate."[457] It should be noted that, this provision notwithstanding, presidents continued to make numerous recess appointments to fill vacancies that predated the recess.[458] A series of attorney general opinions informed presidents that these appointees could not be paid until they were confirmed by the Senate.[459] (After the passage of the 1905 revisions to the Anti-Deficiency Act, discussed in the previous chapter, such voluntary government service became legally questionable; presumably, the justification would be that the Pay Act's seeming acceptance of the service of such appointees without pay means that the voluntary service is "authorized by law" for Anti-Deficiency Act purposes.)[460] In 1940, Congress amended the Pay Act to provide for three exceptions: a recess appointee to a position that had been vacant before the recess began could still be paid if (a) the vacancy arose in the last thirty days of the preceding session, (b) a nomination to fill that vacancy was pending at the close of the session and that nominee had not previously been recess appointed to that position, or (c) a nominee was rejected in the last thirty days of the preceding session and the recess appointment went to someone other than the rejected nominee. Moreover, if a recess appointee was paid under any of those three exceptions, then the president must submit a nomination for that position to the Senate in the first forty days of its next session.[461] Finally, in a series of appropriations riders, Congress has forbidden the payment of any salary to a person filling a position to which that person has been nominated but been rejected by the Senate.[462] Congress has thus acknowledged that there are some situations in which a recess appointment is tolerable, even where the vacancy antedated the recess. But it has also used its power of the purse to limit presidents' ability to use recess appointments as an end run around Senate confirmation. In Mike Gerhardt's apt phrasing, "When presidents have used temporary or recess appointments . . . to bypass the confirmation process, senators have invariably used their other powers, particularly oversight and appropriations, to put pressure on those choices."[463] Likewise, senators may hold up the confirmation of other nominees as a protest against the overuse of recess appointments, as Senator Byrd did in response to President Reagan's use of the recess appointments power in 1985.[464] When the question came before the Supreme Court in the 2014 case *NLRB v. Noel Canning*, Justice Breyer, for a closely divided Court, held that the recess appointments power extends to any vacancy that exists during a recess. He pointed to the Pay Act both as evidence that the Senate had acquiesced in this interpretation and as demonstrating the Senate's ability to prevent the president from abusing this power without judicial intervention.[465]

There is also the question of whether only intersession recesses trigger the recess appointments power or whether intrasession recesses of some length suffice as well. The term "recess" is ambiguous—it can refer to either sort of break. Prior to the Civil War, Congress seldom took intrasession recesses of more than three days, preferring instead to take longer intersession recesses.[466] Beginning with the Andrew Johnson administration, lengthier intrasession recesses became the norm; it is not a coincidence that Johnson was the first president to make intrasession recess appointments.[467] As Justice Breyer noted in *Noel Canning*, it is telling that, despite the fact that Johnson was impeached largely over personnel matters, intrasession recess appointments did not merit any expression of congressional disapproval.[468] Given that today there are routinely intrasession recesses that are longer than intersession recesses, it would be odd if recess appointments during the former were categorically banned and those during the latter were categorically permitted. Indeed, if anything, the true oddity is the idea that intersession recesses categorically allow for recess appointments—relying on this notion, Theodore Roosevelt in 1903 made more than 160 recess appointments in an infinitesimally short intersession recess.[469] The Senate Judiciary Committee protested vigorously.[470]

Relying in part on this history, the Court in *Noel Canning* held that sufficiently lengthy intrasession recesses do indeed give rise to opportunities for recess appointments. Breyer suggested that an intrasession recess of less than ten days was "presumptively" too short to allow for recess appointments, although that presumption might be overcome by "some very unusual circumstance."[471] Importantly, the Court also held that it was up to the Senate itself, not the president or the courts, to determine whether the Senate was in session; by holding "pro forma" sessions every few days, the Senate could forestall an intrasession adjournment of sufficient length to trigger the recess appointments power.[472] The Court's solution in *Noel Canning* can be seen as an attempt to preserve the tools available to each branch for contestation in the recess appointments context. As long as there is some minimum recess length, below which recess appointments are impermissible, and as long as the Senate has the ability to hold pro forma sessions, then the Senate can block the president's ability to make recess appointments. (This is all the more so if the ten-day floor applies to intersession recesses as well as intrasession ones; the *Noel Canning* opinion is opaque on this question.) Thus, presidents whose party also controls the Senate will find it easier to make recess appointments than presidents whose party does not. Once again, broader electoral support for one party's agenda translates into greater ease of enacting that agenda.

There is also the possibility of a role for the House here. Any adjournment of either house of Congress lasting more than three days requires the consent of the other house.[473] Should the houses be unable to agree on "the Time of Adjournment," however, the president is empowered to "adjourn them to such Time as he shall think proper."[474] No president in American history has ever used this power, but one can envision the following scenario.[475] The president's party controls the House but not the Senate. The Senate is obstructing all, or nearly all, of the president's nominees, to the consternation of the House majority as well as the president. The House could then propose an adjournment of more than ten days—long enough for the president to make recess appointments. If the Senate refused, the president could unilaterally adjourn both houses for more than ten days—again, long enough to make recess appointments. This would, of course, enrage the Senate majority; the House and the president could assume that they would not have the Senate's cooperation on much of anything in the aftermath of such a move. But, once again, it is a constitutional mechanism that calibrates institutional power to public support. A president whose party controls neither house of Congress can be prevented from making recess appointments altogether; a president whose party controls at least one house will be able to make recess appointments at least some of the time.

Removals

Getting people into office is only half the story of personnel and of responsible government; getting them out is the other half. The issue of removals from office raises two major questions for congressional power. First, can Congress remove officials? And second, can Congress limit the president's ability to remove officials? As to the first question, we have already seen a number of congressional removals. Consider, for instance, that a number of statutes contain automatic removal provisions by setting a time limit on officeholders. So, for example, the 1801 Organic Act for the District of Columbia specified that Washington justices of the peace were to serve for five years, at the end of which they would lose their offices unless they were renominated and reconfirmed. Likewise, the 1820 Tenure of Office Act not only created four-year tenures for a number of executive offices, it also established expiration dates for currently serving officers, thus effecting a removal of existing officers. Today, to take just one example among many, members of the Board of Governors of the Federal Reserve serve fourteen-year, nonrenewable terms.[476] It is also the case that, from the Founding on, Congress has enacted numerous examples of what Sai Prakash calls "contingent removal provisions"—that is, provisions for officeholders to be deprived of their office automatically upon the occurrence of some event, generally their conviction for some sort of official misconduct.[477] (Indeed, as we have seen, a number of the pre-1787 state constitutions also contained such provisions.) Finally, Congress has, from the early days of the Republic, eliminated offices, thereby terminating the tenure of the officeholders. In 1792, for instance, Congress eliminated the office of assistant to the secretary of the treasury (who, by the terms of the organic act for the Treasury was appointed by the secretary)[478] and created in its stead the commissioner of the revenue, appointed by the president with consent of the Senate.[479] Although Washington appointed Tench Coxe, who had been the assistant to the secretary, as the new commissioner of the revenue,[480] it is clear that he need not have—indeed, in the days before his nomination to the new post, Coxe wrote an angst-ridden letter to Hamilton expressing his fears that "I, and my family will be left without an Establishment."[481] Moreover, all three sorts of statutes discussed above (that is, tenure-limitation provisions, contingent-removal provisions, and office-elimination provisions) have been acquiesced in by presidents from Washington onward.[482] Indeed, given the difficulty of passing legislation over a presidential veto, any form of congressional removal instantiated in a statute would likely have received a presidential signature. In the 1986 case of *Bowsher v. Synar*, the Supreme Court, relying on dicta from *Myers*, held that any "direct congressional role in the removal of officers charged with the execution of the laws beyond [impeachment] is inconsistent with separation of powers."[483] But given that Congress can clearly eliminate offices and thereby effect a removal of incumbent officeholders, it could easily engage in a removal two-step: first, it statutorily eliminates the office, thereby ending the tenure of the incumbent; then, it creates a new, nearly identical office. It seems odd, at best, to deny Congress the power to do in one step what it can clearly do in two.

Indeed, as we have seen, Congress has even used its office-elimination power to remove judges, in the 1802 Repeal Act. In response to Federalist complaints that doing so violated the midnight judges' good-behavior commissions, Republicans asserted that the judges had not been removed; they had simply fallen victim to Congress's undoubted authority to structure the lower federal courts. As we have seen, the Federalist-dominated Supreme Court acquiesced in this argument in *Stuart v. Laird*. At least three factors allowed the Republicans to win the constitutional politics of the 1802 controversy. First, Republicans had a strong electoral mandate, arising out of their victories in both the 1800 elections and the 1802 midterms. Second, the 1801 Judiciary Act was widely seen to be an illegitimate power grab by a repudiated political coalition. And finally, Republicans pressed their advantage judiciously, not maximally. They did not abolish the circuit judges and then create new circuit judges, which would have given Jefferson a number of appointments; rather, they abolished the circuit judges and returned circuit-court staffing to the status quo ante: a

combination of district judges and Supreme Court justices. The result of these
canny political maneuvers was the removal of the midnight judges and a constitutional victory for Jefferson.

The lesson of the 1802 controversy is that the surrounding politics matters
greatly. Consider a more recent example of congressional restructuring of the
federal judiciary. Until 1980, the United States Court of Appeals for the Fifth
Circuit covered most of the Deep South: Texas, Louisiana, Mississippi,
Alabama, Georgia, and Florida. It was therefore, unsurprisingly, at the center of
many of the major controversies surrounding the civil rights revolution and the
fight against Jim Crow.[484] With the economic and demographic growth in the
South, the circuit was also the busiest federal appellate court in the nation
throughout the 1960s and 1970s.[485] More judges were clearly needed, but some
influential jurists believed that a collegial court could not operate effectively
with more than nine judges, to which number the Fifth Circuit had expanded in
1961. Beginning in the 1950s, then, there were proposals, continuing throughout
the 1960s and 1970s, to split the court in two.[486] But against the backdrop of
civil rights struggles, it was nearly impossible to divide up the circuit in a way
that would receive sufficiently widespread support to be enacted into law.[487] It
was only with the decreasing salience of civil rights in the late 1970s that the
necessary political coalition for dividing the circuit became possible.[488] In 1980,
President Carter signed into law the bill dividing the old Fifth Circuit into
today's Fifth and Eleventh Circuits.[489] Note that this law significantly reduced
the jurisdiction of sitting federal judges—where once their rulings had possessed
the force of law from El Paso to the Florida Keys, now they had to content
themselves with either El Paso to Biloxi or Mobile to the Keys. In the right
political context—that is, one in which it did not appear to be motivated by the
desire to influence the outcome of a particular class of cases—this diminution
in jurisdiction was possible. Of course, it might be possible in other political
contexts as well. Imagine a scenario in which the vast majority of the nation
had staked out a position on some civil rights issue, but a single revanchist
court was holding the line against it. In that situation, too, it might be conceivable that judicial reorganization would be used to deprive that court of power—
this time, precisely *because* of how it would influence particular cases.
Reorganization, of course, does not generally mean removal, but the lesson of
1802 is that reorganization can be used to effect removal, and certainly jurisdictional diminution is on a continuum with removal.

It is, therefore, clearly the case that Congress itself has various removal mechanisms at its command. It should be noted that, unlike most of the other powers discussed in this book, these mechanisms require *legislation*—that is, they require bicameralism and presentment. From the beginning, the default rule (recognized in the Decision of 1789) was that the president could unilaterally remove executive officials as well. But there is a remaining question about whether Congress can, by legislation, defeat that default rule. That is, to what extent can Congress limit the president's removal power? In the earliest years of the Republic, when there were very few federal officials total, the power to remove and the power to appoint were almost inextricably linked. Recall Hamilton's claim in *Federalist No. 77* that Senate consent was necessary "to displace as well as to appoint."[490] With so few extant offices, a president simply could not remove an officer if he was unsure about getting a replacement confirmed; he would therefore have to consider the likelihood of Senate approval of a replacement before unilaterally firing an officer. With the growth of the federal government, such pressures eased, and Jefferson, especially, showed no qualms about unilaterally removing Federalists from office. Nevertheless, as we have seen, there was a widespread view in the early Republic that Congress could choose to create executive offices with tenure other than at the pleasure of the president. Recall that the Organic Act for the District of Columbia provided five-year terms for Washington justices of the peace; that the Supreme Court in *Marbury* insisted that those five-year terms precluded presidential removal; and that Jefferson, in renominating William Hammond Dorsey and Thomas Peter, can plausibly be said to have acquiesced in the view that, because their commissions had been delivered, they were entitled to their five-year terms. Of course, the most sustained effort at congressional limitation of presidential removal authority came with the 1867 Tenure of Office Act, which Andrew Johnson asserted was unconstitutional. The one-vote acquittal in his impeachment trial could be read as vindication of this position—but it should be remembered that he served out the rest of his term severely weakened, that Congress was especially assertive in personnel matters for the rest of his term (and, indeed, for most of the rest of the nineteenth century), and that Republicans won the next four consecutive presidential elections. Johnson's acquittal was hardly a resounding victory for him.

Perhaps more importantly, the postbellum growth of the administrative state saw two major developments limiting presidential removal powers. The first was civil service reform. The Pendleton Act itself was premised on the idea that, if "the *front-door* [that is, appointments] were properly tended, the *back-door* [that is, removals] would take care of itself" because a competitive examination system for new appointees would eliminate partisan incentives to remove officials.[491] But the logic of reform pushed further: President McKinley in 1897 issued an executive order permitting classified civil servants to be dismissed only for just cause, and a series of subsequent orders over the next decade narrowed the scope of just cause for dismissal.[492] In 1912, the Lloyd–La Follette Act (passed as a rider to an appropriations bill) statutized tenure protection, providing that "no person in the classified civil service . . . shall be removed therefrom except for such cause as will promote the efficiency of said service and for reasons given in writing," and specifying the procedures for dismissal.[493] In the subsequent century, these protections have been strengthened still further.[494] Even in *Myers*, the Supreme Court went out of its way to insist that nothing in its holding there would affect the civil service system. Non-Senate-confirmed officials could be "entirely removed from politics" with tenure protections, the Court said; it was the fact that Frank Myers was Senate confirmed that was dispositive.[495]

But even Senate-confirmed nonjudicial officers can be given tenure other than at the pleasure of the president, as the Court confirmed in 1935 in *Humphrey's Executor*. This, of course, brings us to the second aspect of the administrative state that limits presidential removal power: the growth of independent agencies. As we have already seen, a great deal depends on whether an office is characterized as "executive," in which case the Court places it in the *Myers* category and demands an unfettered presidential removal power, or as "quasi-legislative and quasi-judicial," in which case the Court applies *Humphrey's Executor* and allows for tenure protection. And it should be clear that there is no principled way to divine *a priori* which offices should be characterized in which way.[496] From the Restoration through the colonial and early state legislatures and into the early Congresses, we have seen that the Treasury was regarded as not fully executive. We have seen Parliament and colonial assemblies using various formal and informal mechanisms to assert varying degrees of authority over various types of civil and military officials. We have seen early state constitutions in which both appointment and removal powers (as well as the veto and other powers) were parceled out among institutions in a bewildering variety of ways. Indeed, the principal point of continuity has been the contingency of taxonomies of powers. Why should the secretary of the treasury (not to mention a first-class postmaster) be regarded as executive, while federal trade commissioners and governors of the Federal Reserve are regarded as quasi-legislative and quasi-judicial? All of those offices could be said to "execute" federal law; likewise, all could be said to be vested with certain quasi-legislative discretionary authority to fashion policy and certain quasi-judicial authority to interpret and apply rules. What principle, other than respect for Congress's chosen structure, allows us to declare some of them to be "executive" and others "independent"?

One could, of course, take a highly formalistic approach and insist that *Humphrey's Executor* was wrong, that there can be no independent agencies. This approach generally goes by the name "unitary-executive theory."[497] The reasoning behind the theory is relatively simple: the Constitution creates three branches, and the enumeration of those three suggests that no others are permissible. Therefore, any legitimate government official who is not in the legislative or judicial branches must be in the executive branch.[498] Article II vests the executive power in "a President" alone; therefore, the president must have full authority over every legitimate function of the federal government that is not legislative or judicial, and this authority must entail the ability to fire underlings who do not perform according to his wishes.[499] It is worth noting that the same train of formalist reasoning would seem to suggest that government employees are impermissible—they are nowhere listed in the textual trinity of principal officers, inferior officers, and recess appointees!—which both flies in the face of early practice and suggests the impossibility of civil service protections. Such formalism would seem to have the Jacksonian spoils system as its end point. More importantly, it would seem to rob Congress of central elements of its ability to structure and monitor government offices. From the Treasury Department's organic statute on, Congress has placed demands on specific officers, demands that may come into conflict with the president's wishes. From the District of Columbia's organic statute on, Congress has created offices whose incumbents do not serve at the president's pleasure. For the entire postbellum period, there has been a widespread recognition that the spoils system is inadequate to the needs of government and that there should be a large category of government employees who do not serve at the president's pleasure. Simultaneously, there has been a widespread recognition that certain functions should be housed in agencies whose members, although appointed by the president with the consent of the Senate, do not serve at the president's pleasure. (When one contemplates the possibility of, say, interest rate manipulation timed around presidential elections, one sees the wisdom in such judgments.)

Far more palatable than unitary-executive theory is an approach that keeps in mind that such questions arise from the desire to create responsible government. And the history of responsible government, from the seventeenth century to the present, is one of constantly shifting and adjusting arrangements over who answers to whom, and how much. It is a mistake to regard agency independence as a mistake, or even as a *Myers/Humphrey's Executor* binary: different agencies have different degrees and types of independence. The agencies are created and structured by Congress, and Congress can provide varying measures of tenure protection when it does so.

Impeachment

We end by returning, briefly, to where we began. As we have seen, impeachment played a major role in the early development of responsible government; it has been resorted to far less frequently in recent centuries, although its shadow may well affect officeholders' behavior in unseen ways. There is also a massive literature on the topic (one to which I have contributed), and I shall not attempt anything like a systematic treatment here.[500] Instead, I shall limit this section to a few brief notes on the impeachment power.

First, although in theory impeachment applies to "all civil Officers of the United States" in addition to the president and vice president,[501] in practice it is likely to remain limited to presidents, vice presidents, and federal judges—in other words, officers whom there is no other way to remove. (Sai Prakash and Steven Smith have argued that Congress can create non-impeachment mechanisms for judging "good behavior" and therefore for removing federal judges.[502] But, with the exception of the 1802 Repeal Act, impeachment is the only mechanism that has been used to remove judges in American history, and, at this point, it would take an extraordinary set of political circumstances for Congress to consider creating the type of mechanism that Prakash and Smith suggest.) Nineteen officers have been impeached by the House of Representatives in American history.[503] The first impeachment was of Senator William Blount in 1797 for conspiring with the British and Indian tribes to seize Spanish territory in Florida and Louisiana. The Senate decided that members of Congress were not "civil Officers" and therefore not impeachable; instead, they expelled him by a vote of twenty-five to one.[504] Of the subsequent eighteen impeachments, two have been of presidents, fifteen have been of judges, and one has been of a cabinet officer. The cabinet officer, Secretary of War William Belknap, resigned from office before the House voted to impeach him in 1876. The House impeached him anyway, both to make a point and in an attempt to disqualify him from future officeholding. The Senate acquitted him, with a number of the votes for acquittal seemingly premised on a belief that his resignation had deprived the Senate of jurisdiction to try him.[505] The Belknap case points to why impeachment is likely to be both rare and used only against presidents, vice presidents, and judges. It is likely to be rare across the board, because, if there is sufficient consensus in both houses to impeach and convict, an officer is likely to resign first (as, for instance, President Nixon did). And it is likely to be even rarer for officers who serve at the president's pleasure, because, should they refuse to resign, the president is likely to fire them rather than have her administration dragged through impeachment proceedings. Indeed, even independent agency officials can generally be dismissed by the president for malfeasance (we have seen, for instance, that the federal trade commissioners in *Humphrey's Executor* could be removed for "inefficiency, neglect of duty, or malfeasance in office" and that Federal Reserve governors today can be removed "for cause"). An offense that could garner a majority in the House to impeach and a supermajority in the Senate to convict would almost certainly satisfy the standards for dismissal by the president. In addition to Belknap's pre-impeachment resignation, three other impeached officials (Judges Mark Delahay, George English, and Samuel Kent) have resigned after impeachment but before trial. Only eight officials, all of them federal judges, have been convicted in Senate trials.[506] In addition to losing their offices, only three (Judge Humphreys in 1862, Judge Archbald in 1912, and Judge Porteous in 2010) were disqualified from holding future office.[507] There might be circumstances under which the desire to send a strong message or the desire to disqualify would lead the Senate to hold a trial for someone who had resigned or been fired, but those would be quite extreme circumstances. American impeachment has, thus far, been used almost exclusively against those who cannot be fired.

Second, impeachment carries—and has long carried—a distinct taint of malfeasance, not just political disagreement or even incompetence. Concerns that impeachment embodied, not simply a determination that someone should not hold office, but also a determination that he was guilty of serious crimes, led the Lords to refuse to convict Strafford in 1640–1641, even as they were willing to pass a bill of attainder against him. Indeed, the subsequent development of responsible government depended on the creation of mechanisms for turning officials out of office without the threat to their life, liberty, property, or honor inherent in impeachment. In the American context, the acquittal of Samuel Chase in 1805—an acquittal that required some Republican votes—embodied a judgment that impeachment was to be reserved for especially serious offenses. It was not considered an appropriate tool of normal partisan contestation, even in the partisan cauldron of the early nineteenth century, and even against as polarizing a figure as Chase. Indeed, at the Philadelphia convention, Benjamin Franklin compared presidential impeachment to an assassination (and I have elsewhere explored what this might mean as far as substantive standards for presidential impeachability are concerned).[508] Conviction upon impeachment has, in fact, been reserved for serious official misconduct: Judge Pickering, as we have already seen, was removed in 1804 for misconduct on the bench; six of the remaining seven were removed for offenses related to corruption, tax evasion, or perjury. Judge West Humphreys was convicted in 1862 for supporting the Confederacy.[509]

The Constitution's high structural bar for impeachment serves to ensure that it will be used only in such serious, and largely uncontroversial, cases of misconduct. The requirement that the Senate hold a trial serves to impress upon senators' minds the punitive nature of the endeavor; more importantly, the requirement of a two-thirds vote to convict significantly increases the likelihood of acquittal in close cases or cases brought from partisan motives. Indeed, there were majorities to convict both Samuel Chase and Andrew Johnson; it was the supermajoritarian safeguard that prevented their removal.

We should not read the procedural difficulty or low incidence of impeachment as an indication that it is unimportant. As of this writing, two of our forty-four presidents have been impeached, and a third surely would have been had he not resigned. Although the two impeached presidents were acquitted, there is no doubt that the mere fact of impeachment hobbled them in important ways for the remainder of their presidencies. Others have no doubt been influenced in at least some ways by the possibility of impeachment. At the same time, we should be careful not to overstate the importance of impeachment or to focus myopically on it, either. Impeachment is one mechanism among many, surveyed in this chapter, for maintaining congressional influence over personnel, and thereby for ensuring some measure of responsible government.

The personnel power has been hard fought and deeply contested in Anglo-American government for centuries. It was intimately tied to the struggle for responsible government in England, and that struggle significantly shaped political thought and practice across the Atlantic. This chapter has aimed to trace the development of legislative power over the personnel of the state and to think about what different distributions and configurations of that power mean for legislative power more broadly.

The various mechanisms of congressional control over appointment, removal, and impeachment, if used judiciously, can increase congressional power and further the ends of responsible government. Of course, if used injudiciously, they can have the opposite effect, harming congressional standing with the public by making it look mindlessly obstructionist or showing it to be zealously pursuing unpopular goals. To the extent, however, that the tools of responsible government are used in ways that are responsible, not just to Congress, but, through it, to the broader public, it will tend to redound to Congress's credit.

5

Contempt of Congress

GATHERING INFORMATION IS NOT A PERIPHERAL PART of Congress's job; it is central to the legislature's identity and function. Information is, of course, necessary for Congress to legislate effectively—as well as for it to appropriate, consider nominees, and perform all of the other functions considered in this book. Equally importantly, holding hearings and releasing information to the press and the public is an essential means by which houses and members make arguments in the public sphere and attempt to shape the public discourse. Hearings give members of Congress opportunities to express their displeasure or disagreements with nominees, to grill administration officials, and to present sympathetic witnesses, all in an attempt to move the conversation, both in Washington and around the country, in their preferred direction. Hearings might even (as we shall see in the next chapter) be used to release secret information, under the veil of the Constitution's Speech or Debate Clause.

But what happens when witnesses refuse to cooperate with a congressional investigation, either by refusing to testify or by refusing to turn over documents? Each house of Congress may issue subpoenas, but what if those subpoenas are defied? This chapter considers each house's power to hold outsiders—and especially outsiders from other branches of the federal government—in contempt of Congress (or its historical close relative, in breach of congressional privilege),[1] along with the mechanisms by which a finding of contempt (or breach) can be enforced.

Historical Development

The offense of contempt of Parliament dates to the institution's inception. Befitting the early Parliament's status as an advisory body meant to assist the monarch in the administration of his kingdom,[2] the earliest contempts were treated as offenses against the Crown, and the contemnors faced royal justice.[3] In 1433, Henry VI gave royal assent to a statute making double damages, fine, and ransom the punishments for all cases of assault upon a member of Parliament, an especially vexing form of contempt.[4] The fact that the fine and ransom were paid to the Crown, as well as the fact that they were dispensed through the mechanisms of royal justice, make it clear that the offense was against the king. The fifteenth-century Parliament did not yet have sufficient institutional independence for the assault on a member to be considered a matter for the House's own cognizance.[5]

Beginning in the sixteenth century, however, the houses themselves began to punish contempts. In 1543, George Ferrers, a member of Parliament from Plymouth, was arrested in London pursuant to an action in the King's Bench to recover a debt (for which Ferrers served as a surety). Upon being notified of Ferrers's arrest, the House of Commons sent its sergeant to demand his release. Rather than surrender him, however, the jailers, "after many stout words, . . . forcibly resisted" the sergeant's demands. In the resulting melee, the sergeant "was driven to defend himself with his mace of armes, and had the crown thereof broken by bearing off a stroke, and his man stroken down." The London sheriffs arrived on the scene but promptly sided with the jailers against the sergeant. The sergeant returned to the House of Commons and reported; the Commons took the matter "in so ill part, that they all together . . . rose up wholly, and retired to the Upper House," where they acquainted the Lords with their grievances.[6]

The House of Lords, "judging the contempt to be very great, referred the punishment thereof to the order of the Commons House."[7] The Lord Chancellor, a Crown official, offered to arm the sergeant with a royal writ, but "the Commons House refused, being of a clear opinion, that all commandments and other acts proceeding from the [House of Commons], were to be done and executed by their Serjeant without writ, only by shew of his mace, which was his warrant."[8] Meanwhile, the London sheriffs, having received word of "how haynously the matter was taken" and having decided that discretion was the better part of valor, decided to turn Ferrers over without a fight when the sergeant returned.

The sergeant, upon securing Ferrers's release, charged the sheriffs, jailers, and the person upon whose suit Ferrers was arrested in the first place to appear before the House of Commons the next morning to answer for their contempt of Parliament.[9]

When they appeared in the House, they were denied counsel. After they spoke in response to the contempt charge, the sheriffs and the person who instituted the suit were committed to the Tower of London, and the arresting officer and most of the jailers were sent to Newgate prison.[10] The jailer who started the physical confrontation with the sergeant was committed to the Little Ease dungeon of the Tower of London.[11] The House released its prisoners three days later, but only after "humble suit made by the Mayor of L[ondon] and other their friends."[12]

In addition to being a member of the House of Commons, Ferrers was a servant of Henry VIII. After the Commons released the sheriffs and jailers, the king called prominent members of the House before him.

First commending their wisdome in maintaining the Privileges of the House (which he would not have to be infringed in any point) alledged that he, being head of the Parliament, and attending in his own person upon the business thereof, ought in reason to have Privilege for him, and all his servants attending there upon him. So that if the said Ferrers had been no Burgess, but only his servant, that in respect thereof he was to have the Privilege, as well as any other. For I understand, quoth he, that you, not only for your own persons, but also for your necessary servants, even to your cooks and horsekeepers, enjoy the said Privilege. . . . And further, we be informed by our Judges, that we at no time stand so highly in our Estate Royal, as in the time of Parliament; wherein we as Head, and you as Members, are conjoin'd and knit together into one Body Politick, so as whatsoever offence or injury (during that time) is offered to the meanest Member of the House, is to be judg'd as done against our Person and the whole Court of Parliament; which prerogative of the Court is so great (as our learned Counsel informeth us) as all acts and processes coming out of any other inferior Courts, must for the time cease and give place to the highest.[13]

Beneath the superficial pleasantries lay a struggle over the role of Parliament in the English constitutional order. The Commons' refusal to accept the Lord Chancellor's proffered writ constituted an assertion that the House's contempt power was independent of royal authority. The sergeant needed only show his mace, the symbol of the authority vested in him *by the House*, in order to free

Ferrers and imprison those who held him. The king, by contrast, attempted to reassert Parliament's role as his advisory body. His claim that his servants should be accorded parliamentary privilege was a claim that privilege was intended to help members of Parliament serve the king.

Henry's words notwithstanding, it was the House's deeds that set the tone for the future. Without royal assistance, the House of Commons had freed Ferrers and imprisoned those who had violated the House's privileges. Henceforth, it would be the House, and the House alone, that would punish contempts. By punishing these contempts itself, the House asserted an institutional identity independent from the Crown: contempts were no longer interferences with the functioning of royal governance; rather, they were interferences with the House's ability to do its own business.

One important consequence of this change was that it became conceivable to hold Crown officers—indeed, even monarchs themselves—in contempt. When Parliament was just one instrument of royal governance, a dispute between Parliament and some (other) Crown official was determinable by reference to what the monarch wanted. But with Parliament beginning to assert institutional powers distinct from the Crown, it became possible to conceive of contempts committed by Crown officials, as a number of cases, beginning in the late sixteenth century, made clear.

In 1566, a joint committee of the Lords and Commons sent Queen Elizabeth a petition requesting both that she "dispose [herself] to marry, where it shall please [her], with whom it shall please [her], and as soon as it shall please [her]" and that she settle the matter of succession in case she should die unmarried and without heirs.[14] The queen sent back a brief reply assuring Parliament that all would be settled in due course.[15] A number of members of the House of Commons were unsatisfied and spoke critically of the queen's refusal to address their concerns directly.[16] In response, Elizabeth summoned thirty members of the House of Commons, as well as the Lords who had served on the joint committee that drafted the petition, to appear before her. When they appeared, she delivered "a smart reproof," albeit one in which "she mixed some sweetness with maj[esty]." She "promised them to manage things not only with the care of a prince, but the tenderness of a parent." And she forbade them to discuss issues of succession any further.[17]

In the House of Commons, Paul Wentworth raised the issue of whether forbidding further discussion of a topic constituted a breach of privilege.[18] This question was extensively debated on the day it was raised, and the next day, the Speaker of the House of Commons was again summoned to appear before the queen, who commanded him to allow no further discussion of the matter.[19] This command was ineffectual—the House immediately appointed a committee to draft a response.[20] The document produced by this committee suggested that, in ordering the House to cease debate, the queen had infringed upon its traditional liberties, and it urged her to lift the restraint.[21] Although this petition was never presented to the queen, the Commons did request a meeting with her to discuss their privileges.[22] Realizing that, as long as the Commons believed that she was infringing on their liberties, the House would refuse to attend to other business, Elizabeth gave in.[23] Two weeks after ordering the House to suspend discussion of the succession issue, the queen revoked that command, although she made it known that she "desired the house to proceed no further in the matter at that time."[24] This incident is important, not simply because of the outcome—that is, in a dispute framed in the language of royal prerogative versus parliamentary privilege, the latter won—but also precisely because it was framed in those terms. That is, both the House and the queen herself thought it conceivable that the queen could breach parliamentary privilege. Moreover, the House was willing to use its other levers of power, such as refusing to turn to other business that the queen wanted passed, in order to give effect to its constitutional position.

A similar pattern, in which the House won a contest that pitted claims of prerogative against those of privilege, played out only a few years later, in 1571. That year, William Strickland, a member of the House of Commons, was summoned before the Queen's Council and ordered not to attend the House because he had introduced a bill moving for the reformation of the Book of Common Prayer.[25] (As head of the Church of England, Elizabeth considered all matters of religion to fall within her royal prerogative and, therefore, outside Parliament's purview.)[26] Several members argued that this interference of the Crown in Strickland's performance of his parliamentary duties constituted a breach of privilege.[27] Christopher Yelverton insisted that Strickland's arrest created a "perilous" precedent, and that the House had a right to debate "all matters not treason, or too much to the derogation of the imperial crown." He concluded that "it was fit for princes to have their prerogatives; but yet the same to be straitened within reasonable limits."[28] The next day the queen yielded, and Strickland was again allowed to attend the House.[29]

In a familiar pattern, it was during the reign of the House of Stuart that clashes between royal prerogative and parliamentary privilege really came to the fore. In 1621, for example, James I ordered the House of Commons to stop meddling in the "mysteries of state" when it questioned his desire to marry off the Prince of Wales to the Spanish Infanta.[30] When the House replied that freedom of speech and debate was part of its "ancient and undoubted right," James claimed that all privileges derived from royal grace—but insisted that he would be glad to show the House this grace, so long as it refrained from encroaching on royal prerogative.[31] When the House replied by passing a resolution reasserting the claim that its privileges were its "ancient and undoubted birthright," James responded by sending for the Commons' *Journal*, tearing out the House's protestation, declaring it "invalid, annulled, void, and of no effect," imprisoning some of the parliamentary ringleaders, sending others off to Ireland as royal commissioners, and dissolving Parliament.[32]

James's fights with Parliament were nothing, however, as compared to those of his son. Indeed, Charles I's clashes with Parliament are of particular interest because they were often framed as clashes between royal prerogative and legislative privilege. Some of these clashes look rather familiar to modern eyes, as when Charles repeatedly asserted a right, grounded in royal prerogative, to withhold documents from Parliament and to prevent his advisers from having to testify before Parliament. Indeed, one lens through which to view the English Civil War is as the victory of parliamentary privilege over such claims of royal prerogative—indeed, as the ultimate finding of contempt of Parliament.[33]

As we saw in the previous two chapters, Charles was at loggerheads with the House of Commons from the beginning of his reign, and these disputes frequently revolved around money: Charles wanted it, and the House was unwilling to grant it until its grievances had been redressed. After dissolving his first Parliament in despair and subsequently collecting taxes without parliamentary authorization,[34] growing financial necessity (created, in large part, by ill-advised and ill-managed military adventuring) forced Charles to call his second Parliament, in 1626.[35] In an attempt to ensure that this Parliament went more smoothly for him, Charles appointed six of the more charismatic leaders of the previous Parliament to the post of sheriff, which made them legally ineligible to sit in the new Parliament (a technique known as "pricking for sheriff").[36] Many members of the Commons, however, resented this perceived invasion of their privileges, and the issue was debated (without conclusive resolution) throughout the short life of the 1626 Parliament.[37]

Simultaneously, parliamentary opposition to the first Duke of Buckingham was growing, as described in chapter 4. Recall Charles's insistence that "I will not allow any of my servants to be questioned amongst you, much less such as are of eminent place, and near unto me. . . . I see you specially aim at the duke of Buckingham. . . . [I] can assure you, he hath not meddled, or done any thing concerning the public or common wealth, but by special directions and appointment, and as my servant."[38] When the House refused to back down, Charles summoned both houses to appear before him, and, after thanking the Lords for their "care of the state of the kingdom," he turned to chastising the Commons for behaving in an "unparliamentary" manner.[39] The Lord Keeper, speaking on the king's behalf, then made it clear that Charles would "by no means suffer [royal prerogative] to be violated by any pretended colour of parliamentary liberty; wherein his maj. doth not forget that the parliament is his council, and therefore ought to have the liberty of a council; but his maj. understands the difference betwixt council and controlling, and between liberty and the abuse of liberty."[40] The king was particularly outraged by the ongoing proceedings against Buckingham, and the Lord Keeper declared that Charles regarded any attack on the duke as an attack on himself.[41] Accordingly, Charles ordered the Commons to "yield obedience unto those directions which you have formerly received, and cease this unparliamentary inquisition."[42] Charles also took exception to the House's presuming to question his counselors and to its having "sent a general warrant to his signet-office, and commanded his officers, not only to produce and shew the records, but their books and private notes, which they made for his maj.'s service."[43] The House of Commons, in his view, had no business summoning royal officials to testify and ordering them to produce documents. He concluded by repeating the demand for an immediate and unconditional grant of supply.[44]

In reply, the Commons asserted that "it hath been the antient, constant, and undoubted right and usage of parliaments, to question and complain of all persons, of what degree soever, found grievous to the common-wealth, in abusing the power and trust committed to them by their sovereign."[45] In other words, the parliamentary power of investigation trumped assertions of royal prerogative. The Commons then set aside all other business—including the king's request for funds—to proceed against Buckingham.[46] On May 10, 1626, the Commons presented thirteen articles of impeachment against Buckingham to the House of Lords.[47]

The Lords were, at the time, locked in their own struggle with the Crown over their privileges and were therefore perhaps less inclined to look favorably on Buckingham than they might otherwise have been. Several months earlier, Charles had committed the Earl of Arundel to the Tower of London.[48] Although the king did not immediately give a reason, some thought that the cause was the marriage of the earl's eldest son to a relative of the king's—a match of which the monarch did not approve.[49] Others noted, however, that Arundel was one of Buckingham's arch-opponents in the House of Lords and suggested that this factor explained his imprisonment.[50] Whatever the king's reasons, the House of Lords, concerned that Arundel's imprisonment might constitute an attack on its privileges, began looking into the matter.[51] Upon learning of the House's inquiry, the king sent the Lord Keeper to communicate to the House that "the earl of Arundel was restrained for a misdemeanor which was personal to his majestie, and lay in the proper knowledge of his majestie, and had no relation to matters of Parliament."[52] The House of Lords then formed a subcommittee to inquire into the matter.[53] Upon learning of this, the king sent a second message, assuring the House that he had acted "justly" and had "not diminished the privilege of the house."[54] The House was unconvinced, however, and resolved that "no lord of Parliament, sitting the Parliament, or within the usual times of privilege of Parliament, is to be imprisoned, or restrained, without sentence or order of the house; unless it be for treason or felony, or for refusing to give surety for the peace."[55] There followed a month of messages sent back and forth between the king and the House, in which the House pressed its privilege claim and demanded an immediate answer and Charles insisted that an answer would be forthcoming in due course.[56] Finally, when the House's patience was exhausted, it suspended all other business "that consideration might be had how their privileges may be preserved unto posterity."[57] (Among the business that did not proceed while the Lords were pondering their privileges was the Duke of Buckingham's attempt to respond to the impeachment charges.)[58] The king sent word that he was "resolved, to satisfy your lordships fully in what you then desired," but the Lords adjourned, refusing to do any business until they were satisfied.[59] When the House reconvened a week later, the king again tried to postpone replying to its assertion of privilege.[60] The Lords again resolved "all other business to cease, but this of the earl of *Arundel's* concerning the privilege of the house."[61] Five days later, on June 8, 1626, Arundel was released.[62] Once again, the Crown was forced to acquiesce in the assertion by a house of Parliament that the king's actions constituted a breach of privilege.

Four days after Arundel's release, the king's supporters in the House of Commons made one final attempt to get the House to provide the funds the king sought. The attempt went nowhere, and on June 15 Charles dissolved his second Parliament, before the Lords could try Buckingham.[63] The Crown's need for funds continued to increase,[64] however, and with Charles unwilling to make the compromises necessary to receive a parliamentary grant of supply, he turned to prerogative taxation. Most notably, he ordered his Treasury officials to collect the customs duties of tonnage and poundage, despite the fact that Parliament had refused to grant him this right,[65] and he ordered the collection of a "forced loan"—that is, he required that his subjects provide a loan proportional to the value of their property.[66] These two devices led to widespread public resistance.[67] When Randolph Crewe, the chief justice of the King's Bench, refused to bless the legality of these measures, Charles summarily dismissed him and replaced him with someone more compliant.[68] The new chief justice, Nicholas Hyde, promptly denied habeas petitions by those who had been imprisoned for refusing to pay the forced loan.[69]

The growing resistance to the Crown's use of prerogative powers to raise funds, combined with the increasing need for funds, forced Charles in 1628 to call his third Parliament.[70] In the hopes of convincing the new Parliament to be generous, Charles released all those who had been imprisoned for refusing to pay the forced loan. Of the seventy-six who had been imprisoned for that reason, twenty-seven were elected to the new Parliament.[71] As Conrad Russell has noted, this Parliament assembled "with the conscious and deliberate aim of vindicating English liberties."[72] After Charles assented to the Petition of Right (in which, among other things, he promised to levy no more forced loans),[73] the Commons voted him subsidies, but not tonnage and poundage,[74] and drew up a remonstrance warning Charles against attempting to collect the duties on his own.[75] Before that remonstrance (and another one on the evils of the Duke of Buckingham) could be presented to him, however, Charles prorogued the Parliament.[76] It was during this prorogation that Buckingham was assassinated, as discussed in the previous chapter.[77] During the prorogation, Charles also continued to collect tonnage and poundage without parliamentary sanction. London merchants, many of whom were either members of Parliament or friends of members, openly rebelled, at one point breaking into the royal customs warehouse and taking back goods that had been impounded because of their refusal to pay the duties.[78] When Parliament reconvened on January 20, 1629, Charles was facing a "full-fledged merchant revolt."[79]

Two days into the new session, the House of Commons impaneled a committee to look into the complaints of John Rolle, a merchant and member of the House.[80] The gist of Rolle's complaint was that "his goods were seized by the officers of the customs, for refusing to pay the rates by them demanded."[81] Two days later, Charles addressed both houses of Parliament, telling them that the best way to ensure that the collection of tonnage and poundage without parliamentary approval would not become a precedent for future expansive interpretations of royal prerogative would be to retroactively authorize tonnage and poundage from the beginning of his reign.[82] The House did not take this suggestion well, refusing even to debate a bill granting tonnage and poundage.[83] The king was displeased—he sent a message expressing his hope that the House would take up the bill, followed the next day by another message expressing his expectation that the House would do so and pointedly noting that he "expect[ed] rather thanks than a remonstrance."[84] The House chose not to proceed with tonnage and poundage.

On February 10, Rolle came before the House and complained that his warehouse had been locked and he had been served with a subpoena to appear in the Star Chamber.[85] Sir Robert Philips told his colleagues in the House that such actions made them "the subject of scorn and contempt" and insisted that the House inquire "by whose procurement this subpoena was taken forth: if those that throw these scorns upon us may go unquestioned, it is in vain to sit here."[86] When the customs official who had seized Rolle's goods came before the House, he explained that he had seized the goods under royal authority. Moreover, he reported that "the king sent for him on Sunday last, and commanded him to make no further answer" to the House.[87] The House was outraged. John Selden thundered, "If there be any near the king that misinterpret our actions, let the curse light on them, and not on us: I believe it is high time to right ourselves; and until we vindicate ourselves in this, it will be vain for us to sit here."[88] The next day, the royal warrant by which the duties were collected was laid before the House. In it, Charles ordered the customs officials to collect tonnage and poundage "as they were in the time of our . . . father. . . . And if any person refuse to pay, then our will is, that the lords of the council and the treasurer shall commit to prison such so refusing."[89] In other words, the warrant asserted Charles's prerogative powers to collect the same tonnage and poundage duties that his father had collected, despite the fact that Parliament had specifically authorized James to collect tonnage and poundage and had specifically denied Charles that right. As Philips remarked, "Thus you see how fast the prerogative of the king doth intrench on the liberty of the subject, and how hardly it is recovered."[90] There was some debate as to whether the House should construe the royal warrant as authorizing the collection of the duties against members of Parliament, or whether the House should assume that the customs officials had acted outside the scope of the warrant.[91] Nathaniel Rich welcomed the possibility of asserting that the customs officials had acted outside the scope of the warrant, saying that it provided "a way open to go to this question, without relation to the king's commission or command."[92] Charles, however, was spoiling for a fight: he dispatched Sir John Cooke to inform the House that the customs officials acted "by his own direct orders and command, or by order of the council-board, his maj. himself being present; and, therefore, would not have it divided from his act."[93] Charles thereby forced the House's hand: either it would have to back down and allow tonnage and poundage to be collected, even from its own members, on the strength of royal prerogative powers alone, or it would have to assert that the king himself had breached parliamentary privilege.

The House chose the latter route and passed a resolution expressing its belief that parliamentary privilege extended to members' goods.[94] John Eliot read in the House a proposed remonstrance to the Crown, in which he asserted that the collection of tonnage and poundage without parliamentary consent was "a breach of the fundamental liberties of this kingdom, and contrary to your majesty's royal Answer to the Petition of Right."[95] When Eliot finished reading his proposed remonstrance, he moved for a vote on presenting it to the king.[96] The Speaker refused, claiming that the king had commanded him to rise from the Speaker's chair, thereby adjourning the House.[97] At this point, several members of the House forcibly held the Speaker in his chair (an incident that is discussed in more detail in the next chapter), while the House passed three resolutions, one of which read, "Whosoever shall counsel, or advise, the taking and levying of the subsidies of Tunnage and Poundage, not being granted by parliament; or shall be an actor or instrument therein, shall be . . . reputed an innovator in the government, and a capital enemy to this kingdom and commonwealth."[98]

Meanwhile, the king, having heard that the House continued to sit against his express command, sent for troops to break down the door of the House, but the House adjourned before the troops arrived.[99]

On the day that the House reconvened after this adjournment, the king dissolved Parliament. In his statement of reasons, he laid the blame entirely at the feet of the Commons, reserving special umbrage for the House's position on the issue of tonnage and poundage.[100] He complained specifically that, in the course of investigating his levying of the duties, the members of the House "send for the officers of the customs, enforcing them to attend, day after day, by the space of a month together; they cause them to produce their letters patent under our great seal, and the warrants made by our privy council, for levying of those duties. They examine the officers upon what questions they please, thereby to entrap them for doing our service and commandment."[101] Even more outrageous to Charles was that the House "sent messengers to examine our attorney general, (who is an officer of trust and secrecy) touching the execution of some commandments of ours, of which, without our leave first obtained, he was not to give account to any but ourself."[102] That is, he considered it a breach of his royal prerogative to have his subordinates and their records examined by the House. He was, finally, outraged at the extension of privilege to members' goods, a privilege he proclaimed that he would "never admit."[103]

Charles governed without Parliament for the next eleven years, until a Scottish revolt and the ensuing Bishops' Wars once again forced him to convene Parliament in April 1640 for the purpose of raising money.[104] The Commons, however, refused to consider granting any funds until Charles addressed their grievances—chief among which were the Crown's continuing use of prerogative taxation (including tonnage and poundage)[105] and (as the next chapter discusses) the House's insistence that its privileges had been breached in 1629 both by the Crown's order to the Speaker to adjourn the House and by the subsequent prosecution of the members who held the Speaker in his chair in order to allow House business to continue.[106] Charles, outraged, dissolved the Short Parliament a mere three weeks after it had assembled.[107]

As we saw in the previous chapter, the Long Parliament, called later that year, assembled in no mood to kowtow to the Crown. The clash came to a head after the passage of the Grand Remonstrance in December 1641. The next month, Charles accused five members of the House of Commons and one member of the House of Lords of treason and had his attorney general bring accusations against them before the House of Lords.[108] Simultaneously, royal officers had gone to the homes of the accused members and sealed their studies.[109] Both houses were outraged. The Commons immediately passed a resolution stating that "the several Parties now sealing up the Trunks or Doors, or seizing the Papers of . . . any . . . Member of this House, that the Serjeant shall be informed of, shall be forthwith apprehended, and brought hither, as Delinquents; And that the Serjeants shall have Power to break open the Doors, and to break the Seals off from the Trunk."[110] The Commons further resolved that if "any Person whatsoever shall offer to arrest or detain the Person of any Member of this House, without first acquainting this House therewith, and receiving further Order from this House, [then] it is lawful for such Member, or any Person to assist him, to stand upon his and their Guard of Defence, and to make Resistance, according to the Protestation taken to defend the Privileges of Parliament."[111] In other words, the House authorized armed resistance to Crown officers acting on the king's behalf, on the grounds that such actions were a breach of parliamentary privilege. The Lords likewise resolved that the sealing of the members' studies was a breach of privilege and that there should be armed guards around Parliament.[112] Charles, meanwhile, sent a message to the Commons demanding that the five accused members of that house be delivered into his custody.[113] The House replied that it would consider the matter and get back to him.[114]

The next day, by order of the Commons, the five accused members attended the House.[115] The Commons *Journal* entry for that day ends abruptly with the notation:

> His Majesty came into the House; and took Mr. Speaker's Chair.
> "Gentlemen,"
> "I AM sorry to have this Occasion to come unto you
> * * * *
> *Resolved*, upon the Question, That the House shall adjourn itself
> till To-morrow One of Clock.[116]

Fortunately, other sources fill in where the overwhelmed *Journals* clerk left off. John Rushworth, who was, at the time, the clerk-assistant to the House of Commons, recounted that, as soon as the accused members assembled in the House, news arrived that "his Majesty was coming with a Guard of Military Men, Commanders and Souldiers."[117] In order to avoid violence, the House ordered the five members to leave immediately. Shortly thereafter, the door of the House was "thrown open," and Charles entered, attended by his troops. Not seeing any of the five members in attendance, he ascended to the Speaker's chair and informed the House that, when he had the previous day sent a messenger demanding that the five members be delivered to him, he "did expect Obedience, and not a Message." He insisted that parliamentary privilege did not protect members against charges of treason and that he would expect them to be delivered as soon as they returned to the House.[118] When he demanded to know where the members had gone, Speaker William Lenthall rather courageously replied,

> May it please your Majesty,
> I Have neither Eyes to see, nor Tongue to speak in this place, but as the House is pleased to direct me, whose Servant I am here, and humbly beg your Majesties Pardon, that I cannot give any other Answer than this, to what your Majesty is pleased to demand of me.[119]

The king then left the chamber; as he was going out "many Members cryed out, aloud so as he might hear them, *Priviledge! Priviledge!*"[120]

The next day, the House of Commons passed a resolution declaring the king's action to have been "a high Breach of the Rights and Privilege of Parliament, and inconsistent with the Liberties and Freedom thereof: And therefore this House doth conceive, they cannot, with the Safety of their own Persons or the Indemnity of the Rights and Privilege of Parliament, sit here any longer without a full Vindication of so high a Breach, and a sufficient Guard wherein they may confide."[121] As the king was walking along the streets of London later that day, "some People did cry out aloud *Priviledges of Parliament! Priviledges of Parliament!*"[122] Five days later, Charles left London, first moving his court to Hampton Court and then to York.[123] Within two days, the House declared that anyone who arrested a member of Parliament "by Pretence or Colour of any Warrant issuing out from the King only, is guilty of the Breach of the Liberties of the Subject, and of the Privilege of Parliament, and a publick Enemy to the Commonwealth."[124] By the next month the conflict had spread, and the Civil War was at hand.[125]

After the ensuing six years of bloody struggle, the House of Commons, on January 6, 1649, created a High Court of Justice to try Charles for treason.[126]

The preamble to the charges against Charles asserted broadly that he had acted "out of a wicked design to erect and uphold in himself an unlimited and tyrannical power to rule according to his will, and to overthrow the rights and liberties of the people, yea, to take away and make void the foundations thereof, and of all redress and remedy of misgovernment, which by the fundamental constitutions of this kingdom were reserved on the people's behalf in the right and power of frequent and successive Parliaments, or national meetings in Council."[127] Charles, who refused to recognize the legitimacy of the High Court, was convicted on January 27, 1649, and executed on January 30.[128] Parliament would govern without a king until the Restoration in 1660.

Importantly, many of the complaints leveled against Charles—including the event that precipitated his departure from London in 1642—were characterized as contempts of Parliament or breaches of parliamentary privilege. Everything from Charles's illegal collection of tonnage and poundage, to his attempt to keep troublemakers out of Parliament by appointing them sheriffs, to his attempts to protect Buckingham, to his arrest of Arundel, to his violation of the Petition of Right, to his seizure of Rolle's goods, to his attempt to arrest the five members accused of treason was framed by the House in terms of contempt and breach of privilege. Indeed, we have even seen examples of what might somewhat anachronistically be called clashes between executive privilege and parliamentary privilege, as when Charles repeatedly refused to allow his ministers and close advisers to be questioned by Parliament, or when he complained about the House's demands that Crown officers turn over certain documents. Most dramatically, of course, the House used its privileges not only as a shield to protect the five members accused of treason in 1642 but also as a sword to justify resistance to Charles after he barged into their chamber in search of the members. Charles's flight from London was precipitated by Parliament's—and much of the political nation's—outrage over that breach of privilege.

Although the House of Commons' rule without king or Lords was short lived, the Restoration Parliaments were determined not to countenance a return to claims of unfettered royal prerogative. Thus, in response to Charles II's appointment of Edmund Jennings, a member of the House, as sheriff of York in 1675, the Commons passed a resolution declaring it to be a "Breach of the Privilege of this House, for any Member thereof to be made a Sheriff during the Continuance of the Parliament."[129] That is, the House (even at a time of relative harmony between Crown and Parliament, as noted in chapter 3) found impermissible Charles II's use of the same procedure for removing members from the House that his father had used in 1626.

A number of aspects of the Revolution Settlement responded to many of the exact royal behaviors that had prompted Stuart Parliaments to resort to charges of contempt or breach of privilege. The new Coronation Oath required monarchs to swear, first and foremost, to "Governe the People of this Kingdome . . . according to the Statutes in Parlyament Agreed on and the Laws and Customs of the same,"[130] and the Bill of Rights forbade prerogative taxation and the Crown's asserted power to suspend or dispense with the laws.[131] More generally, the Revolution Settlement, by tightening parliamentary control over the purse (as traced in chapter 3) and over personnel (as traced in chapter 4) largely obviated the need for contempt or breach of privilege as a means of controlling the Crown. More direct mechanisms of control, such as confidence votes, increasingly became available.[132] Across the Atlantic, however, the American colonies and states carried on the tradition of using breach of privilege and contempt proceedings as a means of controlling the executive.

We have already seen that the colonial American legislatures tended to model themselves on the House of Commons—particularly in matters relating to their privileges and procedures. And while the emergence of new and stronger methods of ministerial accountability meant that the eighteenth-century metropolitan Parliament had less need to rely on contempt and breach of privilege in order to keep the Crown in line, colonial legislatures had a relationship with the Crown that more closely mirrored that of the seventeenth-century Parliament. Thus, in the struggle between executive and legislative authority, contempt and breach of privilege remained valuable tools for the legislatures.

Certainly the contempt power was a familiar one to colonial assemblies. For instance, in 1654 the Virginia House of Burgesses held William Hatcher in contempt for asserting that the House's Speaker was a blasphemer and an atheist. Hatcher was fined and forced to apologize before the House on bended knee.[133] Perhaps most famously, in 1722 the young Benjamin Franklin was given his first chance at running a newspaper when the *New England Courant*, published by his brother James, to whom Benjamin was apprenticed, ran an article that "gave Offence to the [Massachusetts] Assembly." James was "taken up, censur'd and imprison'd for a Month by the Speaker's Warrant."[134] This use of the contempt power against private citizens was quite common in the colonies, as it was in England.[135]

But the colonial assemblies did not limit their use of the contempt power to private citizens: they were quite willing to hold Crown officers in contempt as well. The South Carolina House of Commons (which, as we saw in the previous two chapters, was particularly feisty) was especially active in this regard—it arrested the provost marshal in 1726 for ignoring an order of the House, the chief justice in 1728 for refusing to appear before the House, the council clerk for insolence in 1729, and the surveyor general and his deputy in 1733 for contradicting its orders.[136] In 1771, at the height of the Wilkes Fund Controversy, it held the two colonial treasurers in contempt and ordered them jailed when they refused (on the orders of the governor and council) to disburse funds that the House had appropriated on its sole authority.[137] Nor was South Carolina unique in this regard. In 1722, the Massachusetts House of Representatives fought a "long-drawn-out controversy with the Governor" over the House's right to call before it the two heads of the colonial forces in Maine.[138] The House finally secured their presence and, having determined that the two had acted culpably, "brought about the[ir] retirement."[139] When one of them continued exercising the functions of his office nonetheless, the House ordered him taken into custody.[140] In 1733, the North Carolina Assembly arrested a receiver of the powder money for refusing to submit his accounts to the House, and it attempted to arrest the chief justice for presenting a petition that displeased it.[141] And in 1749, the Virginia House of Burgesses arrested the public printer for printing a resolution of the council that the House found offensive.[142]

Indeed, on occasion, assemblies were even willing to accuse royal governors themselves of breach of privilege. In the midst of a dispute with Governor George Clinton in 1747, the New York House of Representatives passed a series of resolutions accusing Clinton of breaching its privileges and asserted, "Whoever advised his Excellency to send this message . . . has attempted to . . . subvert the Constitution of this Colony, and is an Enemy to the inhabitants thereof."[143] The House also drew up a lengthy remonstrance, which Clinton forbade the public printer to print.[144] When the printer was brought before the House and produced the governor's warrant, the House declared the warrant "arbitrary and illegal" and ordered him to print the remonstrance.[145] In 1763, in the midst of a dispute over whether the governor had the authority to determine that certain members of the assembly were ineligible to serve, the South Carolina House of Commons resolved that "his Excellency the governor, by having repeatedly and contemptuously denied the just claims of this house (solely to examine and determine the validity of the elections of their own members) hath violated the rights and privileges of the commons house of assembly of this province." The House further resolved not to "enter in any further business with him, until his excellency shall have done justice to this house."[146] In 1767, the New York House of Representatives was insistent that Richard Jackson, a colonial official, be fired. The governor made it clear that he would not assent to the dismissal until some payment was also granted to Jackson. The House declared that such a demand was "an unconstitutional exercise of [the governor's] power, and in breach of the privilege of the House." Although the House members earnestly desired Jackson's firing, "[W]e are not disposed to purchase it at the expence of our privileges as well as of our money."[147] And another New World colonial legislature, the Jamaican Assembly, declared the governor guilty of a "high breach of privilege" for taking notice of proceedings in the legislature not properly presented to him.[148]

Indeed, contempt findings against Crown officials played an important role in two states at the dawn of the Revolution. In June 1775, as the siege of Boston was under way, Lord Dunmore, the royal governor of Virginia, fearing for his safety, left Williamsburg in the middle of the night and took refuge on a British warship in the James River.[149] There, he summoned the House of Burgesses to attend upon him; the House unanimously passed a resolution declaring this a "high breach of the rights and privileges of this House."[150] Just under a year later, in June 1776, the New Jersey Provincial Congress declared that the proclamation of royal governor William Franklin (illegitimate son of Benjamin) summoning a meeting of the General Assembly "ought not to be obeyed" and constituted a "direct contempt and violation" of resolutions of the Continental Congress.[151] It immediately stopped Franklin's salary and soon afterward had him arrested.[152] With the approval of the Continental Congress, Franklin was sent to Connecticut, where he was held hostage until he was exchanged for Governor John McKinly of Delaware, a patriot being held by the British.[153]

The colonial legislatures thus largely picked up where the pre–Glorious Revolution Parliaments left off. They had no hesitation in using their breach of privilege and contempt powers against colonial governors and other royal officials, and they had methods ranging from censure to arrest to the withholding of salary in order to give teeth to their contempt findings. The suspicion of executive authority evident in these colonial clashes was reflected in the sorts of executives that the newly independent Americans began creating in 1776.[154]

Under the Continental Congress, as we have seen, there was no independent executive that might incur the wrath of the legislature. The Continental Congress was, however, familiar with contempt procedures, as several findings of contempt against private citizens demonstrate.[155]

In their revolutionary constitutions, a number of states specifically provided for investigation and contempt powers. The 1776 Pennsylvania Constitution created a unicameral legislature with the power to "administer oaths or affirmations on examination of witnesses" as well as "all other powers necessary for the legislature of a free state or commonwealth."[156] The 1777 and 1786 Vermont Constitutions were largely patterned on the Pennsylvania model and had nearly identical provisions.[157] Maryland's 1776 Constitution had two relevant provisions. The first gave the House of Delegates the power to "inquire on the oath of witnesses, into all complaints, grievances, and offences, as the grand inquest of this State . . . [and to] call for all public or official papers and records, and send for persons, whom they may judge necessary in the course of their inquiries, concerning affairs relating to the public interest."[158] Second, both houses of the legislature were given the power to "punish, by imprisonment, any person who shall be guilty of a contempt in their view . . . by any obstruction to their proceedings. They may also punish, by imprisonment, any person who shall be guilty of a breach of privilege."[159] Georgia's 1777 Constitution also specifically mentioned the legislature's ability to call executive officers to account.[160] Massachusetts's 1780 Constitution gave both houses of the state legislature the "authority to punish by imprisonment every person, not a member, who shall be guilty of disrespect to the house, by any disorderly or contemptuous behavior in its presence."[161] The 1784 New Hampshire Constitution, which took the Massachusetts Constitution as a model, had a nearly identical provision.[162]

Other early state constitutions said nothing about a contempt power but were interpreted as implicitly containing such a power. South Carolina's 1776 and 1778 Constitutions both provided that the state legislature "shall enjoy all other privileges which have at any time been claimed or exercised by the commons house of assembly [that is, the South Carolina colonial legislature],"[163] which, as we have seen, included a right to hold executive officers in contempt or breach of privilege. Similarly, the 1777 New York Constitution provided that the assembly would "enjoy the same privileges, and proceed in doing business in like manner as the assemblies of the colony of New York of right formerly did."[164] As we have seen, the right to hold the governor himself in breach of privilege was one of those privileges claimed by the New York colonial assembly. Finally, as discussed further in chapter 8, a number of states had generic provisions allowing the legislative houses to determine the rules of their own proceedings.[165] But even those states that merely had generic rules-of-proceedings clauses understood themselves to have the contempt power— and, moreover, understood that power to run against executive officials. Thus, in 1781 the Virginia House of Delegates ordered the arrest of a clerk in the Treasury Department upon rumors that he had engaged in misconduct.[166] And in 1786, the same house had its sergeant arrest Martin Pickett, a county sheriff, on the grounds that he had failed to report who had won an election.[167] Pickett protested that he had, in fact, made the report; after a committee investigated the matter, it determined that he was right and released him.[168] Thus, we see not only that many of the early American state constitutions explicitly gave state legislatures broad contempt powers but also that even those states that did not explicitly mention contempt or breach of privilege in their constitutions understood their legislatures to have such powers, even against state executives.

Unlike the congressional houses' authority to punish their members (which is discussed in chapter 7), their authority to punish nonmembers has no explicit textual basis in the federal Constitution. At the Philadelphia Convention, Charles Pinckney of South Carolina proposed a provision reading: "Each House shall be the Judge of its own privileges, and shall have authority to punish by imprisonment every person violating the same."[169] His proposal was committed to the Committee of Detail, where it died without recorded debate.[170] No further mention seems to have been made of the houses' ability to punish nonmembers, in either the Philadelphia Convention, the state ratifying conventions, or the press.

The issue was, however, touched upon by several early nineteenth-century commentators on the Constitution. Joseph Story remarked that each house's "power to make rules would be nugatory, unless it was coupled with a power to punish for disorderly behaviour, or disobedience to those rules."[171] Story found it "remarkable" that the Constitution did not explicitly mention a power to punish nonmembers, "yet it is obvious," he wrote, "that, unless such a power, to some extent, exists by implication, it is utterly impossible for either house to perform its constitutional functions."[172] Story, moreover, concluded that in America, as in Britain, "the legislative body was the proper and exclusive forum to decide, when the contempt existed, and when there was a breach of its privileges; and, that the power to punish followed, as a necessary incident to the power to take cognizance of the offence."[173] The houses' power to imprison, however, was limited to punishment during the legislative session; at the end of a session, anyone imprisoned by the house had to be released.[174] Story was not the only commentator who thought that although the Constitution's text was silent on the houses' power to hold nonmembers in contempt, sound structural and historical reasoning dictated that such a power must exist. James Kent likewise noted that such a power "was founded on the principle of self preservation."[175] Thomas Jefferson noted the arguments both for and against such a power and declared himself agnostic.[176]

Almost from the beginning the houses of Congress have, in fact, punished nonmembers. In December 1795, three members of the House of Representatives reported that a man named Robert Randall had approached them offering a bribe for their support of a proposal to grant Randall and his associates about twenty million acres of western lands. Other members reported similar contacts with Randall, as well as with an associate of his named Charles Whitney. Although the matter had already been communicated to the executive branch, and, indeed, there were reports that Randall was already in the custody of the Philadelphia city marshal, the House ordered its sergeant-at-arms to take Randall and Whitney into custody, and it appointed a committee to consider what to do with them.[177] After some debate as to the proper mode of procedure, the House finally agreed that the two were to be tried at the bar of the House.[178] Randall was tried first, and, after a three-day trial, the House voted seventy-eight to seventeen that Randall was "guilty of a contempt to, and a breach of the privileges of, this House, by attempting to corrupt the integrity of its members."[179] The House additionally resolved that Randall was to be kept in the sergeant's custody "until further order of this House."[180] The House released him a week later.[181] Whitney was discharged from custody without any determination of innocence or guilt.[182]

The early Senate, too, was willing to use its contempt power against nonmembers. In March 1800, the Federalist-dominated Senate resolved that certain articles published in the *Aurora*, a Republican newspaper, contained "assertions and pretended information respecting the Senate and the committee of the Senate, and their proceedings, which are false, defamatory, scandalous, and malicious, tending to defame the Senate of the United States, and to bring them into contempt and disrepute, and to excite against them the hatred of the good people of the United States; and . . . the said publication is a high breach of the privileges of this House."[183] The Senate ordered the publisher, William Duane, to attend at the bar of the house.[184] Duane appeared and requested counsel, and his request was granted.[185] However, Duane thereafter refused to appear.[186] The Senate then voted him guilty of a contempt for this refusal and ordered its sergeant to take him into custody.[187] The sergeant never succeeded in doing so, however, and the Senate proceedings expired at the end of the session. Vice President Thomas Jefferson presided over the Senate throughout the proceedings.[188]

In 1821, the Supreme Court lent its imprimatur to the chambers' power to hold nonmembers in contempt. After the House of Representatives found John Anderson guilty of contempt and breach of privilege for attempting to bribe a member,[189] Anderson sued the sergeant-at-arms for assault and battery and false imprisonment.[190] Justice William Johnson, for a unanimous Supreme Court, framed the issue as follows: "[W]hether the House of Representatives can take cognisance of contempts committed against themselves, under any circumstances?"[191] His answer was a resounding "yes"—the alternative, he wrote,

> obviously leads to the total annihilation of the power of the House of Representatives to guard itself from contempts, and leaves it exposed to every indignity and interruption that rudeness, caprice, or even conspiracy, may meditate against it. This result is fraught with too much absurdity not to bring into doubt the soundness of any argument from which it is derived. That a deliberate assembly, clothed with the majesty of the people, and charged with the care of all that is dear to them, composed of the most distinguished citizens, selected and drawn together from every quarter of a great nation, whose deliberations are required by public opinion to be conducted under the eye of the public, and whose decisions must be clothed with all that sanctity which unlimited confidence in their wisdom and purity can inspire, that such an assembly should not possess the power to suppress rudeness, or repel insult, is a supposition too wild to be suggested.[192]

Johnson also made reference to unbroken practice, stretching back to England, as support for the existence of such a power, and he noted that those same precedents also limited the houses' punishment powers to the duration of the session.[193] And although subsequent judicial decisions have tinkered with the permissible scope of congressional contempt against nonmembers, no case has doubted its existence.[194]

Shortly after *Anderson*, a house of Congress used the language of breach of privilege against a president himself for the first time. On March 28, 1834, in response to President Jackson's removal of federal money from the Bank of the United States and deposit of that money into state banks,[195] the Senate (the same Senate that twice rejected Jackson's nomination of Roger Brooke Taney to high offices, in large part because of his role in the transfer of the federal funds) adopted a resolution proclaiming that "the President, in the late Executive proceedings in relation to the public revenue, has assumed upon himself authority and power not conferred by the constitution and laws, but in derogation of both."[196] Jackson replied with a lengthy message of protest, claiming that the only constitutional checks on the presidency were impeachment, criminal trial, civil suit, and public opinion.[197] As the Senate's resolution was none of the above, he insisted that the Senate resolution was "wholly unauthorized by the constitution, and in derogation of its entire spirit."[198] The Senate was not amused at having its own words thrown back in its face. After some debate, it passed a series of resolutions asserting that the president had overstepped his constitutional authority and usurped powers belonging to Congress, that he had no right to make formal protests against votes or proceedings in a house of Congress, and that his protest constituted "a breach of the privileges of the Senate."[199] As we have seen, this language came freighted with enough historical baggage for us to be certain that it was not coincidental: just as Parliament had accused monarchs ranging from Elizabeth I to Charles I and Charles II of breach of privilege, so too Congress accused "King Andrew I"[200] of the same offense. (In 1837, after the Democrats had picked up seven additional Senate seats and as Jackson was on his way out of office, the resolution censuring him was officially "expunged" from the Senate *Journal*.)[201]

Several years later, the House borrowed the Senate's language in asserting that another president had breached legislative privilege. On August 9, 1842, President John Tyler, who had already been expelled from the Whig Party, vetoed a tariff and land distribution bill.[202] The next day, the Whig-dominated House created a select committee to consider the president's objections.[203] The committee, chaired by John Quincy Adams, returned with a scathing report, which began by referring to the veto message as "the last of a series of executive measures, the result of which has been to defeat and nullify the whole action of the legislative authority of this Union, upon the most important interests of the nation,"[204] and got more combative from there. The report ended by recommending a constitutional amendment that would allow Congress to override a presidential veto by a bare majority.[205] Tyler replied with a protest message, complaining that the House's report charged him with serious offenses without giving him the opportunity to defend himself.[206] The House then resolved that the president had no right to make a protest against its votes or proceedings and that the protest message constituted a "breach of the privileges of this House."[207]

As the congressional workload increased during the nineteenth century, it became increasingly onerous for the chambers to hold hearings and dole out punishments in run-of-the-mill contempt cases—that is, contempt cases against private citizens, rather than executive officials.[208] In 1857, therefore, Congress passed a law providing that anyone who refused to obey a congressional subpoena would be criminally liable "in addition to the pains and penalties now existing."[209] When a witness failed to comply with a congressional subpoena, the Speaker of the House or president of the Senate could certify the matter to the district attorney for the District of Columbia, "whose duty it shall be to bring the matter before the grand jury for their action."[210] With the exception of the words "in addition to the pains and penalties now existing," which were omitted when the language was reworked in 1938,[211] the statutory contempt mechanism remains on the books today.[212]

This statutory mechanism, however, was clearly meant to supplement the chambers' own inherent contempt power, not replace it.[213] This was crucial because, if a house wished to use its contempt power to go after an executive-branch official, the president could thwart statutory contempt by ordering the U.S. attorney not to prosecute (or to prosecute lackadaisically). So, for instance, in 1866 the House of Representatives itself handled the contempt proceedings against James Fry, the provost marshal general of the army. In April of that year, Representative James Blaine laid before the House a letter from Fry responding to a speech made several days earlier by Representative Roscoe Conkling.[214] Although Blaine and Conkling were both Republicans, they were long-time personal and political enemies. In the speech, Conkling had referred to Fry as "an undeserving public servant" and asserted that, during the Civil War, the Provost Marshal General's Bureau had "turned the business of recruiting and drafting into one carnival of corrupt disorder, into a paradise of coxcombs and thieves."[215] (This was a somewhat ironic accusation coming from Conkling, who, as we saw in the previous chapter, would come to control federal patronage in New York and lead the Stalwart wing of the Republican Party.) In response, Fry wrote, inter alia, that the enmity between Conkling and himself "arose altogether from my unwillingness to gratify him in certain matters in which he had a strong personal interest. It is true, also, that he was foiled in his efforts to obtain undue concessions from my bureau, and to discredit me in the eyes of my superiors."[216] After the letter was read, the House created a select committee to inquire into the matter.[217] The committee reported back two resolutions, which were overwhelmingly adopted by the House. The first proclaimed that Fry's allegations of corruption by Conkling were "wholly without foundation in truth."[218] The second determined that "General Fry, an officer of the government of the United States, and head of one of its military bureaus, in writing and publishing these accusations . . . which, owing to the crimes and wrongs which they impute to a member of this body, are of a nature deeply injurious to the official and personal character, influence, and privileges of such member, and their publication originating, as in the judgment of the House they did, in no misapprehension of facts, but in the resentment and passion of their author, was guilty of a gross violation of the privileges of such member and of this house, and his conduct in that regard merits and receives its unqualified disapprobation."[219] The Provost Marshal General's Bureau was abolished the next month.[220]

In 1879, the House of Representatives actually had its sergeant arrest an executive-branch officer for contempt. In 1878, the House Committee on Expenditures in the State Department received a communication from John C. Myers, a former consul general to Shanghai, alleging that George F. Seward,[221] then the Minister to China, was guilty of malfeasance during his time as Shanghai consul general.[222] The committee determined that certain books that "contained original entries of fees received at the consulate at Shanghai from the year 1863 to 1871, had not been transmitted to the State Department" but had been taken with Seward when he moved to Peking. The committee believed that the books were "necessary to a thorough and complete investigation of the receipts and expenditures at the Shanghai consulate." Myers, who succeeded Seward in Shanghai, alleged in an affidavit to the committee that the books would show that Seward had misappropriated large sums of money from the consulate.[223]

On February 19, 1879, the committee subpoenaed Seward both to appear and to bring the books with him.[224] Seward, who had returned from China for the hearings, appeared the next day; his counsel argued that the committee had no authority to compel production of the books. In response, the committee adopted a number of resolutions asserting that the books were public property and that Seward had no right to withhold them from the committee.[225] In response to the committee's renewed demands for Seward either to produce the books or to testify as to their contents, Seward's counsel asserted that such demands violated Seward's right against compelled self-incrimination.[226] The committee did not accept this argument, asserting that "an investigation before a congressional committee is not *a criminal case*, within the meaning of the Constitution."[227] The committee accordingly recommended that the sergeant be ordered to "take into custody forthwith, wherever to be found, the body of George F. Seward, and him bring to the bar of the House, to show cause why he should not be punished for contempt; and, in the mean time keep the said George F. Seward in his custody to abide the further order of the House."[228] On February 27, the House adopted the committee's proposed order by a vote of 105 to 47.[229]

On February 28, the sergeant brought Seward to the bar of the House. In response to the Speaker's inquiring whether he was ready to cooperate, Seward presented a written statement contending that the committee's investigation was leading to impeachment charges and that he therefore had a right not to be a witness against himself.[230] The House voted to commit his reply to the Judiciary Committee, and he was released on his own recognizance while that committee deliberated.[231] On March 1, the Committee on Expenditures in the State Department reported articles of impeachment against Seward.[232] The session ended two days later, without a vote on the impeachment articles. On the final day of the session, the Judiciary Committee reported that Seward should not be compelled to incriminate himself when there were ongoing impeachment proceedings against him.[233] That report was never voted on by the House.

The House again arrested an executive-branch official in 1916. In December 1915, Representative Frank Buchanan accused U.S. district attorney for the Southern District of New York H. Snowden Marshall of high crimes and misdemeanors. Two weeks later, a federal grand jury convened by Marshall indicted Buchanan for violations of the Sherman Antitrust Act.[234] Buchanan then introduced a resolution calling for the appointment of a committee to investigate alleged misconduct by Marshall; on February 1, 1916, a subcommittee of the Judiciary Committee was appointed for this task.[235] While the subcommittee was investigating, an article appeared in a newspaper accusing the subcommittee of attempting to frustrate the grand jury investigation.[236] When the reporter refused to name his sources to the subcommittee, he was threatened with contempt proceedings.[237] At that point, Marshall wrote a letter to the subcommittee acknowledging that he was the source for the article; the letter went on to restate the charges in language which the Supreme Court later described as "certainly unparliamentary and manifestly ill-tempered, and which was well calculated to arouse the indignation not only of the members of the subcommittee, but of those of the House generally."[238] Marshall also released the letter to the press.[239] The House then adopted a resolution declaring the letter "defamatory and insulting" and asserting that it "tends to bring the House into public contempt and ridicule, and that the said H. Snowden Marshall, by writing and publishing the same, is guilty of contempt of the House of Representatives of the United States because of the violating of its privileges, its honor, and its dignity."[240] The sergeant-at-arms was dispatched to New York to take Marshall into custody.[241] The sergeant arrested Marshall "at his desk in the Federal Building," although Marshall immediately secured a writ of habeas corpus from federal district judge Augustus Hand. While the habeas petition was pending, Marshall was free on his own recognizance.[242] Marshall's habeas petition was subsequently dismissed by Augustus Hand's cousin, fellow district judge Learned Hand, who returned Marshall to the sergeant's custody.[243] Hand subsequently stayed his decision pending appeal, leaving Marshall free on his own recognizance.[244] In his opinion for the Supreme Court, Chief Justice Edward Douglass White expressed no doubt that the House possessed "a power implied to deal with contempt in so far as that authority was necessary to preserve and carry out the legislative authority given" in the Constitution.[245] Nor did White find it necessary to consider whether the scope of the contempt power was different when applied to executive-branch officials: he simply treated as given that the power extended to them. The Court ordered Marshall released from custody, however, because

> the contempt was deemed to result from the writing of the letter, not because of any obstruction to the performance of legislative duty resulting from the letter, or because the preservation of the power of the House to carry out its legislative authority was endangered by its writing, but because of the effect and operation which the irritating and ill-tempered statements made in the letter would produce upon the public mind, or because of the sense of indignation which it may be assumed was produced by the letter upon the members of the committee and of the House generally. But to state this situation is to demonstrate that the contempt

relied upon was not intrinsic to the right of the House to preserve the means of discharging its legislative duties, but was extrinsic to the discharge of such duties, and related only to the presumed operation which the letter might have upon the public mind and the indignation naturally felt by members of the committee on the subject. But these considerations plainly serve to mark the broad boundary line which separates the limited implied power to deal with classes of acts as contempts for self-preservation and the comprehensive legislative power to provide by law for punishment for wrongful acts.[246]

That is, the House would have had full power to punish Marshall for obstructing its proceedings, but the contempt power does not extend to mere dignitary offenses that do not affect the House's proceedings. Neither the House nor the Court seemed to have any doubt that the House could arrest and hold a federal prosecutor for actions which were truly within the scope of Congress's contempt power, rightly construed.

The historical development traced above tees up several enduring questions surrounding the houses' contempt powers. First, most broadly, do the houses have the power to discipline nonmembers? Second, if they do, does this power extend to members of the executive branch? And, if so, how might such a contempt finding be enforced? Must the houses turn to the courts, or do they have recourse to mechanisms of their own—and what are the costs and benefits of using different enforcement mechanisms? And speaking of the courts, is it possible to conceive of a contempt-of-Congress finding against federal judges? Might it ever be desirable? The remainder of this chapter is devoted to those questions.

Contempt against Outsiders Generally

Although, as we have seen, there is no explicit textual basis for the authority of the houses of Congress to hold nonmembers in contempt of Congress or breach of privilege, it has been widely accepted from the earliest years of the Republic that the houses do, in fact, have such a power. Indeed, we have seen Anglo-American legislatures exercising a power to punish nonmembers since the sixteenth century. This power crossed the Atlantic and was widely used in the American colonies and states prior to the drafting of the federal Constitution. Perhaps most tellingly, even in those states whose constitutions did not explicitly grant their legislatures the power to hold nonmembers in contempt, the legislatures did, in fact, exercise this power.

And it is not hard to see why these legislatures have regarded the contempt power as so important: for a legislative house to be able effectively to perform any of its functions, it must have access to information. In Senator J. William Fulbright's words, "The power to investigate is one of the most important attributes of the Congress. It is perhaps also the most necessary of all the powers underlying the legislative function."[247] If those in possession of the necessary information could not be made to give it up, then Congress would have at its disposal only the information that witnesses wanted it to have— hardly an effective means of carrying out its functions. As Allen Moreland put it, "The investigative power of Congress is intimately related to its power to punish for contempt. In practical terms, the inquisitorial authority of the Congress ends at the point where a witness will be excused . . . for refusing to obey a congressional summons to appear or to produce papers, or for refusing to answer questions posed by a member or committee of Congress."[248] Indeed, if it is essential that courts have the power to compel testimony and evidence in order to render justice in particular cases, then it must be at least as essential for the houses of Congress to have this power, whether they are pondering impeachment, judging the elections, returns, and qualifications of members, conducting oversight, appropriating, considering legislation, or carrying out any of their other functions. Although "the public" in Lord Hardwicke's famous maxim that "the public . . . has a right to every man's evidence"[249] is frequently used to refer to courts,[250] it applies at least as well to Congress. This was precisely the structural reasoning appealed to by Story and Kent. Nor is it only Congress that has recognized the necessity for a congressional contempt power: the other two branches have blessed the practice, in the form of judicial decisions beginning in the early nineteenth century and two OLC memos in the twentieth century.[251]

Moreover, it should be clear that defiance of a subpoena qualifies as contempt. If the contempt power is justified by the structural necessity of Congress's effective functioning, and if the effective functioning of Congress requires that Congress be able to acquire information, even from unwilling sources, then it is clear that refusing to turn over information subpoenaed by Congress is appropriately punishable as contempt. Although the analogy between contempt of Congress and contempt of court is not perfect, it is, of course, the case that an unexcused failure to comply with a subpoena is grounds for a finding of contempt of court.[252]

Executive-Branch Contempt of Congress

Is there any reason to think that the houses' general contempt power over outsiders must operate differently when the outsider in question happens to be a member of the executive branch? Is there any reason to think that contempt must operate differently when the defense to the contempt charge is executive privilege, as opposed to something else?[253] The answer to both of those questions is "no"—although, of course, the politics surrounding contempt by a member of the executive branch will inevitably be different from the politics surrounding other contempts.

Indeed, for most contempts, the houses of Congress will be satisfied with the statutory contempt mechanism dating back to 1857. After all, most congressional investigations do not implicate the executive branch at all, and, in the vast majority of situations, the president will not want to anger a house of Congress by refusing to prosecute someone for contempt. The clear exception, however, occurs when the contemnor is a member of the executive branch. In that situation, it is likely that the president will direct the U.S. attorney not to prosecute. If that were the end of the matter, then the contempt power would have lost all ability to constrain the executive.[254]

But, of course, that is not the end of the matter. As we've already seen with the Fry, Seward, and Marshall contempts, the houses continued to use their inherent contempt mechanism to go after executive officials, even after the statutory contempt mechanism was put into place. Indeed, the case for an inherent contempt authority is, if anything, stronger in the case of executive-branch officials than in that of ordinary citizens. As we have seen, parliaments used contempt and breach of privilege findings against monarchs to assert their authority as early as Elizabeth's reign. When Charles I tried to dispense with Parliament and rule by royal prerogative alone, it was, among other things, a claim of breach of privilege and contempt of Parliament that drove him from his throne. It was, in many cases, such claims that the American colonists used to keep their royal governors in line, and that the states used to cabin executive power in the early Republic. And we have seen Congress make use of breach of privilege and contempt proceedings against executive-branch officials— including presidents themselves—numerous times in our nation's history. Once again, we can see why such a power is so important to Congress's ability to assert itself in the public sphere: in order for legislative oversight to be effective in rooting out executive-branch malevolence and incompetence, Congress must have access to precisely that information that the executive does not wish to turn over—that is, it must have the power to hold executive-branch officials in contempt.

But in recent years, rather than using their power over the personnel of the executive branch (as they did when they eliminated Fry's office) or their sergeant-at-arms (as they did when they arrested Seward and Marshall) or their power of the purse, the houses have turned to the courts to enforce their inherent contempt citations. Once again, Watergate marked a significant turning point. In 1973, the Senate Select Committee on Presidential Campaign Activities demanded five tapes of White House conversations between President Nixon and his aide John Dean. When Nixon, asserting executive privilege, refused to turn the tapes over, the committee went to court, seeking a declaratory judgment that it had a right to the tapes and an injunction ordering Nixon to turn them over.[255] The district court dispensed with justiciability concerns in a brief paragraph, noting that the D.C. Circuit had recently held that an assertion of executive privilege against a grand jury subpoena was justiciable and insisting that the reasoning in that case "is equally applicable to the subpoena of a congressional committee."[256] The court then proceeded to balance the public interest in the president's privilege claim against the public interest in disclosure to the committee, and it determined that "[i]t ha[d] not been demonstrated to the Court's satisfaction" that the latter outweighed the former.[257] The court was especially concerned that disclosure of the tapes might harm "the integrity of the criminal trials arising out of Watergate."[258] Noting that the tapes were available to the grand juries investigating Watergate, the court concluded: "To suggest that at this juncture the public interest requires pretrial disclosure of these tapes either to the Committee or to the public is to imply that the judicial process has not been or will not be effective in this matter."[259] The court accordingly dismissed the complaint.

The D.C. Circuit, sitting en banc, affirmed.[260] It did not discuss the issue of justiciability at all. Instead, noting that presidential conversations are "presumptively privileged,"[261] it claimed that the committee had shown no interest sufficiently compelling so as to defeat the presumption.[262] The court reasoned that because the House Judiciary Committee, which was considering articles of impeachment, already had the tapes, the select committee's need for them was "merely cumulative."[263] And, the court suggested, any potential legislative use the committee had for the tapes was of a lesser weight than a grand jury's need for the tapes (which the court had previously upheld against an assertion of executive privilege).[264] Two months after the D.C. Circuit's opinion, the Supreme Court unanimously ordered the tapes to be turned over to the district court in which White House officials were being tried for their involvement in Watergate.[265] Within days of that decision, the House Judiciary Committee adopted articles of impeachment against Nixon,[266] and he resigned less than two weeks later.

The result of the suite of executive privilege cases arising out of Watergate, then, was an assertion by the courts that executive privilege claims are stronger against Congress than they are against criminal process. The consequences of this assertion of power by the judiciary are far reaching. As we have seen, institutions accrete power by demonstrating trustworthiness in the public sphere—and overcoming partisan divisions in pursuit of a broader public good is a potent means of demonstrating trustworthiness. As Robert Burt has noted, the conduct of the House of Representatives in the Nixon impeachment inquiry was meant to demonstrate such trustworthiness, in sharp contrast to Nixon's behavior: "In the conduct of its deliberations, the [House Judiciary] Committee worked assiduously to avoid the actuality or the appearance of partisan divisions. In its decision to subpoena the Nixon tapes on its own authority, without recourse to judicial enforcement proceedings, the Committee signified that it would not admit that the judiciary had become the sole institutional repository of impartial judgment."[267] But "[t]he Supreme Court's intervention in the *Nixon Tapes* case aborted this redemptive process,"[268] by hastily and immodestly swooping in and demanding that the tapes be turned over to the courts. Although Burt does not discuss it, the *Senate Select Committee* case makes his argument that much stronger—not only did the courts demand that the tapes be turned over to themselves, they denied that Congress had a right to them as well. In insisting that they, and only they, could stand up to Nixon, the courts reinforced the notion that Congress was impotent at best, corrupt at worst—that, in Gerald Gunther's words, "somehow it is the Court's special obligation to save the nation in episodes of constitutional crisis."[269] The courts thus made themselves the heroes of the Watergate story, and in the process they sent the message that Congress was not up to the task. The more frequently such messages are absorbed by the public, of course, the lower Congress's standing in the public sphere falls, and the less able it is to assert a strong institutional role in the future.

Of course, most contempt disputes never make it as far as any sort of formal sanction: since the mid-1970s, committees or subcommittees of Congress have voted to hold a number of cabinet officers and other high-ranking executive-branch officials in contempt, and those disputes have generally ended in disclosure of the requested information before any floor votes on the contempt citation were held.[270] Some of these cases did, however, involve substantial confrontation before a settlement was reached. Consider the contempt proceedings against Anne Gorsuch, Reagan's EPA administrator.[271] In 1982, the House Public Works Committee's Subcommittee on Investigations and Oversight served Gorsuch with a subpoena seeking a number of documents related to the EPA's treatment of various Superfund sites.[272] On President Reagan's instructions, Gorsuch withheld certain documents related to ongoing enforcement actions, asserting that they were privileged.[273] The committee referred the matter to the full House, which cited Gorsuch for contempt on December 16, 1982. That same day, Gorsuch brought an action seeking a declaratory judgment that she had acted lawfully in withholding the documents.[274] The next day, the Speaker certified the matter to the U.S. attorney for prosecution under the 1857 criminal contempt statute; the U.S. attorney refused to prosecute so long as the civil suit was pending.[275]

The district court exercised its discretion under the Declaratory Judgment Act not to hear the case. Arguing that "judicial intervention should be delayed until all possibilities for settlement have been exhausted," the court found that there was still an opportunity for the parties to compromise.[276] Shortly thereafter, the parties did just that: they reached an agreement under which the House withdrew the contempt citation and the EPA granted the subcommittee limited access to the documents.[277] Thereafter, the U.S. attorney presented the contempt citation to a grand jury, which unanimously returned a no bill.[278] Gorsuch resigned a little more than a month after the district court's decision not to hear the civil case, before the agreement with the subcommittee was reached.[279]

The Gorsuch controversy also occasioned the executive branch's most extensive meditations on the interplay between congressional contempt and executive privilege, in the form of two OLC memos. A 1984 memo written by Theodore Olson concluded both that the executive branch could properly exercise its discretion not to prosecute under the criminal contempt statute and that the criminal contempt statute did not apply at all to executive-branch officials asserting executive privilege.[280] In support of this latter proposition, the memo offered some brief snippets of evidence from the legislative history of the criminal contempt statute,[281] but it placed primary emphasis on a separation-of-powers argument: "[I]f executive officials were subject to prosecution for criminal contempt whenever they carried out the President's claim of executive privilege, it would significantly burden and immeasurably impair the President's ability to fulfill his constitutional duties."[282] This is because it would put the president in the position of either placing one of his subordinates at risk of going to prison or surrendering his ability to make executive privilege arguments, even when he thought they were necessary to the performance of his constitutional role.[283] Olson instead argued that Congress should file civil suits to enforce its subpoenas.[284] He also insisted that Congress "has never arrested an executive official for contempt of Congress for failing to produce subpoenaed documents."[285] As we have seen, this is incorrect—the House arrested George Seward for precisely that reason. A 1986 OLC memo, written by Charles Cooper, concurred that the criminal contempt statute was inapplicable, but it went further in asserting that Congress's inherent contempt power might be inapplicable against an executive-branch official as well.[286] Aside from general claims about the unlikeliness of a house of Congress sending its sergeant-at-arms to arrest an executive-branch official and the Supreme Court's recent skepticism about congressional power in other contexts, the memo offers very little reasoning for this point. According to the Cooper memo, then, Congress's *only* remedy for contempt by a member of the executive branch is a civil suit.[287]

The houses of Congress themselves have appeared to accept that conclusion in the two most recent executive-branch contempt of Congress cases, one from the George W. Bush administration and one from the Obama administration. After the Bush administration's politically motivated dismissal of a number of U.S. attorneys in 2006, the Democrat-controlled House and Senate Judiciary Committees sought testimony and documents from various executive-branch officials.[288] In March 2007, White House Counsel Fred Fielding told the Senate Judiciary Committee that the White House would allow the Judiciary Committees to conduct private interviews with several White House officials, so long as the interviews were conducted behind closed doors, with no transcript taken, and with no oath having been administered; the committees would also have to agree not to subpoena those officials in the future. The White House also offered to turn over certain communications regarding the dismissals, but not any communications between White House officials.[289] The committees rejected the offer, and two days later the House Judiciary Committee voted to authorize subpoenas for the testimony and documents. Although the subpoenas were authorized, the committee did not vote to issue them, in the hopes that the matter would be resolved through further negotiation with the White House.[290]

On June 13, 2007, after almost three months of fruitless discussions, the House Judiciary Committee issued two subpoenas: one to former White House counsel Harriet Miers, directing her to testify and produce certain documents, and the other to White House chief of staff Joshua Bolten, directing him to produce documents.[291] (The Senate committee on the same day subpoenaed former White House political director Sara Taylor.)[292] President Bush asserted executive privilege and informed the committees that the executive branch would neither produce the requested documents nor make the officials available to testify.[293]

When Miers and Bolten failed to respond to the subpoenas, the House Judiciary Committee adopted a resolution recommending that they be cited for contempt of Congress.[294] After several more months of failed attempts at a negotiated settlement, the House voted to hold them in contempt on February 14, 2008.[295] The House also adopted two resolutions: one provided for the Speaker to certify the Judiciary Committee's report to the U.S. attorney for the District of Columbia "to the end that [Miers and Bolten] be proceeded against in the manner and form provided by law,"[296] while the other authorized the chairman of the Judiciary Committee to file suit in federal court, seeking "declaratory judgments affirming the duty of any individual to comply with any subpoena . . . issued to such individual by the Committee as part of its investigation into the firing of certain United States Attorneys and related matters, and to seek appropriate ancillary relief, including injunctive relief."[297] Two weeks later, Speaker Nancy Pelosi certified the contempt report to Jeffrey Taylor, the U.S. attorney for the District of Columbia, and she called on Attorney General Michael Mukasey to ensure that Taylor filed criminal contempt charges against Miers and Bolten.[298] The next day, Mukasey replied that because (in the Justice Department's view) Bolten and Miers had properly invoked executive privilege in refusing to comply with the subpoenas, "noncompliance by Mr. Bolten and Ms. Miers with the Judiciary Committee subpoenas did not constitute a crime, and therefore the Department will not bring the congressional contempt citations before a grand jury or take any other action to prosecute Mr. Bolten or Ms. Miers."[299]

The Judiciary Committee then filed suit in federal court, seeking a declaratory judgment that Miers and Bolten were in contempt and an injunction ordering them to comply with the congressional subpoenas.[300] On the question of whether the case should be in the hands of the judiciary at all, Judge John Bates found the case resolvable for two reasons: "(1) in essence, this lawsuit merely seeks enforcement of a subpoena, which is a routine and quintessential judicial task; and (2) the Supreme Court has held that the judiciary is the final arbiter of executive privilege, and the grounds asserted for the Executive's refusal to comply with the subpoena are ultimately rooted in executive privilege."[301] For this second point, the court relied on the Supreme Court's decision in the *Nixon Tapes Case*, the D.C. Circuit's opinion in *Senate Select Committee v. Nixon*, and the views of the executive branch, as expressed in the two OLC memos from the 1980s.[302]

Bates also suggested that Congress's own enforcement powers were not an adequate substitute for judicial resolution, because

> imprisoning current (and even former) senior presidential advisors and prosecuting them before the House would only exacerbate the acrimony between the two branches and would present a grave risk of precipitating a constitutional crisis. Indeed, one can easily imagine a stand-off between the Sergeant-at-Arms and executive branch law enforcement officials concerning taking Mr. Bolten into custody and detaining him. Such unseemly, provocative clashes should be avoided, and there is no need to run the risk of such mischief when a civil action can resolve the same issues in an orderly fashion. [And] even if the Committee did exercise inherent contempt, the disputed issue would in all likelihood end up before this Court, just by a different vehicle—a writ of habeas corpus brought by Ms. Miers and Mr. Bolten. In either event there would be judicial resolution of the underlying issue.[303]

Moreover, Bates noted that negotiations between the branches had reached a "stalemate" and were therefore unlikely to be resolved by the usual process of interbranch "accommodation and negotiation."[304]

Finally, Bates rejected Miers and Bolten's claim that the court should exercise its equitable discretion to dismiss the suit.[305] He asserted that "the judiciary is the ultimate arbiter of claims of executive privilege," and therefore that the political branches take "the availability of ultimate judicial intervention in exactly this sort of controversy" as a background assumption.[306] (Indeed, the court referred to itself as the "ultimate arbiter" of executive privilege claims five times over the course of the opinion.)[307] In short, the court proclaimed, "only judicial intervention can prevent a stalemate between the other two branches that could result in a particular paralysis of government operations."[308] In the few remaining pages of his opinion, Bates concluded that neither Miers nor Bolten was protected by absolute executive privilege, but that both could still make specific claims of privilege against specific demands by the committee.[309]

Miers and Bolten appealed, but the D.C. Circuit never reached the merits.[310] On March 4, 2009—a month and a half into the Obama administration and two months into the 111th Congress—an agreement was reached under which Miers (and Karl Rove) would testify under oath in closed proceedings and a number of documents would be turned over to the committee.[311] After Miers and Rove did so, the D.C. Circuit dismissed the case.[312]

A similar incident occurred in the Obama administration, with the political parties reversed (that is, a Democrat in the White House and Republicans controlling the House of Representatives). In 2009, the Bureau of Alcohol, Tobacco, Firearms and Explosives began a "gunwalking" operation along the Mexican border (an operation in which illegal firearms were allowed to "walk" across the border, in the hopes of tracing them to their end purchasers), codenamed "Operation Fast and Furious."[313] At least some of the weapons eluded detection once in Mexico and were used to commit serious crimes, including the murder of a U.S. Border Patrol agent. In October 2011, the Republican-controlled House Oversight and Government Reform Committee subpoenaed a number of internal Justice Department documents related to the operation; the Department turned over some of the documents while withholding others, with President Obama claiming that the withheld documents were covered by executive privilege. In June 2012, the committee recommended that Attorney General Eric Holder be held in contempt for refusing to turn the documents over, and the House did so that same month.[314] The House again both certified the matter to the U.S. attorney for the District of Columbia and authorized the filing of a civil suit.[315] A poll taken in the immediate aftermath of the contempt vote suggests that the House Republicans were successfully making their case to the public: Holder's unfavorable ratings were up; people approved of the contempt citation by a margin of 53 percent to 33 percent; and 69 percent of respondents thought the administration should drop all claims of privilege and answer the committee's questions. This was all despite the fact that 61 percent of respondents thought the investigation was motivated by congressional Republicans' desire to gain a political advantage, rather than by genuine policy concerns.[316]

As in the *Miers* case, the Justice Department declined to prosecute,[317] and again the House filed suit. In September 2013, the district court denied Holder's motion to dismiss.[318] In September 2014—the same month that Holder announced that he was stepping down as attorney general—the two sides were still fighting over how much information the Justice Department had to provide to the court about each item over which it was claiming privilege, so that the district judge could adjudicate each individual privilege claim.[319] The next month, asserting that Holder had not complied with the judge's orders to produce materials, the House asked that he be held in contempt of court and face monetary fines and possible incarceration.[320] The court denied that motion but ordered Holder to deliver documents over which the Department of Justice did not assert privilege.[321] Loretta Lynch took over from Holder as attorney general in April 2015, but the district court case continued to chug along.[322] Finally, in January 2016, Judge Amy Berman Jackson held that the administration had to turn over most of the records sought by the committee. (Among other factors, Jackson noted that a public report by the Department of Justice inspector general had already "described in detail" the documents responsive to the committee's subpoena.)[323] In April 2016, as both parties narrowed in on their nominees for that year's election to succeed Obama, the administration released the records ordered by Jackson. The committee indicated that it still intended to appeal the portions of Jackson's opinion that allowed the administration to withhold some of the subpoenaed records; as this book goes to press, that appeal is ongoing, with a briefing schedule that extends to the day before the 2017 presidential inauguration.[324]

While the *Holder* case was pending, in May 2014 the House also held former Internal Revenue Service official Lois Lerner in contempt for refusing to answer questions about whether her office improperly targeted conservative tax-exempt groups for higher levels of scrutiny, and it again certified the case to the U.S. attorney.[325] Lerner asserted her Fifth Amendment privilege against compelled self-incrimination.[326] Again, the government declined to prosecute. The House, however, did use its power of the purse: as noted in chapter 3, the IRS budget was chopped in both 2014 and 2015, which was intended to send a message of Republican displeasure over the perceived targeting.[327]

Clearly, the houses of Congress have, in recent years, reinvigorated the contempt power as a tool of interbranch conflict. More than the holding of additional hearings or a press conference, a formal finding of contempt increases the salience of a particular conflict. If the polling in the aftermath of the Holder contempt citation is any indication, it can also move public opinion. The mere finding of contempt can be an important political weapon—this likely explains why the Senate and House used the forceful language of breach of privilege against Presidents Jackson and Tyler, respectively.

But aside from publicity, what other options are available to a congressional house that wishes to enforce a contempt citation against an executive-branch official? We have already seen that criminal proceedings are unlikely to be available. Congress then faces the question of whether to file a civil suit or use some other means of enforcement. The question is one of institutional power: executive-branch officials are likely to make a defense to contempt charges— for example, that their refusal to produce documents was justified because it was pursuant to a proper invocation of executive privilege. Which enforcement route Congress chooses will determine who decides whether the invocation of executive privilege was proper: the house of Congress or the courts.

Until the late twentieth century, the legislative house was generally understood to be the final judge of legislative contempts. Certainly neither the houses of Parliament nor the British monarchs ever considered submitting their disputes to the courts. The same was true of the colonial and early state legislatures, and, indeed, of the houses of Congress in their disputes with Jackson, Tyler, Fry, and Seward. The reason is both very simple and very important: these were disputes over the relative balance of executive and legislative power. Each side was contending for more power vis-à-vis the other. To invoke the aid of a third party is to admit weakness—to admit in the public sphere that one's own authority is insufficient to get what one wants. This is why it is so important to view the disputes between executive authority and the legislative contempt power in their broader historical and political context: these disputes are, at their heart, about the basic contours of the constitutional division of powers.

When Elizabeth and James I ordered Parliament not to discuss certain topics, they were asserting that there were areas of national policy in which Parliament could have no say. In asserting a privilege of unfettered speech and debate— and then asserting that the monarch had breached that privilege—Parliament reasserted its institutional authority. When Charles I attempted to collect taxes

despite Parliament's refusal to grant them to him, when he attempted to withhold royal records and officials from Parliament, when he refused to justify his
imprisonment of Arundel, when he seized John Rolle's goods and attempted to
extort a grant of supply in exchange for their return, and when, after governing
without Parliament for more than a decade, he accused members of treason and
brought an armed guard into the House of Commons to arrest them, he was
asserting in the most strident terms an absolutist constitutional vision. When
the houses reacted against this vision with repeated findings that he had
breached privilege, when they refused to proceed to other business until he
redressed their grievances, when they authorized armed resistance to breaches
of privilege, and when ultimately they rebelled, deposed, tried, and executed
Charles, the houses insisted upon a different understanding of the constitutional
division of powers. And this insistence came in the language of breach of privilege and contempt of Parliament.

These clashes, of course, were not limited to the Old World. When the colonial legislatures wanted to ensure that governors and other officials appointed
in London paid attention to the local concerns that the legislatures represented,
they were not shy about using their contempt powers. And they had a number
of means at their disposal for enforcing their contempt findings, ranging from
censure to arrest to the withholding of salary. Recognizing the importance of
this tool, a number of state constitutions written in the years between independence and the drafting of the federal Constitution explicitly provided the legislature with the power to hold executive officials in contempt. But even in those
states whose constitutions did not explicitly provide for such a power, the legislature understood the power to exist, and made use of it.

And, finally, we have seen the houses of Congress make use of the contempt
power in the context of disputes with the executive branch. The Senate used it
in the context of a dispute with Andrew Jackson, and the House used it in the
context of disputes with John Tyler, James Fry, George Seward, and H. Snowden
Marshall. Until Watergate, the courts never inquired into a contempt judgment
against an executive-branch official that the house of Congress was jurisdictionally competent to make.

It is true that the Supreme Court held that the House had improperly imprisoned Marshall.[328] But that is best understood as a ruling on the scope of the
House's *jurisdiction* rather than a ruling on the *merits*. That is, the House could
punish Marshall for obstructing its proceedings, and the Court never suggested

that it would review a determination by the House that someone had, in fact, obstructed its proceedings. But the House did not purport to make that claim; rather, it punished Marshall for a mere dignitary offense, and that, the Court said, was outside of the House's power to punish for contempt. (In this regard, *Marshall* may be thought of as analogous to *Powell v. McCormack*, in which the Court held that the House could not add qualifications for a member of Congress[329] but never suggested that it would review a determination by the House on the merits—for example, a determination that a claimant was, in fact, under twenty-five years of age.)[330]

Indeed, it was not until Watergate that the courts purported to determine the merits of a contempt claim against an executive-branch official,[331] and it is probably not a coincidence that Watergate was also the first time that a house of Congress had voluntarily gone to court, seeking enforcement of a subpoena against an executive official.[332] Moreover, the Watergate cases may be read as a cautionary tale for those inclined to press claims of congressional power through the judiciary. Judges are (unsurprisingly) inclined to take a court-centric view of the world. Thus, although they were happy to order Nixon to turn the tapes over to the courts,[333] they found that congressional committees had a lesser interest in the tapes, an interest that was outweighed by the president's privilege claims.[334] Both the district court and the court of appeals thought that Congress had less need for the tapes than the courts did,[335] and the district court even worried that turning the tapes over to Congress might harm ongoing grand jury investigations[336]—the implication being that the congressional committee's duties were of a lesser weight than the grand jury's. The court of appeals suggested that its understanding of congressional procedure was superior to that of the committee, dismissing the committee's need for the tapes as "merely cumulative," since another congressional committee already had the tapes.[337] The court of appeals did not consider the issue of justiciability at all, and the district court simply held that, because a claim of executive privilege in resistance to a grand jury subpoena is justiciable, so must be a claim of executive privilege in resistance to a congressional subpoena.[338] But this ignores a key distinction: in holding that an executive privilege claim in defiance of a grand jury subpoena is justiciable, a court is essentially saying, "We, the branch that issued the subpoena, will not give you, the executive branch, carte blanche to defy it, but we will hear you out as to your reasons for defying it." The analogue in the case of a congressional subpoena would be a willingness *on the part of the congressional committee* to hear out the executive's privilege claim. The judges, however, took the opportunity presented by Watergate to press their own branch's claim to enhanced power in the public sphere by implicitly asserting that (only) their own processes were dignified and apolitical. By going to the courts in the first place, the Senate committee invited this increase in judicial power at its own expense.[339]

Finally, it must be noted that courts tend to move at a pace that is poorly suited to Congress's need for timely information: even if, at the end of the day, the courts order an executive-branch official to turn over information to Congress, it will frequently come too late for Congress's purposes.[340] In this regard, consider the contempt proceedings against Miers and Bolten: although a settlement was eventually reached, the Congress that originally issued the subpoenas had ended, as had the administration that the subpoenas were intended to help Congress oversee. To the extent that enforcement of congressional subpoenas is left to the courts, future administrations now know that they can delay compliance for years.[341] Holder, too, successfully ran out the clock—although he served for almost two and a half years after the House held him in contempt, judicial proceedings were still ongoing when he left office. Indeed, despite the fact that the subpoenas were issued in the middle of Obama's first term, the administration did not release (most of) the documents the committee sought until near the end of his second.

What subpoena-enforcement options does Congress have, then, that might better serve its purposes? First, and most crudely, each house has a sergeant-at-arms, and the Capitol building has its own jail. The sergeant can be sent to arrest contemnors and, if necessary, hold them in his custody until either their contempt is purged or the congressional session ends. Indeed, we have seen that a house of Congress has twice arrested and held executive-branch officials (Seward and Marshall), even if neither of them ultimately wound up being jailed.[342] Undoubtedly, the contemnor would then seek habeas relief from a court, but here the congressional house would come before the court, not as a supplicant, but as a powerful institution already enforcing its own prerogatives using its own tools. From this position, the house could compellingly argue that the court, like the *Marshall* and *Powell* courts, should limit its inquiry to the question of whether the house was jurisdictionally competent to hold the contemnor—that is, whether she was, in fact, accused of something that properly qualifies as a contempt of Congress. Given that defiance of a congressional subpoena has long been understood as falling within Congress's contempt power, the court would have a powerful reason not to interfere.

As we saw in Holder's case, the mere finding of contempt can have significant consequences for an actor's standing in the public sphere, and surely legislative houses would not have bothered with findings of breach or contempt against everyone from Elizabeth I to Andrew Jackson if they did not think those findings were of some consequence. But a house seeking some medicine stronger than mere condemnation but weaker than sending its sergeant out trolling the streets still has a number of options. It can use its personnel power by refusing to confirm administration nominees, impeaching contumacious officeholders, or eliminating their offices entirely. Alternatively, it can turn to its power of the purse, zeroing out officials' salaries or reducing the funding of the agencies in which they work. Finally, Congress can, like the House of Lords during the Arundel controversy, simply refuse to turn to matters that the president cares about until its concerns are addressed. Importantly, none of these options requires cooperation from another branch. None of them constitutes a concession by Congress that it is unable to carry out its constitutional role without help.

In the *Miers* case, Judge Bates was concerned about the possibility of "a stand-off between the Sergeant-at-Arms and executive branch law enforcement officials concerning taking Mr. Bolten into custody and detaining him. Such unseemly, provocative clashes should be avoided, and there is no need to run the risk of such mischief when a civil action can resolve the same issues in an orderly fashion."[343] Note the unstated premise here: the executive might resist the House sergeant, but it would never dare resist a court order. Why risk political "mischief" when everything can be handled in a nice, neat, orderly, "civil," judicial manner? Bates was apparently unaware that the executive branch sometimes disobeys even the judiciary.[344] Presumably such disobedience would be met with a finding of contempt of court—followed, perhaps, by a "stand-off between [judicial marshals] and executive branch law enforcement officials." Indeed, this dynamic played out in the *Holder* case, with the House asking the court to find Holder in contempt of court for his conduct during the adjudication of the contempt of Congress finding. Even if, as an empirical matter, the executive branch is more likely to obey a court order than a congressional one, it is a mistake to treat this fact as somehow exogenous to the branches' behavior. Judges have an institutional interest in presenting courts as the only institutions that make reasoned, principled judgments; to the extent that self-presentation is accepted, it stands to reason that people will come to trust the courts more than the other branches. In going to the courts as supplicants in contempt cases, the houses of Congress thus simultaneously diminish their own standing in the public sphere and enhance the courts' standing.

Judicial Contempt of Congress?

In 2011, former House Speaker Newt Gingrich (then running for the Republican presidential nomination) made waves when he suggested that judges who issued "radical" opinions could be subpoenaed by a house of Congress to explain themselves and could be arrested for contempt if they refused to comply.[345] The backlash against Gingrich was intense, with *Slate* legal columnist Dahlia Lithwick declaring herself unable to imagine "a dumber idea" and "tempted to open up a can of lofty rhetorical whoopass to explain" why Gingrich's comments "offend[] the basical constitutional principles of separation of powers, and judicial independence."[346]

But were the former Speaker's comments really so far off the mark? Certainly there are precedents. In 1621, the House of Commons passed a bill aiming to protect subjects against false imprisonment.[347] The bill provided, inter alia, that any judge who wrongfully committed a subject to prison would be brought before Parliament and censured.[348] Edward Coke—often regarded as the great champion of judicial independence, due to his earlier conflicts with James I (discussed in the previous chapter)—served on the committee that reported out the bill.[349] Indeed, Coke's only objection to the bill seems to have been that it went too far in restricting the authority of the Privy Council to imprison for reasons of state.[350] The bill was ultimately a victim of the standoff between James and Parliament: the House of Commons refused to proceed with any business—including the sending of already passed bills to the Lords—in protest against James's insistence that it had no right to discuss foreign policy. As we have already seen, James soon dissolved Parliament in a rage, tore up its *Journal*, and shipped a number of parliamentarians, including Coke, off to Ireland.

But this was not the only time that the House of Commons went after judges. In 1641, as we shall see in the next chapter, the Long Parliament declared judges of the King's Bench guilty of a breach of privilege for convicting and imprisoning John Eliot and his colleagues who had forced the Speaker to keep the House in session in 1629. Indeed, the House of Commons resolved that the judges owed reparations to the parliamentarians they had convicted.[351] In 1682, after the dissolution of the last Parliament of Charles II, John Topham, the sergeant of the House of Commons, was sued in the King's Bench for taking into custody several people that the House had ordered him to arrest. Topham argued that his actions by order of the House were not examinable in the common-law courts; the judges disagreed and ruled against him.[352] As we have already seen, the House met only very briefly during James II's reign, but Topham was patient and brought the matter up when Parliament convened in 1689 after the Glorious Revolution. The House resolved that the judgments against Topham were a breach of parliamentary privilege, and they summoned two of the judges who had sat on the case, Francis Pemberton and Thomas Jones.[353] Both judges insisted that they did not remember the case, but both also gave lengthy speeches attempting to justify their ruling.[354] The House was unconvinced: it ordered them taken into custody, where they were held until the next prorogation of Parliament—a little over three months.[355] Indeed, as late as the 1830s, Parliament arrested for contempt sheriffs who were carrying out court orders and threatened to arrest the judges who issued those orders.[356] And we have seen that royal judges were among those held in contempt by colonial legislatures.

Nor is subpoenaing a sitting judge unknown under the federal Constitution. In 1949, Justices Frankfurter and Reed were subpoenaed (and testified) as character witnesses for Alger Hiss in his first perjury trial.[357] That was, of course, a judicial subpoena, but there is no immediately obvious reason why a congressional subpoena should be treated differently. In 1953, the House Un-American Activities Committee subpoenaed Justice Tom Clark to testify about decisions he had made as attorney general. The committee simultaneously subpoenaed former president Truman, which was immediately and widely recognized as a political blunder.[358] Both Truman and Clark refused to testify (on similar grounds of executive and judicial independence from Congress), although Clark announced that he would answer written questions; in the resulting political firestorm, the committee declined to put questions to him or to proceed against either him or Truman.[359]

Is there any reason to think that it would be categorically inappropriate today to bring judges before congressional committees? As this book has emphasized from the outset, judges *are* political actors, although they of course inhabit political roles different from, say, those of executive-branch officials. These different roles may make it politically dicey for a house of Congress to subpoena them—but this is not categorically different from any other subpoena. After all, HUAC lost the political fight over subpoenaing Truman, and the following year, Joseph McCarthy's Senate Permanent Subcommittee on Investigations was to lose the political fight arising out of the Army-McCarthy hearings (an incident to which we return in chapter 7). This does not make subpoenas categorically inappropriate, of course; it simply means that the power must be exercised judiciously. Gingrich himself recognized this: in the very interview that drew such critical reactions, he insisted that the congressional response to a judicial decision should "depend[] on the severity of the case. I'm not suggesting that the Congress and the president review every decision."[360] Confronting judges about their rulings is a highly contentious step.

But surely this does not mean that it is never permissible. Consider the Fifth Circuit panel, discussed in the prelude to part I, that ordered the Obama administration to file a letter on the constitutional status of judicial review. This homework assignment for the attorney general was clearly not meant to aid the panel in its consideration of the case before it; it was a bit of political theater by an oppositional panel of judges, meant to make the news. In such a context, why should the other two branches be forbidden to use their tools to fight back? Judges have no explicit protection from being questioned in Congress—in contrast to members of Congress, who are, as we shall see in the next chapter, privileged against being questioned "in any other Place" for their official activity[361]—so it is only by inducing an overriding, free-standing constitutional principle of judicial independence that one could argue that they are categorically immune from congressional subpoena. But why should we make such an inductive step for judges, *especially* given the other, explicit independence-protecting measures? Gingrich's critics have provided no convincing answer.

Congressional hearings and other mechanisms of gathering and disseminating information serve at least two key functions. First, for Congress to carry out its manifold functions intelligently and effectively, it needs to base its behavior on accurate information. Second, and equally important, the mechanisms of gathering and releasing information—hearings, reports, and so on—are themselves important tools for congressional interactions in the public sphere. The aggressive questioning of an official, a nominee, or a private citizen, or the releasing of a critical (or supportive) report are mechanisms by which the congressional houses can make the public case for their own trustworthiness, and therefore for augmenting their own power.

Most of the time, the information that Congress seeks for either of these functions is voluntarily provided. When it is not, the houses' contempt powers come into play. When the alleged contemnor is a private party, the houses can generally count on the aid of the other branches. But when the alleged contemnor is a part of one of the other branches, then the houses must turn to their inherent contempt authority. For centuries, the inherent contempt power has served Anglo-American legislatures well in their clashes with executive (and, sometimes, judicial) authorities. Even in recent years, we have seen evidence of the efficacy of the houses' inherent contempt powers, as when the finding of contempt damaged Eric Holder's public standing or when the contempt finding against Lois Lerner played into reductions of the IRS's budget. But the post-Watergate era has also seen a judicial turn in contempt enforcements, and it is a contention of this chapter that this turn has tended to benefit the other two branches at Congress's expense. Congress has its own enforcement powers—including the authority to arrest, but also including mechanisms ranging from public censure to defunding to refusing to confirm nominees or pass legislation. For contempt to be a truly effective tool in interbranch conflicts, Congress should strongly consider leaning more heavily on its own enforcement mechanisms.

PART THREE

CONGRESSIONAL SOFT POWERS

6

The Freedom of Speech or Debate

THE ABILITY OF MEMBERS OF CONGRESS TO ENGAGE discursively in the public sphere would be seriously hampered, of course, if they could be held liable or punished elsewhere for the performance of their congressional duties. More dangerously, their ability to confront the other branches publicly would be significantly reduced if they could be haled before or punished by those branches. Protecting against such danger is the Constitution's Speech or Debate Clause, and this chapter is dedicated to an examination of that protection and a consideration of how its judicious use can enhance congressional power.

Historical Development

As with several of the other legislative powers discussed thus far, the protection of legislative speech begins in earnest in the mid-Tudor era. But, as with those other powers, there are isolated earlier incidents to which later parliamentarians looked as precedents. From at least the mid-fourteenth century, the Speaker prayed at the opening of each new Parliament that if he or the House offended the king, he or it would be forgiven, as no offense would be intended.[1] Clearly, this is not a full-throated demand for liberty of speech, but equally clearly, it is an early indication that the House was cognizant of both its potential to offend and the importance of wide-ranging discussion. In 1397, Thomas Haxey tested the limits of royal tolerance when he authored a bill introduced in the House of Commons condemning the extravagance of Richard II's household. At Richard's insistence, the House of Lords declared Haxey a traitor and condemned him to death, although the sentence was not carried out. Two years later, after Henry IV had deposed Richard, both Haxey and the House of Commons petitioned the new king to reverse the judgment as a violation of the traditional liberties of the Commons. Henry granted the request.[2] More importantly, the Commons that same year sought to ensure that accounts of their debates would be kept from the king. Noting that "it might happen that one of their companions, to please the king and to advance himself," would report on their internal deliberations, the House prayed that the king "should not receive any such person wishing to tell him of such matters, nor listen to him, nor give him any faith or credence in this matter." Henry, after expressing his desire that the House "should take deliberation and advice in order to debate and treat of all their business amongst themselves, in order to reach a better outcome and conclusion, in their opinion, for the good and honour of the king and all his realm," assented to their request.[3]

The king's promise not to pay attention to unauthorized accounts of parliamentary proceedings was far more important than the reversal of Haxey's conviction. J. E. Neale has argued that the *Haxey* case was not about the free-speech privilege at all but rather was an instance of parliamentary objection to Richard II's innovations in treason law and procedure.[4] And, indeed, it is important to note that parliamentary privilege was assuredly not a defense to treason, as the bishop of Carlisle discovered when he was imprisoned in 1399 for insisting in open Parliament that Richard, not Henry, was the rightful king.[5] But if word of such comments never reached the king, then freedom of speech would be protected as a practical, even if not as a theoretical, matter.

In 1451, Thomas Young, a member for Bristol, proposed in open Parliament that Richard, Duke of York, should be declared heir to the throne. For his meddling, he was thrown into the Tower of London. By 1455, Richard was Protector (Henry VI having suffered a mental breakdown), and Young prayed for redress, on the grounds that his imprisonment had violated the "olde liberte and fredom of the Comyns of this Lande . . . enjoyed . . . fro the tyme that no mynde is" that members of Parliament "ought to have theire fredom to speke and sey in the Hous of their assemble, as to theym is thought convenyent or resonable, withoute eny maner chalange, charge or punycion therefore to be leyde to theym in eny wyse."[6] He also complained that the reports that had reached the king of his 1451 speech were "untrewe sinistre reportes."[7] The king—or, rather, York, in the king's name—ordered the Lords to compensate Young, at their discretion.[8] As Neale has noted, we should be careful not to overread this incident: the fact that Richard compensated his political ally at the dawn of the Wars of the Roses does not indicate widespread acceptance of the broader free-speech principle that Young espoused.[9] Still, the fact that a political operator like Young thought that he could plausibly make such an argument suggests that a recognition of parliamentary free speech was at least latent.[10]

This principle became less latent as a result of the 1512 controversy over Richard Strode. Strode represented a tin-mining borough in southwestern Devon, and he introduced several bills to regulate the tin industry in that region. For his temerity, a fellow tinner brought suit against him in the stannary courts—long-standing courts in Devon and Cornwall with jurisdiction over tin miners in all but the most serious matters[11]—which fined Strode £160 and imprisoned him.[12] When Parliament reconvened shortly thereafter, it issued both a writ of habeas corpus, ordering Strode to be delivered to Parliament, and a writ of supersedeas, taking jurisdiction of the case itself and thereby relieving the stannary courts of jurisdiction.[13] If that were the end of Strode's case, then it would be plausible to conclude, with Neale, that this was a jurisdictional fight and nothing more.[14] But it was not the end of the case: Strode immediately introduced, and Parliament passed, what came to be known as Strode's Act. The act not only annulled the stannary courts' judgment against Strode, it also went on to speak in more general language, announcing that "all suits, accusements, condemnations, executions, fines, amerciaments, punishments, corrections, grants, charges, and impositions, put or had, or hereafter to be put or had unto or upon the said *Richard*, and to every other of the person or persons afore specified, that now be of this present parliament, or that of any parliament hereafter shall be, for any bill, speaking, reasoning, or declaring of any matter or matters, concerning the parliament to be communed and treated of, be utterly void and of none effect."[15] The act also provided a cause of action against anyone who "vexed or troubled" a member in one of the prohibited manners.[16]

By the middle of the sixteenth century, moreover, the form of the Speaker's petition to the monarch at the beginning of a new Parliament had changed. Instead of begging forgiveness for any offense that their words might cause, as Speakers had since the mid-fourteenth century, they began to pray for liberty of speech.[17] The change is significant: whereas the older formulation presupposed a transgression and sought to be spared punishment, the newer one sought assurances that parliamentary speech would not be considered a transgression at all. Thus, beginning in the mid-Tudor period,[18] there was a turn toward

conceptualizing free speech as a right of parliamentarians, rather than as something emerging from royal neglect or forbearance.

This expanding conception of parliamentary free speech was tested
throughout Elizabeth's reign, especially by a parliamentarian named Peter
Wentworth. Elizabeth's great conflicts with her Parliaments centered around
the related issues of succession and religion, both of which the queen believed
lay entirely within her royal prerogative. The previous chapter discussed
Elizabeth's early conflicts with Paul Wentworth (Peter's brother) in 1566 over
the House's right to discuss the issue of succession and with William Strickland
in 1571 over the House's right to debate religious matters. In each of those
cases, the queen yielded to parliamentary claims that she had breached their
privilege by interfering with their liberty of speech. In 1576, however, the more
bombastic Wentworth, Peter, arrived on the scene. Concerned that members
were being silenced on crucial matters, he gave a blistering defense of free
speech, declaring that "there is nothing so necessary for the preservation of the
Prince and State as free Speech, and without it is a scorn and mockery to call it
a Parliament House, for in truth it is none, but a very School of Flattery and
Dissimulation, and so a fit place to serve the Devil and his Angels in, and not to
glorify God and benefit the Common-Wealth."[19] Had that been the extent of his
remarks, he might have escaped punishment, but he then went on to criticize the
bishops and the queen herself, whom he declared had "committed great fault."[20]
The House, "out of a reverent regard of her Majesty's Honour," stopped his
speech and arrested him.[21]

The House appointed a committee, which included all the Privy Councillors
who sat in the House, to question Wentworth. When their questions were put to
him, Wentworth replied: "If your Honours ask me as Councellors to her Majesty,
you shall pardon me; I will make you no Answer: I will do no such injury to the
place from whence I came; for I am now no private Person, I am a publick, and
a Councellor to the whole State in that place where it is lawful for me to speak
my mind freely, and not for you as Councellors to call me to account for any
thing I do speak in the House; and therefore if you ask me as Councellors to her
Majesty, you shall pardon me, I will make no Answer; but if you ask me as
Committees from the House, I will make you the best Answer I can."[22] The
questioners assured him that they asked as a committee of the House, and he
replied accordingly.[23] How satisfying those answers were, however, can be
grasped from the comment of one member of the committee: "Mr. *Wentworth*

will never acknowledge himself to make a fault, nor say that he is sorry for any thing that he doth speak, you shall hear none of these things come out of his mouth."[24] Wentworth remained in the Tower for more than a month, until the queen told the House that she was "graciously pleased to remit her just occasioned displeasure for the said offence," and the House released him.[25]

Importantly, even on Wentworth's own understanding of the free-speech privilege, his arrest did not violate it. After all, he was held by order of the House itself, and he was scrupulous to ensure that he was questioned by a House committee, rather than by outsiders. And Wentworth's understanding of the privilege's scope was extreme, even among his fellow Puritans. Still, it is worth emphasizing that he got himself into trouble by offering a full-throated defense of the parliamentary privilege of free speech, a topic that he would continue pressing for the rest of his parliamentary career. For instance, in 1587 he handed the Speaker a list of questions about the scope of the House's privileges; he intended these questions to be put to the House and the replies to serve as rulings on the scope of parliamentary privilege.[26] The questions included "whether free speache and free doinges, or dealinges be not graunted to euerye on of the parliament howse by lawe," but also, even more pointedly, "whether it be not an Iniurye to the whole state, and against the law, that the prince or priuie councell" should punish members for their speeches.[27] The questions were never put to the House; instead, Wentworth and several other members were imprisoned in the Tower by royal officials.[28] Neale has suggested that the members, Wentworth included, were arrested, not for any speech in Parliament, but rather because they had held private meetings to plan parliamentary strategy. In Neale's words, they had "discussed matters of state outside parliament where there could be no question of privilege, and their imprisonment concerns, not the liberty of speech of members in the house of commons, but the liberty of speech of the general public outside."[29] As early as the 1580s, then, questions arose about what it meant for speech to take place "in" Parliament and what the scope of the privilege was.[30] At this early date, the Crown enforced its own view; the members were evidently held in the Tower for quite some time.[31]

Wentworth was again arrested in 1591 and held for nearly six months—all of it between Parliaments—after it came to the Privy Council's attention that he intended to agitate on the succession question at the next Parliament. The Privy Council issued a warrant to search his house, specifically seeking "all letters, bookes, or writings whatsoever that may concern . . . matter that hath bene or may be intended to be moved in Parliament, and especially suche notes, collections, books or papers as conteine matter towchinge the establishing of the succession."[32] At the opening of the 1593 Parliament, when Edward Coke presented the traditional Speaker's petition for liberty of speech he was met with a sharp reply by the Lord Keeper, on behalf of the queen:

> Liberty of Speech is granted you: but how far this is to be thought on, there be two things of most necessity, and those two do most harm, which are wit and speech: the one exercised in invention, and the other in uttering things invented. Privilege of speech is granted, but you must know what privilege you have; not to speak every one what he listeth, or what cometh in his brain to utter that; but your privilege is, *aye* or *no*. Wherefore, mr. Speaker, her maj.'s pleasure is, That if you perceive any idle heads, which will not stick to hazard their own estates; which will meddle with reforming the Church, and transforming the Common-wealth; and do exhibit any bills to such purpose, that you receive them not, until they be viewed and considered by those, who it is fitter should consider of such things, and can better judge of them.[33]

The message was lost on Wentworth, who arranged a meeting at a chambers in Lincoln's Inn with a number of others (some members of Parliament, some not) to discuss the succession question. Wentworth previewed for them a characteristically pugnacious speech that he was planning to give in the House. Word of the meeting leaked, and Wentworth was again arrested by order of the Privy Council; when the Privy Councillors demanded to see a copy of his draft speech, he refused, on the ground that it was privileged.[34] After nearly five years in the Tower, Wentworth died there in 1597.[35]

    On the one hand, Wentworth's parliamentary career may appear a failure: after all, he was repeatedly imprisoned, and he failed to convince either a majority of his colleagues or the queen of the rightness of his position. On the other hand, he provided an alternative vision of the free-speech privilege, one that was "widely divergent" from the Crown's (as exemplified by the Lord Keeper's claim that the privilege was limited to voting "*aye* or *no*")[36] and that therefore was available as a model for subsequent parliamentary agitators. Thus, as we saw in the previous chapter, when James I in 1621 ordered the House of Commons to stay away from the "mysteries of state" (that is, his desire to marry his son to the Spanish Infanta), the House actively pushed back, insisting that freedom of speech over all matters was its "ancient and undoubted right."[37] Coke, now back in the House of Commons, claimed that the privilege was an "ancient inheritance," and he insisted that the House "stand upon the defence of our privileges in this point."[38] In other words, what had been the idiosyncratic view of Wentworth and a few other troublemakers when Coke was a young parliamentarian had become the majority view in the body as he became a septuagenarian.[39]

The previous chapter also discussed the controversy over the seizure of John Rolle's goods by officers of Charles I, early in 1629. After several heated exchanges between the House and the Crown over the matter, John Eliot read an incendiary proposed remonstrance in the House. When he finished reading it, the Speaker refused to allow a vote on presenting the remonstrance to the Crown, claiming that the king had commanded him to adjourn the House.[40] Denzil Holles and Benjamin Valentine forcibly held the Speaker in his chair, keeping the House in session, while the House passed three resolutions, two of which named both those who counseled levying and those who paid the taxes of tonnage and poundage when not authorized by Parliament as "capital enem[ies] to this kingdom and commonwealth."[41] Eliot, Holles, and Valentine were subsequently prosecuted in the King's Bench; the charges against them specified that "the Defendants, by confederacy aforehand, spake a long and continued speech . . . in which were divers malicious and seditious words, of dangerous consequence."[42] The defendants, relying on Strode's Act and other precedents, argued that the court had no jurisdiction, as actions in the House could only be punished by the House.[43] The judges disagreed, insisting that Strode's Act applied only to Strode's case, and that criminal offenses occurring in Parliament—even crimes, like sedition, that were entirely verbal in character—fell outside the scope of privilege.[44] The members were all fined and "imprisoned during the king's pleasure." Interestingly, Eliot received the highest fine and was the only one imprisoned in the Tower, on the grounds that he was "the greatest offender, and the ringleader."[45] In other words, the speech was a greater offense than the assault upon the Speaker.

Charles had dissolved Parliament immediately after the incident with Eliot, Holles, and Valentine, and he then ruled without it for the next eleven years.[46] Holles made his apologies and was released soon after the judgment; Eliot died in the Tower in 1632; and Valentine, unrepentant, remained in prison until 1640, when Charles released him ahead of the opening of the Short Parliament, in an attempt to curry public favor.[47] The gambit did not succeed: when

Parliament assembled in April 1640, it turned immediately to its grievances. It resolved that "the Speaker's refusing to put Questions, after a verbal Command by his Majesty, signified to this House by the Speaker, to adjourn, and no Adjournment made by this House, is a Breach of Privilege of this House."[48] In other words, the malefactors eleven years earlier had been the Speaker and the king, not the members who refused to adjourn and held the Speaker in his chair. Likewise, when several days later the House gathered all of its grievances into a list, it included "Punishing Men, out of Parliament, for things done in Parliament," a clear reference to Eliot, Holles, and Valentine.[49]

The demand for the king to redress grievances like these before Parliament would grant him supply was what led Charles to make the Short Parliament short, but the need for money did not disappear with the dissolution. In July 1641, the Long Parliament returned to the topic, passing a series of resolutions declaring that the proceedings against Eliot, Holles, and Valentine were breaches of parliamentary privilege and specifically pronouncing a number of Crown officers, including judges of the King's Bench, guilty of these breaches of privilege. Indeed, one of the resolutions even declared that Eliot, Holles, and Valentine "ought to have Reparation for their respective Damages and Sufferings" against both members of the Privy Council and judges of the King's Bench.[50]

Even the Civil War and the Restoration did not dim parliamentary zeal to redress this particular grievance. In 1667—as parliamentary opposition to Charles II was picking up steam, and less than three weeks before Clarendon was forced into exile—the House of Commons resolved that Strode's Act was "a general Law, extending to indemnify all and every the Members of both Houses of Parliament, in all Parliaments, for and touching any Bill, speaking, reasoning, or declaring of any Matter or Matters in or concerning the Parliament, to be communed and treated of; and is a declaratory Law of the ancient and necessary Rights and Privileges of Parliament."[51] A few days later, it resolved that the King's Bench judgment against Eliot, Holles, and Valentine was "an illegal Judgment, and against the Freedom of Privileges of Parliament."[52] The next month, the Lords noted their agreement with both of these resolutions.[53] And the following year, the Lords, sitting in their capacity as the highest appellate court in the realm, reversed the King's Bench judgment of nearly four decades earlier.[54]

It is worth noting that, unlike the Short and Long Parliaments of Charles I, parliamentary privilege and the *Eliot* case were not matters that the Restoration

Parliament felt compelled to take up immediately. Rather, they were taken up after frictions, traced in previous chapters, began to emerge between Charles II and his Parliament. In this regard, the actions by both houses in 1667–1668 can be regarded as a warning to the monarch not to repeat his father's mistakes.

The warning was not entirely heeded. In 1680, as the furor over the "Popish Plot" was at its height,[55] and as the House of Commons was attempting to exclude James, the Duke of York (the king's brother and a Catholic) from the succession, a petty criminal and all-around rogue named Thomas Dangerfield came forward with a story of a Catholic plot against the Crown.[56] After hearing his story, the House ordered its Speaker to find some suitable printer to publish Dangerfield's testimony.[57] The testimony implicated the Duke of York in a scheme to put forward evidence of a fake "Presbyterian Plot" to foment insurrection in the north, thereby bringing opprobrium on the duke's opponents and furthering the Catholic cause.[58] The whole thing was made up, and in 1685, long after his story had been discredited, Dangerfield was tried (before Lord Chief Justice Jeffreys, whom we met in chapter 4) and convicted of libels against York, who by then had become King James II. While his punishment (a series of floggings) was ongoing, Dangerfield was killed during an argument.[59] Still alive, however, was William Williams, the Speaker of the House of Commons who had ordered Dangerfield's narrative to be printed. Indeed, the cover page of the printed version proclaims in large letters: "Perused and Signed to be Printed, According to the Order of the House of Commons, by me, *William Williams*, Speaker."[60] This attracted James's attention, and in 1684 Williams was haled before the King's Bench on a charge of seditious libel. By the time the verdict came down in 1686, James was king, and the King's Bench was presided over by Lord Chief Justice Edward Herbert (Jeffreys having been promoted to Lord Chancellor in 1685, immediately on the heels of the Bloody Assizes). When Williams's counsel attempted to argue that he had simply acted in accordance with the orders of the House, Herbert cut him off: "Can the order of the House of Commons justify the scandalous, infamous, flagitious libel?"[61] Williams was fined £10,000, although the fine was reduced to £8,000 when he agreed to pay in cash.[62] In an ill-timed bit of political opportunism, Williams spent the two years preceding the Glorious Revolution cozying up to James, who knighted Williams and made him solicitor general almost exactly a year before losing his crown and fleeing to France. Williams's subsequent attempts to ingratiate himself with the new monarchs were unsuccessful.[63]

Even so, Williams, along with Eliot, Holles, and Valentine, was very much in parliamentarians' minds as they crafted the Revolution Settlement. The list of grievances prefacing the Bill of Rights complained of "Prosecutions in the Court of King's Bench for Matters and Causes cognizable onely in Parlyament," and Article 9 accordingly provided that "the Freedome of Speech and Debates or Proceedings in Parlyament ought not to be impeached or questioned in any Court or Place out of Parlyament."[64] During the parliamentary debates over the Bill of Rights, Sir George Treby explained: "This Article was put in for the sake of one, once in your place [that is, the Speaker], Sir *William Williams*, who was punished out of Parliament for what he had done in Parliament."[65] In July 1689, the House resolved that the judgment against Williams was "an illegal Judgment, and against the Freedom of Parliament."[66] Perhaps because of Williams's later actions on James's behalf, an attempt to reverse the judgment by law and refund his fine went nowhere.[67]

The Bill of Rights enshrined a strong conception of the speech or debate privilege in England, and that conception was picked up across the Atlantic as well. Some of the North American colonial legislatures followed the House of Commons' practice by petitioning the governor for their privileges. Sometimes these privileges were left unspecified; sometimes they explicitly asked for freedom of speech.[68] As in the mother country, legislatures figured that the best way to keep executives from interfering in their deliberations was to keep executives from learning of those deliberations. In Virginia, for instance, the oath traditionally administered to the clerk of the House of Burgesses swore him to "Keep Secret all proceedings of the said House of Burgesses so far as shall by the said House be found necessary."[69] In 1688, Baron Howard of Effingham, the royal governor of Virginia, attempted to remove this provision from the new clerk's oath. The resulting backlash from the chamber forced Effingham to back down and include the secrecy provision.[70] As early as 1701, the South Carolina assembly referred to members' freedom of speech as "their undoubted right."[71] In 1727, the governor of New York dissolved the assembly after an especially fractious session. During the dissolution, some members were "called by an high Hand to give an account of the Proceedings of that House," and one was imprisoned for insisting that only the house could call him to answer for things done in the house.[72] When a new assembly convened in 1728, it unanimously resolved that the harassment of the members of its predecessor was "the highest Violation of the Priviledges of General Assemblies; and that the Liberties and

Properties of the People would be rendred extream Precarious, if ever those who represent them be called to an Account for what they do when they are convened in General Assembly."[73] The assembly accordingly resolved, in language that will sound familiar, that "for any Act, Matter or Thing done in General Assembly, the Members thereof are Accountable and Answerable to the House Only, and to no other Person or Persons whatsoever."[74] Likewise, in the context of a petty spat with Governor Thomas Bladen over whether his harsh words and "scornful and insulting looks" had been intended to prevent members of the Maryland assembly from voting their consciences, the assembly insisted in 1745 that "Liberty of speech on every debate and matter in assembly is and ought to be free, and no member ought to be questioned or impeached for anything said or done in discharge of his duty in the house of delegates by any person whatever, or in any manner whatever other than by the house itself."[75] As Mary Patterson Clarke summarized it, "In all the colonies, freedom of speech . . . was constantly recognized as a fundamental privilege without which the right to deliberate would be of little value."[76]

This recognition carried over into the early republican constitutions, five of which explicitly protected legislative speech and debate.[77] Two other states— New York and South Carolina—had general legislative privilege clauses, providing that their state legislatures were to exercise the same privileges claimed by their colonial predecessors (both of which, as we have already seen, had long asserted a robust free-speech privilege).[78] The Articles of Confederation contained a Speech or Debate Clause as well.[79]

Perhaps because of the deep familiarity of the privilege by this point, its inclusion in the American Constitution was almost wholly uncontroversial.[80] Article I provides that, "for any Speech or Debate in either House, [Senators and Representatives] shall not be questioned in any other Place."[81] In his famous 1791 Lectures on Law, James Wilson (one of the principal drafters of the Constitution and one of the first Supreme Court justices) justified the clause on the grounds that, "[i]n order to enable and encourage a representative of the publick to discharge his publick trust with firmness and success, it is indispensably necessary, that he should enjoy the fullest liberty of speech, and that he should be protected from the resentment of every one, however powerful, to whom the exercise of that liberty may occasion offence."[82]

Thomas Jefferson also had an early opportunity to weigh in on the speech or debate privilege, occasioned by the Cabell affair. In 1797, a federal grand jury sitting in Richmond issued a presentment (akin to an indictment, but at the grand jury's own initiative, rather than the prosecutor's) against Samuel J. Cabell, a Republican member of the federal House of Representatives from Virginia. The presentment charged Cabell with common-law seditious libel for a circular letter to his constituents in which he vigorously attacked the Adams administration, accusing it of violating American treaty obligations with France by being partial toward Britain in the ongoing war between the two powers.[83] In an anonymously authored petition to the Virginia House of Delegates asking it to look into the matter and to punish the grand jurors, Vice President Jefferson (who was one of Cabell's constituents) offered a vigorous defense of the necessity of unfettered communication between members of Congress and their constituents: "[I]n order to give to the will of the people the influence it ought to have, and the information which may enable them to exercise it usefully, . . . their representatives, in the discharge of their functions, should be free from the cognizance or coercion of the co-ordinate branches, Judiciary and Executive; and . . . their communications with their constituents should of right, as of duty also, be free, full, and unawed by any."[84] Jefferson went on to paint a vivid picture of the effects of judicial interference in communication between legislators and their constituents:

> [F]or the Judiciary to interpose in the legislative department between the constituent and his representative, to control them in the exercise of their functions or duties towards each other, to overawe the free correspondence which exists and ought to exist between them, to dictate what communications may pass between them, and to punish all others, to put the representative into jeopardy of criminal prosecution, of vexation, expense, and punishment before the Judiciary, if his communications, public or private, do not exactly square with their ideas of fact or right, or with their designs of wrong, is to put the legislative department under the feet of the Judiciary, is to leave us, indeed, the shadow, but to take away the substance of representation.[85]

Jefferson recommended that the offending grand jurors be impeached and punished,[86] but the final petition presented to the House seems to have dropped this request in favor of the more nebulous suggestion that the House "pursue such steps, as may secure to the citizens of this commonwealth, their constitutional right, that their representatives shall, in the exercise of their functions, be free and independent of the other departments of government."[87] The House ordered a thousand copies of the petition to be printed,[88] and it resolved that the grand jury's presentment was "a violation of the fundamental principles of representation, incompatible with that independence between the co-ordinate branches of government, meditated both by the general and state constitutions."[89] Cabell was never prosecuted on the presentment.

The Cabell affair may be seen as a dress rehearsal for reactions against the Sedition Act, which became law a little more than six months after the Virginia House of Delegates passed its resolution dealing with Cabell.[90] It is well known that the chief Republican responses to the act came in the form of resolutions (secretly authored by Jefferson and Madison) passed by the legislatures of Kentucky and Virginia.[91] There were many reasons, of course, to have Republican-controlled state legislatures lead the charge against this Federalist overreach, but one of them was surely that it was the safest forum for dissent. Criticism of the Sedition Act in the press or elsewhere might have resulted in the critic's prosecution under that very act, but criticism in the legislature seemed far less likely to result in legal peril. Although the federal Constitution's Speech or Debate Clause applies only to Congress, politically engaged actors in the late eighteenth century had sufficiently internalized the history traced thus far that it was highly unlikely that anyone would attempt to prosecute state legislators for how they debated or voted.

However, the consensus against prosecuting someone for actions taken within the statehouse does not necessarily indicate a consensus in favor of Jefferson's more expansive conception of the privilege. Consider the 1798 conviction of Vermont Republican Matthew Lyon under the Sedition Act. Lyon was not the most temperate of congressmen—that same year, he was nearly expelled from the House of Representatives for spitting in another member's face and brawling on the floor.[92] His Sedition Act trial concerned two publications: in one, he accused the Adams administration of "an unbounded thirst for ridiculous pomp, foolish adulation, and selfish avarice," and in the other, he reprinted a letter from an American in France accusing the administration and its Federalist allies of "bullying," "stupid[ity]," and "borrowing the language of Edmund Burke" with regard to the French revolutionary government.[93] Lyon, who defended himself, argued that the Sedition Act was unconstitutional, but he did not argue that he was privileged under the Speech or Debate Clause. Justice Paterson, riding circuit, instructed the jury that it had "nothing whatever to do with the constitutionality or unconstitutionality of the sedition law,"[94] a

milder version of the sort of instruction that would soon lead to the impeachment of Justice Chase, as we saw in chapter 4. Lyon was convicted and
sentenced to four months' imprisonment and a fine of $1,000.[95] Vermonters
protested the conviction vigorously and reelected Lyon while he was imprisoned.[96] For the second time in two years, Federalists then introduced a motion
to expel Lyon from the House, and Lyon's defenders turned, among other arguments, to the inappropriateness of expelling a member for expressing his views
to his constituents. John Nicholas of Virginia insisted, "We are . . . sent here to
form an opinion, and, when we return home, we are expected to deliver that
opinion to our constituents." In fact, he insisted, it was even more important for
a member to give his views to his constituents "in proportion as such opinions
may be offensive to the administrators of the Government."[97] Albert Gallatin
went even further, arguing that "it was the duty of this House to have sent the
Sergeant-at-Arms for [Lyon], and demanded him from confinement, that he
might have attended to his duty in this House."[98] Although a majority voted to
expel Lyon, it failed to clear the two-thirds bar, and he remained in the House,
serving several more terms before retiring in 1811. In 1840, on the petition of
his heirs, the government refunded his fine, with interest, on the grounds that
the Sedition Act was unconstitutional.[99]

With the decisive repudiation of the Federalists and the Sedition Act in the
1800 election, the Speech or Debate Clause entered a period in which it worked
almost entirely below the surface. This is not to suggest that the clause was not
important throughout the nineteenth century; it is simply to note that no major
controversies over the privilege arose for quite some time, perhaps because it
was sufficiently well understood that no one thought it worthwhile to test its
limits. Indeed, it was not until 1876 that another major controversy surrounding
the clause arose, and this time it was in the context of a suit by a private citizen,
not a prosecution by the executive. Still, the incident is worth considering for
the light it sheds on how the privilege was understood in the late nineteenth
century. In 1876, Hallett Kilbourn refused to answer questions put to him by a
select committee of the House of Representatives that was investigating the
bankruptcy of a bank into which a significant sum of federal money had been
deposited.[100] Kilbourn was held in contempt and imprisoned for forty-five
days.[101] He subsequently filed a false-imprisonment suit against the sergeant-at-
arms, the Speaker, and the members of the select committee, and the case made
its way to the Supreme Court. Most of Justice Samuel Miller's opinion for the

Court was devoted to holding that the House had no authority to hold Kilbourn in contempt in this situation.[102] But the Court then, relying heavily on an 1808 case dealing with the free-speech privilege in the Massachusetts legislature,[103] went on to hold that the Speaker and committee members were immune from suit under the Speech or Debate Clause. Although the suit was not, in the most literal sense, about speech or debate on the floor, "[i]t would be a narrow view of the constitutional provision to limit it to words spoken in debate. The reason of the rule is as forcible in its application to written reports presented in that body by its committees, to resolutions offered, which, though in writing, must be reproduced in speech, and to the act of voting, whether it is done vocally or by passing between the tellers. In short, to things generally done in a session of the House by one of its members in relation to the business before it."[104] In the understanding of the *Kilbourn* Court, then, "speech or debate" had to be understood as synecdoche for a member's official duties. This broad understanding of "speech or debate," however, was tempered by limiting the privilege's applicability narrowly to senators and representatives themselves.

The history traced thus far leaves us with two broad classes of questions at the interface of the speech or debate privilege and the separation of powers. First, how does the Speech or Debate Clause interact with some conception of state secrets? Elizabeth and James both insisted that certain matters were beyond parliamentary competence and therefore unfit for parliamentary discussion. Today, that claim is often heard with respect to discussions of "national security" or "classified information." To what extent does the privilege immunize members against prosecution for releasing such information? And second, to what extent should the speech or debate privilege be understood as protecting legislators' communications with their constituents? This question arose as early as the debate over whether Peter Wentworth could be punished for holding meetings outside Parliament to plan parliamentary opposition, and it continues to arise with some regularity. The following sections consider these two issues in turn.

State Secrets

In thinking about state secrets, it makes sense to begin with the most iconic leak of such secrets, the *Pentagon Papers* case. For most lawyers, the name conjures *New York Times v. United States*,[105] in which the heroic Supreme Court stood up for freedom of the press against a secrecy-obsessed executive branch.[106] But, in fact, a little-known senator from Alaska beat the judiciary to the punch. Within days of the *New York Times* and *Washington Post*'s beginning to run stories based on the *Papers*[107] in mid-June 1971, federal courts in New York and Washington issued temporary restraining orders to stop them.[108] Injunctions against publishing the material remained in effect in both jurisdictions until the Supreme Court ruled, seventeen days after the first *Times* article had appeared.[109]

The night before the Supreme Court's ruling, however, Democrat Mike Gravel, a first-term senator, had placed forty-one hundred pages of the *Pentagon Papers* into the public record. Daniel Ellsberg, the same RAND Corporation analyst who had leaked the *Papers* to the press, had given them to Gravel as well.[110] After an attempt to read them on the floor of the Senate failed due to lack of a quorum,[111] Gravel convened a 9:45 P.M. meeting of the Buildings and Grounds Subcommittee of the Senate's Environment and Public Works Committee.[112] Gravel, the subcommittee chair, was the only senator in attendance; an antiwar House member was rounded up to serve as the "witness" whose "testimony" would provide the impetus for Gravel's reading the *Papers* into the record.[113] Gravel read aloud from the *Papers* until approximately 1:00 A.M. the next morning, at which point he broke down in tears.[114] He then entered the remaining pages into the subcommittee record.[115] By the time he returned to his office, his staff was already photocopying the "subcommittee record" and handing it out to reporters.[116] By the time the Court ruled, roughly twelve hours later,[117] the *Papers* could not, as a practical matter, have been removed from the public sphere.

Even after the Court's ruling, Gravel came to the conclusion that some combination of the threat of criminal prosecution[118] and newsroom cowardice had led the newspapers to publish too little of the *Papers*.[119] He accordingly arranged to have the entire "4,100-page subcommittee record" published by Beacon Press.[120] Subsequently, in the course of the grand jury investigation into the leaking of the *Papers*, one of Gravel's aides, Leonard Rodberg, was subpoenaed, as was the director of the MIT Press, where Gravel had tried to publish his edition of the *Papers*.[121] Gravel intervened with a motion to quash the subpoenas on Speech or Debate Clause grounds.[122] The case eventually reached the Supreme Court, at which point the Senate passed a resolution authorizing a bipartisan group of Senators to file an amicus brief on behalf of the chamber and authorizing the payment of Gravel's litigation expenses by the Senate.[123]

The amicus brief, overseen by an ad hoc committee of four Democrats and four Republicans and coauthored by towering constitutional scholar Philip Kurland, boldly asserted that "[t]he purpose of this brief is to establish the position of the United States Senate that the attempt to subpoena an aide to a Senator to testify before a grand jury as to his activities and those of the Senator whom he serves is an invasion of the Senate's constitutional privilege. . . . [T]his brief is filed on behalf of the Congressional privilege. It is not a defense of Senator Gravel or his aide, nor is it a defense of their conduct in this case. If there were misconduct on their part, they must answer to the Senate itself."[124] Moreover, in language echoing Jefferson's concerns about putting the legislature under the boot of the other branches, the Senate insisted that publication, too, was a matter for the senator himself, answerable only to the Senate: "It is not for the Executive to challenge nor for the Judiciary to judge a Member's choice of issues to publicize or methods of publication regardless of whether they may be considered ill-advised. The Senate as a whole may or may not approve the exercise of the privilege by Senator Gravel in this case. But it joins in Senator Gravel's assertion of the privilege."[125]

The Court, per Justice Byron White, was partially convinced. It found it "incontrovertible" that Gravel himself would be privileged against "questioning elsewhere than in the Senate, with respect to the events occurring at the subcommittee hearing at which the Pentagon Papers were introduced into the public record."[126] And given that Gravel was privileged, Rodberg must have been, too, because "it is literally impossible, in view of the complexities of the modern legislative process, with Congress almost constantly in session and matters of legislative concern constantly proliferating, for Members of Congress to perform their legislative tasks without the help of aides and assistants; . . . the day-to-day work of such aides is so critical to the Members' performance that they must be treated as the latter's alter egos; and . . . if they are not so recognized, the central role of the Speech or Debate Clause—to prevent intimidation of legislators by the Executive and accountability before a possibly hostile judiciary—will inevitably be diminished and frustrated."[127] The Court went on to hold, however, that Gravel's agreement to publish the *Papers* was not privileged, on the grounds that "private publication by Senator Gravel through the cooperation of Beacon Press was in no way essential to the deliberations of the Senate; nor does questioning as to private publication threaten the integrity or independence of the Senate by impermissibly exposing its deliberations to executive influence."[128]

In other words, the Court allowed for the possibility of criminal prosecution by the executive branch of members of Congress for publishing more widely material that they had already released in the course of congressional proceedings. It is hard to see this holding of the Court's as anything other than futile. After all, the release of classified information will almost always draw substantial public notice, and the *Congressional Record* and committee reports have long been widely available. Advances since Gravel's release of the *Pentagon Papers* in 1971, including the online availability of the *Congressional Record*, committee reports, and the entire C-SPAN video archive, mean that, even in the absence of a republication agreement, theretofore secret information released by members of Congress will be picked up, reported upon, and read by the public.

Nor is Senator Gravel alone in having made use of his Speech or Debate Clause protections to release secret information. An instance occurring just a few years later is instructive. At the request of Michael Harrington, a liberal Massachusetts Democrat, a foreign affairs subcommittee of the House of Representatives held a hearing in October 1973 about CIA activities in Chile, where a military coup had deposed President Salvador Allende the previous month. William Colby, the director of central intelligence, refused to testify, insisting that he would only testify in closed session before the CIA subcommittee of the Armed Services Committee.[129] After Colby did so, Harrington requested and received the transcript of Colby's testimony before that subcommittee, which described the CIA's interference in the 1970 Chilean election.[130] After unsuccessfully attempting to persuade the chairs of the House and Senate Foreign Relations Committees to take up the matter, Harrington leaked the substance of Colby's testimony to the press.[131] The "storm of criticism" resulting from the disclosure that the CIA had interfered in foreign elections was a significant factor in the passage of the Hughes-Ryan Amendment in December 1974, which expanded both presidential and congressional oversight of the CIA.[132] The House Ethics Committee voted against punishing Harrington for the disclosure, on the grounds that the subcommittee meeting at which Colby testified had been procedurally irregular and therefore that normal House rules governing the release of such information did not apply.[133] By contrast, to this day no court has ever accepted a defense of improper classification when an individual has been criminally charged with leaking classified information.[134]

Eight days before President Ford signed the Hughes-Ryan Amendment into law, the *New York Times* published a front-page story by Seymour Hersh detailing a huge number of illegal activities by the CIA during the Nixon admin-istration.[135] These activities were just a subset of those described in what came to be known as the "Family Jewels," a 693-page dossier that Director of Central Intelligence James Schlesinger had ordered produced in mid-1973 as a compre-hensive list of past CIA activities that were illegal or had the potential to embar-rass the agency.[136] By the time the dossier was produced, Schlesinger had become secretary of defense and Colby had been nominated as the new director of central intelligence. Before his confirmation hearings, Colby informed the chairmen of the House and Senate Armed Services Committees and the chairmen of the CIA subcommittees of the existence of the Family Jewels; the members agreed to keep quiet about it.[137] Their revelation in the *Times*, then, came as a shock to most members of Congress (as well as to the White House, which had not been told of their existence at all).[138]

Concerned that the CIA subcommittees had proven ineffectual at best, and been captured at worst, both chambers in early 1975 established ad hoc commit-tees to investigate CIA abuses. The Senate committee was chaired by Democrat Frank Church—the same Frank Church who had coauthored the Cooper-Church and Case-Church Amendments discussed in chapter 3. The House committee was initially chaired by Lucien Nedzi, but he was pressured to step aside when it was reported that, as chairman of the CIA subcommittee of the House Armed Services Committee, he had known about the Family Jewels for more than a year. Nedzi was replaced by fellow Democrat Otis Pike.[139] Over the following year, both the Pike Committee and the Church Committee released information over the objections of the Ford administration.[140] The Church Committee also released its final report; the Pike Committee voted to do likewise but was over-ridden by the full House. The Pike Committee report was leaked to the press, and a subsequent House Ethics Committee investigation failed to uncover the source.[141] These revelations helped push forward the politics of intelligence reform, resulting in the creation of the intelligence committees in both chambers in 1976 and 1977 and, on the recommendations of those committees, the Intelligence Oversight Act of 1980.[142] These developments substantially strengthened congressional oversight of the intelligence community.[143]

Nor were such releases limited to the political tumult of the early and mid-1970s. In 1992, Henry Gonzalez, the Democratic chairman of the House Banking Committee, repeatedly read aloud from classified documents on the floor and placed a number of those documents in the legislative record. The documents, which Republican congressional aides claimed added up to the largest release of classified information since the Vietnam War, indicated that senior officials in the George H. W. Bush administration had been cozying up to the Iraqi regime as late as early 1990, mere months before Iraq's invasion of Kuwait.[144] When the administration vigorously objected, Gonzalez insisted that "the American people have a right to know [the facts], and piddling, phony charges about national security won't stop me."[145] Republican Larry Combest, who introduced a resolution requesting that the Ethics Committee investigate Gonzalez, retorted: "Of course, it is practically impossible for laymen to grasp all of the possible ramifications which may result from the disclosure of classified information."[146] Combest's resolution failed on a party-line vote.[147] A few years later, in 1995, Democrat Robert Torricelli, a member of the House Intelligence Committee, revealed to the press that the CIA was covering up the involvement of one of its paid informants in murders in Guatemala. The Ethics Committee found that Torricelli had violated House rules but recommended no punishment.[148] The State Department employee who told Torricelli about the CIA's behavior, by contrast, had his security clearance revoked and resigned from his job.[149]

In late 2004, in open session of the Senate, two Democrats (and therefore minority members) on the Intelligence Committee, John D. Rockefeller IV and Ron Wyden, announced that they would oppose the conference report on the intelligence authorization bill that had come out of their committee. Rockefeller's opposition was, in his words, "based solely on my strenuous objection—shared by many in our committee—to a particular major funding acquisition program that I believe is totally unjustified and very wasteful and dangerous to national security. Because of the highly classified nature of the programs contained in the national intelligence budget, I cannot talk about them on the floor. . . . [The conference report] fully authorizes funding for this unjustified and stunningly expensive acquisition. I simply cannot overlook that."[150] Wyden added, "I wish more of my colleagues knew of the details of this program and understood why we are so convinced that it should be canceled. I encourage you to request a briefing, to come to the Intelligence Committee and let our staff explain why we believe we are right about this program."[151] In publicly making these statements, Rockefeller and Wyden took what David Pozen has termed "deep secrets"—that is, secrets that we did not even know existed—and made them shallower.[152] In less than a week, the *New York Times* ferreted out and reported on what the acquisition program was: "a new $9.5 billion spy satellite system that could take photographs only in daylight hours and in clear weather."[153] It was the largest single item in the intelligence budget.[154] The Justice Department investigated the leaks, but of course the Speech or Debate Clause precluded it from pursuing Rockefeller or Wyden, whose floor speeches had tipped off the press that there was something worth looking into.[155] Although the 2004 conference report passed and became law, the program was terminated in 2007 by the director of national intelligence.[156]

Wyden was back at it again in 2011, joined by his Intelligence Committee colleague and fellow Democrat Mark Udall. During debates over reauthorizing portions of the PATRIOT Act, they announced on the Senate floor that the Obama administration had adopted a secret, implausible interpretation of portions of the act dealing with domestic surveillance, although they did not release the details of this secret interpretation.[157] Once again, making the secrets shallower spurred on other actors: Wyden and Udall's disclosure prompted the American Civil Liberties Union and the *New York Times* to file Freedom of Information Act requests, seeking to strip the interpretation of even its shallow secrecy.[158] In response, the government produced some documents,[159] but not enough to satisfy the ACLU or the *Times*, both of which filed suit (ultimately unsuccessfully) in federal court.[160] When the government moved to dismiss the suits, Senators Wyden and Udall released an open letter to Attorney General Holder. The letter reiterated their concern over the secret legal interpretation, arguing that "most Americans would be stunned to learn the details of how these secret court opinions have interpreted section 215 of the Patriot Act." The letter went on not only to argue that policy makers in the executive branch were too deferential to intelligence officers, but also to express the senators' skepticism about the substantive merits of the "intelligence collection operation" that the administration claimed would be compromised by releasing the secret legal interpretations.[161]

In 2013 the details of that "intelligence collection operation" became clearer, as documents leaked to the press by Edward Snowden revealed that the National Security Agency had been relying on section 215 as legal authority to collect the metadata from huge numbers of domestic phone calls since 2006. The ACLU then filed another suit, seeking to have the program declared illegal. In May 2015, a federal appeals court did so, holding that section 215 did not give the NSA the statutory authority to collect telephone metadata indiscriminately.[162] Section 215 subsequently sunset on June 1 of that year and was renewed with significant new limitations on the NSA's surveillance authority.[163] We can see here how the Speech or Debate Clause fits into a powerful "ecology of transparency,"[164] working together with the press, civil society organizations, the courts, and subsequent legislative actions. The senators' initial disclosure made the secret interpretation shallow enough that the *Times* and the ACLU could file a FOIA request and subsequent lawsuit; the government's conduct in the course of the FOIA suit prompted the senators to amplify and elaborate upon their concerns publicly, drawing further media attention. The Snowden leaks drew still more notice,[165] which allowed the ACLU to win a subsequent suit, and the changes in public opinion that had been attendant upon all of this enabled a significant curtailment of NSA authority when section 215 sunset and was reauthorized in a far more limited form.

Wyden and Udall's role in this process made them folk heroes to many civil libertarians, who urged them to continue releasing evidence of government wrongdoing. Bruce Ackerman encouraged them to reveal information they had learned in closed Intelligence Committee briefings, in the interest of having an informed debate on legislative responses to the surveillance program.[166] After Udall lost his seat in the 2014 election, and while the Senate and the White House were still sparring over how much of a Senate Intelligence Committee report on CIA torture to release, Mike Gravel publicly encouraged Udall to put the report into the congressional record, as Gravel had done with the *Pentagon Papers* more than forty years earlier.[167] Udall did not do so, but the committee itself released a redacted version of the nearly 550-page executive summary of the report a month later. News stories noted that the "milestone" report[168] contained a "sweeping indictment" of CIA interrogation practices and lies to the White House, Congress, and the public about the efficacy of those practices.[169] When a private publishing house released paperback and digital versions of the report, the paperback edition immediately sold out its initial print run of fifty thousand copies.[170] Even if concerns about unilateral action by Udall did not speed the release—and, to be clear, there is no evidence that they did—it is still the case that Wyden and Udall (along with Senate colleagues like Republican Rand Paul and Democrat Martin Heinrich)[171] contributed to growing public skepticism toward the intelligence community,[172] and this skepticism undoubtedly played a role in the tone of the report and the amount of it that was released to the public.[173]

Of course, congressional disclosure is not necessarily a good thing. Like all political behavior in the public sphere, it can be done injudiciously, and such injudicious disclosures may well harm both national interests and Congress's institutional interests. If, for instance, Senate Democrats had released portions of the Intelligence Committee report that named covert operatives still working in the field, then the disclosure might well have resulted in significant harm (to those operatives, to American interests abroad, and to the Democrats' political futures as well). But there is no good reason to think that Congress is especially prone to injudicious disclosures. Senator Gravel, after all, released only about forty-one hundred of the *Pentagon Papers'* seventy-eight hundred total pages, and he excised various names from the pages he did release.[174] Many of the other disclosures discussed above revealed past misconduct—embarrassing to the intelligence community, no doubt, but likely without adverse consequences for national security. Indeed, many of these revelations have come to be understood as deeply important and patriotic acts. Today, for instance, we rightly consider the release of the *Pentagon Papers* to be an important milestone in the checking of an imperial presidency at war.[175] And despite the Nixon administration's hyperventilation at the time, their release did not harm American national interests (as distinct from the interests of the Nixon administration). Indeed, Erwin Griswold, Nixon's solicitor general who argued the *Pentagon Papers Case* for the government, repeatedly said as much,[176] and the preeminent historian of the *Papers* concurs.[177] Likewise, the bipartisan consensus that developed around reform of the NSA's surveillance methods suggests that Wyden and Udall's disclosures were judicious as well. In addition to choosing *when* to spill secrets, members have been careful about precisely *what* they spill: in addition to Senator Gravel's redacting of the *Pentagon Papers* before releasing them, Senators Rockefeller, Wyden, and Udall chose to make deep secrets shallower, not to lift the veil of secrecy entirely.

By contrast, the two major indiscriminate disclosures in recent history—those by Chelsea Manning and Edward Snowden—have come from people with executive-branch ties.[178] Indeed, it is at least possible that if members of Congress were more willing to evaluate and consider releasing classified information, future Mannings and Snowdens might be willing to leak to them rather than engaging in indiscriminate public releases.[179] In that case, at least the final decision on releasing information to the public would be made by a democratically accountable official, who would be likely to exercise at least some measure of care—as Senator Gravel did—to avoid releasing especially damaging information.

More importantly, perhaps, the question of what disclosures count as damaging depends crucially on a politically constructed understanding of our national security interests. As David Pozen has demonstrated in a groundbreaking article, the extant regime regulating disclosure of secret information—a cocktail of massive overclassification, the availability of draconian penalties, and the infrequency of actual enforcement actions—suits executive-branch interests quite nicely.[180] The regime allows high-level executive officials to control the public narrative and advance their own agendas by selectively releasing information without fear of prosecution by their own underlings. At the same time, the release of information by individuals working at cross-purposes to the administration (like the State Department official who gave information to Representative Torricelli) can be punished severely. This regime makes apparent a very important fact: *"secret" is a political category, not a natural one.* Facts in isolation do not cry out for secrecy; facts within a specific political context do.[181] Treating "secrecy" as something that inheres in a piece of information itself simply privileges the actor who made the initial determination of secrecy. In that regard, Representative Combest's claim that "it is practically impossible for laymen to grasp all of the possible ramifications which may result from the disclosure of classified information"[182] plays much the same role as James I's insistence that certain matters were "mysteries of state," beyond Parliament's competence.[183] In a context in which the executive makes the initial secrecy determinations (and is loath to declassify much of anything)[184] and the courts are unwilling to accept improper classification as a defense, the Speech or Debate Clause gives members of Congress the authority to challenge the executive's construction of national security interests without having to worry about the threat of criminal sanctions. In a separation-of-powers scheme characterized by a multiplicity of legitimate power centers competing publicly with one another for public support, ensuring that members of Congress are able publicly to contest the executive's construction of national security interests is vital.

Importantly, this power to disclose information is centrally located in the public sphere. When Congress responsibly releases to the public information that the public wants, it enhances its own prestige and, hence, its power. It may simultaneously knock the president down a peg by showing the American people what he sought to withhold from them. The power to reveal information is a soft power, and, as such, its potency depends entirely on how well the member of Congress using it gauges public sentiment. A member releasing, say, the names of covert operatives would likely find her public standing diminished, not bolstered. But, as the aftermath of the release of the *Pentagon Papers* shows, a member who uses the power properly can enhance her own, and her branch's, stature, especially in relation to an executive branch that appears to be fighting to keep its own failures and misdeeds out of the public eye.

Information Flows

Of course, spilling secrets is far from the only way that legislators engage in the public sphere, and it is therefore not the only form of their public communication that requires protection. Legislators communicate with the broader public on all sorts of matters, and there are many ways in which that communication can be subject to outside interference. For the Speech or Debate Clause adequately to protect members' ability to contest for decision-making authority in the public sphere, it must shield their communication from such interference.

As we have seen, the privilege was not always conceived of in this way. In its earliest incarnations, it was entirely inward-looking.[185] This made sense in an English milieu in which Parliament was understood as a component of *royal* government, a resource on which the monarch called in order to help govern his realm more effectively.[186] Thus, the fourteenth-century Speaker's petition prayed, not a right to speak freely, but rather forgiveness for offensive speech, as an underling today might begin a speech with "No offense intended, boss, but . . ." As the conception of Parliament's role in the state gradually changed, however, so too did the role that the speech or debate privilege was understood to play. The evolution of the Speaker's petition, from begging forgiveness to asserting a right, is some evidence of this change. So, too, is the nature of the claims that Peter Wentworth made in defense of his right freely to discuss religion and succession. As we have seen, Wentworth's confrontations with the Crown directly raised the question of where speech had to take place in order to be protected: it was the private meetings he held in order to plan parliamentary strategy that got Wentworth into trouble.

Of course, Wentworth *did* get into trouble—which is to say, he died in the Tower of London for his words. But the alternative, stronger understanding of the speech or debate privilege that he advocated came increasingly to dominate over the next century. The way in which parliamentarians, over the course of decades, tenaciously refused to let go of the breach of privilege associated with the prosecution of Eliot, Holles, and Valentine signaled this shift; moreover, the fact that Article 9 of the Bill of Rights was presented as a reaction to the *Williams* case—which arose out of the publication of Dangerfield's narrative—indicates that by the end of the seventeenth century the privilege was understood to apply broadly, including to communication with the public.

In the early American Republic, this position was taken by both James Wilson and Thomas Jefferson. Recall that, for Jefferson, the "free correspondence" between representatives and their constituents was absolutely essential to free government. And Jefferson's arguments fit nicely with the principles underlying the multiplicity-based approach to the separation of powers. After all, if legislators' communications with the public can be interfered with by another branch, then it is hard to see how they can compete effectively for public support.

And yet this is not how the courts have understood the privilege in recent decades. (The role of the courts here is perhaps greater than their role in dealing with any other congressional power discussed in this book, because the "other Place" in which members are most likely to be "questioned" is a courtroom.) The courts have indeed protected speech that was strictly among legislators and internal to congressional institutions. For instance, in 1930 the Court of Appeals of the District of Columbia threw out a slander suit against a senator for words spoken on the Senate floor, finding that such speech was absolutely privileged.[187] In 1967, the Supreme Court held, in *Dombrowski v. Eastland*, that James Eastland, the chairman of the Internal Security Subcommittee of the Senate Judiciary Committee, was immune from a tort suit arising out of an investigation conducted by his subcommittee. Louisiana state courts had already found that a series of raids carried out against the Southern Conference Educational Fund, a civil rights group, violated the Fourth Amendment, and the group sued Eastland and the subcommittee's counsel, alleging that they had conspired with the Louisiana authorities who carried out the raids.[188] The Supreme Court held that the suit had to be dismissed against Eastland, but that it could proceed against the subcommittee counsel.[189] Similarly, in the 1969 *Powell v. McCormack* case, the Court held that the Speech or Debate Clause barred a suit against a number of members for the refusal to seat an elected member, but that cameral employees who carried out the decision of the chamber (the sergeant-at-arms, the doorkeeper, and the clerk) had no such immunity.[190] In 1975, Senator Eastland was back before the Court, after the United States Servicemen's Fund had sued him, nine other members of his subcommittee, and the subcommittee's chief counsel in an attempt to enjoin the implementation of a subpoena issued by the subcommittee. The Court held that the Speech or Debate Clause absolutely immunized all of the defendants—including the chief counsel, who benefited from *Gravel*'s "alter ego" language—against the suit.[191]

But the courts' fairly robust protection of behavior within the halls of power has not been matched by an equally robust commitment to protecting legislators' speech in the public sphere. In dicta in the 1934 *Long v. Ansell* case, the Court of Appeals of the District of Columbia insisted that Senator Huey P. Long was not immune from a libel suit for reprinting and mailing copies of a speech he delivered on the Senate floor. The court claimed that the libel "consists not in what was said in the Senate, but in the publication and circularizing of the libelous documents."[192] In its 1960 decision in *McGovern v. Martz*, the federal District Court for the District of Columbia took up the *Long* dicta, holding that the "reason for the rule [of speech or debate immunity]—complete and uninhibited discussion among legislators—is not . . . served" by republication of speeches.[193] Then the Supreme Court got in on the action, first in its 1972 *Gravel* holding that republication of the *Pentagon Papers* was not privileged, and again the following year in *Doe v. McMillan*. In that case, a House subcommittee looking into Washington, D.C., public schools issued a report, which the House subsequently ordered printed by the Government Printing Office.[194] The report contained unredacted documents about specific students, and those students' parents filed an invasion-of-privacy suit against the chairman and members of the House Committee on the District of Columbia, various employees of the committee (the clerk, staff director, and counsel, as well as a consultant and an investigator), the superintendent of documents and the public printer, and various officials of the Washington, D.C., schools system.[195] The Court held that the members and employees of the committee were absolutely immune,[196] but that the superintendent of documents and the public printer were not:

[W]e cannot accept the proposition that in order to perform its legislative function Congress not only must at times consider and use actionable material but also must be free to disseminate it to the public at large, no matter how injurious to private reputation that material might be. We cannot believe that the purpose of the

Clause—to prevent intimidation of legislators by the Executive and accountability before a possibly hostile judiciary—will suffer in the slightest if it is held that those who, at the direction of Congress or otherwise, distribute actionable material to the public at large have no automatic immunity under the Speech or Debate Clause but must respond to private suits to the extent that others must respond in light of the Constitution and applicable laws.[197]

In short, it was unimaginable to the Court majority that members' communication with the public was as integral to their legislative duties—and therefore as deserving of protection against being questioned before the judiciary—as their communication with other members.

The Court took this line of reasoning to its logical conclusion in its 1979 decision in *Hutchinson v. Proxmire*, holding that a member himself could be sued for communicating with his constituents. Senator William Proxmire created a "Golden Fleece of the Month Award" to publicize what he considered wasteful government spending, and in 1975 he awarded it to three federal agencies that had funded the work of Ronald Hutchinson, a behavioral scientist who studied aggression. Proxmire gave a speech on the Senate floor about the "award," and the speech was included in a press release (with the addition of introductory and concluding sentences). Proxmire also "repeated the essence" of his floor speech in newsletters to his constituents and in a television interview. In addition, Proxmire's aide contacted the agencies that funded Hutchinson's work— Hutchinson claimed these calls were intended to pressure the agencies to withdraw the funding; the aide claimed that they were simply to discuss the subject. Hutchinson sued both Proxmire and the aide, claiming defamation, interference with contractual relationships, and violations of privacy.[198] The Court held that "neither the newsletters nor the press release was essential to the deliberations of the Senate and neither was part of the deliberative process";[199] indeed, they were "primarily means of informing those outside the legislative forum."[200] Accordingly, neither was privileged under the Speech or Debate Clause.

The courts have thus taken a very narrow view of the scope of the clause. Unlike Jefferson, who, in the midst of the Cabell affair, wrote that it was essential that legislators' communications with their constituents be "free, full, and unawed by any,"[201] the Supreme Court seems to view communication between legislators and constituents as peripheral to *real* legislative activity, which it understands as occurring wholly within the confines of the Capitol. The multiplicity-based understanding of the separation of powers helps us to see how stunted this view is: real legislative authority is, in fact, largely constructed through the processes of public engagement, and the Speech or Debate Clause ought to be understood to facilitate those processes.[202]

To bring this into sharper relief, consider a foreign policy spat that arose after Republicans took control of the Senate in 2015. A number of Republicans were concerned that negotiations between Iran and a United States–led coalition over the status of the former's nuclear program would lead to unacceptable compromises on the part of the United States. In March 2015, forty-seven Republican senators signed an open letter, drafted by Senator Tom Cotton and addressed to "the Leaders of the Islamic Republic of Iran."[203] The letter noted that any agreement concluded without congressional assent would be a "mere executive agreement," and that "[t]he next president could revoke such an executive agreement with the stroke of a pen and future Congresses could modify the terms of the agreement at any time."[204] The letter was clearly meant to undermine the ongoing negotiations by suggesting to the Iranians that any deal they struck would be likely to unravel. The reaction against the letter was swift: Vice President Joe Biden said that the letter "undercut[s] our President and circumvent[s] our constitutional system";[205] the *New York Daily News* printed the word "TRAITORS" underneath pictures of Senate Republicans;[206] and others accused the letter's signatories of violating the Logan Act.[207] That last accusation is worth considering in some detail, because it makes salient the separation-of-powers implications of limiting the speech or debate privilege to matters "internal" to the Capitol. The Logan Act, passed in 1799 (and never enforced), is a criminal statute prohibiting any American citizen "without authority of the United States" from communicating with any foreign government in an attempt to influence that government "in relation to any disputes or controversies with the United States, or to defeat the measures of the United States."[208] Note the subsumed premise of any discussion about prosecuting members of Congress under the act: it presupposes that members lack the "authority of the United States"— which is another way of saying that only the president possesses that authority, and that only she determines the "measures of the United States." In Biden's words, any attempt to "undercut" the president's construction of American interests abroad is equated to "circumvent[ing] our constitutional system."

Such claims rely on and reinforce the so-called sole organ doctrine, the claim that the president is "the sole organ of the federal government in the field of international relations."[209] This doctrine has, for obvious reasons, proven appealing to presidents, who have relied on it for everything from the authority to trade destroyers to the British in exchange for the right to establish bases in the Atlantic before the United States' formal entrance into World War II[210] to the authority for National Security Agency wiretapping.[211] And, since the *Curtiss-Wright* decision in 1936, the courts have been on board as well.[212] As a number of scholars have noted, the doctrine's historical pedigree—it purports to derive from a speech John Marshall made in the House of Representatives in 1800—is shaky, at best.[213] Perhaps more importantly, it is nonsensical as a descriptive matter: as we saw in chapter 3, Congress can pull the purse strings in matters of foreign policy, refusing to fund embassy construction or providing that no money be used to travel to meetings with, say, representatives of the Iranian regime. Top-level diplomats require Senate confirmation, and, as we saw in chapter 4, Congress can use its personnel power to rein in executive diplomacy. Attempts to circumvent these measures could spark congressional investigations and, perhaps, contempt citations, as discussed in chapter 5. Quite simply, there is no "sole organ" of American diplomacy.[214] There is a multiplicity of organs jointly engaged—sometimes cooperatively, sometimes not—in defining and implementing American diplomatic policy.

The fact that multiple institutions of government—most definitely including the members and houses of Congress—take part in conducting foreign relations means that we should be deeply skeptical of any attempt to give the president the sole authority to define, construct, and delimit American interests or positions on the world stage. But it is hard to see how members of Congress could play an effective role in that process if they had to worry about criminal prosecution by agents of the president, tried before the judges, any time that they articulated a conception of American interests, priorities, or values that was at odds with the president's articulation. Such a prosecution would be an almost literal rerun of the Cabell affair, which also concerned the authority of a member of Congress to speak out on matters of foreign policy. The Speech or Debate Clause should be understood precisely to protect such attempts by members of Congress to challenge the construction of national interests by the executive.

But what of the fact that the Cotton letter was addressed, not to the signers' constituents, but rather to the leaders of Iran? Why not simply publish the contents of the letter as an op-ed? First, note that, under *Hutchinson v. Proxmire*, the courts would have no particular reason to distinguish between an op-ed and a letter. Second, and more importantly, the epistolary form itself carries meaning that an op-ed lacks. By purporting to write directly to the Iranian regime, the signatories to the letter asserted that they were, in fact, entitled to a seat at the diplomatic table, rather than being relegated to sniping from the sidelines. A speech or debate privilege that did not support the senators' claim to a privileged role in the public construction of American policy would be a substantially impoverished one.

For Congress to compete effectively with the other branches in the public sphere, it must be able to communicate with the public. This means that its members must be able to air their views publicly, without the threat of prosecution by and in front of the other branches. This is true even, or perhaps especially, with regard to their views on matters that the other branches do not wish to have aired, matters they have chosen to label as "secret." The Speech or Debate Clause, by protecting members' ability to do just that, is therefore one of the key constitutional provisions enabling the functioning of our multiplicity-based separation-of-powers regime.

7

Internal Discipline

WITH GREAT POWER, OF COURSE, comes great responsibility.[1] Accordingly, provisions like the Speech or Debate Clause that empower the houses and members of Congress should be read *in pari materia* with a provision that encourages them to exercise that power responsibly: the authority granted to each house to "punish its Members for disorderly Behaviour, and, with the Concurrence of two thirds, expel a Member."[2] Self-policing is often viewed as a duty of legislatures (one that they may carry out more or less assiduously). But it can also be a source of soft power: when exercised responsibly, it can build or restore public trust in the institution, thus enhancing its ability to engage successfully in the public sphere.[3]

Historical Development

As with many of the legislative powers discussed in the preceding chapters, it was around the mid-sixteenth century that Parliament began taking responsibility for disciplining its own members. On January 21, 1549—the same day that the House of Commons passed the Act of Uniformity, establishing the Book of Common Prayer as the form of worship in England[4]—John Story spoke out against the Book. Story, who was both a well-regarded civil-law scholar and a notoriously difficult person,[5] paraphrased Ecclesiastes on the House floor: "Wo unto thee, O England, when thy king is a child."[6] The king at the time was the eleven-year-old Edward VI. As soon as Story made those remarks, the House ordered him arrested by its sergeant and held incommunicado;[7] three days later, it sent him to the Tower.[8] He remained there for more than five weeks, until he apologized and the House released him.[9] Importantly, even though Story's insult had been directed at the king (or perhaps more precisely, at the king's uncle, the Duke of Somerset, the Protector), it was the House itself that both punished and released him; indeed, the House's resolution releasing Story even purported to assert authority over the Crown, "requir[ing] the King's Majesty to forgive him his Offences in this Case towards his Majesty and his Council."[10]

A number of early cases of parliamentary discipline likewise dealt with positions taken or words spoken or written by members. In 1581, Arthur Hall became the first member to be expelled from the House of Commons,[11] when he was held in contempt for publishing a book containing "Matter of Infamy of sundry good particular Members of the House, and of the whole State of the House in general; and also of the Power and Authority of this House."[12] When Hall was brought to the bar of the House, the *Journals* noted, he did not behave "in such humble and lowly wise, as the State of One in that Place to be charged and accused requireth."[13] For his contempt, he was not only expelled; he was also imprisoned in the Tower for more than seven weeks and fined five hundred marks.[14]

Just a few years later, cameral discipline was once again a hot issue. William Parry, who had spent parts of the 1570s and 1580s as a government agent on the Continent, spying on English Catholics in exile, was elected to the House of Commons from Queensborough in Kent in 1584. His dealings with Continental Catholics were convoluted, and there is a high likelihood that he was a double, and perhaps a triple, agent.[15] Shortly after taking his seat, Parry was the only member of either house to speak against the Bill Against Jesuits, Seminary Priests, and Such Like Disobedient Subjects,[16] the gist of which is apparent from its title. Parry declared the act to be "full of blood, danger, despair and terrour or dread to the English Subjects of this Realm," and he intimated that its passage was motivated by the desire of members of both houses to acquire the property of exiled priests and other Catholics. He further insisted he would explain his reasons only to the queen herself, not to the House.[17] The House ordered him into the sergeant's custody; the following day, he was brought to the bar of the House, where he knelt and acknowledged that he had "very undutifully misbehaved himself, and had rashly and unadvisedly uttered those Speeches he used, and was with all his heart very sorry for it," blaming his inexperience and unfamiliarity with parliamentary procedures for the lapse (and promising that "if ever after he should give any just cause of offence again to this House or any Member thereof, he would then never after crave any more favour of them").[18] The House, after some debate, readmitted him.[19] Alas, the harmony was not to last: Parry was found in February 1585 to be plotting the assassination of the queen.[20] The House immediately expelled him and petitioned the queen (even before his trial began) for permission to make a law "for his Execution after his Conviction, as may be thought fittest for his so extraordinary and most horrible kind of Treason."[21] No such law was passed, and after Parry's conviction, he was hanged, drawn, and quartered—the usual punishment for treason.[22]

This tradition of using internal discipline to punish members for unpopular positions (especially when intemperately expressed) certainly continued through the seventeenth century. In a 1607 debate over a possible union with Scotland, Christopher Pigott, a member from Buckinghamshire, "entered into By-matter of Invective against the *Scotts* and the *Scottish* Nation, using many Words of Scandal and Obloquy."[23] This did not sit well with James I, only recently arrived from Scotland, who communicated his displeasure to the House. After substantial debate, in which it was "resolutely" resolved that "he might not in this Case be punished by any other means," he was expelled and committed to the Tower,[24] where he remained for twelve days.[25] It is worth noting that, even while acceding to royal wishes that Pigott be punished, the House first insisted on vindicating its speech or debate privilege that he not be punished anywhere else. We can thus see this first Parliament of the Stuart reign using its disciplinary power to carefully position itself vis-à-vis the Crown: it punished Pigott for his enmity toward James but also went out of its way to insist (with James as the clearly intended audience) that *only* it could punish Pigott for his words on the floor.

As opposition to James increased over the next two decades, the particular sentiments for which a member might get into trouble began to shift: in 1621, Thomas Sheppard was expelled for his vehement opposition to a bill for keeping the Sabbath, in which he referred to the member who introduced the bill as "a perturber of the peace, and a Puritan."[26] The Puritans and their friends in the House were not amused, with John Pym leading the charge in his first recorded speech, and Edward Coke chiming in with points both theological ("Whatsoever hindereth the observation of the sanctification of the Sabbath is against the scripture") and procedural (expressing his desire "to have such birds crushed in the shell; for, if it be permitted to speak against such as prefer [that is, intro-duce] bills, we should have none preferred").[27] Likewise, at the end of the century, four members were expelled for being insufficiently anti-Catholic: Edward Sackville was expelled (and briefly committed to the Tower) in 1679 for (correctly, as it turned out) denying the existence of the Popish Plot and calling Titus Oates "a lying rogue,"[28] and three others were expelled in 1680 for being too sympathetic toward the Duke of York (the future James II).[29]

But the seventeenth century also saw a broadening of the uses of parliamentary discipline. Three expulsions in 1621 mark this phenomenon. John Bennet was expelled for taking bribes and excessive fees in his simultaneous role as a judge in prerogative courts;[30] Robert Lloyd was expelled for zealously exercising and promoting his royal patent for the engrossing of wills;[31] and Giles Mompesson was expelled after he had fled to France while under arrest by the House for his use and abuse of royal patents.[32] These expulsions actually partake of two distinct trends: first, they mark the beginning of expulsions for conduct that was not undertaken as part of the members' parliamentary duties, and, second, they mark the beginning of a turn toward something like modern ethical standards. As to the first, although Bennet, Lloyd, and Mompesson were all clearly punished for activities taking place outside their parliamentary duties, the ties to parliamentary concerns are actually closer than they appear at first glance, especially in the cases of Lloyd and Mompesson. As we saw in previous chapters, Parliament in the 1620s was increasingly concerned that the Stuart kings sought to rule without it. The granting of patents was a source of revenue for the Crown independent of parliamentary taxation; patents were therefore a threat to parliamentary power, which partially explains why Parliament was so diligent in attacking their abuse. Patentees were, in some sense, undermining Parliament as an institution, so it is not entirely surprising that the House of Commons objected to some of the most egregious patentees sitting as its members. Still, the expulsions of Bennet, Lloyd, and Mompesson came to serve as precedent for the proposition that one could be expelled for conduct "external" to Parliament.[33]

Perhaps more importantly, they represent the beginning of the practice of the House of Commons' taking responsibility for the ethical standards of its own members. In 1628, while the House was looking into the participation of Edmund Sawyer, one of its members, in the drawing up of a new book of rates, Sawyer went to the home of a witness and told him that, since the House would not examine him under oath, "he should not need to speak of any thing which had passed between them." For witness tampering, Sawyer was expelled, sent to the Tower, and declared "unworthy ever to serve as a Member of this House."[34] After the Restoration, the House even began—cautiously, of course—navigating the line between (unacceptable) bribery and (acceptable) patronage in relation to parliamentary duties. In 1667, John Ashburnham was expelled for receiving £500 "from the *French* Merchants" (who were, in fact, English merchants seeking a license to import prohibited French wines).[35] In an illustration of how fuzzy the ethical lines between patronage and bribery remained, Ashburnham's defenders asserted that he took the money "not . . . as a member of the House of Commons but as a Courtier."[36] The House didn't buy it, and he was expelled. A little more than a decade later, when contemplating the expulsion of Thomas Wancklyn for selling parliamentary protections,[37] Henry Coventry remarked of Ashburnham: "There was no law against his taking that bribe. . . . He was a worthy Gentleman, and yet you expelled him the House. He was no Judge, and you judged that taking a bribe."[38] Coventry, at least, perceived the disapproval of bribery to be a judicial standard that had been, perhaps improperly, imported into the legislative realm. In the end, though, Wancklyn too was expelled.[39]

Three bribery cases in 1695 brought the issue squarely to the forefront of the House's attention. First, Henry Guy, a member of the Tory inner circle responsible for managing the court's business in the Commons, was sent to the Tower in mid-February for accepting a bribe from the officers of a certain army regiment, in exchange for help in passing a bill securing back pay for the regiment.[40] A vote to expel Guy narrowly failed two months later,[41] but he remained in the Tower until the end of the parliamentary session in early May.[42] Simultaneously, some members were increasingly concerned that the City of London and the East India Company were both using their considerable financial resources to advance legislation that they favored.[43] While Guy was in the Tower, John Trevor, the Speaker of the House, was expelled for taking a thousand guineas from the City in order to aid the passage of the 1694 Orphans Act, which resulted in a much-needed infusion of money into the City's coffers.[44] Ten days later, John Hungerford was expelled for receiving a (mere) twenty-guinea bribe from the City for the same purpose.[45] The House clearly perceived bribery to be a significant enough problem in mid-1695 that, the day before it was prorogued (thus releasing Guy from the Tower), it resolved that "the Offer of any Money, or other Advantage, to any Member of Parliament, for the promoting of any Matter whatsoever, depending, or to be transacted, in Parliament, is a high Crime and Misdemeanor, and tends to the Subversion of the *English* Constitution."[46]

As we saw in chapter 4, the beginning of the eighteenth century marked the rise of responsible government, with the leadership of the party with a parliamentary majority increasingly determining state policy. As a result, there was little benefit in bribing a member who did not also hold some office of state. Many eighteenth-century cases of parliamentary discipline, therefore, dealt with members who had received bribes in their capacities as such officers. To take just a few examples, Richard Jones, the Earl of Ranelagh (an Irish title which neither entitled him to sit in the House of Lords nor disqualified him from the House of Commons), was expelled from the House in 1703 for "misappl[ying] several sums of the public money" in his role as paymaster-general of the army;[47] and Robert Walpole was expelled and sent to the Tower in 1712 for allegedly orchestrating a kickback scheme for army foraging contracts when he was secretary of war.[48] Walpole had been a key player in the Whig government that was ousted by the Tories (with Queen Anne's support) in 1710, and his expulsion and imprisonment were seen as partisan in their motivation. His imprisonment made him a celebrity, and he was reelected the following year and held his seat for nearly three decades more, including two decades as prime minister.[49] Even as the transition to responsible government was proceeding, some backbenchers did continue to get caught up in parliamentary scandals: in 1721, for instance, seven members were expelled (one even after he had attempted to resign) for their roles in improprieties related to the South Sea Company. Of the seven, five were disqualified from future public service; six were heavily fined; and two were sent to the Tower.[50]

But parliamentary discipline maintained a broader scope than just bribery or abuse of office. In 1675, John Fagg, a member of the House of Commons, was the defendant in a lawsuit. In the normal course of appeals, the suit came before the House of Lords; the lower house believed that it was a breach of privilege for any of its members to be made to answer before the upper. Fagg appeared in the Lords to defend himself, leading his own house to have him arrested and sent to the Tower for breach of privilege.[51] Two days later, Fagg apologized and was released.[52] In 1707, John Asgill was expelled from the House for blasphemy, for arguing in a pamphlet that true Christians could be "translated" into eternal life without the necessity of dying first.[53] And in 1716, three members were expelled for participating in or supporting the Jacobite rebellion of the previous year.[54] Parliamentary discipline thus continued to be used for a wide variety of purposes, including speech that the House disdained (Asgill), actions that might damage the House's standing vis-à-vis other institutions (Fagg), or supporting a pretender to the throne (the Jacobites).

Undoubtedly the most prominent use of parliamentary discipline in the eighteenth century concerned John Wilkes, the notorious troublemaker whom we met briefly in chapter 3's discussion of the Wilkes Fund Controversy. Wilkes had incensed both the Tory prime minister, the Earl of Bute, and his patron, George III, with his attacks on Crown policy in the *North Briton No. 45* in 1763.[55] Wilkes was arrested and his house ransacked on a general warrant, and he was charged with seditious libel; he was subsequently released from the Tower after asserting the parliamentary privilege against arrest, and he won two trespass suits arising out of the search of his home. He soon became a folk hero, with "Wilkes and Liberty!" serving as a rallying cry for many, especially in London—and in the American colonies.[56] After Samuel Martin, an ally of Bute's whom Wilkes had also attacked in print, referred to Wilkes as "a coward, and a malignant scoundrel" in debate on the floor of the House of Commons, Wilkes challenged him to a duel.[57] Injured in the resulting duel, Wilkes fled to Paris. The House ordered him to attend upon it; when he sent his regrets from Paris, he was held in contempt.[58] He was then, in January 1764, expelled by the House for having published the *North Briton No. 45*, which the House concluded was "a false, scandalous, and seditious libel, containing expressions of the most unexampled insolence and contumely towards his Majesty, the grossest aspersions upon both Houses of Parliament, and the most audacious defiance of the authority of the whole legislature; and most manifestly tending to alienate the affections of the people from his Majesty, to withdraw them from their obedience to the laws of the realm, and to excite them to traitorous insurrections against his Majesty's government."[59] After returning from France in 1768, Wilkes stood for election to Parliament from Middlesex, and he received the most votes for the seat. But the House declared him ineligible for membership and refused to seat him, instead issuing a writ for a new election. Wilkes got the most votes in that election, and in the subsequent two reruns as well. After the fourth round of voting, the House simply seated his opponent.[60] As his conflicts with the House (and the Crown) grew, so too did his popularity, with Burke concluding that Wilkes "is the object of persecution. . . . [H]e is pursued . . . for his unconquerable firmness, for his resolute, indefatigable, strenuous resistance against oppression."[61] Finally, in 1774, when Wilkes was again returned for Middlesex (and after sixty thousand people had petitioned on his behalf), he was seated.[62] And, after moving the resolution every year for eight years, in 1782 he finally succeeded in having the records of his repeated exclusions expunged from the House's *Journals*, "as being subversive of the rights of the whole body of electors of this kingdom" to have their choice of representative respected.[63]

As we have already seen with the Wilkes Fund Controversy, the Wilkes saga was followed avidly in the colonies, where he was seen as a fellow struggler against an oppressive ministry.[64] But the colonists did not take from Wilkes the lesson that parliamentary discipline was inherently problematic. After all, as Mary Patterson Clarke has noted, the power of the colonial assemblies to discipline their members was sufficiently pervasive that it was "more or less assumed" to exist everywhere, although a number of colonies also made it explicit in one way or another.[65] Moreover, this assumption did not lie dormant: colonial assemblies "over and over again" disciplined their members for offenses ranging from absenteeism to "scandalous" papers to unparliamentary conduct, and the assemblies' power to do so went largely unquestioned.[66] Indeed, as Clarke pointed out, the famous 1765 speech in which Patrick Henry suggested that George III might "profit by [the] example" of Caesar and Charles I, who had their Brutus and Cromwell, respectively,[67] was immediately followed by Henry's begging the pardon of the Speaker and the House.[68] Even the hotheaded Henry recognized that his language had been unparliamentary and might subject him to cameral discipline.[69] And punishments by the assembly chambers frequently involved not only expulsion but also refusing to seat expelled members who had been reelected.[70]

But it should not be thought that the Wilkes case did not make a significant mark on American legislative procedure. Of the five early republican state constitutions that explicitly mentioned a power of expulsion, four prohibited either a second expulsion for the same offense or an expulsion for any reason that was known to the member's constituents at the time of his election,[71] and, given the prominence of the Wilkes affair in the colonial constitutional imagination only a decade earlier, it seems highly likely that these provisions were written with his case in mind.[72] Moreover, the provision in the fifth instance— that of South Carolina in 1776—makes it clear that the power of disciplining members was understood to be one of the privileges that Anglo-American legislative houses were assumed to possess even in the absence of such provisions: the two legislative houses "shall enjoy all other privileges which have at any time been claimed or exercised by the commons house of assembly, but the [upper house] shall have no power of expelling their own members."[73] This made sense, because the membership of the upper house was chosen by the lower house;[74] when, two years later, the state's new constitution created an elected upper house, the prohibition on its expelling its own members was dropped.[75] The provision that the houses would enjoy "all other privileges" that their colonial ancestors had enjoyed clearly, at least in the case of South Carolina, included a power to expel. And a number of other states included general provisions protecting the privileges of their legislative houses and/or allowing those houses to determine the rules of their own proceedings.[76] These provisions almost certainly would have sufficed to empower the legislative houses to make use of disciplinary powers up to and including expulsion. Moreover, unlike members of the British Parliament, whose terms could last as long as seven years under the 1716 Septennial Act,[77] members of the Revolutionary state legislatures served extremely short terms,[78] which may have made recourse to expulsion seem unnecessary. After all—and especially if an intervening election washed away most punishable offenses—the voters would have their say soon enough.

At the Constitutional Convention, the delegates clearly had the state constitutional provisions regarding expulsion in mind. An early draft out of the Committee of Detail gave the "house of delegates . . . power over its own members" but also contained a question for further discussion: "quaere. how far the right of expulsion may be proper."[79] In a subsequent draft, the committee came to a tentative conclusion: "Each House shall have Authority . . . to punish its own Members for disorderly Behaviour. Each House may expel a Member, but not a second Time for the same Offence."[80] The provision had become less detailed, however, by the time the committee reported to the full convention: "Each House . . . may punish its members for disorderly behaviour; and may expel a member."[81] When it came up for debate, Madison "observed that the right of expulsion . . . was too important to be exercised by a bare majority of a quorum: and in emergencies of faction might be dangerously abused. He moved that 'with the concurrence of 2/3' might be inserted between may & expel."[82] With very little subsequent debate, Madison's proposed addition passed overwhelmingly, and the provision, thus amended, passed as well.[83] Without any further debate in the Philadelphia Convention, the state ratifying conventions, or the press,[84] the provision assumed its final form: "Each House may . . . punish its Members for disorderly Behaviour, and, with the Concurrence of two thirds, expel a Member."[85]

Two influential early commentators made brief mention of the provision for legislative discipline. In his 1791 *Lectures on Law*, James Wilson tied the houses' disciplinary powers to their free-speech privilege: "When it is mentioned, that the members shall not be questioned in any *other* place; the implication is strong, that, for their speeches in either house, they may be questioned and censured by that house, in which they are spoken. Besides; each house . . . has an express power given it to 'punish its members for disorderly behavior.' "[86] Wilson went on to note that one of the available punishments was expulsion, but that the federal Constitution, unlike the constitution of his home state of Pennsylvania, did not explicitly prohibit reexpulsion for the same offense.[87] Joseph Story, in his 1833 *Commentaries on the Constitution*, tied the disciplinary power, not to the free-speech privilege, but rather to the power of each house to determine its own rules of proceeding (which is discussed in the next chapter): "[T]he power to make rules would be nugatory, unless it was coupled with a power to punish for disorderly behaviour, or disobedience to those rules."[88] Moreover, for those situations in which a member is "so lost to all sense of dignity and duty, as to disgrace the house by the grossness of his conduct, or interrupt its deliberations by perpetual violence or clamour," expulsion is available as a last resort.[89] The two-thirds requirement for expulsion serves to ensure that the power—"so summary, and at the same time so subversive of the rights of the people"—could not be "exerted for mere purposes of faction or party, to remove a patriot, or to aid a corrupt measure."[90]

As Story suggested, Madison had been prescient about faction: almost as soon as partisan conflict began to emerge under the Constitution, so too did issues of congressional discipline. In 1795, backlash against the Citizen Genêt affair allowed Federalist Humphrey Marshall (who was both the first cousin and the brother-in-law of future chief justice John Marshall) to win a Senate seat in Republican-dominated Kentucky. Unhappy with the results, Kentucky's governor and House delegation in 1796 asked the Senate to investigate charges by two Republican judges that Marshall had committed perjury in a lawsuit eighteen months before being elected to the Senate. At Marshall's request, the matter was referred to a committee, which reported that no evidence had been presented to the Senate that showed any fault on Marshall's part. In addition, the committee concluded that the Senate had no jurisdiction over matters occurring before a member was elected and having nothing to do with his congressional service. The full chamber agreed with its committee on a straight party-line vote.[91]

Of course, clear instances of misconduct could swamp partisan considerations. In 1797, President Adams transmitted to Congress evidence that Senator William Blount, a Republican from Tennessee, was promoting a scheme to help the British and Native American tribes seize Spanish Florida and Louisiana. The select committee impaneled by the Senate to investigate recommended that he be expelled. The following day, the Senate received an impeachment of Blount from the House, and the day after that, the Senate expelled Blount by a vote of twenty-five to one. Although Blount promised he would remain in town for his impeachment trial, he in fact hightailed it back to Tennessee. The Senate sent its sergeant-at-arms after him, but Blount's home-state supporters dissuaded the sergeant from attempting to take him back to Philadelphia. In January 1799, the Senate concluded that Blount was not an impeachable officer, and there has never been any attempt since to impeach a member of Congress.[92] Discipline by one's own house, rather than impeachment, which has a role for both, has thus been the sole mechanism of congressional control over members' behavior.

In January 1798, while the House was selecting managers for the Blount impeachment, Roger Griswold, a Federalist from Connecticut, and Matthew Lyon, a Republican from Vermont, began arguing. Griswold referred to allegations that Lyon had behaved in a cowardly manner during the Revolutionary War; Lyon responded by spitting in Griswold's face. While a committee was considering what to do about this, the House passed a resolution declaring that it would "consider it a high breach of privilege if either of the Members shall enter into any personal contest until a decision of the House shall be had thereon."[93] A vote to expel Lyon garnered a majority but fell short of two-thirds. Shortly thereafter, Griswold attacked Lyon with a cane on the floor of the House; Lyon grabbed the tongs from the fireplace and fought back. While a motion to expel both men was pending before a committee, they pledged themselves before the Speaker to keep the peace. The committee then recommended against expelling them, and the House concurred.[94] As we saw in the previous chapter, Lyon again narrowly escaped expulsion the next year, following his

Sedition Act conviction. In addition to the free-speech arguments noted in the previous chapter, several of Lyon's defenders suggested that, since his conviction had been public knowledge prior to his most recent election to the House, it would be inappropriate to expel him for it.[95] Although there was once again a majority to expel Lyon, it was a smaller majority than there had been to expel him for spitting at Griswold, and, in any case, far short of two-thirds.

The difficulty of meeting the two-thirds threshold was again on display in 1807–1808, when Senator John Smith, a Republican from Ohio, was implicated in Aaron Burr's treason conspiracy. Burr had allegedly sought to carve an independent nation, which he would rule, out of the newly acquired Louisiana territory. The ensuing trial was presided over by John Marshall riding circuit, with President Jefferson micromanaging the prosecution from afar. Burr was acquitted after Marshall issued a ruling excluding much of the government's evidence.[96] The charges against Smith, who had been indicted for providing supplies to Burr, were dropped after Burr's acquittal. Nevertheless, Samuel Maclay introduced a resolution calling for his expulsion, and John Quincy Adams authored the select committee report, which began by noting that, the verdict in the Burr trial notwithstanding, the existence of the Burr Conspiracy was "established by . . . a mass of concurring and mutually corroborative testimony"; moreover, the report stated, participation in the conspiracy should be incompatible with service in the Senate.[97] The report was at pains to differentiate expulsion proceedings from criminal ones: whereas the latter err on the side of acquitting the guilty, the presumption flips for the former: "It is not better that ten traitors should be members of this Senate than that one innocent man should suffer expulsion."[98] The committee also submitted to the Senate evidence that Smith was indeed part of the conspiracy. After extensive debate, including allowing Smith to be heard by counsel (Francis Scott Key, as it turned out), the final Senate vote was nineteen to ten for expulsion—one vote short of the requisite two-thirds. Republicans were split, and no Federalist voted to expel.[99] (Adams, who had been kicked out of the Federalist Party the previous year for his support of various Jeffersonian policies, did vote to expel.) Two weeks later, Smith resigned his seat.[100]

Expulsion, however, was not the only option available to the houses, and lesser punishments did not have to clear the two-thirds bar. Thus, in 1810, Massachusetts Federalist Timothy Pickering violated a Senate rule by reading a confidential document aloud in public session. On the motion of Republican

Henry Clay, the Senate passed a resolution declaring that Pickering had "committed a violation of the rules of this body," thus making Pickering the first member of Congress to be censured by his chamber.[101] The House followed suit, censuring its first member in 1832. William Stanbery, while criticizing a ruling from the chair, said: "[T]he eyes of the Speaker are too frequently turned from the chair you occupy toward the White House."[102] For his unparliamentary language, Stanbery was censured by his colleagues.[103]

Members could also take advantage of disciplinary procedures as a way of clearing their name. In 1835, President Jackson was nearly assassinated while attending a funeral in the House chamber. Although the attempted assassin was clearly mentally ill, reactions to the attempt were immediately and divisively partisan.[104] Rumors soon began circulating that Senator George Poindexter, a former Jackson ally who had a dramatic falling out with the president, had engineered the attack—and Jackson indicated that he found the rumors plausible. Poindexter requested that the Senate impanel a committee to investigate him and expel him if the charges were found to be accurate. After taking extensive testimony, the select committee concluded that the charges were baseless, and the full chamber unanimously exonerated Poindexter.[105] This official cameral determination of Poindexter's innocence played publicly to Jackson's opponents, "as the entire affair seemed to offer additional proof of the incompetence and corruption of the Jackson administration."[106]

These partisan tensions would become increasingly violent as sectional rivalry grew in intensity through the middle of the nineteenth century. Between 1838 and 1856, the chambers (especially the House) began small-scale dress rehearsals for the Civil War, with at least ten violent physical altercations between members. Seven of these conflicts pitted a Democrat against a Whig (or a Unionist or Opposition Party member, between the collapse of the Whigs and the rise of the Republicans).[107] These included the 1838 killing of Democratic representative Jonathan Cilley by Whig representative William Graves in a duel[108] and the infamous 1856 caning of Opposition Party senator Charles Sumner by Democratic representative Preston Brooks, aided by fellow Democrats Laurence Keitt and Henry Edmundson, in retribution for Sumner's "Crime against Kansas" speech on the Senate floor.[109] And at least one of the intraparty fights was clearly sectional: after Missouri Democratic senator Thomas Hart Benton said on the floor in 1850 that "the country has been alarmed without reason and against reason; . . . there is no design in the

Congress of the United States to encroach upon the rights of the South, nor to aggress upon the South," his Democratic colleague from Mississippi Henry Foote called it "a direct attack upon myself, and others with whom I am proud to stand associated." Benton then approached Foote, who responded by drawing and cocking a loaded pistol.[110]

Of these ten physical altercations, no punishment at all was meted out in nine (including the fatal Graves-Cilley duel, which led to the enactment of an anti-dueling law for the District of Columbia in 1839[111] but never resulted in any punishment for Graves). An expulsion resolution against Brooks for the attack on Sumner failed, but Keitt was censured by the House (a censure resolution against Edmundson also failed). Brooks and Keitt then resigned their seats, and both were immediately reelected and seated.[112] In the Benton-Foote imbroglio, the special committee, which recommended that no action be taken against either senator, laid blame at the feet of the entire Senate, which, "for some time past, and, until very recently, departed in its practice from the strict rules of order in debate, and tolerated [personal verbal attacks], which were increasing in frequency and violence."[113]

One member who was punished by the House during this period was Joshua Giddings, an Ohio Whig and staunch abolitionist. In violation of the House's "gag rule," a cameral rule adopted in 1840 providing that the House would refuse to receive any petition seeking the abolition of slavery or of the interstate slave trade,[114] Giddings offered a series of resolutions in 1842 approving of the slave revolt on the ship *Creole*, which had been carrying its human cargo from Richmond to New Orleans, and declaring that the "persons on board the said ship, in resuming their natural rights of personal liberty, violated no law of the United States, incurred no legal penalty, and are justly liable to no punishment."[115] A resolution, authored by Virginia Whig John Botts, was then passed declaring Giddings's conduct in offering the resolutions "altogether unwarranted and unwarrantable, and deserving the severe condemnation of the people of this country, and of this body in particular."[116] The day after receiving this censure, Giddings resigned his seat. He was immediately reelected and took his seat again.[117] In that same session, John Quincy Adams pressed the limits of the gag rule by presenting a petition from constituents calling for the peaceful dissolution of the Union, on the grounds that "a vast proportion of the resources of one section of the Union is annually drained to sustain the views and course of another section without any adequate return."[118] Several resolutions were offered censuring Adams; after much debate, the whole matter was tabled.[119] In 1844, Adams succeeded in having the gag rule repealed.[120]

The Civil War itself naturally led to a number of disciplinary cases. In the House, because of the biennial election schedule, many Southern states simply did not return any members for the Thirty-seventh Congress, and what controversies there were (as, for instance, when Unionists in seceding states held their own elections and sent members to Washington) were settled through the chamber's power to judge the elections, returns, and qualifications of members.[121] The border states, however, presented the expulsion problem squarely: two House members (one from Missouri and one from Kentucky) were expelled from the Thirty-seventh Congress for "having taken up arms against" and being "in open rebellion against" the federal government; one other member-elect from Missouri was expelled for the same reason.[122] The Senate, of course, had to deal with a number of members from seceding states whose terms had not expired. After some debate as to how to deal with the announced "withdrawals" of a number of members, the new Republican-dominated Senate declared six seats vacant (including that previously held by Jefferson Davis) when it met in special session in March 1861.[123] After Fort Sumter, the language hardened: when the Senate expelled ten more members from seceding states that July, it declared that they were "engaged in [a] conspiracy for the destruction of the Union and Government, or, with full knowledge of such conspiracy, have failed to advise the Government of its progress or aid in its suppression," and it explicitly used the word "expelled."[124] Over the next year, the Senate expelled four members from non-seceding states as well, because of their support of the Confederacy: John Breckinridge of Kentucky (formerly vice president under Buchanan) was declared a "traitor" and expelled after becoming a general in the Confederate Army; both Missouri senators were expelled after backing the secessionist forces in their state; and Jesse Bright of Indiana was expelled for writing a letter of introduction to "His Excellency Jefferson Davis, President of the Confederation of States," on behalf of a Texas arms dealer.[125] But the chamber was not indiscriminate: attempts to expel Benjamin Stark of Oregon and Lazarus Powell of Kentucky (both Democrats) for their insufficiently pro-war views both failed.[126] Likewise, attempts to expel Democrats Alexander Long of Ohio and Benjamin Harris of Maryland from the House failed, and both were instead declared "unworthy Member[s]" and censured for their speeches advocating recognition of the Confederacy.[127]

Unsurprisingly, the contentiousness of the Civil War spilled over into the Reconstruction Congresses. In May 1866, Democratic Representative John Chanler of New York was censured for introducing a resolution lauding President Johnson's vetoes of the "wicked and revolutionary acts of a few malignant and mischievous men"—that is, the Reconstruction bills passed by the Republican-dominated Congress.[128] The following month, Representative Lovell Rousseau of Kentucky—who had been a Union general during the war and was a self-described "Andrew Johnson man"[129]—gave a long speech chastising the Republican majority for foot-dragging in readmitting the Southern states.[130] In the course of the speech, he referred derisively to "some northern non-combatants, stay-at-home patriots."[131] In response, Josiah Grinnell, a Republican from Iowa, described Rousseau as "assum[ing] the air of a certain bird that has a more than usual extremity of tail, wanting in the other extremity," and asked, "[H]is military record, who has read it? In what volume of history is it found?"[132] Three days later, Rousseau attacked Grinnell with a cane on the portico of the Capitol.[133] The committee appointed to look into the matter recommended that Rousseau be expelled for the assault and that Grinnell be censured for improperly imputing cowardice to Rousseau.[134] The motion to expel Rousseau failed to garner the necessary two-thirds supermajority, and the motion to censure Grinnell was then tabled. A subsequent motion to censure Rousseau passed; Rousseau resigned but was censured at the bar nonetheless.[135] He was then reelected to fill his own vacancy.[136] Over the next decade, several other Democrats were censured for unparliamentary language in opposition to Reconstruction measures.[137] As the sectional conflict receded, the use of discipline for unparliamentary language or brawling dissipated, although it did not completely die out.[138] Indeed, a 1902 brawl between Senators John McLaurin and Benjamin Tillman, both Democrats from South Carolina, triggered by the debate over Philippine annexation, led to both men being censured and to a change in Senate rules governing decorum. Thenceforth, it was a violation of cameral rules to impute to a colleague "any conduct or motive unworthy or unbecoming a Senator" or to "refer offensively to any State of the Union."[139]

Of course, issues surrounding the Civil War and Reconstruction were not the only matters for which members of Congress faced discipline in the mid-nineteenth century. For instance, in 1844, Senator Benjamin Tappan of Ohio, like Senator Pickering three decades earlier, was censured for publicly releasing secret information—in this case, a message from President Tyler describing the terms of an annexation agreement with Texas.[140] The issue that would come to dominate congressional discipline in postbellum America, however, was corruption. Although federal statutes regulated corruption by officers and employees of the other branches from the earliest days of the Republic,[141] it was not until the middle of the nineteenth century that a law regulating the conduct of members of Congress was passed. An 1853 statute both forbade members of Congress to receive pay for prosecuting any claim against the United States and forbade them to receive anything of value that was given with intent to influence their vote or decision on any matter before them (or potentially before them) in their official capacity. Punishment for both offenses involved fines and imprisonment; punishment for receiving a bribe also involved disqualification from holding "any office of honor, trust, or profit, under the United States" in the future.[142] An 1862 law expanded the scope of the antibribery provision, no longer requiring that the compensation be given with "intent to influence [the member's] vote or decision," but now encompassing also compensation accepted for "attention to, [or] services, action, vote, or decision [on]," any actual or potential matter pending before Congress, as well as "procuring, or aiding to procure, any contract, office, or place, from the government of the United States or any department thereof, or from any officer of the United States, for any person or persons whatsoever."[143] And an 1864 law tightened the prohibition on lobbying by legislators, forbidding compensation for any services rendered "in relation to any proceeding, contract, claim, controversy, charge, accusation, arrest, or other matter or thing in which the United States is a party, or directly or indirectly interested, before any department, court-martial, bureau, officer, or any civil, military, or naval commission whatever."[144] No further statutes regulating corruption by members of Congress were passed for nearly a century.[145]

But the paucity of criminal provisions did not mean that the chambers themselves were inattentive to corruption. In 1857, a House select committee recommended that four members be expelled for various acts of corruption, ranging from agreeing to support various bills in exchange for bribes to attempting to bribe other members to support bills.[146] The worst of the bunch was Orsamus Matteson of New York, who not only recommended that the president of a railroad company bribe a number of members (to the tune of $100,000 total) to secure the passage of a bill but also stated that twenty to thirty members of the House had agreed with one another not to vote for any bill granting money or lands unless they were all bribed to do so.[147] The committee reported that it could find no evidence of such a widespread conspiracy, but it noted that it was in the interests of certain people ("broker[s] in congressional corruption") to spread such rumors, which were then disseminated by a sensationalizing press (whose members were "particularly anxious to be the first in giving to the public some piece of 'startling intelligence' or 'astounding development'").[148] The committee also reported out a bill that would have banned any lobbying for compensation[149]—which, perhaps needless to say, failed to pass. The recommended expulsions, however, had more traction: the House found insufficient evidence to proceed against William Welch of Connecticut, but the other three, including Matteson, all resigned while the expulsion resolutions were pending.[150] Even after his resignation, however, the House passed two resolutions censuring Matteson and declaring him "unworthy to be a Member" of the chamber.[151] Matteson (but not the other two resigners) ran for and was reelected to his seat; after some debate as to whether he should be expelled for his previous offense, a select committee decided that expulsion would be "inexpedient," and he was seated.[152] None of the four members ever faced criminal proceedings. Similarly, in 1862, Senator James Simmons, a Republican from Rhode Island, resigned while facing an expulsion resolution for using his influence to secure a war contract for two rifle manufacturers in exchange for a promised $50,000. Simmons's case led to the passage of the 1862 law described above, but Simmons, too, faced no judicial proceeding after leaving office.[153] And in 1870, three representatives were censured for taking money in exchange for appointments to the academies at West Point and Annapolis (two of the three were censured even after they had resigned),[154] but no action was taken against them in the courts.

The great scandals of the Gilded Age were also handled altogether internally. The Crédit Mobilier scandal centered on Representative Oakes Ames, a Republican from Massachusetts who was also an officer of Crédit Mobilier, a dummy construction company designed to skim off profits from government grants to build the Union Pacific Railroad. Ames distributed shares of the company to fellow members of Congress at below-market-value prices, in exchange for votes that would keep the money flowing into the Union Pacific coffers.[155] The stock had been handed out in 1867, but the gifts did not come to light until the *New York Sun* broke the story in 1872. A number of members of both houses (as well as Treasury Secretary George Boutwell and Vice Presidents

Schuyler Colfax and Henry Wilson) were implicated, but most were exonerated by the congressional committees set up to investigate. (Many of these members had made negligible profits and had returned the stock when the scandal became public.)[156] However, the House committee recommended the expulsion of both Ames and James Brooks, a Democrat from New York.[157] The committee majority was not troubled by the fact that the gifts had been received before the election of the investigating Congress, since they had theretofore remained secret, and thus the members' reelections could not be regarded as approbation or forgiveness on the part of their constituents.[158] The House Judiciary Committee, however, came to the opposite conclusion, arguing that members could never be punished by the House for actions prior to their most recent election.[159] In the end, the chamber split the difference, "absolutely con-demn[ing]" the behavior of Ames and Brooks but not expelling either.[160] The Congress ended shortly thereafter, and both men passed away within months of their censure.[161] In the Senate, the select committee recommended the expulsion of James Patterson, Republican of New Hampshire, and the censure of James Harlan, Republican of Iowa, but their terms expired before any action was taken.[162] No formal action was taken against any other senators, although Vice President Colfax was so thoroughly implicated and disgraced that his career was effectively ended.[163]

The other major congressional scandal of the Gilded Age involved the payment of bribes by the Pacific Mail Steamship Line in 1872 in a (successful) attempt to increase its annual subsidy from Congress for carrying mail. The scandal began to come to light in late 1874, and the House Ways and Means Committee investigation of it ran right up to the end of the Forty-third Congress in March 1875. The committee issued a report noting that William King, who had been the postmaster of the House in the Forty-third Congress (thus putting him in a uniquely good position to distribute bribes) and had been elected as a Republican from Minnesota to be a member of the Forty-fourth Congress, and John Schumaker, a Democrat from New York, had obstructed its investigation. The committee recommended both that the evidence it had collected be laid before the new House when it convened and also that it be sent to the federal district attorney for Washington, D.C.[164] Both men were indicted in 1875,[165] although apparently never prosecuted. Meanwhile, the House Judiciary Committee of the Forty-fourth Congress reported that it had no jurisdiction over offenses in previous Congresses, and the matter was apparently left to lie there.[166]

Schumaker may have been the first person indicted for conduct directly tied to his behavior as a member (as opposed to, say, Matthew Lyon or John Smith, who were indicted for what was understood to be extracurricular activity), but it would still be three decades before a member would be convicted for such behavior. In 1904, Senator Joseph Burton, a Republican from Kansas, became the first member of Congress to be convicted of a crime stemming from his legislative service. He had taken money for interceding with postal officials regarding an ongoing mail-fraud investigation, thereby violating the 1864 statute forbidding members to receive compensation for services rendered before governmental agencies.[167] In appealing his conviction to the Supreme Court, he argued that the statute was unconstitutional insofar as it interfered with the disciplinary powers of his house; the Court, per Justice Harlan, disagreed, noting that the Senate still had all of its disciplinary powers intact.[168] The Senate, which had held expulsion proceedings in abeyance while Burton's appeals were pending, ordered its Committee on Privileges and Elections to resume consideration of the matter after the Supreme Court's decision; Burton short-circuited the issue by resigning.[169] He then served five months in prison, at the end of which he was welcomed back to his Kansas hometown with a celebration that the *New York Times* described as being "in the nature of a triumphal procession."[170] The night of his return, Burton gave a speech to a sold-out auditorium seating nine hundred people (with proceeds going to support the local library), in which he excoriated his fellow Republican President Theodore Roosevelt. Burton insisted that Roosevelt had persecuted him because he had stood up for the domestic beet sugar industry and opposed Roosevelt's attempts to lower the tariffs on Cuban cane sugar, which Burton portrayed as having been undertaken at the behest of the powerful Sugar Trust.[171] In Burton's words, "I mortally offended Roosevelt. ... Roosevelt never forgave me." Burton claimed that Roosevelt had told Kansas's other senator, Chester Long (also a Republican), "I may indict Senator Burton." His political disagreements with Roosevelt, Burton claimed, were "why I was first struck down; why I was hounded for years for a crime I never committed; why all the vast energy of the Government was brought against me; ... why every crime that can surround a court of justice was committed to hunt me to death."[172]

The second conviction of a senator, under the same statute, led to similar accusations. John Mitchell, Republican of Oregon, was convicted in 1905 of violating the 1864 statute by receiving money to intercede with the General

Land Office (headed by fellow Oregonian Binger Hermann) on behalf of the key players in the Oregon Land Frauds scandal. He died while the case was on appeal, and while he remained a member of the Senate.[173] Although the press largely considered the verdict to be just, there were dissenters. The Salem *Capital Journal*, for instance, evinced "profound sympathy" for Mitchell: "For two years the Government secret service men have followed on his trail and pursued the methods of the Russian spies and detectives. . . . The *Journal* does not believe in the methods that are being employed by the Government. . . . It believes the jurors are terrorized by the press and the Government."[174] Friends of Mitchell's would assert that the prosecution was payback from President Roosevelt for Mitchell's insistence that the Interoceanic Canal Committee, which he chaired, not be rushed in its consideration of the Panama Canal (Mitchell had supported a Nicaraguan route). As one friend put it, Roosevelt had "concluded to get Senator Mitchell out of the way—no matter how." From this vantage, the appointment of a special prosecutor in the Oregon Land Frauds case was not an assurance of independence from local patronage networks but rather an assurance that the prosecution would be handled by a "generalissimo," aided by a "gang of jury-fixing detectives," who, at the behest of the president, assembled a "packed jury, everyone of whom was for years a bitter political enemy of Senator Mitchell, and thereby ma[de] sure of a verdict of guilty."[175] Likewise, the fact that the trial was presided over by a California-based district judge sitting by designation, after the only Oregon-based federal district judge (who had been seen as reluctant to go after Mitchell) had died, was viewed as a form of fixing the trial.[176]

In contrast to the alleged use of prosecution to sully the reputations of members, some members continued actively seeking internal investigations as a way of clearing their own names. In 1904, Senator Charles Dietrich, a Republican from Nebraska, submitted a resolution asking that a committee be appointed to investigate allegations that he had behaved corruptly as governor of Nebraska (allegations on which he had been indicted, but the charges had subsequently been dismissed).[177] In approving the resolution, the Senate appeared to take the position that it could investigate matters occurring before a member was elected; the select committee impaneled to investigate reported that there was no basis to the allegations.[178] As illustrated by the headline in the next day's *Washington Post*—"Dietrich Free From Guilt"—he received the public exoneration that he sought.[179]

Several issues are particularly salient in the history of the congressional disciplinary power traced thus far. First, partisanship has clearly been important—although by no means determinative—in who got punished and how. Second, members who believed themselves to be innocent of wrongdoing have sometimes actively sought investigations as a means of clearing their names. Third, members whose behavior subjected them to the disciplinary procedures of their houses have often resigned before the houses could act. These resignations fall into two broad categories: some members have slunk away, effectively admitting guilt but largely avoiding the official judgment of their peers, while others have resigned and then stood for reelection, effectively taking their case to the people. Finally, prosecution in the courts for violations of congressional ethical standards is a relatively late development, and its early uses were marked by accusations of political payback and interbranch meddling. Each of these issues in one way or another makes salient the functioning of congressional discipline in the public sphere.

Congressional Discipline and Congressional Ethics

One of the most prominent trends in the development of the congressional disciplinary power is its increasing use for what we would today call "ethics" matters—that is, attempts to prevent members from being influenced by factors that are believed to corrupt their judgment.[180] Studies have consistently shown that involvement in a publicized scandal harms a member's reelection chances.[181] Recent work has also indicated that the effects of scandals cut a wider swath, decreasing trust in government generally,[182] as well as harming all candidates from the party most closely identified with the scandal.[183] Importantly, studies have also found that scandals cause more negative public evaluations of Congress as an institution.[184]

How politicians *respond* to these scandals can be quite important in shaping the subsequent public reaction. (Indeed, in some cases their response will determine whether certain actions get publicly coded as "scandals" at all.) Between 2004 and 2006, there was a steadily increasing drumbeat of news about the lavish gifts that lobbyist Jack Abramoff had provided to certain members of Congress in exchange for their support on issues important to his clients. Even though the scandal implicated members of both parties, Democrats made concerted efforts to publicize Republicans' roles in the scandal and to make ethics reform a central plank of their 2006 midterm elections platform. As a result of this successful engagement in the public sphere, they forced Republicans to "own" the Abramoff scandal, with one study finding that voters punished Republican incumbents who received money from Abramoff but not Democratic incumbents.[185] Another study of the same election found that Republicans were harmed by the Mark Foley scandal (as a member, he had sent sexually suggestive messages to underage House pages). The study speculated that the incident harmed the party as a whole because "evidence surfaced to implicate a substantial number of party members of sheltering Mark Foley for political gain."[186] Scandals, then, have the potential to cause a significant amount of collateral damage—particularly if the public perceives the scandalous behavior to have been tolerated or facilitated by other members. As we saw in chapter 1, institutional trust is a significant source of institutional power; insofar as scandals damage public trust in Congress as an institution—as the studies cited above strongly suggest that they do—then they are damaging to congressional power as well. It is thus in the collective, institutional interests of the houses of Congress for their members to "[e]ngag[e] in fewer scandals."[187]

But, of course, this presents a collective action problem: the benefits of remaining largely scandal free are diffuse and can be undermined by just a few members. By contrast, the benefits of engaging in scandalous behavior (at least, in the period before it becomes publicly known) accrue entirely and immediately to the individual. What is needed, then, is a coordinating mechanism, whereby the chamber as an institution can enforce cooperation with a no-scandal norm and thereby ensure that it receives the institutional benefits that come with being (relatively) scandal free. Properly structured and properly functioning, the congressional disciplinary power can serve as such a mechanism.

This mechanism would, at the very least, have to involve the houses' taking primary responsibility for policing the ethics of their members. As we have seen, this was the case for quite some time. The House of Commons was long jealous of its exclusive ability to police its members; indeed, the law courts did not have jurisdiction over members of Parliament accused of bribery until 2010.[188] In America, as we have seen, no member was indicted for conduct related to service as a member until John Schumaker in 1875, and no one was convicted until Joseph Burton in 1904. Moreover, the first two members convicted—Burton and John Mitchell the following year—both asserted, persuasively to many, that their prosecution was political payback from

President Roosevelt. Regardless of the truth of those assertions, they point to two important concerns with the other branches' policing of members' ethics: first, there is the possibility that the president and the courts will use that authority as a means of influencing legislators, and, second, even if they are not in fact doing so, they are likely to be accused of it, making it harder to figure out who has acted improperly.

But even (or perhaps especially) where there is no plausible claim of improper interbranch meddling, greater involvement of the other branches in congressional ethics has significant soft-power implications. When congressional ethics violations are prosecuted by the executive and adjudicated by the courts, those branches get to play the heroes as they ferret out corruption by powerful actors in the name of the public interest. Meanwhile, congressional enforcement is relegated to the status of an also-ran, coming either after the other branches have acted or when the issue is too minor to warrant their attention. The message sent to the public is that Congress protects its own, handing out slaps on the wrist at most, and that only the executive and the courts can be trusted to keep politics clean. And to the extent that this lesson is internalized by the public, it fosters a narrative that Congress is *institutionally* corrupt. To the extent that only the executive and the judiciary act to root out corruption, the public will come to see them as trustworthy and Congress as untrustworthy. In refusing to clean up its own messes, then, Congress sacrifices its soft power.

This is precisely what has happened in recent decades. Beginning with the convictions of Burton and Mitchell in the first decade of the twentieth century, primary responsibility for ethics enforcement began steadily shifting away from the houses and into the executive and the courts. This transition was not immediate; for instance, when allegations surfaced in 1913 that the National Association of Manufacturers had bribed a number of members of Congress, the House appointed a special committee to investigate. The committee exonerated all but one of the accused members; it recommended that Representative James McDermott, Democrat of Illinois, be censured, although McDermott resigned before the House could vote on the resolution.[189] McDermott was subsequently reelected to his seat, and he was never indicted. In 1929, the Senate censured Hiram Bingham, a Republican from Connecticut, for placing on his Senate staff a lobbyist who was simultaneously being paid by the Manufacturers' Association of Connecticut.[190] And members convinced of their innocence continued for some time to seek vindication through cameral disciplinary processes. Senator

Burton Wheeler, Democrat of Montana, had been harshly critical of Attorney General Harry Daugherty's failure to prosecute officials involved in the Teapot Dome scandal, leading to Daugherty's resignation in March 1924. The next month, Wheeler learned that he had been indicted by a Montana grand jury for violating the 1864 law prohibiting members of Congress from representing paying clients before federal agencies. Wheeler insisted that he was being framed as a matter of political payback from the Justice Department, and he asked for a Senate investigation. The special committee appointed to investigate, consisting of three Republicans and two Democrats, voted four to one (with South Dakota Republican Thomas Sterling in the minority) to exonerate Wheeler, finding that he had handled only state litigation for a client while a senator-elect. The Senate overwhelmingly agreed with the committee, and the following year the Montana jury acquitted Wheeler as well.[191]

But this proactive congressional role was already in decline when Wheeler sought exoneration from his colleagues. That same year, it came to the House's attention that a grand jury in Illinois had reported to the court that it had evidence involving the payment of money to two members of Congress. The House resolved to ask the attorney general to name the members and specify the charge against them, but the attorney general refused. Meanwhile, the two members (John Langley of Kentucky and Frederick Zihlman of Maryland, both Republicans) were identified in the press and took to the House floor to deny the charges. Rather than continue to press the attorney general or proceed on its own, the House simply requested that the attorney general proceed with the case expeditiously. Both members were subsequently indicted, and Langley was convicted of using his influence with federal officials as part of a conspiracy to violate the Prohibition Act. Even after his conviction, he remained in the House (although he took no part in any official business) until all of his appeals were exhausted. Only then did he resign, the House never having taken any action against him; Zihlman was acquitted and remained in the House.[192]

It is certainly a long way from John Quincy Adams's claim in 1807–1808 that the Senate could expel John Smith for participation in the Burr conspiracy even after the court case against him had been dropped to the House's determination in 1924 that a convicted member would simply be held in limbo until all of his appeals were exhausted. The predictable consequence was that members who had engaged in serious improprieties often did not face any proceedings at all in their chambers. Thus, Harry Rowbottom of Indiana was sentenced to a year in Leavenworth in 1931 for taking bribes from people seeking postal appointments,[193] but, because Rowbottom lost his seat in the 1930 election, one searches the *Congressional Record* and committee reports in vain for any mention whatsoever of his illicit behavior. Indeed, there were no disciplinary proceedings at all (not even ones resulting in no action being taken) in the House between 1926 and 1967 and none in the Senate between 1929 and 1951,[194] and yet a substantial number of members were indicted and convicted during this period.[195]

Congress was not wholly silent on the ethics of its members during this period: in 1958, prompted by an influence-peddling scandal in the Eisenhower administration, the two houses adopted a one-page "Code of Ethics for Government Service" that applied to its own members as well as other government officials and employees.[196] As the Senate committee report accompanying it noted, the code "creates no new law; imposes no penalties; identifies no new type of crime; and establishes no legal restraints on anyone. It does, however, etch out a charter of conduct against which those in public service may measure their own actions and upon which they may be judged by those whom they serve."[197] In 1962, Congress, for the first time in a century, updated the bribery, unlawful gratuity, and conflict-of-interest laws as they applied to members, giving them the form that they largely retain today.[198] In 1964 and 1966, the Senate and House, respectively, created standing Ethics Committees for the first time.[199] And in 1968, both chambers, at the behest of their new Ethics Committees, adopted formal ethics codes.[200] But it had still been decades since either chamber had actually pursued any member for ethical violations. This was the context in which muckrakers Drew Pearson and Jack Anderson, in their 1968 book *The Case against Congress*, wrote that "Washington's neoclassic temples of government shelter petty thieves and bold brigands—the political Pharisees of modern America."[201]

Exhibit A for Pearson and Anderson was Senator Thomas Dodd, Democrat of Connecticut,[202] who became the subject of the first investigation by the Senate Ethics Committee in 1966–1967.[203] The committee found that Dodd had used campaign funds for personal expenses, and it recommended censure. Although there was widespread agreement that Dodd had not broken any laws, the Senate voted ninety-two to five to censure him.[204] The *New York Times* the next day applauded the Senate's performance of this "necessary, if disagreeable, public service" and noted that members of the Ethics Committee "ha[d] earned respect for a difficult job well done."[205] In particular, the *Times* noted that, "[e]ven though they are not explicitly forbidden in any code or statute book, there are some things that a man in public life knows he should not do," and it voiced its approval of the Senate's decision to punish Dodd for doing them, while simultaneously recommending the adoption of such a code.[206] The paper also noted that, despite the fact that the censure imposed no additional punishment, Dodd "is now finished as a useful member of the body. . . . No member can hope to survive such condemnation of his peers, and although Mr. Dodd has said he will run again, it is doubtful whether the Connecticut Democrats will let him."[207] Indeed, Dodd was denied the Democratic nomination in 1970; he then ran as an independent and finished third.[208]

The House also returned to the ethics field in 1966–1967 with the Adam Clayton Powell case. Powell, a Democrat from New York, had faced widespread accusations of financial improprieties and other misconduct during the Eighty-ninth Congress (1965–1967). (It should be noted that Powell was an African American and a civil rights leader, and, while he was likely guilty of misconduct, it is also undoubtedly true that some of his antagonists were motivated by racism.) At the opening of the Ninetieth Congress in 1967, a resolution was introduced to appoint a special committee to consider whether Powell was entitled to his seat.[209] The committee recommended that Powell be censured, fined, and stripped of seniority, but when the committee's proposed resolution came to the floor, it was amended to exclude Powell from membership in the Ninetieth Congress, and the amended resolution passed by an overwhelming vote of 307 to 116.[210] Importantly, this was done, not as an exercise of the House's power to expel, but rather as an exercise of its power to judge the qualifications of a member, which it decides by simple majority vote.[211] In the 1969 case *Powell v. McCormack*, the Supreme Court, per Chief Justice Earl Warren, held that the House had acted improperly because the ability to judge qualifications (and therefore to exclude from the body anyone lacking the requisite qualifications) was limited to those qualifications spelled out in the Constitution itself—in short, that the House could not circumvent the supermajority requirement for expulsion by purporting to exclude instead.[212] The Court also held that the fact that the exclusion vote passed the two-thirds bar was immaterial; it would not read an exclusion vote as a constructive expulsion vote.[213] Regardless, the damage to Powell was done: although he was reelected to the Ninetieth Congress (to fill the vacancy caused by his own exclusion), he did not seek to be sworn in; he was then elected to the Ninety-first Congress while his case was pending, but he lost the 1970 Democratic primary to Charlie Rangel, who had challenged Powell's long absences (and, implicitly, the cause for them) from the Capitol.[214]

But the houses' return to the ethics field in the late 1960s came too late to prevent the courts from stepping up and reaping the public relations benefits of serving as the primary ethics enforcers. The Supreme Court initially expressed some reticence to involve itself in such matters: in the 1966 *United States v. Johnson* case, the Court held that the Speech or Debate Clause barred the government from introducing evidence about why former representative Thomas Johnson had made a floor speech—a holding that made it rather difficult for the government to prove that he made the speech because he had been bribed.[215] But the Court quickly changed course, holding in *United States v. Brewster* in 1972 that evidence that former senator Daniel Brewster had solicited and received bribes in exchange for his vote on postage-rate legislation was admissible. Chief Justice Burger, for the Court, wrote that "[t]aking a bribe is, obviously, no part of the legislative process or function; it is not a legislative act. It is not, by any conceivable interpretation, an act performed as a part of or even incidental to the role of a legislator."[216] Accordingly, evidence of bribe taking was not barred by the Speech or Debate Clause. In dissent, Justice White (joined by two colleagues) argued that this was not a job for the judiciary: "The Speech or Debate Clause does not immunize corrupt Congressmen. It reserves the power to discipline in the Houses of Congress. I would insist that those Houses develop their own institutions and procedures for dealing with those in their midst who would prostitute the legislative process."[217] But White's call has not been heeded—since *Brewster*, although the courts have recognized that the Speech or Debate Clause imposes some limits on admissible evidence in such cases,[218] they have nevertheless been broadly willing to treat criminal proceedings as the primary forum for enforcement of congressional ethics.[219]

The houses have largely accepted this role for the courts. Consider a resolution reported out by the House Ethics Committee in 1972: it expressed the sense of the House that a member who had been convicted of a crime that carried a sentence of at least two years' imprisonment should refrain from participating in committee or floor business until either the conviction was overturned or the member was reelected.[220] The report accompanying the proposed resolution noted that it was the Ethics Committee's stated position to take a back seat on ethics enforcement: "[W]here an allegation involves a possible violation of statutory law, and the committee is assured that the charges are known to and are being expeditiously acted upon by the appropriate authorities, the policy has been to defer action until the judicial proceedings have run their course."[221] (The proposed resolution failed to pass in 1972, but a nearly identical resolution passed in 1975.)[222] This, of course, is precisely the opposite of Justice White's argument that the houses should develop their own procedures for dealing with corruption; instead, the House Ethics Committee explicitly declared the executive branch and the courts to be the "appropriate authorities" to deal with congressional corruption.

It will come as little surprise, then, that in recent major ethics scandals the other branches have routinely acted first, with action by the chambers themselves coming later, if at all. Consider the "Abscam" scandal, which played out from 1978 to 1982. It began as an FBI sting operation designed to ensnare forgers and art thieves and subsequently, based on information from informants, expanded to include political corruption. It culminated with undercover agents, posing as Arab sheiks, attempting to bribe legislators. In 1980, the media reported that the FBI had video evidence of seven members of Congress—six House members and one senator, all Democrats except Representative Richard Kelly of Florida—agreeing to accept bribes in exchange for various favors, ranging from introducing special immigration bills to steering government contracts.[223] All seven were indicted in 1980 and convicted between 1980 and 1982, but only one ever faced discipline from his house. Four of the seven were defeated in reelection bids in November 1980, "in large part because of Abscam."[224] Representative Raymond Lederer of Pennsylvania won his reelection bid in 1980 while under indictment and was convicted in January 1981. After the House Ethics Committee recommended expulsion in April, Lederer resigned.[225] Likewise, Senator Harrison Williams of New Jersey was convicted in May 1981; the Ethics Committee recommended expulsion in August; and he resigned in March 1982, once it became apparent that the Senate would vote to expel him.[226] Only Representative Michael Myers of Pennsylvania was actually disciplined by his chamber—he was expelled a month after being convicted on bribery charges.[227]

Nor is Abscam an outlier. Indeed, the only member of Congress to have been expelled since Myers is Representative James Traficant, Democrat of Ohio, who was expelled in 2002 after he had been convicted on ten counts of bribery, racketeering, and corruption.[228] Other members charged with or even convicted of crimes have been allowed to resign or have lost their seats with no formal action by the House.[229] For instance, Representative Mario Biaggi, Democrat from New York (and a former New York City police officer), was convicted in two separate corruption trials in 1987 and 1988, one of which carried a thirty-month prison sentence and the other of which carried an eight-year sentence. He resigned in 1988, as colleagues were preparing to expel him.[230] In 1994, powerful Illinois Democrat Dan Rostenkowski was indicted on seventeen counts, including misuse of official funds and obstruction of justice. At the request of the Justice Department, the House Ethics Committee deferred proceedings;[231] Rostenkowski lost his seat in the 1994 Republican wave, and he pled guilty to two counts of mail fraud in 1996.[232] The same pattern holds for Duke Cunningham, Republican of California, who resigned from the House in 2005 and was sentenced to more than eight years in prison for accepting millions in bribes,[233] and for the two House members (Bob Ney, Republican of Ohio, and Tom DeLay, Republican of Texas) convicted in the Jack Abramoff scandal in 2006–2007:[234] none of them was subject to any sort of formal cameral discipline. Similarly, Representative William Jefferson, Democrat of Louisiana, was indicted in 2007 on sixteen corruption charges—the evidence against him included $90,000 in cash that was found stuffed in frozen-food containers in his home freezer. He lost his reelection bid in 2008 and was convicted on eleven counts in 2009.[235] Again, the Ethics Committee held its own investigation in abeyance while the criminal investigation was ongoing.[236] The pattern largely holds even for scandals that do not give rise to criminal charges: in the 1989–1991 "Keating Five" Senate scandal, although the Ethics Committee found that all five senators involved (four Democrats and one Republican) were guilty of at least "poor judgment" in intervening with regulators on behalf of a savings and loan, the worst punishment handed out was a "reprimand" to Senator Alan Cranston (three of the five, including Cranston, retired at the end of their term). The lack of any more severe punishments led to significant public criticism.[237] Likewise, although the House took no formal action against any of the members who had overdrawn their accounts in the 1991–1992 House banking scandal, Republican leaders pressured Democratic Speaker Tom Foley to ensure that the names of the members who had overdrawn their accounts were made public. Subsequently, a huge number of House members either retired or lost their seats in the 1992 elections, at least in part due to the scandal.[238]

Insofar as trust in Congress as an institution is significantly affected by how Congress *reacts* to ethics violations—and I have argued above that it is—this pattern is a problem for the institution. The chambers have so thoroughly ceded the ethics-policing role to the other two branches that they are willing to allow members to remain in the chamber for years after they have been indicted on serious ethical violations—indeed, in some cases even after they have been convicted, while the convictions are on appeal. Only members who have the poor manners to refuse to resign once their convictions have become final seem to face discipline from their chambers. Indeed, the ethics committees even hold fact-finding in abeyance while criminal proceedings play out. The inevitable appearance is that Congress has almost no interest in policing its members; only the executive and the courts appear to have the will to keep politics clean. To the extent that this lesson is received by the public, it furthers the narrative that Congress is *institutionally* corrupt, which, in turn, decreases public trust in Congress, while increasing trust in the executive and the courts. In failing to keep its own houses in order, Congress sacrifices its soft power.

Of course, it is understandable why many members are reluctant to pursue their colleagues. Some might have good reason to fear that the scrutiny would subsequently be turned on them; others may simply feel uncomfortable investigating and punishing their colleagues and friends. Still, incentives cut the other way, too: from Theodore Roosevelt to Newt Gingrich, politicians have made national reputations as corruption fighters. And, of course, there are always partisan motivations to bring the misdeeds of one's political opponents to light. So, what institutional reforms might make the houses more likely to pursue wrongdoing vigorously, which would, in turn, redound to the institution's benefit?

In 2008, the House took a tentative step in that direction, creating the Office of Congressional Ethics (OCE), an internal entity charged with reviewing allegations of misconduct and recommending action to the House Ethics Committee.[239] The OCE's board is made up of nonmembers, with an equal number appointed by the Speaker and the minority leader. Lobbyists and officers and employees of the federal government are prohibited from serving as OCE board members.[240] The OCE receives complaints from the public and also takes notice of press reports and other sources of information about potential wrongdoing; if two board members agree that there is a reasonable basis to proceed, it can then open a thirty-day preliminary review into allegations of misconduct. At the end of the preliminary review, if at least three board members find probable cause to believe that there has been a violation, then the investigation proceeds to a second-phase review. Whether the investigation proceeds to a second-phase review or not, the OCE must notify both the Ethics Committee and the individual under investigation of its decision. If the investigation does proceed, then the OCE has forty-five days (extendable for an additional fourteen days) to conduct the second-phase investigation, at the end of which it must transmit its findings and recommendation to the Ethics Committee.[241]

The Ethics Committee remains responsible for making any recommendations to the full House. But it must act on any recommendations received from the OCE within forty-five days. At the end of forty-five days, the committee must publicly release both its own actions and the OCE report and findings, unless the chair and ranking member jointly agree, or a majority of the committee votes, to withhold the information for an additional forty-five days. However, if the committee agrees with an OCE recommendation to dismiss the complaint, or if the committee dismisses it when the OCE left the case unresolved, then the committee need not (although it can) make a public disclosure. A deadlocked committee results in the disclosure of the OCE report and findings. And at the end of each Congress any theretofore undisclosed OCE reports are released.[242]

The structure of the OCE is important. Unlike the Ethics Committees, it receives complaints from nonmembers, so someone with knowledge of wrongdoing need not get the attention of a member in order to begin the ethics process. Moreover, any time the OCE recommends further inquiry by the Ethics Committee, that recommendation will become public. Even though all final decisions are made by the Ethics Committee and then by the full House, the knowledge that an OCE recommendation of further inquiry must be publicly released will necessarily put pressure on the Ethics Committee either to recommend disciplinary action or to have a very good reason why such action is not necessary. At the same time, since any disciplinary action will, in fact, be taken by the House itself, the institutional benefits of keeping one's own house in order will accrue to the chamber. Given these institutional features, it is unsurprising that the OCE has received highly favorable reviews, both in the press and from the public-watchdog groups that pressed for its creation.[243] A report for Public Citizen found that the OCE had "unquestionably . . . helped boost the case record of the Ethics Committee" in punishing wrongdoing.[244] Moreover, the office has sufficient public cachet that a surprise move by the Republican majority to eliminate it at the opening of the 115th Congress in January 2017 sparked substantial backlash and was hastily abandoned.

The OCE is unquestionably a move in the right direction, but its structure could be improved still further.[245] First, and most basically, the OCE exists only for the House; attempts to create a similar institution in the Senate have failed to gain traction so far. Insofar as the office works well in the House, an analogue would likely work well in the Senate.[246] Second, the OCE currently lacks subpoena power, and one of the most frequent recommendations is that it be given that power.[247] Third, the public-disclosure requirements could be strengthened: any investigation making it to second-phase review should be disclosed, even where the OCE recommends dismissal and the Ethics Committee concurs. The requirement that it make it to second-phase review would serve to weed out the most frivolous complaints, and the expanded disclosure would demonstrate, at the very least, that all complaints are taken seriously.

Finally, both the OCE and the Ethics Committees lack jurisdiction over former members.[248] As a result, members frequently resign (or simply run out the clock and do not seek reelection) and thereby escape any discipline from their chambers. The forcing of resignations is not trivial—indeed, we have seen that one outcome of a vigorous cameral disciplinary process has long been that the wrongdoer slinks away in shame. In many cases, this will suffice to show that the house has effectively policed itself. In still other cases, resignation has been used as a means of submitting members' conduct to their constituents—when a member resigns and immediately seeks reelection, the people can decide whether his conduct makes him unworthy to be a member or not.[249] But there may well be certain cases in which allowing a member to slink quietly away is insufficient. I have argued elsewhere that the House has the authority to refuse to accept the resignations of members and that it might wish to do so in circumstances in which it wants to send a message by expelling them instead.[250] But even if it chooses not to go that far (and in the case of the Senate, from which resignations are explicitly contemplated in the Constitution's text), the chambers could still censure or (using their contempt powers) even imprison former members who had violated ethical rules and then resigned to escape cameral punishment.

Congressional Discipline and Cameral Order

Cameral discipline is not only appropriate for what we would today call ethics violations; it is also an important means of preventing members from unilaterally hijacking or otherwise disrupting the proceedings of their chamber. Recall, in this regard, that Joseph Story treated the disciplinary power as necessary to give effect to the houses' rule-making powers. For an instance of this sort of use of the houses' disciplinary powers, consider the Senate's censure of

Joseph McCarthy in the aftermath of the 1954 Army-McCarthy hearings. After Ralph Flanders, Republican of Vermont, introduced a censure resolution (declaring a broad swath of McCarthy's conduct "unbecoming a Member of the United States Senate, . . . contrary to senatorial traditions, and tend[ing] to bring the Senate into disrepute"),[251] the Senate impaneled a special committee, composed of three Democrats and three Republicans, all of them éminences grises of the chamber, and chaired by Republican Arthur Watkins of Utah. The committee reviewed more than forty allegations of misconduct by McCarthy[252] and ultimately boiled them down to thirteen allegations, grouped into five general categories. These categories ranged from his noncooperation with and contempt of a subcommittee that had investigated him in the previous Congress for misconduct,[253] to his improper use of classified information,[254] to his "abuses of colleagues in the Senate."[255] After taking substantial amounts of testimony and issuing detailed findings, the committee reported mere days after the 1954 midterm elections, which swung control of both houses to the Democrats, a result partially attributable to public disgust with McCarthy.[256] The Watkins Committee report concluded that two of the five categories of charges justified censure: those dealing with contempt of the previous investigation and those dealing with his abuse of Army General Ralph Zwicker when Zwicker testified before McCarthy's Permanent Subcommittee on Investigations.[257] When the resolution came to the Senate floor, the charge relating to Zwicker was dropped and replaced with a charge that McCarthy had abused the Watkins Committee itself. By a vote of sixty-seven to twenty-two, the Senate censured McCarthy for his abuse of the two committees in two successive Congresses.[258]

The next day, the *New York Times* editorialized that, in voting overwhelmingly to censure McCarthy, "the Senate of the United States has done much to redeem itself in the eyes of the American people and to give new assurance of its faithfulness to the principles of orderly democratic government and individual liberty under law."[259] The *Washington Post* declared the censure "a vindication of the Senate's honor."[260] Writing the following year, anti-McCarthyite journalist Alan Barth celebrated the Watkins Committee hearings as "in almost every important respect the antithesis of the procedure followed" by McCarthy himself in conducting Permanent Subcommittee on Investigations hearings.[261] The Senate's censure "reflected a sense of honor on the part of the Senate, and a revived regard for that honor. It revealed a recognition, too long suppressed, that the Senate as an institution is the inheritor and the trustee of a great tradition. . . . 'The honor of the Senate' may be undefined and undefinable, but it is nonetheless real; and it was essentially for the violation of this honor, rather than for any breach of specific rules, that McCarthy was at last called to account. The Senate's action bespoke an awareness of the moral obligation that inescapably accompanies authority."[262] The censure effectively ended McCarthy's political prominence, with his attempts at provocation increasingly ignored. Within three years, he drank himself to death.[263]

The McCarthy censure was publicly effective in large part because of the bipartisan nature of both the Watkins Committee and the final Senate vote. Contrast this with the 2009 "resolution of disapproval" passed against South Carolina Representative Joe Wilson, a Republican, for shouting "You lie!" at President Obama while the president was addressing a joint session of Congress.[264] The House was under Democratic control at the time, and, although the resolution of disapproval was intended to be a milder measure than a censure, only seven Republicans voted in favor of the resolution (and twelve Democrats voted against). Press reports described the vote as "largely party-line,"[265] and there was no widespread editorializing in support of the chamber's action. Indeed, the whole incident raised Wilson's profile in his party, making him a highly sought-after fundraiser for fellow Republicans.[266] He was handily reelected in 2010.

Maintaining public trust on an institutional level requires that the houses combat—and be seen to combat—abuses in their midst. This is true both for ethical violations, like bribery, and for significant violations of cameral order and decorum. The houses have at times used their disciplinary powers over their members in ways that enhance their soft power with the public. But far too frequently, they have failed to do so, and in recent decades, in particular, they have far too readily ceded this form of soft power to the other branches. Still, recent developments like the House's creation of the Office of Congressional Ethics offer some hope that the chambers will begin to take more advantage of this means of building public trust.

8

Cameral Rules

LURKING IN THE BACKGROUND OF NEARLY every topic covered thus far has been the authority of each house to "determine the Rules of its Proceedings."[1] Without that authority, the chambers would not be able to structure their budget deliberations, issue subpoenas for testimony or documents, issue contempt citations when those subpoenas were defied, create an Office of Congressional Ethics, or, indeed, do much of anything. The ability of each chamber to determine its own cameral rules can be thought of as its authority to create its own constitution: the rules constitute it as a certain type of body with certain powers and procedures for exercising those powers, as well as certain constraints on its powers. Depending upon the deftness with which they are promulgated and implemented, these rules can be more or less effective in facilitating their house's engagement in the public sphere.

Historical Development

The House of Commons recognized from an early period that its internal ordering could significantly impact its interactions with the Crown. As we saw in chapter 6, the House in 1399 successfully petitioned Henry IV to promise not to pay attention to any accounts of parliamentary proceedings not authorized by the House. The ability to keep deliberations secret was an important step in the development of free parliamentary speech, and therefore in the development of the House's ability to confront the Crown. Just two years later, in 1401, the House again attempted to use its internal deliberative structure to its institutional advantage, requesting of Henry "that they might be informed as to the replies to their petitions before any . . . grant [of money would be] made."[2] The order of business was obviously important: once Parliament granted funds to the Crown, it had no other leverage with which to negotiate redress of grievances. Conversely, the king might be inclined to be more accommodating with respect to petitions if he knew that the funds he sought were still hanging in the balance. Henry, understanding this dynamic as well, declined the House's request, but it was the Commons who actually won the underlying debate. As Redlich notes, the principle that redress of grievances preceded supply "speedily became a customary right, inasmuch as the kings acquiesced in the practice adopted by the Commons, of putting off their grant of supply to the last day of the session."[3] In previous chapters, we saw that timing used to good effect, especially in the seventeenth century, with concessions extracted from the Stuart monarchs before supply was granted.

A subsequent fifteenth-century procedural innovation was also an important step in evolving Crown-Parliament relations. Through the reign of Henry IV, as the House's request above indicates, most parliamentary business was carried out via petition: members presented a petition—either on behalf of those they represented or on their own initiative—seeking from the Crown some sort of redress or alteration in the status quo.[4] During the reigns of Henry V and Henry VI, however, petitions slowly came to be replaced by bills.[5] As a consequence, legislation ceased to take the form of a request to the Crown for some action; it now took the form of a draft of the proposed change, "free from any formula of asking."[6] The result was a more assertive conception of Parliament's role in the state: it was now an initiator of action, not a mere supplicant.

By the middle of the sixteenth century, when the House of Commons began keeping its *Journals*, one can see evidence of a "highly developed" and specific (if largely customary) procedure, including the requirement of three readings of a bill, the requirement that members address the Speaker rather than one another, the proscription of unparliamentary language, the prohibition on the Speaker's taking part in debate, voting procedures, and so on.[7] One can also see evidence of the appointment of select committees for a variety of purposes, ranging from drafting bills to deciding disputed elections, and by the late-sixteenth century one can find early versions of what would become the "grand" standing committees, which came into their final form in the 1620s.[8]

The Speaker is an especially interesting case study for the importance of cameral ordering upon the House's relationships with the other branches. A central component of the Speaker's role was to speak for the House—that is, to represent the chamber in its dealings with the monarch (including, of course, delivering the prayer for the House's traditional liberties at the opening of a new Parliament, as described in chapter 6). As a result, the monarch had the right to refuse the House's choice of a Speaker, which meant that the Speaker was long understood to have dual loyalties, at best—and to be an agent of the Crown, at worst.[9] Indeed, as Hatsell noted, the Speaker sometimes simultaneously "held a considerable office" under the Crown.[10] Edward Coke, for instance, was simultaneously the Speaker of the House of Commons and Elizabeth's solicitor general in 1592–1593.[11] Because the Speaker, as presiding officer of the House, also had significant agenda-setting power,[12] he was an important mechanism of Crown influence in the House.

Early in the reign of the Stuarts, the House responded to the power of the Speaker with a procedural innovation: the Committee of the Whole House. This "committee" consisted of the entire membership of the chamber, but, because it was a committee, it was presided over not by the Speaker but rather by another member chosen by the body. Moreover, rules limiting members to one speech per debate on the floor did not apply in the Committee of the Whole, and the proceedings were not recorded in the *Journals*.[13] It has long been suggested that the development of the Committee of the Whole was intended to reduce the power of the Speaker by removing his ability to set the agenda and control the progress of debate.[14] Of course, the desirability of removing control of proceedings from the Speaker varied as a function both of the state of Crown-Commons relations at any given moment and of the degree to which any individual Speaker tended to kowtow to the Crown,[15] but it is worth noting that those chosen to chair the Committee of the Whole were usually not Privy Councillors and, by the 1620s, were often central figures in the incipient parliamentary opposition to James and Charles.[16] But getting the Speaker out of the chair was not the only important procedural reason for going into Committee of the Whole: at least as significant was that the rule against a member speaking twice on the same matter did not apply in the committee.[17] The relaxation of this rule had significant implications outside the chamber. Supporters of Crown policy had less need to engage in running detailed rebuttals of their opponents' arguments; after all, they had the power of the Crown and the agenda-setting authority of the Speaker on their side. Unfettered debate was more helpful to developing opposition and moving the debate away from the terms set by the Crown. And committee procedures allowed the rising class of parliamentarians more control over the workings of their chamber.[18]

Nor was the development of the Committee of the Whole the only significant procedural innovation of the early Stuart period. The first decades of the seventeenth century saw a dramatic rise in formal cameral rulemaking, as procedures that had theretofore been matters of custom or tradition were codified into explicit orders of the House. Indeed, the opening months of the 1604 Parliament—the first of James's reign—saw a remarkable outpouring of such rules.[19] Only a week into that Parliament, we find the Commons passing both a motion "against Hissing" and noting, "[a]s an ancient Rule of the House, that, upon any Conference [with the Lords], the Number of the Commons named for the said Conference, are always double to those of the Lords; and the Place and Time of Meeting appointed by the Lords."[20] Given the difference in status, it is understandable that the Commons would consider it important to have the advantage of numbers when meeting with the Lords to iron out disagreements. Additional rules passed in this session governed everything from decorum in debate[21] to the prevention of dilatory tactics (including one forbidding members from offering "any superfluous Motion, or tedious Speech")[22] to the phrasing of questions and the procedures for voting on them.[23] All of these rules demonstrate an increasingly active desire to engage with the substance and forms of self-regulation; for that reason alone, they bespeak an increasingly active and self-aware House.[24]

Several other rules passed in 1604 had the more direct goal of combatting Crown authority, much as the rule governing conferences with the Lords, discussed above, had the goal of reining in the authority of the upper chamber. In late April, the House agreed to a rule allowing the Speaker to "explain" a bill, "but not to sway the House with Argument or Dispute."[25] As we have already seen, the Speaker was viewed as an arm of the Crown; the Speaker chosen in 1604, Sir Edward Phelips, was considered especially close to the new monarch, and his election to the chair was unusually contentious within the House.[26] The limitation on his taking substantive part in debate, then, was clearly a means of restricting Crown influence over the course of debates. Indeed, the following month, after Phelips had, on his own initiative, sent the king a draft of a bill that James had refused to return to the House, the House declared that the Speaker could not "deny to read a Bill, which he receiveth; to withdraw it out of the House; to inform the King, or any other, before the House be made acquainted with it."[27] One can even see the concern to limit Crown authority in the determination that, "if Two stand up to speak to a Bill, he against the Bill . . . to be the first heard."[28] Given the extent to which agents of the Crown (the Speaker, as well as other Privy Councillors in the House) still controlled the course of proceedings at this point, bills brought to the floor were likely to have been introduced at the behest of the Crown. Allowing opponents of a bill to speak first, then, would generally have functioned as a means of giving them some ability to establish the terms of the debate.

At around the same time, the *Journals* were becoming increasingly detailed— the result, Redlich suggested, of the House's desire "to take care that precedents as to procedure and privilege were safeguarded against forgetfulness and preserved for future use."[29] In other words, the House was increasingly investing its energy in institutional capacity building. In the previous five chapters, we saw much of what this increased institutional capacity allowed the House to do in the first half of the seventeenth century: obviously, these procedural moves did not *cause* the House to be increasingly assertive, but they most certainly did enable and channel that assertiveness, which manifested itself in fights over money, personnel, free parliamentary speech, and so on. Recall, for instance, the 1629 incident, described in chapter 6, in which John Eliot, Denzil Holles, and Benjamin Valentine were prosecuted in the King's Bench for holding the Speaker in his chair while the House passed resolutions against the Crown's use of prerogative taxation. Here was a moment in which the Speaker, acting as a loyal agent of the Crown, attempted to use his authority to prevent a cameral majority from effecting its will. And when the Short Parliament convened in 1640, after eleven years in which no Parliament sat, one of the grievances for which it immediately demanded redress was the Speaker's unilateral attempt to adjourn the House, on the king's orders—in other words, the violation of cameral authority over its own proceedings.[30]

Of course, not all Speakers saw their role as serving primarily the Crown. Most famously, as described in chapter 5, Speaker William Lenthall refused to tell Charles where to find several members accused of treason, insisting, "I Have neither Eyes to see, nor Tongue to speak in this place, but as the House is pleased to direct me, whose Servant I am here."[31] (Lenthall would go on to serve as Speaker of the Rump Parliament and the Commonwealth Parliaments

under Cromwell.)[32] Just as cameral rules could help members get around a
Speaker who was too solicitous of the Crown, they could also be used by a
Speaker to justify his own pushback against the king.

Moreover, as resistance to Charles kicked into high gear in 1641–1642, we
see the House taking additional steps to ensure that its proceedings would
become known and disseminated only on its own terms. In July 1641, it resolved
both that "all the Members of the House are enjoined to deliver out no Copy or
Notes of any thing that is brought into the House, propounded, or agitated in the
House" and that all printers were required to keep track of and make available
to the House the names of the authors and conveyors of anything brought in to
be printed.[33] The fact that these two resolutions were passed back to back is
surely no coincidence: the latter was, at least partially, a means of enforcing the
former. In March of the following year, the House simultaneously sent its
sergeant out to arrest a number of printers for unauthorized publications and
resolved that "what Person soever shall print [or] sell any Act or Passages of
this House . . . without the particular Licence of this House, shall be reputed a
high Contemner and Breaker of the Privilege of Parliament, and so punished
accordingly."[34] The House would reassert this principle—and enforce it with
contempt citations and arrests—numerous times across the seventeenth, eighteenth, and even nineteenth centuries; indeed, it was not until 1971 that the
House formally announced that it would no longer consider the publication of
(open session) debates a contempt.[35] Again, we should not be surprised to see
this tightening of cameral rules in a time of high conflict between Parliament
and the Crown: by preventing the unauthorized dissemination of its proceedings, the House could not only keep Charles off-guard; it could also exercise a
greater degree of control over its own public image. And, as we saw in previous
chapters, managing public perception was crucial for the House of Commons in
the run up to the Civil War.

After the Restoration, debates over procedural rules continued to flare up at
times of conflict between the Crown and the House. Recall from previous chapters that the House's relationship with Charles II, which had recovered somewhat after the Second Anglo-Dutch War, soured again in the aftermath of the
Third Anglo-Dutch War. By the late 1670s, this newfound hostility manifested
itself in a number of ways, including the proliferation of specific appropriations
and auditing provisions, addresses against and impeachments of Crown officers,
and breach of privilege accusations against the Crown. It also manifested itself

in conflicts over cameral procedure. In 1677, at the king's command, Speaker Edward Seymour (described in the nineteenth century as "the most arrogant man that ever presided over the deliberations of the House of Commons")[36] adjourned the House, even as members still desired to speak.[37] When Parliament convened again the following January, William Sacheverell launched a blistering attack on Seymour, beginning, " '[T]is time to right ourselves upon you, Mr Speaker. . . . It seems you will undertake to be bigger than the House, and, contrary to . . . known rights of the House, will undertake to violate them upon your own authority."[38] The issue was rather technical in nature: all agreed that the king might unilaterally adjourn the House, but Sacheverell and others insisted that the forms to do so had not been followed here and that therefore only the House could have adjourned itself.[39] But Seymour's opponents were quick to broaden the debate from the technicalities to the House's ability to assert itself against the Crown. As Henry Powle told the Speaker, "If we do not preserve form, we shall lose substance. The Question is plainly, by what authority do you assume to yourself to do what the King commands us to do? . . . By the same reason that you adjourned the House, you may put by any Question."[40] Powle also explicitly compared the Speaker's unilateral adjournment to Charles I's order to adjourn in 1629, which Eliot, Holles, and Valentine had forcibly resisted.[41] Others amplified the connection to the free-speech privilege. In Thomas Clarges's words, " 'Tis our birth-right to speak; and we are not so much as a part of a Parliament, if that be lost."[42] Allowing unilateral adjournment was, in the words of William Coventry, "dangerous to the whole constitution of Parliament."[43] Ultimately, by a narrow vote, the House moved on and did not punish Seymour;[44] later that year, however, it resolved as a standing rule that "Mr. Speaker shall not, at any time, adjourn the House, without a Question first put, if it be insisted upon."[45]

By December 1678, Seymour had regained his popularity in the House, largely thanks to his increasingly strident attacks on Catholicism. At the same time, however, he had lost the support of the Earl of Danby, due to his inability (or perhaps disinclination) to prevent Danby's impeachment (described in chapters 3 and 4).[46] At the beginning of the new Parliament in 1679, the House overwhelmingly reelected Seymour as Speaker, but the king, having been lobbied by Danby, refused to accept him. The House, outraged, refused to elect the alternative candidate put forward by the Court, leading the king to prorogue Parliament for a few days. After this cooling-off period, both sides settled on a third candidate, William Gregory.[47] In Seymour's Speakership, then, we can see both the concerns that parliamentarians had about royal influence over the Speaker and the ways in which they used their cameral rulemaking authority to attempt to minimize this danger.

As norms of responsible government began solidifying and taking root in the aftermath of the Glorious Revolution (a process traced in chapter 4), the importance of cameral rulemaking shifted somewhat. This shift is best exemplified by Arthur Onslow, who served as Speaker for a third of the eighteenth century (1728 to 1761). Onslow is, in many ways, the creator of the modern British Speakership, with a focus on impartiality and nonpartisanship.[48] This transition is best understood as an adaptation of the Speakership to the new constitutional reality of responsible government. If the struggle of the seventeenth century was to free the Speaker from allegiance to the Crown and make him responsible to the House, then the struggle of the eighteenth century became to free the Speaker from allegiance to the House majority (and therefore to the government of the day) and make him a neutral arbiter between government and opposition. In both cases, the underlying purpose was to preserve a space for opposition to Crown policy. Onslow himself justified punctilious adherence to cameral rules on the grounds that "nothing tended more to throw power into the hands of Administration, and those who acted with the majority of the House of Commons, than a neglect of, or departure from, these rules."[49]

Once again the behavior of the American colonies in this same period had more in common with the House of Commons in the seventeenth century than with the contemporaneous Commons. The colonial legislatures, like the seventeenth-century House, made significant use of cameral rules as a means of protecting their power in interbranch disputes. Indeed, some of the earliest examples of more assertive behavior by colonial assemblies arose directly out of the English Civil War. For instance, during the Interregnum, the Virginia House of Burgesses arrogated to itself the authority to elect those officials formerly appointed by the Crown.[50] After turning out one governor in 1655 and having another depart for London the following year, the House appointed Samuel Mathews, the callow scion of an influential, if somewhat unpopular, Virginia family.[51] By 1658, relations had deteriorated, and Mathews attempted to dissolve the House; the House, declaring that he lacked the power to do so, refused to disband and ordered its members to remain in town. It also ordered that its deliberations would proceed in secret and that the Speaker could "signe nothing" without the House's consent.[52] It moreover appointed a committee to investigate the precedents and issue a report; the resulting report declared that no one but the House could dissolve the House. After accepting the committee's report, the House passed three further measures: the first required the House's sergeant to act only according to orders signed by the Speaker; the second required the secretary of the colony to turn over all public records to the Speaker's custody; and the third required the governor, secretary, and all other councillors to swear new oaths of office before the House, as the price of being reelected for two more years.[53] As Warren Billings noted, "Mathews and the Council had no choice but to give way."[54]

Of course, the burgesses were able to be unusually assertive during the Interregnum, but even after the Restoration, colonial assemblies were intent on preserving the power to determine their own rules, including rules enjoining secrecy.[55] Several conflicts between assemblies and Crown officers over those rules may prove instructive. A number of these controversies involved the requirement for a quorum. In 1641, the English House of Commons set the quorum at forty members, where it remains today.[56] Some of the colonies, however, preferred a larger quorum (a large quorum for doing business was sometimes coupled with a much smaller quorum for adjourning from day to day, so that the absence of a quorum would not result in a dissolution.)[57] This sometimes brought the assemblies into conflict with royal governors, who wished to be able to carry on business with fewer members. Indeed, governors at various points accused members of skipping town deliberately in an effort to break the quorum.[58] This dispute came to a head in North Carolina in 1758. A 1715 colonial statute (which was, in turn, based on the 1663 proprietary charter) specified that a quorum of the lower house of the assembly consisted of half of the members. On the complaint of Governor Gabriel Johnston, the royal attorney general and solicitor general in 1753 questioned whether a practice so at odds with that of the House of Commons was necessary. The following year, the instructions given to the new governor, Arthur Dobbs, specified that a quorum should consist of fifteen members. After acquiescing for a few years, the lower house changed course, simply refusing to carry on any business unless at least half of the membership was present. Although Dobbs and his successors could (and did) complain bitterly, both to the assembly itself and to officials in London, there was nothing they could do about it, so long as the house remained united in its refusal to transact business.[59]

Perhaps a greater source of tension between colonial legislatures and governors was over who had the authority to appoint the Speaker. Just as the Speakers of the House of Commons had to be presented to the monarch for approval, so the Speakers of the colonial assemblies had to be presented to royal governors. As Jack Greene noted, governors' ability to "influence affairs in the house depended largely upon the degree of their control over the[] officers [of the house], whom they tried to use to direct legislative proceedings into channels favorable to the executive."[60] While gubernatorial approval of Speakers was the norm, it was by no means guaranteed. In 1705, Governor Joseph Dudley of Massachusetts refused to give his approval to the colonial House of Representatives' choice of Speaker; the House simply ignored the governor and proceeded to business with the Speaker that it had chosen. Dudley protested, but to no avail.[61] Fifteen years later, Governor Samuel Shute also rejected a Massachusetts Speaker. Once again, the House refused to back down; this time, the governor dissolved the House, and the new House, which convened in 1721, chose a more acceptable Speaker.[62] The most sustained conflict over the issue came in Georgia in the early 1770s. In 1771, Governor James Wright rejected the colonial House of Commons' choice of Speaker, Noble Wymberly Jones. The following day, the House resolved that the governor's rejection of its Speaker was a breach of privilege; Wright, enraged, dissolved the House. When the House reconvened a year later, it again chose Jones as its Speaker, and he was again rejected. The Commons chose Jones once more, and he was rejected yet again. The Commons then chose him *again*—this time, Jones declined the position, and another was elected in his stead. But the acting governor (Wright was in London) insisted that the House expunge its third election of Jones from its journals. When the House declined, he dissolved it.[63] During the dissolution, there was a lively debate in the press, with pro-House pamphleteer John Joachim Zubly describing the power of choosing a Speaker as an essential part of the legislative toolbox, alongside the power of the purse and the freedom of speech and debate.[64] Referring to Seymour, Zubly archly noted that "the only instance where a Speaker appears rejected by the Crown was in the reign of a *Stuart*, when there was a settled design against the religion and liberties of the nation, which is far from being a presumption favourable to such a claim."[65] When the Georgia House of Commons next convened, it again elected Jones as Speaker. He declined again; the House chose another in his stead; and the acting governor accepted the replacement.[66] Neither side could claim a clear victory, but the very fact that colonial politics was convulsed for nearly two years by the conflict demonstrates both an increased assertiveness on the part of the assembly and a recognition that the issue of who chose the Speaker was worth vigorously contesting. For similar reasons, we saw in previous chapters that the legislative houses were also zealous to maintain authority over their clerks.

The 1760s and 1770s also saw significant conflict between governors and colonial assemblies over the location of the legislative seat. In 1769, as protests in Boston against the Townshend duties became more strident, British troops were quartered in the city. Royal governor Francis Bernard called the assembly to meet in Cambridge, rather than Boston, citing the need to protect the safety of members. Assembly members—some of whom, like Samuel Adams, were leaders of the opposition to the Townshend Acts—objected strenuously to the move, but to no avail.[67] A similar situation arose in South Carolina in 1772. In an effort to break the opposition during the Wilkes Fund Controversy, Governor Lord Montagu repeatedly called the legislature to meet in Beaufort, rather than Charleston, and he dissolved the House four times in eighteen months.[68] And, as we saw in chapter 5, the Virginia House of Burgesses unanimously declared that Lord Dunmore breached its privileges when, in 1775, he summoned it to meet on a British warship in the James River.

Some of these grievances surrounding Crown meddling in legislative procedure found an airing in the Declaration of Independence. In three successive paragraphs, it complained that George III

> has called together Legislative Bodies at Places unusual, uncomfortable, and distant from the Depository of their public Records, for the sole Purpose of fatiguing them into Compliance with his Measures.
>
> He has dissolved Representative Houses repeatedly, for opposing with manly Firmness his Invasions on the Rights of the People.
>
> He has refused for a long Time, after such Dissolutions, to cause others to be elected. . . .[69]

Note that calling assemblies in distant locations is presented, not simply as an inconvenience to the members or an attempt to keep them apart from their power base, but also as an attempt to keep them away from their records—the depositories of accumulated precedents in defense of their privileges. And, as we have seen in nearly every chapter thus far, the Crown's ability to dissolve

Parliament and colonial assemblies at will was a significant source of Crown power and of legislative grievance.

These concerns were, of course, of less moment under the Articles of Confederation, which did not create an independent executive with which the Continental Congress might have to contend. Nevertheless, the Articles did include a few provisions responsive to the concerns that had arisen during the colonial period. Specifically, the Articles gave Congress the authority to adjourn itself—but never for longer than six months—and it gave it the authority to determine the place of its meeting.[70] It also gave Congress the authority to appoint its presiding officer and whatever committees it deemed necessary.[71] Jointly, these can be seen as responsive to Crown meddling in legislative houses' choice of speakers and location of sitting, as well as unconstrained royal authority to dissolve the legislative houses.

The early republican state constitutions were more emphatic about maintaining legislatures' control over their procedures. With the exception of the (very cursory, and soon superseded) New Hampshire Constitution of 1776, every single state constitution promulgated between 1776 and 1787 explicitly empowered legislative houses to choose their own presiding officer (and generally other officers as well).[72] Six state constitutions contained an explicit rules of proceedings clause, and nearly all specified a quorum.[73] Perhaps most importantly, the early republican constitutions were keen to limit the state executive's power over when the legislature would sit. Delaware, South Carolina, and Virginia explicitly forbade their executives to exercise any role in the adjournment, prorogation, or dissolution of the legislative chambers;[74] Georgia, North Carolina, and the 1776 New Hampshire Constitution each gave the legislative houses (either severally or jointly) the power to adjourn themselves, thereby implying without stating that the executive was to have no role.[75] New Jersey, Pennsylvania, and Vermont all gave their houses the power to "sit on their own adjournments," again without any mention of a role for the executive in adjourning them.[76] Only four states appeared to give the executive any role at all in proroguing or dissolving the legislature: in New York, the governor could prorogue the assembly, "provided such prorogations shall not exceed sixty days in the space of any one year."[77] And in Maryland, Massachusetts, and New Hampshire (under its 1784 constitution, which was patterned on the Massachusetts Constitution), the executive could adjourn or prorogue the legislature for a strictly limited amount of time, and only if the houses could not agree between themselves on an adjournment.[78] Maryland, Massachusetts, and New Hampshire were also the only three states whose constitutions explicitly addressed the issue of location, forbidding the governor from unilaterally altering where the legislature was to meet, except in cases of extreme threats to the health or safety of the members.[79] In sum, the early republican state constitutions by and large evince a keen desire to keep the executive from meddling in legislative procedures.

It is perhaps unsurprising, then, that the U.S. Constitution, drafted against the backdrop of those state constitutions, evinces a similar desire. The House of Representatives is given the authority to "chuse [its] Speaker and other Officers."[80] The vice president is given the presidency of the Senate, although he is forbidden to vote, except to break ties.[81] This decision occasioned some opposition in both the Philadelphia Convention and the ratification debates: Elbridge Gerry complained, "We might as well put the President himself at the head of the Legislature. The close intimacy that must subsist between the President & vice-president makes it absolutely improper," and George Mason declared it to be "an encroachment on the rights of the Senate."[82] Luther Martin was concerned that the state of which the vice president was a citizen would receive outsized influence in the Senate.[83] On the other hand, Roger Sherman suggested that, "[i]f the vice-President were not to be President of the Senate, he would be without employment."[84] William Davie, who had been a delegate to the Philadelphia Convention, told the North Carolina ratifying convention that, in the likely event of a tie vote in the Senate, "[i]t would then be necessary to have some person who should determine the question as impartially as possible." A presiding officer drawn from the body's own membership, he suggested, would be under the "local influence" of his state; by contrast, the national constituency of the vice presidency would ensure the greatest possible degree of impartiality.[85] Alexander Hamilton, writing as Publius, and later Joseph Story both made similar points.[86] This concern over who would break tie votes was not misplaced: John Adams wound up breaking twenty ties in his eight years as president of the Senate,[87] including, as we saw in chapter 4, a tie-breaking vote in the "Decision of 1789" debates over presidential removal powers. The Senate was, however, given the authority to choose all of its other officers, including a president pro tempore to serve when the vice president was unavailable.[88]

The Constitution also requires that Congress assemble at least once per year,[89] and each house is forbidden to adjourn for more than three days or to a different location without the consent of the other house.[90] As was discussed briefly in chapter 4, if the houses cannot agree among themselves as to the time of adjournment, the president can unilaterally adjourn them "to such Time as he shall think proper,"[91] subject, of course, to the requirement that they assemble at least once a year. Hamilton suggested that only someone with an "insatiable avidity for censure" could object to these provisions,[92] and, indeed, they seem to have occasioned little controversy. Joseph Story noted that the British king had the authority to prorogue or dissolve Parliament at any time, and "[u]nder the colonial governments, the undue exercise of the same power by the royal governors constituted a great public grievance, and was one of the numerous cases of misrule, upon which the declaration of independence strenuously relied. . . . It was natural, therefore, that the people of the United States should entertain a strong jealousy on this subject, and should interpose a constitutional barrier against any such abuse by the prerogative of the executive."[93]

Finally, the Constitution both imposes a quorum requirement (a majority of each house, with a smaller number authorized to adjourn from day to day and to compel the attendance of absent members) and, most broadly, allows each house to "determine the Rules of its Proceedings."[94] Story insisted that "[n]o person can doubt the propriety" of allowing each chamber to determine its cameral rules, for, "[i]f the power did not exist, it would be utterly impracticable to transact the business of the nation, either at all, or at least with decency, deliberation, and order."[95]

The Constitution's quorum requirement posed a problem for both houses right from the beginning. Although Congress was scheduled to convene in New York City on March 4, 1789, it was not until early April that either house had enough members in attendance to transact business.[96] Upon achieving a quorum, the chambers' first actions were to elect their officers and establish their standing rules. The House elected Frederick Muhlenberg of Pennsylvania as its first Speaker and also chose various other officers (including a clerk, a doorkeeper, and a sergeant).[97] The Senate elected John Langdon of New Hampshire as its first president pro tempore and also selected other officers.[98] Each chamber then appointed a committee to determine its standing rules; within a few days, the committees had reported and the rules were adopted.[99] Both sets of standing rules evinced some concern with overly lengthy or obstructive debate, limiting members' abilities to speak multiple times in the same debate and providing for the chair to call members to order.[100] In the *Manual of Parliamentary Practice* that Thomas Jefferson compiled throughout his legislative career and published in 1801 to aid future presidents of the Senate, we find a more blunt statement: "No one is to speak impertinently or beside the question, superfluously or tediously."[101]

Still, from the very beginning, there were complaints about the pace of legislative proceedings. An incident from August 1789 is worth considering in some detail. As William Maclay, a senator from Pennsylvania and a rather persistent thorn in the side of Washington, Adams, and Hamilton, noted in his invaluable diary, President Washington called on the Senate in person to receive its advice and consent for the instructions to be given to commissioners negotiating a treaty with native tribes. Maclay, determining that there was "no chance of a fair investigation of subjects while the President of the U.S. sat there with his Secretary at War, to support his Opinions and over awe the timid and neutral part of the Senate," called first for the reading of various papers, and then for the commitment of the whole matter to a select committee. In Maclay's telling, the president listened with "an aspect of Stern displeasure," then "started up in a Violent fret. *This defeats every purpose of my coming here*, were the first words that he said," and he then left the chamber. Maclay impishly noted that "had it been any other, than the Man who I wish to regard as the first Character in the World, I would have said with sullen dignity."[102] Washington may or may not have exclaimed that "he would be damned if he ever went [to the Senate chamber] again" as he left,[103] but he did indeed return two days later. After some "tedious debate" (in Maclay's words), the Senate voted on the various questions posed by the president—a number of which were altered, and some of which were voted down entirely.[104] The president's subsequent instructions to the treaty commissioners "conformed to the Senate's answers."[105] In the earliest days of Congress, then, members were already exploring the ways in which cameral procedure could be used to enhance the chambers' power vis-à-vis the executive. Against the overawing presence of George Washington, Maclay turned to obstruction and to committee consideration, both of which frustrated Washington immensely but both of which also gave the Senate room to consider the matter and to alter the president's proposals.

It is also worth noting why we are reliant on Maclay's diary for the recounting of this incident: the Senate met secretly for most of its first six years, with its doors closed and without any published accounts of its debates.[106] Openness was, by contrast, the default in the House. (Both chambers have always understood the Constitution's Journals Clause[107] to require only a bare-bones account of actions taken. Newspapers covered the House from the beginning and the Senate from 1795. Some of these newspaper accounts were subsequently collected by Gales and Seaton and published as the *Annals of Congress*, beginning in 1834. It was not until the birth of the *Congressional Record* in 1873 that Congress began printing its own debates.)[108] The Senate's closed-door policy was controversial from the beginning, with observers regarding it as antirepublican.[109] Perhaps more importantly, closed Senate proceedings "caused popular interest to center on the House."[110] For the Senate to compete effectively for institutional power in the public sphere, it would have to let the public in. Starting in 1794, it did.

As the back-and-forth between Maclay and Washington also indicated, committees were an important part of cameral ordering from the beginning.[111] Indeed, both chambers' 1789 standing rules provided for the appointment of committees: in the Senate, all committees were to be appointed by ballot of the full chamber; in the House, the Speaker appointed committees of up to three members, with larger committees being appointed by ballot.[112] Nine months later, the House revised its rules so that all committees (including committee chairmen) were appointed by the Speaker, "unless otherwise specially directed by the House."[113] The fact that the House very quickly gave this power to the Speaker, whereas the Senate retained it in the full body, may well reflect different levels of comfort with the presiding officer: after all, the House chose its own Speaker, while the Senate had a presiding officer, the vice president, foist upon it.[114]

The earliest House rules provided for a Committee of the Whole, specifying that "[t]he rules of proceeding in the House shall be observed in committee, so far as they may be applicable, except that limiting the times of speaking."[115] In the first few Congresses, the House debated general principles in the Committee of the Whole and then appointed select committees to reduce the agreed-upon principles to specific legislative language.[116] Such referrals were always to *select* committees—that is, committees appointed specifically for that purpose. The House had only a single standing committee in the First Congress, the Committee of Elections, which had jurisdiction over elections and qualifications disputes, not over legislation.[117] As Thomas Skladony has noted, there was some continuity of membership across various select committees addressing similar topics, allowing members to specialize somewhat,[118] but as a general matter, ad hoc committee consideration was the rule of the day. This meant, of course, that opportunities to build expertise or information-gathering capacity were limited; unsurprisingly, then, these earliest Congresses relied heavily on the executive branch. We saw in chapter 3 the extent to which early appropriations laws both relied heavily upon estimates prepared by Treasury Secretary Alexander Hamilton and also delegated significant spending discretion by dividing the appropriations into only a very small number of general categories. Nor was Hamilton the only cabinet secretary to take an active part in legislative matters: in the First Congress, we also see bills drafted by Secretary of War Henry Knox and Secretary of State Thomas Jefferson, among others.[119]

But as partisan competition began to pick up in the mid-1790s, the influence of Hamilton, in particular, in the House of Representatives began to attract attention and discontentment.[120] After the Jeffersonian faction gained the upper hand in the House, the chamber created a standing Committee on Ways and Means, led by Albert Gallatin, as we saw in chapter 3. As Harlow notes, this was clearly seen as an interbranch counterweight: "The Republicans now planned to bring about the proper balance between the different branches, by broadening at once the scope of the operations of the House, and restricting the executive."[121] Subsequent Congresses saw a rapid growth of both standing committees and what Skladony labeled "semi-standing" committees: select committees kept in existence for long periods of time to which numerous matters were referred over the course of a session.[122] Through the first decade of the nineteenth century, the House continued to develop the legislative infrastructure of standing committees, but the fact that both houses of Congress and the presidency were firmly in the hands of the Jeffersonians meant that the administration (in which Gallatin was now the treasury secretary) largely called the shots in Congress.[123]

But the infrastructure was getting thicker throughout this period, so that when there arose some desire to make the House a counterweight to the administration, the necessary machinery was in place.[124] Thus, when the 1810 elections returned a number of "War Hawks"—Republicans eager to go to war against Britain, ostensibly over British impressment of American sailors and violations of American maritime rights—they put one of their own, the young Henry Clay, in the Speaker's chair on his very first day as a member of the chamber.[125] It quickly became clear that Clay's ascension marked the beginning of a new era for the chamber: he was the first to employ his power of appointing committees toward his own clearly identified ideological ends, as distinct from those of the president.[126] Because he recognized that strong committees, under the control of his ideological allies, could win "for the Speakership a new measure of independence as a power base in the American political system,"[127] Clay oversaw the firm entrenchment of the system of standing committees.[128] In the first session of the Tenth Congress (1807–1808), before Clay became Speaker, there were a total of eight standing committees in the House, and there were eighty-four select committees appointed during that session. Clay's speakership covered most of the period from 1811 to 1825; by the first session of the Twentieth Congress (1827–1828), there were twenty-seven standing committees and only eighteen select committees.[129] The increasing use of standing committees, and the concomitant development of expertise, was accompanied by an increasing amount of power delegated to those committees. In 1815, committees were for the first time given blanket authority to report out bills; up to that point, standard procedure had been for standing committees to issue reports, and special permission from the House was needed for a committee to report a bill.[130] By the middle of Clay's Speakership, then, standing committees were newly prominent, newly powerful, and "avowedly made up in the interests of the dominant party."[131] As a result, the majority party in the House had the ability to form an effective counterweight to the executive, when it was inclined to do so.

The Senate made a similar transition, but much more suddenly. Until 1816, the Senate had only four standing committees, all of which were concerned primarily with internal organizational matters rather than legislation.[132] Then, in December 1816, the Senate, perhaps in imitation of the House, created twelve standing committees; almost immediately, the standing committees became responsible for the vast bulk of the legislative activity of the chamber.[133] As Walter Kravitz has noted, this development allowed the Senate, like the House, to move away from reliance on the president: "Until James Madison's administrations, the legislature habitually relied upon the chief executive and his associates for the initiative on much significant legislation. Congress lost its traditional agenda-maker ... because of the deep and bitter estrangement between Madison and his Congresses and turned to standing committees to fill the vacuum."[134]

There continued to be a crucial difference between the chambers, however, with regard to how committees were appointed. In the Senate, between 1816 and the 1830s, "party control of the standing committees was notably haphazard."[135] Not infrequently, the minority party in the chamber held a majority on some committees; also not infrequently, some committees consisted entirely of members of the majority party in the chamber. But with the rise of the Second Party System, there developed a norm in the mid-1830s of "[s]ystematic majority party domination" of committees.[136] The practice from the earliest days was that committees were appointed in the Senate by ballot. In 1823, the chamber experimented with allowing its presiding officer to name committees, but it revoked the power three years later when it did not like how Vice President John C. Calhoun was using it. It then tried giving the power to its president pro tempore, but that experiment was soon given up as well. Between 1833 and 1845, the rule was that committees were appointed by ballot, but in practice unanimous consent was often given to allow the presiding officer to make appointments. Finally, in 1845, the chamber inaugurated the practice of party committee lists: each party would put forward its roster of members for each committee, and the chamber would adopt the lists wholesale.[137] This, in turn, allowed for the emergence of a strong seniority system, to which the parties committed themselves, as a general, albeit not inviolable, rule. The twin pillars of the seniority system were, first, that a senator, once appointed to a committee, had a right to remain on that committee for as long as he wished, and second, that each party's hierarchy within each committee was determined by length of service in the chamber.[138] This naturally tended toward a certain diffusion of power, as committee chairmanships could not be doled out or withheld as rewards or punishments, nor could the leaders of even the majority party ensure that the members of their party on a particular committee would toe the party line.

In the House, by contrast, "the Speakers that followed Clay wielded their appointment power as a major political resource for achieving their legislative ends and for dealing with other Representatives."[139] Speakers exercised wide latitude to name both the members of committees and their chairs.[140] Especially as committees grew in influence across the nineteenth century, Speakers' committee appointment powers translated into significantly broader power over the business of the House.[141] A development in the second half of the nineteenth century demonstrates especially vividly the ways in which the Speaker's power over committees radiated outward. Beginning in 1858, the Speaker appointed himself as chairman of the Rules Committee, a select committee.[142] In the general revision of House standing rules in 1880, the Rules Committee was made into a standing committee, still chaired by the Speaker.[143] It was, moreover, long-standing practice (although not codified in House rules until 1890) that Rules Committee reports were privileged—that is to say, that it was always in order to call up a Rules Committee report on the floor of the House.[144] In 1883, Representative Thomas Reed, a Republican member of the Rules Committee, offered as a matter of privilege a resolution, to be passed by majority vote, making it in order to consider sending a specified bill to conference committee. That is, he introduced a resolution that would have the effect of overriding the standing calendaring rules and bringing a specific piece of business to the front of the queue. When a Democrat raised a point of order against Reed's resolution, Republican Speaker (and, of course, Rules Committee chair) J. Warren Keifer overruled the point of order, a ruling that was sustained (as all rulings from the chair can be) by majority vote in the chamber.[145] This was a crucial innovation: under the background calendaring rules, many significant measures (such as the matter before the House here) would never make their way to the front of the legislative queue before the end of a Congress. The normal procedure for dealing with this problem had been the motion to suspend the rules, but that required a two-thirds vote, which meant that it would fail on many controversial issues, as indeed it had already failed in this case. As a consequence, the House by the mid-1880s was widely considered to be sclerotic, and obstruction in that chamber was of increasing concern to political observers.[146] In 1884, Senator Richard Coke of Texas could confidently state, "It is well known . . . that bills are passed much more rapidly and with much more facility through the Senate than through the House on account of the difference in the constitution of the two bodies, the one small and compact and the other large and unwieldy."[147] Reed's 1883 resolution and Keifer's ruling from the chair marked the beginnings of a procedural solution to this sclerosis: now the Rules Committee had the general power to report a special order that, when passed by simple majority on the House floor, provided for the consideration of a piece of pending legislation that would have been out of order under the standing rules. That is, the ruling allowed a simple majority to set the agenda. More specifically, because of the Speaker's tight control over the Rules Committee, the ruling allowed the Speaker to exercise almost unfettered discretion over what came to the floor and when.[148] Use of this new procedural device remained halting at first, but beginning around 1890, it increasingly became the principal means of bringing a matter to the floor. By 1896, one observer described "giving very large power to a small committee of five men, the committee on Rules" as a central component of the "irresistible" consolidation of cameral power in the Speaker.[149]

Thomas Reed would go on to serve two stints as Speaker (1889–1891 and 1895–1899), earning the nickname "Czar Reed" (an appellation that perhaps carried more force before the Russian Revolution than it does today). At the beginning of his first term in the Speaker's chair, with Republicans holding only a very slim majority in the "large and unwieldy" House, Democrats took to employing a "disappearing quorum." Taking advantage of the Constitution's majority requirement for a quorum, as well as long-standing precedents requiring that a member actually cast a vote in order to be counted for quorum purposes, Democrats simply refused to vote. If more than a handful of Republicans were absent, the result would be the absence of a quorum and the inability of the chamber to do business.[150] (This was especially vexing to a Republican Party that, as Richard Valelly has demonstrated, hoped to grow its majority in future Houses by enacting legislation providing for stringent federal oversight of Southern elections.)[151] In response, in January 1890 Reed ordered the clerk to record the names of those present but refusing to vote and to count them for quorum purposes.[152] When Democrats objected vociferously and moved to adjourn, Reed refused to entertain the motion, asserting that "[t]he object of a parliamentary body is action, and not stoppage of action. Hence, if any member or set of members undertakes to oppose the orderly progress of business, even by the use of the ordinarily recognized parliamentary motions, it is the right of the majority to refuse to have those motions entertained, and to cause the public business to proceed." An appeal of Reed's ruling was then tabled by a unanimous vote of those Republicans present (and with Reed counting the Democrats who refused to vote for quorum purposes).[153] The House subsequently codified these and other anti-obstruction measures (including reducing the quorum requirement in the Committee of the Whole to one hundred members) in the "Reed Rules" of 1890.[154] Eric Schickler has described the Reed Rules as "without question one of the most significant events in the institutional development of the Congress," because "[n]o single change did more to secure majority rule in the House."[155] Democrats campaigned against the Reed Rules in the 1890 elections, and they won decisively. In 1892, the new Democratic majority repealed the Reed Rules, even though doing so meant diminishing their own power as the majority.[156] Remarkably, in 1894 Reed, now the minority leader, led an obstructionist campaign with the sole aim of restoring his (anti-obstructionist) rules. Reed won both the policy and the politics: Democrats caved in and reinstated the Reed Rules, and Republicans won the 1894 elections, returning the Speakership to Reed.[157]

By the early twentieth century, the Speaker's control of committee appointments, chairmanships, and referrals, combined with his control of floor proceedings via the Rules Committee, made the Speaker immensely powerful. The zenith of the office's powers came under Speaker Joseph Cannon, a conservative Republican from Illinois, who was speaker from 1903 to 1911.[158] A decidedly snippy *New York Times* profile from 1908 referred to Cannon as "the greatest absolute monarch on earth": "[I]n Russia, the Czar is hedged about by bureaus; in Persia, the Shah holds his throne by main strength; the President of the United States has to take counsel with Cabinet, Senate, and House, and the boss of Tammany Hall with his district leaders; but the 'Yes' of the Speaker of the House of Representatives passes a bill and makes a law, and the 'No' kills it."[159] Actual floor proceedings were but a "sad comedy" and an "empty pageant"; the real action took place in "the throne room of Uncle Joe."[160] But pushback was not far off: progressive Republicans joined with Democrats in 1909 to pressure Cannon to create "Calendar Wednesdays," a procedure whereby, every Wednesday, the standing committees would be called alphabetically and allowed to bring legislation within their jurisdiction to the floor, thereby circumventing the Rules Committee. Calendar Wednesdays proved a disappointment to the reformers, however, as the entire legislative day wound up being consumed by just one or two committee reports.[161] In 1910, progressive Republican George Norris of Nebraska rose as a matter of privilege and presented a motion to change the standing rules of the House. A Cannon deputy raised a point of order, insisting that the motion was not, in fact, privileged; after a lengthy debate, the Speaker ruled the motion out of order. Cannon's ruling was appealed to the floor and overturned by a cross-partisan majority of the House, consisting of nearly all of the Democrats and a sizable number of progressive Republicans. A similar coalition then passed the change to the standing rules.[162] The new rule provided that the Rules Committee would be expanded to ten members; it forbade the Speaker to serve on the Rules Committee; and it provided that the members of the Rules Committee would be elected by ballot and would then elect their own chairman.[163] In the immediate aftermath of the vote, Cannon pouted that "the assault upon the Speaker of the House by the minority, supplemented by the efforts of the so-called insurgents, shows that the Democratic minority, aided by a number of so-called insurgents . . . is now in the majority, and that the Speaker of the House is not in harmony with the actual majority of the House."[164] He mused about the possibility of resigning but declined to do so because it might have been taken as "a confession of weakness or mistake or an apology for past actions." Instead, he announced his intention to entertain at any time a privileged motion "to vacate the office of the Speakership and choose a new Speaker . . . so that power and responsibility may rest with the Democratic and insurgent Members who, by the last vote, evidently constitute a majority of this House."[165] Democrat Albert Burleson of Texas immediately took Cannon up on the offer, but the progressive Republican "insurgents" were not prepared to turn over control of the chamber to the Democrats: the motion was defeated by a nearly forty-vote margin.[166]

Cannon did not hold on to the Speakership for long: the Democrats won a decisive victory in the 1910 House elections, and he was forced to hand over his gavel to Champ Clark of Missouri. But it was a much-diminished Speakership that Clark inherited: not only did he not control the Rules Committee but also, beginning in 1911, House rules provided that the members and chairs of all standing committees were to be elected by ballot, not selected by the Speaker.[167] In practice, the House moved to a procedure, similar to the procedure instituted by the Senate in the mid-nineteenth century, of simply ratifying committee lists prepared in advance by the parties.[168] Republicans soon gave the job of working out committee assignments to a Republican Conference Committee on Committees; Democrats for a long time lodged the power in the Democratic membership of the House Ways and Means Committee, before transferring it to the caucus Steering and Policy Committee in the 1970s.[169] Within committees, a strong seniority system soon took hold: the chairman and ranking member were those members of the majority and minority party, respectively, with the longest service on the committee, with the proviso that no one should chair more than one committee.[170] And the Rules Committee, freed from the Speaker's control, became a power center in its own right.[171]

In the Senate, the most significant procedural innovation of the early twentieth century was the adoption of cloture. Just as a period of heightened frustration with obstructionism in the House had preceded the Reed Rules, so too concerns about obstructionism in the Senate began to increase around the turn of the twentieth century. In the aftermath of a 1917 filibuster of a bill that would have armed merchant ships against German U-boat attacks, the Senate allowed debate to be cut off with a two-thirds vote.[172]

From the history traced thus far, it is apparent that cameral rules have significant implications, not simply for the distribution of power within a chamber, but also for the power dynamics between a chamber and other constitutional actors. Used effectively, cameral control over internal procedures can build institutional capacity, thus allowing the chamber to compete more effectively in the public sphere, as by, for example, pushing back against budgets or other legislation proposed by the executive. Used ineffectively, however, cameral rules can disadvantage a chamber, allowing other institutions to poach its power. It is to an examination of these possibilities that this chapter now turns.

The Promise of Cameral Organization

We have already seen several examples of how increasing institutional sophistication—what Nelson Polsby called "institutionalization"[173]—has enabled legislative chambers to assert themselves more forcefully. This is apparent as early as the reign of Henry IV, when the House of Commons used its cameral rules both to maintain deliberative secrecy and to ensure that the Crown would respond to petitions before the House voted on supply. Likewise, many of the innovations of the seventeenth century, ranging from the development of committee structures to the preservation of precedents in increasingly detailed *Journals* to the attempts to reduce the power of the Speaker through the Committee of the Whole, can be seen as attempts by the House to develop the capacity for greater independence from the Crown. Likewise, in the American colonies, legislative chambers' insistence on appointing their own Speakers, determining their own meeting places, and setting their own quorums were largely attempts to resist perceived meddling by royal officials and thereby to preserve space for independent legislative action. These concerns were reflected, first in the Declaration of Independence, then in the early republican state constitutions, and finally in various provisions of the federal Constitution.

One of the central lessons to be drawn from this historical development is that legislative houses' authority over their own rules, procedures, and organization can, if used judiciously, be an important source of cameral power. But, as with the other powers surveyed thus far, the judiciousness of any particular use of the power is highly sensitive to the surrounding politics. The issue of legislative secrecy provides an interesting case study in the ways in which the same institutional imperative can lead to very different policies in different political situations. For the House of Commons, as early as the late fourteenth century and especially in the seventeenth-century conflicts with the Stuart Crown, cameral power was best protected by ensuring secrecy. After all, monarchs could not interfere in business that they did not know was occurring. But when the early American Senate instituted a secrecy regime, it undermined its own power by alienating the public. When it became clear that the Senate was losing public esteem to the more open House, it reversed course.

Nor is openness the only way in which the houses of Congress have attempted to use their power over their own rules to carve out policy-making space. Consider the question of agenda-setting power: because the vice president was made the Senate's presiding officer, there was a special fear of executive interference. The Senate from its earliest days reacted to this by ensuring the weakness of the chair: committees and their chairs were appointed by ballot from the beginning, and the brief experiment with giving that power to the vice president was quickly quashed. Moreover, the vice president has never exercised significant agenda-setting authority in the Senate. The early House had no such worries—and, in fact, it created structures of deference to the executive, allowing cabinet secretaries to play an important role in the drafting of legislation. But with the development of partisan contestation, the House began to develop its own infrastructure, and, beginning with Clay, it created a strong Speakership to oversee that infrastructure.[174] The development of a strong chair in the House served much the same function as the *lack* of a strong chair in the Senate: both allowed the chambers to resist the intrusion of executive authority into cameral affairs.

The rapid growth of the administrative state in the first decades of the twentieth century posed a new—or, perhaps more accurately, the recurrence of an old—problem for the houses. Just as the chambers in their earliest years lacked institutional infrastructure and were therefore forced to rely on the executive branch, so too the expansion of the administrative state led to the chambers' having insufficient resources to form an effective counterweight. We saw one manifestation of this shifting institutional balance in chapter 3: the 1921 Budget Act ended the era of congressional domination of the budget process both by giving the White House the authority to set the initial terms of the budget proposal and by enhancing executive institutional capacity, in the form of the Budget Bureau (later OMB). This change was in large part motivated by the recognition that Congress's piecemeal approach to budgeting was insufficient for the large and growing American state.

Likewise, the expansion of the administrative state put new strains on congressional staff. The Senate Finance Committee had been authorized to employ a clerk starting in the 1840s, and in 1857 that right was extended to all standing committees.[175] The House got a later start: it first authorized the Ways and Means Committee to employ clerks in 1856, and other committees were authorized to employ staff at various points throughout the remainder of the nineteenth century.[176] In the final decade and a half of the nineteenth century, individual members were permitted to hire a clerk.[177] The growth in both the size of Congress itself and the number of staffers led to the construction of the first two congressional office buildings (now called the Cannon and Russell Buildings), both of which opened in the first decade of the twentieth century.[178] Nevertheless, congressional staffing remained anemic: committees from both houses frequently "borrowed" staffers from various administrative agencies, a practice that became especially prevalent with the proliferation of committees and subcommittees during the Second World War.[179] In just a four-month period at the end of 1944, fourteen Senate committees reported borrowing ninety-five staffers from twenty-five different government agencies.[180] These borrowings presented two distinct concerns: first, they suggested that committees were understaffed, and, second, they raised the specter of conflicts of interest. Senator Kenneth Wherry, a Republican from Nebraska, expressed a concern that such staffers were "loyal to the organization" that employed them: "[B]eing employed by a department, to a certain degree they have a loyalty to that department which otherwise they might give to the Senate committee in a study of the problems covered in the investigations."[181] As Wherry's statement indicates, dual loyalties were a special problem in the context of committees' oversight functions. Inadequate internal resources were likely to give rise to inadequate ability to push back against the executive.

In response to such concerns about congressional capacity, Congress (by strong, bipartisan majorities) passed the Legislative Reorganization Act of 1946, with the explicit aim of modernizing Congress to allow it to play a more forceful role in the increasingly robust American state.[182] The act had a number of goals, but two of the most important were reorganizing committee structures and enhancing staffing in both chambers. On the committee front, the act eliminated more than half of the standing committees in each chamber and (for the first time) formally codified and delineated the jurisdiction of each, including the oversight jurisdiction.[183] As for personnel, the law significantly increased the number of staffers for both members and committees, and it increased staffers' pay.[184] As Senator Byrd later noted, Francis Wilcox, a political scientist who in the aftermath of the 1946 act became the first chief of staff of the Senate Foreign Relations Committee, "epitomized the kind of professional civil servant" that the act contemplated.[185] Wilcox had originally sought a more modest title for his new position, but Senator Arthur Vandenberg, the committee chairman and a Republican, wanted a title that would "make an impression on [Truman's] State Department. . . . [Chief of Staff] sounds bigger and better and stronger. . . . I want you to be an important figure."[186] Wilcox would indeed be a significant figure in debates over the creation of NATO and the Marshall Plan.[187] Or consider the staff that the House Judiciary Committee assembled in 1974 to investigate Watergate. Chairman Peter Rodino, a Democrat from New Jersey, went out of his way to signal independence and fairness by appointing John Doar, a Republican civil rights lawyer, as chief counsel, a move that Patrick Sandman describes as "help[ing to] elevate the inquiry's credibility."[188] At the same time, by assembling "the largest Congressional investigative staff" in history, Rodino and Doar projected strength and ensured that the White House would not be able simply to outgun the committee.[189] Doar in particular is emblematic of a broader post-1946 trend in which both parties—often working together—used their increased committee staff resources to engage in investigations aimed at checking the executive and defending congressional power.[190] Nor is the importance of congressional staffing limited to those who work directly for members or committees: the 1946 act also significantly enhanced the nonpartisan staffing of both chambers, directing more resources to both the Legislative Reference Service (now the Congressional Research Service) and the Offices of Legislative Counsel, which provide technical assistance with bill drafting.[191]

The 1946 act's reforms were not entirely successful: in what might be termed a Law of Conservation of Chairmanships, the reduction in the number of committees led to a dramatic increase in the number of subcommittees.[192] Moreover, not every member or committee took advantage of the new staffing money to hire well-trained experts; some "clung to the old ways, appointing political cronies or low-paid employees of limited capabilities."[193] And a third major category of reforms attempted in the act—reconfiguring the budget process—was more or less stillborn;[194] those reforms would have to wait until the 1970s. Nevertheless, the act clearly strengthened both committees in general and committee chairmen in particular, and the result was an increased ability of the chambers to confront the executive.[195] As Eric Schickler has noted, "[T]he Act strengthened committee chairs—by bolstering their jurisdictions and providing them with the staff to help formulate policy—making them central actors in the policy process. The executive branch would have to deal with these chairmen as co-equal competitors and partners over the next several decades."[196]

If anything, there may have been a concern that the 1946 act made the committee chairs too powerful—one of the goals of the Legislative Reorganization Act of 1970 (which, like the 1946 act, was passed by large, bipartisan majorities) was to curb their power by requiring that committees adopt and publish written rules and by strengthening the ability of committee majorities to circumvent obstruction by the chair.[197] The act also contained a number of antisecrecy provisions, providing for greater openness (and broadcasting) of committee hearings and, most importantly, allowing twenty members of the House to demand that votes in the Committee of the Whole be recorded.[198] Since most of the floor business in the House in fact takes place in the Committee of the Whole, the creation of a mechanism by which a member's votes in Committee of the Whole could be recorded was a significant step toward openness. The 1970 act (and subsequent cameral resolutions in 1974 and 1975) also enhanced committee staffing and staff training and gave increased committee personnel to the minority party.[199] In addition, it authorized the production of a new compilation of House precedents (the last one having been completed in 1936); it gave new auditing authority to the congressionally controlled General Accounting Office (now the Government Accountability Office), which had been created as part of the 1921 Budget Act; it changed the name of the Legislative Reference Service to the Congressional Research Service and gave it increased responsibilities and staffing; and it authorized the modernizing of the House galleries and the provision of free public tours of the Capitol.[200] The 1970 act, though not as ambitious as its predecessor, thus shared some of the same goals: the building of institutional capacity (by increasing committee staff, creating a compilation of House precedents, and bulking up institutions, like GAO and CRS, that aid members in their work) and the attempt to engage more effectively with the public (through antisecrecy provisions and tours).[201] Piecemeal reforms throughout the 1970s also built on the 1970 act's antisecrecy provisions by requiring more committee activities to be open—a development that was brought even further by C-SPAN, which began airing House proceedings in 1979 and Senate proceedings in 1986.[202] Both chambers thus rediscovered in the late twentieth century what the Senate had first learned in the late eighteenth: the logic of public engagement pushes toward greater openness.

Perhaps one of the most significant of the 1970 reforms was the attack on the power of committee chairs. These efforts were furthered in both chambers as both parties moved away from strict seniority rules in the 1970s.[203] At the same time, the House Rules Committee once again came increasingly under the thumb of the majority party leadership, a process that coincided with the rise of closed and restricted special rules, meant to maintain the leadership's control over a bill once it reached the floor.[204] The increased power of leadership, combined with the diminishment of committee chairs as autonomous power bases, led to greater concentration and centralization of power, especially in the House. The result was a stronger Speaker, who was therefore capable of serving more vigorously as a counterweight to presidents in the following decades.[205]

Not all of these adventures in cameral procedure were beneficial to their houses, of course. Some were ineffective; others aimed at goals other than increasing cameral power (for instance, some of the minority-empowering reforms); and others still had unintended consequences (as, for example, when the reduction in the number of committees led to the rise of subcommittees). As for antisecrecy provisions, the degree to which openness redounds to the houses' credit will obviously depend on the extent to which the public likes what it sees. And there is evidence that openness itself has had the unintended consequences of making negotiations more difficult and compromises more elusive.[206] Still, many of these procedural changes, like the changes wrought to the budget process during the 1970s traced in chapter 3, had the effect of enhancing congressional standing. Increased resources for committee-based oversight—a key feature of both the 1946 act and the 1970 act—has led to a Congress that is able to monitor the executive branch far more actively, and studies attempting to quantify the level of oversight bear this out.[207] Unsurprisingly, congressional oversight is greater under conditions of divided government[208]—a situation that seems normatively attractive if we understand divided government as indicating a lack of full public trust in either of the political parties (an understanding explored in chapter 2). And the procedural reforms that have led to stronger and more centralized leadership in the chambers have served (as also explored in chapter 2) to combat the president's advantage of univocality by creating a clear counter-spokesperson.

The Pitfalls of Cameral Organization

Of course, as with every power traced in this book, cameral rulemaking authority can also, if used injudiciously, work to the detriment of the chamber. Consider rules that allow a minority to obstruct the business of the chamber. In some situations, this might be good for the institution: we have seen how Senator William Maclay in 1789 used procedural tactics to slow down consideration of President Washington's proposed instructions to treaty negotiators. This delay allowed the Senate to consider the matter free from the imposing physical presence of Washington and his secretary of war, which, in turn, gave it the breathing room to critique and alter the president's proposals.

More sustained obstruction may have the opposite effect, however, allowing other political actors to make a compelling case in the public sphere that they are more worthy of trust than "dysfunctional" legislative houses. As we have already seen, when obstructionist tactics have threatened to undermine a chamber's effectiveness and public standing—in the House in the 1880s and in the Senate in the first decades of the twentieth century—there has been institutional reform aimed at combatting those tactics (the rise of the Rules Committee and the Reed Rules in the House and cloture in the Senate). In 1975, the Senate engaged in another round of such reform by lowering the cloture threshold to three-fifths of the membership for most matters.[209] But the Senate reforms of the mid-1970s backfired: instead of reducing obstruction, they led to the routinization of the filibuster. By the turn of the twenty-first century, it was clear that the filibuster had come to operate as a standing supermajority requirement for doing business, rather than as a debate- or deliberation-forcing device.[210] Once again, public discourse began to coalesce around the notion of a hopelessly dysfunctional Senate.[211]

One significant effect of this routinization of the filibuster was to transfer power away from Congress and to the executive. As the filibuster came to operate as an absolute bar to the passage of measures that commanded the support of fewer than sixty senators, many measures with broad and deep support nonetheless failed to pass. This gave presidents a strong rhetorical ploy: a matter of such importance, they could argue, deserves at the very least an up-or-down vote, but congressional "dysfunction" and "stalemate" have made this impossible, thus necessitating strong executive action.

Consider the fate of legislative attempts to combat global warming. In 2009, after significant arm-twisting by Democratic Speaker Nancy Pelosi, the House of Representatives passed a bill by a vote of 219 to 212 that would have created a "cap-and-trade" system for greenhouse gases.[212] Although it enjoyed strong support from President Obama, the bill never received a vote in the Democrat-controlled Senate. When West Virginia senator Jay Rockefeller was asked about the Senate version of the bill (which was sponsored by his fellow Democratic senators John Kerry and Joseph Lieberman), he responded: "I think there is a dominant concern [which is] 'What's the point of doing anything without 60 votes?' . . . And I think that there's some feeling that you don't spend time on the floor trying to figure out if you have got 60 votes. You have to understand before you go to the floor that you have got 60 votes."[213] When asked whether he thought Kerry's bill could get sixty votes, Rockefeller replied: "I don't think so. But I think John [Kerry] does."[214] Rockefeller was right, and Kerry was wrong—the sixty votes never materialized, and the bill was never brought to the Senate floor.

But this did not spell the end of the government's attempt to combat global warming. The Supreme Court had ruled in 2007 that the Clean Air Act required the Environmental Protection Agency to consider whether greenhouse gases constituted an air pollutant that endangered public health or welfare.[215] In the waning years of the Bush administration, the EPA was in no hurry to complete this review,[216] but the Obama administration issued an endangerment finding in late 2009.[217] The threat of EPA regulation had been enough to convince some House members to vote for the cap-and-trade bill, in order to ensure that they had a say in environmental policy.[218] Some observers expected a similar dynamic to play out in the Senate.[219] But while that motivation was strong enough to secure a House majority, it was not strong enough to secure a Senate supermajority—that is, it was not strong enough to overcome the filibuster.

In May 2010, the EPA issued its first regulation pursuant to the endangerment finding, raising vehicle fuel economy standards.[220] The next month, the filibuster again protected executive power when fifty-three senators supported a measure to strip the EPA's authority to regulate greenhouse gases.[221] Because this fell short of the sixty votes needed to end a filibuster, the measure failed,[222] and the EPA continues to set government policy on greenhouse gases. Indeed, in October 2015 the Obama administration, claiming existing authority under the Clean Air Act, published the final rule for the Clean Power Plan, a wide-ranging and ambitious regulation aimed at reducing carbon pollution from power plants.[223] In the face of congressional inaction, polls have consistently shown high levels of public support for greenhouse gas regulation by the EPA.[224]

Notice the effect of the filibuster here. By making it significantly more difficult to pass legislation, the filibuster simply shifted the locus of policy making to the executive branch. Rather than have environmental policy made through the process of intra- and intercameral negotiation and deliberation, the policy is now made in its entirety by the EPA. Of course, the EPA has less leeway in regulating than Congress does in legislating, and the courts have not always been entirely hospitable to EPA regulations.[225] But they by and large refrained from significant interference with environmental regulations during the Obama administration.[226] And this phenomenon is not limited to environmental policy. President Obama, seizing on claims of legislative obstruction, embarked on a wide range of aggressive administrative actions in fields ranging from immigration to education, using the catchphrase "We can't wait"—and prominent academic commentators have begun to provide theoretical justifications for the claim that congressional obstruction justifies executive aggrandizement.[227]

Nor is this executive aggrandizement limited to the substitution of regulation for legislation: Senate obstruction also for a time served as a justification for aggressive expansions of the president's unilateral appointment powers. In April 2010, President Obama nominated Donald Berwick to be administrator of the Centers for Medicare and Medicaid Services, a job with significant responsibilities for implementing the Affordable Care Act, which had been passed the previous month.[228] When it became apparent that Berwick's nomination would be successfully filibustered, the president instead used a recess appointment to install him in the post.[229] Similarly, having determined that a nomination of Elizabeth Warren to head the newly created Consumer Financial Protection Bureau would "linger without Senate action for months,"[230] Obama instead in 2010 appointed her a special assistant to the president and special adviser to the secretary of the treasury, in which capacity she was in charge of setting up the new agency but did not have to face a Senate confirmation battle.[231] A number of Warren's supporters subsequently urged the president to use a recess appointment to put Warren into the directorship,[232] although he ultimately opted to nominate Richard Cordray.[233] Cordray, too, was filibustered, and the Senate conducted pro forma sessions in December 2011 and January 2012 in an attempt to prevent a recess appointment.[234] President Obama, relying on an opinion from the Office of Legal Counsel, then took the unprecedented step of declaring that a Senate recess existed, the pro forma sessions notwithstanding, and he installed Cordray in the directorship.[235] Obama's public justification for this move was squarely grounded on the filibuster: "For almost half a year, Republicans in the Senate have blocked Richard [Cordray]'s confirmation. They refused to even give Richard an up-or-down vote. . . . But when Congress refuses to act, and as a result, hurts our economy and puts our people at risk, then I have an obligation as President to do what I can without them. I've got an obligation to act on behalf of the American people. And I'm not going to stand by while a minority in the Senate puts party ideology ahead of the people that we were elected to serve."[236] Politically sympathetic commentators were quick to seize on the same rationale: Larry Tribe justified Cordray's recess appointment on the grounds that the filibuster of nominees created "transparent and intolerable burdens on [presidential] authority."[237] Matt Stephenson more broadly suggested that the Senate should be deemed to have consented to an appointment so long as it did not actively vote down the nominee.[238] Note again how much rhetorical work the claim of minority obstruction does here. It would be politically very difficult for a president to recess appoint a nominee who had previously been defeated in the Senate—and, as noted in chapter 4, it would be illegal for a recess appointee to draw a salary under those circumstances. But when the president can claim that his nominees are not even receiving a vote, he is significantly freer to act unilaterally without facing the same degree of political backlash.

In November 2013, the Democratic majority in the Senate, by a vote of fifty-two to forty-eight, successfully appealed a ruling from the chair and established the principle that cloture for all nominations other than to the Supreme Court could be achieved by majority vote.[239] The rationale—which supporters called the "constitutional option" and opponents called the "nuclear option"— was that the existing cloture rules were unconstitutional and therefore did not have to be followed.[240] As a result, nominees whom the Democratic majority in the chamber wished to prioritize were able to get confirmed.[241] This, of course, did not mean that all of Obama's nominees were confirmed—as Senate leadership made decisions about which nominations to prioritize, some nominees actually faced longer delays and experienced higher failure rates.[242] Moreover, one controversial nomination—that of Debo Adegbile to head the Civil Rights Division of the Department of Justice—failed to achieve cloture on the Senate floor, even under the new majoritarian rules, when seven Democrats joined all of the Republican senators in voting against him.[243] Although Obama was clearly disappointed—he called the vote "a travesty"[244]—he did not seek to install Adegbile via recess appointment. Indeed, in the aftermath of the rules change, it appears that Obama ceased making recess appointments altogether.[245] This is especially noteworthy because Republicans took control of the Senate in January 2015, thus making confirmation of nominees significantly more difficult. But Obama did not attempt to resort to recess appointments—that is, he reacted to a majoritarian holdup very differently from a supermajoritarian one. Thus, by the time the Supreme Court held, in *NLRB v. Noel Canning* (discussed in chapter 4), that recess appointments made while the Senate was conducting pro forma sessions (like the one received by Cordray) were invalid,[246] Senate rules had already changed so as to make the issue far less politically salient.[247]

For appointments, then, the Senate has followed the pattern of earlier instances of congressional obstruction: once it became clear that minority obstruction tactics were diminishing the chamber's power, it acted to limit those tactics and restore its authority. For legislation (and Supreme Court nominations), however, the filibuster remains available as this book goes to press.[248] At least a few senators, spurred by the "growing sense that something serious needs to be done to make the Senate more functional, or its public image will continue to decline," recently proposed further reforms, with a procedural twist.[249] A year before the 2016 elections, Senator Lamar Alexander and other Republicans (who were in the majority) were working on a proposed package of institutional reforms with a *sunrise* provision: they would not take effect until January 2017. With neither party particularly confident that it would have the majority then, Alexander's thinking was that proposed rule changes could be evaluated behind a sort of veil of ignorance, with an eye toward the interests of the institution rather than those of a party.[250] Although nothing came of Alexander's reform efforts in 2015–2016, the fact that the 2016 elections resulted in Republican control of the House,

Senate, and presidency, read alongside the historical patterns traced above, would lead us to think that further obstruction-reducing reforms are likely in the short-to-medium term. Alternatively, if unified government does not result in filibuster reform, one would expect the use of minority obstruction to continue to serve as a justification for executive aggrandizement. In structuring its rules so as to allow for indefinite minority obstruction, the Senate costs itself power.

It should be noted that although the executive branch is the most obvious beneficiary of the filibuster, the judiciary may stand to benefit as well. One of the standard defenses of "dynamic" or "updating" theories of judicial statutory interpretation is that legislative inertia prevents Congress from updating statutes itself.[251] Of course, some amount of legislative inertia is inevitable in any system, and a great deal more is hardwired into our constitutional structure through the mechanisms of bicameralism and presentment. But the filibuster adds yet another inertial obstacle to the mix: the status quo is insulated against change unless a proposal to alter it can garner the support of a supermajority of the Senate in addition to that of a majority of the House plus the president. To the extent that inertia justifies judicial updating, then more inertia will mean more updating, and Congress will have still less say in the operation of the law.

We can thus see how each house's authority over its own internal rules can either enhance or diminish its power vis-à-vis the other branches. When that authority is used to strengthen institutional capacity to push back against the other branches and to compete effectively for public support, then it enhances the power of the chamber. But when a house uses its power in a way that leads to a narrative of irresponsibility, gridlock, or dysfunction, then it provides a justification for the other branches to step in and poach congressional power. As we have seen, the other branches have been all too happy to do so.

Conclusion: Toward
a Normative Evaluation

THIS BOOK HAS BEEN LARGELY ANALYTIC IN APPROACH, offering a new framework for thinking about the American separation-of-powers scheme and arguing that Congress has a powerful suite of tools at its disposal, giving it the potential to engage effectively within that scheme. Through detailed developmental accounts of these tools, it has argued that, used judiciously—which is to say, with real sensitivity to the surrounding politics—they can not only be effective in getting Congress what it wants in the moment, they can also increase congressional power vis-à-vis the other branches in the long run.

But is that really a desirable goal? After all, recent years have seen a rising chorus of criticisms of the American separation-of-powers regime. Prominent scholars tell us that it is a "failure,"[1] having been "overwhelmed . . . almost from the outset" by the rise of political parties.[2] Our politics is alleged to be hopelessly broken, characterized by little more than gridlock and sclerosis. The Madisonian republic is gone; the only question is whether we should make ourselves comfortable with executive dominance[3] or come up with some new institutional design.[4] If our institutional structure is as defective as these criticisms suggest, then a discussion of how Congress can best engage in the public sphere within the confines of that structure may well seem beside the point—an exercise in rearranging the deck chairs on the *Titanic*.

Clearly, a different normative evaluation underlies this book. By way of conclusion, then, it may be helpful to pull back the lens to the separation-of-powers system more broadly and offer some general normative thoughts about it. To be clear, these thoughts are meant to be preliminary, and they certainly should not be read as attempting a comprehensive defense, much less a claim that the American separation-of-powers system is optimal (whatever that might mean).[5] Rather, my more modest aim here is simply to suggest that the American separation-of-powers system has significant virtues that recent scholarly attacks may have substantially underappreciated. In particular, this conclusion argues that separation-of-powers multiplicity has at least three distinct, but interrelated, virtues: it is more fully representative, more deliberation promoting, and more resistant to assertions of tyrannical or autocratic power than constitutional structures with less built-in capacity for conflict. To the extent that these virtues are indeed characteristic of the system, they are reasons to cheer a more effective Congress, which is to say, a Congress that makes use of the tools discussed in this book to play a robust role in the American governing structure.

Representation

The concept of representation is tremendously complex, and it is well beyond the scope of this brief discussion to attempt anything like a systematic treatment.[6] But we can attempt to draw out and evaluate some of the salient aspects of representation under conditions of separation-of-powers multiplicity.

To begin, I take it that any plausible modern conception of political representation must make some reference to the interests of the represented.[7] To be clear: I mean "interest" broadly as anything in which a person is interested. This includes material interests, of course, but it also includes policy- and value-based interests. Opponents of abortion have an interest in antiabortion policies even if no one they know has ever had or sought to have an abortion; proponents of increased aid to Haiti have an interest in the aid, even if they've never met a Haitian. To focus on the representation of interests is not to take a position on the question of whether there exist public interests that are irreducible to aggregated private interests. Nor is it to take a position on whether the represented are the best judges of their own interests. It is simply to say that, when we speak of representative government—that is, government that makes present in some sense that which is literally absent[8]—what we expect to be made present is (some conception of) the interests (broadly understood) of the represented.

Second, I take it that Walt Whitman is not the only one who contains multitudes.[9] Our interests are plural and frequently incommensurate. My interests may simultaneously include deriving pleasure from eating french fries and enhancing my health and lifespan by losing weight. More exaltedly, they may simultaneously include donating my limited resources to the victims of a natural disaster and saving those resources to pay for my child's college education. Our interests vary across a number of dimensions, of course, but three of the most fundamental are space, time, and (what for lack of a better term I shall call) principledness. Spatially, my interests radiate outward from the most local (myself, my family, my community) to the global. Temporally, my interests range from the most immediate to the most distant, including those interests that account for unborn generations. On the principledness axis, my interests range from the purely material (my interests in my own safety, comfort, wealth) to the highly abstract (my interest in living in the type of society that I believe to be morally best). My french fry decision involves temporal trade-offs: my immediate gustatory interest conflicts with my longer-term health interest. My decision about whether to send money to disaster victims or save it for my child's education involves spatial trade-offs: my local interest in the well-being of an immediate family member conflicts with my global interest in alleviating the suffering of strangers. A decision about whether to jump into a fast-moving river in an attempt to save a drowning stranger involves principledness trade-offs: my material concern for my own safety conflicts with my belief that one ought to aid those in dire need. And, of course, a single decision can involve trade-offs on multiple dimensions: the college education versus disaster relief trade-off also has a temporal dimension, insofar as my child's college education may be years away, but disaster victims will receive the benefit of my donation immediately. And it has a principledness trade-off, insofar as my child's well-being may be more materially immediate to me than the stranger's.

Sometimes our various interests will be compatible; sometimes they will be in tension; and sometimes they will be outright incompatible. And we have no widely agreed upon master principle that allows us to assign ordinal priority to some interests over others.[10] Even the most dedicated devotee of healthy living is unlikely to think that she should never eat a french fry, and even the most dedicated glutton is likely to recognize some limits. Most of us, of course, fall somewhere in between the health nut and the glutton; given that we will never be able to satisfy all of our interests maximally, we negotiate with ourselves, we make trade-offs, we compromise, and we engage our faculties of practical reasoning to chart a way forward.[11] Charles Taylor has compellingly described these trade-offs in narrative terms: we make local, one-off choices between incommensurate goods in an attempt to construct the sort of life that we would like to lead.[12]

As with my individual interests, so too with our collective interests: we may have interests both in allowing individuals to make their own dietary choices free from government interference and in combatting an obesity epidemic, both in funding disaster relief and in funding college scholarships. And these interests are frequently incommensurate. Our collective interests may be in inherent tension: we value both personal autonomy (which counsels in favor of letting people make their own food choices) and public health (which counsels in favor of some measure of food paternalism). Local interests in enforcing communal standards of behavior may conflict with more permissive norms in the larger communities in which the local community is embedded. For that matter, the same community may be devoted both to certain standards of behavior and to a libertarian conception of the role of government. In other contexts, it may be resource scarcity that causes a tension to arise: there simply may not be enough money available fully to fund both college scholarships and disaster relief. And, of course, there are interaction effects between values and resources: how much money is "available" for collective purposes itself involves a trade-off between our immediate interests in low taxes and lavish government spending and our longer-term interests in fiscal sustainability.

And there is no *a priori* determinable rule for resolving these conflicts— almost no one would seriously advocate always choosing the immediate over the long term (or vice versa) or the global over the local (or vice versa) or the principled over the material (or vice versa).[13] The political community, like the individual, must use its practical reasoning to negotiate these trade-offs. It, too, must construct a collective self-identity by choosing among incommensurate goods.[14] It too, to return to Taylor's formulation, must decide what sort of (communal, political) existence it wishes to have.

While as individuals we may figuratively contain multitudes, as a polity we literally do. This, of course, adds a new dimension of complexity to our attempts to figure out what to do—we now have to contend, not only with each individual's trade-offs, but also with how to make trade-offs between the competing interests that different people have and the very different lives that they seek to lead. Fortunately, along with this new complexity come new resources for addressing these trade-offs. Specifically, we can attempt to structure our institutions of collective decision making in such a way as to help us engage in collective practical reasoning. We can attempt, that is, to shape our institutions in such a way as to have them represent what are likely to be some of the different facets of our collective interests.

While no institutional arrangement could possibly hope to capture all of our collective complexity—and while I do not claim to know how we would determine an *optimal* set of institutional arrangements—the American separation-of-powers regime, with its multiplied, overlapping, and nonhierarchical authority claims, does a pretty good job of fostering collective practical reasoning under conditions of multiple and incommensurate interests. Consider the ways in which the constituencies and timetables of the different national institutions, discussed in chapter 2, map onto different points along the axes of our interests. The House of Representatives, elected from the smallest constituencies[15] and facing the voters at the most frequent intervals,[16] is best suited to represent our (relatively) local and (relatively) immediate interests. A small but geographically concentrated group can generally be assured of at least the attention, if not the wholehearted fealty, of its representative. And an interest group or movement that arises quickly (think of the rise of the Tea Party in 2009) can make its impact felt quickly as well (think of the 2010 congressional elections). Moreover, as chapter 8 traced, the cameral rules and practices of the House have developed with an emphasis on expediting the passage of measures favored by the majority party, which tends to promote a discourse centered around efficiency and inevitability, with much of the actual argumentation taking place within the majority party caucus. The Senate, of course, is very differently organized, with larger, statewide constituencies[17] and six-year terms.[18] Importantly, those six-year terms are staggered, with only a third of the chamber up for reelection every two years. This means that a flash-in-the-pan movement might be able to capture the House and a number of Senate seats, but unless it persists, it will not be able to capture a Senate majority. The Senate as a body is thus institutionally structured to focus on longer-term and geographically larger and more general interests. Moreover, the Senate's smaller size and tradition of unlimited debate (also discussed in chapter 8) may tend to promote a more wide-ranging discourse, with greater necessity of persuading across party lines.[19] The president has a nationwide constituency (as refracted through the odd prism of the Electoral College), a four-year term, and a two-term limit.[20] The presidency is thus structured to be responsive to the geographically widest concerns and medium-term temporal concerns in the first term, shifting to much longer-term concerns ("legacy" is the word often used) in the second term. This also means that second-term presidents are better able to move somewhat toward the abstract-principle end of the principledness spectrum. Finally, the federal judiciary has its own distinct institutional structure.[21] Nominated by the president and confirmed by the Senate, federal judges must be acceptable to actors representing a nationwide constituency; yet judges tend to resist the formulation that they, themselves, have a constituency, instead claiming fidelity to the law.[22] Of course, the law is not something wholly distinct from politics; rather, courts are themselves political actors, broadly understood. Nevertheless, widely shared norms and practices of legal discourse and argumentation do constrain judges in ways that they do not constrain presidents or members of Congress,[23] forcing them to speak a certain sort of language of principle.[24] And, of course, judges have good-behavior tenure,[25] which may allow them to take a temporally longer view of things—although good-behavior tenure should certainly not be confused with complete disregard for public opinion, as the discussion of the healthcare cases in part I stressed.[26]

In short, the four major constitutional actors—House, Senate, president, and courts—are structured to be responsive to different sets of interests held by the public, varying across space, time, and principledness. To the extent, then, that chapter 1 was correct in describing our separation-of-powers regime as one in which claims of institutional authority multiply and overlap in a nonhierarchical order, what we have are institutions, each of which represents some part of our collective interests in all of their incommensurate complexity, empowered to fight it out with one another in the making of national policy.[27] House members whose two-year terms serve to focus their attention on the immediate public mood must negotiate with senators who will have to face the consequences of policy choices four years later, as well as with a president who may be focused on his historical legacy. Controversial policies are then likely to face judicial challenges, and the judges are made to juggle their long-term jurisprudential goals against the constraints on their decisions imposed by the forms of legal discourse and the need to maintain the conditions of their public legitimacy. Policy choices that survive this gauntlet are unlikely to reflect the "pure" perspective of any of these actors. Just as in making choices about how to lead our individual lives we negotiate between short-term and long-term, local and global, materially concrete and abstract interests, so too in our collective political life the clash between these institutions ensures that various points along the various dimensions of our collective interests are all represented. Again, there is no hierarchical ordering, nor should there be. We do not always prefer the short term over the long term (or vice versa), nor do we always prefer the global over the local (or vice versa), nor do we always prefer the abstractly principled over the immediately material (or vice versa). These different institutions, representing these different aspects of our plural and frequently incommensurate interests, negotiate and compromise locally, policy choice by policy choice, in the process constructing and ratifying a collective identity.

In order for these representational benefits to accrue to the polity, the different constitutional actors must be willing to press—albeit judiciously—their distinct representational claims. Assertions that actors should categorically refrain from using the tools available to them in interbranch confrontations become claims that some other actor's form of representation should be absolutely prioritized over theirs. Consider the claim, encountered in chapter 4, that the Senate should consider only "qualifications," not "ideology," in confirmation battles. As we have seen, this reduces to a claim that appointee ideology should be unilaterally determined by the president. Or consider the claim that it is categorically improper for members of Congress to spill "state secrets," which (as we saw in chapter 6) allows the executive a free hand in unilaterally constructing our national security interests. Or consider the claim, encountered in chapter 5, that the houses of Congress should always turn to the courts to enforce subpoenas against a recalcitrant executive, a claim that allows the judiciary to position itself as the only "grown-up" branch in the constitutional room. In each of these cases (and many more that we have seen throughout the book), the claim that Congress ought categorically to renounce aggressive uses of its constitutional tools as against the other branches amounts to a claim that the other branches' modes of representation ought to be given lexical priority over Congress's. Such arguments seek to reduce multiplicity to a hierarchy, and in doing so they seek to flatten the represented interests into a single spatial, temporal, or discursive type. But to the extent that we understand our collective political interests to be frequently incommensurate and resistant to hierarchicalization, we should prefer a multiplicity-based separation-of-powers system. That is, we should prefer a political process that represents our interests in their spatial, temporal, and discursive complexity, recognizing that there is no *a priori* hierarchy of them, but rather forcing them to compromise in a manner analogous to the compromises that individuals work out among them in making decisions on a daily basis.

Deliberation

A second virtue of the multiplicity-based separation-of-powers regime is that it helps to promote public deliberation on matters of policy. This is related to, but distinct from, the representativeness virtue. Just as chapter 1 argued that political power is largely endogenous to politics, this section argues that political interests are always, at least to some extent, endogenous to politics. Conflict in the public sphere can be enlightening, both increasing the salience of policy disagreements and allowing all sides to be heard.

Mariah Zeisberg and Jeff Tulis have properly emphasized the ways in which our separation-of-powers regime can enhance deliberation among different governmental actors.[28] Tulis notes that the branches are structured so as to "behave and 'think' quite differently from each other."[29] Zeisberg elaborates: "Each branch can be expected to express different understandings on how [governmental] power should be used; likewise, each branch is required to grapple with the perspectives of the other branches if it cares about seeing its visions enacted. This grappling creates the possibility of interbranch deliberation, and that interbranch deliberation is a crucial component . . . in the right functioning of the American constitutional polity."[30] This interbranch "grappling"—which takes place through both word and deed[31]—generates "continuous public assertions of disagreement with public policies," which, in turn, "help to reveal the truth about the common good."[32] This is all quite right as far as it goes: the expression of diverse viewpoints enhances the quality of deliberation.[33] The expression of nondiverse viewpoints, by contrast, can have the opposite effect, further polarizing discussants.[34] Precisely because of the different temporal, geographic, and role-based scopes of representation discussed above, the American Constitution makes it more likely that the government as a whole will be ideologically diverse. That is to say, the "grappling" between the House, Senate, presidency, and courts is likely to result in the expression of diverse views, which, in turn, is likely to enhance the quality of deliberation among those institutions, as compared with institutional structures that do not foster such diversity. In this regard, consider the ways in which congressional pushback against the activities of the intelligence agencies, traced in chapter 6, has led to greater oversight of, and stricter limitations on, those agencies.

But we can go even further: precisely because institutional actors must make arguments to the American public if they are to win an interbranch battle, arguments between the branches can enhance the quality of public deliberation as well.[35] Recall that the Bork hearings, discussed in chapter 1, moved public opinion, not just opinion within the Senate. In watching the nightly television news or reading the morning newspaper, Americans were exposed to the arguments made both by supporters and by opponents of the Bork nomination, and our regime of separated powers gave both supporters and opponents institutional platforms from which to make their arguments. Supporters, led by the White House, insisted that Bork was eminently qualified and possessed an attractive judicial philosophy; opponents, based largely in the Democratic-controlled Senate, claimed that he was an out-of-touch extremist. Debates about broad constitutional philosophy, about the proper role of judges, and about specific legal issues were aired in detail. The more they were talked about in the Senate—and the more heatedly they were talked about—the more it signaled to the press that it should report on this and to the public that it should pay attention. And as the public learned more about Bork, it came to oppose his nomination in higher numbers. Clearly, the debates taking place within the Senate and between the Senate and the White House, as filtered by the media, were influencing public debate. The public debate, in turn, influenced the Senate debates, emboldening opponents of the nomination. In the end, the nomination was defeated—and the public deliberation fostered by the separation of powers was largely responsible.

Tyranny Prevention

The final virtue of the multiplicity-based conception of the separation of powers is also perhaps the most familiar. The multiple, overlapping, and nonhierarchical authority claims that the American constitutional regime fosters help to ensure that no one branch is able to exert tyrannical control over the nation. Again, the reasoning sounds in each branch's interactions in the public sphere: by encouraging conflicting claims of authority, the Constitution allows the people to choose their champion, thereby empowering that branch at the expense of the others. Political actors who want to maintain or gain power are thus incentivized to compete for the affections of the people from their various institutional bases. The result is likely to be an equilibrium in which no actor is able to exercise tyrannical power.

The multiplication of power centers as a means of keeping power in check was a central structural strategy of the Constitution's drafters. In the context of federalism,[36] Alexander Hamilton explained that, "[p]ower being almost always the rival of power, the general government will at all times stand ready to check the usurpations of the state governments, and these will have the same disposition towards the general government. The people, by throwing themselves into either scale, will infallibly make it preponderate."[37] Madison concurred, writing that, if "the people should in future become more partial to the federal than to the State governments, the change can only result from such manifest and irresistible proofs of a better administration as will overcome all their antecedent propensities. And in that case, the people ought not surely to be precluded from giving most of their confidence where they may discover it to be most due."[38] And James Wilson told his fellow delegates at the Constitutional Convention that "[a] private citizen of a State is indifferent whether power be exercised by the Genl. or State Legislatures, provided it be exercised most for his happiness."[39] Wilson accordingly thought that the states and the federal government would view each other "with the eye of a jealous rival."[40]

Likewise, in the separation-of-powers context, "[a]mbition must be made to counteract ambition."[41] Accordingly, the Constitution's "constant aim is to divide and arrange the several offices in such a manner as that each may be a check on the other—that the private interest of every individual may be a sentinel over the public rights."[42] Note that for the separation of powers to produce this virtuous effect it is not necessary for the branches actually to engage in constant conflict: as chapter 1 emphasized, the multiplicity-based separation-of-powers system privileges judicious, rather than maximal, combativeness—and negotiation and compromise are often the judicious path. Nor is it necessary to posit that an individual's primary loyalty is to her branch: as chapter 2 emphasized, the separation-of-powers structure provides institutional homes and tools for actors to use in the process of publicly contesting for decision-making authority, regardless of what actually *motivates* them to engage in that contestation.[43] The tyranny-prevention argument simply presupposes that there is likely to be *some* actor, or group of actors, motivated by something—whether it be their own power lust, partisan animosity, ideological disagreement, a genuine attachment to a certain balance of institutional powers, or anything else—that will seek to oppose other political actors attempting to maximize their own powers. The fact that the American separation-of-powers system multiplies the opportunities for tension and conflict means that there will often be an institutionally housed actor with the motivation and the means to oppose other actors.[44] When this is the case, any actor attempting to aggrandize her power beyond tolerable limits can expect to find herself opposed by other actors, with their own constitutional tools at their disposal. If those actors are housed in Congress, those tools will range from tugging on the purse strings to impeachment to spilling state secrets—in short, the powers described in parts II and III of this book.

(In)Stability and (Un)Predictability

The obvious rejoinder to this normative defense of the multiplicity-based separation-of-powers regime is that it is all quite messy. It undermines stability and predictability, important legal values. Indeed, Larry Alexander and Fred Schauer base their defense of judicial interpretive supremacy—an antithesis of the multiplicity-based understanding—entirely on the supposed need for authoritative settlement of constitutional questions.[45] And it cannot be denied that stability, predictability, and certainty have significant legal appeal. They can be efficiency enhancing (for example, we might be more willing to engage in mutually beneficial transactions when we can be certain of the background rules against which those transactions will be judged)[46] and fairness promoting (for example, we may consider it fundamentally unfair to hold people accountable for violating legal rules of which they lacked reasonable notice).[47] But these virtues of certainty and stability may be overstated,[48] and there may be other values served by uncertainty, instability, and unpredictability.[49]

In the context of the separation of powers, the efficiency and fairness concerns that tend to favor a highly stable and certain regime are relatively weak. A person who has been deprived of liberty or property when it was not possible for him to discover in advance the legal rules governing his conduct presents to most of us the very paradigm of injustice; his case is literally the stuff out of which Kafkaesque nightmares are made.[50] Josef K's experience—unable to determine either the substantive law he is charged with violating or the procedures by which his case will proceed—strikes at the very heart of his autonomy, and this steady erosion of his moral personhood can end in nothing but his death. By contrast, institutional actors whose powers are subject to the play of politics have a significantly weaker pull on our sympathies. A president whose nominees are subject to more strenuous questioning than another president's or a House majority that finds itself with relatively weaker bargaining power over spending priorities than previous majorities enjoyed does not seem to present us with a grievous wrong—especially if we are aware of the historically contingent nature of these relationships, as traced in parts II and III. This is because we tend to view the distribution of governmental power in instrumental terms: we ask whether a certain distribution of authority makes us a better- or a worse-governed polity. This is not to deny that political actors may feel unfairly treated at times—one certainly suspects that Robert Bork did. It is simply to say that when the issue at hand is the distribution of governmental authority, we tend to regard the fairness concerns of the participants as significantly less important than the good-governance concerns of the polity at large. Fairness concerns are thus less compelling in the separation-of-powers context than in, say, the criminal-law or tort-law context.

Likewise, efficiency concerns are weaker in this context than they are in, say, contract law, because the goal of the allocation of governmental authority is not to facilitate private exchanges among the actors. The aim is not to smooth the way for a mutually beneficial transaction between Congress, the president, and the courts. Rather, it is to foster the sort of representation and interbranch deliberation that will result in better governance for the nation as a whole. As chapter 1 highlighted, inefficiencies and redundancies are deliberately built in, as a means of promoting the opportunities for interbranch tension and conflict. Ours is an intentionally inefficient system.[51]

It is true, of course, that these inefficiencies, especially when they manifest in outright interbranch hostility or seemingly implacable obstruction, can appear unattractive. Indeed, complaints about gridlock, sclerosis, and petty squabbling abound. This is nothing new—Machiavelli devoted a section of his *Discourses* to refuting "those who allege that the republic of Rome was so tumultuous and so full of confusion that, had not good fortune and military virtue counterbalanced these defects, its condition would have been worse than that of any other republic."[52] Machiavelli, to the contrary, insisted that "those who condemn the quarrels between the nobles and the plebs, seem to be cavilling at the very things that were the primary cause of Rome's retaining her freedom, and . . . they pay more attention to the noise and clamour resulting from such commotions than to what resulted from them, i.e. to the good effects which they produced."[53] Indeed, it was precisely the "clash" between the interests of the two classes that was responsible for "all legislation favourable to liberty."[54] Or, in Jeremy Waldron's perceptive summary, we should not be "fooled into thinking that calmness and solemnity are the mark of a good polity, and noise and conflict a symptom of political pathology."[55] Conflict, tension, and tumult may be precisely what produces good government; easy, authoritative resolution may be the mark of dysfunction.

Why is this? The simple answer is that, in a diverse political community, politics is our peaceable means for dealing with deep and persistent conflicts. As Bernard Crick has suggested, politics is "the activity by which differing interests within a given unit of rule are conciliated by giving them a share in power in proportion to their importance to the welfare and the survival of the whole community."[56] Importantly, as we have seen, those interests are frequently incommensurate. Politics therefore both "arises from the problem of diversity, and does not try to reduce all things to a single unity."[57] Politics thus necessarily involves opposition; the elimination of opposition is not political rule but rather autocracy.[58] But if we abjure autocracy and instead seek to use our collective practical reason to navigate among and negotiate between the different, and often incommensurate, interests in the polity—that is, if we are to engage in politics—then we must accustom ourselves to messiness and discord. As Robert Post has put it, politics inevitably "appears anarchic and disorganized. That is because politics is the practice we use when we agree to continue to disagree."[59] Stability and predictability in politics can be achieved only by repressing that disagreement, which is to say, only by repressing the underlying diversity of interests in the polity. Or, to put it differently, insofar as the Constitution "proliferat[es] the modes of representation governing normal politics"[60] because of its judgment that "*no* legal form can transubstantiate *any* political institution of normal politics into We the People of the United States,"[61] it also deliberately and necessarily proliferates the points of tension and conflict, noise and clamor.

The tools analyzed in this book allow Congress, its houses, and its members to make their noise and take part in the general clamor. As we have seen throughout, institutional authority is something built by successful public engagement through time. It neither arises nor disappears instantaneously. Congressional authority at any particular historical moment is in part a function of the success or failure of Congress's public engagements in past historical moments and in part a function of how adroitly congressional members and leaders make use of historical reservoirs of authority in the present to create a future congenial to them. This requires the skillful deployment of political judgment both in evaluating the political circumstances and in crafting public engagement that suits those circumstances while furthering the actor's goals. For a member of Congress, this means not only having a holistic sense of the suite of powers available to the institution but also understanding that they *are* a suite, that any one of a number of different tools, deployed more or less vigorously, might conduce to the desired end.

We have seen Congress use its tools effectively in a number of instances across American history, ranging from pulling on the purse strings to bring some administrative agency into line, to using the appointments process to force substantive concessions from the executive, to changing institutional rules in order to enhance its capacity to oversee and confront the other branches. We have also seen numerous ill-advised uses of congressional power, ranging from ineffectual budget brinksmanship, to turning to the courts to enforce contempt citations, to encouraging a reputation for institutional venality by failing to discipline members. The fact that we have found examples of both effective and ineffective engagement ranging across the breadth of American history should further demonstrate the point, first advanced in chapter 2, that claims that Congress is somehow structurally doomed to be the least effective branch are mistaken. Congress has all the institutional powers it needs to allow it to play a vigorous role in American governance. To the extent that we care about collective self-government, these powers, and their judicious use, are something to be celebrated.

NOTES

Introduction

1. Letter from Fisher Ames to George Richards Minot (May 27, 1789), in 1 *Works of Fisher Ames* 44, 44–45 (Seth Ames ed., Boston, Little, Brown 1854).
2. Letter from John Adams to Abigail Adams (Dec. 14, 1794), in 10 *Adams Family Correspondence* 304, 304 (Margaret A. Hogan et al. eds., 2011).
3. Letter from Fisher Ames to Thomas Dwight (May 30, 1796), in 1 *Works of Fisher Ames*, *supra* note 1, at 194, 194.
4. For my own take on gridlock, including citations to some sources worrying about its prevalence, see Josh Chafetz, *The Phenomenology of Gridlock*, 88 Notre Dame L. Rev. 2065 (2013).
5. Michael J. Teter, *Gridlock, Legislative Supremacy, and the Problem of Arbitrary Inaction*, 88 Notre Dame L. Rev. 2217, 2217 (2013); *see also* Thomas E. Mann & Norman J. Ornstein, *The Broken Branch: How Congress Is Failing America and How to Get It Back on Track* (rev. ed. 2008).
6. On the executive, see, e.g., Arthur M. Schlesinger Jr., *The Imperial Presidency* (1973); Eric A. Posner & Adrian Vermeule, *The Executive Unbound: After the Madisonian Republic* (2010). On the judiciary, see, e.g., Raoul Berger, *Government by Judiciary: The Transformation of the Fourteenth Amendment* (2d ed. 1997); Cass R. Sunstein, *Radicals in Robes: Why Extreme Right-Wing Courts Are Wrong for America* 1–78 (2005).
7. This should not be understood as downplaying the importance of statutes. For a ground-breaking recent examination of the importance of statutory law in our constitutional life, see William N. Eskridge Jr. & John Ferejohn, *A Republic of Statutes: The New American Constitution* (2010). For Eskridge and Ferejohn, the reason that certain statutes—their examples range from the Social Security Act of 1935 to the Civil Rights Act of 1964—are able to fundamentally alter our constitutional life is precisely because of buy-in from numerous institutionally situated political actors. *See id.* at 7–8, 105, 111. But their account tells us very little about how institutions might contend with one another for

constitutional authority when they *disagree*. In other words, they tell us very little about the sources of constitutional leverage that Congress has in attempting to press for the types of policy changes it desires.

8. Richard E. Neustadt, *Presidential Power and the Modern Presidents: The Politics of Leadership from Roosevelt to Reagan* 29 (1990).

9. Joseph S. Nye Jr., *Soft Power and American Foreign Policy*, 119 Pol. Sci. Q. 255, 256 (2004).

10. Joseph S. Nye Jr., *Bound to Lead: The Changing Nature of American Power* 32 (1990).

11. Nye, *supra* note 9, at 256.

12. *Id.*; *see also* Nye, *supra* note 10, at 32 (associating soft power with "intangible power resources such as culture, ideology, and institutions").

13. *See* Nye, *supra* note 9, at 257 ("It is not smart to discount soft power as just a question of image, public relations, and ephemeral popularity. . . . [I]t is a form of power. . . . When we discount the importance of our attractiveness to other countries, we pay a price."); *see also* Harold Hongju Koh, *Can the President Be Torturer in Chief?*, 81 Ind. L.J. 1145, 1153 n.38 (2006) ("[W]e cannot accomplish our goals [in the War on Terror] without diplomacy and international law—soft power tools that were developed precisely so that countries would not have to rely exclusively on force all the time.").

14. Karen Orren & Stephen Skowronek, *The Search for American Political Development* 1 (2004).

15. *Id.* at 11; *see also* Brian J. Glenn, *The Two Schools of American Political Development*, 2 Pol. Stud. Rev. 153, 154 (2004) ("[T]he goals that actors choose to pursue, and those that they are able to pursue effectively, are shaped by the institutional arrangements through which they and other political actors must operate. . . . [Therefore,] the outcomes of an earlier era will influence the strategies and assessments of later groups operating within the same policy spectrum."); Ira Katznelson, *Historical Approaches to the Study of Congress: Toward a Congressional Vantage on American Political Development*, in *The Oxford Handbook of the American Congress* 115, 120–21, 127 (Eric Schickler & Frances E. Lee eds., 2011); Eric Schickler, *Disjointed Pluralism: Institutional Innovation and the Development of the U.S. Congress* 15–18, 252–54, 267 (2001).

16. 1 Mark A. Graber & Howard Gillman, *The Complete American Constitutionalism* 26 (2015).

17. *See* Orren & Skowronek, *supra* note 14, at 184–94.

18. Jack P. Greene, *Negotiated Authorities: Essays in Colonial Political and Constitutional History* 189–90 (1994).

19. *Id.* at 199 (quoting a 1728 address of the Pennsylvania Assembly to the lieutenant governor).

20. Jack N. Rakove, *Original Meanings: Politics and Ideas in the Making of the Constitution* 20 (1996); *see also* 1 Graber & Gillman, *supra* note 16, at xviii (noting that "the American colonists borrowed heavily from the constitutional claims made during" the "seventeenth-century controversies between Parliament and the Stuart monarchs," and that "the eventual parliamentary victory helps explain the course of both British and American constitutional development"); *id.* at 49 ("What Otis, Franklin, Adams, and other colonists described as well-established liberties and governing practices were largely consequences of political struggles in seventeenth-century England.").

21. *See* Greene, *supra* note 18, at 197 (noting that colonial legislatures looked to English sources for "a whole set of generalized and specific institutional imperatives for representative bodies, a particular pattern of behavior for their members, and a concrete program of political action"); Warren M. Billings, *A Little Parliament: The Virginia General Assembly in the Seventeenth Century* 36–38 (2004) (noting that, "[i]n tone and substance," the procedural rules of the Virginia House of Burgesses "bore marked resemblance to orders then in force in the House of Commons"); Daniel J. Hulsebosch, *Constituting Empire: New York and the Transformation of Constitutionalism in the Atlantic World, 1664–1830*, at 55 (2005) (noting that, in the New York colonial assembly, "[l]egislative procedure followed parliamentary lines"); J. R. Pole, *Political Representation in England and the Origins of the American Republic* 31 (1966) (noting that colonial "[a]ssemblies adopted for themselves the theory of the British House of Commons and modelled themselves on its precedents and procedures"); John Phillip Reid, *The Concept of Representation in the Age of the American Revolution* 29 (1989) ("American constitutional theory was generally the same as British constitutional theory. Americans thought of their representatives as checks on executive authority and as the voices of grievances.").

Prelude

1. Citizens United v. Fed. Election Com'n, 558 U.S. 310 (2010).
2. *Id.* at 365.
3. U.S. Const. art. II, § 3.
4. Jeffrey Toobin, *The Oath: The Obama White House and the Supreme Court* 196 (2012).
5. President Barack Obama, Remarks by the President in State of the Union Address (Jan. 27, 2010), http://www.whitehouse.gov/the-press-office/remarks-president-state-union-address ("Applause" notations omitted).
6. Robert Barnes, *Alito Dissents on Obama Critique of Court Decision*, Wash. Post, Jan. 28, 2010, at A6.
7. *See, e.g.*, Robert Barnes, *In the Court of Public Opinion, No Clear Ruling*, Wash. Post, Jan. 29, 2010, at A1 ("[L]egal experts said they had never seen anything quite like it, a rare and unvarnished showdown between two political branches during what is usually the careful choreography of the State of the Union Address."); Editorial, *Obama v. the Supremes*, Wall St. J., Jan. 29, 2010, at A14 ("In the case of Barack Obama v. Supreme Court of the United States, that was some oral argument on Wednesday night. With the Justices arrayed a few feet in front of him in the House chamber, President Obama blistered their recent decision defending free political speech for corporations and unions."); David G. Savage, *Obama-Alito Tensions Rise to the Surface: There's a History Behind the Justice's Public Reaction to the President's Criticism of a High Court Ruling*, L.A. Times, Jan. 29, 2010, at A20 ("If there was ever an era of good feelings between President Obama, a Harvard Law School grad and former law professor, and the justices of the Supreme Court, it apparently ended this week.").
8. Toobin, *supra* note 4, at 198.
9. Andrew Cohen, *For Barack Obama, Law Professor, the Time to Lecture Is Now*, Atlantic Online, Apr. 4, 2012, http://www.theatlantic.com/politics/archive/2012/04/for-barack-obama-law-professor-the-time-to-lecture-is-now/255396/.

10. *See, e.g.*, Charles Krauthammer, *Obama v. SCOTUS*, Wash. Post, Apr. 6, 2012, at A15; *see also* Warren Richey, *Questions about Chief Justice's Health-Care Ruling Could Have Lasting Impact*, Christian Sci. Monitor, July 3, 2012, http://www.csmonitor.com/ USA/Justice/2012/0703/Questions-about-chief-justice-s-health-care-ruling-could-have-lasting-impact (noting that the rhetoric before the decision came down clearly warned the justices that "[t]he Supreme Court and the justices themselves were about to become fair game in the president's campaign for reelection").

11. Editorial, *Obama vs. Marbury v. Madison*, Wall St. J., Apr. 3, 2012, at A14.

12. Ruth Marcus, *Disorder in the Court*, Wash. Post, Apr. 5, 2012, at A15.

13. Letter from Attorney General Eric Holder to Judges Smith, Garza, and Southwick, at 1 (Apr. 5, 2012), *available at* http://legaltimes.typepad.com/files/doj_letter_smith.pdf.

14. *Id.* at 2–3.

15. *See, e.g.*, Brian Beutler & Sahil Kapur, *Conservatives Bristle at Federal Court's Retaliatory Move at Obama*, TPM, Apr. 4, 2012, http://tpmdc.talkingpointsmemo. com/2012/04/conservatives-bristle-at-judges-punching-back-at-obama-over-health-care-law.php; John H. Cushman Jr., *Administration Tells a Court It Doesn't Deny Its Powers*, N.Y. Times, Apr. 6, 2012, at A11.

16. Adam Liptak & Allison Kopicki, *Approval Rating for Justices Hits Just 44% in Poll*, N.Y. Times, June 8, 2012, at A1.

17. *Id.*

18. *Id.*

19. Michael Tomasky, *Democrats Should Come Out Swinging against the Court*, The Daily Beast, June 24, 2012, http://www.thedailybeast.com/articles/2012/06/24/michael-tomasky-democrats-should-come-out-swinging-against-the-court.html; *see also* Erwin Chemerinsky, *Political Ideology and Constitutional Decisionmaking: The Coming Example of the Affordable Care Act*, 75 Law & Contemp. Probs., no. 3, 2012, at 1, 14 ("A consequence of the Court effectively nullifying the Affordable Care Act hopefully would be that finally people would perceive that the real judicial activism today is from the right."); Richard L. Hasen, *A Court of Radicals*, Slate, Mar. 30, 2012, http://www.slate. com/articles/news_and_politics/politics/2012/03/supreme_court_and_obamacare_will_ the_court_s_conservatives_strike_down_the_affordable_care_act_.html (suggesting that, if the Court struck down the healthcare law, "for the first time a Democratic candidate may be able to run for president against the Supreme Court").

20. Toobin, *supra* note 4, at 286.

21. Jeffrey Rosen, *Roberts's Rules*, Atlantic, Jan./Feb. 2007, at 104, 105.

22. *Id.* at 111.

23. *Id.* at 111–12, 113.

24. 132 S. Ct. 2566 (2012).

25. Jan Crawford, *Roberts Switched Views to Uphold Health Care Law*, CBS News, July 1, 2012, http://www.cbsnews.com/8301-3460_162-57464549/roberts-switched-views-to-uphold-health-care-law/.

26. *See* Josh Blackman, *Unprecedented: The Constitutional Challenge to Obamacare* 225–33 (2013); Ross Douthat, *John Roberts's Political Decision*, N.Y. Times Evaluations Blog, June 28, 2012, http://douthat.blogs.nytimes.com/2012/06/28/john-roberts-political-

decision/; Ronald Dworkin, *Why Did Roberts Change His Mind?*, N.Y. Rev. of Books Blog, July 9, 2012, http://www.nybooks.com/blogs/nyrblog/2012/jul/09/why-did-roberts-change-his-mind/; Dan Ernst, *"My Whole Life" Redux*, Legal History Blog, June 29, 2012, http://legalhistoryblog.blogspot.com/2012/06/my-whole-life-redux.html; Charles Krauthammer, *Why Roberts Did It*, Wash. Post, June 29, 2012, at A19.

27. Crawford, *supra* note 25.

28. Adam Liptak, *Roberts's Delicate Twist*, N.Y. Times, June 29, 2012, at A1.

29. Linda Greenhouse, *A Justice in Chief*, N.Y. Times Opinionator, June 28, 2012, http://opinionator.blogs.nytimes.com/2012/06/28/a-justice-in-chief/.

30. Jeffrey Rosen, *Welcome to the Roberts Court: How the Chief Justice Used Obamacare to Reveal His True Identity*, New Republic Online, June 29, 2012, http://www.tnr.com/blog/plank/104493/welcome-the-roberts-court-who-the-chief-justice-was-all-along; *see also* Jeffrey Rosen, *Big Chief*, New Republic, Aug. 2, 2012, at 13, 14 ("Roberts set aside his ideological preference to protect the Court from a decision along party lines that would have imperiled its legitimacy.").

31. Thomas L. Friedman, *Taking One for the Country*, N.Y. Times, July 1, 2012, at SR11.

32. David L. Franklin, *Why Did Roberts Do It?*, Slate, June 28, 2012, http://www.slate.com/articles/news_and_politics/jurisprudence/2012/06/john_roberts_broke_with_conservatives_to_preserve_the_supreme_court_s_legitimacy.html.

33. *See* Toobin, *supra* note 4, at 294.

34. Andrew Ross Sorkin, *Investors in Health Care Seem to Bet on Incumbent*, N.Y. Times, Aug. 21, 2012, at B1.

35. *We Believe in America: 2012 Republican Platform* 32 (2012), *available at* http://www.gop.com/wp-content/uploads/2012/08/2012GOPPlatform.pdf.

36. *ABC World News with Diane Sawyer* (television broadcast Nov. 8, 2012), *available at* 2012 WLNR 23923008.

37. 159 Cong. Rec. S6841–42 (daily ed. Sept. 24, 2013) (statement of Sen. McCain) ("[The Affordable Care Act] was a major issue in the campaign. . . . Well, the people spoke. They spoke, much to my dismay, but they spoke and reelected the President of the United States. . . . [E]lections have consequences and those elections were clear in a significant majority. The majority of the American people supported the President of the United States and renewed his stewardship of this country. . . . I think all of us should respect the outcome of the elections which reflects the will of the people.").

38. Sam Baker, *Poll Finds Support for Repealing Obama Health Law at Record Low*, The Hill, Nov. 13, 2012, http://thehill.com/blogs/healthwatch/politics-elections/267577-poll-support-for-healthcare-repeal-hits-record-low.

39. For the story of the website's problems, see Sheryl Gay Stolberg & Michael D. Shear, *Inside the Race to Rescue a Health Site, and Obama*, N.Y. Times, Dec. 1, 2013, at A1. For the story of how they got fixed, see Steven Brill, *Code Red*, Time, Mar. 10, 2014, at 26.

40. *See* Jonathan Weisman, *G.O.P.'s Assault on Health Law Fades in Races*, N.Y. Times, Nov. 1, 2014, at A1.

41. Greg Jaffe, *Obama Criticizes Supreme Court Because He Can*, Wash. Post, June 21, 2015, at A2.

42. 135 S. Ct. 2480 (2015).

Chapter 1. Political Institutions in the Public Sphere

1. *See* U.S. Const. art. III, § 2, cl. 1.

2. *See id.* art. I, § 9, cl. 7.

3. *See* Philip Bobbitt, *Constitutional Fate: Theory of the Constitution* 3–119 (1982) (the canonical account of the principal modalities of constitutional interpretation).

4. On the concept of underdeterminacy in law, see Lawrence B. Solum, *On the Indeterminacy Crisis: Critiquing Critical Dogma*, 54 U. Chi. L. Rev. 462, 473 (1987) ("The law is *underdeterminate* with respect to a given case if and only if the set of results in the case that can be squared with the legal materials is a nonidentical subset of the set of all imaginable results.").

5. Readers who detect an Aristotelian slant to this understanding of politics are not mistaken. For a brief discussion of the tie to Aristotelian political theory, see Josh Chafetz, *The Political Animal and the Ethics of Constitutional Commitment*, 124 Harv. L. Rev. F. 1, 6–7 (2011).

6. That narrower conception of politics is reflected in statements like the following: "Society will maintain respect for the rule of law if people believe that judges make decisions based on promulgated rules and free from political considerations, interpreting the law based on an honest legal judgment and applying that judgment to the facts of each case." Wm. Grayson Lambert, Note, *The Real Debate over the Senate's Role in the Confirmation Process*, 61 Duke L.J. 1283, 1317 (2012). This claim, of course, presupposes that legal decision making can generally be separated from "political considerations."

7. My distinction between politics and partisanship largely tracks Balkin and Levinson's distinction between "high politics" and "low politics." *See* Jack M. Balkin & Sanford Levinson, *Understanding the Constitutional Revolution*, 87 Va. L. Rev. 1045, 1062–63 (2001).

8. This is not meant to privilege "structural" provisions over "rights" provisions. Rather, it is meant to build upon Akhil Amar's observation that they are, in fact, superficially distinct ways of performing very similar functions. *See generally* Akhil Reed Amar, *The Bill of Rights as a Constitution*, 100 Yale L.J. 1131 (1991); *see also* Daryl J. Levinson, *Rights and Votes*, 121 Yale L.J. 1286 (2012).

9. This is importantly different from Bruce Ackerman's definition of constitutional politics as "the series of political movements that have, from the Founding onward, tried to mobilize their fellow Americans to participate in the kind of engaged citizenship that, when successful, deserves to carry the special authority of We the People of the United States." Bruce Ackerman, *Constitutional Politics/Constitutional Law*, 99 Yale L.J. 453, 462 (1989). Ackerman's understanding is tied to his theory of "constitutional moments," those rare occasions on which a successful social movement changes our deep constitutional commitments in a lasting way. In contrast, because I understand our constitutional order to involve continual contestation for, and shifting of, political authority, I view constitutional politics as a continuous phenomenon. Ackerman's understanding of constitutional politics is a subset of my understanding, but my understanding also includes less grandiose moments, like President Obama's back-and-forth with the courts.

10. In this, I am calling upon Bruce Ackerman's famous discussion of dualist democracy. *See* Bruce A. Ackerman, *The Storrs Lectures: Discovering the Constitution*, 93 Yale L.J. 1013, 1039–43 (1984).

11. *See* U.S. Const. art. I, § 2, cl. 5; *id.* § 3, cl. 6.

12. *See id.* art. II, § 2, cl. 2.

13. For a comparative discussion of such interbranch defense mechanisms, see N. W. Barber, *Self-Defence for Institutions*, 72 Cambridge L.J. 558 (2013).

14. *See* U.S. Const. art. I, § 6, cl. 1; Josh Chafetz, *Democracy's Privileged Few: Legislative Privilege and Democratic Norms in the British and American Constitutions* 134–43 (2007) (describing this privilege).

15. *See* U.S. Const. art. I, § 6, cl. 1; Chafetz, *supra* note 14, at 87–110.

16. *See* U.S. Const. art. II, § 1, cl. 7 (president); *id.* art. III, § 1 (judges).

17. *Cf.* William N. Eskridge Jr. & John Ferejohn, *A Republic of Statutes: The New American Constitution* 114 (2010) (defining "entrenchment" as "beyond partisan debate").

18. This is not to deny that, in Jack Balkin's evocative language, constitutional claims that are today considered "off the wall" can come to be "on the wall" through the play of constitutional politics. *See* Jack M. Balkin, *Constitutional Redemption: Political Faith in an Unjust World* 12, 88–90, 177–86 (2011). But politics, including constitutional politics, is (as the following pages argue in some detail) a discursive practice; to be successful, constitutional claims must be at least plausible, and the language of the Constitution may foreclose the plausibility of certain claims. *Cf.* John Hart Ely, *Gerrymanders: The Good, the Bad, and the Ugly*, 50 Stan. L. Rev. 607, 632 (1998) ("Call me a troglodyte, but I don't see how anyone can function as a lawyer (or even a law professor) without believing that on (admittedly rare) occasions the language of the controlling document can foreclose certain outcomes. . . ."). Thus, to take just one example, even commentators who abhor the equal representation of the states in the Senate take the Constitution's precise command ("The Senate of the United States shall be composed of two Senators from each State. . . ." U.S. Const. art. I, § 3, cl. 1; *id.* amend. XVII, cl. 1.) to be dispositive. *See* Sanford Levinson, *Our Undemocratic Constitution* 50–52 (2006); Jeffrey W. Ladewig, *One Person, One Vote, 435 Seats: Interstate Malapportionment and Constitutional Requirements*, 43 Conn. L. Rev. 1125, 1143 (2011) ("[I]f an amendment is [politically] possible, then the first order of business should be to change the vastly more egregious interstate malapportionment of the U.S. Senate."); Suzanna Sherry, *Our Unconstitutional Senate*, in *Constitutional Stupidities, Constitutional Tragedies* 95, 95 (William N. Eskridge Jr. & Sanford Levinson eds., 1998) ("[W]ere this provision [requiring equal state representation in the Senate] not unequivocally enshrined in the Constitution itself (Article V), it would undoubtedly be unconstitutional. . . ."). Indeed, even as they point out that the "plain meaning" of various constitutional provisions is often an artifact of constitutional interpretation, rather than a precondition for it, Curt Bradley and Neil Siegel treat equal representation in the Senate as ironclad. Curtis A. Bradley & Neil S. Siegel, *Constructed Constraint and the Constitutional Text*, 64 Duke L.J. 1213, 1234 (2015). In the very long term, perhaps even an argument for the unconstitutionality of equal state representation in the Senate could come to be "on the wall," but in any reasonably foreseeable time frame, this seems highly unlikely. I refer to constitutional provisions with that degree of stability as "determinate."

19. The term "multiplicity" is adopted from Alison L. LaCroix, *The Ideological Origins of American Federalism* 6–9 (2010). I first began applying it in the separation-of-powers context in my review of her book. Josh Chafetz, *Multiplicity in Federalism and the Separation of Powers*, 120 Yale L.J. 1084 (2011). Bryan Garsten deploys similar language. *See* Bryan Garsten, *Representative Government and Popular Sovereignty*, in *Political Representation* 90, 103–04 (Ian Shapiro et al. eds., 2009).

20. As Bill Eskridge has noted, "formalism" and "functionalism" are not single unified theories but rather familial groupings. *See* William N. Eskridge Jr., *Relationships between Formalism and Functionalism in Separation of Powers Cases*, 22 Harv. J.L. & Pub. Pol'y 21, 21–22 (1998) (describing three different ways of characterizing the formalism/functionalism divide).

21. *See id.* at 21 (identifying formalism with "bright-line rules that seek to place determinate, readily enforceable limits on public actors" that can be deduced from "authoritative constitutional text, structure, original intent, or all three working together"); John F. Manning, *Separation of Powers as Ordinary Interpretation*, 124 Harv. L. Rev. 1939, 1958 (2011) (identifying formalism with "readily ascertainable and enforceable rules of separation").

22. *See* Christopher L. Eisgruber, *The Most Competent Branches: A Response to Professor Paulsen*, 83 Geo. L.J. 347, 353–54 (1994) (advocating "the principle of comparative institutional competence, which stands for the proposition that interpretive authority belongs to the branch that, by virtue of its structural characteristics, is best able to interpret the Constitution"); *see also* Eskridge, *supra* note 20, at 22 (noting that functionalism emphasizes "efficacy").

23. Abraham Lincoln, Speech at Chicago, July 10, 1858, in *The Political Debates between Abraham Lincoln and Stephen A. Douglas* 38, 54 (George Haven Putnam ed., 1912).

24. *Id.* at 56.

25. For an example similar to this phenomenon, consider *Western Tradition Partnership, Inc. v. Attorney General*, 271 P.3d 1 (Mont. 2011), in which the Montana Supreme Court seemed to offer an implausible reading of *Citizens United* in the course of coming out differently in a very similar case. *See generally* Adam Liptak, *Unsigned Opinions, and Citizens United*, N.Y. Times, June 12, 2012, at A14. And, indeed, the Supreme Court summarily reversed the Montana Supreme Court. Am. Tradition P'ship v. Bullock, 132 S. Ct. 2490 (2012) (per curiam). Pam Karlan views *Bullock* as evidence of the Court's "deep distrust of democratic process." Pamela S. Karlan, *The Supreme Court, 2011 Term—Foreword: Democracy and Disdain*, 126 Harv. L. Rev. 1, 28 (2012); *see also id.* at 35–39.

26. *See* U.S. Const. art. III, § 1.

27. *Id.* art. VI, cl. 2 (providing that federal law trumps state law).

28. The fact that these institutional settlements do not give rise to normatively binding legal rules to govern future disputes is a key distinction between the multiplicity-based view of the separation of powers and the "historical gloss" view championed by Curt Bradley, Trevor Morrison, and Neil Siegel. *See* Curtis A. Bradley & Trevor W. Morrison, *Historical Gloss and the Separation of Powers*, 126 Harv. L. Rev. 411 (2012); Curtis A. Bradley & Trevor W. Morrison, *Presidential Power, Historical Practice, and Legal Constraint*, 113 Colum. L. Rev. 1097 (2013); Curtis A. Bradley & Neil S. Siegel, *After*

Recess: Historical Practice, Textual Ambiguity, and Constitutional Adverse Possession, 2014 Sup. Ct. Rev. 1; Curtis A. Bradley & Neil S. Siegel, *Historical Gloss, Constitutional Conventions, and the Judicial Separation of Powers*, 105 Geo. L.J. (forthcoming 2016).

29. *Cf.* Confirmation Hearing on the Nomination of John G. Roberts, Jr., To Be Chief Justice of the United States Before the S. Comm. on the Judiciary, 109th Cong. 55 (2005) (statement of John G. Roberts Jr.) ("Nobody ever went to a ballgame to see the umpire.").

30. David R. Mayhew, *America's Congress: Actions in the Public Sphere, James Madison through Newt Gingrich* 7–9 (2000). Mayhew, of course, takes the phrase from Habermas. *See generally* Jürgen Habermas, *The Structural Transformation of the Public Sphere* (Thomas Burger trans., MIT Press 1989) (1962). In using the phrase as Mayhew does, I mean to remain agnostic on many of Habermas's particular historical and sociological claims.

31. David R. Mayhew, *Partisan Balance: Why Political Parties Don't Kill the U.S. Constitutional System*, at xviii (2011).

32. Mayhew catalogues forty-three different types of congressional actions in the public sphere, with the final one being the catchall "unusual." Mayhew, *supra* note 30, at 67–69 tbl.2.6. The number would clearly be higher if he were focused on all political actors, not just members of Congress.

33. Even two scholars for whom public opinion is quite important have referred to the "mysterious process by which public opinion forms" and determines which branch will "prevail" in interbranch conflict. Eric A. Posner & Adrian Vermeule, *Constitutional Showdowns*, 156 U. Pa. L. Rev. 991, 1006 (2008).

34. *Cf.* Daniel Yankelovich, *Coming to Public Judgment: Making Democracy Work in a Complex World*, at xii (1991) ("Most public opinion polls are misleading because they fail to distinguish between people's top-of-the-mind, offhand views (mass opinion) and their thoughtful, considered judgments (public judgment).").

35. Catherine Roach has perceptively called attention to the ambiguity of the word "engagement" in a different context, noting that it "can alternately refer to an intimate union (a promise between two individuals) or a hostile encounter (a contest between two armies)." Catherine Roach, *The Turner Inheritance*, 34 Art Hist. 594, 595 (2011). Engagements among political elites and between elites and their publics can, likewise, fall almost anywhere along the spectrum from cooing lovers to hostile warriors.

36. *See generally* Richard E. Neustadt, *Presidential Power and the Modern Presidents: The Politics of Leadership from Roosevelt to Reagan* 76 (1990) ("The weaker [the president's] apparent popular support, the more his cause in Congress may depend on negatives at his disposal like the veto or 'impounding.' He may not be left helpless, but his options are reduced, his opportunities diminished, his freedom for maneuver checked in the degree that Washington conceives him unimpressive to the public."); Douglas Rivers & Nancy L. Rose, *Passing the President's Program: Public Opinion and Presidential Influence in Congress*, 29 Am. J. Pol. Sci. 183, 194 (1985) (finding that "public opinion is an important source of presidential influence in Congress"). On judicial nominations specifically, see George L. Watson & John A. Stookey, *Shaping America: The Politics of Supreme Court Appointments* 88–89 (1995). Indeed, a president riding particularly low in public support may even face opposition from within his own party, as demonstrated by Republican resistance to George W. Bush's failed nomination of Harriet Miers to the

Supreme Court in 2005. *See* Jan Crawford Greenburg, *Supreme Conflict: The Inside Story of the Struggle for Control of the United States Supreme Court* 263–84 (2007).

37. Paul Burstein, *The Impact of Public Opinion on Public Policy: A Review and an Agenda*, 56 Pol. Res. Q. 29, 29 (2003).

38. Marc J. Hetherington, *Why Trust Matters: Declining Political Trust and the Demise of American Liberalism* 53 (2005).

39. Richard F. Fenno Jr., *Home Style: House Members in Their Districts* 154 (1978).

40. *Id.*

41. This is, of course, true even for institutions whose members do not face the voters directly. Thus, for instance, Justice Breyer spent the first third of a recent book discussing the importance of public trust to the working of the Supreme Court, *see* Stephen Breyer, *Making Our Democracy Work: A Judge's View* 1–72 (2010), and Justice Sotomayor has made significant efforts at public outreach, *see* David Fontana, *The People's Justice?*, 123 Yale L.J. F. 447 (2014), http://www.yalelawjournal.org/forum/the-peoples-justice. Despite these efforts, there is some evidence that the Court is losing public trust. *See* Brian Christopher Jones, *Disparaging the Supreme Court: Is SCOTUS in Serious Trouble?*, 2015 Wis. L. Rev. Forward 53; Eric Posner, *The Supreme Court's Loss of Prestige*, Slate, Oct. 7, 2015, http://www.slate.com/articles/news_and_politics/view_from_chicago/2015/10/the_supreme_court_is_losing_public_approval_and_prestige.html.

42. Philip Pettit, *The Cunning of Trust*, 24 Phil. & Pub. Aff. 202, 209–10 (1995) (footnote omitted).

43. Hetherington, *supra* note 38, at 67.

44. This likely explains why, conventional wisdom to the contrary notwithstanding, politicians appear to try very hard to carry through on their campaign promises. *See, e.g.*, Jeff Fishel, *Presidents and Promises: From Campaign Pledge to Presidential Performance* (1985); Michael G. Krukones, *Promises and Performance: Presidential Campaigns as Policy Predictors* (1984); Ian Budge & Richard I. Hofferbert, *Mandates and Policy Outputs: U.S. Party Platforms and Federal Expenditures*, 84 Am. Pol. Sci. Rev. 111 (1990); Evan J. Ringquist & Carl Dasse, *Lies, Damned Lies, and Campaign Promises? Environmental Legislation in the 105th Congress*, 85 Soc. Sci. Q. 400 (2004); Carolyn M. Shaw, *President Clinton's First Term: Matching Campaign Promises with Presidential Performance*, 25 Cong. & Presidency 43 (1998); Glen Sussman & Byron W. Daynes, *Party Promises and Presidential Performance: Social Policies of the Modern Presidents, FDR–Clinton*, 28 Southeastern Pol. Rev. 111 (2000).

45. Mayhew, *supra* note 30, at 18.

46. *Id.* at 96. In the executive context, Richard Neustadt described this as the president's "teaching" role, Neustadt, *supra* note 36, at 84, and other scholars have discussed the ways in which rhetorical framing allows the president to serve as a policy "choice architect" under certain circumstances, Oren Gross & Fionnuala Ní Aoláin, *The Rhetoric of War: Words, Conflict, and Categorization Post-9/11*, 24 Cornell J.L. & Pub. Pol'y 241, 244–64 (2014). As I argue in the following pages, although there are certain structural features of the presidency that facilitate its role as a choice architect, that role is available to other political actors as well.

47. Mayhew, *supra* note 30, at 19.

48. *Id.* at 20.

49. Balkin & Levinson, *supra* note 7, at 1070.

50. Stephen L. Carter, *The Confirmation Mess: Cleaning Up the Federal Appointments Process* 6 (1994). Carter's comment may have been intended to be tongue in cheek, but it is no less true for that.

51. Elena Kagan, *Confirmation Messes, Old and New*, 62 U. Chi. L. Rev. 919, 940 (1995).

52. Balkin & Levinson, *supra* note 7, at 1070.

53. Al Kamen, *Bork Fails to Catch Public's Eye: Opinion Is Split among the Informed*, Wash. Post, Aug. 7, 1987, at A18.

54. Edward Walsh, *Public Opposition to Bork Grows: In Shift, Plurality Objects to Confirmation, Post-ABC Poll Finds*, Wash. Post, Sept. 25, 1987, at A1.

55. Edward Walsh & Richard Morin, *Majority Opposes Bork, Poll Shows*, Wash. Post, Oct. 16, 1987, at A10.

56. David S. Broder, *President's Credibility Rises in Poll*, Wash. Post, Aug. 7, 1987, at A1 (noting that Reagan's "overall approval rating is at the 50 percent level, where it has hovered since the issue became public last November"); *see also* Watson & Stookey, *supra* note 36, at 47 fig.2.3 (showing where Reagan's popularity registered at the time of the Bork nomination, as plotted against the popularity of presidents from Eisenhower to Clinton at the time of Supreme Court nominations).

57. *See, e.g.*, Jeffrey K. Tulis, *The Rhetorical Presidency* (1987); Lee Epstein & Jeffrey A. Segal, *Advice and Consent: The Politics of Judicial Appointments* 78 (2005) (describing the presidential strategy of "going public" in an attempt to get judicial nominees confirmed).

58. This is related to Aziz Huq's observation that much of the structural Constitution is "negotiated," rather than fought over. *See* Aziz Z. Huq, *The Negotiated Structural Constitution*, 114 Colum. L. Rev. 1595 (2014). I regard negotiation and conflict as part of the same process—first a conflict arises, then a local settlement is worked out through a more-or-less conciliatory process. A judicious actor is adept at knowing when to be more conciliatory and when to be less.

59. *See generally* Dan Balz & Scott Clement, *Poll Finds Major Damage to GOP after Shutdown*, Wash. Post, Oct. 22, 2013, at A1.

60. *See generally* James D. Morrow, *Game Theory for Political Scientists* 160–87 (1994).

61. *See id.* at 60 ("Information sets express a player's knowledge of prior moves when it must decide. When a player reaches an information set with more than one node . . . it knows that it must make a decision and that it is at one of the nodes in that information set. Information sets with multiple nodes reflect the player's ignorance of prior moves in the game tree.").

62. *See id.* at 173 ("A belief for a given node is the conditional probability that the node is reached if the information set containing the node is reached during play of the game.").

63. *See* Jill E. Fisch, *Retroactivity and Legal Change: An Equilibrium Approach*, 110 Harv. L. Rev. 1055, 1101 (1997) ("An unstable equilibrium . . . will not endure or return if disturbed but moves readily to a different equilibrium position.").

64. For an insightful analysis and defense of the practice of judicial statesmanship, see Neil S. Siegel, *The Virtue of Judicial Statesmanship*, 86 Tex. L. Rev. 959 (2008).

65. *Cf.* Mark Tushnet, *Why the Constitution Matters* 1 (2010) ("The Constitution matters because it provides a structure for our politics.").

Chapter 2. The Role of Congress

1. *See* Staff of the Wash. Post, *Landmark: The Inside Story of America's New Health-Care Law and What It Means for Us All* 15–16 (2010) (noting that one of the lessons that Obama's team took from the Clinton administration's failed attempt at healthcare reform was "Do not write a bill. Members of Congress view that as their job. . . ."); *id.* at 50–51 (reporting that the Obama administration came to regret "giving up so much control to Congress"); Jackie Calmes, *A Policy Debacle and Its Lessons*, N.Y. Times, Sept. 6, 2009, at A1 ("Mr. Obama got a faster start than Mr. Clinton by not repeating his mistake of trying to write the law for the lawmakers. . . . Mr. Obama went to the other extreme. He produced no plan, only fairly specific directives. . . . While Congressional Democrats welcomed the partnership, some now wonder if the president did not 'overlearn the lessons of 1994 by giving Congress too much leeway,' as Mr. Cooper of the Blue Dog Coalition put it.").

2. Daryl J. Levinson & Richard H. Pildes, *Separation of Parties, Not Powers*, 119 Harv. L. Rev. 2311, 2313 (2006) (quoting *The Federalist No. 51*, at 321–22 (James Madison) (Clinton Rossiter ed., 1961)) (alteration and ellipsis in original).

3. *Id.* at 2318.

4. *Id.* at 2313.

5. *Id.* at 2368–69.

6. *See id.* at 2315.

7. *See* Josh Chafetz, *The Unconstitutionality of the Filibuster*, 43 Conn. L. Rev. 1003, 1008–11 (2011) (tracing the routinization of the filibuster for most matters of Senate business).

8. Barry Cushman, *The Man on the Flying Trapeze*, 15 U. Pa. J. Const. L. 183, 183 (2012).

9. *See* Business Roundtable v. SEC, 647 F.3d 1144 (D.C. Cir. 2011); *see also* John C. Coffee Jr., *The Political Economy of Dodd-Frank: Why Financial Reform Tends to Be Frustrated and Systemic Risk Perpetuated*, 97 Cornell L. Rev. 1019, 1049, 1065–67 (2012).

10. *See* EME Homer City Generation v. EPA, 696 F.3d 7 (D.C. Cir. 2012), *rev'd*, 134 S. Ct. 1584 (2014); *see also* Julie D. Carter, Note, EME Homer City Generation, L.P. v. EPA: *The D.C. Circuit Strikes Down Another EPA Attempt to Make Good Neighbors through Interstate Air Pollution Regulation*, 26 Tulane Envtl. L.J. 123 (2012).

11. *See* Nat'l Ass'n of Mfrs. v. NLRB, 717 F.3d. 947 (D.C. Cir. 2013), *overruled by* Am. Meat Inst. v. U.S. Dep't of Ag., 760 F.3d 18 (D.C. Cir. 2014) (en banc).

12. *See* Noel Canning v. NLRB, 705 F.3d 490 (D.C. Cir. 2013), *aff'd on other grounds*, 134 S. Ct. 2550 (2014); *see also* Peter Strauss, *The Pre-Session Recess*, 126 Harv. L. Rev. F. 130 (2013); Cass R. Sunstein, *Originalism v. Burkeanism: A Dialogue over Recess*, 126 Harv. L. Rev. F. 126 (2013).

13. *See* Jessica Bulman-Pozen, *Federalism as a Safeguard of the Separation of Powers*, 112 Colum. L. Rev. 459, 500–03 (2012); Jessica Bulman-Pozen, *Partisan Federalism*, 127 Harv. L. Rev. 1077 (2014).

14. *See* Levinson & Pildes, *supra* note 2, at 2324.

15. *See* Stephen Ansolabehere & Philip Edward Jones, *Dyadic Representation*, in *The Oxford Handbook of the American Congress* 293, 296 (Eric Schickler & Frances E. Lee

eds., 2011) ("Indeed, it is not uncommon for Members of the U.S. Congress to take a strong stand against their own party's president on critically important legislation in response to reactions to that legislation by constituents."). This is related to Mariah Zeisberg's observation that the forms in which partisanship manifests itself are historically contingent. *See* Mariah Zeisberg, *War Powers: The Politics of Constitutional Authority* 249–50 (2013). *See also* Eric Schickler, *Disjointed Pluralism: Institutional Innovation and the Development of the U.S. Congress* 258–61 (2001) (noting that the strength of partisan motivations for congressional reform has varied both across time and between the House and the Senate).

16. President George W. Bush, Address Before a Joint Session of the Congress on the State of the Union (Feb. 2, 2005), http://www.presidency.ucsb.edu/ws/index.php?pid=58746. By my count, the speech comprised 5,032 words, of which 1,112 were devoted to Social Security.

17. Jim VandeHei & Peter Baker, *Social Security: On with the Show*, Wash. Post, Mar. 12, 2005, at A3.

18. *See* Richard W. Stevenson & Elisabeth Bumiller, *President Bush's News Conference: The Overview; Bush Cites Plan That Would Cut Social Security*, N.Y. Times, Apr. 29, 2005, at A1.

19. Todd S. Purdum, *President Bush's News Conference: News Analysis; After 99 Days, Testing Winds*, N.Y. Times, Apr. 29, 2005, at A1.

20. *See* Richard W. Stevenson, *Seeking Support, Bush Offers Assurances on Retirement Cuts*, N.Y. Times, May 4, 2005, at A18 (noting that, in a series of CNN/USA Today/ Gallup polls, "Mr. Bush's approval rating for his handling of Social Security generally remained stuck at 35 percent, where it has been for the last two months, down from 43 percent just after his State of the Union address in February").

21. *See id.*

22. *See* Patrick O'Connor, *Social Security in Limbo: Whip's Summer Agenda Leaves Out Keynote Reform*, The Hill, June 1, 2005, at 1.

23. *See* Josh Chafetz, *Multiplicity in Federalism and the Separation of Powers*, 120 Yale L.J. 1084, 1125 n.244 (2011) (briefly describing the political dynamics surrounding the Miers nomination and defeat).

24. *See* Josh Chafetz, *Congress's Constitution*, 160 U. Pa. L. Rev. 715, 777 & n.345 (2012).

25. *See* Annie Lowrey & Binyamin Appelbaum, *Summers out of Running for Federal Reserve Chief*, N.Y. Times, Sept. 16, 2013, at A1.

26. *See, e.g.*, Charlie Savage, *Senators Say Patriot Act Is Being Misinterpreted*, N.Y. Times, May 27, 2011, at A17 (noting that the two senators disclosed on the Senate floor the existence of an administration secret legal interpretation of the PATRIOT Act); Michael D. Shear & Scott Shane, *Congress to Get Classified Memo on Drone Strike*, N.Y. Times, Feb. 7, 2013, at A1 (describing pressure by Wyden and others that forced the administration to release its legal memo justifying the use of unmanned drones to kill American citizens abroad).

27. Political scientists have long noted that members of Congress pursue a number of disparate goals. *See, e.g.*, Richard F. Fenno Jr., *Congressmen in Committees* 1 (1973). As Eric Schickler has noted, one of those goals is the building of institutional capacity; indeed, at various points (especially following periods of presidential aggrandizement),

this has been a particularly prominent goal. Schickler, *supra* note 15, at 7–8, 257, 263–64.

28. U.S. Const. art. II, § 2, cl. 2.

29. *See* Oona A. Hathaway, *Treaties' End: The Past, Present, and Future of International Lawmaking in the United States*, 117 Yale L.J. 1236, 1286 (2008) ("Congressional-executive agreements have been in use since the very beginning of the republic.").

30. *See id.* at 1288–1305 (tracing the history of the use of congressional-executive agreements).

31. Curtis A. Bradley & Trevor W. Morrison, *Historical Gloss and the Separation of Powers*, 126 Harv. L. Rev. 411, 468 (2012).

32. *Id.* at 473–74; Hathaway, *supra* note 29, at 1240; Peter J. Spiro, *Treaties, Executive Agreements, and Constitutional Method*, 79 Tex. L. Rev. 961, 996–1002 (2001).

33. Bradley & Morrison, *supra* note 31, at 473–74.

34. *Id.* at 474; Spiro, *supra* note 32, at 996–97.

35. Phillip R. Trimble & Jack S. Weiss, *The Role of the President, the Senate and Congress with Respect to Arms Control Treaties Concluded by the United States*, 67 Chi.-Kent L. Rev. 645, 661–62 (1991).

36. *See* Associated Press, *Carter Is Warned on SALT Treaty*, Wash. Post, Aug. 25, 1978, at A6 (noting that Democratic senators Alan Cranston, Dick Clark, and Gary Hart insisted that SALT II be sent to the Senate as a treaty); Robert G. Kaiser, *Byrd Warns Administration SALT Pact Must Be a Treaty*, Wash. Post, Aug. 26, 1978, at A2 (noting similar insistences by Democratic senator Henry Jackson and Democratic Senate majority leader Robert Byrd).

37. Quoted in Kaiser, *supra* note 36, at A2 (alteration in original).

38. Trimble & Weiss, *supra* note 35, at 662.

39. *See* Bradley & Morrison, *supra* note 31, at 474–75; *see generally* Phillip R. Trimble & Alexander W. Koff, *All Fall Down: The Treaty Power in the Clinton Administration*, 16 Berkeley J. Int'l L. 55 (1998).

40. Bradley & Morrison, *supra* note 31, at 475.

41. Letter from Joseph R. Biden Jr. & Jesse Helms to Colin Powell (Mar. 2002), *reprinted in* Curtis A. Bradley & Jack L. Goldsmith, *Foreign Relations Law* 590 (4th ed. 2011).

42. *Id.*

43. *See* Peter Baker, *Some Skepticism but Little Opposition on Arms Treaty*, N.Y. Times, May 19, 2010, at A7.

44. Harold Hongju Koh, *Remarks: Twenty-First-Century International Lawmaking*, 101 Geo. L.J. 725, 728 (2013).

45. *Id.*

46. Bradley & Morrison, *supra* note 31, at 476.

47. U.S. Const. art. I, § 7, cl. 1.

48. For an example, see H.R. Res. 1653, 111th Cong. (2010) (returning six measures to the Senate for Origination Clause violations). For a discussion of the practice, see *Report on the Legislative and Oversight Activities of the Committee on Ways and Means during the 113th Congress*, H.R. Rep. No. 113-723, at 126–27 (2015) [hereinafter *Ways and Means Report*].

49. *Ways and Means Report, supra* note 48, at 127–30. It is worth noting that there is a minor error in the committee's table. It lists three blue slips for the 107th Congress, *id.* at 128. However, only the first of these (H. Res. 240, 107th Cong. (2001)) occurred in the 107th Congress; the other two are actually from the 106th Congress (H. Res. 393, 106th Cong. (1999); H. Res. 249, 106th Cong. (1999)).

50. Each blue slip sent one measure back, except for H. Res. 1653, 111th Cong. (2010), which returned six.

51. Tabulated from *Ways and Means Report, supra* note 48, at 127–30.

52. *Id.*

53. More precisely, the Republicans held both houses from 1995 to 2001. The 2000 elections resulted in a fifty–fifty split in the Senate, so there was a Democratic majority from January 3 to January 20, 2001 (i.e., as long as Al Gore remained vice president), which then became a Republican majority on January 20 with the installation of Dick Cheney as president of the Senate. On May 24, 2001, Jim Jeffords of Vermont left the Republican Party and became an independent who caucused with the Democrats, returning the majority to them. In the 2002 elections, Republicans regained a slim majority in the upper chamber, which they held until January 2007.

54. As a result, in the nineteen elections between 1980 and 2016 (inclusive), there were only either three or four occasions (depending on how one counts) on which more than one of the House, Senate, and presidency simultaneously switched partisan control. There were no occasions on which all three switched simultaneously. *See* Josh Chafetz, *A Fourth Way? Bringing Politics Back into Recess Appointments (and the Rest of the Separation of Powers, Too)*, 64 Duke L.J. Online 161, 170 & n.39 (2015) (noting this pattern through the 2014 elections).

55. The canonical work on the prevalence and workings of divided government remains David R. Mayhew, *Divided We Govern: Party Control, Lawmaking, and Investigations, 1946–2002* (2d ed. 2005).

56. Jessica Bulman-Pozen makes an analogous argument in the federalism context, suggesting that the states provide actors who are motivated by partisanship with the "institutional terrain" and "durable and robust scaffolding" for opposing the programs of the federal government. Bulman-Pozen, *Partisan Federalism, supra* note 13, at 1080–81.

57. Terry M. Moe & William G. Howell, *The Presidential Power of Unilateral Action*, 15 J.L. Econ. & Org. 132, 133 (1999).

58. Cooper-Church Amendment, Pub. L. No. 91-652, § 7(a), 84 Stat. 1942, 1943 (1971) (prohibiting the use of funds to introduce ground troops or military advisers into Cambodia); Case-Church Amendment, Pub. L. No. 93-52, § 108, 87 Stat. 130, 134 (1973) (prohibiting the use of any funds for any combat activities in Vietnam, Laos, or Cambodia after August 15, 1973). *See also* Zeisberg, *supra* note 15, at 163–68 (noting the Nixon administration's resistance to these and other antiwar congressional measures, as well as the efficacy of those measures).

59. Moe & Howell, *supra* note 57, at 140.

60. Eric A. Posner & Adrian Vermeule, *The Executive Unbound: After the Madisonian Republic* 4 (2010).

61. Moe & Howell, *supra* note 57, at 138.

62. Posner & Vermeule, *supra* note 60, at 5.

63. David R. Mayhew, *Congress as a Handler of Challenges: The Historical Record*, 29 Stud. Am. Pol. Dev. 185, 211 (2015) (internal footnote omitted).

64. *See* Aziz Z. Huq, *Binding the Executive (by Law or by Politics)*, 79 U. Chi. L. Rev. 777, 777–80 (2012) (reviewing Posner & Vermeule, *supra* note 60).

65. *Id.* at 781.

66. *See* Mark Landler & Jonathan Weisman, *Obama Delays Syria Strike to Focus on a Russian Plan*, N.Y. Times, Sept. 11, 2013, at A1; Charlie Savage, *President Tests Limits of Power in Syrian Crisis*, N.Y. Times, Sept. 9, 2013, at A1.

67. William G. Howell & Jon C. Pevehouse, *Presidents, Congress, and the Use of Force*, 59 Int'l Org. 209, 217–28 (2005).

68. Huq, *supra* note 64, at 781.

69. Posner & Vermeule, *supra* note 60, at 4–5.

70. For a discussion of the power and importance of entrepreneurial members (including, sometimes, entrepreneurial backbenchers), see Schickler, *supra* note 15, at 14–15, 250–52.

71. John R. Hibbing & Elizabeth Theiss-Morse, *Congress as Public Enemy: Public Attitudes Toward American Political Institutions* 62–105 (1995).

72. *Id.* at 19.

73. *See, e.g.*, Timothy E. Cook, Book Review, 60 J. Pol. 249, 250 (1998) (arguing that the level of dissatisfaction with Congress may have been an artifact of the moment at which Hibbing and Theiss-Morse gathered their data); Molly E. Shaffer, Book Review, 33 Harv. J. on Legis. 617, 622 (1996) (suggesting that another possible explanation for Hibbing and Theiss-Morse's results is that "people know compromise when they see it and they see too little of it in Congress"); Eric M. Uslaner, Book Review, 61 Pub. Opinion Q. 667, 669 (1997) (explaining dislike of Congress in terms of partisan animosity).

74. Office of Pers. Mgmt., Historical Federal Workforce Tables: Executive Branch Civilian Employment Since 1940, https://www.opm.gov/policy-data-oversight/data-analysis-documentation/federal-employment-reports/historical-tables/executive-branch-civilian-employment-since-1940/.

75. Office of the Asst. Sec'y of Def., Readiness & Force Mgmt., Dep't of Defense, Defense Manpower Requirements Report 2 tbl.1-1 (2014), *available at* http://prhome.defense.gov/Portals/52/Documents/RFM/TFPRQ/docs/F15%20DMRR.pdf.

76. Recent scholarship has found that even cabinet members may have significant differences in ideology from their appointing president. *See* Anthony M. Bertelli & Christian R. Grose, *The Lengthened Shadow of Another Institution? Ideal Point Estimates for the Executive Branch and Congress*, 55 Am. J. Pol. Sci. 767 (2011).

77. *See generally* David E. Pozen, *The Leaky Leviathan: Why the Government Condemns and Condones Unlawful Disclosures of Information*, 127 Harv. L. Rev. 512 (2013).

78. *See* Kimberley A. Church, Note, *Espionage 2.0: Protecting Human Intelligence Sources in the Digital Age*, 85 S. Cal. L. Rev. 1183, 1188–94 (2012).

79. *See* Mark Mazzetti & Michael S. Schmidt, *Ex-C.I.A. Worker Says He Disclosed U.S. Surveillance*, N.Y. Times, June 10, 2013, at A1.

80. *See* Michiko Kakutani, *Glimpses of Obama among 'Friends,'* N.Y. Times, Sept. 19, 2011, at C1 (book review) ("Why have so many people in the Obama administration vented to Mr. Suskind in the first place, when the president was only partway through his first term? Like many of Bob Woodward's sources a lot of them are motivated by spin, score settling and second-guessing.").

81. *See* Jon D. Michaels, *An Enduring, Evolving Separation of Powers*, 115 Colum. L. Rev. 515, 529–51 (2015).

82. *See generally* Adrian Vermeule, *Conventions of Agency Independence*, 113 Colum. L. Rev. 1163 (2013).

83. Matthew N. Green, *The Speaker of the House: A Study of Leadership* 182 (2010); *see generally id.* at 179–83 (describing the strategy of "going public" by Speakers).

84. For a graphical representation of this over the period 1966–1994, see Hibbing & Theiss-Morse, *supra* note 71, at 32 fig.2.1; *see also* Samuel C. Patterson & Gregory A. Caldeira, *Standing Up for Congress: Variations in Public Esteem Since the 1960s*, 15 Legis. Stud. Q. 25, 26 (1990) ("The fact is that 'standing up for Congress' waxes and wanes. Since pollsters began to take regular readings of the public pulse in the early 1960s, congressional popularity has fluctuated a great deal.").

85. Hibbing & Theiss-Morse, *supra* note 71, at 158.

86. The classic texts are Richard F. Fenno Jr., *If, as Ralph Nader Says, Congress Is "the Broken Branch," How Come We Love Our Congressmen So Much?*, in *Congress in Change: Evolution and Reform* 277 (Norman J. Ornstein ed., 1975), and Glenn R. Parker & Roger H. Davidson, *Why Do Americans Love Their Congressmen So Much More Than Their Congress?*, 4 Legis. Stud. Q. 53 (1979). *See also* Hibbing & Theiss-Morse, *supra* note 71, at 117–18.

87. Justin Crowe, *Building the Judiciary: Law, Courts, and the Politics of Institutional Development* 17 (2012).

88. *See id.* at 2 (noting that, in the aftermath of *Bush v. Gore*, it was plausible to describe the Supreme Court as sitting "at the apex of not just the American judiciary but the entire American political system"). In this vein, consider also Neal Katyal's description of the Supreme Court decision in *Hamdan v. Rumsfeld*, 548 U.S. 557 (2006):

> "*Hamdan v. Rumsfeld* challenges law schools, courts, the President, and Congress to rethink their practices of the past several years. It would be fitting for each entity to begin thinking about a response worthy of what the Court did on June 29, 2006. For on that day, the Court said something profound about America. A man with a fourth-grade education from Yemen, accused of conspiring with one of the world's most evil men, sued the most powerful man in the nation (if not the world), took his case to the highest court in the land, and won. The Court's profound commitment to the rule of law is a beacon for other countries around the world. In no other country would such a thing be possible."

Neal Kumar Katyal, Hamdan v. Rumsfeld: *The Legal Academy Goes to Practice*, 120 Harv. L. Rev. 65, 122 (2006). The fact that Katyal uses excessively purple prose to describe the case, in which he was the victorious counsel of record, should not distract from the accuracy of the claim that the Court is a far more powerful actor in the American political system than high courts are in almost any other.

Chapter 3. The Power of the Purse

1. *See* U.S. Const. art. I, § 9, cl. 7 ("No Money shall be drawn from the Treasury, but in Consequence of Appropriations made by Law. . . .").

2. *See id.* § 7, cl. 2 ("Every Bill which shall have passed the House of Representatives and the Senate, shall, before it become a Law, be presented to the President. . . .").

3. *See id.* (providing that a two-thirds vote in each house can override a presidential veto).

4. On the concept of "vetogates," see William N. Eskridge Jr., *Vetogates, Chevron, Preemption*, 83 Notre Dame L. Rev. 1441, 1444–48 (2008). I refer to bicameralism and presentment as *absolute* vetogates because, unlike some of the items to which Eskridge points (e.g., substantive congressional committees, the House Rules Committee, and conference committees), they are not simply major legislative chokepoints, but are, in fact, hardwired constitutional requirements that cannot be circumvented.

5. F. W. Maitland, *The Constitutional History of England* 309 (H. A. L. Fisher ed., 1908). Kantorowicz locates the seeds of English modernity in the growing recognition of "the difference between the king as a personal liege lord and the king as the supra-individual administrator of a public sphere—a public sphere which included the fisc that 'never died' and was perpetual because no time ran against it." Kantorowicz puts the genesis of that recognition in the thirteenth century. Ernst H. Kantorowicz, *The King's Two Bodies: A Study in Mediaeval Political Theology* 191 (rev. ed. 1997). But it was still quite a bit longer—a bit more than four centuries, in fact—until the publicness of the public fisc became fully dominant over the private revenues of the king-as-liege-lord.

6. William Blackstone, 1 *Commentaries* *271; *see also* Maitland, *supra* note 5, at 433–34.

7. *See generally* William Blackstone, 1 *Commentaries* *272–96.

8. *Id.* at *297 ("[E]xtraordinary grants are usually called by the synonymous names of aids, subsidies, and supplies. . . .").

9. *See* J. R. Maddicott, *The Origins of the English Parliament, 924–1327*, at 119–26 (2010); Maitland, *supra* note 5, at 66–68.

10. *See* Jeffrey Goldsworthy, *The Sovereignty of Parliament: History and Philosophy* 69 (1999).

11. For an excellent, detailed history of the development of Parliament in its earliest years, see Maddicott, *supra* note 9. For an extremely abbreviated summary, see Josh Chafetz, *"In the Time of a Woman, Which Sex Was Not Capable of Mature Deliberation": Late Tudor Parliamentary Relations and Their Early Stuart Discontents*, 25 Yale J.L. & Human. 181, 183–85 (2013).

12. *See* Maddicott, *supra* note 9, at 108, 182.

13. *See id.* at 182 ("Behind appropriation lay the view that taxes should be spent on the purposes for which they had been granted. . . .").

14. Simon Payling, *The Later Middle Ages*, in *The House of Commons: Seven Hundred Years of British Tradition* 48, 51 (Robert Smith & John S. Moore eds., 1996).

15. *See* Maitland, *supra* note 5, at 184 (noting several instances of this in the fourteenth century and that it "continued with increasing elaboration under the Lancastrian kings"); Theodore F. T. Plucknett, *Taswell-Langmead's English Constitutional History, from the Teutonic Conquest to the Present Time* 160, 169, 186 (11th ed. 1960).

16. 4 Rot. Parl. 302 (1425).

17. Maitland, *supra* note 5, at 309. This calls upon the traditional idea of "Tudor despotism"— the cowing of Parliament by the Tudor monarchs. As I have argued elsewhere, the picture is somewhat more complicated than that; while the Crown certainly maintained the upper hand in matters of state throughout the Tudor period, innovations in parliamentary procedure in the late Tudor period paved the way for parliamentary pushback against the Stuart monarchs. *See* Chafetz, *supra* note 11, at 188–95. But issues of taxing and spending were among those great matters of state in which the Tudors can rightly be said to have, in Wallace Notestein's memorable phrase, held "the whip hand." Wallace Notestein, *The Winning of the Initiative by the House of Commons* 13 (1926).

18. *See, e.g.*, Chafetz, *supra* note 11, at 195–201 (tracing the Stuart reaction against the innovations in parliamentary procedure made in the late Tudor period and the parliamentary attempts to hold firm to their institutional gains).

19. Conrad Russell, *The Causes of the English Civil War* 161–84 (1990).

20. *Id.* at 166.

21. *See* Conrad Russell, *King James VI & I and His English Parliaments* 16–18 (Richard Cust & Andrew Thrush eds., 2011) (noting England's precarious financial situation upon James I's ascension).

22. Russell, *supra* note 19, at 171.

23. *See* Josh Chafetz, *Impeachment and Assassination*, 95 Minn. L. Rev. 347, 369–83 (2010).

24. *See generally* Chafetz, *supra* note 11.

25. Russell, *supra* note 19, at 185.

26. I have traced this vicious cycle in some detail in Chafetz, *supra* note 23, at 369–84; Josh Chafetz, *Executive Branch Contempt of Congress*, 76 U. Chi. L. Rev. 1083, 1100–16 (2009).

27. Maitland, *supra* note 5, at 310; *see also* Plucknett, *supra* note 15, at 428 ("The complete authority exercised by the commons, during the late Civil War and Commonwealth, over the whole receipts and expenditure of the national treasury had accustomed the House to regulate the disbursement of the sums which they granted. . . .").

28. *See* Maitland, *supra* note 5, at 310 ("This precedent [of specific appropriations] was followed in some, but not all, . . . cases under Charles II.").

29. *See* Tenures Abolition Act, 12 Car. 2, c. 24 (1660); *see also* Maitland, *supra* note 5, at 434–35.

30. *See* Subsidy Act, 12 Car. 2, c. 4 (1660) (life grant); Excise Act, 12 Car. 2, c. 23 (1660) (life grant); Tenures Abolition Act, 12 Car. 2, c. 24, § 14 (1660) (perpetual grant); Arrears of Excise Act, 13 Car. 2, stat. 1, c. 13 (1661) (perpetual grant); Taxation Act, 14 Car. 2, c. 10 (1662) (perpetual grant); Wine Licenses Act, 22 & 23 Car. 2, c. 6 (1670) (perpetual grant).

31. *See* Annabel Patterson, *The Long Parliament of Charles II*, at 5 (2008) (noting the "joyful subservience" of Parliament to the new monarch upon the Restoration).

32. Taxation Act, 12 Car. 2, c. 9 (1660); Taxation Act, 12 Car. 2, c. 20 (1660); Taxation Act, 12 Car. 2, c. 27 (1660). On the disbanding of the Republican army generally, see Joyce Lee Malcolm, *Charles II and the Reconstruction of Royal Power*, 35 Hist. J. 307, 315–17 (1992).

33. *See* Taxation Act, 12 Car. 2, c. 21 (1660); Taxation Act, 12 Car. 2, c. 29 (1660); An Act for a Free and Voluntary Present to his Majesty, 13 Car. 2, stat. 1, c. 4 (1661); Taxation Act, 13 Car. 2, stat. 2, c. 3 (1661); Taxation Act, 15 Car. 2, c. 9 (1663); Taxation Act, 16 & 17 Car. 2, c. 1 (1664).

34. Patterson, *supra* note 31, at 89.

35. *See id.* at 73–74.

36. 11 H.L. Jour. 625 (Nov. 24, 1664).

37. Taxation Act, 16 & 17 Car. 2, c. 1 (1664); *see also* 8 H.C. Jour. 568 (Nov. 25, 1664) (noting the narrow, 172 to 102, vote in favor of granting the funds).

38. Taxation Act, 17 Car. 2, c. 1, § 5 (1665).

39. *Id.* (requiring "That there be provided and kepte in His Majestyes Exchequer (to witt) in the Office of the Auditor of the Receipt one Booke or Register in which Booke or Register all Moneyes that shall be paid into the Exchequer by this Act shall be entered [& registered] apart and distinct from the Moneyes paid or payable to Your Majestie on the before mentioned Act and from all other Moneyes or Branches of Your Majesties Revenue whatsoever[.] And that alsoe there be one other Booke or Registry provided or kepte in the said Office of all Orders and Warrants to be made by the Lord Treasurer and Under Treasurer or by the Comissers of the Treasury for the time being for payment of all and every Summe and summes of money to all persons for moneyes lent Wares or Goods bought or other payments directed by His Majestie relateing to the service of this Warr.") (first alteration in original indicating interlineation on the parliamentary roll).

40. *Id.* § 7 (providing that any person willing to lend money to the Crown is to have "accesse unto and [the right to] view and peruse all or any of the said Bookes for their Information of the state of those Moneyes").

41. Taxation Act, 18 & 19 Car. 2, c. 1, § 33 (1666).

42. *Id.* § 34.

43. *Id.* § 31.

44. *See* Brian Harwood, *Chivalry & Command: 500 Years of Horse Guards* 37–39 (2006); Clifford Walton, *History of the British Standing Army* 1–14 (London, Harrison & Sons 1894).

45. *See* John Childs, *The Army of Charles II*, at 13–20 (1976).

46. When Clarendon was impeached in 1667, the first proposed article of impeachment charged that he "designed a Standing Army to be raised, and to govern the Kingdom thereby." 9 H.C. Jour. 16 (Nov. 6, 1667). This article, however, did not pass the House of Commons.

47. 12 H.L. Jour. 114 (July 29, 1667). For an account of the rumors that were swirling at the time to the effect that Charles meant to rule by standing army, see Patterson, *supra* note 31, at 78–80.

48. Taxation Act, 18 & 19 Car. 2, c. 13, § 6 (1667); Taxation Act, 19 & 20 Car. 2, c. 6, §§ 23–25 (1668).

49. Taxation Act, 18 & 19 Car. 2, c. 13, §§ 10–11 (1667).

50. Accounts of Public Moneys Act, 19 & 20 Car. 2, c. 1 (1667).

51. Patterson, *supra* note 31, at 89.

52. *See* Taxation Act, 22 Car. 2, c. 3 (1670); Taxation Act, 22 Car. 2, c. 4 (1670); Taxation Act, 25 Car. 2, c. 1 (1672). A counterexample can be found in Taxation Act, 22 & 23 Car.

2, c. 3, § 51 (1670) (appropriating the supply for repayment of debts and "other the occasions aforesaid," which presumably refers to the broad statement of purposes set out in section 1 of the act).

53. Taxation Act, 29 Car. 2, c. 1, §§ 35, 39, 43–47 (1677); Taxation Act, 29 & 30 Car. 2, c. 1, §§ 58, 61–66, 68 (1678); Taxation Act, 30 Car. 2, c. 1, §§ 15, 19, 22–23, 74 (1678); Billeting Act, 31 Car. 2, c. 1, §§ 21–22 (1679). One customs duty statute from this period was only partially appropriated, Taxation Act, 29 Car. 2, c. 2, §§ 4–8 (1677) (setting aside one-fifth of the raised funds as security for loans to the Crown), and another customs duty statute made no appropriation at all, Taxation Act, 30 Car. 2, c. 2 (1678).

54. 9 H.C. Jour. 562 (Dec. 21, 1678).

55. Mark Knights, *Osborne, Thomas, First Duke of Leeds (1632–1712)*, Oxford Dict. Nat'l Biog. (2008), http://www.oxforddnb.com/view/article/20884.

56. 13 H.L. Jour. 724 (Dec. 21, 1680).

57. *Id.*

58. D. W. Hayton, *Seymour, Sir Edward, Fourth Baronet (1633–1708)*, Oxford Dict. Nat'l Biog. (2009), http://www.oxforddnb.com/view/article/25162.

59. *See* Plucknett, *supra* note 15, at 438.

60. *See* Revenue Act, 1 Jac. 2, c. 1 (1685).

61. Taxation Act, 1 Jac. 2, c. 3 (1685).

62. Taxation Act, 1 Jac. 2, c. 4 (1685).

63. Taxation Act, 1 Jac. 2, c. 5 (1685).

64. *Id.* § 1.

65. It is worth noting that this financial comfort was not primarily due to the few extraordinary grants that Parliament had made him; rather, it was primarily due to economic developments that greatly increased the value of the perpetual grants to the Crown that had been made at the Restoration in lieu of the more traditional sources of ordinary revenue. *See* Steve Pincus, *1688: The First Modern Revolution* 160 (2009).

66. *See* Maitland, *supra* note 5, at 328 (finding that "James seems to have had above 16,000 men"); Plucknett, *supra* note 15, at 440 (putting the number of regular troops at James's command at "about 20,000"); *see also* Pincus, *supra* note 65, at 181–83 (discussing James's determination to maintain a standing army).

67. *See* 9 H.C. Jour. 755–56 (Nov. 9, 1685) (reprinting James's speech to the houses of Parliament announcing his intention to dispense with the Test Act); Plucknett, *supra* note 15, at 440–43.

68. *See* Pincus, *supra* note 65, at 182 ("Many English people loathed and feared James II's modern army. Within months the new standing army had become a national grievance.").

69. 9 H.C. Jour. 757 (Nov. 13, 1685).

70. 9 H.C. Jour. 761 (Nov. 20, 1685).

71. Bill of Rights, 1 W. & M., sess. 2, c. 2, § 1, cl. 4–5 (1689).

72. *Id.* § 2, cl. 4, 6, 13.

73. The hearth tax had been granted to Charles II, his "Heires and Successors." Taxation Act, 14 Car. 2, c. 10, § 1 (1662). It was repealed by Hearth Money Act, 1 W. & M., c. 10 (1689). The land tax—which was originally a general property tax but was quickly limited to real property to ease enforcement—was inaugurated in Taxation Act, 1 W. &

M., c. 20 (1689); *see also* Taxation Act, 4 W. & M., c. 1 (1692); Taxation Act, 5 W. & M., c. 1 (1693); etc. The land tax took on its final form as a tax on real property only—the form that it was to maintain throughout the eighteenth century—early in the reign of Queen Anne. *See* Land Tax Act, 2 & 3 Ann., c. 1 (1703); Land Tax Act, 3 & 4 Ann., c. 1 (1704); etc.

Historians have written incisively about the political economy arguments attending the shift from a hearth tax to a land tax. *See, e.g.*, Pincus, *supra* note 65, at 384–85; Colin Brooks, *Public Finance and Political Stability: The Administration of the Land Tax, 1688–1720*, 17 Hist. J. 281 (1974). For our purposes here, however, it is the *duration* of the tax that is more interesting than its form—after all, the perpetual hearth tax could have been replaced with a perpetual land tax. (Indeed, this is precisely what Pitt's government did at the end of the eighteenth century. Perpetual Land Tax Act, 38 Geo. 3, c. 60 (1798).) Parliament's choice to make it a one-year grant from the Glorious Revolution through the end of the eighteenth century is clearly, in itself, meant to be a form of parliamentary control over the government.

74. Taxation Act, 2 W. & M., c. 4, § 1 (1690). As Gill notes, these were "the mainsprings of government finance." Doris M. Gill, *The Treasury, 1660–1714*, 46 Eng. Hist. Rev. 600, 610 (1931).
75. *See, e.g.*, Taxation Act, 2 W. & M., c. 3 (1690).
76. William Blackstone, 1 *Commentaries* *296.
77. G. M. Trevelyan, *The English Revolution, 1688–1689*, at 96 (1965).
78. *See* Maitland, *supra* note 5, at 310, 433; Plucknett, *supra* note 15, at 428; *see also* Gerhard Casper, *Appropriations of Power*, 13 U. Ark. Little Rock L. Rev. 1, 4 (1990).
79. *See* Gill, *supra* note 74, at 610–22.
80. *See id.* at 614–20.
81. Clayton Roberts, *The Growth of Responsible Government in Stuart England* 261 (1966).
82. 1 W. & M., c. 5, §§ 2, 8 (1689).
83. *See, e.g.*, Mutiny Act, 2 W. & M., sess. 2, c. 6 (1690); Mutiny Act, 4 W. & M., c. 13 (1692); *see also* Frederick Bernays Wiener, *Civilians under Military Justice: The British Practice Since 1689 Especially in North America* 8 & n.9 (1967) (noting that, "[e]xcept only during the years 1698–1702, an annual Mutiny Act was always in force" between 1688 and 1879).
84. *See* Roberts, *supra* note 81, at 245–378; Basil Williams, *The Whig Supremacy, 1714–1760*, at 30–40 (rev. C. H. Stuart, 2d ed. 1960).
85. Maitland, *supra* note 5, at 385.
86. *Id.* at 446.
87. *Id.* at 446 n.1; *see also* A. V. Dicey, *Introduction to the Study of the Law of the Constitution* 203 (Liberty Fund 1982) (8th ed. 1915) ("[N]ot a penny of revenue can be legally expended except under the authority of some Act of Parliament.").
88. Maitland, *supra* note 5, at 310 ("Before the end of William's reign, a certain annual sum is assigned to the king for his own use; we begin to have what is afterwards called a civil list; the residue of the money is voted for this purpose and for that—so much for the navy, so much for the army."); *see also id.* at 435 (referring to this process as "the gradual separation of . . . the king's private pocket-money from the national revenue"); William Blackstone, 1 *Commentaries* *321–22 (describing the civil list).

89. *See* Jack P. Greene, *The Quest for Power: The Lower Houses of Assembly in the Southern Royal Colonies, 1689–1776*, at 51 (1963).

90. *Id.* at 87–107.

91. *Id.* at 87.

92. *Id.* at 107.

93. *Id.*

94. *See id.* at 88, 90, 96, 98, 102.

95. Jack P. Greene, *Bridge to Revolution: The Wilkes Fund Controversy in South Carolina, 1769–1775*, 29 J. Southern Hist. 19, 20–21 (1963).

96. *Id.* at 20.

97. On Wilkes's fights with both houses of Parliament, see Josh Chafetz, *Democracy's Privileged Few: Legislative Privilege and Democratic Norms in the British and American Constitutions* 155–58 (2007); for a discussion of American colonial lionization of Wilkes, see Pauline Maier, *John Wilkes and American Disillusionment with Britain*, 20 Wm. & Mary Q. 373 (1963); for a discussion of Wilkes as a libertarian hero, see Chafetz, *supra* note 23, at 389–90 & n.334; for a full account of Wilkes's life, see Arthur H. Cash, *John Wilkes: The Scandalous Father of Civil Liberty* (2006).

98. Greene, *supra* note 95, at 26.

99. *Id.* at 26–28.

100. *Id.* at 28–29.

101. *Id.* at 26–50.

102. *Id.* at 52.

103. Warren M. Billings, *A Little Parliament: The Virginia General Assembly in the Seventeenth Century* 183 (2004).

104. *Id.* at 187–88.

105. 3 Herbert L. Osgood, *The American Colonies in the Eighteenth Century* 156–57 (1958).

106. *See* Evarts Boutell Greene, *The Provincial Governor in the English Colonies of North America* 191–92 (1966).

107. 4 Osgood, *supra* note 105, at 123.

108. More precisely, it charged the salary to the quit-rent fund. *Id.* at 124. On the survival of this feudal charge on land in the American colonies, see Beverley W. Bond Jr., *The Quit-Rent System in the American Colonies*, 17 Am. Hist. Rev. 496 (1912).

109. *See* Greene, *supra* note 89, at 129–47.

110. Declaration of Independence, para. 11 (1776).

111. Greene, *supra* note 89, at 138.

112. *See* Greene, *supra* note 106, at 173–75 (giving further examples).

113. Articles of Confederation, art. 9, § 5.

114. *Id.* art. 8; *see also* E. James Ferguson, *The Power of the Purse: A History of American Public Finance, 1776–1790*, at 220–50 (1961); Jack N. Rakove, *The Beginnings of National Politics: An Interpretive History of the Continental Congress* 275–96, 337–42 (1979).

115. Articles of Confederation, art. 9, §§ 5–6.

116. 4 *Journals of the Continental Congress* 223 (Mar. 21, 1776) (appropriating $12,000 for that purpose).

117. 7 *id.* at 294 (Apr. 23, 1777) (appropriating "115 30/90 dollars" for that purpose).

118. 27 *id.* at 704 (Dec. 23, 1784) (appropriating up to $100,000 for that purpose).
119. Del. Const. of 1776, art. 7 (The president "may draw for such sums of money as shall be appropriated by the general assembly, and be accountable to them for the same. . . ."); Mass. Const. of 1780, pt. 2, ch. 2, § 1, art. 11 ("No moneys shall be issued out of the treasury of this commonwealth, and disposed of (except such sums as may be appropriated for the redemption of bills of credit or treasurer's notes, or for the payment of interest arising thereon) but by warrant under the hand of the governor for the time being, with the advice and consent of the council, for the necessary defence and support of the commonwealth; and for the protection and preservation of the inhabitants thereof, agreeably to the acts and resolves of the general court."); N.H. Const. of 1784, pt. 2, Executive, para. 14 ("No monies shall be issued out of the treasury of this state, and disposed of (except such sums as may be appropriated for the redemption of bills of credit or treasurers' notes, or for the payment of interest arising thereon) but by warrant under the hand of the president for the time being, by and with the advice and consent of the council, for the necessary support and defence of this state, and for the necessary protection and preservation of the inhabitants thereof, agreeably to the acts and resolves of the general court."); N.C. Const. of 1776, art. 19 ("[T]he Governor, for the time being, shall have power to draw for and apply such sums of money as shall be voted by the general assembly, for the contingencies of government, and be accountable to them for the same."); Penn. Const. of 1776, Frame of Gov't, § 20 (The president and council "may draw upon the treasury for such sums as shall be appropriated by the house [of representatives]. . . ."); S.C. Const. of 1778, art. 16 (providing "that no money be drawn out of the public treasury but by the legislative authority of the State"); Vt. Const. of 1786, ch. 2, § 11 (The governor and council "may draw upon the Treasurer for such sums as may be appropriated by the House of Representatives."). An earlier Vermont republican constitution contained a similar provision. *See* Vt. Const. of 1777, ch. 2, § 18.
120. Md. Const. of 1776, art. 13; Mass. Const. of 1780, pt. 2, ch. 2, § 4, art. 1; N.H. Const. of 1784, pt. 2, Secretary, Treasurer, Commissary-General, &c., para. 1; N.J. Const. of 1776, art. 12; N.Y. Const. of 1777, art. 22; N.C. Const. of 1776, art. 22; Penn. Const. of 1776, Frame of Gov't, § 9; S.C. Const. of 1778, art. 29; Va. Const. of 1776, para. 17. Vermont had an elected treasurer, but if no candidate received a majority, then the legislature appointed one. Vt. Const. of 1786, ch. 2, § 10.
121. Ga. Const. of 1777, art. 49.
122. Ga. Const. of 1798, art. 1, § 24. *See also* Richard D. Rosen, *Funding "Non-Traditional" Military Operations: The Alluring Myth of a Presidential Power of the Purse*, 155 Mil. L. Rev. 1, 62–64 (1998) (noting the pattern that, when governors became stronger, state constitutions became more explicit about legislative control over appropriations).
123. Casper, *supra* note 78, at 8; *see also* Rosen, *supra* note 122, at 57 ("Late eighteenth century Americans unquestionably understood that the powers to tax and spend were legislative, not executive, powers.").
124. Mass. Const. of 1780, pt. 2, ch. 2, § 1, art. 13; S.C. Const. of 1778, art. 37.
125. N.H. Const. of 1784, pt. 2, Executive, para. 17.
126. *Id.* para. 16.
127. Bill of Rights, 1 W. & M., sess. 2, c. 2, § 2, cl. 13 (1689).
128. *See* U.S. Const. art. I, § 4, cl. 2; *id.* amend. XX, § 2.

129. *See* Rosen, *supra* note 122, at 69–73.

130. U.S. Const. art. I, § 9, cl. 7.

131. *Id.* art. II, § 1, cl. 7 (presidential salaries); *id.* art. III, § 1 (judicial salaries); *id.* amend. XXVII (congressional salaries).

132. *See* Declaration of Independence, para. 13 (1776) (complaining that the king "has kept among us, in Times of Peace, Standing Armies, without the consent of our Legislatures"); Md. Const. of 1776, Dec. of Rts., art. 26 ("[S]tanding armies are dangerous to liberty, and ought not to be raised or kept up, without consent of the Legislature."); Va. Const. of 1776, Bill of Rts., § 13 ("[S]tanding armies, in time of peace, should be avoided, as dangerous to liberty; and . . . in all cases the military should be under strict subordination to, and governed by, the civil power.").

133. U.S. Const. art. I, § 8, cl. 12.

134. Hamilton, writing as Publius, made this point explicit when he noted that building an army "so large as seriously to menace" the liberties of the people would take a great deal of time. Given the requirement of biennial congressional elections and the prohibition on military appropriations lasting for more than two years, he thought it improbable that an oppressive standing army could be constructed. *The Federalist No. 26*, at 172 (Alexander Hamilton) (Clinton Rossiter ed., 1961).

135. U.S. Const. art. I, § 8, cl. 13.

136. *Id.* amend. III.

137. William Blackstone, 1 *Commentaries* *405.

138. *The Federalist No. 41* (James Madison), *supra* note 134, at 260–61.

139. 3 *The Debates in the Several State Conventions on the Adoption of the Federal Constitution* 58–59 (Jonathan Elliot ed., 2d ed. 1907).

140. *Id.* at 393.

141. 2 *id.* at 349.

142. *See generally* Rosen, *supra* note 122, at 78–83.

143. *See* Gerhard Casper, *An Essay in Separation of Powers: Some Early Versions and Practices*, 30 Wm. & Mary L. Rev. 211, 239–42 (1989); *see also* House Comm. on House Admin., *History of the United States House of Representatives, 1789–1994*, H.R. Doc. No. 103-324, at 23–24 (1994).

144. An Act for Establishing an Executive Department, to be Denominated the Department of Foreign Affairs, ch. 4, 1 Stat. 28 (1789); An Act to Establish an Executive Department, to be Denominated the Department of War, ch. 7, 1 Stat. 49 (1789).

145. An Act to Establish the Treasury Department, ch. 12, § 1, 1 Stat. 65, 65 (1789).

146. *Id.* §§ 2, 4, 1 Stat. at 65–66.

147. Casper, *supra* note 143, at 241; *see also* Ralph Volney Harlow, *The History of Legislative Methods in the Period before 1825*, at 132–33 (1917) ("It seems evident that [in creating the Treasury] Congress planned to create an agent, not for the executive, but for itself.").

148. Appropriations Act, ch. 23, 1 Stat. 95, 95 (1789).

149. *See, e.g.*, Invalid Pensioners Act, ch. 24, 1 Stat. 95, 95 (1789); Appropriations Act, ch. 4, 1 Stat. 104, 104 (1790); Appropriations Act, ch. 6, 1 Stat. 190, 190 (1791); Appropriations Act, ch. 3, 1 Stat. 226, 226 (1791).

150. *See* Casper, *supra* note 78, at 10.

151. Appropriations Act, ch. 23, 1 Stat. 95, 95 (1789).

152. Appropriations Act, ch. 4, § 1, 1 Stat. 104, 104 (1790).

153. *Id.* § 3, 1 Stat. at 105.

154. *See* Casper, *supra* note 78, at 12–14 (tracing this process).

155. *See* David P. Currie, *The Constitution in Congress: The Federalist Period, 1789–1801*, at 165–67 (1997); Casper, *supra* note 78, at 14–15.

156. Albert Gallatin, *A Sketch of the Finances of the United States* (1796), in 3 *The Writings of Albert Gallatin* 69, 111 (Henry Adams ed., Philadelphia, J. B. Lippincott & Co. 1879). As David Currie explains it, for Hamilton to have followed Giles's understanding of the law "would apparently have required him to transport one sum of money home from Europe and another back to take its place." Currie, *supra* note 155, at 166.

157. *See* Raymond Walters Jr., *Albert Gallatin: Jeffersonian Financier and Diplomat* 88–89 (1957); Norman K. Risjord, *Partisanship and Power: House Committees and the Powers of the Speaker, 1789–1801*, 49 Wm. & Mary Q. 628, 640–43 (1992).

158. *See* Casper, *supra* note 78, at 16–17.

159. An Act Further to Amend the Several Acts for the Establishment and Regulation of the Treasury, War, and Navy Departments, ch. 28, § 1, 2 Stat. 535, 535–36 (1809). *See also* Noble E. Cunningham Jr., *The Process of Government under Jefferson* 114–17 (1978) (describing Gallatin's role in the passage of this legislation and its place in his larger financial thinking).

160. *See generally* Rosen, *supra* note 122, at 103–10.

161. For extensive analyses of these statutes and their modern forms, see Kate Stith, *Congress' Power of the Purse*, 97 Yale L.J. 1343, 1363–77 (1988).

162. Miscellaneous Receipts Statute, ch. 110, § 1, 9 Stat. 398, 398–99 (1849).

163. *See* Stith, *supra* note 161, at 1371–72.

164. Appropriations Act, ch. 251, § 7, 16 Stat. 230, 251 (1870).

165. Anti-Deficiency Act, ch. 1484, § 4, 33 Stat. 1214, 1257–58 (1905) (emphasis added).

166. Rebecca Kysar has attacked sunset provisions on a number of fronts. *See* Rebecca M. Kysar, *Lasting Legislation*, 159 U. Pa. L. Rev. 1007, 1051–65 (2011). The merits of Kysar's particular attacks are beyond the scope of this chapter, but it should be noted that none of her arguments addresses the separation-of-powers implications of sunset provisions, which are my focus here.

167. *See* U.S. Const. art. I, § 7, cl. 2.

168. *See* USA PATRIOT Act, Pub. L. No. 107-56, § 224(a), 115 Stat. 272, 295 (2001) ("[T]his title and the amendments made by this title . . . shall cease to have effect on December 31, 2005."). As Republican Representative Dan Lungren put it, "An integral aspect of the logic of sunsets was that they would entail a vigorous exercise of the oversight function of Congress. . . . The pendency of an expiration date provides additional incentives for the exercise of oversight and scrutiny." Daniel E. Lungren, *A Congressional Perspective on the Patriot Act Extenders*, 26 Notre Dame J.L. Ethics & Pub. Pol'y 427, 432 (2012).

169. See Beryl A. Howell, *Seven Weeks: The Making of the USA PATRIOT Act*, 72 Geo. Wash. L. Rev. 1145, 1172, 1178–79 (2004) (noting that the Bush administration preferred a bill lacking a sunset clause).

170. Staff of S. Comm. on the Budget, 105th Cong., *The Congressional Budget Process: An Explanation* 5 (Comm. Print 1998); see also Allen Schick, *The Federal Budget: Politics,*

Policy, Process 57 (3d ed. 2007) ("Direct spending is not controlled by annual appropriations but by the legislation that establishes eligibility criteria and payment formulas, or otherwise obligates the government.").

171. Staff of S. Comm. on the Budget, *supra* note 170, at 5.

172. *See id.* at 5–6, 56.

173. *See id.* at 6 ("Most of the actual operations of the Federal Government are funded by discretionary spending.").

174. *See* Office of Mgmt. & Budget, *Budget of the U.S. Government, Fiscal Year 2017*, at 120 tbl.S-4 (2016) (recording that, for fiscal year 2016, total spending was projected to be $3.952 trillion, of which $2.727 trillion would go to mandatory spending and net interest).

175. *See* Robert C. Byrd, *The Control of the Purse and the Line Item Veto Act*, 35 Harv. J. on Legis. 297, 314 (1998) (noting the considerable growth in mandatory spending since the 1960s).

176. *See* Alan L. Feld, *The Shrunken Power of the Purse*, 89 B.U. L. Rev. 487, 492 (2009) (noting that the prevalence of "permanent fiscal legislation limits Congress's ability to review and change priorities through the appropriation process").

177. *See* Louis Fisher, *Constitutional Conflicts between Congress and the President* 195 (5th ed. 2007).

178. Allen Schick, *Whose Budget? It All Depends on Whether the President or Congress Is Doing the Counting*, in *The Presidency and the Congress: A Shifting Balance of Power* 96, 97 (William S. Livingston et al. eds., 1979).

179. Schick, *supra* note 170, at 10–14.

180. Pub. L. No. 67-13, 42 Stat. 20.

181. 31 U.S.C. § 1105(a) (2006) ("On or after the first Monday in January but not later than the first Monday in February of each year, the President shall submit a budget of the United States Government for the following fiscal year.").

182. *See* Jacob E. Gersen & Eric A. Posner, *Soft Law: Lessons from Congressional Practice*, 61 Stan. L. Rev. 573, 589 (2008) (noting the "first-mover advantage [that] . . . accrues from the President's ability to propose an initial budget"); *see also* Fisher, *supra* note 177, at 195, 199 (noting the executive-empowering features of the 1921 act); Schick, *supra* note 170, at 14 (suggesting that the 1921 act ushered in an era of "presidential dominance" of the budget process).

183. Budget and Accounting Act of 1921 §§ 207–17, 42 Stat. at 22–23.

184. Louis Fisher, *Congressional Abdication: War and Spending Powers*, 43 St. Louis U. L.J. 931, 945–46 (1999).

185. Fisher, *supra* note 177, at 196.

186. *See generally* Elena Kagan, *Presidential Administration*, 114 Harv. L. Rev. 2245, 2272–2319 (2001); Eloise Pasachoff, *The President's Budget as a Source of Agency Policy Control*, 125 Yale L.J. 2182 (2016).

187. Budget and Accounting Act of 1921 §§ 301–17, 42 Stat. at 23–27.

188. *See* Eric Schickler, *Disjointed Pluralism: Institutional Innovation and the Development of the U.S. Congress* 89–94 (2001).

189. *See* Schick, *supra* note 170, at 14–18.

190. *See* Schick, *supra* note 178, at 99–100.

191. Pub. L. No. 93-344, 88 Stat. 297.

192. On the 1974 act, see Fisher, *supra* note 177, at 202–04; Schick, *supra* note 170, at 18–20; Schick, *supra* note 178, at 104–08; Schickler, *supra* note 188, at 195–200; Staff of S. Comm. on the Budget, *supra* note 170, at 8–9.

193. On the subsequent statutes, see Fisher, *supra* note 177, at 204–06.

194. Thomas Jefferson, Third Annual Message to Congress (Oct. 17, 1803), in 1 *A Compilation of the Messages and Papers of the Presidents* 345, 348 (James D. Richardson ed., New York, Bureau of Nat'l Lit. 1897). For just a few examples referring to this as the first instance of impoundment, see, e.g., Arthur M. Schlesinger Jr., *The Imperial Presidency* 235 (1973); Robert J. Delahunty & John C. Yoo, *Dream On: The Obama Administration's Nonenforcement of Immigration Laws, the Dream Act, and the Take Care Clause*, 91 Tex. L. Rev. 781, 841 n.384 (2013); Louis Fisher, *Presidential Spending Discretion and Congressional Controls*, 37 Law & Contemp. Probs. 135, 159 (1972).

195. An Act to Provide Additional Armament, ch. 11, § 3, 2 Stat. 206, 206 (1803).

196. 21 Op. Att'y Gen. 414, 415 (1896).

197. *See* Wm. Bradford Middlekauff, Note, *Twisting the President's Arm: The Impoundment Control Act as a Tool for Enforcing the Principle of Appropriation Expenditure*, 100 Yale L.J. 209, 211 (1990) ("It makes little sense for Congress to challenge the executive when money is impounded because the original purpose of the appropriation no longer exists or because efficiencies can be achieved."); *see also* Fisher, *supra* note 194, at 160 (noting that, when the president engages in such routine impoundments, "few legislators are likely to challenge him").

198. *See* Schlesinger, *supra* note 194, at 236; Fisher, *supra* note 177, at 199–200.

199. *See* Schlesinger, *supra* note 194, at 237–38 (Nixon "embarked on an impoundment trip unprecedented in American history."); Fisher, *supra* note 177, at 200 ("On an entirely different order were the impoundments carried out by the Nixon administration. They set a precedent in terms of magnitude, severity, and belligerence."); Schick, *supra* note 178, at 103 ("Far from administrative routine, Nixon's wholesale impoundments in late 1972 and 1973 were intended to rewrite national priorities at the expense of congressional power and preferences."); Middlekauff, *supra* note 197, at 212 ("The Nixon Administration changed the unwritten rules of the impoundment battle.").

200. Schick, *supra* note 178, at 103.

201. Middlekauff, *supra* note 197, at 212.

202. 420 U.S. 35 (1975).

203. *See* Fisher, *supra* note 177, at 200 (discussing these cases).

204. Pub. L. No. 93-344, §§ 1001–17, 88 Stat. 297, 332–39 (1974), *codified at* 2 U.S.C. §§ 681–88 (2006).

205. 2 U.S.C. § 683 (2006).

206. Impoundment Control Act § 1013, 88 Stat. at 334–35.

207. 462 U.S. 919 (1983).

208. City of New Haven v. United States, 809 F.2d 900 (D.C. Cir. 1987).

209. Pub. L. No. 100-119, § 206, 101 Stat. 754, 785–86 (1987), *as codified at* 2 U.S.C. § 684 (2006).

210. Middlekauff, *supra* note 197, at 218–19.

211. *Id.* at 219.

212. *Id.*

213. Schick, *supra* note 178, at 109–10.

214. Line Item Veto Act, Pub. L. No. 104-130, 110 Stat. 1200 (1996).

215. Clinton v. City of New York, 524 U.S. 417 (1998).

216. Schick, *supra* note 170, at 19; *see also* Fisher, *supra* note 177, at 202.

217. *The Federalist No. 58* (James Madison), *supra* note 134, at 359.

218. Charles L. Black Jr., *The Working Balance of the American Political Departments*, 1 Hastings Const. L.Q. 13, 15 (1974).

219. Mike Dorf, who suggested the air conditioning hypothetical in conversation, is also the source of the hypothetical about cutting the salaries of judicial staff. *See* Michael C. Dorf, *Fallback Law*, 107 Colum. L. Rev. 303, 331 (2007). Dorf raises the possibility that such cuts would be an unconstitutional violation of a free-floating structural principle of judicial independence, but he does not take a position on the question. *See id.* at 331–32. *See also* Adrian Vermeule, *The Constitutional Law of Official Compensation*, 102 Colum. L. Rev. 501, 531 (2002) ("Congress may curtail the judiciary's physical facilities and fringe benefits as it pleases; nothing in the Constitution would bar Congress from turning the Supreme Court building into a museum and sending the Justices to hear cases in, say, the basement of the Smithsonian.").

220. *See* U.S. Const. art. II, § 1, cl. 7 ("The President shall . . . receive for his Services, a Compensation, which shall neither be increased nor diminished during the Period for which he shall have been elected. . . .").

221. *See id.* art. III, § 1 ("The Judges, both of the supreme and inferior Courts . . . shall . . . receive for their Services, a Compensation, which shall not be diminished during their Continuance in Office.").

222. J. Gregory Sidak, *The President's Power of the Purse*, 1989 Duke L.J. 1162, 1162; *see also id.* at 1208–14 (giving specific examples from the appropriations legislation for fiscal year 1990).

223. Act of May 1, 1810, ch. 44, § 2, 2 Stat. 608, 608.

224. *See, e.g.*, 4 Asher C. Hinds, *Hinds' Precedents of the House of Representatives of the United States* §§ 3681–86, 3699, 3917–26, 3942–46, 3948–54, at 449–53, 461–62, 617–21, 636–47 (1907) (giving examples from the late nineteenth and early twentieth-century House).

225. *See, e.g.*, L. Anthony Sutin, *Check, Please: Constitutional Dimensions of Halting the Pay of Public Officials*, 26 J. Legis. 221, 224–28 (2000) (giving several examples).

226. Consular and Diplomatic Appropriations Act, ch. 125, § 7, 15 Stat. 319, 322 (1869).

227. *See, e.g.*, Sidak, *supra* note 222, at 1202–43; Sutin, *supra* note 225, at 232–39, 255–58.

228. 328 U.S. 303 (1946).

229. *Id.* at 313–14.

230. Sai Prakash reads *Lovett* similarly. *See* Saikrishna Prakash, *Removal and Tenure in Office*, 92 Va. L. Rev. 1779, 1800–1801 (2006).

231. The current version of the Anti-Deficiency Act provides that "[a]n officer or employee of the United States Government or of the District of Columbia government may not accept voluntary services for either government or employ personal services exceeding that authorized by law except for emergencies involving the safety of human life or the

protection of property." 31 U.S.C. § 1342. "Essential" government personnel—that is, those deemed necessary to protect life or property—continue to report for work, even during government "shutdowns," although they cannot be paid until the government reopens. The executive branch has interpreted "essential" government personnel expansively, but it is nevertheless the case that "shutdowns" have a pervasive impact on government operations. *See* Auth. to Employ the Servs. of White House Office Emps. During an Appropriations Lapse, 19 Op. O.L.C. 235, 235 (1995); Auth. for the Continuance of Gov't Functions During a Temp. Lapse in Appropriations, 5 Op. O.L.C. 1, 11–12 (1981).

232. *See* Ari Hoogenboom, *Rutherford B. Hayes: Warrior and President* 392–94 (1995).

233. *See id.* at 396–402.

234. *See id.* at 399, 402.

235. *Id.* at 402.

236. For the first seventeen, see Sharon S. Gressle, *Shutdown of the Federal Government: Causes, Effects, and Process*, CRS Report for Cong. No. 98-844, at 6 (2001). For the eighteenth, see Jonathan Weisman & Ashley Parker, *Shutdown Is Over*, N.Y. Times, Oct. 17, 2013, at A1.

237. *See generally* Elizabeth Drew, *Showdown: The Struggle between the Gingrich Congress and the Clinton White House* 330–41, 355–67 (1996) (describing the shutdowns); Gressle, *supra* note 236, at 2–3 (same).

238. *See* Richard S. Conley, *President Clinton and the Republican Congress, 1995–2000: Political and Policy Dimensions of Veto Politics in Divided Government*, 31 Cong. & Presidency 133, 151 (2004) ("By early January 1996 it became clear that the public was beginning to ascribe far greater blame to the Congress than to the president for the policy confrontation and stalemate.").

239. *See, e.g.*, Chris McGreal, *Midterms 2010: Lessons of 1994*, Guardian (London), Nov. 4, 2010, at 13 (suggesting, based on the evidence of the 1995 shutdown alone and without regard to context, that the president enjoys a significant advantage in a budget shutdown); Steve Benen, *Norquist Thinks the GOP Will Win from Another Shutdown*, Wash. Monthly Pol. Animal Blog (Nov. 19, 2010), http://www.washingtonmonthly.com/archives/individual/2010_11/026718.php (noting that some Republicans "seriously believe that the public would credit Republicans for shutting down the government" and asking "whether Republican leaders are crazy enough to think this is a good idea").

240. Jennifer Steinhauer, *Last Shutdown Is a Lesson Lost on Capitol Hill as a New Crisis Looms*, N.Y. Times, Sept. 29, 2013, at A18.

241. Steven M. Gillon, *The Pact: Bill Clinton, Newt Gingrich, and the Rivalry That Defined a Generation* 159 (2008).

242. *See* Ann Devroy & Eric Pianin, *Talks on 7-Year Balanced Budget 'Goal' Collapse*, Wash. Post, Nov. 18, 1995, at A1 (discussing the president's slipping public approval ratings and the mounting pressure from House Democrats who "urg[ed] passage of a new continuing resolution and instruct[ed] the President to work with Congress to develop a seven-year balanced budget 'without preconditions'"); Todd S. Purdum, *President and G.O.P. Agree to End Federal Shutdown and to Negotiate a Budget*, N.Y. Times, Nov. 20, 1995, at A1 (stating that, "[w]hile early public opinion polls" favored the president, "[t]he consensus on Capitol Hill was that Mr. Clinton would have had a

hard time sustaining a veto if Democrats were given another chance to vote on" "a stopgap spending measure . . . that . . . included the goal of balancing the budget in seven years"). It is also worth noting that Clinton's approval ratings did suffer in the shutdowns' aftermath, although not as much as Congress's did. *See* Tim Groseclose & Nolan McCarty, *The Politics of Blame: Bargaining before an Audience*, 45 Am. J. Pol. Sci. 100, 112 n.29 (2001).

243. During the shutdown, Gingrich publicly complained about the seating arrangements for a flight on Air Force One. Gillon, *supra* note 241, at 160. As Gillon notes, "Gingrich's childish verbal tirade was a public relations disaster for the Republicans. Coming in the second day of the shutdown when public opinion was still malleable, it made the Republicans seem petulant and stubborn. . . ." *Id.*

244. *See id.* at 170 ("Gingrich could have declared victory at a number of points [during budget negotiations]. . . . [But] Gingrich misinterpreted the results of the 1994 election and oversold the revolution."); Conley, *supra* note 238, at 151 ("[T]he Republican leadership had overestimated support for the Contract [with America] following the 1994 elections. . . .").

245. Peter Baker & Carl Hulse, *The Great Divide: Obama and G.O.P.*, N.Y. Times, Nov. 4, 2010, at A1.

246. *See* Peter Baker, *Washington Worries about Its New Power Couple*, N.Y. Times, Nov. 10, 2010, at A24.

247. *See* Further Additional Continuing Appropriations Amendments, 2011, Pub. L. No. 112-8, 125 Stat. 34; Additional Continuing Appropriations Amendments, 2011, Pub. L. No. 112-6, 125 Stat. 23; Further Continuing Appropriations Amendments, 2011, Pub. L. No. 112-4, 125 Stat. 6; Continuing Appropriations and Surface Transportation Extension Act, 2011, Pub. L. No. 111-322, 124 Stat. 3518 (2010); Act of Dec. 18, 2010, Pub. L. No. 111-317, 124 Stat. 3454; Act of Dec. 4, 2010, Pub. L. No. 111-290, 124 Stat. 3063; Continuing Appropriations Act, 2011, Pub. L. No. 111-242, 124 Stat. 2607 (2010).

248. The final budget deal is embodied in Department of Defense and Full-Year Continuing Appropriations Act, 2011, Pub. L. No. 112-10, 125 Stat. 38.

249. *See* Jennifer Steinhauer, *2011 Budget Bill with Cuts Is Approved by Congress*, N.Y. Times, Apr. 15, 2011, at A1 (spending cuts); Felicity Barringer & John M. Broder, *Congress, in a First, Removes an Animal from the Endangered Species List*, N.Y. Times, Apr. 13, 2011, at A16 ("A rider to the Congressional budget measure . . . dictates that wolves in Montana and Idaho be taken off the endangered species list. . . . The rider is the first known instance of Congress' directly intervening in the list."); Trip Gabriel, *Budget Deal Fuels Revival of School Vouchers*, N.Y. Times, Apr. 15, 2011, at A18 (noting that the budget deal included a provision financing school vouchers in Washington, D.C.); Editorial, *The Crisis Next Time*, N.Y. Times, Apr. 11, 2011, at A24 (noting that a provision in the budget deal prohibited the District of Columbia from spending any public money on abortion provision).

250. *See* James Risen, *Obama Takes on Congress over Policy Czar Positions*, N.Y. Times, Apr. 17, 2011, at A17. In a signing statement, President Obama suggested that this provision of the budget law may be an unconstitutional infringement of his inherent Article II powers. *See Statement on Signing the Department of Defense and Full-Year*

Continuing Appropriations Act, 2011, 2011 Daily Comp. Pres. Doc. 263 (Apr. 15, 2011). On the separation-of-powers tussle over "policy czars," see generally Kevin Sholette, Note, *The American Czars*, 20 Cornell J.L. & Pub. Pol'y 219 (2010).

251. *See* Jackie Calmes & Peter Baker, *Back to Work: Obama Greeted by Looming Fiscal Crisis*, N.Y. Times, Nov. 8, 2012, at A1.

252. *See id.* (noting that "[i]f Mr. Obama got a mandate for anything," it was for raising taxes on the wealthy).

253. *See* Josh Chafetz, *The Phenomenology of Gridlock*, 88 Notre Dame L. Rev. 2065, 2068–72 (2013).

254. *See* Quinnipiac Univ. Polling Inst., *American Voters Reject GOP Shutdown Strategy 3–1*, Oct. 1, 2013, http://www.quinnipiac.edu/institutes-and-centers/polling-institute/national/release-detail?ReleaseID=1958.

255. *See, e.g.*, *Republicans Lose Ground vs. Obama in the Shutdown Blame Game*, ABC News/Wash. Post Poll, Oct. 7, 2013, http://www.langerresearch.com/uploads/1144a 29TheShutdown.pdf; Andrew Dugan, *Republican Party Favorability Sinks to Record Low*, Gallup, Oct. 9, 2013, http://www.gallup.com/poll/165317/republican-party-favorability-sinks-record-low.aspx; Scott Clement & Peyton M. Graighill, *Poll: Republicans Losing No-Win Game*, Wash. Post The Fix, Oct. 14, 2013, http://www.washingtonpost.com/blogs/the-fix/wp/2013/10/14/poll-republicans-losing-no-win-game/.

256. *See* Assoc. Press, *Wall St. Climbs as Hopes for Détente on Debt Emerge*, N.Y. Times, Oct. 10, 2013, at B8.

257. On conservative interest groups, see, e.g., Eric Lipton & Nicholas Confessore, *Kochs and Other Conservatives Split over Strategy on Health Law*, N.Y. Times, Oct. 11, 2013, at A14; Jonathan Weisman, *As Pressure Mounts, House G.O.P. Weighs Short-Term Debt Deal*, N.Y. Times, Oct. 10, 2013, at A19. On opinion leaders, see, e.g., John Podhoretz, *Suicide of the Right*, N.Y. Post Online, Oct. 8, 2013, http://nypost.com/2013/10/08/suicide-of-the-right/; Editorial, *A GOP Shutdown Strategy*, Wall St. J., Oct. 2, 2013, at A12.

258. *See* Weisman & Parker, *supra* note 236.

259. Bipartisan Budget Act of 2013, Pub. L. No. 113-67, 127 Stat. 1165; Jonathan Weisman, *Budget Vote Passes the Details to Two Panels*, N.Y. Times, Dec. 19, 2013, at A26.

260. Bipartisan Budget Act of 2015, Pub. L. No. 114-74, 129 Stat. 584; David M. Herszenhorn, *Congress Strikes a Budget Deal with President*, N.Y. Times, Oct. 27, 2015, at A1.

261. John C. Roberts, *Are Congressional Committees Constitutional? Radical Textualism, Separation of Powers, and the Enactment Process*, 52 Case W. Res. L. Rev. 489, 564 (2001). A recent survey of congressional drafters confirms that they use legislative history in the appropriations context for the explicit purpose of directing agencies and departments in their spending of the appropriated funds. Abbe R. Gluck & Lisa Schultz Bressman, *Statutory Interpretation from the Inside—An Empirical Study of Congressional Drafting, Delegation, and the Canons: Part I*, 65 Stan. L. Rev. 901, 980 (2013); Abbe R. Gluck & Lisa Schultz Bressman, *Statutory Interpretation from the Inside—An Empirical Study of Congressional Drafting, Delegation, and the Canons: Part II*, 66 Stan. L. Rev. 725, 761, 768 (2014).

262. Roberts, *supra* note 261, at 564.

263. 155 Cong. Rec. H7907 (daily ed. July 9, 2009).

264. For the details of this confrontation, see Kristina Daugirdas, *Congress Underestimated: The Case of the World Bank*, 107 Am. J. Int'l L. 517, 547–49 (2013).

265. Roberts, *supra* note 261, at 564.

266. Consolidated Appropriations Act, 2014, Pub. L. No. 113-76, 128 Stat. 5; Consolidated and Further Continuing Appropriations Act, 2015, Pub. L. No. 113-235, 128 Stat. 2130. On the IRS budget, see Howard Gleckman, *IRS Gets Hammered in the 2014 Budget Agreement*, TaxVox, Jan. 14, 2014, http://taxvox.taxpolicycenter.org/2014/01/14/irs-gets-hammered-in-the-2014-budget-agreement/; Ed O'Keefe, *Congressional Leaders Agree on $1.01 Trillion Spending Bill*, Wash. Post, Dec. 10, 2014, at A3.

267. For an earlier generation of works in this vein, see, e.g., Joseph P. Harris, *Congressional Control of Administration* (1964); Michael W. Kirst, *Government without Passing Laws: Congress' Nonstatutory Techniques for Appropriations Control* (1969). For more recent works, see, e.g., Daugirdas, *supra* note 264, at 533–42; Thomas H. Hammond & Jack H. Knott, *Who Controls the Bureaucracy? Presidential Power, Congressional Dominance, Legal Constraints, and Bureaucratic Autonomy in a Model of Multi-Institutional Policy-Making*, 12 J.L. Econ. & Org. 119, 122–26 (1996); Mathew D. McCubbins, Roger G. Noll & Barry R. Weingast, *Administrative Procedures as Instruments of Political Control*, 3 J.L. Econ. & Org. 243 (1987); Barry R. Weingast & Mark J. Moran, *Bureaucratic Discretion or Congressional Control? Regulatory Policymaking by the Federal Trade Commission*, 91 J. Pol. Econ. 765, 780–92 (1983); Note, *Independence, Congressional Weakness, and the Importance of Appointment: The Impact of Combining Budgetary Autonomy with Removal Protection*, 125 Harv. L. Rev. 1822, 1825–27 (2012); Miranda Yaver, *Asserting the Power of the Purse: Institutional Conflict and Regulatory Authority* (draft), http://ssrn.com/abstract=2125438.

268. Morris P. Fiorina, *Control of the Bureaucracy: A Mismatch of Incentives and Capabilities*, in *The Presidency and the Congress*, *supra* note 178, at 124, 125.

269. On the importance of the budget as a signaling device, see Daniel P. Carpenter, *Adaptive Signal Processing, Hierarchy, and Budgetary Control in Federal Regulation*, 90 Am. Pol. Sci. Rev. 283 (1996); *see also* Note, *supra* note 267, at 1825–27 (noting that congressional budget control is accomplished through control of overall spending levels, earmarks and riders, and threats and signaling).

270. 462 U.S. 919 (1983).

271. Anthony M. Bottenfield, Comment, *Congressional Creativity: The Post-*Chadha *Struggle for Agency Control in the Era of Presidential Signing Statements*, 112 Penn. St. L. Rev. 1125, 1138 (2008).

272. Louis Fisher, *The Legislative Veto: Invalidated, It Survives*, 56 Law & Contemp. Probs. 273, 288 (Autumn 1993).

273. Jessica Korn, *The Legislative Veto and the Limits of Public Choice Analysis*, 109 Pol. Sci. Q. 873, 883 (1994–1995).

274. Eugenia Froedge Toma, *Congressional Influence and the Supreme Court: The Budget as a Signaling Device*, 20 J. Legal Stud. 131, 136–46 (1991); Eugenia F. Toma, *A Contractual Model of the Voting Behavior of the Supreme Court: The Role of the Chief Justice*, 16 Int'l Rev. L. & Econ. 433, 439–44 (1996).

275. *See generally* Nicholas R. Parrillo, *Against the Profit Motive: The Salary Revolution in American Government, 1780–1940* (2013).

276. *See id.* at 76–78 (discussing the social and political justifications of negotiation in the late eighteenth century); *id.* at 80–110 (discussing attempts to maintain the fee system while banning negotiation).

277. *Id.* at 273–89.

278. Eric Schmitt, *Troops' Queries Leave Rumsfeld on the Defensive*, N.Y. Times, Dec. 9, 2004, at A1.

279. *See* Matthew L. Wald, *Nuclear Weapons Money Is Cut from Spending Bill*, N.Y. Times, Nov. 23, 2004, at A22.

280. David Mayhew has noted that, "[n]otwithstanding an occasional out-front hawkishness, as in 1898 vis-à-vis Spain, Congress, on occasions when it has differed with the presidency on foreign policy, has ordinarily leaned toward quietude and stasis." In Mayhew's view, Congress's relative resistance to imperial adventuring explains the "relative lack of colonies that came to be physically possessed" by the United States. David R. Mayhew, *Congress as a Handler of Challenges: The Historical Record*, 29 Stud. Am. Pol. Dev. 185, 196–97 (2015). Of course, a resistance to permanent territorial acquisition is itself a limitation on future imperial adventuring.

281. Cooper-Church Amendment, Pub. L. No. 91-652, § 7(a), 84 Stat. 1942, 1943 (1971).

282. Case-Church Amendment, Pub. L. No. 93-52, § 108, 87 Stat. 130, 134 (1973).

283. On Nixon's (and Kissinger's) resistance to these measures, as well as their efficacy in reining in the president, see Mariah Zeisberg, *War Powers: The Politics of Constitutional Authority* 163–68 (2013); *see also* Thomas M. Franck & Edward Weisband, *Foreign Policy by Congress* 13–33 (1979); Amy Belasco et al., *Congressional Restrictions on U.S. Military Operations in Vietnam, Cambodia, Laos, Somalia, and Kosovo: Funding and Non-Funding Approaches*, CRS Report for Cong. No. RL33803, at 1–3 (2007); Rosen, *supra* note 122, at 93.

284. Byrd Amendment, Pub. L. No. 103-139, § 8151(b)(2)(B), 107 Stat. 1418, 1476–77 (1993).

285. Recent Legislation, *National Defense Authorization Act for Fiscal Year 2013, Pub. L. No. 112-239, § 1028, 126 Stat. 1632, 1914–17 (codified at 10 U.S.C. § 801 note (2012))*, 127 Harv. L. Rev. 835, 835–37 (2013); Charlie Savage, *Decaying Guantánamo Defies Closing Plans*, N.Y. Times, Sept. 1, 2014, at A1.

286. On the history of this provision, see Note, *Congressional Control of Foreign Assistance to Post-Coup States*, 127 Harv. L. Rev. 2499, 2502–03 (2014).

287. *Id.* at 2503–09.

288. *Id.* at 2508–09.

289. The strictest language is contained in the 1984 Boland Amendment, Pub. L. No. 98-473, § 8066(a), 98 Stat. 1837, 1935 (1984) (prohibiting "any . . . agency or entity of the United States involved in intelligence activities" from obligating or spending any funds "for the purpose or which would have the effect of supporting, directly or indirectly, military or paramilitary operations in Nicaragua by any nation, group, organization, movement, or individual").

290. Zeisberg, *supra* note 283, at 190–93, 196–202, 211–17.

291. U.S. Const. art. I, § 9, cl. 7.
292. 50 U.S.C. § 3506(a)(1).
293. *See* Fisher, *supra* note 177, at 206–14; *see also* Franck & Weisband, *supra* note 283, at 115–16; Lawrence Rosenthal, *The Statement and Account Clause as a National Security Freedom of Information Act*, 47 Loy. U. Chi. L.J. 1, 3–59 (2015).
294. *See* Ron Wyden, Mark Udall & Martin Heinrich, *End the N.S.A. Dragnet, Now*, N.Y. Times, Nov. 26, 2013, at A25.

Chapter 4. The Personnel Power

1. Mass. Const. of 1780, pt. 1, art. 30.
2. Clayton Roberts, *The Growth of Responsible Government in Stuart England*, at viii (1966).
3. Vernon Bogdanor, *The Monarchy and the Constitution* 14 (1995).
4. *See* Theodore F.T. Plucknett, *Taswell-Langmead's English Constitutional History* 164–65 (11th ed. 1960).
5. Roberts, *supra* note 2, at 7–8.
6. Plucknett, *supra* note 4, at 170–71.
7. *Id*. at 191–92.
8. *See* Samuel Rezneck, *The Early History of the Parliamentary Declaration of Treason*, 42 Eng. Hist. Rev. 497, 509–10 (1927).
9. Roberts, *supra* note 2, at 8.
10. 1 Sir James Fitzjames Stephen, *A History of the Criminal Law of England* 158 (London, Macmillan 1883); *see also* Raoul Berger, *Impeachment: The Constitutional Problems* 29–30 (1974); Roberts, *supra* note 2, at 2–3.
11. *See* Josh Chafetz, *"In the Time of a Woman, Which Sex Was Not Capable of Mature Deliberation": Late Tudor Parliamentary Relations and Their Early Stuart Discontents*, 25 Yale J.L. & Human. 181 (2013).
12. Roberts, *supra* note 2, at 5.
13. 1 Edward Coke, *Institutes* bk. 1, ch. 2, § 13, *19b (1628) ("[I]t is a maxime in Law, That the King can doe no wrong.").
14. 3 William Blackstone, *Commentaries* *254–55.
15. *See* Roberts, *supra* note 2, at 1, 18; Josh Chafetz, *Executive Branch Contempt of Congress*, 76 U. Chi. L. Rev. 1083, 1100 (2009); William R. Stacy, *Impeachment, Attainder, and the 'Revival' of Parliamentary Judicature under the Early Stuarts*, 11 Parl. Hist. 40, 41–46 (1992).
16. *See* Chafetz, *supra* note 11, at 197–98.
17. William Carr, *Michell, Francis (b. c.1556, d. in or after 1628)*, Oxford Dict. Nat'l Biog. (Sean Kelsey rev., 2008), http://www.oxforddnb.com/view/article/18655; Sidney Lee, *Mompesson, Sir Giles (1583/4–1651x63)*, Oxford Dict. Nat'l Biog. (Sean Kelsey rev., 2008), http://www.oxforddnb.com/view/article/18932; Markku Peltonen, *Bacon, Francis, Viscount St Alban (1561–1626)*, Oxford Dict. Nat'l Biog. (2007), http://www.oxforddnb.com/view/article/990.
18. *See* Roberts, *supra* note 2, at 29.
19. *Id*. at 31.

20. Conrad Russell, *Parliaments and English Politics, 1621–1629*, at 148 (1979) ("If there was to be a war, there would have to be a Parliament. . . .").

21. Roberts, *supra* note 2, at 36–39.

22. *Id.* at 38–39; Russell, *supra* note 20, at 198–202.

23. *See* Thomas McSweeney, *English Judges and Roman Jurists: The Civilian Learning behind England's First Case Law*, 84 Temp. L. Rev. 827, 832–33 (2012).

24. *See* Allen Dillard Boyer, *"Understanding, Authority, and Will": Sir Edward Coke and the Elizabethan Origins of Judicial Review*, 39 B.C. L. Rev. 43, 62 (1997) ("Tudor judges were active agents of the royal will, directing the implementation of royal policy and gathering information across their assize circuits."); C. H. McIlwain, *The Tenure of English Judges*, 7 Am. Pol. Sci. Rev. 217, 219 (1913) ("From the earliest patents down to the Long Parliament, [the] tenure [of judges of the King's Bench and Common Pleas] was practically invariable—during the pleasure of the king.").

25. Fuller's Case, 12 Co. Rep. 41, 77 Eng. Rep. 1322 (C.P. 1607).

26. Prohibitions del Roy, 12 Co. Rep. 63, 77 Eng. Rep. 1342, 1342 (K.B. 1607).

27. *See* James R. Stoner Jr., *Common Law and Liberal Theory: Coke, Hobbes, and the Origins of American Constitutionalism* 31 (1992).

28. Prohibitions del Roy, 77 Eng. Rep. at 1343.

29. *See* Catherine Drinker Bowen, *The Lion and the Throne: The Life and Times of Sir Edward Coke* 377–88 (1957); Stoner, *supra* note 27, at 15; Boyer, *supra* note 24, at 87–88.

30. McIlwain, *supra* note 24, at 222.

31. On Buckingham generally, see Roger Lockyer, *Buckingham: The Life and Political Career of George Villiers, First Duke of Buckingham, 1592–1628* (1981).

32. *See* Josh Chafetz, *Impeachment and Assassination*, 95 Minn. L. Rev. 347, 369–76 (2010).

33. 5 David Hume, *The History of England, From the Invasion of Julius Caesar to The Revolution in 1688*, at 158 (Liberty Fund 1983) (1778).

34. John Rushworth, *Historical Collections of Private Passages of State. Weighty Matters in Law. Remarkable Proceedings in Five Parliaments. Beginning the Sixteenth Year of King James, Anno 1618. And Ending the Fifth Year of King Charls, Anno 1629*, at 217 (London, Newcomb 1659).

35. 2 William Cobbett, *Parliamentary History of England* 49–50 (London, Hansard 1806).

36. *Id.* at 58.

37. 3 H.L. Jour. 619–26 (May 15, 1626).

38. Chafetz, *supra* note 32, at 372; Roberts, *supra* note 2, at 54.

39. Chafetz, *supra* note 32, at 372–73.

40. Russell, *supra* note 20, at 343.

41. 3 Car. I, ch. 1 (1628). On the controversy, which dealt with how Charles signaled his assent to the Petition, see 5 Hume, *supra* note 33, at 197–200.

42. Rushworth, *supra* note 34, at 607.

43. *Id.* at 617.

44. *Id.* at 619–26 (reprinting the remonstrance).

45. *Id.* at 631.

46. *See* Chafetz, *supra* note 32, at 374–76; Thomas Cogswell, *John Felton, Popular Political Culture, and the Assassination of the Duke of Buckingham*, 49 Hist. J. 357 (2006).

47. Chafetz, *supra* note 32, at 376.

48. *Id.* at 375.

49. On the events occurring between the reconvening of Parliament following Buckingham's assassination and its dissolution several months later, see Chafetz, *supra* note 15, at 1108–11.

50. *See* Ronald G. Asch, *Wentworth, Thomas, First Earl of Strafford (1593–1641)*, Oxford Dict. Nat'l Biog. (2009), http://www.oxforddnb.com/view/article/29056.

51. On the new grievances that accumulated during Charles's rule without Parliament, see Chafetz, *supra* note 32, at 377–78.

52. *See* Chafetz, *supra* note 15, at 1111–12.

53. Roberts, *supra* note 2, at 77.

54. 4 H.L. Jour. 97 (Nov. 25, 1640).

55. Roberts, *supra* note 2, at 77.

56. *Id.* at 80–81.

57. *See id.* at 91–92; Asch, *supra* note 50.

58. Roberts, *supra* note 2, at 92–93.

59. *Id.* at 96.

60. Godfrey Davies, *The Early Stuarts, 1603–1660*, at 99–100 (1937).

61. Roberts, *supra* note 2, at 97.

62. 5 Hume, *supra* note 33, at 326.

63. 4 H.L. Jour. 130 (Jan. 12, 1641).

64. *Id.* at 132 (Jan. 15, 1641).

65. McIlwain, *supra* note 24, at 223.

66. *See* Roberts, *supra* note 2, at 108–12.

67. 1 John Rushworth, *Historical Collections. The Third Part; in Two Volumes. Containing the Principal Matters Which Happened from the Meeting of the Parliament, November the 3d. 1640 to the end of the Year 1644*, at 438 (London, Chiswell & Cockerill 1692).

68. *See* Chafetz, *supra* note 11, at 181–83.

69. 2 H.C. Jour. 444 (Feb. 19, 1642).

70. 4 H.L. Jour. 700 (April 5, 1642).

71. *See* Roberts, *supra* note 2, at 113.

72. *Id.* at 114–17.

73. *See* Chafetz, *supra* note 32, at 383–88.

74. *See* Roberts, *supra* note 2, at 118–19.

75. *Id.* at 152–53.

76. *Id.* at 153.

77. Paul Seaward, *Hyde, Edward, First Earl of Clarendon (1609–1674)*, Oxford Dict. Nat'l Biog. (2008), http://www.oxforddnb.com/view/article/14328.

78. *Id.*

79. *See* Roberts, *supra* note 2, at 157.

80. *Id.* at 163.

81. Seaward, *supra* note 77.

82. Roberts, *supra* note 2, at 171.

83. 9 H.C. Jour. 293 (Jan. 14, 1674).

84. *Id.* at 303 (Feb. 5, 1674).

85. Roberts, *supra* note 2, at 195.

86. *Id.* at 217.

87. *Id.* at 217–22.

88. *Id.* at 225.

89. *See id.* at 240–41, 244.

90. McIlwain, *supra* note 24, at 223.

91. J. S. Cockburn, *A History of English Assizes, 1558–1714*, at 249 (1972).

92. *Id.* at 249–50.

93. For background, see Jennifer Levin, *The Charter Controversy in the City of London, 1660–1688, and Its Consequences* 1–16 (1969).

94. *Id.* at 27–28; *see also* Stuart Handley, *Saunders, Sir Edmund (d. 1683)*, Oxford Dict. Nat'l Biog. (2008), http://www.oxforddnb.com/view/article/24691.

95. R. v. City of London, 8 How. St. Tr. 1039, 1264–72 (K.B. 1683).

96. Handley, *supra* note 94.

97. *See* G. W. Keeton, *Lord Chancellor Jeffreys and the Stuart Cause* 312–31 (1965); *see also* George Clark, *The Later Stuarts, 1660–1714*, at 120 (2d ed. 1961) ("There has been some dispute about the exact number of executions, but the best opinion seems to be that about 150 persons suffered death and 800 were transported to the hard servitude of the West Indies. In any case it is certain that Jeffreys bore himself so brutally as to raise a lasting resentment. Another unsavoury part of the government's vengeance was the granting to individual courtiers of the rebels who were to be sent as slaves to the plantations." (footnote omitted)); Steve Pincus, *1688: The First Modern Revolution* 4 (2009) ("In late 1685 [James] overreacted to the romantic but hopeless rebellion of his nephew, the Protestant Duke of Monmouth, by judicially murdering hundreds of humble inhabitants of the English West Country in the Bloody Assizes.").

98. *See* Roberts, *supra* note 2, at 245 (suggesting this counterfactual).

99. 10 H.C. Jour. 41 (Mar. 5, 1689).

100. An Act for Reversing the Judgment in a Quo Warranto against the City of London, 2 W. & M., c. 8 (1690).

101. G. M. Trevelyan, *The English Revolution: 1688–1689*, at 88 (1965).

102. Act of Settlement, 12 & 13 Will. 3, c. 2, § 3 (1701).

103. Roberts, *supra* note 2, at 249–50.

104. *Id.* at 267.

105. *Id.* at 268–69.

106. *Id.* at 283–84.

107. *Id.* at 291–95.

108. *Id.* at 296–97

109. *See id.* at 326.

110. *See id.* at 105, 146–47, 237–38, 273, 285.

111. Act of Settlement, 12 & 13 Will. 3, c. 2, § 3 (1701).

112. Regency Act, 4 & 5 Ann., c. 20, §§ 28–30 (1705).

113. For more on these provisions and some aspects of their subsequent operation, see Josh Chafetz, *Leaving the House: The Constitutional Status of Resignation from the House of Representatives*, 58 Duke L.J. 177, 188–95 (2008).

114. Roberts, *supra* note 2, at 351–53.

115. *Id.* at 354–56.

116. *See id.* at 360–61, 398–99.

117. *Id.* at 425.

118. Chequers Estate Act, 7 & 8 Geo. 5, c. 55, sched. (1917); *see also* O. Hood Phillips et al., *Constitutional and Administrative Law* 358 (8th ed. 2001).

119. Roberts, *supra* note 2, at 401–03.

120. Ct. Charter of 1662, paras. 2, 6; R.I. and Providence Plantations Charter of 1663, paras. 4–5.

121. *See* Evarts Boutell Greene, *The Provincial Governor in the English Colonies of North America* 92 (1966).

122. *See id.* at 93, 110.

123. *Id.* at 111–12.

124. *See* Bernard Bailyn, *The Origins of American Politics* 74 (1968).

125. *Id.*

126. *See id.* at 75–76; Jack P. Greene, *The Quest for Power: The Lower Houses of Assembly in the Southern Royal Colonies, 1689–1776*, at 223–50 (1963).

127. Greene, *supra* note 126, at 224.

128. *Id.* at 429–33.

129. *Id.* at 250.

130. *Id.* at 242–43.

131. Greene, *supra* note 121, at 115–16.

132. *See id.* at 113.

133. *Id.* at 134.

134. *Id.* at 134–35.

135. *Id.* at 94–95, 135–36. This stands in some tension with an incident a decade earlier, in which the Privy Council held that New York Chief Justice James DeLancey's grant of good-behavior tenure was valid. The reason seems to be that the commission given to New York Governor William Cosby contained no express instructions as to how he was to commission judges. *See* Daniel J. Hulsebosch, *Constituting Empire: New York and the Transformation of Constitutionalism in the Atlantic World, 1664–1830*, at 127 (2005). Hardy's commission, by contrast, explicitly incorporated by reference his instructions from the Crown, which ordered him to commission judges during pleasure. *See* Greene, *supra* note 121, at 95. The New Jersey good-behavior commissions were accordingly void ab initio.

136. *See* Greene, *supra* note 126, at 341; *see also id.* at 332, 400–401.

137. Declaration of Independence, para. 11 (1776).

138. *Id.* para. 12; *compare with* Exodus 10:14–15.

139. Jack N. Rakove, *The Beginnings of National Politics: An Interpretive History of the Continental Congress* 195–96 (1979).

140. *Id.* at 200–201.

141. 17 *Journals of the Continental Congress* 791 (Aug. 29, 1780).

142. 19 *id.* at 42–44 (Jan. 10, 1781); *id.* at 126–28 (Feb. 7, 1781).

143. Rakove, *supra* note 139, at 282–84, 297.

144. *Id.* at 300.

145. Articles of Confederation, art. 9, § 5.

146. *Id.* art. 9, § 4; *id.* art. 7.

147. *Id.* art. 5, § 2.

148. *Id.* art. 9, §§ 1–2.

149. Gordon S. Wood, *The Creation of the American Republic, 1776–1787*, at 149 (rev. ed. 1998).

150. As Akhil Amar has noted, those states using the title "president" tended to have weaker chief executives than those using the title "governor." Akhil Reed Amar, *America's Constitution: A Biography* 133–34 (2005).

151. N.Y. Const. of 1777, art. 17; Mass. Const. of 1780, pt. 2, ch. 2, § 1, art. 3; N.H. Const. of 1784, pt. 2, Executive Power—President, para. 3; Vt. Const. of 1786, ch. 2, § 10. *See also* Willi Paul Adams, *The First American Constitutions: Republican Ideology and the Making of the State Constitutions in the Revolutionary Era* 266–67, 270 (Rita & Robert Kimber trans., expanded ed. 2001).

152. S.C. Const. of 1776, art. 7. The veto was eliminated entirely in 1778. S.C. Const. of 1778, art. 16. Perhaps unsurprisingly, the states with popularly elected governors tended to create some (limited) veto mechanisms, while the states whose governors were chosen by the legislature did not. *See* Mass. Const. of 1780, pt. 2, ch. 1, § 1, art. 2 (gubernatorial veto with supermajority legislative override); N.Y. Const. of 1777, art. 3 (veto power wielded by a "council of revision" including the governor but with a supermajority legislative override); Vt. Const. of 1786, ch. 2, art. 16 (suspensive veto only, exercised by governor and council jointly).

153. Wood, *supra* note 149, at 148.

154. *Id.*

155. Md. Const. of 1776, art. 48; *id.* art. 13 (treasurers); Penn. Const. of 1776, Frame of Gov't, § 20; *id.* § 9 (treasurer).

156. Md. Const. of 1776, art. 48; *id.* art. 26.

157. Penn. Const. of 1776, Frame of Gov't, § 19; *see also* Wood, *supra* note 149, at 149 n.41.

158. *See* Mass. Const. of 1780, pt. 2, ch. 2, § 1, arts. 9–10; *id.* § 3, art. 2; Va. Const. of 1776, paras. 8, 10, 12.

159. N.Y. Const. of 1777, art. 23.

160. Del. Const. of 1776, art. 18; Ga. Const. of 1777, art. 17; Md. Const. of 1776, art. 37; Mass. Const. of 1780, pt. 2, ch. 6, art. 2, para. 3; N.H. Const. of 1784, pt. 2, Oaths, para. 15; N.J. Const. of 1776, art. 20; N.C. Const. of 1776, arts. 27–30; Penn. Const. of 1776, Frame of Gov't, §§ 19, 23; S.C. Const. of 1776, art. 10; S.C. Const. of 1778, art. 20; Vt. Const. of 1786, ch. 2, § 23; Va. Const. of 1776, para. 12.

161. Mass. Const. of 1780, pt. 2, ch. 6, art. 2, para. 3; *id.* amend. 27.

162. For good-behavior provisions, see Del. Const of 1776, art. 12; Md. Const. of 1776, art. 40; Mass. Const. of 1780, pt. 2, ch. 3, art. 1; N.H. Const. of 1784, pt. 2, Judiciary Power, para. 1; N.C. Const. of 1776, art. 13; S.C. Const. of 1776, art. 20; S.C. Const. of 1778, art. 27; Vt. Const. of 1777, ch. 2, § 27; Va. Const. of 1776, para. 12. For fixed-tenure provisions, see N.J. Const. of 1776, art. 12; Penn. Const. of 1776, Frame of Gov't, § 23.

For New York's good-behavior tenure with mandatory retirement, see N.Y. Const. of 1777, art. 24.

163. *See* Md. Const. of 1776, art. 40 (giving good-behavior tenure to the attorney general, clerks of various courts, registers of the land office, and registers of wills, as well as judges).

164. Penn. Const. of 1776, Frame of Gov't, § 34.

165. N.Y. Const. of 1777, art. 24.

166. S.C. Const. of 1776, art. 19; S.C. Const. of 1778, art. 26.

167. *See* Wood, *supra* note 149, at 141–42.

168. N.Y. Const. of 1777, arts. 32–33.

169. Mass. Const. of 1780, pt. 2, ch. 1, § 2, art. 8; *id.* § 3, art. 6.

170. Penn. Const. of 1776, Frame of Gov't, § 22; Vt. Const. of 1777, ch. 2, § 20; Vt. Const. of 1786, ch. 2, § 21.

171. The language quoted is from Va. Const. of 1776, para. 14, although nearly identical language appears at Del. Const. of 1776, art. 23.

172. Del. Const. of 1776, art. 23.

173. Md. Const. of 1776, Dec. Rts., art. 30.

174. Penn. Const. of 1776, Frame of Gov't, § 23; Vt. Const. of 1777, ch. 2, § 27.

175. Mass. Const. of 1780, pt. 2, ch. 3, art. 1; N.H. Const. of 1784, pt. 2, Judiciary Power, para. 1.

176. S.C. Const. of 1776, arts. 20, 22

177. S.C. Const. of 1778, arts. 27, 29.

178. *See* Michael J. Gerhardt, *The Federal Appointments Process: A Constitutional and Historical Analysis* 18 (rev. ed. 2003).

179. U.S. Const. art. II, § 2, cl. 2–3.

180. *Id.* art. I, § 8, cl. 9; *id.* art. III, § 1.

181. *See* Martin H. Redish & Curtis E. Woods, *Congressional Power to Control the Jurisdiction of Lower Federal Courts: A Critical Review and a New Synthesis*, 124 U. Pa. L. Rev. 45, 52–56 (1975).

182. U.S. Const. art. I, § 6, cl. 2.

183. *Id.* art. II, § 4.

184. *Id.* art. I, § 2, cl. 5; *id.* art. I, § 3, cl. 6–7; *id.* art. II, § 2, cl. 1; *id.* art. II, § 4; *id.* art. III, § 2, cl. 3.

185. *Id.* art. III, § 1.

186. *The Federalist No. 76*, at 455 (Alexander Hamilton) (Clinton Rossiter ed. 1961).

187. *Id.* at 455–56.

188. Luther Martin, *The Genuine Information* (1788), in 2 *The Complete Anti-Federalist* 19, 67 (Herbert J. Storing ed., 1981).

189. *The Federalist No. 76* (Alexander Hamilton), *supra* note 186, at 456.

190. *Id.* at 457–58.

191. *The Federalist No. 77* (Alexander Hamilton), *supra* note 186, at 459.

192. Seth Barrett Tillman, *The Puzzle of Hamilton's* Federalist No. 77, 33 Harv. J.L. & Pub. Pol'y 149 (2010).

193. An Act for Establishing an Executive Department, to be Denominated the Department of Foreign Affairs, ch. 4, 1 Stat. 28 (1789); An Act to Establish an Executive Department,

to be Denominated the Department of War, ch. 7, 1 Stat. 49 (1789); An Act to Establish the Treasury Department, ch. 12, § 1, 1 Stat. 65, 65 (1789).

194. *See* Tillman, *supra* note 192, at 157–58.

195. *See id.* at 158.

196. *See* Saikrishna Prakash, *New Light on the Decision of 1789*, 91 Cornell L. Rev. 1021, 1029–30 (2006).

197. An Act to Establish the Treasury Department, ch. 12, § 7, 1 Stat. 65, 67 (1789); *see also* An Act for Establishing an Executive Department, to be Denominated the Department of Foreign Affairs, ch. 4, § 2, 1 Stat. 28, 29 (1789); An Act to Establish an Executive Department, to be Denominated the Department of War, ch. 7, § 2, 1 Stat. 49, 50 (1789).

198. *See* Prakash, *supra* note 196, at 1029–42.

199. *Contrast* David P. Currie, *The Constitution in Congress: The Federalist Period, 1789–1801*, at 40–41 (1997) (no majority), *and* Myers v. United States, 272 U.S. 52, 284–85 (1926) (Brandeis, J., dissenting) (same), *with* Prakash, *supra* note 196, at 1067–70 (majority for constitutional removal power in the president), *and Myers*, 272 U.S. at 114–15 (same).

200. 11 *Documentary History of the First Federal Congress* 1083 (Charlene Bangs Bickford et al. eds., 1992) (statement of Rep. Madison, June 29, 1789).

201. *See* Prakash, *supra* note 196, at 1070–72.

202. *See id.* at 1033–34.

203. An Act Making Alterations in the Treasury and War Departments, ch. 37, § 8, 1 Stat. 279, 281 (1792).

204. Amendment Act, ch. 21, 1 Stat. 415 (1795).

205. Stanley Elkins & Eric McKitrick, *The Age of Federalism* 539 (1993).

206. Gerard H. Clarfield, *Pickering, Timothy*, Am. Nat'l Biog. (2000), http://www.anb.org/articles/03/03-00380.html; Gaspare J. Saladino, *McHenry, James*, Am. Nat'l Biog. (2000), http://www.anb.org/articles/02/02-00229.html.

207. Judiciary Act of 1801, ch. 4, §§ 6, 7, 21, 2 Stat. 89, 90–91, 96–97.

208. *See* Alison L. LaCroix, *The Ideological Origins of American Federalism* 202–10 (2010).

209. *See* Jed Glickstein, Note, *After Midnight: The Circuit Judges and the Repeal of the Judiciary Act of 1801*, 24 Yale J.L. & Human. 543, 547 (2012).

210. Organic Act for the District of Columbia, ch. 15, § 11, 2 Stat. 103, 107 (1801).

211. Michael W. McConnell, *The Story of* Marbury v. Madison*: Making Defeat Look Like Victory*, in *Constitutional Law Stories* 13, 16 (Michael C. Dorf ed., 2004).

212. 1 Sen. Exec. Jour. 388 (Mar. 2, 1801).

213. *Id.* at 390 (Mar. 3, 1801).

214. *See* McConnell, *supra* note 211, at 16–18.

215. Repeal Act, ch. 8, 2 Stat. 132 (1802).

216. Judiciary Act of 1802, ch. 31, § 4, 2 Stat. 156, 157–58.

217. *See* Glickstein, *supra* note 209, at 549–50.

218. Although the margin of the Republican victory in 1800 may sometimes be overstated, there is no gainsaying the facts that the election was hard-fought and that it generated intense public interest and engagement. *See* John Ferling, *Adams vs. Jefferson: The Tumultuous Election of 1800*, at 169–74 (2004). The resulting shift in power—in both

Congress and the presidency—from Federalists to Republicans thus both was and was perceived to be a watershed moment in the young Republic.

219. Judiciary Act of 1802, § 1, 2 Stat. at 156 (Supreme Court term); *id.* § 4, 2 Stat. at 157–58 (circuit court terms).

220. *See* Glickstein, *supra* note 209, at 551–53.

221. *Id.* at 563.

222. *See id.* at 554–55.

223. Stuart v. Laird, 5 U.S. (1 Cranch) 299, 308–09 (1803).

224. Jed Glickstein traces this series of events with great care in Glickstein, *supra* note 209, at 556–74.

225. McConnell, *supra* note 211, at 26.

226. Marbury v. Madison, 5 U.S. (1 Cranch) 137, 154–62 (1803).

227. *Id.* at 162–80.

228. *Id.* at 173–80. For canonical observations of the strained nature of Marshall's reading of the statute, see, e.g., Akhil Reed Amar, Marbury*, Section 13, and the Original Jurisdiction of the Supreme Court*, 56 U. Chi. L. Rev. 443, 456–61 (1989); David P. Currie, *The Constitution in the Supreme Court: The Powers of the Federal Courts, 1801–1835*, 49 U. Chi. L. Rev. 646, 653 (1982); William W. Van Alstyne, *A Critical Guide to Marbury v. Madison*, 1969 Duke L.J. 1, 15–16.

229. *See* McConnell, *supra* note 211, at 28.

230. *Id.* at 31.

231. *Marbury*, 5 U.S. at 155; *see also id.* at 167, 172.

232. *Id.* at 162.

233. *See* David F. Forte, *Marbury's Travail: Federalist Politics and William Marbury's Appointment as Justice of the Peace*, 45 Cath. U.L. Rev. 349, 399–400 (1996).

234. *See* 1 Sen. Exec. J. 404 (Jan. 6, 1802), *as corrected by id.* at 417 (Apr. 5, 1802).

235. *See id.* at 404 (Jan. 6, 1802) (nominating the original fifteen), *updated by id.* at 417 (Apr. 5, 1802) (naming replacements).

236. Forte, *supra* note 233, at 401.

237. *Id.*

238. *Id.* at 401 n.269.

239. Although Forte mistakenly describes Peter as one of Jefferson's substitutes (noting that "[i]t is not known why Jefferson nominated" someone from a "family of prominent Federalist merchants"), Forte, *supra* note 233, at 401 n.270, it is clear that Peter was originally nominated by Adams, 1 Sen. Exec. Jour. 388 (Mar. 2, 1801). On Peter's politics, see Harold Donaldson Eberlein & Cortlandt Van Dyke Hubbard, *Historic Houses of George-Town and Washington City* 125–31 (1958).

240. Thomas Jefferson, Tables of Justices of the Peace for the District of Columbia (before Mar. 16, 1801), in 36 *The Papers of Thomas Jefferson* 314 (Barbara B. Oberg ed., 2009).

241. *Id.* The "Commissions given out" category has seven names in it, four of which also appear in the "Commissions not given" list. The editors suggest that Jefferson moved some names from the second column to the first (without crossing them out of the second) when he decided that he wanted to reappoint them. *See id.* at 315 (editors' note).

242. *See* Saikrishna Bangalore Prakash, *The Appointment and Removal of William J. Marbury and When an Office Vests*, 89 Notre Dame L. Rev. 199, 209–11 (2013) (making this argument).

243. *See generally* Carl E. Prince, *The Passing of the Aristocracy: Jefferson's Removal of the Federalists, 1801–1805*, 57 J. Am. Hist. 563 (1970).

244. Peter Charles Hoffer & N. E. H. Hull, *Impeachment in America, 1635–1805*, at 207–08 (1984).

245. 4 H.R. Jour. 383–84 (Mar. 3, 1803).

246. 13 Annals of Cong. 320–22 (Jan. 4, 1804).

247. Hoffer & Hull, *supra* note 244, at 212.

248. *See id.* at 210–16.

249. 13 Annals of Cong. 367–68 (Mar. 12, 1804).

250. *See* Hoffer & Hull, *supra* note 244, at 228–29.

251. *See* Akhil Reed Amar, *The Bill of Rights: Creation and Reconstruction* 98–102 (1998).

252. Hoffer & Hull, *supra* note 244, at 230.

253. 13 Annals of Cong. 1180–81 (Mar. 12, 1804); *id.* at 1237–40 (Mar. 26, 1804).

254. 14 *id.* at 726–63 (Nov. 30–Dec. 4, 1804).

255. *Id.* at 728–31 (Dec. 3, 1804).

256. *See* Hoffer & Hull, *supra* note 244, at 260.

257. *See id.* at 238–52.

258. *Id.* at 253.

259. 14 Annals of Cong. 665–69 (Mar. 1, 1805).

260. Hoffer & Hull, *supra* note 244, at 254.

261. As Mark Graber has noted, the Court remained "quite docile" for the remainder of the Jefferson administration and then proceeded to rule in a manner broadly consistent with "moderate Republican" principles for the remainder of Marshall's life. Mark A. Graber, *Federalist or Friends of Adams: The Marshall Court and Party Politics*, 12 Stud. Am. Pol. Dev. 229, 232–33 (1998).

262. For evidence of this intraparty harmony in the judicial appointments context, note how few of Jefferson's, Madison's, and Monroe's appointments to the bench failed; note, moreover, that what failures those presidents did experience all resulted from declined seats, not from the Senate's refusal to confirm. *See* Michael J. Gerhardt & Michael Ashley Stein, *The Politics of Early Justice: Federal Judicial Selection, 1789–1861*, 100 Iowa L. Rev. 551, 559–60 tbl. (2015).

263. Tenure of Office Act, ch. 102, § 1, 3 Stat. 582, 582 (1820).

264. *Id.* § 2, 3 Stat. at 582.

265. *See* Saikrishna Prakash, *Removal and Tenure in Office*, 92 Va. L. Rev. 1779, 1797–98 (2006) (noting this feature of the act).

266. *See* Daniel Walker Howe, *What Hath God Wrought: The Transformation of America, 1815–1848*, at 331–34 (2007).

267. *See* Richard J. John, *Affairs of Office: The Executive Departments, The Election of 1828, and the Making of the Democratic Party*, in *The Democratic Experiment: New Directions in American Political History* 50, 62 (Meg Jacobs et al. eds., 2003).

268. *See* Howe, *supra* note 266, at 332–33.

269. *See id.* at 333–34.

270. *See* Gerhardt, *supra* note 178, at 91.

271. *See id.* at 92–93; Howe, *supra* note 266, at 385.

272. *See* Gerhardt, *supra* note 178, at lxi, lxxix, tbls.5 & 7; Howe, *supra* note 266, at 388–89.

273. Howe, *supra* note 266, at 392, 441.

274. *Id.* at 390.

275. *See* Michael J. Gerhardt, *The Forgotten Presidents: Their Untold Constitutional Legacy* 26–27 (2013).

276. *Id.* at 25–35.

277. *See id.* at 41–47; Howe, *supra* note 266, at 590–95.

278. Gerhardt, *supra* note 275, at 58.

279. Gerhardt, *supra* note 178, at 54.

280. *Id.* at 55.

281. There remains some debate as to how involved Lincoln was with the choice of his 1864 running mate, but it is clear at least that he was not opposed to Johnson. *See* Hans L. Trefousse, *Andrew Johnson: A Biography* 177–79 (1989).

282. *See* Chafetz, *supra* note 32, at 401–13.

283. An Act to Provide Circuit Courts for the Districts of California and Oregon, ch. 100, § 1, 12 Stat. 794, 794 (1863) (expanding the Court to ten justices); An Act to Fix the Number of Judges of the Supreme Court of the United States, ch. 210, § 1, 14 Stat. 209, 209 (1866) (reducing the Court to seven justices).

284. Tenure of Office Act, ch. 154, 14 Stat. 430 (1867).

285. Army Appropriations Act, ch. 170, § 2, 14 Stat. 485, 486–87 (1867).

286. *See* Chafetz, *supra* note 32, at 404–05.

287. *See id.* at 405–07.

288. *See id.* at 407–08.

289. *Id.* at 409.

290. *See* Trefousse, *supra* note 281, at 335, 340.

291. *See* Floyd M. Riddick, *Senate Procedure: Precedents and Practices* 991 (1981).

292. 61 Sen. Jour. 340, 344–45 (Mar. 25, 1868).

293. Vacancies Act, ch. 45, 12 Stat. 656 (1863).

294. Vacancies Act, ch. 227, §§ 1–3, 15 Stat. 168, 168 (1868).

295. Vacancies Amendment Act, ch. 113, 26 Stat. 733 (1891).

296. Jerry L. Mashaw, *Creating the Administrative Constitution: The Lost One Hundred Years of American Administrative Law* 235–36 (2012).

297. An Act to Amend the Judicial System of the United States, ch. 22, § 1, 16 Stat. 44, 44 (1869).

298. Appropriations Act, ch. 114, § 9, 16 Stat. 495, 514–15 (1871).

299. *See* Mashaw, *supra* note 296, at 237–38; Leonard D. White, *The Republican Era: 1869–1901: A Study in Administrative History* 282–84 (1958).

300. Hans L. Trefousse, *Rutherford B. Hayes* 94 (2002). On Hayes's emphasis on civil service reform while campaigning for the presidency, see *id.* at 70.

301. *See id.* at 94–96, 107.

302. *Id.* at 107.

303. Allan Peskin, *Charles Guiteau of Illinois: President Garfield's Assassin*, 70 J. Ill. St. Hist. Soc'y 130, 134, 136, 139 (1977).

304. *See* Amanda Schaffer, *A President Felled by an Assassin and 1880's Medical Care*, N.Y. Times, July 25, 2006, at F5.

305. *The Assassination*, N.Y. Times, July 3, 1881, at 6.

306. *A Lesson*, N.Y. Times, July 4, 1881, at 4.

307. Pendleton Act, ch. 27, §§ 1–2, 22 Stat. 403, 403–04 (1883).

308. *Id.* § 6, 22 Stat. at 405–06.

309. *Id.* § 2, paras. 5–6, 22 Stat. at 404; *id.* §§ 5, 9–14, 22 Stat. at 405–07.

310. Stephen Skowronek, *Building a New American State: The Expansion of National Administrative Capacities, 1877–1920*, at 69 (1982). For a detailed breakdown of the expansion of classified positions, see *id.* at 70–71 tbl.1.

311. *See* Mashaw, *supra* note 296, at 239; Ari Hoogenboom, *The Pendleton Act and the Civil Service*, 64 Am. Hist. Rev. 301, 303–04 (1959).

312. Skowronek, *supra* note 310, at 69, 72.

313. *Id.* at 74.

314. Gerhardt, *supra* note 178, at 277.

315. Skowronek, *supra* note 310, at 82.

316. *See* Edmund Morris, *The Rise of Theodore Roosevelt* 397–409, 412–13, 422–25, 433–37, 443–44, 446–52, 472–73 (1979).

317. Wayne E. Fuller, *The American Mail: Enlarger of the Common Life* 314 (1972).

318. *Id.* at 294–96, 324–25.

319. Robert K. Murray, *The Harding Era: Warren G. Harding and His Administration* 305 (1969).

320. *Id.* Sai Prakash mistakenly views this as evidence of Wilson's "partially revers[ing] course from the partisan tack he had taken in his first term." Saikrishna Prakash, *The Story of* Myers *and Its Wayward Successors: Going Postal on the Removal Power*, in *Presidential Power Stories* 165, 169 (Christopher H. Schroeder & Curtis A. Bradley eds., 2009). In fact, viewed in light of the long-standing practice of making patronage appointments and then classifying positions, this was a continuation of Wilson's partisanship, not a repudiation of it.

321. Postal Appropriations Bill, ch. 179, § 6, 19 Stat. 78, 80 (1876).

322. *See* Prakash, *supra* note 320, at 165–67.

323. *See id.* at 178.

324. Myers v. United States, 272 U.S. 52, 117 (1926).

325. *Id.* at 114.

326. *Id.* at 116.

327. *Id.* at 131–34.

328. Repeal Act, ch. 353, 24 Stat. 500 (1887).

329. *Myers*, 272 U.S. at 165–70.

330. *Id.* at 177 (Holmes, J., dissenting).

331. *Id.* at 178 (McReynolds, J., dissenting); *id.* at 240 (Brandeis, J., dissenting).

332. Humphrey's Ex'r v. United States, 295 U.S. 602, 618–20 (1935).

333. *Id.* at 621–26.

334. *Id.* at 626.

335. *Id.* at 624.

336. *Id.* at 628.

337. *Id.* at 629–32.

338. *Id.* at 632.

339. Prakash, *supra* note 320, at 191.

340. U.S. Const. art. II, § 2, cl. 2.

341. *See* 5 U.S.C. § 2105(a)(1)(D) (recursively defining "employee" to include, inter alia, anyone appointed in the civil service by any employee).

342. Collections Act, ch. 5, § 1, 1 Stat. 29, 35 (1789) (authorizing the (Senate-confirmed) port collectors to appoint "one or more searchers or inspectors, as may be necessary for the security of the revenue"); *id.* § 5, 1 Stat. at 37 (requiring collectors to "employ proper persons as weighers, gaugers, measurers and inspectors at the several ports within his district, together with such persons as shall be necessary to serve in the boats which may be provided for securing the collection of the revenue"); *id.* § 6, 1 Stat. at 37 (authorizing collectors to appoint deputies); *id.* § 26, 1 Stat. at 43 (recognizing the existence of "officers . . . appointed *or employed* by virtue of this act" (emphasis added)).

343. Morrison v. Olson, 487 U.S. 654, 671–72 (1988).

344. *Id.* at 719 (Scalia, J., dissenting).

345. *See* Janet Reno, *Statement of Janet Reno, Attorney General, Before the Committee on Governmental Affairs, United States Senate, Concerning the Independent Counsel Act* (Mar. 17, 1999), *available at* http://www.justice.gov/archive/ag/testimony/1999/aggovern031799.htm.

346. Edmond v. United States, 520 U.S. 651, 662 (1997).

347. *See* Ronald C. Moe, *Senate Confirmation of Executive Appointments: The Nixon Era*, 32 Proc. Acad. Pol. Sci. 141, 144–47 (1975).

348. Paperwork Reduction Act of 1980, Pub. L. No. 96-511, §2(a), 94 Stat. 2812, 2814–15.

349. Appropriations Act, Pub. L. No. 99-500, § 813(a), 100 Stat. 1783, 1783-336 (1986).

350. Omnibus Crime Control and Safe Streets Act, Pub. L. No. 90-351, § 1101, 82 Stat. 197, 236 (1968).

351. Gerhardt, *supra* note 178, at 61.

352. One study finds similar manipulation with respect to lower courts. *See* John M. de Figueiredo & Emerson H. Tiller, *Congressional Control of the Courts: A Theoretical and Empirical Analysis of Expansion of the Federal Judiciary*, 39 J.L. & Econ. 435 (1996) (finding that Congress is significantly more likely to expand the federal judiciary when doing so would give the nominations to a same-party president—that is, when doing so would promote congressional preferences).

353. Gerhardt, *supra* note 178, at 157.

354. Jed Handelsman Shugerman, *The Creation of the Department of Justice: Professionalization without Civil Rights or Civil Service*, 66 Stan. L. Rev. 121, 131 (2014).

355. Bruce Ackerman, *The Decline and Fall of the American Republic* 152–55 (2010).

356. On the present-day staffing of agencies, see Anne Joseph O'Connell, *Vacant Offices: Delays in Staffing Top Agency Positions*, 82 S. Cal. L. Rev. 913, 923–27 (2009).

357. Civil Service Reform Act, Pub. L. No. 95-454, 92 Stat. 1111 (1978). For a discussion of its various provisions, see *Developments in the Law—Public Employment*, 97 Harv. L. Rev. 1611, 1632–50 (1984).

358. U.S. Const. art. I, § 6, cl. 2.
359. *See* John F. O'Connor, *The Emoluments Clause: An Anti-Federalist Intruder in a Federalist Constitution*, 24 Hofstra L. Rev. 89, 122–34 (1995).
360. Judiciary Act, ch. 20, § 35, 1 Stat. 73, 93 (1789).
361. *See* Ronald J. Krotoszynski Jr. et al., *Partisan Balance Requirements in the Age of New Formalism*, 90 Notre Dame L. Rev. 941, 962–83 (2015) (describing the history of partisan balance requirements in federal law).
362. Pendleton Act, ch. 27, § 1, 22 Stat. 403, 403 (1883).
363. Justice Brandeis compiled a list of qualifications in his *Myers* dissent. *See* Myers v. United States, 272 U.S. 52, 265–74 (1926) (Brandeis, J., dissenting). *See also* Mitchel A. Sollenberger, *Statutory Qualifications on Appointments: Congressional and Constitutional Choices*, 34 Pub. Admin. Q. 202, 202–03 (2010) (discussing conflict-of-interest prohibitions as statutory officeholding requirements).
364. *See* Louis Fisher, *Constitutional Conflicts between Congress and the President* 26 (5th ed. 2007).
365. *Id.*
366. Gerhardt, *supra* note 178, at 41.
367. Scalia was found dead on the morning of February 13, 2016. That same day, both Senate majority leader Mitch McConnell and Judicary Committee chairman Chuck Grassley insisted that the next president should nominate Scalia's replacement. *See* Mark Landler & Peter Baker, *Battle Begins over Successor as Obama Vows to Press On*, N.Y. Times, Feb. 14, 2016, at A1.
368. *See id.*
369. Michael D. Shear, Julie Hirschfeld Davis & Gardiner Harris, *Obama Pick Engages Supreme Court Battle*, N.Y. Times, March 17, 2016, at A1.
370. *See, e.g.*, David Wasserman, *House Republicans Staring into the Abyss: 10 Ratings Changes Favor Democrats*, Cook Pol. Rep't, March 18, 2016, http://cookpolitical.com/story/9382.
371. *See* Seung Min Kim & Burgess Everett, *More Republicans Agree to Meet with Garland*, Politico, March 31, 2016, http://www.politico.com/story/2016/03/republicans-meet-merrick-garland-supreme-court-221432.
372. For an analysis of these dynamics written before the Garland nomination was announced, see Josh Chafetz, *What the Constitution Has to Say about the Supreme Court Vacancy*, The Hill, Feb. 16, 2016, http://thehill.com/blogs/pundits-blog/the-judiciary/269486-what-the-constitution-has-to-say-about-the-supreme-court.
373. *See, e.g.*, Amar, *supra* note 150, at 194.
374. Sheryl Gay Stolberg & Philip Shenon, *Bush to Appoint Ex-Judge as Head of Justice Dept.*, N.Y. Times, Sept. 17, 2007, at A1.
375. *See* David Johnston, *Bush May Name Former Federal Judge to Succeed Gonzales*, N.Y. Times, Sept. 16, 2007, at 23 (noting announced Democratic opposition to Michael Chertoff and Theodore Olson).
376. *Id.*
377. Carl Hulse, *Mukasey Wins Vote in Senate, Despite Doubts*, N.Y. Times, Nov. 9, 2007, at A1.

378. Fisher, *supra* note 364, at 32. For a discussion of the history of senatorial courtesy, see Dorothy Ganfield Fowler, *Congressional Dictation of Local Appointments*, 7 J. Pol. 25 (1945).

379. *See* Gerhardt, *supra* note 178, at 64.

380. *See* Fisher, *supra* note 364, at 28 ("Under these circumstances, it is the President who is placed in the position of giving his 'advice and consent.'"); *see also* Janet M. Box-Steffensmeier et al., *Advising, Consenting, Delaying, and Expediting: Senator Influences on Presidential Appointments*, 30 Stud. Am. Pol. Dev. 19, 20 (2016) (studying all Senate blue slips between 1933 and 1960 and concluding that they "provided senators with significant agenda control over nominations from their states," which, in turn, strengthened the Senate as an institution in appointments-related negotiations with the president).

381. *See* Will Weissert, *Report: Vacant Texas Federal Judgeships Languish*, Assoc. Press, Apr. 2, 2014.

382. *See* Ben Kamisar, *Obama Names Three Texas Judges in Apparent Deal with Cornyn and Cruz*, Dallas Morning News Trail Blazers Blog, June 26, 2014, http://trailblazersblog.dallasnews.com/2014/06/obama-names-three-texas-judges-in-apparent-deal-with-cornyn-and-cruz.html/.

383. *See* Josh Chafetz, *Multiplicity in Federalism and the Separation of Powers*, 120 Yale L.J. 1084, 1117–18 (2011) (giving examples of scholars, senators, and members of the media taking this position).

384. Senator Roman Hruska (in)famously expressed the contrary view, when, in response to the claim that Supreme Court nominee Harrold Carswell was a mediocre nominee, he noted, "There are a lot of mediocre judges and people and lawyers . . . and they are entitled to a little representation, aren't they?" 116 Cong. Rec. 7881 (Mar. 18, 1970) (reprinting a *Washington Post* editorial quoting Sen. Hruska).

385. *See* Adrian Vermeule, *Should We Have Lay Justices?*, 59 Stan. L. Rev. 1569 (2007).

386. *See, e.g.*, Robert Barnes, *High Court Nominee Never Let Lack of Experience Hold Her Back*, Wash. Post, May 10, 2010, at A5; Robert Barnes & Anne E. Kornblut, *Obama Picks Kagan for Supreme Court; Solicitor General Would Be Break with Tradition as a Non-Judge*, Wash. Post, May 10, 2010, at A1; Jeff Zeleny & Carl Hulse, *Democrats Express Praise; Republicans Are Cautious*, N.Y. Times, May 11, 2010, at A16.

387. *See* Josh Chafetz, *Governing and Deciding Who Governs*, 2015 U. Chi. Legal F. 73, 76–90.

388. *See* Rob Robinson, *Executive Branch Socialization and Deference on the U.S. Supreme Court*, 46 Law & Soc'y Rev. 889 (2012).

389. Charles M. Cameron, Albert D. Cover & Jeffrey A. Segal, *Senate Voting on Supreme Court Nominees: A Neoinstitutional Model*, 84 Am. Pol. Sci. Rev. 525, 530 (1990).

390. *See* Chafetz, *supra* note 383, at 1118 n.206.

391. Letter from George Washington to Timothy Pickering (Sept. 27, 1795), in 13 *The Writings of George Washington* 106, 107 (Worthington Chauncey Ford ed., New York, Putnam 1892).

392. Gerhardt & Stein, *supra* note 262, at 554.

393. George L. Watson & John A. Stookey, *Shaping America: The Politics of Supreme Court Appointments* 21 (1995).

394. *See* Lee Epstein & Jeffrey A. Segal, *Advice and Consent: The Politics of Judicial Appointments* 108 (2005); *see also* Watson & Stookey, *supra* note 393, at 41–47 (discussing the impact of public and Senate support for the president on the success of nominees).
395. *See* Jan Crawford Greenburg, *Supreme Conflict: The Inside Story of the Struggle for Control of the United States Supreme Court* 263–84 (2007).
396. On Bush's standing in the polls, see Chafetz, *supra* note 383, at 1125 n.244.
397. *See* Glickstein, *supra* note 209, at 568.
398. *See* Gerhardt, *supra* note 178, at 85–86, 108–09, 125, 305, 333 (giving examples).
399. *See* Jackie Calmes & Binyamin Appelbaum, *Push for Yellen to Lead at Fed Gathers Steam*, N.Y. Times, Sept. 17, 2013, at A1; Annie Lowrey, *Summers Seen as Costly in Political Terms*, N.Y. Times, Sept. 17, 2013, at B1. On the term of office of the Fed chair (and, indeed, all members of the Fed's Board of Governors), see 12 U.S.C. § 242.
400. Jonathan Martin, *Warren Is Now Hot Ticket of the Populist Left, but Resists a Presidential Run*, N.Y. Times, Sept. 30, 2013, at A13.
401. In addition to those candidates who are never nominated, there is also a significant pool of "forced withdrawals"—nominated candidates who withdraw from consideration when facing likely defeat. *See* Gerhardt, *supra* note 178, at 165–67.
402. 159 Cong. Rec. S5626 (July 11, 2013).
403. *See* David C. Nixon, *Separation of Powers and Appointee Ideology*, 20 J.L. Econ. & Org. 438 (2004); B. Dan Wood & Richard W. Waterman, *The Dynamics of Political Control of the Bureaucracy*, 85 Am. Pol. Sci. Rev. 801 (1991).
404. *See* Morgan Thomas, *Atomic Energy and Congress* 137, 173–74 (1956).
405. *See* Richard Allan Baker, *A Slap at the "Hidden-Hand Presidency": The Senate and the Lewis Strauss Affair*, 14 Cong. & Presidency 1, 4, 7–8 (1987).
406. *Id.* at 2, 5–6.
407. *Id.* at 7–8.
408. *Id.* at 9.
409. *Id.* at 10.
410. Quoted in *id.* at 13.
411. Editorial, *The Strauss Debate*, Wash. Post, June 20, 1959, at A10.
412. *Id.*
413. Moe, *supra* note 347, at 143.
414. *Id.* at 142.
415. Gerhardt, *supra* note 178, at 178–79.
416. *See* Ed O'Keefe & Aaron Blake, *Senator Holds Long Filibuster to Oppose Obama's Drone Policy*, Wash. Post, Mar. 7, 2013, at A2; Rand Paul, *My 13 Hours Were Just the Beginning*, Wash. Post, Mar. 10, 2013, at B1.
417. Peter Finn & Aaron Blake, *CIA Chief Confirmed after Debate over Drones*, Wash. Post, Mar. 8, 2013, at A1.
418. *Id.*
419. *See* Charlie Savage, *Rand Paul Sues over Phone Program*, N.Y. Times, Feb. 13, 2014, at A19.
420. Rand Paul, *Show Us the Drone Memos*, N.Y. Times, May 12, 2014, at A23.
421. N.Y. Times v. U.S. Dep't of Justice, 752 F.3d 123 (2d Cir. 2014).

422. *See* Jeremy W. Peters, *Judicial Nominee's Memos on Drones Stirring Bipartisan Concern in the Senate*, N.Y. Times, May 6, 2014, at A14.

423. *See* Ashley Parker, *U.S. to Release Rationale in Drone Killing of Citizen*, N.Y. Times, May 21, 2014, at A12; Charlie Savage, *Court Releases Large Parts of Memo Approving Killing of American in Yemen*, N.Y. Times, June 24, 2014, at A17. The memo is appended to N.Y. Times v. U.S. Dep't of Justice, 756 F.3d 100, 124–51 (2d Cir. 2014).

424. *See, e.g.*, Editorial, *A Thin Rationale for Drone Killings*, N.Y. Times, June 24, 2014, at A26; Kenneth Anderson, *Readings: Civilian Intelligence Agencies and the Use of Armed Drones by Ian Henderson*, Lawfare, June 27, 2014, https://www.lawfareblog.com/readings-civilian-intelligence-agencies-and-use-armed-drones-ian-henderson; Steve Vladeck, *The Constitutional Question the Drone Memo Didn't—and Couldn't—Answer*, Just Security, June 24, 2014, http://justsecurity.org/12086/drone-memo-constitution/.

425. Walter J. Oleszek, *Congressional Procedures and the Policy Process* 232 (8th ed. 2011).

426. Gerhardt, *supra* note 178, at 65, 152–53.

427. *See* John H. Cushman Jr., *Senate Stops Consumer Nominee*, N.Y. Times, Dec. 9, 2011, at B1.

428. *See* Jonathan Weisman & Jeremy W. Peters, *Senate Confirms Nominees as G.O.P. Discontent Rises*, N.Y. Times, July 19, 2013, at A14.

429. *See* Paul David Nelson, *Lincoln, Levi*, Am. Nat'l Biog. (2000), http://www.anb.org/articles/03/03-00282.html.

430. *See* David P. Currie, *The Constitution in Congress: The Jeffersonians, 1801–1829*, at 187 (2001); Michael B. Rappaport, *The Original Meaning of the Recess Appointments Clause*, 52 UCLA L. Rev. 1487, 1516 & n.80 (2005).

431. Vacancies Act, ch. 227, § 2, 15 Stat. 168, 168 (1868).

432. 5 U.S.C. § 3345.

433. *Id.* § 3345(a)(3).

434. *Contra* Currie, *supra* note 430, at 187 (asserting that the current statutory scheme "require[s] that the officer designated [as a potential acting officer] already hold an office for which Senate consent was required").

435. *See* 1 Sen. Jour. 427–28 (Apr. 17, 1792) (passage of the bill without recorded vote); 1 H.R. Jour. 601 (May 7, 1792) (passage of the bill, as amended, without recorded vote); 1 Sen. Jour. 441 (May 7, 1792) (accepting House amendments with one alteration, without recorded vote); 1 H.R. Jour. 603 (May 7, 1792) (accepting Senate amendment without recorded vote). None of the back-and-forth appears to have concerned the acting appointments provision.

436. *See* Rappaport, *supra* note 430, at 1515 (making this argument).

437. Presidential Transitions Effectiveness Act, Pub. L. No. 100-398, § 7, 102 Stat. 985, 988 (1988). On the desire to avoid agency evasion of the Vacancies Act, see S. Rep. No. 100-317, at 14 (1988).

438. *See* Gerhardt, *supra* note 178, at 267–69; Brannon P. Denning, *Article II, the Vacancies Act and the Appointment of "Acting" Executive Branch Officials*, 76 Wash. U. L.Q. 1039, 1052–55 (1998).

439. Pub. L. No. 105-277, div. C, title I, § 151, 112 Stat. 2681, 2681-611 to 2681-615 (1998).

440. *Id.* § 151(b), 112 Stat. at 2681-612, codified at 5 U.S.C. § 3346.

441. *Id.*, 112 Stat. at 2681-613, codified at 5 U.S.C § 3347.

442. *Id.*, 112 Stat. at 2681-614 to 2681-615, codified at 5 U.S.C. § 3349.

443. For more detailed discussion of the act's specific provisions, see Joshua L. Stayn, Note, *Vacant Reform: Why the Federal Vacancies Reform Act of 1998 is Unconstitutional*, 50 Duke L.J. 1511, 1522–25 (2001).

444. *See* 5 U.S.C. § 3349c.

445. Under the Vacancies Act, the acting officer must be either the first assistant to the officer, some other Senate-confirmed officer, or some high-ranking civil servant who served in the relevant agency within the past year. 5 U.S.C. § 3345(a).

446. Thomas A. Curtis, Note, *Recess Appointments to Article III Courts: The Use of Historical Practice in Constitutional Interpretation*, 84 Colum. L. Rev. 1758, 1775 (1984).

447. *Id.* at 1775–76.

448. Henry B. Hogue, *The Law: Recess Appointments to Article III Courts*, 34 Pres. Stud. Q. 656, 659–61 (2004).

449. S. Res. 334, 86th Cong. (1960), reprinted at 106 Cong. Rec. 18,145 (Aug. 29, 1960).

450. Hogue, *supra* note 448, at 659–61.

451. James M. Hobbs, Case Note, *The Future of Recess Appointments after the Decision of the D.C. Circuit in* Noel Canning v. NLRB, 162 U. Pa. L. Rev. Online 1, 27–28 & n.189 (2013), http://www.pennlawreview.com/online/162-U-Pa-L-Rev-Online-1.pdf.

452. Hogue, *supra* note 448, at 659.

453. *See* Akhil Reed Amar, *America's Unwritten Constitution: The Precedents and Principles We Live By* 345 (2012) (arguing that "long-standing usage" is the "strongest argument in support of the constitutionality" of recess appointments of federal judges).

454. William Wirt, *Executive Authority to Fill Vacancies*, 1 Op. Att'y Gen. 631, 633 (1823).

455. *Id.*

456. S. Rep. No. 37-80, at 6 (1863).

457. Army Appropriations Act, ch. 25, § 2, 12 Stat. 642, 646 (1863).

458. The solicitor general compiled a noncomprehensive, "illustrative" list of such appointments in his brief in *Noel Canning. See* Brief for the Petitioner at 65a, 71a-79a, NLRB v. Noel Canning, 134 S. Ct. 2550 (2014) (No. 12-1281) (listing some recess appointments to fill vacancies that preexisted the recess in the period 1863–1940).

459. *See, e.g.*, C. B. Ames, *Payment of Salaries to Recess Appointees*, 32 Op. Att'y Gen. 271 (1920); Benjamin Harris Brewster, *Appointment to Office*, 17 Op. Att'y Gen. 521 (1883); Charles Devens, *Appointments during Recess of the Senate*, 16 Op. Att'y Gen. 522, 531–32 (1880).

460. Anti-Deficiency Act, ch. 1484, § 4, 33 Stat. 1214, 1257 (1905).

461. Recess Appointees Pay Act, ch. 580, 54 Stat. 751 (1940), codified at 5 U.S.C. § 5503.

462. *See* Fisher, *supra* note 364, at 42; Josh Chafetz, *Congress's Constitution*, 160 U. Pa. L. Rev. 715, 766 n.287 (2012).

463. Gerhardt, *supra* note 178, at 174.

464. *See* Patrick Hein, *In Defense of Broad Recess Appointment Power: The Effectiveness of Political Counterweights*, 96 Calif. L. Rev. 235, 253–54 (2008).

465. NLRB v. Noel Canning, 134 S. Ct. 2550, 2567–73 (2014).

466. *See id.* app. at 2579–80.

467. *Id.* app. at 2580–88.

468. *Id.* at 2562.

469. *See* Hogue, *supra* note 448, at 671.

470. *See* 39 Cong. Rec. 3823–24 (Mar. 2, 1905) (reprinting the Judiciary Committee's report).

471. *Noel Canning*, 134 S. Ct. at 2567.

472. *Id.* at 2573–77.

473. U.S. Const. art. I, § 5, cl. 4.

474. *Id.* art. II, § 3.

475. This scenario is described in more detail in Josh Chafetz, *A Fourth Way? Bringing Politics Back into Recess Appointments (and the Rest of the Separation of Powers, Too)*, 64 Duke L.J. Online 161, 168–71 (2015).

476. 12 U.S.C. § 242.

477. *See* Prakash, *supra* note 265, at 1795–96.

478. An Act to Establish the Treasury Department, ch. 12, § 1, 1 Stat. 65, 65 (1789).

479. Act Making Alterations in the Treasury and War Departments, ch. 37, § 6, 1 Stat. 279, 280 (1792).

480. *See* 1 Sen. Exec. Jour. 124 (May 8, 1792) (nomination and confirmation of Coxe as commissioner of revenue). On Coxe's previous position as assistant to the secretary of the treasury, see Letter from Alexander Hamilton to Tench Coxe (May 10, 1790), in 6 *The Papers of Alexander Hamilton* 411 (Harold C. Syrett ed., 1962).

481. Letter from Tench Coxe to Alexander Hamilton (May 6, 1792), in 11 *The Papers of Alexander Hamilton, supra* note 480, at 364, 365. More precisely, Coxe seems to have been promised the new position in advance, but he seems to have been deeply offended at the diminution of his authority that would have resulted from an early draft of the bill. Hamilton intervened on his behalf, and Coxe was satisfied with the final outcome. *See* Jacob E. Cooke, *Tench Coxe and the Early Republic* 240–42 (1978).

482. *See* Prakash, *supra* note 265, at 1798–99.

483. 478 U.S. 714, 723 (1986).

484. *See* Harvey C. Couch, *A History of the Fifth Circuit, 1891–1981*, at 105–39 (1984).

485. Deborah J. Barrow & Thomas G. Walker, *A Court Divided: The Fifth Circuit Court of Appeals and the Politics of Judicial Reform* 2–4 (1988).

486. *Id.* at 5–6.

487. For instance, a 1964 proposal from a committee of the federal Judicial Conference was unacceptable to pro-civil-rights jurists, because it divided the staunchest supporters of civil rights evenly, thus depriving them of significant power on either proposed court. *See id.* at 65.

488. As Barrow and Walker note, "[T]he supporters of division had placed a high priority on convincing the House subcommittee that the civil rights issue was not relevant in the context of 1977. . . . Even the opponents believed that the core issue was no longer the civil rights question." *Id.* at 202–03. Only in a context in which such an argument could be convincing to the Democratic majorities in both chambers and to President Carter could the proposal for division be enacted.

489. Fifth Circuit Court of Appeals Reorganization Act of 1980, Pub. L. No. 96-452, 94 Stat. 1994.

490. *The Federalist No. 77* (Alexander Hamilton), *supra* note 186, at 459.

491. Paul P. Van Riper, *History of the United States Civil Service* 102 (1958).

492. *See Developments in the Law*, *supra* note 357, at 1630.

493. Lloyd–La Follette Act, ch. 389, § 6, 37 Stat. 539, 555 (1912).

494. Current tenure protections for civil service employees are codified at 5 U.S.C. § 7513.

495. Myers v. United States, 272 U.S. 52, 173–74 (1926).

496. *See generally* Kirti Datla & Richard L. Revesz, *Deconstructing Independent Agencies (and Executive Agencies)*, 98 Cornell L. Rev. 769 (2013) (finding that no single feature or set of features distinguishes agencies usually thought of as "independent" from those usually thought of as "executive" and therefore rejecting a sharp binary between the two categories).

497. *See, e.g.*, Steven G. Calabresi & Saikrishna B. Prakash, *The President's Power to Execute the Laws*, 104 Yale L.J. 541 (1994).

498. *See id.* at 566–68.

499. *See id.* at 570–99.

500. For my own contribution, see Chafetz, *supra* note 32. For just a smattering of the other important contributions, see Berger, *supra* note 10; Charles L. Black Jr., *Impeachment: A Handbook* (1974); Michael J. Gerhardt, *The Federal Impeachment Process: A Constitutional and Historical Analysis* (2d ed. 2000); Hoffer & Hull, *supra* note 244; Jonathan Turley, *Senate Trials and Factional Disputes: Impeachment as a Madisonian Device*, 49 Duke L.J. 1 (1999).

501. U.S. Const. art. II, § 4.

502. *See generally* Saikrishna Prakash & Steven D. Smith, *How to Remove a Federal Judge*, 116 Yale L.J. 72 (2006).

503. Mike Gerhardt lists sixteen in Gerhardt, *supra* note 500, at 201 n.3. His list omits Judge Mark Delahay, who was impeached in 1873. Two additional impeachments have occurred since Gerhardt's book was published: those of Judge Samuel Kent in 2009 and Judge Thomas Porteous in 2010.

504. *Id.* at 47–48; Josh Chafetz, *Democracy's Privileged Few: Legislative Privilege and Democratic Norms in the British and American Constitutions* 218 (2007).

505. Gerhardt, *supra* note 500, at 51–52.

506. Gerhardt lists the first seven at *id.* at 201 n.4. The eighth was Judge Porteous in 2010.

507. *Id.*; Jennifer Steinhauer, *Senate, for Just the 8th Time, Votes to Oust a Federal Judge*, N.Y. Times, Dec. 9, 2010, at A27.

508. *See generally* Chafetz, *supra* note 32.

509. Gerhardt, *supra* note 500, at 201 n.4; Steinhauer, *supra* note 507.

Chapter 5. Contempt of Congress

1. On the historical kinship between contempt and breach of privilege, see Mary Patterson Clarke, *Parliamentary Privilege in the American Colonies* 206 (1943) ("Often [contempt] was synonymous with breach of privilege, and the House of Commons, as well as a colonial assembly, might use the two terms interchangeably. . . . Indeed, there is logically a very close relation between the two. Anything that was a recognized breach of the assembly's privilege might be considered contemptuous; and any expression of contempt was

in clear violation of the 'undoubted right' of the assembly to be treated with dignity."); *see also Erskine May's Treatise on the Law, Privileges, Proceedings and Usage of Parliament* 75 (William McKay et al. eds., 23d ed. 2004) (noting that breach of privilege technically applies to violations of specific rights, whereas contempt applies to "actions which, while not breaches of any specific privilege, obstruct or impede [Parliament] in the performance of its functions, or are offences against its authority or dignity").

2. *See* Josh Chafetz, *"In the Time of a Woman, Which Sex Was Not Capable of Mature Deliberation": Late Tudor Parliamentary Relations and Their Early Stuart Discontents,* 25 Yale J.L. & Human. 181, 183–85 (2013).

3. *See id.* at 191–92; Josh Chafetz, *Democracy's Privileged Few: Legislative Privilege and Democratic Norms in the British and American Constitutions* 194 (2007) [hereinafter Chafetz, *Democracy's Privileged Few*]; Josh Chafetz, *Executive Branch Contempt of Congress,* 76 U. Chi. L. Rev. 1083, 1093–95 (2009) [hereinafter Chafetz, *Contempt*].

4. Assault on Lords or Commoners, 1433, 11 Hen. 6, c. 11.

5. For other examples of pre-sixteenth-century Parliaments appealing to the Crown to vindicate their privileges, see Chafetz, *Democracy's Privileged Few, supra* note 3, at 112–16, 145–47 (describing the House of Commons' reliance on the Crown to enforce its privileges); Josh Chafetz, *Leaving the House: The Constitutional Status of Resignation from the House of Representatives,* 58 Duke L.J. 177, 185 (2008) (noting that resignation from Parliament required the king's permission).

6. 1 John Hatsell, *Precedents of Proceedings in the House of Commons* 53–54 (London, Hansard rev. ed. 1818).

7. *Id.* at 54.

8. *Id.*

9. *Id.* at 54–55.

10. *Id.* at 55.

11. *Id.* The Little Ease was a cell so small that a prisoner could not fully stretch out in any direction. "He was obliged to sit in a squatting position and was kept confined there." L. A. Parry, *The History of Torture in England* 80 (1933).

12. 1 Hatsell, *supra* note 6, at 55.

13. *Id.* at 56–57.

14. 1 William Cobbett, *Parliamentary History of England* 711 (London, Hansard 1806).

15. *Id.* at 714–15 ("[I]f I can bend my liking to your need, I will not resist such a mind.").

16. Cobbett records that some members spoke "with much heat and great insolence" and that they were "so audacious as to back their pertness with invectives and abuses." *Id.* at 715.

17. *Id.* at 716. For a different version of this address, albeit one with the same tenor, see 1 J. E. Neale, *Elizabeth I and Her Parliaments, 1559–1581,* at 146–50 (1953).

18. 1 Cobbett, *supra* note 14, at 716.

19. *Id.*

20. 1 Neale, *supra* note 17, at 154.

21. *Id.* at 155–56 (protesting that surely "your Majesty meant not . . . to diminish our accustomed lawful liberties").

22. *Id.* at 156.

23. *Id.*

24. 1 Cobbett, *supra* note 14, at 716.

25. *Id.* at 761–62, 765. For background on the dispute between Elizabeth and the 1571 Parliament over religious reforms, see generally J. E. Neale, *Parliament and the Articles of Religion, 1571*, 67 Eng. Hist. Rev. 510 (1952).

26. *See* G. R. Elton, *The Tudor Constitution: Documents and Commentary* 334 (1960) (describing Elizabeth's belief in strong personal supremacy over the church).

27. 1 Cobbett, *supra* note 14, at 761–63.

28. *Id.* at 762.

29. *Id.* at 765.

30. *Id.* at 1326–27.

31. *Id.* at 1335, 1344.

32. *Id.* at 1361–71. *See also* 2 Hannis Taylor, *The Origin and Growth of the English Constitution* 249 (1898).

33. There are, of course, many lenses through which to view the Civil War. *See* Chafetz, *supra* note 2, at 185–86 & nn.35–40 (cataloging some of these lenses).

34. *See* 2 Cobbett, *supra* note 14, at 6; F. W. Maitland, *The Constitutional History of England* 307 (H. A. L. Fisher ed., 1908); Theodore F. T. Plucknett, *Taswell-Langmead's English Constitutional History from the Teutonic Conquest to the Present Time* 363 (11th ed. 1960); John Rushworth, *Historical Collections of Private Passages of State, Weighty Matters in Law, Remarkable Proceedings in Five Parliaments, Beginning the Sixteenth Year of King James, Anno 1618, and Ending the Fifth Year of King Charls, Anno 1629*, at 191 (London, Newcomb 1659); Conrad Russell, *Parliaments and English Politics, 1621–1629*, at 229 (1979).

35. *See* Roger Lockyer, *The Early Stuarts: A Political History of England, 1603–1642*, at 25–26 (1989); Plucknett, *supra* note 34, at 363; Russell, *supra* note 34, at 262–67.

36. 1 Edward Porritt, *The Unreformed House of Commons: Parliamentary Representation before 1832*, at 383–84 (1903); Harold Hulme, *The Sheriff as a Member of the House of Commons from Elizabeth to Cromwell*, 1 J. Mod. Hist. 361, 367–70 (1929). Porritt mistakenly lists Miles Fleetwood as among the "opposition" leaders pricked for sheriff; in fact, Fleetwood was neither in opposition nor pricked for sheriff. *See* 4 Andrew Thrush & John P. Ferris, *The House of Commons, 1604–1629*, at 286–89 (2010).

37. 2 Cobbett, *supra* note 14, at 45–49; Hulme, *supra* note 36, at 368–70.

38. 2 Cobbett, *supra* note 14, at 49–50.

39. *Id.* at 56.

40. *Id.* at 57.

41. *Id.* at 58.

42. *Id.*

43. *Id.*

44. *Id.* at 59–60.

45. *Id.* at 69.

46. *Id.* at 79 (resolving that "setting all other business aside, they would proceed in the great Affair of the duke of Buckingham, morning and afternoon, till it was done").

47. 3 H.L. Jour. 619–26 (May 15, 1626).

48. Henry Elsynge, *The Manner of Holding Parliaments in England* 192 (London, Richardson & Clark 1768).

49. 1 Hatsell, *supra* note 6, at 142.

50. Vernon F. Snow, *The Arundel Case, 1626*, 26 Historian 323, 327–37 (1964).

51. Elsynge, *supra* note 48, at 192.

52. *Id.* at 193.

53. *Id.*

54. *Id.* at 194.

55. *Id.* at 223.

56. *Id.* at 224–38.

57. *Id.* at 238.

58. *See id.* at 239 (noting that Buckingham tried to raise an issue about his defense, but "the lords would not hear him, because they would entertain no business").

59. *Id.*

60. *Id.* at 240 (detailing the king's message to the House, which stated that the king "hath endeavoured as much as may be to ripen [the issue], but cannot yet effect it").

61. *Id.*

62. *Id.* at 242.

63. 2 Cobbett, *supra* note 14, at 193–200.

64. Russell, *supra* note 34, at 328–30 (noting the drift toward war with France and the corresponding need for more money).

65. *See* Commission for Raising Tonnage and Poundage with Impositions (July 26, 1626), in *The Constitutional Documents of the Puritan Revolution, 1625–1660*, at 49 (Samuel Rawson Gardiner ed., 1906) [hereinafter *Documents*].

66. *See* The Commission and Instructions for Raising the Forced Loan in Middlesex (Sept. 23, 1626), in *Documents*, *supra* note 65, at 51.

67. *See* Lockyer, *supra* note 35, at 223 (noting that the forced loan was "parliamentary taxation without parliamentary sanction, and as such it ran counter to many Englishmen's most deeply-held beliefs"); D. Lindsay Keir, *The Constitutional History of Modern Britain 1485–1937*, at 190 (1938) (noting the "disastrous political cost" attendant on Charles's fundraising methods).

68. For a decidedly partial, but nonetheless generally accurate, description of Crewe's conflict with Charles, see 1 John Lord Campbell, *The Lives of the Chief Justices of England: From the Norman Conquest till the Death of Lord Mansfield* 374–75 (London, John Murray 1849).

69. The Five Knights' Case, 3 How. St. Tr. 1, 51–59 (K.B. 1627).

70. *See* 2 Cobbett, *supra* note 14, at 217.

71. Plucknett, *supra* note 34, at 366.

72. Russell, *supra* note 34, at 343.

73. Petition of Right, 1628, 3 Car. 1, c. 1, § 8.

74. *See* Lockyer, *supra* note 35, at 338, 345.

75. Rushworth, *supra* note 34, at 629–30.

76. 1 H.C. Jour. 919 (June 26, 1628).

77. *See* Josh Chafetz, *Impeachment and Assassination*, 95 Minn. L. Rev. 347, 374–76 (2010).

78. Linda S. Popofsky, *The Crisis over Tonnage and Poundage in Parliament in 1629*, 126 Past & Present 44, 59 (1990).

79. *Id.* at 61.

80. 1 H.C. Jour. 921 (Jan. 22, 1629).

81. 2 Cobbett, *supra* note 14, at 437.

82. *Id.* at 443 (noting that, "by passing the bill [granting tonnage and poundage] as my ancestors have had it, my by-past actions will be concluded, and my future proceedings authorized").

83. *Id.*

84. *Id.* at 449, 453.

85. *Id.* at 461.

86. *Id.* at 461–62.

87. *Id.* at 477.

88. *Id.* at 478.

89. *Id.*

90. *Id.* at 480.

91. *Id.* at 479–82.

92. *Id.* at 481.

93. *Id.* at 482.

94. *Id.*

95. *Id.* at 490.

96. *Id.*

97. *Id.*

98. *Id.* at 490–91.

99. *Id.* at 491.

100. *Id.* at 492–96.

101. *Id.* at 499.

102. *Id.* at 500.

103. *Id.* at 501.

104. *See* Lockyer, *supra* note 35, at 354.

105. *Id.* at 355–56.

106. 2 H.C. Jour. 11 (Apr. 24, 1640) (listing, as one of the Commons' grievances, the "[p]unishing [of] Men, out of Parliament, for things done in Parliament"—a reference to punishing the members who held the Speaker in his chair); 2 H.C. Jour. 7 (Apr. 20, 1640) (resolving that the adjournment order was a breach of parliamentary privilege). *See also* Plucknett, *supra* note 34, at 390–91 (describing the heads of the Commons' complaints); Keir, *supra* note 67, at 210 (noting that the Commons "made it evident that a Scottish invasion was in their eyes less important than the invasion of English liberties in the name of Prerogative," and listing the liberties that the House believed had been infringed).

107. 2 H.C. Jour. 19 (May 5, 1640). Charles's statement of his reasons for dissolving Parliament is reprinted in 2 Cobbett, *supra* note 14, at 572–79 (claiming that a few men "endeavoured nothing more than to bring into contempt and disorder all government and magistracy").

108. *See* Chafetz, *supra* note 2, at 181–83. The specific accusations are printed at 4 H.L. Jour. 500–01 (Jan. 3, 1642) (including, for example, accusations that the members encouraged a foreign power to invade England, sought to "alienate the Affections" of the people for their king, and conspired to levy war against the king).

109. 2 Cobbett, *supra* note 14, at 1007.

110. 2 H.C. Jour. 366 (Jan. 3, 1642).

111. *Id.*

112. 4 H.L. Jour. 502 (Jan. 3, 1642).

113. 2 H.C. Jour. 367 (Jan. 3, 1642).

114. *Id.*

115. 2 H.C. Jour. 368 (Jan. 4, 1642).

116. *Id.*

117. 1 John Rushworth, *Historical Collections. The Third Part; In Two Volumes. Containing the Principal Matters Which Happened from the Meeting of the Parliament, November the 3d. 1640. To the End of the Year 1644*, at 477 (London, Chiswell & Cockerill 1692).

118. *Id.* at 477–78.

119. *Id.* at 478.

120. *Id.*

121. 2 H.C. Jour. 368 (Jan. 5, 1642).

122. 1 Rushworth, *supra* note 117, at 479.

123. *Id.* at 484.

124. 2 H.C. Jour. 373 (Jan. 12, 1642).

125. Christopher Hill, *The Century of Revolution: 1603–1714*, at 112 (1961).

126. The Act Erecting a High Court of Justice for the King's Trial, 1649, reprinted in *Documents*, *supra* note 65, at 357 (passed Jan. 6, 1649). The court was created by the Commons alone because the House had, two days earlier, declared itself "the Supreme Power in this Nation," thus obviating the need for the consent of the Lords or the Crown to any piece of legislation. 6 H.C. Jour. 111 (Jan. 4, 1649).

127. The Charge against the King, in *Documents*, *supra* note 65, at 372 (Jan. 20, 1649).

128. *See generally* Chafetz, *supra* note 77, at 383–84; Trial of King Charles I, 4 How. St. Tr. 1045 (1649) (reprinting many of the relevant documents of the trial, including the Journal of the High Court).

129. 9 H.C. Jour. 378 (Nov. 16, 1675).

130. Coronation Oath Act, 1 W. & M., c. 6, § 3 (1689).

131. Bill of Rights, 1 W. & M., sess. 2, c. 2, §§ 1–2 (1689).

132. This is not to say, however, that Parliament has wholly ceased using contempt proceedings against Crown officials. In 1963, the House of Commons held John Profumo, the secretary of state for war, in contempt for lying about his relationship with an attaché at the Soviet Embassy. After he resigned, the House decided not to punish Profumo. For the report of the government inquiry into the matter, see generally Alfred Denning, *Lord Denning's Report* (1963). For all the tawdry details, see generally Anthony Summers & Stephen Dorril, *Honeytrap* (1987).

133. *See* Warren M. Billings, *A Little Parliament: The Virginia General Assembly in the Seventeenth Century* 37–38 (2004).

134. Benjamin Franklin, *The Autobiography of Benjamin Franklin* (1793), reprinted in *The Autobiography and Other Writings* 1, 20 (Kenneth Silverman ed., Penguin Books 1986).

135. For the colonies, see Clarke, *supra* note 1, at 206–07; Ernest J. Eberling, *Congressional Investigations: A Study of the Origin and Development of the Power of Congress to Investigate and Punish for Contempt* 17–21 (1928) (citing instances of private citizens

held in contempt for bribing corrupt officials and printing criticisms of a legislative house); C. S. Potts, *Power of Legislative Bodies to Punish for Contempt*, 74 U. Pa. L. Rev. 691, 700–712 (1926) (providing examples of arrests for legislative contempt in the colonies for offenses ranging from arresting members of a legislative house (or their servants), to insulting members, to refusing to testify before the assembly). For England, see Chafetz, *Democracy's Privileged Few*, *supra* note 3, at 193–206 (discussing Parliament's use of the contempt power against private subjects).

136. Jack P. Greene, *The Quest for Power: The Lower Houses of Assembly in the Southern Royal Colonies 1689–1776*, at 215–16 (1963).

137. Jack P. Greene, *Bridge to Revolution: The Wilkes Fund Controversy in South Carolina, 1769–1775*, 29 J. Southern Hist. 19, 34 (1963).

138. Potts, *supra* note 135, at 708.

139. *Id.* at 708 n.53.

140. *Id.*

141. Greene, *supra* note 136, at 216.

142. Elmer I. Miller, *The Legislature of the Province of Virginia: Its Internal Development* 151 (1907).

143. 4 Herbert L. Osgood, *The American Colonies in the Eighteenth Century* 188 (1958).

144. *Id.* at 188–89.

145. *Id.* at 190.

146. *Extract of a Letter from South Carolina*, reprinted in Boston Post-Boy, Mar. 28, 1763, at 3.

147. *Resolution of the New York House of Representatives*, reprinted in Boston Post-Boy, Feb. 23, 1767, at 2.

148. Clarke, *supra* note 1, at 231.

149. Allan Nevins, *The American States during and after the Revolution, 1775–1789*, at 77 (1924).

150. Va. House of Burgesses J. 281 (June 24, 1775).

151. *Resolution of the Provincial Congress of New Jersey*, reprinted in Pa. Packet, June 17, 1776, at 3.

152. *See* Sheila L. Skemp, *William Franklin: Son of a Patriot, Servant of a King* 202–12 (1990).

153. *See id.* at 212–26.

154. *See* Gordon S. Wood, *The Creation of the American Republic, 1776–1787*, at 135–36 (rev. ed. 1998) (describing the ways in which fear of concentrated authority led to a significant weakening of the powers of state executives in the early Republic).

155. *See, e.g.*, 8 *Journals of the Continental Congress* 458–61, 466–67 (reporting Gunning Bedford's contempt in June 1777); 4 *id.* at 188, 190 (reporting Isaac Melchior's contempt in March 1776).

156. Penn. Const. of 1776, Frame of Gov't, § 9.

157. Vt. Const. of 1777, ch. 2, § 8; Vt. Const. of 1786, ch. 2, § 9.

158. Md. Const. of 1776, art. 10.

159. *Id.* art. 12.

160. Ga. Const. of 1777, art. 49 ("Every officer of the State shall be liable to be called to account by the house of assembly.").

161. Mass. Const. of 1780, pt. 2, ch. 1, § 3, art. 10 (providing this power for the House of Representatives); *id.* art. XI (providing the same power for the Senate).

162. N.H. Const. of 1784, pt. 2, House of Reps., para. 12.

163. S.C. Const. of 1776, art. 7; S.C. Const. of 1778, art. 16.

164. N.Y. Const. of 1777, art. 9.

165. *See, e.g.*, Del. Const. of 1776, art. 5 (providing that each legislative house could "settle its own rules of proceedings" and exercise "all other powers necessary for the legislature of a free and independent State"); Va. Const. of 1776, para. 4 (allowing each house to "settle its own rules of proceedings").

166. Potts, *supra* note 135, at 716–17.

167. Va. House of Delegates J. 35 (Nov. 11, 1786).

168. *Id.* at 36 (Nov. 13, 1786).

169. 2 *The Records of the Federal Convention of 1787*, at 341 (Max Farrand ed., rev. ed. 1966).

170. *Id.* at 342.

171. 2 Joseph Story, *Commentaries on the Constitution of the United States* § 835, at 298 (Boston, Hilliard, Gray 1833).

172. *Id.* § 842, at 305.

173. *Id.* § 844, at 308.

174. *Id.* § 846, at 316.

175. 1 James Kent, *Commentaries on American Law* 221 (New York, Halsted 1826).

176. Thomas Jefferson, *A Manual of Parliamentary Practice* 7–11 (Cosimo Classics 2007) (1801).

177. 5 Annals of Cong. 166–70 (Dec. 28–29, 1795).

178. *Id.* at 171–95 (Dec. 29, 1795–Jan. 1, 1796).

179. 2 H.R. Jour. 405 (Jan. 6, 1796).

180. *Id.* at 406.

181. *Id.* at 414 (Jan. 13, 1796).

182. *Id.* at 407 (Jan. 7, 1796).

183. 3 S. Jour. 54 (Mar. 20, 1800).

184. *Id.*

185. *Id.* at 56 (Mar. 24, 1800).

186. *Id.* at 58 (Mar. 26, 1800).

187. *Id.* at 60 (Mar. 27, 1800).

188. *See, e.g.*, *id.* at 60–61 (Mar. 27, 1800) (reprinting the warrant, signed by Jefferson, authorizing the Senate sergeant-at-arms to take Duane into custody).

189. 11 H.R. Jour. 154 (Jan. 16, 1818).

190. Anderson v. Dunn, 19 U.S. (6 Wheat.) 204, 204 (1821).

191. *Id.* at 224–25.

192. *Id.* at 228–29.

193. *See id.* at 231–32.

194. The case law has proceeded in ebbs and flows. The Court's most narrowly cabined view of the contempt power came in *Kilbourn v. Thompson*, 103 U.S. 168 (1881), in which the Court struck down a contempt citation against a witness who refused to testify at a hearing regarding the loss of federal funds in an investment scheme. The Court

determined that such hearings were not legislative in nature and were therefore outside the House's purview. *Id.* at 192. Subsequent decisions again broadened the scope of the houses' contempt powers. *See In re* Chapman, 166 U.S. 661, 672 (1897) (upholding a contempt conviction for refusing to answer questions from a committee regarding corruption in the passage of a bill); McGrain v. Daugherty, 273 U.S. 135, 180 (1927) (upholding a contempt citation where a witness refused to testify in front of a committee seeking information for the purpose of drafting legislation); Jurney v. MacCracken, 294 U.S. 125, 151 (1935) (upholding a contempt citation against a person who allowed papers subpoenaed by a Senate committee to be destroyed). With the coming of the McCarthy era, the Court somewhat narrowed the scope of the congressional contempt power. *See* United States v. Rumely, 345 U.S. 41, 47–48 (1953) (overturning a contempt citation on the grounds that a congressional committee had exceeded the scope of its authorizing resolution).

195. *See* 10 Reg. Deb. 1185–87 (Mar. 28, 1834) (Senator Gabriel Moore explaining his reasoning for voting for the resolutions). The bank's charter was due to expire in 1836, and Jackson had already, in 1832, vetoed a bill to renew the charter. He sought to kill the bank off even earlier by removing all federal deposits in 1834. *See generally* Bray Hammond, *Jackson, Biddle, and the Bank of the United States*, 7 J. Econ. Hist. 1 (1947).

196. 23 S. Jour. 197 (Mar. 28, 1834).

197. *See* 10 Reg. Deb. 1317–36 (Apr. 17, 1834).

198. *Id.* at 1318.

199. 23 S. Jour. 252–53 (May 7, 1834).

200. *See* Akhil Reed Amar, *America's Constitution: A Biography* 175 (2005) (reprinting an 1833 cartoon referring to Jackson as "King Andrew the First" and showing him trampling on the Constitution while holding a veto message in his hand).

201. 26 S. Jour. 123–24 (Jan 16, 1837). *See* David P. Currie, *The Constitution in Congress: Democrats and Whigs, 1829–1861*, at 73–75 (2005) (describing the debate over expunging the Senate *Journal*).

202. 37 H.R. Jour. 1242–47 (Aug. 9, 1842).

203. *Id.* at 1254 (Aug. 10, 1842).

204. Cong. Globe, 27th Cong., 2d Sess. 894–96 (Aug. 16, 1842).

205. *Id.* at 896.

206. John Tyler, Protest (Aug. 30, 1842), in 4 *A Compilation of the Messages and Papers of the Presidents, 1797–1897*, at 190, 191–92 (James D. Richardson ed., 1897).

207. 37 H.R. Jour. 1464 (Aug. 30, 1842).

208. For examples of such cases, see Chafetz, *Democracy's Privileged Few, supra* note 3, at 222–34.

209. An Act More Effectually to Enforce the Attendance of Witnesses on the Summons of Either House of Congress, and to Compel Them to Discover Testimony, ch. 19, § 1, 11 Stat. 155, 155 (1857).

210. *Id.* § 3.

211. Joint Resolution Relating to Congressional Investigations, ch. 594, § 102, 52 Stat. 942, 942 (1938).

212. 2 U.S.C. §§ 192–94.

213. *See* Todd Garvey & Alissa M. Dolan, *Congress's Contempt Power and the Enforcement of Congressional Subpoenas: Law, History, Practice, and Procedure*, CRS Report for Cong. No. RL34097, at 18 (2014) ("It is clear from the floor debates and the subsequent practice of both Houses that the legislation was intended as an *alternative* to the inherent contempt procedure, not as a substitute for it.").

214. Cong. Globe, 39th Cong., 1st Sess. 2292–93 (Apr. 30, 1866).

215. *Id.* at 2151 (Apr. 24, 1866).

216. *Id.* at 2293 (Apr. 30, 1866).

217. 63 H.R. Jour. 639 (Apr. 30, 1866).

218. *Id.* at 1056–57 (July 19, 1866).

219. *Id.* at 1057.

220. An Act to Increase and Fix the Military Peace Establishment of the United States, ch. 299, § 33, 14 Stat. 332, 337 (1866) (ordering the closure of the Provost Marshal General's Bureau within thirty days).

221. Seward also happened to be the nephew of Lincoln's and Johnson's secretary of state, William H. Seward. For an overview of George Seward's career—albeit one that omits all mention of his tussles with the House—see generally Paul Hibbert Clyde, *Attitudes and Policies of George F. Seward, American Minister at Peking, 1876–1880*, 2 Pac. Hist. Rev. 387 (1933).

222. 8 Cong. Rec. 1771 (Feb. 22, 1879).

223. *Id.* at 1771–72.

224. *Id.* at 1772.

225. *Id.*

226. *Id.* at 1773.

227. *Id.* at 1774.

228. *Id.* at 1775.

229. *Id.* at 2016 (Feb. 27, 1879).

230. *Id.* at 2138–41 (Feb. 28, 1879).

231. *Id.* at 2143–44.

232. *Id.* at 2350–51 (Mar. 3, 1879).

233. The Judiciary Committee's report is reprinted in 3 Asher C. Hinds, *Hinds' Precedents of the House of Representatives of the United States* § 1700, at 59–61 (1907).

234. Marshall v. Gordon, 235 F. 422, 424–25 (S.D.N.Y. 1916).

235. *Id.* at 425.

236. *See* Marshall v. Gordon, 243 U.S. 521, 531 (1917).

237. *Id.*

238. *Id.* at 531–32. The letter is reprinted in *Marshall*, 235 F. at 423–24.

239. *Marshall*, 243 U.S. at 532.

240. *Id.*

241. *Id.*

242. *Writ for Marshall after His Arrest*, N.Y. Times, June 27, 1916, at 9.

243. *Marshall*, 235 F. at 433; *Orders Marshall Back into Custody*, N.Y. Times, July 20, 1916, at 17.

244. *Stay for Marshall; The House Wins, Too*, N.Y. Times, July 22, 1916, at 10.

245. *Marshall*, 243 U.S. at 541.

246. *Id.* at 545–46.
247. J. W. Fulbright, *Congressional Investigations: Significance for the Legislative Process*, 18 U. Chi. L. Rev. 440, 441 (1951). *See also* James M. Landis, *Constitutional Limitations on the Congressional Power of Investigation*, 40 Harv. L. Rev. 153, 209 (1926) ("To deny Congress power to acquaint itself with facts is equivalent to requiring it to prescribe remedies in darkness."); *id.* at 205 ("[K]nowledge is not an *a priori* endowment of the legislator. His duty is to acquire it, partly for the purposes of further legislation, partly to satisfy his mind as to the adequacy of existing laws. Yet the ultimate basis for the duty is the broader presupposition of representative government that the legislator is responsible to his electorate for his actions. Responsibility means judgment, and judgment, if the word implies its intelligent exercise, requires knowledge.").
248. Allen B. Moreland, *Congressional Investigations and Private Persons*, 40 S. Cal. L. Rev. 189, 189 (1967).
249. 12 Cobbett, *supra* note 14, at 693.
250. *See, e.g.*, Branzburg v. Hayes, 408 U.S. 665, 688 (1972); Kastigar v. United States, 406 U.S. 441, 443 (1972).
251. *See* Response to Cong. Requests for Information Regarding Decisions Made under the Indep. Counsel Act, 10 Op. O.L.C. 68 (1986) [hereinafter Cooper OLC Memo]; Prosecution for Contempt of Cong. of an Exec. Branch Official Who Has Asserted a Claim of Exec. Privilege, 8 Op. O.L.C. 101, 124 (1984) [hereinafter Olson OLC Memo].
252. Fed. R. Civ. P. 45(e); Fed. R. Crim. P. 17(g).
253. Todd Peterson acknowledges a general power of contempt over nonmembers, and even against executive-branch officials, but he seems to think that only a finding that is (a) explicitly *called* contempt, (b) enforced by arrest, and (c) against an official claiming executive privilege counts as a precedent for an inherent contempt authority against an executive official asserting such a privilege. *See* Todd Davis Peterson, *Contempt of Congress v. Executive Privilege*, 14 U. Pa. J. Const. L. 77, 121–30, 139 (2011) (dismissing one case after another for lacking at least one of those components). But that seems to me exactly backwards. If the general power exists, then we need a reason for carving out an exception. Is there any special reason to think that Congress suddenly started meaningfully differentiating between contempt and breach of privilege? If not, then why should the use of one phrasing rather than the other matter? Is there any special reason to think that a defense of executive privilege should be treated differently from any other defense to a contempt charge? If not, then why should executive privilege claims be subject to a different rule? Is there any reason to think that certain contemnors are exempt from arrest while others are not? If not, then why exempt them?
    Peterson seems to be motivated by a desire to keep contempt of Congress thoroughly walled off from other separation-of-powers tools. Thus, he insists that the Andrew Jackson case "does not even involve the use of Congress's contempt power at all; it is simply a garden variety separation of powers dispute between Congress and the President, where each side argues for the supremacy of its own constitutional prerogatives." *Id.* at 126. As we have seen repeatedly, however, breach of privilege and legislative contempt are very closely related and frequently used interchangeably, and the Senate's choice to deploy the language of breach of privilege against Jackson was undoubtedly a conscious

nod to this power. Indeed, the rarity of such language suggests that this was anything but "garden variety." More to the point, I agree that this was a separation-of-powers dispute involving each side asserting the primacy of its own authority. Indeed, as chapter 1 made clear, this book is largely motivated by the claim that separation-of-powers disputes cannot be neatly categorized, that the powers overlap and combine to provide each branch with its own distinct toolbox, and that conflicts making use of these tools always involve the branches publicly contending for power vis-à-vis one another. It is unclear what Peterson hopes to gain by artificially separating these mechanisms and then pronouncing upon whether a given case counts as contempt or not.

254. In the aftermath of Watergate, a statute gave the Senate (but not the House) explicit authority to file a civil suit seeking enforcement of a congressional subpoena. Ethics in Government Act, Pub. L. No. 95-521, § 705, 92 Stat. 1824, 1878–80 (1978), codified as amended at 2 U.S.C. § 288d; 28 U.S.C. § 1365. However, the statute explicitly exempts subpoenas issued to officers or employees of the executive branch acting in their official capacities. 28 U.S.C. § 1365(a).

255. Senate Select Comm. on Presidential Campaign Activities v. Nixon, 370 F. Supp. 521, 521–22 (D.D.C. 1974).

256. *Id.* at 522 (citing Nixon v. Sirica, 487 F.2d 700, 712 (D.C. Cir. 1973)).

257. *Id.*

258. *Id.* at 523.

259. *Id.* at 524.

260. Senate Select Comm. on Presidential Campaign Activities v. Nixon, 498 F.2d 725, 726 (D.C. Cir. 1974) (en banc).

261. *Id.* at 730 (quoting *Nixon*, 487 F.2d at 717).

262. *Senate Select Comm.*, 498 F.2d at 731.

263. *Id.* at 732.

264. *Id.*

265. United States v. Nixon, 418 U.S. 683, 706 (1974).

266. *Articles of Impeachment*, H.R. Rep. No. 93-1305 (1974).

267. Robert A. Burt, *The Constitution in Conflict* 325 (1992).

268. *Id.*

269. Gerald Gunther, *Judicial Hegemony and Legislative Autonomy: The* Nixon *Case and the Impeachment Process*, 22 UCLA L. Rev. 30, 33 (1974).

270. *See* Garvey & Dolan, *supra* note 213, at 40 (noting thirteen such contempt citations between 1975 and 2014).

271. This conflict is described in Olson OLC Memo, *supra* note 251, at 103–10; *see also* Garvey & Dolan, *supra* note 213, at 35–36; Todd D. Peterson, *Prosecuting Executive Branch Officials for Contempt of Congress*, 66 N.Y.U. L. Rev. 563, 571–74 (1991); Peter M. Shane, *Legal Disagreement and Negotiation in a Government of Laws: The Case of Executive Privilege Claims against Congress*, 71 Minn. L. Rev. 461, 508–14 (1987).

272. The text of the subpoena is reprinted in United States v. U.S. House of Representatives, 556 F. Supp. 150, 151 (D.D.C. 1983).

273. *Id.*; Olson OLC Memo, *supra* note 251, at 106–07.

274. *U.S. House of Representatives*, 556 F. Supp. at 151.

275. Peterson, *supra* note 271, at 573.

276. *U.S. House of Representatives*, 556 F. Supp. at 152–53.

277. Olson OLC Memo, *supra* note 251, at 110.

278. *Id.*

279. The decision was handed down on February 3, 1983. *U.S. House of Representatives*, 556 F. Supp. at 150. Gorsuch resigned on March 9. Douglas Martin, *Anne Gorsuch Burford, 62, Reagan E.P.A. Chief, Dies*, N.Y. Times, July 22, 2004, at C13. The contempt citation was withdrawn August 3. Olson OLC Memo, *supra* note 251, at 110.

280. Olson OLC Memo, *supra* note 251, at 114–15, 118–42.

281. *Id.* at 129–32.

282. *Id.* at 134.

283. *Id.* at 136.

284. *Id.* at 137.

285. *Id.* at 141.

286. Cooper OLC Memo, *supra* note 251, at 83–86.

287. *Id.* at 87–89.

288. This discussion is condensed from Chafetz, *Contempt, supra* note 3, at 1086–93.

289. Sheryl Gay Stolberg, *Bush in Conflict with Lawmakers on Prosecutors*, N.Y. Times, Mar. 21, 2007, at A1.

290. *Id.*; Carl Hulse, *Panel Approves Rove Subpoena on Prosecutors*, N.Y. Times, Mar. 22, 2007, at A1.

291. Comm. on the Judiciary v. Miers, 558 F. Supp. 2d 53, 61 (D.D.C. 2008) (detailing the timeline of the requests).

292. Dan Eggen & Paul Kane, *2 Former Aides to Bush Get Subpoenas*, Wash. Post, June 14, 2007, at A1.

293. Michael Abramowitz & Amy Goldstein, *Bush Claims Executive Privilege on Subpoenas*, Wash. Post, June 29, 2007, at A1.

294. 153 Cong. Rec. D1055 (daily ed. July 25, 2007).

295. 154 Cong. Rec. H962 (daily ed. Feb. 14, 2008) (noting that the final vote was 223 to 32).

296. H.R. Res. 979, 110th Cong. (2008).

297. H.R. Res. 980, 110th Cong. (2008).

298. Letter from Speaker Nancy Pelosi to Jeffrey A. Taylor, U.S. Att'y for D.C. (Feb. 28, 2008), http://www.democraticleader.gov/newsroom/pelosi-letter-to-attorney-general-mukasey-on-contempt-citations-of-miers-and-bolten/; Letter from Speaker Nancy Pelosi to Att'y Gen. Michael B. Mukasey (Feb. 28, 2008), http://www.democraticleader.gov/newsroom/pelosi-letter-to-attorney-general-mukasey-on-contempt-citations-of-miers-and-bolten/.

299. Letter from Att'y Gen. Michael B. Mukasey to Speaker Nancy Pelosi (Feb. 29, 2008), http://www.documentcloud.org/documents/373620-mukasey-letter-to-pelosi-feb-29-2008.html.

300. *Miers*, 558 F. Supp. 2d at 55, 63–64.

301. *Id.* at 71.

302. *Id.* at 74–77.

303. *Id.* at 92 (quotation marks and citations omitted).

304. *Id.* at 92–93.

305. *Id.* at 94–99.

306. *Id.* at 96.

307. *See id.* at 56, 76, 96, 103, 107.

308. *Id.* at 99.

309. *Id.* at 99–108.

310. It did, however, stay the district court's decision and deny a request for expedited review. Comm. on the Judiciary v. Miers, 542 F.3d 909 (D.C. Cir. 2008) (per curiam).

311. Carrie Johnson, *Deal Clears Rove, Miers to Discuss Prosecutor Firings*, Wash. Post, Mar. 5, 2009, at A8.

312. Comm. on the Judiciary v. Miers, No. 08-5357, 2009 WL 3568649 (D.C. Cir. Oct. 14, 2009).

313. This paragraph is based on the timelines of relevant events at CNN Library, *Eric Holder Fast Facts*, CNN, Nov. 2, 2014, http://edition.cnn.com/2013/02/21/us/eric-holder-fast-facts/; NRO Staff, *Fast and Furious: A Timeline*, Nat'l Rev. Online, June 28, 2012, http://www.nationalreview.com/article/304215/fast-and-furious-timeline-nro-staff.

314. H.R. Res. 711, 112th Cong. (2012).

315. *Id.* (providing for the matter to be certified to the U.S. attorney); H.R. Res. 706, 112th Cong. (2012) (authorizing the filing of a civil suit).

316. CNN-ORC Poll 2–3 (July 9, 2012), http://i2.cdn.turner.com/cnn/2012/images/07/09/rel6d.pdf.

317. Sari Horwitz, *Justice Dept.: Holder Won't Be Prosecuted*, Wash. Post, June 30, 2012, at A2.

318. Comm. on Oversight & Gov't Reform v. Holder, 979 F. Supp. 2d 1 (D.D.C. 2013).

319. *See* Comm. on Oversight & Gov't Reform v. Holder, No. 12-1332 (D.D.C. Sept. 9, 2014), *available at* http://images.politico.com/global/2014/09/10/jacksonholderorder.pdf; Josh Gerstein, *House Seeks New Contempt for Eric Holder*, Politico, Oct. 2, 2014, http://www.politico.com/story/2014/10/eric-holder-new-contempt-fast-and-furious-111572.html.

320. Comm.'s Motion for Entry of Order Directing the Att'y Gen. to Show Cause Why He Should Not Be Found in Contempt, Comm. on Oversight & Govt. Reform v. Holder, No. 12-1332 (D.D.C. Oct. 2, 2014), *available at* http://images.politico.com/global/2014/10/02/holdercontemptfiling.pdf.

321. *See* Comm. on Oversight & Gov't Reform v. Holder, No. 12-1332 (D.D.C. Oct. 6, 2014), *available at* http://images.politico.com/global/2014/10/06/holdernocontemptord.pdf.

322. *See* Josh Chafetz, *Furious, Perhaps, but Certainly Not Fast*, The Hill, Apr. 27, 2015, http://thehill.com/blogs/pundits-blog/the-administration/240134-furious-perhaps-but-certainly-not-fast.

323. Comm. on Oversight & Gov't Reform v. Lynch, 156 F. Supp. 3d 101, 105–06 (D.D.C. 2016).

324. *See* Josh Gerstein, *Obama Relents in Fight over Fast and Furious Documents*, Politico, Apr. 8, 2016, http://www.politico.com/story/2016/04/obama-relents-in-fight-over-fast-and-furious-documents-221741; *see also* Docket, Comm. on Oversight v. Lynch, No. 16-5078 (D.C. Cir. 2016).

325. H.R. Res. 574, 113th Cong. (2014).
326. David S. Joachim, *Oversight Committee Censures Ex-I.R.S. Official for Refusal to Take Questions*, N.Y. Times, Apr. 11, 2014, at A20.
327. *See* Ed O'Keefe, *Congressional Leaders Agree on $1.01 Trillion Spending Bill*, Wash. Post, Dec. 10, 2014, at A3 (noting that the reduction in IRS funding was paired with a provision prohibiting it from targeting groups based on ideology).
328. Marshall v. Gordon, 243 U.S. 521, 548 (1917) (granting Marshall's habeas petition and ordering his discharge from custody).
329. Powell v. McCormack, 395 U.S. 486, 521–48 (1969).
330. *See id.* at 521 n.42 ("[F]ederal courts might still be barred by the political question doctrine from reviewing the House's factual determination that a member did not meet one of the standing qualifications. This is an issue not presented in this case and we express no view as to its resolution."); *id.* at 548 ("Art. I, § 5, is at most a 'textually demonstrable commitment' to Congress to judge only the qualifications expressly set forth in the Constitution." (internal citation omitted)). For an argument that a judgment by a house of Congress on the merits of a qualifications claim would be nonjusticiable, see Chafetz, *Democracy's Privileged Few*, *supra* note 3, at 55–56 ("The Court nowhere suggests [in *Powell*] that it could review the *content* of an exclusion decision."); Akhil Reed Amar & Josh Chafetz, *How the Senate Can Stop Blagojevich*, Slate, Dec. 31, 2008, http://www.slate.com/id/2207754.
331. In *Kilbourn v. Thompson*, 103 U.S. 168 (1881), the Supreme Court did undertake a probing and skeptical review of a congressional contempt citation against a *private citizen*. Even there, however, the Court phrased its holding in jurisdictional language. *See id.* at 190 (holding that the House of Representatives had no jurisdiction to inquire into Kilbourn's "private affairs"). The Court soon moved away from this narrow interpretation. *See* Chafetz, *Democracy's Privileged Few*, *supra* note 3, at 231–33. Elsewhere, I have criticized the *Kilbourn* holding as unduly narrow. *See id.* at 229–30. Even within the *Kilbourn* framework, however, it is clear that Congress would be jurisdictionally competent to hold executive-branch officials in contempt for defying subpoenas related to their official duties.
332. Tara Grove and Neal Devins argue that there is a lengthy history of congressional houses litigating disputes over subpoenas. Tara Leigh Grove & Neal Devins, *Congress's (Limited) Power to Represent Itself in Court*, 99 Cornell L. Rev. 571, 575, 597–603 (2014). But their argument curiously elides the distinction between a house's being haled into court (by, say, a habeas petition) and a house's filing suit. They point to no pre-Watergate cases in which a house served as a plaintiff in an attempt to enforce a subpoena against an executive official.
333. *See* United States v. Nixon, 418 U.S. 683, 712 (1974); Nixon v. Sirica, 487 F.2d 700, 712 (D.C. Cir. 1973).
334. Senate Select Comm. on Presidential Campaign Activities v. Nixon, 498 F.2d 725, 732 (D.C. Cir. 1974); Senate Select Comm. on Presidential Campaign Activities v. Nixon, 370 F. Supp. 521, 522–23 (D.D.C. 1974).
335. *Senate Select Comm.*, 498 F.2d at 732; *Senate Select Comm.*, 370 F. Supp. at 523–24.
336. *Senate Select Comm.*, 370 F. Supp. at 523–24.
337. *Senate Select Comm.*, 498 F.2d at 732.

338. *Senate Select Comm.*, 370 F. Supp. at 522 (citing *Nixon*, 487 F.2d at 700).

339. It should be clear, of course, that the courts neither are nor could be any more "apolitical" than any other branch. Commentators who argue that the courts must serve as "neutral" arbiters in separation-of-powers disputes are simply accepting uncritically the judges' own institutionally partisan framing. *See, e.g.*, Timothy T. Mastrogiacomo, Note, *Showdown in the Rose Garden: Congressional Contempt, Executive Privilege, and the Role of the Courts*, 99 Geo. L.J. 163 (2010); Peterson, *supra* note 253, at 147; *see also* Kenneth A. Klukowski, *Making Executive Privilege Work: A Multi-Factor Test in an Age of Czars and Congressional Oversight*, 59 Clev. St. L. Rev. 31, 48 (2011) (calling my argument here "odd," "absurd on its face," and "intrinsic[ally] flaw[ed]"). Indeed, this discussion should make clear that no institutional design could invariably prevent the possibility of partial decision makers. *See* Adrian Vermeule, *Contra* Nemo Iudex in Sua Causa*: The Limits of Impartiality*, 122 Yale L.J. 384 (2012); Jeremy Waldron, *The Core of the Case against Judicial Review*, 115 Yale L.J. 1346, 1400–01 (2006).

340. *See* Stanley M. Brand & Sean Connelly, *Constitutional Confrontations: Preserving a Prompt and Orderly Means by Which Congress May Enforce Investigative Demands against Executive Branch Officials*, 36 Cath. U. L. Rev. 71, 81, 84 (1986) (noting the effect of delay in the Gorsuch case).

341. *See* Josh Chafetz, *Should Boehner Arrest Holder?*, Wash. Post, June 22, 2012, at A15.

342. For contemporary discussions of this possibility, see *id.*; David Grant, *Could Congress Jail Attorney General Eric Holder for Contempt?*, Christian Sci. Monitor Online, June 29, 2012, http://www.csmonitor.com/USA/DC-Decoder/Decoder-Buzz/2012/0629/Could-Congress-jail-Attorney-General-Eric-Holder-for-contempt.

343. Comm. on the Judiciary v. Miers, 558 F. Supp. 2d 53, 92 (D.D.C. 2008) (citation omitted).

344. President Jefferson defied, on executive privilege grounds, a subpoena issued by Chief Justice John Marshall, riding circuit, in the treason trial of Aaron Burr, *United States v. Burr*, 25 F. Cas. 187, 189 (C.C.D. Va. 1807). *See* John C. Yoo, *The First Claim: The Burr Trial*, United States v. Nixon*, and Presidential Power*, 83 Minn. L. Rev. 1435, 1446–63 (1999). In response to *Worcester v. Georgia*, 31 U.S. (6 Pet.) 515 (1832), President Jackson is reported to have exclaimed, "John Marshall has made his decision, now let him enforce it." (Although the quotation is quite likely apocryphal, the dismissiveness toward judicial authority that it expresses was quite real.) *See* Gerard N. Magliocca, *Andrew Jackson and the Constitution: The Rise and Fall of Generational Regimes* 49 (2007). President Abraham Lincoln famously ignored Chief Justice Roger Taney's ruling in *Ex parte Merryman*, 17 F. Cas. 144, 153 (C.C.D. Md. 1861) (ordering that "the civil process of the United States"—in particular, the writ of habeas corpus—"be respected and enforced"). *See* William Baude, *The Judgment Power*, 96 Geo. L.J. 1807, 1853–61 (2008).

345. *Face the Nation* (CBS News television broadcast Dec. 18, 2011).

346. Dahlia Lithwick, *Courting Disaster*, Slate, Dec. 19, 2011, http://www.slate.com/articles/news_and_politics/jurisprudence/2011/12/what_logic_could_possibly_be_behind_newt_gingrich_s_crazy_attacks_on_the_federal_courts_.html. Lithwick's article also collects other critical reactions to Gingrich's comments.

347. 1 H.C. Jour. 652 (Nov. 30, 1621).

348. *See* 3 *Commons Debates 1621*, at 323–24 (Wallace Notestein et al. eds. 1935) (entry for May 28, 1621); 2 *id.* at 477–78 (entry for Nov. 30, 1621).

349. *See* 1 H.C. Jour. 610 (May 5, 1621) (appointing Coke to the committee).

350. *See* 3 *Commons Debates 1621*, *supra* note 348, at 172–73, 323–24 (entries for May 5 & 28, 1621).

351. *See* 2 H.C. Jour. 200–201 (July 6, 1641); *id.* at 202–03 (July 8, 1641).

352. Jay v. Topham, 12 How. St. Tr. 821, 821–22 (H.C. 1689).

353. *Id.* at 822–23.

354. *Id.* at 823–33.

355. They were taken into custody on July 19, 1689. *Id.* at 827, 834. The next prorogation came on October 21 of that year. 10 H.C. Jour. 272 (Oct. 21, 1689).

356. *See* Chafetz, *Democracy's Privileged Few*, *supra* note 3, at 77–78, 196 (recounting the facts of the *Stockdale v. Hansard* controversy).

357. Craig Alan Smith, *Tom Clark under Fire: The Consequences of Congressional Investigations of Supreme Court Justices*, 38 J. Sup. Ct. Hist. 139, 140–41 (2013).

358. *Id.* at 154–55.

359. *Id.* at 156–57.

360. *Face the Nation*, *supra* note 345.

361. U.S. Const. art. I, § 6, cl. 1.

Chapter 6. The Freedom of Speech or Debate

1. *See* J. E. Neale, *The Commons' Privilege of Free Speech in Parliament*, in 2 *Historical Studies of the English Parliament* 147, 150 (E. B. Fryde & Edward Miller eds., 1970).

2. *See* Josh Chafetz, *Democracy's Privileged Few: Legislative Privilege and Democratic Norms in the British and American Constitutions* 69 (2007); Henry Elsynge, *The Manner of Holding Parliaments in England* 179–80 (London, Richardson & Clark 1768); A. K. McHardy, *Haxey's Case, 1397: The Petition and Its Presenter Reconsidered*, in *The Age of Richard II*, at 93, 100–109 (James L. Gillespie ed., 1997).

3. 3 Rot. Parl. 456 (1399).

4. Neale, *supra* note 1, at 149.

5. Chafetz, *supra* note 2, at 69.

6. 5 Rot. Parl. 337 (1455); *see also* Neale, *supra* note 1, at 154–55.

7. 5 Rot. Parl. 337 (1455).

8. *Id.*

9. *See* Neale, *supra* note 1, at 155.

10. *See id.* (suggesting that "a certain, or more probably a very uncertain, freedom of speech had evidently come to be regarded as a customary right").

11. *See generally* George Randall Lewis, *The Stannaries: A Study of the English Tin Miner* 85–130 (1908).

12. 3 S. T. Bindoff, *The House of Commons, 1509–1558*, at 399–400 (1982).

13. *Id.* at 400.

14. Neale, *supra* note 1, at 160 n.45.

15. Strode's Act, 4 Hen. 8, c. 8 (1512).

16. *Id.*

17. Neale, *supra* note 1, at 157–58.
18. I have elsewhere identified this period as one in which the House of Commons became more cognizant of and more assertive about its institutional privileges. Josh Chafetz, *"In the Time of a Woman, Which Sex Was Not Capable of Mature Deliberation": Late Tudor Parliamentary Relations and Their Early Stuart Discontents*, 25 Yale J.L. & Human. 181 (2013).
19. Simonds D'Ewes, *The Journals of All the Parliaments During the Reign of Queen Elizabeth* 237 (Paul Bowes ed., London, Starkey 1682).
20. *Id.* at 239.
21. *Id.* at 241.
22. *Id.*
23. *Id.* at 242.
24. *Id.* at 243.
25. *Id.* at 259.
26. *See* J. E. Neale, *Peter Wentworth, Part I*, 39 Eng. Hist. Rev. 36, 47–48 (1924).
27. *Id.* at 48.
28. *Id.* at 49.
29. *Id.* at 52.
30. I have elsewhere argued that the conception of privilege that existed at this point was "geographical," which is to say, deeply concerned with what happened "within the physical confines of the House." Chafetz, *supra* note 2, at 5 (describing the Blackstonian conception of privilege); *id.* at 70–72 (noting that the Elizabethan confrontations took place during the period in which the Blackstonian conception was dominant).
31. Neale, *supra* note 26, at 54.
32. Quoted in J. E. Neale, *Peter Wentworth, Part II*, 39 Eng. Hist. Rev. 175, 184–85 (1924).
33. *The Lord Keeper's Further Answer*, in 3 *The Selected Writings of Sir Edward Coke* 1190 (Steve Sheppard ed., 2003). Neale discovered a slightly different version of the speech in a manuscript in the British Museum, but the tenor is the same. J. E. Neale, *The Lord Keeper's Speech to the Parliament of 1592/3*, 31 Eng. Hist. Rev. 128, 136–37 (1916).
34. Neale, *supra* note 32, at 187–91.
35. *Id.* at 202.
36. *Id.*
37. 1 William Cobbett, *Parliamentary History of England* 1326–27, 1335, 1361 (London, Hansard 1806); *see also* Chafetz, *supra* note 2, at 72–73.
38. 1 Cobbett, *supra* note 37, at 1349.
39. Thus late Tudor parliamentary precedents, in the free-speech area as in many others, formed the basis for parliamentary pushback against the Stuart Crown. *See generally* Chafetz, *supra* note 18.
40. 2 Cobbett, *supra* note 37, at 490.
41. *Id.* at 490–91.
42. R. v. Eliot, Hollis & Valentine, 3 How. St. Tr. 293, 293–94 (K.B. 1629).
43. *Id.* at 295–305.
44. *Id.* at 306–08.
45. *Id.* at 310.
46. 2 Cobbett, *supra* note 37, at 492.

47. 4 Andrew Thrush & John P. Ferris, *The House of Commons, 1604–1629,* at 199, 757 (2010); 6 *id.* at 602.

48. 2 H.C. Jour. 7 (Apr. 20, 1640).

49. *Id.* at 11 (Apr. 24, 1640).

50. The resolutions are laid out at *id.* at 200–201 (July 6, 1641); *id.* at 202–03 (July 8, 1641).

51. 9 *id.* at 19 (Nov. 12, 1667).

52. *Id.* at 25 (Nov. 23, 1667).

53. 12 H.L. Jour. 166 (Dec. 11, 1667).

54. *Id.* at 223 (Apr. 15, 1668).

55. *See generally* John Kenyon, *The Popish Plot* (1972).

56. On Dangerfield generally, see Alan Marshall, *Dangerfield, Thomas (1654–1685),* Oxford Dict. Nat'l Biog. (2008), http://www.oxforddnb.com/view/article/7109.

57. 9 H.C. Jour. 648–49 (Nov. 9, 1680) (ordering "That all the Informations already given in at the Bar of this House, in Writing, relating to the Popish Plot, be entered upon the Journal of this House: And that all the said Informations be printed, being first perused and signed by Mr. Speaker: And that Mr. Speaker nominate and appoint the Persons to print the same: And that Mr. Dangerfeild [*sic*] have the Benefit of the Printing the said Information").

58. Thomas Dangerfield, *The Information of Thomas Dangerfield, Gent. Delivered at the Bar of the House of Commons* (London, Newcomb & Hills 1680).

59. Marshall, *supra* note 56.

60. Dangerfield, *supra* note 58, at title page.

61. R. v. Williams, 13 How. St. Tr. 1369, 1437 (K.B. 1686).

62. *Id.;* James Alexander Manning, *The Lives of the Speakers of the House of Commons* 381 (London, George Willis 1851).

63. *See* Manning, *supra* note 62, at 381–82; Paul D. Halliday, *Williams, Sir William, First Baronet (1633/4–1700),* Oxford Dict. Nat'l Biog. (2004), http://www.oxforddnb.com/view/article/29555.

64. Bill of Rights, 1 W. & M., sess. 2, c. 2, § 1, cl. 8 (1689); *id.* § 2, cl. 9.

65. 9 Anchitell Grey, *Debates of the House of Commons* 81 (London, Henry, Cave & Emonson 1763).

66. 10 H.C. Jour. 215 (July 12, 1689).

67. *See* 10 H.C. Jour. 284, 289–90 (Nov. 12 & 19, 1689) (noting the introduction and first reading of a bill to reverse the judgment); Manning, *supra* note 62, at 382 (noting that the bill failed to pass).

68. *See* Mary Patterson Clarke, *Parliamentary Privilege in the American Colonies* 62–92 (1943).

69. Warren M. Billings, *A Little Parliament: The Virginia General Assembly in the Seventeenth Century* 122 (2004).

70. *Id.* at 122–23.

71. Clarke, *supra* note 68, at 94.

72. *A Journal of the Votes & Proceedings of the General Assembly of His Majesty's Colony of New-York, Which Began the 23d of July, 1728,* at 6 (July 30, 1728).

73. *Id.*

74. *Id.*

75. Clarke, *supra* note 68, at 96–97.

76. *Id.* at 97.

77. Md. Const. of 1776, Decl. of Rts., art. 8; Mass. Const. of 1780, pt. 1, art. 21; N.H. Const. of 1784, pt. 1, art. 30; N.C. Const. of 1776, Form of Gov't, art. 45; Vt. Const. of 1786, ch. 1, art. 16.

78. N.Y. Const. of 1777, art. 9; S.C. Const. of 1776, art. 7; S.C. Const. of 1778, art. 16.

79. Articles of Confederation, art. 5, § 5.

80. *See* Chafetz, *supra* note 2, at 87–88.

81. U.S. Const. art. I, § 6, cl. 1.

82. James Wilson, *Lectures on Law, Part Two: Of the Constitutions of the United States and of Pennsylvania—Of the Legislative Department* (1791), in 1 *The Works of James Wilson* 399, 421 (Robert Green McCloskey ed., 1967).

83. For the offending letter, see Circular Letter from Samuel J. Cabell (Jan. 12, 1797), in 1 *Circular Letters of Congressmen to Their Constituents, 1789–1829*, at 67 (Noble E. Cunningham Jr. ed., 1978). For some historical background, see *id.* at xxxvii–xxxix; Noble E. Cunningham Jr., *In Pursuit of Reason: The Life of Thomas Jefferson* 210–11 (1987); Adrienne Koch & Harry Ammon, *The Virginia and Kentucky Resolutions: An Episode in Jefferson's and Madison's Defense of Civil Liberties*, 5 Wm. & Mary Q. (3d ser.) 145, 152–53 (1948); Joseph McGraw, *"To Secure These Rights": Virginia Republicans on the Strategies of Political Opposition, 1788–1800*, 91 Va. Mag. Hist. & Biog. 54, 67–68 (1983).

84. Thomas Jefferson, Petition to Virginia House of Delegates (Aug. 1797), in 8 *The Works of Thomas Jefferson* 322, 322 (Paul Leicester Ford ed., 1904).

85. *Id.* at 325–26.

86. *See id.* at 329–30.

87. *Journal of the House of Delegates of the Commonwealth of Virginia, Begun and Held at the Capitol, in the City of Richmond, on Monday, the Fourth Day of December, One Thousand Seven Hundred and Ninety Seven* 62 (Dec. 28, 1797).

88. *Id.* at 61.

89. *Id.* at 63. The resolution was adopted by a vote of 92 to 53. *Id.* at 64.

90. Sedition Act, ch. 74, 1 Stat. 596 (1798).

91. On the Kentucky and Virginia resolutions, see generally Josh Chafetz, *Multiplicity in Federalism and the Separation of Powers*, 120 Yale L.J. 1084, 1107–11 (2011); Koch & Ammon, *supra* note 83.

92. *See* Chafetz, *supra* note 2, at 214; David P. Currie, *The Constitution in Congress: The Federalist Period, 1789–1801*, at 263–65 (1997); Joanne B. Freeman, *Affairs of Honor: National Politics in the New Republic* 173–75 (2001).

93. Lyon's Case, 15 F. Cas. 1183, 1183–84 (C.C.D. Vt. 1798) (No. 8,646).

94. *Id.* at 1185.

95. *Id.*

96. *Id.* at 1189.

97. 9 Annals of Cong. 2963–64 (Feb. 22, 1799).

98. *Id.* at 2970.

99. An Act to Refund a Fine Imposed on the Late Matthew Lyon, ch. 45, 6 Stat. 802 (1840); H.R. Rep. No. 26-86 (1840).

100. Chafetz, *supra* note 2, at 229.

101. *Id.* at 95, 229.

102. For criticism of this holding, see *id.* at 230.

103. Coffin v. Coffin, 4 Mass. 1 (1808). For a discussion of *Coffin* and its afterlife, see Chafetz, *supra* note 2, at 93–97.

104. Kilbourn v. Thompson, 103 U.S. 168, 204 (1880).

105. N.Y. Times Co. v. United States (Pentagon Papers), 403 U.S. 713 (1971) (per curiam).

106. Lionization of *New York Times v. United States* is widespread. See, e.g., Christopher L. Eisgruber, *Constitutional Self-Government* 73 (2001) (listing it as one of the Court's four "greatest moments" in the second half of the twentieth century); J. M. Balkin & Sanford Levinson, *The Canons of Constitutional Law*, 111 Harv. L. Rev. 963, 974 n.43 (1998) (listing it as one of only eighteen "truly canonical" American constitutional law cases).

107. The *Pentagon Papers* is the popular name for the top secret Pentagon study prepared between 1967 and 1969 and officially titled "History of U.S. Decision Making Process on Vietnam Policy." The complete study was more than seven thousand pages long and was bound in forty-seven volumes. Only parts of it were leaked. *See* David Rudenstine, *The Day the Presses Stopped: A History of the Pentagon Papers Case* 2, 27 (1996).

108. United States v. Wash. Post Co., 446 F.2d 1322, 1323 (D.C. Cir. 1971) (per curiam); United States v. N.Y. Times Co., 328 F. Supp. 324, 325 (S.D.N.Y. 1971).

109. For a fuller time line, see Josh Chafetz, *Congress's Constitution*, 160 U. Pa. L. Rev. 715, 746–47 (2012).

110. Daniel Ellsberg, *Foreword* to Mike Gravel & Joe Lauria, *A Political Odyssey: The Rise of American Militarism and One Man's Fight to Stop It* 9, 9–10 (2008).

111. Gravel & Lauria, *supra* note 110, at 27–29.

112. *Id.* at 30.

113. *Id.*

114. *Id.* at 35–36.

115. *Id.* at 38.

116. *Id.*

117. *See* N.Y. Times Co. v. United States (Pentagon Papers), 403 U.S. 713 (1971) (per curiam); *see also* Rudenstine, *supra* note 107, at 302 (noting that the Court announced its judgment at 2:30 P.M. on June 30).

118. The Supreme Court majority held simply that the government's requested injunction would constitute an impermissible prior restraint. 403 U.S. at 714. But three justices dissented, *id.* at 748 (Burger, C.J., dissenting); *id.* at 752 (Harlan, J., joined by Burger, C.J., and Blackmun, J., dissenting), and two justices in the majority explicitly held open the possibility of post-publication criminal sanction, *id.* at 730 (Stewart, J., concurring); *id.* at 733, 740 (White, J., concurring). It was thus perfectly plausible that the newspapers, their reporters, and their editors might still be criminally prosecuted for publishing the *Papers*, and, indeed, the Justice Department briefly pursued such prosecutions before ultimately abandoning them. *See* Rudenstine, *supra* note 107, at 339–43 (describing the unsuccessful prosecutions of Daniel Ellsberg and Anthony Russo and considering why no further criminal charges were brought in connection with the *Papers*).

119. *See* Gravel & Lauria, *supra* note 110, at 49–50 (suggesting that the newspapers stopped publishing portions of the *Papers* in response to legal pressure).

120. *Id.* at 50–51; *see also* 5 *The Pentagon Papers: The Senator Gravel Edition* 314–15 (1972) (describing the text of the Gravel edition of the *Papers*).

121. Rudenstine, *supra* note 107, at 340–41.

122. *See* Gravel v. United States, 408 U.S. 606, 608–09 (1972).

123. S. Res. 280, 92d Cong. (1972).

124. Brief for the Senate of the United States as Amicus Curiae at 3, *Gravel*, 408 U.S. 606 (1972) (No. 71-1026).

125. *Id.* at 6.

126. *Gravel*, 408 U.S. at 615.

127. *Id.* at 616–17 (citation omitted).

128. *Id.* at 625.

129. L. Britt Snider, *The Agency and the Hill: CIA's Relationship with Congress, 1946–2004*, at 31 (2008).

130. *Id.* at 31–32.

131. Cecil V. Crabb Jr. & Pat M. Holt, *Invitation to Struggle: Congress, the President and Foreign Policy* 146 (1980).

132. Hughes-Ryan Amendment, Pub. L. No. 93-559, § 32, 88 Stat. 1795, 1804 (1974). On the Harrington releases as a spur to the Hughes-Ryan Amendment, see Crabb & Holt, *supra* note 131, at 146; Snider, *supra* note 129, at 32–33.

133. House Comm. on Standards of Official Conduct, *Summary of Activities, Ninety-Fourth Congress*, H.R. Rep. No. 94-1792, at 3–4 (1977); *see also* Crabb & Holt, *supra* note 131, at 150. On the normal rules governing the release of information, see Josh Chafetz, *Whose Secrets?*, 127 Harv. L. Rev. F. 86, 90–91 (2013).

134. David E. Pozen, *The Leaky Leviathan: Why the Government Condemns and Condones Unlawful Disclosures of Information*, 127 Harv. L. Rev. 512, 523 (2013).

135. Seymour M. Hersh, *Huge C.I.A. Operation Reported in U.S. Against Antiwar Forces, Other Dissidents in Nixon Years*, N.Y. Times, Dec. 22, 1974, at 1.

136. Snider, *supra* note 129, at 30.

137. *Id.* at 30–31.

138. *Id.* at 33–34.

139. *Id.* at 34, 37–38.

140. Kathleen Clark, *Congress's Right to Counsel in Intelligence Oversight*, 2011 U. Ill. L. Rev. 915, 943–44.

141. Snider, *supra* note 129, at 37–39.

142. *Id.* at 51–60.

143. *See id.* at 75–76; *see also* Thomas M. Franck & Edward Weisband, *Foreign Policy by Congress* 125–29 (1979).

144. *See* George Lardner Jr., *Gonzalez's Iraq Exposé: Hill Chairman Details U.S. Prewar Courtship*, Wash. Post, Mar. 22, 1992, at A1.

145. 138 Cong. Rec. 25449 (Sept. 17, 1992) (Rep. Combest quoting Gonzalez).

146. *Id.*

147. *See* Assoc. Press, *Congressman Avoids Inquiry into U.S.-Iraq Disclosures*, N.Y. Times, Sept. 20, 1992, at 11; Clark, *supra* note 140, at 945.

148. Clark, *supra* note 140, at 945–46.

149. *Id.* at 946.

150. 150 Cong. Rec. S11957 (daily ed. Dec. 8, 2004).

151. *Id.* at S11958.

152. *See generally* David E. Pozen, *Deep Secrecy*, 62 Stan. L. Rev. 257 (2010).

153. Douglas Jehl, *New Spy Plan Said to Involve Satellite System*, N.Y. Times, Dec. 12, 2004, at 1.

154. *Id.*

155. *See* David Johnston, *Justice Dept. May Explore Leak on Spy Satellites*, N.Y. Times, Dec. 15, 2004, at A28.

156. Mark Mazzetti, *Spy Director Ends Program on Satellites*, N.Y. Times, June 22, 2007, at A16.

157. *See* Chafetz, supra note 109, at 750–51.

158. *See* Jameel Jaffer, *Unmasking "Secret Law": New Demand for Answers about the Government's Hidden Take on the Patriot Act*, ACLU Blog of Rights, May 31, 2011, http://www.aclu.org/blog/national-security/unmasking-secret-law-new-demand-answers-about-governments-hidden-take-patriot.

159. These are archived at http://www.aclu.org/national-security/section-215-patriot-act-foia.

160. ACLU v. FBI, 2015 WL 1566775 (S.D.N.Y. Mar. 31, 2015); ACLU v. FBI, 59 F. Supp. 3d 584 (S.D.N.Y. 2014); N.Y. Times v. U.S. Dep't of Justice, 872 F. Supp. 2d 309 (2012).

161. Letter from Sens. Wyden and Udall to Attorney General Holder, Mar. 15, 2012, *available at* https://www.documentcloud.org/documents/325953-85512347-senators-ron-wyden-mark-udall-letter-to.html.

162. ACLU v. Clapper, 785 F.3d 787 (2d Cir. 2015).

163. USA Freedom Act, Pub. L. No. 114-23, 129 Stat. 268 (2015); *see also* Jennifer Steinhauer & Jonathan Weisman, *U.S. Surveillance in Place Since 9/11 is Sharply Limited*, N.Y. Times, June 3, 2015, at A1. On the sunsetting of the NSA's authority, see Josh Chafetz, *A Beautiful Sunset (Provision) for NSA Surveillance*, The Hill, May 27, 2015, http://thehill.com/blogs/pundits-blog/homeland-security/243169-a-beautiful-sunset-provision-for-nsa-surveillance.

164. The term is borrowed from Seth F. Kreimer, *The Freedom of Information Act and the Ecology of Transparency*, 10 U. Pa. J. Const. L. 1011 (2008).

165. For Snowden's victory lap, see Edward J. Snowden, *The World Says No to Surveillance*, N.Y. Times, June 5, 2015, at A27.

166. Bruce Ackerman, *Breach or Debate*, Foreign Pol'y (Aug. 1, 2013), http://foreignpolicy.com/2013/08/01/breach-or-debate/.

167. Dan Froomkin, *Senator Who Put Pentagon Papers into Public Record Urges Udall to Do Same with Torture Report*, The Intercept, Nov. 10, 2014, https://firstlook.org/theintercept/2014/11/10/mike-gravel-senator-put-pentagon-papers-public-record-urges-udall-torture-report/.

168. Spencer Ackerman et al., *Senate Report on CIA Torture Claims Spy Agency Lied about 'Ineffective' Program*, Guardian, Dec. 9, 2014, http://www.theguardian.com/us-news/2014/dec/09/cia-torture-report-released.

169. Mark Mazzetti, *Senate Panel Faults C.I.A. over Brutality and Deceit in Terrorism Investigations*, N.Y. Times, Dec. 10, 2014, at A1.

170. Rachel Deahl, *Melville House Sells Out of 'Torture Report'*, Publishers Wkly., Dec. 30, 2014, http://publishersweekly.com/pw/by-topic/industry-news/publisher-news/article/65149-melville-house-sells-out-of-torture-report.html.

171. *See, e.g.*, Jeremy Herb, *Intelligence Chief Clapper Apologizes for 'Erroneous' Statement to Congress*, The Hill, July 3, 2013, at 3; Ron Wyden, Mark Udall & Martin Heinrich, *End the N.S.A. Dragnet, Now*, N.Y. Times, Nov. 26, 2013, at A25.

172. *See* Peter Baker, *Patriot Act II*, N.Y. Times, June 2, 2015, at A1; Scott Shane, *Spy Agencies under Heaviest Scrutiny Since Abuse Scandal of the '70s*, N.Y. Times, July 26, 2013, at A15.

173. It was no secret that the Senate Intelligence Committee and the CIA were fighting in the weeks leading up to the release about how much of it to redact. *See* Greg Miller, *Senate, CIA Clash over Report on Interrogations*, Wash. Post, Aug. 6, 2014, at A6; Jason Leopold, *'Comprehensive' CIA Torture Report Won't Even Name Well-Known Architects of Torture Program*, Vice News, Aug. 21, 2014, https://news.vice.com/article/comprehensive-cia-torture-report-wont-name-well-known-architects-of-torture-program. The CIA was not pleased with the amount that was ultimately released. *See* Mazzetti, *supra* note 169 ("The release of the report was severely criticized by current and former C.I.A. officials.").

174. *See* Chafetz, *supra* note 109, at 751.

175. *See Inside the Pentagon Papers* 183 (John Prados & Margaret Pratt Porter eds., 2004) ("[T]he Pentagon Papers revelation 'lent credibility to and finally crystalized the growing consensus that the Vietnam War was wrong and legitimized the radical critique of the war.' The leak also began a period of militancy on the part of the press."); Heidi Kitrosser, *What If Daniel Ellsberg Hadn't Bothered?*, 45 Ind. L. Rev. 89, 93 (2011) ("[T]he leak . . . is invoked in judicial opinions and in public debates alike for the proposition that it is dangerous to defer heavily to executive branch judgments, including executive claims that certain information is too dangerous to release. It is highly plausible that this social learning effect imposes practical constraints on the executive's ability to take legal action against classified information leaks and publications."); *id.* at 100 ("The Papers thus helped to disrupt the momentum of the national security state and the imperial presidency. It forced a crisis in the culture of deference and trust on which these phenomena relied.").

176. *See* Erwin N. Griswold, *Ould Fields, New Corne: The Personal Memoirs of a Twentieth Century Lawyer* 310 (1992) ("As far as I know, . . . none of the material which was 'objectionable' from my point of view was ever published by anyone, including the newspapers, until several years later."); Erwin N. Griswold, *'No Harm Was Done,'* N.Y. Times, June 30, 1991, at E15 ("In hindsight, it is clear to me that no harm was done by publication of the Pentagon Papers."); Erwin N. Griswold, *Secrets Not Worth Keeping*, Wash. Post, Feb. 15, 1989, at A25 ("I have never seen any trace of a threat to the national security from the publication. Indeed, I have never seen it even suggested that there was such an actual threat.").

177. *See* Rudenstine, *supra* note 107, at 327–28 (noting that neither Nixon nor Kissinger claimed any damages from the *Papers'* publication in their memoirs and concluding

that "[t]here is no evidence" that the release of the *Papers* "harmed the U.S. military, defense, intelligence, or international affairs interests").

178. For a brief summary of Manning's and Snowden's leaks, see Margaret B. Kwoka, *Leaking and Legitimacy*, 48 U.C. Davis L. Rev. 1387, 1397–99 (2015).

179. Indeed, Daniel Ellsberg initially approached Senators Fulbright, McGovern, and Mathias with the *Pentagon Papers*, hoping that they would hold hearings on them. Although those senators were initially supportive, their eventual "cold feet" led Ellsberg to approach the press. He subsequently learned that Senator Gravel shared his antiwar leanings and approached him. Ellsberg insists that, from the beginning, he preferred legislative hearings over release to the newspapers. *See* Ellsberg, *supra* note 110, at 9–10.

180. *See generally* Pozen, *supra* note 134.

181. In this regard, it is helpful to think in terms of what Mariah Zeisberg has called "security orders"—political constructs that "specif[y] and enact[] the content of a national security interest; what will be construed as threats to that interest; and a supportive construction of constitutional war authority." Mariah Zeisberg, *War Powers: The Politics of Constitutional Authority* 95 (2013). To the extent that a certain piece of information "must be" secret for national security reasons, that imperative arises only in the context of, and with respect to the terms of, a particular security order. *See also* Aziz Rana, *Who Decides on Security?*, 44 Conn. L. Rev. 1417, 1451–90 (2012) (tracing the twentieth-century rise of a security order emphasizing executive expertise).

182. *See supra* text accompanying note 146.

183. *See supra* text accompanying note 37.

184. *See* Steven Aftergood, *Reducing Government Secrecy: Finding What Works*, 27 Yale L. & Pol'y Rev. 399, 401–07 (2009) (summarizing the literature on overclassification).

185. I have previously referred to this inward-facing conception of privilege as "Blackstonian." *See* Chafetz, *supra* note 2, at 4–10, 69–77.

186. *See* Chafetz, *supra* note 18, at 183–85.

187. Cochran v. Couzens, 42 F.2d 783 (D.C. Cir. 1930), *cert. denied*, 282 U.S. 874 (1930).

188. The details of the claims are laid out in the court of appeals' decision, Dombrowski v. Burbank, 358 F.2d 821 (D.C. Cir. 1966).

189. Dombrowski v. Eastland, 387 U.S. 82, 84–85 (1967) (per curiam).

190. Powell v. McCormack, 395 U.S. 486, 501–06 (1969). For more on the Speech or Debate Clause holding in *Powell*, see Josh Chafetz, *The Unconstitutionality of the Filibuster*, 43 Conn. L. Rev. 1003, 1036–37 (2011).

191. Eastland v. U.S. Servicemen's Fund, 421 U.S. 491 (1975).

192. Long v. Ansell, 69 F.2d 386, 389 (D.C. Cir. 1934), *aff'd on other grounds*, 293 U.S. 76 (1934).

193. McGovern v. Martz, 182 F. Supp. 343, 347 (D.D.C. 1960).

194. Doe v. McMillan, 412 U.S. 306, 307–08 (1973).

195. *Id.* at 309.

196. *Id.* at 312–13.

197. *Id.* at 316 (internal quotation marks and citations omitted).

198. Hutchinson v. Proxmire, 443 U.S. 111, 114–18 (1979).

199. *Id.* at 130.

200. *Id.* at 133.

201. Jefferson, *supra* note 84, at 322.

202. For arguments along similar lines, see Chafetz, *supra* note 2, at 91–92, 98–105; Michael L. Shenkman, *Talking about Speech or Debate: Revisiting Legislative Immunity*, 32 Yale L. & Pol'y Rev. 351, 384–98 (2014).

203. Open Letter from 47 Senators to the Leaders of the Islamic Republic of Iran (Mar. 9, 2015), *available at* https://s3.amazonaws.com/s3.documentcloud.org/documents/1683798/the-letter-senate-republicans-addressed-to-the.pdf.

204. *Id.*

205. Statement by the Vice President on the March 9 Letter from Republican Senators to the Islamic Republic of Iran (Mar. 9, 2015), *available at* https://www.whitehouse.gov/the-press-office/2015/03/09/statement-vice-president-march-9-letter-republican-senators-islamic-repu.

206. *See* Editorial, *Un-Patriot Games: GOP Senators' Letter to Iran is a Treacherous Betrayal of the U.S. Constitutional System*, N.Y. Daily News, Mar. 10, 2015, http://www.nydailynews.com/opinion/editorial-un-patriot-games-article-1.2143378.

207. *See* Peter Spiro, *GOP Iran Letter Might Be Unconstitutional. Is It Also Criminal?*, Opinio Juris, Mar. 9, 2015, http://opiniojuris.org/2015/03/09/gop-iran-letter-might-be-unconstitutional-is-it-also-criminal/.

208. Logan Act, ch. 1, 1 Stat. 613 (1799), codified as amended at 18 U.S.C. § 953.

209. United States v. Curtiss-Wright Export Corp., 299 U.S. 304, 320 (1936).

210. Acquisition of Naval and Air Bases in Exchange for Over-Age Destroyers, 39 Op. Att'y Gen. 484, 486–87 (1940).

211. Legal Authorities Supporting the Activities of the National Security Agency Described by the President, 2006 WL 6179901, at *7, *15, *28 (O.L.C. Jan. 19, 2006).

212. 299 U.S. 304 (1936). For a more recent example, see Zivotofsky v. Kerry, 135 S. Ct. 2076 (2015).

213. *See, e.g.*, Louis Fisher, *The Law: Presidential Inherent Power: The "Sole Organ" Doctrine*, 37 Pres. Stud. Q. 139 (2007); Michael P. Van Alstine, *Taking Care of John Marshall's Political Ghost*, 53 St. Louis U. L.J. 93 (2008).

214. *See* Sarah H. Cleveland, *Crosby and the 'One-Voice' Myth in U.S. Foreign Relations*, 46 Vill. L. Rev. 975, 984–89 (2001).

Chapter 7. Internal Discipline

1. *Cf.* Stan Lee et al., *Amazing Fantasy No. 15*, at 11 (1962), *reprinted in* 1 *The Essential Spider-Man* (2004) ("[W]ith great power there must also come—great responsibility!").

2. U.S. Const. art. I, § 5, cl. 2.

3. My argument here may be viewed as a loose congressional analogue to the claims that some administrative law scholars have made about the ways in which "executive self-binding" can, in the long run, enhance presidential power. *See* Eric A. Posner & Adrian Vermeule, *The Executive Unbound: After the Madisonian Republic* 137–50 (2010); David E. Pozen, *The Leaky Leviathan: Why the Government Condemns and Condones Unlawful Disclosures of Information*, 127 Harv. L. Rev. 512, 573–77 (2013).

4. 2 & 3 Edw. 6, c. 1 (1549). On the House's passage, see 1 H.C. Jour. 6 (Jan. 21, 1549).
5. *See* 3 S. T. Bindoff, *The House of Commons, 1509–1558*, at 386–87 (1982).
6. 2 Gilbert Burnet, *The History of the Reformation of the Church of England* 517–18 (Nicholas Pocock ed., Oxford, Clarendon Press rev. ed. 1865); *see also* Ecclesiastes 10:16.
7. 1 H.C. Jour. 6 (Jan. 21, 1549).
8. *Id.* (Jan. 24, 1549).
9. *Id.* at 9 (Mar. 2, 1549).
10. *Id.*
11. On his status as the first expellee, see 2 P. W. Hasler, *The House of Commons, 1558–1603*, at 241 (1981).
12. 1 H.C. Jour. 125 (Feb. 14, 1581). For more details about the contents of the book, see *id.* at 122 (Feb. 4, 1581).
13. *Id.* at 125 (Feb. 14, 1581).
14. *Id.* at 125–26 (Feb. 14, 1581); 2 Hasler, *supra* note 11, at 241.
15. For as much detail as can be sussed out of the available sources, see 3 Hasler, *supra* note 11, at 180–84.
16. 1 William Cobbett, *Parliamentary History of England* 822–23 (London, Hansard 1806); Simonds D'Ewes, *The Journals of All the Parliaments During the Reign of Queen Elizabeth* 340 (Paul Bowes ed., London, Starkey 1682). For the act itself, see 27 Eliz., c. 2 (1584).
17. D'Ewes, *supra* note 16, at 340–41.
18. *Id.* at 342.
19. *Id.*
20. *See* 3 Hasler, *supra* note 11, at 183.
21. D'Ewes, *supra* note 16, at 352, 355.
22. 3 Hasler, *supra* note 11, at 184.
23. 1 H.C. Jour. 333 (Feb. 13, 1607).
24. *Id.* at 335–36 (Feb. 16, 1607).
25. *Id.* at 344 (Feb. 28, 1607) (ordering Pigott to be freed from the Tower but not readmitted to the House).
26. 1 Cobbett, *supra* note 16, at 1190.
27. *Id.* at 1191–92.
28. 9 H.C. Jour. 576 (Mar. 25, 1679); *id.* at 581 (Apr. 1, 1679); 4 Cobbett, *supra* note 16, at 1118.
29. *See* 4 Cobbett, *supra* note 16, at 1174–75 (noting the exclusions of Robert Cann for denying the existence of the Popish Plot and asserting the existence of a Presbyterian Plot and of Francis Wythens for petitioning against the summoning of the Exclusion Bill Parliament); *id.* at 1233–34 (noting the expulsion of Robert Peyton for associating with York).
30. 1 H.C. Jour. 586–88 (Apr. 23, 1621).
31. *Id.* at 565–67 (Mar. 21, 1621).
32. *Id.* at 535–36 (Mar. 3, 1621).
33. *See* 1 Andrew Thrush & John P. Ferris, *The House of Commons, 1604–1629*, at 62 (2010).

34. 1 H.C. Jour. 917 (June 21, 1628).

35. 9 H.C. Jour. 24 (Nov. 22, 1667); 1 Basil Duke Henning, *The House of Commons, 1660–1690*, at 552–53 (1983).

36. *The Diary of John Milward* 132 (Caroline Robbins ed., 1938).

37. Freedom from civil arrest is one of the traditional privileges of Parliament, and that privilege extended to members' servants until 1770. A "protection" was a document issued by a member—usually sold—claiming another person as his servant, and thus offering that person immunity from civil arrest. The sale of protections was a problem for the House throughout the seventeenth and eighteenth centuries. *See* Josh Chafetz, *Democracy's Privileged Few: Legislative Privilege and Democratic Norms in the British and American Constitutions* 124–30 (2007).

38. 5 Anchitell Grey, *Debates of the House of Commons* 53–54 (London, Henry, Cave & Emonson 1763).

39. 9 H.C. Jour. 430–31 (Feb. 1, 1678).

40. 11 *id.* at 236 (Feb. 16, 1695); 4 Eveline Cruickshanks, Stuart Handley & D. W. Hayton, *The House of Commons, 1690–1715*, at 127–28 (2002).

41. 11 H.C. Jour. 307 (Apr. 17, 1695).

42. *Id.* at 333 (May 3, 1695) (proroguing Parliament); 4 Cruickshanks et al., *supra* note 40, at 128–29 (noting that Guy remained in the Tower until the end of the session).

43. *See* 5 Cruickshanks et al., *supra* note 40, at 685.

44. For the expulsion, see 11 H.C. Jour. 274 (Mar. 16, 1695). For the Orphans Act, see 5 & 6 W. & M., c. 10 (1694). For a brief description of the act, see Francis Sheppard, *London: A History* 141–42 (1998).

45. 11 H.C. Jour. 283 (Mar. 26, 1695).

46. *Id.* at 331 (May 2, 1695).

47. 6 Cobbett, *supra* note 16, at 126.

48. *Id.* at 1067–68.

49. *See* 5 Cruickshanks et al., *supra* note 40, at 780–84.

50. *See* 1 Romney Sedgwick, *The House of Commons, 1715–1754*, at 409, 534–35, 541–42 (1970) (John Aislabie, George Caswall, and Robert Chaplin); 2 *id.* at 20, 171–72, 409–10, 499 (Francis Eyles, Theodore Janssen, Jacob Sawbridge, and Thomas Vernon).

51. The incident is recounted in more detail in Chafetz, *supra* note 37, at 30–31.

52. 9 H.C. Jour. 352 (June 3, 1675).

53. 6 Cobbett, *supra* note 16, at 600–601.

54. 1 Sedgwick, *supra* note 50, at 531 (John Carnegie); 2 *id.* at 45–46, 371–72 (Thomas Forster and Lewis Pryse).

55. The discussion of Wilkes that follows relies on Chafetz, *supra* note 37, at 155–58.

56. *See* Pauline Maier, *John Wilkes and American Disillusionment with Britain*, 20 Wm. & Mary Q. (3d ser.) 373 (1963).

57. 15 Cobbett, *supra* note 16, at 1356–57 n.*; 3 Lewis Namier & John Brooke, *The House of Commons, 1754–1790*, at 116 (1964).

58. 15 Cobbett, *supra* note 16, at 1388–91.

59. *Id.* at 1393.

60. Chafetz, *supra* note 37, at 157.

61. Edmund Burke, *Thoughts on the Cause of the Present Discontents* (1770), in 1 *The Works of the Right Honorable Edmund Burke* 433, 501 (Boston, Little, Brown 3d ed. 1869).

62. *See* Chafetz, *supra* note 37, at 158.

63. 22 Cobbett, *supra* note 16, at 1407–11.

64. *See generally* Maier, *supra* note 56.

65. Mary Patterson Clarke, *Parliamentary Privilege in the American Colonies* 184 (1943).

66. *Id.* at 185–90.

67. As often related, the quotation is "Caesar had his Brutus—Charles the first his Cromwell, and George the third . . . *may profit by their example.* If *this* be treason, make the most of it." *Yale Book of Quotations* 355 (Fred R. Shapiro ed., 2006). A likely more accurate rendition was discovered in the 1920s. *Journal of a French Traveler in the Colonies, 1765, I*, 26 Am. Hist. Rev. 726, 745 (1921) [hereinafter *Journal of a French Traveler*]. On the importance of the assassinations of Caesar and Charles I for the founding generation generally, see Josh Chafetz, *Impeachment and Assassination*, 95 Minn. L. Rev. 347, 347–88 (2010).

68. *Journal of a French Traveler*, *supra* note 67, at 745 (Henry "said that if he had afronted the speaker, or the house, he was ready to ask pardon, and he would shew his loyalty to his majesty King G. the third, at the Expence of the last Drop of his blood, . . . [and] again, if he said any thing wrong, he beged the speaker and the houses pardon.").

69. *See* Clarke, *supra* note 65, at 191–94.

70. *See id.* at 194–96.

71. Del. Const. of 1776, art. 5 (prohibiting reexpulsion for the same offense); Md. Const. of 1776, art. 10 (same); Penn. Const. of 1776, Frame of Gov't, § 9 (same); Vt. Const. of 1786, ch. 2, § 9 (prohibiting expulsion for "causes known to their constituents antecedent to their election").

72. Peter Hoffer has recently insisted that the Wilkes case "was not seen as a legal precedent for any of the revolutionary acts and died with the death of the imperial connection." Indeed, if anything, the Wilkes case would have been considered "a negative precedent, for the state constitutional writers and the delegates to the federal constitutional convention regarded the Parliament of the 1760's as thoroughly corrupt—bought and paid for by the crown." Peter Charles Hoffer, *The Pleasures and Perils of Presentism: A Meditation on History and Law*, 33 Quinnipiac L. Rev. 1, 2–3 (2014). But, of course, that's precisely why the colonists were so interested in Wilkes—as Maier demonstrated, they viewed Wilkes as a fellow struggler against the thoroughly corrupt Parliament and ministry. *See* Maier, *supra* note 56. Wilkes's constituents' struggle to be represented by the person of their choice in Parliament mirrored the colonists', and it seems highly implausible that a group of people so thoroughly invested in Wilkes in the 1760s, as Maier has shown, would have forgotten him—and yet still written constitutional provisions embodying the principle for which he had fought—the following decade. Hoffer's standard of proof—a "smoking gun" or it didn't happen!, Hoffer, *supra*, at 5—is simply too strict. Wilkes had foregrounded the issue of repeated expulsions and exclusions being used to thwart the will of the people, and the issue clearly remained salient for Americans of the early Republican period. Of course, it would be a mistake to assume too much familiarity—the exact twists and turns of the Wilkes struggle were

likely not on the Americans' minds. But it is equally mistaken to assume too little familiarity.

73. S.C. Const. of 1776, art. 7.

74. *Id.* art. 2.

75. S.C. Const. of 1778, arts. 12, 16.

76. For general legislative privilege protections in addition to the two South Carolina provisions mentioned above, see Mass. Const. of 1780, pt. 2, ch. 1, § 3, art. 11; N.Y. Const. of 1777, art. 9. For rules-of-proceedings provisions, see Del. Const. of 1776, art. 5; Ga. Const. of 1777, art. 7; Mass. Const. of 1780, pt. 2, ch. 1, § 2, art. 7; *id.* § 3, art. 10; N.H. Const. of 1784, pt. 2, Senate, para. 12; *id.* House of Representatives, para. 12; Va. Const. of 1776, para. 4.

77. 1 Geo. 1, stat. 2, c. 38 (1716).

78. *See* Akhil Reed Amar, *America's Constitution: A Biography* 75 (2005) (noting that, under their Revolutionary constitutions, "[t]wo states held elections for the lower house twice a year, ten others ran annual elections, and only one—South Carolina—gave lower-house members two-year terms. Although several state upper houses featured multiyear terms, none exceeded five years."); *see also* Willi Paul Adams, *The First American Constitutions: Republican Ideology and the Making of the State Constitutions in the Revolutionary Era* 241–43 (Rita & Robert Kimber trans., Rowman & Littlefield, expanded ed. 2001) (1973) (describing the brief legislative terms in the Revolutionary state constitutions).

79. 2 *The Records of the Federal Convention of 1787*, at 140 (Max Farrand ed., rev. ed. 1966).

80. *Id.* at 156. The first sentence quoted originally ended with "punish its own Members." The committee added "for disorderly and indecent Behavior." It then crossed out "and indecent." Textual notations of these insertions and deletions have been omitted from the quotation above.

81. *Id.* at 180.

82. *Id.* at 254.

83. *Id.*

84. *See* Chafetz, *supra* note 37, at 208.

85. U.S. Const. art. I, § 5, cl. 2.

86. James Wilson, *Lectures on Law, Part Two: Of the Constitutions of the United States and of Pennsylvania—Of the Legislative Department* (1791), in 1 *The Works of James Wilson* 399, 421 (Robert Green McCloskey ed., 1967).

87. *Id.*

88. 2 Joseph Story, *Commentaries on the Constitution of the United States* § 835, at 298 (Boston, Hilliard, Gray 1833).

89. *Id.*

90. *Id.*

91. *See* 5 Annals of Cong. 58–60 (Mar. 22, 1796); Anne M. Butler & Wendy Wolff, *United States Senate Election, Expulsion and Censure Cases, 1793–1990*, at 8–9 (1995); 2 Asher C. Hinds, *Hinds' Precedents of the House of Representatives of the United States* § 1288, at 858–60 (1907); Harry M. Ward, *Marshall, Humphrey*, Am. Nat'l Biog. (2000), http://www.anb.org/articles/03/03-00306.html.

92. *See* 7 Annals of Cong. 33–45 (July 3–10, 1797); 8 *id.* at 2245–2416 (Dec. 17, 1798–Jan. 14, 1799); Butler & Wolff, *supra* note 91, at 13–15; Chafetz, *supra* note 37, at 218.

93. 2 Hinds, *supra* note 91, § 1642, at 1115. *See also* Joanne B. Freeman, *Affairs of Honor: National Politics in the New Republic* 173–75 (2001).

94. *See* 2 Hinds, *supra* note 91, §§ 1642–43, at 1114–16; Chafetz, *supra* note 37, at 214; David P. Currie, *The Constitution in Congress: The Federalist Period, 1789–1801*, at 263–65 (1997); Freeman, *supra* note 93, at 173–75.

95. *See* Chafetz, *supra* note 37, at 221; 2 Hinds, *supra* note 91, § 1284, at 850.

96. United States v. Burr, 25 F. Cas. 55, 159–81 (1807).

97. 2 Hinds, *supra* note 91, § 1264, at 816.

98. *Id.* at 818.

99. *Id.* at 821–22; 17 Annals of Cong. 164–324 (Mar. 15–Apr. 9, 1808).

100. 17 Annals of Cong. 324 n.* (Apr. 25, 1808).

101. 22 *id.* at 65–83 (Dec. 31, 1810–Jan. 2, 1811); Butler & Wolff, *supra* note 91, at 26–28.

102. 2 Hinds, *supra* note 91, § 1248, at 799.

103. *Id.* at 799–801.

104. *See generally* Richard C. Rohrs, *Partisan Politics and the Attempted Assassination of Andrew Jackson*, 1 J. Early Repub. 149 (1981).

105. Butler & Wolff, *supra* note 91, at 38–39.

106. Rohrs, *supra* note 104, at 159.

107. 2 Hinds, *supra* note 91, § 1644, at 1116–19 (Jonathan Cilley (D) and William Graves (W) in 1838); *id.* § 1648, at 1121–22 (John Bell (W) and Hopkins Turney (D) in 1838); *id.* § 1649, at 1122–23 (Rice Garland (W) and Jesse Bynum (D) in 1840); *id.* § 1651, at 1125–26 (George Rathbun (D) and John White (W) in 1844); *id.* § 1652, at 1126–27 (Albert Brown (D) and John Wilcox (Unionist) in 1852); *id.* § 1621, at 1090–94 (Preston Brooks (D), Laurence Keitt (D), and Henry Edmundson (D) against Charles Sumner (Opposition) in 1856); *id.* § 1645, at 1119–20 (Fayette McMullen (D) and Amos Granger (Opposition) in 1856). The three intraparty fights are *id.* § 1650, at 1123–24 (Henry Wise (W) and Edward Stanly (W) in 1841); *id.* § 1647, at 1120–21 (Hugh Haralson (D) and George Jones (D) in 1848); Butler & Wolff, *supra* note 91, at 57–59 (Thomas Benton (D) and Henry Foote (D) in 1850).

108. *See* Chafetz, *supra* note 37, at 214–15.

109. *See id.* at 215–16; 2 Hinds, *supra* note 91, §§ 1621–23, at 1090–96.

110. Cong. Globe, 31st Cong., 1st Sess. 1480 (July 30, 1850).

111. Anti-Dueling Law, ch. 30, 5 Stat. 318 (1839).

112. 2 Hinds, *supra* note 91, §§ 1621, 1211–12, at 1093–94, 779.

113. Cong. Globe, 31st Cong., 1st Sess. 1480 (July 30, 1850).

114. *See* David P. Currie, *The Constitution in Congress: Descent into the Maelstrom, 1829–1861*, at 21–23 (2005).

115. Cong. Globe, 27th Cong., 2d Sess. 342 (Mar. 21, 1842).

116. *Id.* at 345–46 (Mar. 22, 1842).

117. 2 Hinds, *supra* note 91, § 1256, at 808.

118. Cong. Globe, 27th Cong., 2d Sess. 168 (Jan. 25, 1842).

119. 2 Hinds, *supra* note 91, § 1255, at 805–07.

120. Currie, *supra* note 114, at 22.

121. *See* Chafetz, *supra* note 37, at 181–89.

122. 2 Hinds, *supra* note 91, §§ 1261–62, at 812–13.

123. *See* Butler & Wolff, *supra* note 91, at 89–91.

124. *Id.* at 97.

125. *Id.* at 102–08.

126. *Id.* at 109–14.

127. 2 Hinds, *supra* note 91, §§ 1253–54, at 803–05.

128. Cong. Globe, 39th Cong., 1st Sess. 2572–75 (May 14, 1866).

129. *Id.* at 3092 (June 11, 1866).

130. *Id.* at 3090–95.

131. *Id.* at 3094.

132. *Id.* at 3096.

133. *Id.* at 3818–19 (July 14, 1866).

134. *Id.*

135. 2 Hinds, *supra* note 91, § 1656, at 1134–35.

136. Cong. Globe, 39th Cong., 2d Sess. 5 (Dec. 3, 1866).

137. *See, e.g.,* 2 Hinds, *supra* note 91, § 1249, at 801 (John Hunter in 1867); *id.* § 1247, at 798–99 (Fernando Wood in 1868); *id.* § 1251, at 802 (John Brown in 1875).

138. *See, e.g., id.* § 1259, at 810–12 (Rep. William Bynum censured in 1890 for calling a fellow member "a liar and a perjurer").

139. Butler & Wolff, *supra* note 91, at 269–71.

140. *See id.* at 47–48.

141. *See* Duties Act, ch. 5, § 35, 1 Stat. 29, 46–47 (1789) (bribing a customs officer); Crimes Act, ch. 9, § 21, 1 Stat. 112, 117 (1790) (bribing a judge); Crimes Act, ch. 65, §§ 12, 16, 24, 4 Stat. 115, 118–19, 122 (1825) (extortion by an "officer of the United States," embezzlement by an employee of the Bank of the United States, theft by an employee of the mint).

142. An Act to Prevent Frauds Upon the Treasury, ch. 81, §§ 3, 6, 10 Stat. 170, 170–71 (1853); *see* Butler & Wolff, *supra* note 91, at xxvi (noting that this was the first statute "specifically govern[ing] the behavior of members of Congress").

143. An Act to Prevent Members of Congress and Officers of Government of the United States from taking Consideration, ch. 180, 12 Stat. 577 (1862).

144. An Act Relating to Members of Congress, Heads of Departments, and Other Officers of Government, ch. 119, 13 Stat. 123 (1864).

145. *See* Butler & Wolff, *supra* note 91, at xxvi (noting that the next statute governing the conduct of members of Congress was passed in 1958).

146. *Alleged Corrupt Combinations of Members of Congress*, H.R. Rep. No. 34-243, at 3–26 (1857) (reporting the findings against, and recommending the expulsion of: William Gilbert of New York, William Welch of Connecticut, Francis Edwards of New York, and Orsamus Matteson of New York).

147. *Id.* at 24, 26.

148. *Id.* at 32.

149. *Id.* at 38a.

150. 2 Hinds, *supra* note 91, § 1275, at 835–36.

151. *Id.*

152. *See* Chafetz, *supra* note 37, at 221.

153. *See* Butler & Wolff, *supra* note 91, at 115–16.

154. 2 Hinds, *supra* note 91, §§ 1239, 1273–74, at 796, 829–33 (noting the censures of John Deweese of North Carolina (even after his resignation), B. F. Whittemore of South Carolina (also after resigning), and Roderick Butler of Tennessee).

155. *See* Robert V. Remini, *The House: The History of the House of Representatives* 219–21 (2006).

156. *Id.* at 221; *see also* Butler & Wolff, *supra* note 91, at 189–95.

157. 2 Hinds, *supra* note 91, § 1286, at 852–53.

158. *Id.* at 853–54.

159. *Id.* at 855–56.

160. *Id.* at 857. Remini mistakes the voting sequence and therefore erroneously suggests that the censure votes were tinged with partisanship, with many more voting to censure the Democrat Brooks than the Republican Ames. *See* Remini, *supra* note 155, at 221. In fact, Ames was censured by a larger margin than Brooks. *See* 2 Hinds, *supra* note 91, § 1286, at 857; Cong. Globe, 42d Cong., 3d Sess. 1832–33 (Feb. 27, 1873).

161. *See* Remini, *supra* note 155, at 221.

162. Butler & Wolff, *supra* note 91, at 189–95.

163. *Id.* at 194.

164. 2 Hinds, *supra* note 91, § 1283, at 848–49.

165. *See The Indictment of Congressman Schumaker*, Brooklyn Daily Eagle, Mar. 31, 1875, at 2.

166. 2 Hinds, *supra* note 91, § 1283, at 849–50.

167. Butler & Wolff, *supra* note 91, at 275–76.

168. Burton v. United States, 202 U.S. 344, 366–69 (1906).

169. Butler & Wolff, *supra* note 91, at 276.

170. *Roosevelt Plotted to Ruin Me—Burton*, N.Y. Times, Mar. 24, 1907, at 16.

171. *Id.*

172. *Id.*

173. *See generally* John Messing, *Public Lands, Politics, and Progressives: The Oregon Land Fraud Trials, 1903–1910*, 35 Pac. Hist. Rev. 35, 40–57 (1966); Jerry A. O'Callaghan, *Senator Mitchell and the Oregon Land Frauds, 1905*, 21 Pac. Hist. Rev. 255 (1952).

174. Reprinted in *The Verdict in the Mitchell Case*, Morning Oregonian (Portland), July 7, 1905, at 8.

175. William H. Galvani, *Recollections of J. F. Stevens and Senator Mitchell*, 44 Or. Hist. Q. 313, 320–21 (1943).

176. *Id.* at 321 (suggesting that the administration believed that Judge DeHaven "could be more easily managed by [Roosevelt's] generalissimo"); *see also* Messing, *supra* note 173, at 51 (noting that Judge Bellinger, the recently deceased District of Oregon judge, had been "reluctant to tackle the prominent citizens of Oregon").

177. Butler & Wolff, *supra* note 91, at 277.

178. *Charges Affecting the Hon. Charles H. Dietrich*, S. Rep. No. 58-2152, at i–vii (1904).

179. *Dietrich Free From Guilt*, Wash. Post, Apr. 15, 1904, at 4; *see also Dietrich Exonerated by Fellow-Senators*, N.Y. Times, Apr. 15, 1904, at 9.

180. For two insightful recent treatments of the concept of corruption, see Zephyr Teachout, *Corruption in America* (2014), and Laura S. Underkuffler, *Captured by Evil: The Idea of Corruption in Law* (2013).

181. *See, e.g.*, Alan I. Abramowitz, *Incumbency, Campaign Spending, and the Decline of Competition in U.S. House Elections*, 53 J. Pol. 34, 42 (1991); Alan I. Abramowitz, *Explaining Senate Election Outcomes*, 82 Am. Pol. Sci. Rev. 385, 392, 397 (1988); Scott J. Basinger, *Scandals and Congressional Elections in the Post-Watergate Era*, 66 Pol. Res. Q. 385 (2013); Harold D. Clarke et al., *More Time with My Money: Leaving the House and Going Home in 1992 and 1994*, 52 Pol. Res. Q. 67 (1999); Carolyn L. Funk, *The Impact of Scandal on Candidate Evaluations: An Experimental Test of the Role of Candidate Traits*, 18 Pol. Behav. 1 (1996); Gary C. Jacobson & Michael A. Dimock, *Checking Out: The Effects of Bank Overdrafts on the 1992 House Elections*, 38 Am. J. Pol. Sci. 601 (1994); Rodrigo Praino et al., *The Lingering Effect of Scandals in Congressional Elections: Incumbents, Challengers, and Voters*, 94 Soc. Sci. Q. 1045 (2013); *see also* Eric Lipton, *Ethics in Play, Voters Oust Incumbents under Inquiry*, N.Y. Times, Nov. 9, 2012, at A20 (noting how many members under ethical scrutiny lost reelection bids in 2012).

182. *See, e.g.*, Marc J. Hetherington, *Why Trust Matters: Declining Political Trust and the Demise of American Liberalism* 16, 65 (2005); Virginia A. Chanley et al., *The Origins and Consequences of Public Trust in Government: A Time Series Analysis*, 64 Pub. Op. Q. 239, 251, 254 (2000).

183. Two recent articles agree that scandals significantly harmed congressional Republicans in the 2006 midterm elections, although they disagree as to whether the relevant scandal was the Abramoff corruption scandal or the Foley sex scandal. *Contrast* Samuel J. Best et al., *Owning Valence Issues: The Impact of a "Culture of Corruption" on the 2006 Midterm Elections*, 40 Cong. & Presidency 129 (2013), *with* Michael D. Cobb & Andrew J. Taylor, *Paging Congressional Democrats: It Was the Immorality, Stupid*, 47 PS: Pol. Sci. & Pol. 351 (2014).

184. John R. Hibbing & Elizabeth Theiss-Morse, *Congress as Public Enemy: Public Attitudes Toward American Political Institutions* 70–71, 96–97 (1995); Shaun Bowler & Jeffrey A. Karp, *Politicians, Scandals, and Trust in Government*, 26 Pol. Behav. 271, 278–80 (2004).

185. Best et al., *supra* note 183.

186. Cobb & Taylor, *supra* note 183, at 354.

187. Bowler & Karp, *supra* note 184, at 284.

188. *See* Bribery Act, 2010, c. 23, § 12(8). For the treatment of bribery up until the passage of that act, see *Erskine May's Treatise on the Law, Privileges, Proceedings and Usage of Parliament* 254–56 (Malcolm Jack ed., 24th ed. 2011). *See also* Yvonne Tew, *No Longer a Privileged Few: Expense Claims, Prosecution, and Parliamentary Privilege*, 70 Cambridge L.J. 282 (2011).

189. 6 Clarence Cannon, *Cannon's Precedents of the House of Representatives of the United States* §§ 396–98, at 551–60 (1935).

190. Butler & Wolff, *supra* note 91, at 336–38.

191. *Id.* at 309–10; *Senator Burton K. Wheeler*, S. Rep. No. 68-537 (1924).

192. 6 Cannon, *supra* note 189, §§ 238, 402–03, at 405–07, 573–77.

193. *See Rowbottom Guilty in Postal Job Sales*, N.Y. Times, Apr. 16, 1931, at 52.

194. For the House, see Staff of H.R. Comm. on Standards of Official Conduct, *Historical Summary of Conduct Cases in the House of Representatives, 1798–2004*, at 11 (2004), *available at* https://ethics.house.gov/sites/ethics.house.gov/files/Historical_Chart_Final_Version%20in%20Word_0.pdf; for the Senate, see Butler & Wolff, *supra* note 91, at 452.

195. *See Indictments—A Grand Congressional Tradition Since 1798*, L.A. Times, June 5, 1994, at M2 [hereinafter *Indictments*].

196. H.R. Con. Res. 175, 85th Cong. (1958); on the impetus for the code, see Richard Allan Baker, *The History of Congressional Ethics*, in *Representation and Responsibility: Exploring Legislative Ethics* 3, 23–24 (Bruce Jennings & Daniel Callahan eds., 1985).

197. *Code of Ethics for Government Service*, S. Rep. No. 85-1812, at 1 (1958).

198. Bribery Act, Pub. L. No. 87-849, 76 Stat. 1119 (1962) (codified as amended at 18 U.S.C. §§ 201–27).

199. 110 Cong. Rec. 16939–40 (July 24, 1964) (establishing the Senate Select Committee on Standards and Conduct); 112 Cong. Rec. 27713–30 (Oct. 19, 1966) (establishing the House Select Committee on Standards and Conduct).

200. *See* Baker, *supra* note 196, at 25–26.

201. Drew Pearson & Jack Anderson, *The Case against Congress* 11 (1968).

202. *See id.* at 27–97.

203. Butler & Wolff, *supra* note 91, at 413.

204. *Id.* at 414–17.

205. *Censure for Mr. Dodd*, N.Y. Times, June 24, 1967, at 28.

206. *Beyond the Dodd Case*, N.Y. Times, June 25, 1967, at 8E.

207. *Dodd Verdict: 'Dishonor and Disrepute,'* N.Y. Times, June 25, 1967, at 2E.

208. Butler & Wolff, *supra* note 91, at 418.

209. *See* Staff of the Joint Comm. on Cong. Operations, 93d Cong., *House of Representatives Exclusion, Censure and Expulsion Cases from 1789 to 1973*, at 93–94, 104–05 (Comm. Print 1973).

210. *Id.* at 106–09.

211. *See* U.S. Const. art. I, § 5, cl. 1 (making each house "the Judge of the Elections, Returns and Qualifications of its own Members"). I have discussed the houses' power to judge the elections, returns, and qualifications of their members at length in Chafetz, *supra* note 37, at 162–92.

212. 395 U.S. 486 (1969).

213. *Id.* at 506–12.

214. *See* Lawrence Van Gelder, *New York Congressman on the Move: Charles Bernard Rangel*, N.Y. Times, Dec. 12, 1974, at 38.

215. 383 U.S. 169 (1966).

216. 408 U.S. 501, 526 (1972).

217. *Id.* at 563 (White, J., dissenting).

218. *See, e.g.*, United States v. Helstoski, 442 U.S. 477 (1979) (holding that the government could not introduce evidence of past legislative acts in a bribery case); United States v.

Rayburn House Office Bldg. Room 2113, 497 F.3d 654 (D.C. Cir. 2007) (holding that a search of a member's files in his congressional office violated the Speech or Debate Clause and required the return of privileged legislative materials); In re Grand Jury Subpoenas, 571 F.3d 1200 (D.C. Cir. 2009) (holding that statements made by a member to the Ethics Committee could not be subpoenaed).

219. See, e.g., United States v. Renzi, 769 F.3d 731 (9th Cir. 2014); United States v. Renzi, 651 F.3d 1012 (9th Cir. 2011); United States v. Jefferson, 546 F.3d 300 (4th Cir. 2008); United States v. Williams, 644 F.2d 950 (2d Cir. 1981); United States v. Murphy, 642 F.2d 699 (2d Cir. 1980); United States v. Myers, 635 F.2d 932 (2d Cir. 1980).

220. H.R. Res. 933, 92d Cong. (1972).

221. Sense of the House of Representatives with Respect to Actions by Members Convicted of Certain Crimes, H.R. Rep. No. 92-1039, at 2 (1972).

222. 121 Cong. Rec. 10339–45 (Apr. 16, 1975).

223. Julian E. Zelizer, On Capitol Hill: The Struggle to Reform Congress and Its Consequences, 1948–2000, at 200–202 (2004).

224. Id. at 204.

225. Id.; In the Matter of Representative Raymond F. Lederer, H.R. Rep. No. 97-110 (1981).

226. Butler & Wolff, supra note 91, at 434–37.

227. Martin Tolchin, Myers Is Ousted from the House in Abscam Case, N.Y. Times, Oct. 3, 1980, at A1.

228. Alison Mitchell, House Votes, with Lone Dissent from Condit, to Expel Traficant from Ranks, N.Y. Times, July 25, 2002, at A13.

229. See Indictments, supra note 195 (listing the members indicted and the outcome of their cases up to 1994).

230. Robert D. McFadden, Mario Biaggi, 97, Official Undone by Scandals, Dies, N.Y. Times, June 26, 2015, at A25.

231. See Staff of the H.R. Comm. on Standards of Official Conduct, Summary of Activities, H.R. Rep. No. 103-873, at 8 (1994).

232. Keith Schneider, Dan Rostenkowski, 82, Powerful Congressman Touched by Scandal, Is Dead, N.Y. Times, Aug. 12, 2010, at A29.

233. Randal C. Archibold, Ex-Congressman Gets 8-Year Term in Bribery Case, N.Y. Times, Mar. 4, 2006, at A1.

234. Carl Hulse, DeLay is Quitting Race and House, Officials Report, N.Y. Times, Apr. 4, 2006, at A1; Philip Shenon, Ex-Congressman Is Sentenced to 2½ Years in Abramoff Case, N.Y. Times, Jan. 20, 2007, at A8.

235. David Stout, U.S. Jury Convicts Ex-Lawmaker of Bribery, N.Y. Times, Aug. 6, 2009, at A14.

236. See Staff of the H.R. Comm. on Standards of Official Conduct, Summary of Activities, H.R. Rep. No. 110-938, at 17–18 (2009).

237. Zelizer, supra note 223, at 243.

238. See Remini, supra note 155, at 479–82; Zelizer, supra note 223, at 243–44; Clarke et al., supra note 181, at 80–82; Jacobson & Dimock, supra note 181, at 605–19.

239. H.R. Res. 895, 110th Cong. § 1 (2007).

240. Jacob R. Straus, House Office of Congressional Ethics: History, Authority, and Procedures, CRS Report for Cong. No. R40760, at 12, 14 (2015).

241. *Id.* at 18–20.
242. *Id.* at 21.
243. *See, e.g.*, Editorial, *An Ethics Watchdog Survives*, Wash. Post, Dec. 30, 2010, at A14; Eric Lipton, *House Ethics Office Gains, Dismissals Aside*, N.Y. Times, Mar. 23, 2010, at A18; Craig Holman & Victoria Hall-Palerm, Pub. Citizen, *The Case for Independent Ethics Agencies: The Office of Congressional Ethics Six Years Later, and a History of Failed Senate Accountability* (2014).
244. Holman & Hall-Palerm, *supra* note 243, at 7.
245. Shortly before the OCE came into being, I proposed a similar body. While the OCE does indeed incorporate many of the features I recommended, in cases where the two diverge, I continue to believe that the institutional structure I proposed was preferable. *See* Josh Chafetz, *Cleaning House: Congressional Commissioners for Standards*, 117 Yale L.J. 165 (2007); *see also* Josh Chafetz, *Politician, Police Thyself*, N.Y. Times, Dec. 2, 2006, at A15.
246. *See* Holman & Hall-Palerm, *supra* note 243, at 9–14.
247. *See id.* at 14.
248. Straus, *supra* note 240, at 20.
249. Indeed, I have suggested this course of action in the case of a member whose conduct was slimy, but perhaps not so slimy as to be disqualifying. *See* Josh Chafetz, *Run, Anthony, Run*, Slate, June 15, 2011, http://www.slate.com/articles/news_and_politics/politics/2011/06/run_anthony_run.html.
250. Josh Chafetz, *Leaving the House: The Constitutional Status of Resignation from the House of Representatives*, 58 Duke L.J. 177 (2008).
251. 100 Cong. Rec. 12729 (July 30, 1954).
252. *Report of the Select Committee to Study Censure Charges*, S. Rep. No. 83-2508, at 2 (1954) [hereinafter *Report*].
253. *See id.* at 5–31; for a description of the earlier investigation, see Butler & Wolff, *supra* note 91, at 394–98.
254. *See Report*, *supra* note 252, at 39–45.
255. *See id.* at 45–46.
256. *See* Neil MacNeil & Richard A. Baker, *The American Senate: An Insider's History* 257 (2013); Thomas C. Reeves, *The Life and Times of Joe McCarthy* 654 (1982).
257. *See Report*, *supra* note 252, at 47–61, 67–68.
258. Butler & Wolff, *supra* note 91, at 406.
259. Editorial, *Censure*, N.Y. Times, Dec. 3, 1954, at 26.
260. Editorial, *Judgment of the Senate*, Wash. Post, Dec. 3, 1954, at 20.
261. Alan Barth, *Government by Investigation* 210 (1955).
262. *Id.* at 216.
263. MacNeil & Baker, *supra* note 256, at 257; Reeves, *supra* note 256, at 671.
264. H.R. Res. 744, 111th Cong. (2009).
265. Paul Kane, *House Votes to Rebuke Wilson for Interruption*, Wash. Post, Sept. 16, 2009, at A8; *see also* Carl Hulse, *House Formally Rebukes Wilson for Shouting 'You Lie'*, N.Y. Times, Sept. 16, 2009, at A14 ("mainly party line").
266. *See* Assoc. Press, *No Lie, Wilson Is Now a GOP Star*, L.A. Times, Sept. 26, 2009, at 16.

Chapter 8. Cameral Rules

1. U.S. Const. art. I, § 5, cl. 2.
2. 3 Rot. Parl. 458 (1401).
3. 1 Josef Redlich, *The Procedure of the House of Commons: A Study of Its History and Present Form* 10 (A. Ernest Steinthal trans., 1908); *see also* 3 *id.* at 148–49.
4. *See* Charles Howard McIlwain, *The High Court of Parliament and Its Supremacy* 205–09 (1962); 1 Redlich, *supra* note 3, at 8–9.
5. McIlwain, *supra* note 4, at 209; 1 Redlich, *supra* note 3, at 16–20.
6. 1 Redlich, *supra* note 3, at 16.
7. *Id.* at 26, 29–33.
8. 2 *id.* at 205–10.
9. 1 *id.* at 40–42; *see also* 2 *id.* at 157–60.
10. 2 John Hatsell, *Precedents of Proceedings in the House of Commons* 217 (London, Hansard rev. ed. 1818).
11. *Id.*; *see also* James Alexander Manning, *The Lives of the Speakers of the House of Commons* 260–61 (London, George Willis 1851).
12. *See* 1 Redlich, *supra* note 3, at 41.
13. *See* 1 Edward Porritt, *The Unreformed House of Commons: Parliamentary Representation before 1832*, at 531–32 (1903); Conrad Russell, *Parliaments and English Politics, 1621–1629*, at 38 (1979).
14. For an earlier suggestion of this idea, see Wallace Notestein, *The Winning of the Initiative by the House of Commons* 26, 32, 37 (1926). For a more recent (and nuanced) suggestion, see Russell, *supra* note 13, at 38. For a more skeptical take, see Sheila Lambert, *Procedure in the House of Commons in the Early Stuart Period*, 95 Eng. Hist. Rev. 753, 765–67 (1980).
15. *See* Russell, *supra* note 13, at 38–39 (noting that this rationale carried more weight "during the highly partisan Speakership of Sir Edward Phelips" in 1604–1611 than it did in some subsequent Speakerships).
16. Notestein, *supra* note 14, at 37.
17. *See id.* at 39–41; 1 Porritt, *supra* note 13, at 531–32.
18. *See* Notestein, *supra* note 14, at 38.
19. *See* Mary Patterson Clarke, *Parliamentary Privilege in the American Colonies* 174 (1943) ("It is doubtful if any other years can show so large a number of rules being definitely adopted and written as 1604.").
20. 1 H.C. Jour. 152, 154 (Mar. 26, 1604).
21. *See, e.g.,* 1 H.C. Jour. 172 (Apr. 14, 1604) (allowing the Speaker to interrupt any member speaking "impertinently, or besides the Question in Hand"); *id.* at 177 (Apr. 19, 1604) (requiring the Speaker to suppress ad hominem remarks); *id.* at 244 (June 21, 1604) (allowing the Speaker to be heard "without Interruption").
22. *Id.* at 175 (Apr. 16, 1604); *see also, e.g., id.* at 162 (Apr. 2, 1604) (preventing the reraising of a question already decided); *id.* at 214 (May 19, 1604) ("If any Man speak not to the Matter in Question, the Speaker is to moderate."); *id.* at 245 (June 23, 1604) (forbidding members to speak twice on the same bill, even when the previous speech had occurred on a previous day).

23. *See, e.g., id.* at 239–40 (June 15, 1604) (requiring questions to be phrased in the affirmative for "the Adding of any new Thing" and in the negative for "the Continuing of an old," and requiring that, on a division, "the Yea must sit still, and the Noe go forth").

24. *See* 1 Redlich, *supra* note 3, at 43 ("When, at the beginning of the reign of James I, the opposition between Crown and Parliament became acute and the era of severe parliamentary struggle began, it became all the more necessary to define the mode of procedure, to draw up new rules, and to increase the stringency of the regulations that had grown up by custom."). On the use of procedural tools as foundational elements of oppositional politics, see generally Josh Chafetz, *"In the Time of a Woman, Which Sex Was Not Capable of Mature Deliberation": Late Tudor Parliamentary Relations and Their Early Stuart Discontents*, 25 Yale J.L. & Human. 181 (2013).

25. 1 H.C. Jour. 187 (Apr. 27, 1604).

26. *See* 5 Andrew Thrush & John P. Ferris, *The House of Commons, 1604–1629*, at 675 (2010).

27. 1 H.C. Jour. 212 (May 17, 1604).

28. *Id.* at 232 (June 4, 1604).

29. 1 Redlich, *supra* note 3, at 44.

30. 2 H.C. Jour. 7 (Apr. 20, 1640).

31. 1 John Rushworth, *Historical Collections. The Third Part; In Two Volumes. Containing the Principal Matters Which Happened from the Meeting of the Parliament, November the 3d. 1640. To the End of the Year 1644*, at 478 (London, Chiswell & Cockerill 1692).

32. *See* Manning, *supra* note 11, at 320–22.

33. 2 H.C. Jour. 220 (July 22, 1641).

34. *Id.* at 500–501 (Mar. 28, 1642).

35. *See* Josh Chafetz, *Democracy's Privileged Few: Legislative Privilege and Democratic Norms in the British and American Constitutions* 197–98, 201–02 (2007).

36. Manning, *supra* note 11, at 362.

37. *See* 4 Anchitell Grey, *Debates of the House of Commons* 390 (London, Henry, Cave & Emonson 1763).

38. 5 *id.* at 5.

39. *See id.* at 124 (Henry Powle describing the various forms by which the House can be adjourned).

40. *Id.* at 11.

41. *Id.* at 126.

42. *Id.* at 12; *see also id.* at 139 (John Maynard: "When the King opens a Parliament, what does the Speaker first crave? Liberty of Speech.").

43. *Id.* at 143.

44. *Id.* at 144.

45. 9 H.C. Jour. 560 (Dec. 19, 1678).

46. *See* 3 Basil Duke Henning, *The House of Commons, 1660–1690*, at 416 (1983).

47. *Id.*; 2 Redlich, *supra* note 3, at 162–63.

48. On Onslow, see 2 Redlich, *supra* note 3, at 163–64; on the modern conception of the Speakership, see Malcolm Jack, *Erskine May's Treatise on the Law, Privileges, Proceedings and Usage of Parliament* 61 (24th ed. 2011).

49. 2 Hatsell, *supra* note 10, at 237.

50. *See* Warren M. Billings, *A Little Parliament: The Virginia General Assembly in the Seventeenth Century* 35 (2004).

51. *Id.*

52. *Id.* at 36.

53. *Id.*

54. *Id.*

55. *See, e.g.*, Jack P. Greene, *The Quest for Power: The Lower Houses of Assembly in the Southern Royal Colonies, 1689–1776*, at 216 (1963); Clarke, *supra* note 19, at 179.

56. *See* 2 Redlich, *supra* note 3, at 75–76; Jack, *supra* note 48, at 319–20.

57. *See* Clarke, *supra* note 19, at 175.

58. *See* Greene, *supra* note 55, at 217–18.

59. *Id.* at 217–19.

60. *Id.* at 206.

61. Evarts Boutell Greene, *The Provincial Governor in the English Colonies of North America* 150 (1966).

62. *Id.* at 150–51.

63. Greene, *supra* note 55, at 433–35.

64. John Joachim Zubly, *Calm and Respectful Thoughts on the Negative of the Crown on a Speaker Chosen and Presented by the Representatives of the People* 2–3 ([Savannah, J. Johnston] 1772).

65. *Id.* at 21.

66. Greene, *supra* note 55, at 435–36.

67. Leonard Woods Labaree, *Royal Government in America* 194–99 (1958).

68. Greene, *supra* note 55, at 408–09, 451–52.

69. Declaration of Independence, paras. 6–8 (1776).

70. Articles of Confederation, art. 9, § 7.

71. *Id.* § 5.

72. Del. Const. of 1776, art. 5; Ga. Const. of 1777, art. 7; Md. Const. of 1776, arts. 8, 20, 24; Mass. Const. of 1780, pt. 2, ch. 1, § 2, art. 7; *id.* § 3, art. 10; N.H. Const. of 1784, pt. 2, Senate, para. 12; *id.* House of Reps., para. 12; N.J. Const. of 1776, art. 5; N.Y. Const. of 1777, art. 9; N.C. Const. of 1776, art. 10; Penn. Const. of 1776, Frame of Gov't, § 9; S.C. Const. of 1776, art. 9; S.C. Const. of 1778, art. 18; Vt. Const. of 1777, ch. 2, § 8; Vt. Const. of 1786, ch. 2, § 9; Va. Const. of 1776, para. 4.

73. For rules of proceedings clauses, see Del. Const. of 1776, art. 5; Ga. Const. of 1777, art. 7; Md. Const. of 1776, art. 24; Mass. Const. of 1780, pt. 2, ch. 1, § 2, art. 7; *id.* § 3, art. 10; N.H. Const. of 1784, pt. 2, Senate, para. 12; *id.* House of Reps., para. 12; Va. Const. of 1776, para. 4. For quorum provisions, see Ga. Const. of 1777, art. 2; Md. Const. of 1776, arts. 8, 20; Mass. Const. of 1780, pt. 2, ch. 1, § 2, art. 9; *id.* § 3, art. 9; N.H. Const. of 1784, pt. 2, Senate, para. 12; *id.* House of Reps., para. 10; N.J. Const. of 1776, art. 3; N.Y. Const. of 1777, art. 9; Penn. Const. of 1776, Frame of Gov't, § 10; S.C. Const. of 1776, art. 12; S.C. Const. of 1778, arts. 12, 14; Vt. Const. of 1777, ch. 2, § 9; Vt. Const. of 1786, ch. 2, § 9.

74. Del. Const. of 1776, art. 10; S.C. Const. of 1776, art. 8; S.C. Const. of 1778, art. 17; Va. Const. of 1776, para. 7.

75. Ga. Const. of 1777, art. 7; N.H. Const. of 1776, para. 8; N.C. Const. of 1776, art. 10.

76. N.J. Const. of 1776, art. 5; Penn. Const. of 1776, Frame of Gov't, § 9; Vt. Const. of 1777, ch. 2, § 8; Vt. Const. of 1786, ch. 2, § 9.

77. N.Y. Const. of 1777, art. 18.

78. Md. Const. of 1776, art. 29; Mass. Const. of 1780, pt. 2, ch. 2, § 1, art. 6; N.H. Const. of 1784, pt. 2, President, para. 6.

79. Md. Const. of 1776, Dec. of Rts., art. 9; Mass. Const. of 1780, pt. 2, ch. 2, § 1, art. 5; N.H. Const. of 1784, pt. 2, President, para. 6.

80. U.S. Const. art. I, § 2, cl. 5.

81. *Id.* § 3, cl. 4.

82. 2 *The Records of the Federal Convention of 1787*, at 536–37 (Max Farrand ed., rev. ed. 1966) [hereinafter *Farrand's Records*]. For the state conventions, see, e.g., 3 *The Debates in the Several State Conventions on the Adoption of the Federal Constitution* 489–90 (Jonathan Elliot ed., 2d ed. 1907) (James Monroe in the Virginia convention) [hereinafter *Elliot's Debates*]; 4 *id.* at 26 (David Caldwell in the North Carolina convention).

83. Luther Martin, *The Genuine Information* (1788), in 2 *The Complete Anti-Federalist* 19, 67 (Herbert J. Storing ed., 1981).

84. 2 *Farrand's Records, supra* note 82, at 537.

85. 4 *Elliot's Debates, supra* note 82, at 43.

86. *The Federalist No. 68*, at 415 (Alexander Hamilton) (Clinton Rossiter ed., 1961); 2 Joseph Story, *Commentaries on the Constitution of the United States* §§ 735–36, at 209–12 (Boston, Hilliard, Gray 1833).

87. Akhil Reed Amar, *America's Constitution: A Biography* 168 (2005).

88. U.S. Const. art. I, § 3, cl. 5.

89. *Id.* § 4, cl. 2; *id.* amend. XX, § 2.

90. *Id.* art. I, § 5, cl. 4.

91. *Id.* art. II, § 3.

92. *The Federalist No. 77, supra* note 86, at 463 (Alexander Hamilton).

93. 2 Story, *supra* note 86, §§ 841–42, at 304–05.

94. U.S. Const. art. I, § 5, cl. 1–2.

95. 2 Story, *supra* note 86, § 835, at 298.

96. House Comm. on House Admin., *History of the United States House of Representatives, 1789–1994*, H.R. Doc. No. 103-324, at 11 (1994) [hereinafter *House History*]; 1 Robert C. Byrd, *The Senate, 1789–1989: Addresses on the History of the United States Senate*, S. Doc. No. 100-20, at 6 (1988).

97. *House History, supra* note 96, at 13.

98. 1 Byrd, *supra* note 96, at 6–7.

99. *House History, supra* note 96, at 13; 2 Byrd, *supra* note 96, at 45–48.

100. 1 H.R. Jour. 9 (Apr. 7, 1789); 1 Sen. Jour. 13 (Apr. 16, 1789).

101. Thomas Jefferson, *A Manual of Parliamentary Practice* § 17, at 36 (Cosimo Classics 2007) (1801).

102. *The Diary of William Maclay and Other Notes on Senate Debates* 128–30 (Aug. 22, 1789) (Kenneth R. Bowling & Helen E. Veit eds., 1988) [hereinafter *Maclay's Diary*].

103. The only source for the claim is a secondhand report in John Quincy Adams's memoirs. For the debate as to whether Washington really made the statement, see Curtis A.

Bradley & Martin S. Flaherty, *Executive Power Essentialism and Foreign Affairs*, 102 Mich. L. Rev. 545, 634 & n.434 (2004).

104. *Maclay's Diary, supra* note 102, at 131–32 (Aug. 24, 1789).

105. Bradley & Flaherty, *supra* note 103, at 634.

106. *See* 1 Annals of Cong. 15 (editor's note); *see also* Elaine K. Swift, *The Making of an American Senate: Reconstitutive Change in Congress, 1787–1841*, at 58 (1996).

107. U.S. Const. art. I, § 5, cl. 3.

108. *See* 2 Byrd, *supra* note 96, at 311–14.

109. *See* 1 *id.* at 10; David P. Currie, *The Constitution in Congress: The Federalist Period, 1789–1801*, at 10 (1997); Swift, *supra* note 106, at 58–59.

110. Adrian Vermeule, *The Constitutional Law of Congressional Procedure*, 71 U. Chi. L. Rev. 361, 415 (2004); *see also* Swift, *supra* note 106, at 63–64.

111. *See* Norman K. Risjord, *Partisanship and Power: House Committees and the Powers of the Speaker, 1789–1801*, 49 Wm. & Mary Q. 628, 631–32 (1992).

112. 1 H.R. Jour. 9–10 (Apr. 7, 1789); 1 Sen. Jour. 13 (Apr. 16, 1789).

113. 1 H.R. Jour. 140 (Jan. 13, 1790); *see also id.* at 434 (Oct. 24, 1791); *House History, supra* note 96, at 155 (noting that, from 1790 to 1910, the Speaker "generally appointed both the members and the chairmen of all select and standing committees").

114. *Cf.* Vermeule, *supra* note 110, at 401 (noting that the Senate "developed various means of self-defense" to protect itself against executive domination).

115. 1 H.R. Jour. 10–11 (Apr. 7, 1789); *accord* De Alva Stanwood Alexander, *History and Procedure of the House of Representatives* 256 (1916) (suggesting that the purpose of the Committee of the Whole was to allow for "less formal procedure, by means of which the entire membership is enabled to participate in the consideration of a bill, unhampered by roll-calls or the intervention of motions to adjourn, to refer, to postpone, for the previous question, and the like").

116. Ralph Volney Harlow, *The History of Legislative Methods in the Period before 1825*, at 127–28 (1917); *House History, supra* note 96, at 15, 17, 143; Thomas W. Skladony, *The House Goes to Work: Select and Standing Committees in the U.S. House of Representatives, 1789–1828*, 12 Cong. & Presidency 165, 170 (1985).

117. *House History, supra* note 96, at 144.

118. Skladony, *supra* note 116, at 170.

119. Harlow, *supra* note 116, at 134–35.

120. *Id.* at 140–44; Risjord, *supra* note 111, at 638.

121. Harlow, *supra* note 116, at 157.

122. Skladony, *supra* note 116, at 170–71; *see also* Risjord, *supra* note 111, at 639.

123. Harlow, *supra* note 116, at 176.

124. *See id.* at 192–93; *see also* Risjord, *supra* note 111, at 629–30, 650–51.

125. On the War Hawks generally, see Gordon S. Wood, *Empire of Liberty: A History of the Early Republic, 1789–1815*, at 659–61 (2009). On Clay, see *House History, supra* note 96, at 88, 100–102.

126. *See* Harlow, *supra* note 116, at 207–08; *House History, supra* note 96, at 101; Nelson W. Polsby, *The Institutionalization of the U.S. House of Representatives*, 62 Am. Pol. Sci. Rev. 144, 155–56 (1968). For evidence of earlier Speakers' using committee assignments in service of the president's agenda, see Risjord, *supra* note 111, at 648–49.

127. Polsby, *supra* note 126, at 156.

128. Harlow, *supra* note 116, at 208.

129. Skladony, *supra* note 116, at 168 tbl.2.

130. Harlow, *supra* note 116, at 222, 225–26.

131. *Id.* at 250.

132. *See* 2 Byrd, *supra* note 96, at 216.

133. *See* Gerald Gamm & Kenneth Shepsle, *Emergence of Legislative Institutions: Standing Committees in the House and Senate, 1810–1825*, 14 Legis. Stud. Q. 39, 53–57 (1989); Walter Kravitz, *Evolution of the Senate's Committee System*, 411 Annals Am. Acad. Pol. & Soc. Sci. 27, 28–29 (1974).

134. Kravitz, *supra* note 133, at 29–30.

135. *Id.* at 31.

136. *Id.*

137. *Id.* at 32; 2 Byrd, *supra* note 96, at 219.

138. Kravitz, *supra* note 133, at 33; 2 Byrd, *supra* note 96, at 226.

139. *House History*, *supra* note 96, at 95.

140. *Id.* at 155.

141. *See id.* at 164–65.

142. *Id.* at 106.

143. *Id.*

144. *See* 4 Asher C. Hinds, *Hinds' Precedents of the House of Representatives of the United States* § 4621, at 951–52, 952 n.5 (1907).

145. *Id.* § 3160, at 194–95.

146. *See* Josh Chafetz, *The Unconstitutionality of the Filibuster*, 43 Conn. L. Rev. 1003, 1025 (2011); *House History*, *supra* note 96, at 104–05, 173–75.

147. 15 Cong. Rec. 309 (Jan. 9, 1884).

148. 4 Hinds, *supra* note 144, § 3152, at 191–92; *House History*, *supra* note 96, at 186.

149. M. P. Follett, *The Speaker of the House of Representatives* 307 (1896).

150. *House History*, *supra* note 96, at 181–82.

151. *See generally* Richard M. Valelly, *The Reed Rules and Republican Party Building: A New Look*, 23 Stud. Am. Pol. Dev. 115 (2009).

152. 21 Cong. Rec. 949–60 (Jan. 29, 1890).

153. *Id.* at 998–1000 (Jan. 31, 1890).

154. *House History*, *supra* note 96, at 174, 181–82.

155. Eric Schickler, *Disjointed Pluralism: Institutional Innovation and the Development of the U.S. Congress* 32 (2001).

156. *Id.* at 43–46.

157. *Id.* at 46–50.

158. *House History*, *supra* note 96, at 106–07; Robert V. Remini, *The House: The History of the House of Representatives* 267–72 (2006); Schickler, *supra* note 155, at 67–71.

159. *A Glimpse into Speaker Cannon's Famous Red Room*, N.Y. Times Mag., Dec. 13, 1908, at 8.

160. *Id.*

161. Remini, *supra* note 158, at 272.

162. *Id.* at 273–75; 45 Cong. Rec. 3425–36 (Mar. 19, 1910).

163. H.R. Res. 502, 61st Cong. (1910).

164. 45 Cong. Rec. 3437 (Mar. 19, 1910).

165. *Id.*

166. *Id.* at 3438–39.

167. *House History*, *supra* note 96, at 155–56.

168. *Id.* at 156.

169. *Id.* at 156–57.

170. Polsby, *supra* note 126, at 160–61; Nelson W. Polsby, Miriam Gallaher & Barry Spencer Rundquist, *The Growth of the Seniority System in the U.S. House of Representatives*, 63 Am. Pol. Sci. Rev. 787 (1969).

171. *See* Schickler, *supra* note 155, at 82–83, 163–68.

172. Chafetz, *supra* note 146, at 1027.

173. *See generally* Polsby, *supra* note 126.

174. The tie between partisan infrastructure and cameral infrastructure is analyzed in detail in Jeffery A. Jenkins & Charles Stewart III, *Fighting for the Speakership: The House and the Rise of Party Government* (2013).

175. 2 Byrd, *supra* note 96, at 235.

176. *House History*, *supra* note 96, at 164.

177. Appropriations Act, ch. 343, 23 Stat. 388, 390 (1885) (Senate); H.R.J. Res. 21, 52d Cong., 27 Stat. 757 (1893) (House).

178. On the House buildings, see Remini, *supra* note 158, at 261–62, 571 n.44. On the Senate buildings, see Neil MacNeil & Richard A. Baker, *The American Senate: An Insider's History* 6–7 (2013).

179. *See Organization of Congress: Hearing Before the Joint Comm. on the Org. of Cong.*, 79th Cong. 165 (1945) [hereinafter *Organization Hearing*]. The proliferation in the number of committees came largely in the form of special committees. *See* 4 Byrd, *supra* note 96, at 518 tbl.5-1.

180. *Organization Hearing*, *supra* note 179, at 168. For a detailed breakdown of those borrowings, see *id.* at 170–79 tbl.

181. *Id.* at 166–67.

182. Pub. L. No. 79-601, 60 Stat. 812 (1946); *see also* Roger H. Davidson, *The Legislative Reorganization Act of 1946*, 15 Legis. Stud. Q. 357, 360 (1990) ("As big government became a permanent fixture . . . legislators became restive over their inability to manage their workload and review the executive's implementation of laws."); Schickler, *supra* note 155, at 140–50 (noting that concerns about congressional power, particularly vis-à-vis the executive, largely motivated the act's supporters).

183. Davidson, *supra* note 182, at 365.

184. *Id.* at 367–68. To get a sense of the increased number of staffers in the aftermath of the 1946 act, see 4 Byrd, *supra* note 96, at 623–26 tbl.5-10.

185. 2 Byrd, *supra* note 96, at 254.

186. *Id.* at 255.

187. *See Francis O. Wilcox, 76; Ex-State Dept. Official*, N.Y. Times, Feb. 23, 1985, at 10.

188. Patrick P. Sandman, Saved by the 'Smoking Gun': The House Judiciary Committee's Impeachment Inquiry of Richard Nixon 11 (2012) (unpublished M.St. thesis, University of Oxford).

189. *Id.* at 12–14.
190. *See* Schickler, *supra* note 155, at 155–63.
191. Davidson, *supra* note 182, at 368.
192. *See id.* at 366; Kravitz, *supra* note 133, at 35–36.
193. Davidson, *supra* note 182, at 368.
194. *Id.* at 369–70.
195. *See* Polsby, *supra* note 126, at 153.
196. Eric Schickler, *The Development of the Congressional Committee System*, in *The Oxford Handbook of the American Congress* 712, 728 (Eric Schickler & Frances E. Lee eds., 2011).
197. Pub. L. No. 91-510, 84 Stat. 1140 (1970); Walter Kravitz, *The Legislative Reorganization Act of 1970*, 15 Legis. Stud. Q. 375, 376–77 (1990); Schickler, *supra* note 155, at 213–17.
198. Kravitz, *supra* note 197, at 378; 2 Byrd, *supra* note 96, at 259.
199. Kravitz, *supra* note 197, at 378–79, 383, 388; Schickler, *supra* note 155, at 217–20.
200. Kravitz, *supra* note 197, at 381–82, 383, 386, 387, 393–94, 395–96.
201. *See* Schickler, *supra* note 155, at 214 (noting that the desire to enhance congressional capacity was a major driver of the 1970 act).
202. Kravitz, *supra* note 197, at 390; Remini, *supra* note 158, at 461; MacNeil & Baker, *supra* note 178, at 297; Schickler, *supra* note 155, at 209–12, 244.
203. Kravitz, *supra* note 197, at 389–90.
204. *House History*, *supra* note 96, at 190; Kravitz, *supra* note 197, at 391–92; Schickler, *supra* note 155, at 228–30, 234–38; Schickler, *supra* note 196, at 733.
205. *See* Matthew N. Green, *The Speaker of the House: A Study of Leadership* 116–18 (2010); Schickler, *supra* note 155, at 238–42. *See also* Sam Tanenhaus, *The Power of Congress*, New Yorker, Jan. 19, 2015, at 69, 74 ("Under [Speaker Newt] Gingrich, the House of Representatives became, at last, the American House of Commons. 'The Republican Party in the House is the most disciplined political party we have ever seen in the history of America,' [Democratic representative] Barney Frank said at the time.").
206. *See* Sarah A. Binder & Frances E. Lee, *Making Deals in Congress*, in Am. Pol. Sci. Ass'n, *Negotiating Agreement in Politics* 54, 63–64 (Jane Mansbridge & Cathie Jo Martin eds., 2013).
207. *See* Joel D. Aberbach, *Keeping a Watchful Eye: The Politics of Congressional Oversight* 19–47 (1990); Schickler, *supra* note 196, at 731.
208. *See* Douglas Kriner & Liam Schwartz, *Divided Government and Congressional Investigations*, 33 Legis. Stud. Q. 295 (2008).
209. *See* Chafetz, *supra* note 146, at 1026–28.
210. For evidence of and explanations for the routinization of the filibuster, see *id.* at 1008–11. Recent years have seen several important books on the filibuster and Senate obstructionism: Gregory Koger, *Filibustering: A Political History of Obstruction in the House and Senate* (2010); Steven S. Smith, *The Senate Syndrome: The Evolution of Procedural Warfare in the Modern U.S. Senate* (2014); Gregory J. Wawro & Eric Schickler, *Filibuster: Obstruction and Lawmaking in the U.S. Senate* (2006).
211. For just a few especially prominent examples, see Thomas E. Mann & Norman J. Ornstein, *It's Even Worse Than It Looks* 98–100, 166–72, 197 (2012); Joyce Appleby, *Minority Rule in the Senate*, L.A. Times, Dec. 1, 2013, at A34; Thomas Geoghegan, *Mr.*

Smith Rewrites the Constitution, N.Y. Times, Jan. 11, 2010, at A17; Tom Harkin, Letter, *Filibusters, A Threat to Compromise*, Wash. Post, Sept. 30, 2012, at A20; Jeff Merkley, *Why 'Supermajority' No Longer Works in the Senate*, Wash. Post, Nov. 6, 2011, at A21; George Packer, *The Empty Chamber*, New Yorker, Aug. 9, 2010, at 38.

212. American Clean Energy and Security Act of 2009, H.R. 2454, 111th Cong. §§ 721–28 (2009).

213. Ben Geman, *Senate Turns Down Resolution to Block EPA Gas Regulations*, The Hill, June 11, 2010, at 3 (first alteration in original).

214. *Id.* (alteration in original).

215. Massachusetts v. EPA, 549 U.S. 497, 532–35 (2007).

216. *See* Juliet Eilperin, *White House Tried to Silence EPA Proposal on Car Emissions*, Wash. Post, June 26, 2008, at A2 (describing the Bush administration's stifling of greenhouse gas regulation in the wake of *Massachusetts v. EPA*).

217. Endangerment and Cause or Contribute Findings for Greenhouse Gases Under Section 202(a) of the Clean Air Act, 74 Fed. Reg. 66,496 (Dec. 15, 2009).

218. *See* Louis Peck, *A Veteran of the Climate Wars Reflects on U.S. Failure to Act*, Yale Env't 360, Jan. 4, 2011, http://e360.yale.edu/feature/a_veteran_of_the_climate_wars_reflects_on_us_failure_to_act/2356 (Representative Rick Boucher explaining that he supported the bill because "if Congress did not act, EPA would regulate").

219. *See, e.g.*, Bradford Plumer, *Does Obama Need Congress to Act on Climate Change?*, New Republic Online, Dec. 4, 2008, http://www.tnr.com/blog/the-vine/does-obama-need-congress-act-climate-change ("Republicans may not be able to stymie carbon regulations for long, since the choice isn't between something or nothing; it's between Congress capping emissions or Obama doing it for them. As the saying goes, better to sit at the table than find yourself on the menu.").

220. Light-Duty Vehicle Greenhouse Gas Emission Standards and Corporate Average Fuel Economy Standards, 75 Fed. Reg. 25,324 (May 7, 2010) (codified at 40 C.F.R. pts. 85, 86, 600 (2011)).

221. *See* Geman, *supra* note 213, at 3. Of course, even had the bill passed the Senate and the House, it would almost certainly have prompted a presidential veto.

222. *Id.*

223. Clean Power Plan for Existing Power Plants, 80 Fed. Reg. 64,661 (Oct. 23, 2015) (to be codified in scattered parts of 40 C.F.R.); *see also* Joby Warrick, *States Sue to Block EPA's Pollution Rule*, Wash. Post, Oct. 24, 2015, at A2.

224. *See* Colleen Leahy, *Poll: Most Americans Support Clean Power Plan*, Morning Consult, Aug. 13, 2015, http://morningconsult.com/2015/08/poll-most-americans-support-clean-power-plan/ (finding that 63 percent of registered voters support the Clean Power Plan); CNN & Opinion Research Corp., *CNN Opinion Research Poll*, Apr. 9–10, 2011, at 6, http:// i2.cdn.turner.com/cnn/2011/images/04/11/rel6a.pdf (finding that, in April 2011, 71 percent of respondents opposed stripping the EPA of the authority to regulate greenhouse gases); *Washington Post–ABC News Poll*, Wash. Post, June 8, 2010, http://www.washingtonpost.com/wp-srv/politics/polls/postpoll_ 060810.html (finding between 65 percent and 75 percent support for federal government regulation of greenhouse gases in four polls conducted between April 2009 and June 2010).

225. *See, e.g.*, Michigan v. EPA, 135 S. Ct. 2699 (2015).

226. *See, e.g.*, Utility Air Regulatory Group v. EPA, 134 S. Ct. 2427 (2014); EPA v. EME Homer City Generation, 134 S. Ct. 1584 (2014).
227. *See, e.g.*, David E. Pozen, *Self-Help and the Separation of Powers*, 124 Yale L.J. 2 (2014); Cass R. Sunstein, *Partyism*, 2015 U. Chi. Legal F. 1, 21–24.
228. *See* Robert Pear, *President Nominates Professor to Health Job*, N.Y. Times, Apr. 20, 2010, at A13.
229. *See* Robert Pear, *Obama to Bypass Senate to Name Health Official*, N.Y. Times, July 7, 2010, at A11.
230. Jim Kuhnhenn, *Obama Picks Consumer Advocate Warren, Opposed by Big Bankers, Will Build Financial Watchdog Agency*, Houston Chron., Sept. 18, 2010, at A3.
231. Paul Wiseman, *Warren Gets a Lead Role in Consumer Protection: Harvard Professor to Help Set Up Watchdog Agency*, USA Today, Sept. 16, 2010, at 1B.
232. *See* Joseph Williams, *Liberals Push Elizabeth Warren Nomination*, Politico, May 28, 2011, http:// www.politico.com/news/stories/0511/55864.html ("Liberal boosters for consumer advocate Elizabeth Warren are redoubling their pressure on President Barack Obama to pick her to lead a new financial watchdog agency—despite Republicans' all-out attempts to . . . block Obama from giving her the job over the Memorial Day recess.").
233. *See* Binyamin Appelbaum, *Former Ohio Attorney General to Head New Consumer Agency*, N.Y. Times, July 18, 2011, at B1. It is worth noting that President Obama's decision not to recess appoint Warren seems to have had significantly more to do with the fact that "she never won the full support of the president or his senior advisors" than it did with any concern about the recess appointment mechanism. *Id.*
234. Helene Cooper & Jennifer Steinhauer, *Bucking Senate, Obama Appoints Consumer Chief*, N.Y. Times, Jan. 5, 2012, at A1.
235. *Id.* For the OLC memo, see Lawfulness of Recess Appointments During a Recess of the Senate Notwithstanding Periodic Pro Forma Sessions, 36 Op. O.L.C. (2012), *available at* 2012 WL 168645.
236. Remarks at Shaker Heights High School in Shaker Heights, Ohio, 2012 Daily Comp. Pres. Doc. 2–3 (Jan. 4, 2012), available at http://www.gpo.gov/fdsys/pkg/DCPD-201200003/pdf/DCPD-201200003.pdf.
237. Laurence H. Tribe, *Games and Gimmicks in the Senate*, N.Y. Times, Jan. 6, 2012, at A25.
238. *See* Matthew C. Stephenson, *Can the President Appoint Principal Executive Officers without a Senate Confirmation Vote?*, 122 Yale L.J. 940 (2013).
239. 159 Cong. Rec. S8414–28 (daily ed. Nov. 21, 2013); Paul Kane, *Senate Eliminates Filibusters on Most Nominees*, Wash. Post, Nov. 22, 2013, at A1.
240. For one version of this argument, see generally Chafetz, *supra* note 146.
241. For an account of precisely which sorts of nominees the Democratic Senate appeared to prioritize, see Anne Joseph O'Connell, *Shortening Agency and Judicial Vacancies through Filibuster Reform? An Examination of Confirmation Rates and Delays from 1981 to 2014*, 64 Duke L.J. 1645, 1676–79 (2015).
242. *See id.*
243. *See* Michael A. Memoli, *Obama Nominee Blocked in Senate*, L.A. Times, Mar. 6, 2014, at A6.
244. *See id.*

245. No official list of recess appointments is maintained. As of May 2015, the Congressional Research Service tallied that Obama had made thirty-two recess appointments, the last occurring in January 2012. Henry B. Hogue, *Recess Appointments Made by President Barack Obama*, CRS Report for Cong. No. R42329, at 8–10 tbl.3 (2015). Using the same sources as CRS, a research assistant and I have been unable to discover any subsequent recess appointments by Obama.

246. NLRB v. Noel Canning, 134 S. Ct. 2550 (2014).

247. For an expansion of this argument, see Josh Chafetz, *A Fourth Way? Bringing Politics Back into Recess Appointments (and the Rest of the Separation of Powers, Too)*, 64 Duke L.J. Online 161, 166–71 (2015).

248. Indeed, even without control of the presidency, some Republican Senators in 2015 advocated eliminating the filibuster, presumably so as to be able to force Obama to veto measures that could then become election issues. *See* Seung Min Kim, *Republicans Weigh Battle over Filibuster Rules*, Politico, Nov. 5, 2015, http://www.politico.com/story/2015/11/senate-republicans-filibuster-rule-change-215501.

249. Carl Hulse, *G.O.P. Senator Seeks to Forge Path for Change*, N.Y. Times, Nov. 10, 2015, at A13.

250. *See id.*

251. *See* Guido Calabresi, *A Common Law for the Age of Statutes* 120–21 (1982) ("[T]he courts in exercising the power to induce the updating of statutes should only deal in areas of legislative inertia."); William N. Eskridge Jr., *Dynamic Statutory Interpretation* 156–61 (1994) (arguing that dynamic statutory interpretation can help counteract political dysfunction). Rick Hasen has argued that decreasing legislative output in recent decades has increased the power of the courts at the expense of Congress. *See generally* Richard L. Hasen, *End of the Dialogue? Political Polarization, the Supreme Court, and Congress*, 86 S. Cal. L. Rev. 205 (2013); *but see* Matthew R. Christiansen & William N. Eskridge Jr., *Congressional Overrides of Supreme Court Statutory Interpretation Decisions, 1967–2011*, 92 Tex. L. Rev. 1317, 1343–46 (2014) (disputing this account).

Conclusion

1. *See* Bruce Ackerman, *The Failure of the Founding Fathers: Jefferson, Marshall, and the Rise of Presidential Democracy* (2005); *see also* David Fontana, *Government in Opposition*, 119 Yale L.J. 548, 602 (2009) ("[W]hen one political party captures all the levers of power, then the American system of separation of powers fails.").

2. Daryl J. Levinson & Richard H. Pildes, *Separation of Parties, Not Powers*, 119 Harv. L. Rev. 2311, 2313 (2006); *see also* Curtis A. Bradley & Trevor W. Morrison, *Historical Gloss and the Separation of Powers*, 126 Harv. L. Rev. 411, 443 (2012) ("[T]he Madisonian model of interbranch rivalry is especially inaccurate during times of unified government.").

3. *See* Eric A. Posner & Adrian Vermeule, *The Executive Unbound: After the Madisonian Republic* (2010).

4. *See* Bruce Ackerman, *The Decline and Fall of the American Republic* 119–79 (2010); Sanford Levinson & Jack M. Balkin, *Constitutional Dictatorship: Its Dangers and Its Design*, 94 Minn. L. Rev. 1789, 1858–65 (2010).

5. I am skeptical that the design of something as complicated as a constitution is the sort of thing that can be optimized. Aziz Huq has recently concluded that the only meaningful criterion of constitutional success is that it not undermine the very existence or functioning of the state that it is meant to constitute. *See* Aziz Z. Huq, *Hippocratic Constitutional Design*, in *Assessing Constitutional Performance* 39 (Tom Ginsburg & Aziz Huq eds., 2016). If this is the most that one can say as to why one constitutional design is more successful than others (and I share Huq's belief that no more than this can be said), then any talk of optimizing constitutional design should be at an end. I therefore talk instead in terms of the *underappreciated virtues* of the American separation-of-powers system. This is still irreducibly comparative: if representativeness, deliberation promotion, and autocracy resistance are virtues of the American system, it must mean that the American system promotes them better than some alternative. But I resist the belief that there is some underlying metric that will allow us to tally across virtues and declare one constitutional design better than all of the alternatives. (Values being the plural and incommensurate things they are, it seems to me implausible in the extreme that any constitutional design would dominate as against all others.)

6. The classic systematic treatment remains Hanna Fenichel Pitkin, *The Concept of Representation* (1967).

7. *See, e.g., id.* at 209 (offering, as a bare-bones synthesis of views on political representation, the view that representing "means acting in the interest of the represented, in a manner responsive to them").

8. *See id.* at 8–9 ("[R]epresentation, taken generally, means that making present *in some sense* of something which is nevertheless *not* present literally or in fact.").

9. *See* Walt Whitman, *Song of Myself*, in *Leaves of Grass* § 51, at 29, 78 (Small, Maynard & Co. 1903) (1855) ("Do I contradict myself? / Very well then I contradict myself, / (I am large, I contain multitudes.)").

10. Indeed, as Charles Taylor has noted, "it would be absurd and disastrous" to attempt to impose some sort of "statement of systematic priority," abstracted from specific circumstances, upon our values. Charles Taylor, *Leading a Life*, in *Incommensurability, Incomparability, and Practical Reason* 170, 177 (Ruth Chang ed., 1997).

11. For illuminating discussions of practical reasoning, see Gregory S. Alexander, *Pluralism and Property*, 80 Fordham L. Rev. 1017, 1046–49 (2011); Taylor, *supra* note 10, at 178–83.

12. *See* Taylor, *supra* note 10, at 179 (noting that our "sense of good and right" is "not so much a matter of the relative importance of goods, but of a sense of how they fit together in a whole life. In the end, what we are called on to do is not just carry out isolated acts, each one being right, but to live a life, and that means to be and become a certain kind of human being"); *id.* at 180 ("[I]nsofar as we have some sense of our lives, of what we are trying to lead, we will be relating the different goods we seek not just in regard to their differential importance, but also in the way they fit, or fail to fit, together in the unfolding of our lives.").

13. On the latter point, Alexander Bickel incisively noted that "[n]o good society can be unprincipled; and no viable society can be principle-ridden." Alexander M. Bickel, *The Supreme Court, 1960 Term—Foreword: The Passive Virtues*, 75 Harv. L. Rev. 40, 49 (1961).

14. The idea that polities engage in narrative self-construction through their collective choices across time owes a great deal to Jed Rubenfeld's "commitmentarian" account of self-government. *See* Jed Rubenfeld, *Freedom and Time: A Theory of Constitutional Self-Government* 91–102 (2001).

15. Federal law requires House members to be elected from districts, rather than at-large. 2 U.S.C. § 2c.

16. *See* U.S. Const. art. I, § 2.

17. Except in the cases of Alaska, Delaware, Montana, North Dakota, South Dakota, Vermont, and Wyoming, which have one House member each, meaning that their representative and their senators have the same constituency.

18. *See* U.S. Const. art. I, §3; *id.* amend. XVII.

19. Indeed, voters appear to use different criteria to evaluate House and Senate candidates. *See* Arthur H. Miller, *Public Judgments of Senate and House Candidates*, 15 Legis. Stud. Q. 525 (1990).

20. *See* U.S. Const. art. II; *id.* amend. XXII.

21. *See id.* art. III; *id.* art. II, § 2, cl. 2.

22. *Cf.* Philip Pettit, *Varieties of Public Representation*, in *Political Representation* 61, 69–70 (Ian Shapiro et al. eds., 2009) (describing judges as "indicative representers"— that is, as "proxies for the public").

23. *Cf.* W. Bradley Wendel, *Lawyers and Fidelity to Law* (2010) (arguing that fidelity to law, as a particular kind of discourse, structures lawyers' ethical obligations); Mitchell N. Berman, *Constitutional Theory and the Rule of Recognition: Toward a Fourth Theory of Law*, in *The Rule of Recognition and the U.S. Constitution* 269, 282–90 (Matthew D. Adler & Kenneth Einar Himma eds., 2009) (describing law as a type of argumentative practice).

24. The normative push toward judges using this sort of language can be seen in, for example, the Legal Process school's emphasis on "reasoned elaboration" as the foundation of judicial legitimacy, Henry M. Hart Jr. & Albert M. Sacks, *The Legal Process: Basic Problems in the Making and Application of Law* 145–52 (William N. Eskridge Jr. & Philip P. Frickey eds., 1994), and Dworkin's insistence that the courts "should make decisions of principle rather than policy," Ronald Dworkin, *A Matter of Principle* 69 (1985).

25. *See* U.S. Const. art. III, § 1.

26. *See* Barry Friedman, *The Will of the People: How Public Opinion Has Influenced the Supreme Court and Shaped the Meaning of the Constitution* (2009) (arguing that the Supreme Court has always been quite responsive to public opinion); Peter K. Enns & Patrick C. Wohlfarth, *The Swing Justice*, 75 J. Pol. 1089 (2013) (finding that public opinion is a significant driver of the votes of swing justices in closely divided Supreme Court cases); William Mishler & Reginald S. Sheehan, *Public Opinion, the Attitudinal Model, and Supreme Court Decision Making: A Micro-Analytic Perspective*, 58 J. Pol. 169, 170 (1996) ("The evidence that the Court has been responsive to public opinion, even in the absence of changes in its ideological composition, suggests that public opinion can influence the behavior of individual justices, causing at least some justices to alter their decisions or perhaps even change their personal ideologies or beliefs."); Mark Tushnet, *Understanding the Rehnquist Court*, 31 Ohio N.U. L. Rev. 197, 200–201 (2005) (discussing the "Greenhouse effect"—that is, the desire of justices to win the

approval of media elites like (former) *New York Times* Supreme Court reporter Linda Greenhouse). *See also* Neal Devins & Lawrence Baum, *Split Definitive: How Party Polarization Turned the Supreme Court into a Partisan Court* (2013) (manuscript at part IV) (discussing the ways in which their "social environments" push judges in various jurisprudential directions).

27. *Cf.* Victoria Nourse, *The Vertical Separation of Powers*, 49 Duke L.J. 749, 752 (1999) ("The power created by our Constitution comes from more than constitutional description; it comes from the people, aggregated in different kinds of constituencies, commonly distinguished as districts, states, and nation. Thus, every shift in governmental function or task can be reconceived, not simply as a shift in tasks but also as a shift in the relative power of popular constituencies.").

28. *See* Jeffrey K. Tulis, *Deliberation between Institutions*, in *Debating Deliberative Democracy* 200 (James S. Fishkin & Peter Laslett eds., 2003); Mariah Zeisberg, *Constitutional Fidelity and Interbranch Conflict*, 13 Good Soc'y, no. 3, 2004, at 24.

29. Tulis, *supra* note 28, at 208.

30. Zeisberg, *supra* note 28, at 26.

31. Zeisberg rightly emphasizes that deliberation encompasses both "talk" and "the signals that the branches give each other through their actions." *Id.*

32. *Id.* at 28.

33. *See generally* James Surowiecki, *The Wisdom of Crowds* (2004); Josh Chafetz, Comment, *It's the Aggregation, Stupid!*, 23 Yale L. & Pol'y Rev. 577 (2005).

34. *See* Cass R. Sunstein, *Deliberative Trouble? Why Groups Go to Extremes*, 110 Yale L.J. 71 (2000).

35. Tulis views interbranch deliberation as being in some tension with deliberation between a branch and the public; he accordingly sees the move from a State of the Union address aimed primarily at Congress to one aimed primarily at the American people as anti-deliberative. Tulis, *supra* note 28, at 209. By contrast, I view them as part of the same, larger conversation.

36. For further elaboration of this principle with respect to federalism, see Josh Chafetz, *Multiplicity in Federalism and the Separation of Powers*, 120 Yale L.J. 1084, 1092–98 (2011).

37. *The Federalist No. 28*, at 181 (Alexander Hamilton) (Clinton Rossiter ed., 1961).

38. *The Federalist No. 46*, *supra* note 37, at 295 (James Madison).

39. 1 *The Records of the Federal Convention of 1787*, at 344 (Max Farrand ed., rev. ed. 1966).

40. *Id.*

41. *The Federalist No. 51*, *supra* note 37, at 322 (James Madison).

42. *Id.*

43. In a federalism analogue to this argument, Jessica Bulman-Pozen argues that our federal structure provides the tools by which state-level actors can check federal actors, even as something else—partisanship—provides the motive for such checking. Jessica Bulman-Pozen, *Partisan Federalism*, 127 Harv. L. Rev. 1077 (2014).

44. These means, of course, include the ability to make plausible authority claims. *See* Bryan Garsten, *Representative Government and Popular Sovereignty*, in *Political Representation*, *supra* note 22, at 90, 91 ("[R]epresentative government aims (on this

view) to provoke debate about precisely what the popular will is and thereby to prevent any one interpretation of the popular will from claiming final authority. . . . [I]t makes any particular claim to fully represent the people implausible, and it helps to combat the use of such claims to justify the concentration of power.").

45. *See generally* Larry Alexander & Frederick Schauer, *On Extrajudicial Constitutional Interpretation*, 110 Harv. L. Rev. 1359 (1997). It is true that Alexander and Schauer say that settlement is merely "an important function of law," *id.* at 1371, and they even admit that it is "not the only" one, *id.* at 1376. But since they discuss no other functions of law generally or constitutional law in particular, it seems fair to attribute to them the belief that it is, at the very least, the overwhelmingly dominant function of the law. *See also id.* at 1377 ("Thus an important—perhaps *the* important—function of law is its ability to settle authoritatively what is to be done.").

46. *See* Werner Z. Hirsch, *Reducing Law's Uncertainty and Complexity*, 21 UCLA L. Rev. 1233, 1234 (1974) ("In terms of efficient allocation of resources, uncertainty about laws tends to increase the cost to transactors and the efficiency with which society conducts its business.").

47. See BMW of N. Am., Inc. v. Gore, 517 U.S. 559, 574 (1996) ("Elementary notions of fairness enshrined in our constitutional jurisprudence dictate that a person receive fair notice . . . of the conduct that will subject him to punishment. . . .").

48. *See* Mariah Zeisberg, *War Powers: The Politics of Constitutional Authority* 230–35 (2013) (arguing that accounts like Alexander and Schauer's treat "the costs of conflict as intrinsic," whereas they are in fact contingent); Shawn J. Bayern, *Against Certainty*, 41 Hofstra L. Rev. 53, 53 (2012) ("The Article's principal contention is that arguments about certainty are often mistaken, that certainty itself is often misunderstood, and that many defenses of certainty in legal rules are tautological, irrelevant, or substantively overstated.").

49. *See, e.g.*, Zeisberg, *supra* note 48, at 229–30, 235–36 (noting that theories like Alexander and Schauer's fail to account for the ways in which the Constitution "supports interpretive conflict as well as interpretive consensus" and fail to appreciate the importance for institutional maintenance of critique and resistance); Seana Valentine Shiffrin, *Inducing Moral Deliberation: On the Occasional Virtues of Fog*, 123 Harv. L. Rev. 1214 (2010) (arguing that vagueness and opacity can be virtues in legal standards, insofar as they promote moral deliberation among the subjects of the law).

50. *See* Franz Kafka, *The Trial* (Mike Mitchell trans., Oxford World's Classics 2009) (1925).

51. *See* Josh Chafetz, *The Phenomenology of Gridlock*, 88 Notre Dame L. Rev. 2065, 2073–82 (2013); *see also* Bruce Ackerman, *This Is Not a War*, 113 Yale L.J. 1871, 1878 n.20 (2004) (declaring that his "devotion to separation of powers derives precisely from the 'deliberate inefficiencies' that [others] disparage").

52. Niccolò Machiavelli, *The Discourses*, bk. 1, ch. 4, at 113 (Bernard Crick ed., Leslie J. Walker trans., Penguin Books 1998) (1531).

53. *Id.*

54. *Id.*

55. Jeremy Waldron, *The Dignity of Legislation* 34 (1999).

56. Bernard Crick, *In Defence of Politics* 21 (4th ed. 1993).

57. *Id.* at 31.

58. *See id.* at 33–55.
59. Robert Post, *Theorizing Disagreement: Reconceiving the Relationship between Law and Politics*, 98 Calif. L. Rev. 1319, 1338 (2010).
60. Bruce A. Ackerman, *The Storrs Lectures: Discovering the Constitution*, 93 Yale L.J. 1013, 1028 (1984).
61. *Id.* at 1026.

INDEX

New Hampshire, 56, 95, 97, 124–125, 170, 278–279

New Jersey, 93, 95, 96, 169, 278

New START treaty, 32

New York Daily News, 229

New York State, 57, 280; colonial government in, 93, 168, 169, 210; constitution of, 95, 96, 170–171, 211, 278; patronage in, 114, 126, 175–176

New York Sun, 249

New York Times, 12, 114–115, 130, 216, 218–219, 220–222, 251, 257–258, 265, 288

New York Times v. United States (1971), 215–216

Ney, Bob, 261

NFIB v. Sebelius (2012), 11–12, 13, 16, 25, 27, 307

Nicaragua, 75, 252

Nicholas, John, 214

Nixon, Richard: appointments under, 121; budgetary reforms under, 63, 121; CIA misdeeds under, 219; executive privilege asserted by, 182, 187, 192; impeachment inquiry into, 182–183; impoundment by, 64; Pentagon Papers release opposed by, 223; resignation of, 149, 183; Vietnam War waged by, 75

NLRB v. Noel Canning (2014), 140, 141, 300

Norris, George, 288

North Atlantic Treaty Organization (NATO), 293

North Carolina, 93, 95, 168, 275, 278, 279

Oates, Titus, 235

Obama, Barack: Affordable Care Act and, 10–14, 15, 17, 18–19, 25, 27, 197, 298; appointments by, 124, 126, 127, 130, 132–134, 298–300; arms control and, 32; budget battles of, 40, 69–71; *Citizens United* criticized by, 9–10, 19, 27; congressional opposition to, 30, 37, 40, 69–71, 72, 75, 124, 266; environmental policies of, 297–298;

foreign policy of, 133; "gunwalking" operation under, 188–189, 193; intraparty opposition to, 30, 72; national security policies of, 221

Obey, David, 72

Office of Congressional Ethics (OCE), 262–264, 266, 267

Office of Information and Regulatory Affairs (OIRA), 121, 122

Office of Legal Counsel (OLC), 30, 132, 133, 180, 184, 185, 187, 299

Office of Management and Budget (OMB), 63, 76, 121, 122, 292

Oleszek, Walter, 134

Olson, Theodore, 120, 184–185

Onslow, Arthur, 274

"Operation Fast and Furious," 188–189

Oregon Land Frauds, 252

Organic Act for the District of Columbia (1801), 103, 106, 142, 145, 147

Origination Clause, 32–33, 126

Orren, Karen, 4

Osborne, Thomas, Earl of Danby and Duke of Leeds, 49–50, 87–88, 273

Osgood, Herbert, 54

Pacific Mail Steamship Line, 250

Panama Canal, 252

Panetta, Leon, 69

Parliament, 4–5; appropriations powers of, 45–53; breach of privilege in, 155–156, 160, 164–167, 181, 191, 195–196, 208, 226, 237, 272; cameral rules in, 267–274, 275; contempt of, 153–167, 181; dissolution of, 50, 80, 81, 82, 83, 84, 85, 88, 91, 157, 160, 163, 195, 196, 207, 208, 277–278, 280; ethics in, 235–237, 254; impeachments by, 49–50, 79–82, 84–88, 96, 158–159, 273; internal disciplinary power of, 232–239; personnel powers of, 78–92; speech or debate privilege in, 201–210, 225; unified government in, 34

Parrillo, Nicholas, 73

Parry, William, 233–234